MACMILLAN
DICTIONARY
OF
MARKETING AND
ADVERTISING

MACMILLAN DICTIONARY OF

MARKETING AND ADVERTISING

Third Edition

Michael J. Baker

MACMILLAN
Business

First hardcover edition 1984
Paperback first published 1985
Second edition 1990
Reprinted three times
Third edition 1998

Published by
MACMILLAN PRESS LTD
Houndmills, Basingstoke, Hampshire RG21 6XS
and London
Companies and representatives
throughout the world

ISBN 0–333–71565–9 hardback
ISBN 0–333–71566–7 paperback

A catalogue record for this book is available
from the British Library.

This book is printed on paper suitable for recycling and
made from fully managed and sustained forest sources.

10 9 8 7 6 5 4 3 2 1
07 06 05 04 03 02 01 00 99 98

Printed in Great Britain by
Antony Rowe Ltd, Chippenham, Wiltshire

MAJOR CONTRIBUTORS
Michael J Baker
Keith Crosier

OTHER CONTRIBUTORS
George Avlonitis
Ken N Bernard
J A Bound
Kevin A Boyle
A J Brown
Douglas Brownlie
James R Bureau
Marie Clare Cameron
Kenneth R Deans
Sandra Deans
W Donaldson
J L Drayton
Keith Fletcher
Joanna Kinsey
Douglas Leathar
James M Livingstone
Gerald Michaluk
Barry R Moore
Stephen T Parkinson
Graham K Peaston
Margaret D Potts
Michael Saren
Steve K Tagg
Colin N Wheeler
Alan M Wilson

Introduction

Since its first publication in 1984, the upsurge of interest in the subject of marketing which prompted the preparation of a *Dictionary of Marketing and Advertising* has continued unabated. Indeed, if anything, it has gathered momentum and greatly increased the number of persons exposed to terms and phrases which were formerly the preserve of the marketing specialist. At the same time, emphasis upon marketing as a major factor contributing to competitive success and its recognition as a major business function has resulted in a rapid expansion of the vocabulary of the subject.

In 1990 a revised second edition was published. As with the first edition, while the editor took responsibility for many of the entries, the overall work was very much a collaborative effort on the part of members of the Department of Marketing at Strathclyde University. Their names are listed on the title page and their contributions are still identified by their initials following the entries for which they were responsible.

Since 1990 not only have the number of terms and phrases continued to grow but many of the original contributors have moved to other appointments, retired etc. Accordingly, when it was decided to publish a completely revised and updated third edition only two of the original contributors were involved – myself and Keith Crosier. Keith Crosier is the Senior Lecturer responsible for the development of courses in the Department of Marketing in the field of marketing communications, of which advertising is the most important single subject. A substantial number of the original entries were made by him and he has completely revised , updated and added to his original contribution – a fact acknowledged by his identification as Principal Contributor to this Third Edition. For the rest the Editor must take responsibility. A number of entries have been deleted, some revised and over 600 new entries added.

As Editor, I consider the original objective of providing concise but informative definitions still to be the primary goal. The intended audience remains practitioners, managers, students and lay persons in other fields who are exposed to marketing 'jargon' and need a clear explanation of its meaning. However, while considerably more technical terms have been included, no attempt has been made to incorporate the more arcane terminology of the marketing specialist in sub-fields such as advertising, marketing research, P.R., etc. Persons seeking such terms will have to refer to the specialised text books and glossaries which deal with these essentially minority interests.

We all trust you find the new edition a useful addition to your working library and, as before, will welcome comments and suggestions for further improvements.

Michael J Baker

List of Abbreviations

Definitions in CAPITAL LETTERS are included in the Dictionary

AA ADVERTISING ASSOCIATION

AAAA American Association of Advertising Agencies

ABC AUDIT BUREAU OF CIRCULATIONS

a/c ACCOUNT

ACORN A CLASSIFICATION OF RESIDENTIAL NEIGHBOURHOODS

ACT Advance Corporation Tax

ad ante them (after date)

ad hoc for this purpose; type of research

ad referendum for further consideration

addendum an additional mark to be added

ADP Automatic Data Processing

AE ACCOUNT EXECUTIVE

AGB Ltd AUDITS OF GREAT BRITAIN LTD

AGM Annual General Meeting

AID ADVERTISING INVESTIGATION DEPARTMENT; AUTOMATIC INTERACTION DETECTOR

AIDA Attention Interest Desire Action

AIO activities, interests and opinions

AIRC ASSOCIATION OF INDEPENDENT RADIO CONTRACTORS

AMA AMERICAN MARKETING ASSOCIATION

AMSAC ATTWOOD MULTI-SEGMENTED ANALYSIS OF CONSUMERS

AMSO Association of Market Survey Organisations

ANCOVA ANALYSIS OF COVARIANCE

ANOVA ANALYSIS OF VARIANCE

antedate date earlier than arranged

a/o account of

API Advertising Planning Index

A/R All risk

ARB American Research Bureau

A/S ADVERTISING-TO-SALES RATIO

ASA ADVERTISING STANDARDS AUTHORITY

ASBOF ADVERTISING STANDARDS BOARD OF FINANCE

ASSC Accounting Standards Steering Committee

AURA Association of Users of Research Agencies

A/V ad valorem (based on value)

AYCA all you can afford

BARB BROADCASTERS' AUDIENCE RESEARCH BOARD

BBC British Broadcasting Corporation

BDMA BRITISH DIRECT MARKETING ASSOCIATION

B/E BILL OF EXCHANGE; Bill of Entry

BEC British Employers Confederation

BEHA BRITISH EXPORT HOUSES ASSOCIATION

BIM British Institute of Management

B/L BILL OF LADING

BMRB BRITISH MARKET RESEARCH BUREAU LTD

BO Branch Office; Buyer's Option

BOM Beginning of Month

BOT Board of Trade

BOTB BRITISH OVERSEAS TRADE BOARD

bp below proof

BP Bills Payable

BPB Bank Post Bills

BRAD BRITISH RATE AND DATA

BRI Brand Rating Index

BRITE Basic Research in Industrial Technologies for Europe

BRS Business Readership Survey

bs Balance Sheet; Bill of Sale

BSI BRITISH STANDARDS INSTITUTE

bsr BASAL SKIN RESISTANCE

C4 Channel 4

C&E Customs and Excise

C/C Centre to Centre

cc Compte Courant (Account Current)

CA Chartered Accountant; Chief Accountant

CAB CONSUMER ADVICE BUREAU

CAC COGNITIVE, AFFECTIVE, CONATIVE

CAD COMPUTER AIDED DESIGN

CAM Communication, Advertising and Marketing Education Foundation Ltd COMPUTER AIDED MANUFACTURING

CAP capital allowance; Code of Advertising Practice

CAPEX capital expenditure

CAPM Capital Asset Pricing Model

CATI COMPUTER ASSISTED TELEPHONE INTERVIEWING

CBI CONFEDERATION OF BRITISH INDUSTRY

CCTV CLOSED CIRCUIT TELEVISION

CEO Chief Executive Officer

c/f carry forward

CF Carriage and Freight

CIF COST, INSURANCE, FREIGHT

CIFI Cost, Insurance, Freight and Insurance

CIM Chartered Institute of Marketing

CIR Commissioners of Inland Revenue

ck cask

CKD COMPLETELY KNOCKED DOWN

CLS CONSUMER LOCATION SYSTEM

CM Certified Master

CMA Cash Monthly Account

CMEA COUNCIL FOR MUTUAL ECONOMIC ASSISTANCE

c/o care of; Carried Over in the Stock Exchange

COD CASH ON DELIVERY

COI Central Office of Information

COMECON COUNCIL FOR MUTUAL ECONOMIC ASSISTANCE

COMO Committee of Marketing Organisations

COS Charity Organisation Society

CPA CRITICAL PATH ANALYSIS

CPI CALIFORNIA PERSONALITY INVENTORY

CPM Critical Path Method

CPT (UK) / CPM (USA) COST PER THOUSAND

CPU Central Processing Unit

Cr CREDIT; Creditor

CRC CAMERA READY COPY

CRD COMPLETELY RANDOMISED DESIGN

CSO Central Statistical Office

CT With the dividend to come

CTNs confectioners, tobacconists and newsagents

CTT Capital Transfer Tax

CVIF Compound Value Interest Factor

cwo Cash with Order

CWS Cooperative Wholesale Society

DADA DESIGNERS' AND ART DIRECTORS' ASSOCIATION

DAGMAR DEFINING ADVERTISING GOALS FOR MEASURED ADVERTISING RESULTS

DAR DAY AFTER RECALL

db daybook

DBMS DATABASE MANAGEMENT SYSTEM

DBS Direct Broadcast Satellite

DC DOUBLE COLUMN

DCI Direct Computer Interviewing

D/d delivered

DMSSB Direct Marketing Services Standards Board

DMU DECISION MAKING UNIT

D/P Documents against Payment

DP DATA PROCESSING

DPO Distribution Post Office

DPS DOUBLE PAGE SPREAD

DSD Documentary Sight Draft

DSS DECISION SUPPORT SYSTEM

dy delivery

E&OE Errors and Omissions Excepted

ea each

EAN European Article Number

EC EUROPEAN COMMUNITY

ECG extended creativity group

ECGD EXPORT CREDIT GUARANTEE DEPARTMENT

ECI Equity Capital for Industry

ECM EUROPEAN COMMON MARKET

ECO European Coal Organisation

Econ Economical; Economist; Economy; Economics

ECU European Currency Unit

EEA Exchange Equalisation Account

EEC EUROPEAN ECONOMIC COMMUNITY

EFTA EUROPEAN FREE TRADE ASSOCIATION

EFTPOS ELECTRONIC FUND TRANSFER AT POINT OF SALE

EMA European Monetary Agreement

EMF European Monetary Fund

EMV EXPECTED MONETARY VALUE

EPA Environmental Protection Agency

EPD Excess Profits Duty

EPOS ELECTRONIC POINT OF SALE

EPPS Edwards Personal Preference Schedule

EPS earnings per share

EPT Excess Profits Tax

EPU European Payments Union

ERP European Recovery Plan

ESOMAR EUROPEAN SOCIETY FOR OPINION AND MARKETING RESEARCH

ESPRIT European Strategic Programme for Research in Information Technology

ESU Elementary Sampling Unit

EV EXPECTED VALUE

EVAP European Association for Industrial Marketing

ex div without next dividend

ex int without next interest

ex officio by virtue of office

faa Free of All Average

FAQ Fair Average Quality

FAS Fee Alongside Ship; Free Alongside Ship

FCC First Class Certificate

f.co. Fair Copy

FDI foreign direct investment

FIFO FIRST IN, FIRST OUT

FIRA Furniture Industry Research Association

FMCGs FAST MOVING CONSUMER GOODS

fo folio

FOB FREE ON BOARD

FOR Free on Rail

FOT Free on Truck

fpa Free from Particular Average

fpc For Private Circulation

fs Full Size

FTC Federal Trade Commission

FWA Factories and Works Act

GATT GENERAL AGREEMENT ON TARIFFS AND TRADE

GDP Gross Domestic Product

GHI GUARANTEED HOMES IMPRESSIONS

GHR GUARANTEED HOMES RATINGS

GMB Good Merchantable Brands

GNP GROSS NATIONAL PRODUCT

GRP GROSS RATING POINTS

GSR GALVANIC SKIN RESPONSE

GSS Government Statistical Service

guar GUARANTEE; guarantor

HBR Harvard Business Review

H Comm High Commissioner

HP HIRE PURCHASE

HMSO Her Majesty's Stationery Office

IAA INTERNATIONAL ADVERTISING ASSOCIATION

IATA International Air Transport Authority

IBA INDEPENDENT BROADCASTING AUTHORITY

i/c in charge

ICAB International Cargo Advisory Bureau

ICAO International Civil Aviation Organisation

ICC Interstate Commerce Commission

IE INSTITUTE OF EXPORT

IGD Institute of Grocery Distribution

ILC Irrevocable Letter of Credit

ILR Independent Local Radio

IMF International Monetary Fund

IMRA Industrial Marketing Research Association

in toto in total

Inc Incorporated – US equivalent to a private limited company

inst present month

int interest

inv INVOICE

IOU I Owe You

IPA INSTITUTE OF PRACTITIONERS IN ADVERTISING

IR Inland Revenue

IRO Inland Revenue Office

IRR Internal Rate of Return

ISBA INCORPORATED SOCIETY OF BRITISH ADVERTISERS

ISP Institute of Sales Promotion

ITA INDEPENDENT TELEVISION AUTHORITY

ITCA INDEPENDENT TELEVISION COMPANIES ASSOCIATION

ITO International Trade Organisation

ITV INDEPENDENT TELEVISION

IWW International Workers of the World

JICNARS JOINT INDUSTRY COMMITTEE FOR NATIONAL READERSHIP SURVEYS

JICPAS JOINT INDUSTRY COMMITTEE FOR POSTER AUDIENCE SURVEYS

JICRAR JOINT INDUSTRY COMMITTEE FOR RADIO AUDIENCE RESEARCH

JICTAR JOINT INDUSTRY COMMITTEE FOR TELEVISION ADVERTISING RESEARCH

JND JUST NOTICEABLE DIFFERENCE

KD Knocked Down

l/a Letter d'Avis (Letter of advice)

LA Law Agent; Legislative Assembly; Local Authority

LAFTA Latin American Free Trade Association

LAIA LATIN AMERICAN INTEGRATION ASSOCIATION

l/cr LETTER OF CREDIT

LDCs LESS DEVELOPED COUNTRIES

LIFO Last In, First Out

LOTIS Liberalisation of Trade in Services

Ltd Limited

MANOVA Multivariate Analysis of Convariance

MAT Moving Annual Total

MBO Management by Objectives

MBWA MANAGEMENT BY WALKING ABOUT

MCA Market Research Corporation of America

MDF MEDIA DATA FORM

MDS MULTI-DIMENSIONAL SCALING

MEAL Media Expenditure Analysis Ltd

MEU Maximise the Expected Utility

MFN MOST FAVOURED NATION

MINTEL Market Intelligence Reports

MIRS Magazine Impact Readership Service

MIS Management Information System

MITI Ministry of International Trade and Industry (Japan)

MkIS MARKETING INFORMATION SYSTEM

MLR Minimum Lending Rate

mm Mutatis Mutandis (with the necessary changes)

MNC MULTINATIONAL CORPORATION

MNE Multinational Enterprise

mo method of operation (modis operandi)

MORI Market and Opinion Research International

MRG Media Research Group

MRI Mediamark Research Inc

MRP materials requirement planning; manufacturer's recommended price

MRS Market Research Society

MS Management Science

MSI Marketing Science Institute

n/a No Advice; no account; non acceptance; not available

NABM National Association of British Manufacturers

NAC Nielsen Audience Composition

NARDB Newspaper Audience Research Data Bank

NBS National Broadcasting Company (USA)

NCC NATIONAL CONSUMER COUNCIL

NEDC National Economic Development Council

NEDO National Economic Development Office

NIC Newly Industrialising Countries

NICB National Industrial Conference Board

NOMMAD Normative Model of Markets Acceptance Determination

np New paragraph

NPA NEWSPAPER PUBLISHERS' ASSOCIATION

NPD NEW PRODUCT DEVELOPMENT

NPO NON PROFIT ORGANISATION

NPV NET PRESENT VALUE

NRS National Readership Survey

n/s Not Sufficient (money to meet a cheque)

ns not specified

NS NEWSPAPER SOCIETY

NTI Nielsen Television Index

o/a on account

OAA Outdoor Advertising Association of Great Britain Ltd

OAC Outdoor Advertising Council

o/c over charge

OCR Optical Character Recognition

O/D Overdraft; Overdrawn; On Demand

OECD Organisation for Economic Cooperation and Development

OFT OFFICE OF FAIR TRADING

OLRT ON LINE REAL TIME

OM Organisation and Methods

OP Out of Print

OPEC Organisation of Petroleum Exporting Countries

OPM Option Pricing Model

O/R Owner's Risk

OR Operational Research

O/S Outstanding

OTC over the counter

OTs OPPORTUNITIES-TO-SEE

P/A Payment against Acceptance

PAB POSTER AUDIT BUREAU

PAYE Pay as you Earn

PC; pc; P/C percent; personal computer; prices current; petty cash

PD PHYSICAL DISTRIBUTION

PEP Political and Economic Planning; Personal Equity Plan

PERA Production Engineering Research Association

PERT PROJECT EVALUATION AND REVIEW TECHNIQUE

PI per inquiry

PIMS PROFIT IMPACT OF MARKET STRATEGIES

PIP Public Information Panels

PLC PRODUCT LIFE CYCLE, PUBLIC LIMITED COMPANY

POD pay on delivery; proof of delivery

POP POINT OF PURCHASE DISPLAY

POS POINT OF SALE DISPLAY

PPA PERIODICAL PUBLISHERS' ASSOCIATION

PPI Policy Proof of Interest; Personal Purchase Index; Printed Postage Impression

PR PUBLIC RELATIONS

PRO PUBLIC RELATIONS OFFICER; Professional

Proforma a specimen

PSC Pre Selected Campaign

R&D RESEARCH AND DEVELOPMENT

RACE Research in Advanced Communications in Europe

RAJAR RADIO JOINT AUDIENCE RESEARCH (successor to JICRAR)

RBD RANDOMISED BLOCK DESIGN

RFMR Recency Frequency Monetary Ratio

RNAB REGIONAL NEWSPAPER ADVERTISING BUREAU

ROI return on investment

rop RUN OF PAPER

ROW RUN OF WEEK

RPI RETAIL PRICE INDEX

RPM RESALE PRICE MAINTENANCE

RSGB Research Surveys of Great Britain Ltd

RSVP Rating Site Value Points

S4C Channel 4 (Wales)

SBU STRATEGIC BUSINESS UNIT

s.d. sine die (indefinitely)

SDA Scottish Development Agency

SDR Special Drawing Rights

SEC Securities and Exchange Commission

SEF Scottish Enterprise Foundation

SEM Single European Market

SERT Screening Evaluation and Rating Technique

SHEG SCOTTISH HEALTH EDUCATION GROUP

SIC STANDARD INDUSTRIAL CLASSIFICATION

SMP STRATEGIC MARKETING PLANNING

SPRI Science Policy Research Institute

src SELF REFERENCE CRITERION

SWOT STRENGTHS, WEAKNESS, OPPORTUNITIES AND THREATS

TA Transactional Analysis

TABS TELEVISION ADVERTISING BUREAU (SURVEYS) LTD

TAP Total Audience Package

TAT Thematic Apperception Test

TCA TELEVISION CONSUMER AUDIT

TGI TARGET GROUP INDEX

TPI Total Prime Time; Tax and Price Index

TR Total Revenue

TREES Trustees

TSAs Total Survey Areas

TUC TRADES UNION CONGRESS

TVR TELEVISION RATINGS

UNCTAD United Nations Conference on Trade and Development

UVM Universal Vendor Marking

UPC UNIVERSAL PRODUCT CODE

USP UNIQUE SELLING PROPOSITION

VALS VALUES AND LIFESTYLES

VAT VALUE ADDED TAX

VDU Visual Display Unit

VFD VERIFIED FREE DISTRIBUTION

VMS VERTICAL MARKETING SYSTEM

VOPAN Voice Pitch Analysis

WB Way Bill

xc commercial term for x without coupon

xd ex dividend

xep without coupon

A

AA. *See* ADVERTISING ASSOCIATION.

AB. *See* SOCIO-ECONOMIC CLASSIFICATIONS.

ABC. *See* AUDIT BUREAU OF CIRCULATION.

ABC analysis. A technique for the classification of INVENTORY or STOCK in relation to its importance to the stockholder, based on the rank ordering of the cumulative value of usage of individual items over a prescribed period of time (usually one year). The resultant list is then divided conventionally into three groups (A, B and C), making use of PARETO ANALYSIS, such that approximately 70 per cent of cumulative value found is to be derived from about 10 per cent of PRODUCTS or commodities (class A); 20 per cent of cumulative value is derived from the subsequent 20 per cent of products or commodities (class B) and the remaining 10 per cent of cumulative value from the residual 70 per cent of products or commodities (class C).   (KNB)

above-the-line. Defines ADVERTISING MEDIA which pay MEDIA COMMISSION to advertising agencies buying space or time from them. The 'line' is a purely imaginary boundary between those which do and do not, a distinction generally believed to have been first made by Procter & Gamble in the 1950s. Above the line are newspapers, magazines, television, radio, posters and cinema. They are also referred to as the 'major media'. *See also* BELOW-THE-LINE.   (KC)

absolute advantage. A form of COMPARATIVE ADVANTAGE where one country is able to produce goods at a lower cost than any other.   (MJB)

absolute frequency. A raw count of the numbers of occurrence of each value of a variable. (SKT)

absolute income hypothesis. One of three theories which have evolved in an attempt to explain variations in aggregate consumption functions. This theory holds that expenditure/ savings are a function of income. *See also* PERMANENT INCOME HYPOTHESIS and RELATIVE INCOME HYPOTHESIS.
          (MJB)

absolute threshold. The point at which a JUST NOTICEABLE DIFFERENCE becomes apparent.
          (MJB)

absorption costing. *See* FULL COST APPROACH.

accelerated development. The act of speeding up the development of a new product by parallel processing, concurrent engineering etc. so as to shorten the TIME TO MARKET and so increase the likelihood for success.   (MJB)

accelerator. *See* ACCELERATOR PRINCIPLE.

accelerator principle. A principle in business cycle theory which holds that changes in demand for consumer goods will give rise to increased changes in the demand for those capital goods, i.e. investment, which are required to make the consumer goods.   (MJB)

acceptance. (1) In MARKETING COMMUNICATIONS, the integration of incoming information into the long-term memory or COGNITIVE STRUCTURE as positive CONCEPTS related to the PRODUCTS.

(2) The ADOPTION by CONSUMERS of new products. Prediction of acceptance can be made using

DIFFUSION MODELS (e.g. the Bass model of product acceptance), and represented graphically by means of an ADOPTION CURVE.   (GKP)

accessibility. One of the four basic properties a market segment must possess if it is to deserve specific marketing attention. The other three conditions are that it should be measurable, substantial and unique in its response. A fifth condition proposed by Michael Thomas is that segments should be stable in the sense that their behaviour may be predicted in the future. *See also* MARKET SEGMENTATION.   (MJB)

accessory equipment. Tools or other equipment used in the production process in either the factory or office which are not incorporated in the physical output.   (MJB)

account. ADVERTISING AGENCY terminology for an individual piece of business given to it by an advertiser. One agency CLIENT may thus represent several accounts. The vocabulary is, for example, 'Lever Brothers is a client of ours; we have the Persil'. There is no direct connection with 'account' in its financial sense.   (KC)

account executive. The generic job title for an ADVERTISING AGENCY employee whose job is to act as the point of contact for a single ACCOUNT or group of accounts. A more self-explanatory alternative is 'client-service executive', but it is comparatively rare. Account executives (often called 'AEs') need considerable skills of co-ordination, negotiation and diplomacy to discharge their task to best effect. The large agencies annually recruit university graduates for account-executive training; they are generally then termed 'graduate trainees'.   (KC)

accounting. The concept, conventions and procedures used to record and analyse transactions between parties in the exchange of goods and services.   (MJB)

accounting ratios. Tools for performance ANALYSIS often used to evaluate profitability and liquidity. As with all ratios, percentages and yields, they are of little use if viewed in isolation. It is necessary to compare a ratio with some standard, the most common being budgets, previous year's figures, or external industrial AVERAGES, compiled from observing the ratios of companies operating in the same or similar field. The most common ratios used are:

$$\text{return on capital employed} = \frac{\text{profit (before interest) x 100}}{\text{capital employed}}$$

$$\text{acid test/quick ratio/liquidity ratio} = \frac{\text{current assets} - \text{stock}}{\text{current liabilities}}$$

$$\text{current ratio} = \frac{\text{current assets}}{\text{current liabilities}}$$

$$\text{price earnings ratio} = \frac{\text{market price per ordinary share}}{\text{earnings per ordinary share after tax}}$$

Other accounting ratios of most interest to marketing managers are: operating profit/net operating assets; operating profit/sales; production costs/sales; marketing expenses/ sales; distribution expenses/sales; administration expenses/sales; cash/average day's sales; debtors/creditors; STOCK/average day's sales.   (GM)

account planner. An ADVERTISING AGENCY employee who practices the specialized discipline of ACCOUNT PLANNING. The tendency has been to shorten the description to 'planner' in recent years.   (KC)

account planning. One of the two planning functions in a sophisticated FULL-SERVICE ADVERTISING AGENCY, the other being MEDIA PLANNING. 'ACCOUNT' is used here in the specialized advertising sense of the word. Account planners are mostly concerned with research – formative and developmental as well as straightforward market research – and with the theoretical underpinnings of advertising strategy. They are, so to speak, the intellectual wing of the business. The goal of account planning is to understand consumers, audiences, markets and society, and to use that knowledge as a basis for the development of effective advertising campaigns. The role of account planners is thus quite often to influence CREATIVE strategy (media planners doing the same for media strategy). This can in practice cause internal conflict, since key people in the CREATIVE DEPARTMENT are likely to maintain that creativity is an intuitive and personal process, not amenable to design by committee or interpretation by researchers. The job and its title have recently spread beyond the confines of advertising agencies into other marketing communications service providers, particularly DIRECT MARKETING agencies. The tendency has been to shorten the description to 'planning' in recent years.

The account planning discipline seems to be stuck in a prolonged adolescence, not yet really widespread in smaller or less sophisticated advertising agencies. It was 'invented' in Britain, and remains something of a British specialization. There is debate in the business as to whether the credit should be given to Stephen King of the J. WALTER THOMPSON agency of Stanley Pollitt of Boase Massimi Pollitt, since absorbed into BMP DDB Needham. A Californian agency which pioneered the discipline in America in the 1980s, Chiat Day had an Account Planning Department staffed entirely by British expatriates. The Account Planning Group is a professional common-interest group for account planners and ADMAP is the house journal of the discipline. (KC)

Account Planning Group. The professional common-interest group for those working in the ACCOUNT PLANNING function in ADVERTISING AGENCIES. (KC)

accrual accounting. The accrual concept in ACCOUNTING recognizes costs and revenue as they are earned or incurred, and not as money is received or paid, i.e. matching revenue with expenses. *See also* ACCRUALS and PRE-PAID EXPENSES. (GM)

accruals. Charges for items consumed or incurred during the period for which no invoice has yet been received. Common examples of such liabilities incurred but not entered in the accounts ledger are gas, electricity, and telephone charges where the service has been consumed, but not yet billed for. *See also* ACCRUAL ACCOUNTING and PRE-PAID EXPENSES. (GM)

acculturation. The process by which members of one culture learn and adapt to the folkways and mores of another. (MJB)

accumulation. The process through which an inventory is created. (MJB)

accumulation process. The collection of products from many small producers, a process common in agriculture and horticulture. After collection, the products can be more efficiently graded, packed, or processed, ready for distribution to the channels of distribution, or can be marketed as a standard unchanging product with a guarantee of quality. (AJB)

achieved communality. The COMMUNALITY achieved in a FACTOR ANALYSIS. To be contrasted with estimated communalities, which need to be specified in advance. (SKT)

acid test. The acid test, also known as the QUICK RATIO and LIQUIDITY RATIOS, is:

$$\frac{current\ assets - stock}{current\ liabilities}$$

This ratio is a measure of liquidity, and as with all ratios, percentages and yields, is of little use if viewed in isolation. The rationale behind the ratio is that STOCK is often the most difficult current asset to realize at book value in a crisis, and if a company can meet all its liabilities from other current assets, then it will have a good liquidity level. (GM)

ACNielsen.MEAL. Successor to Media Expenditure Analysis Ltd (MEAL), this commercial research company monitors UK advertising volume and expenditure in all five MAJOR MEDIA. A sample of more than 600 PRESS titles includes all national daily and Sunday newspapers, the largest paid-for weekly newspapers, all major consumer magazines and a cross-section of the 'business and professional' category. TELEVISION expenditure on the terrestrial commercial network and the SKY stations is estimated on the basis of BARB data plus figures supplied by a panel of MEDIA BUYERS. RADIO estimates are based on 'post transmission advertising logs' received from 77 participating stations and RAJAR data. In the case of CINEMA, the two main advertising contractors supply details of every national and regional campaign costing more than £4,000. Lastly, OUTDOOR advertising expenditure is estimated from data supplied by a panel of eight major contractors and buying specialists, covering all campaigns in the 'poster' subdivision but none in the 'transport' category. Expenditure on tobacco advertising is also excluded. (KC)

ACORN. A type of socio-economic classification by allocating to a locality in which a respondent lives, one of a number of types derived from Population Census data about the locality. *See* CONSUMER LOCATION SYSTEM, SOCIO-ECONOMIC CLASSIFICATIONS. (JAB)

acquiescence bias (yea-saying). The tendency of questionnaire and interview RESPONDENTS to form a response set: specifically it is a distortion of true responses to increase the number of yes responses, or to be in agreement with the imagined point of view of the researcher or interviewer. (SKT)

acronym. A word formed from the initial letters of other words, e.g. CATI = Computer Assisted Telephone Interviewing. (MJB)

active exposure. Exposure to MARKETING information as a result of an active information search process undertaken by the CONSUMER. Marketers are therefore required to accommodate consumers by providing relevant information in a readily accessible form. *See also* PASSIVE EXPOSURE. (GKP)

activities, interests and opinions. *See* PSYCHOGRAPHICS.

activity based costing. The allocation of costs to the specific activities associated with them rather than by an arbitrary formula. *See also* CONTRIBUTION ANALYSIS. (MJB)

actual product. An American term used to describe the physical attributes of a product and its packaging including such characteristics as design, quality, brand name etc. which taken together define the core product benefits. (MJB)

ad. *See* ADVERTISEMENT.

adaptive planning. An approach to planning by which the decision maker follows an iterative process comprising four phases – situation or SWOT ANALYSIS; evaluation of alternative strategies or LIMITED STRATEGIC ALTERNATIVES; selection of a preferred course of action; implementation. *See also* STRATEGIC MARKETING PLANNING. (MJB)

addendum. An additional mark to be added.

ad hoc. For this purpose; type of research.

Admail. A Post Office redirection response service which allows a firm to quote a local or prestigious address in an ADVERTISEMENT and then have the replies redirected to another address in the UK. (GM)

Admap. A British professional periodical, mainly for planners and researchers in the advertising business, taking the form of an academic journal rather than a trade magazine. (KC)

administered channel system. A set of relationships in ordering, supply and payment between a producer and his channel intermediaries which preserves the autonomy of each channel member while permitting informal and enduring organizational arrangements to improve efficiency and encourage loyalty. The organizational arrangement may be initiated by the retailer (e.g. Marks & Spencer plc) or the wholesaler (pharmaceutical trade ordering systems) or the manufacturer (brewing companies). (AJB)

administered prices. Those prices which can be controlled or set by the seller due to the existence of imperfect competition by contrast with market prices, which are the outcome of the free interplay of the forces of supply and demand under conditions of pure or perfect competition.

While the administration of price is widely accepted as a desirable objective by the entrepreneur who wishes to exercise some control over the market, the existence of administered prices has been the subject of adverse criticism since the 1930s, when research by Gardner Means into more than 700 items in the wholesale price index showed that such prices are inflexible and do not reflect market pressures. Thus it was argued that an unwillingness to lower prices to stimulate demand resulted in an unnecessary prolongation of the Depression. Similarly, it has been argued that administered prices encourage inflation on the grounds that the type of companies which can administer prices (usually those with a dominant market share) do not have any incentive to resist wage inflation as they can pass the additional costs directly to the consumer, thus propagating an inflationary spiral. However, there is significant evidence from several industries in which administered prices exist that the opposite is the case, i.e. employers have resisted wage inflation and kept prices down. (MJB)

adopter categories. A classification of users or buyers of an innovation according to time of adoption. Everett Rogers identified five categories within the ADOPTION CURVE which he described as conceptualizations based on his own observations of the diffusion process. Rogers' categories are defined in terms of percentage groupings within the normal distribution of the adoption curve as follows:

innovators – first 2.5% of all adopters
early adopters – next 13.5% of all adopters
early majority – next 34% of all adopters
late majority – next 34% of all adopters
laggards – last 16% of all adopters

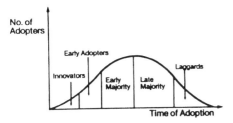

Figure 1: **Adopter categories**

Research has shown that these groups of adopters have different characteristics regarding social class, age, education, ATTITUDES, and other variables. Most attention has been focused on the first group of adopters. The characteristics and behaviour of innovators are studied in order to identify the most likely early purchasers of new products. The desired aim is to target marketing launch efforts more accurately and efficiently towards the most receptive buyers of a new product.   (MS)

adoption. The decision to buy and become a regular user of a product or service.   (MJB)

adoption curve. A graphic representation of the diffusion of an innovation. The curve illustrates the number of adopters who have purchased a new product or service in each time period from the launch date.

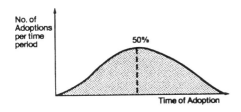

Figure 2: **Adoption curve**

The curve takes the shape of a normal statistical distribution. A small number of people adopt the innovation shortly after it becomes available and this rate of adoption increases until 50 per cent of the potential buyers (or users) have tried it. After this point the number adopting within each time period falls until there are no potential adopters who have not tried the innovation. An alternative method of illustrating the same process is by plotting the cumulative number of adopters against time:

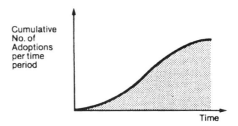

Figure 3: **Adoption curve (cumulative)**

This produces an S-shaped curve, also known as the diffusion curve.   (MS)

adoption process. *See* DIFFUSION PROCESS.

ad referendum. For further consideration.

Adshel. The proprietary name, sometimes used generically, of an advertising site which integrates a POSTER into the structure of a bus shelter. The original 'four sheet' panels (60 in x 40 in) are being steadily supplanted by back-illuminated 'six-sheet' (1.2 m x 1.8 m), 'lightboxes', branded by the two MEDIA OWNERS offering them as Citylight (formerly 'superlite') and Backlight. *See also* OUTDOOR.   (KC)

adspend. Short for ADVERTISING EXPENDITURE.
                                                (KC)

ad valorem duty. A tax imposed on an imported product which is a percentage of its value. *See also* TARIFFS.   (MJB)

advertisement, advert, ad. Alternative terms for the same thing, which scarcely requires precise definition since advertisements are a very familiar feature of contemporary life in western countries. 'Ad' is generally the trade jargon, particularly in America, but enters the public vocabulary in the term 'small ads'. 'Advert' is the lay person's word, not much used within the business and not at all by American writers on advertising. 'Advertisement' is safest.   (KC)

advertisement manager, advertisement sales manager. Not to be confused with an ADVERTISING MANAGER, this is an employee of a press MEDIA OWNER who is responsible for selling advertising space to prospective advertisers. In television and radio, the term 'advertising sales manager' is more common.   (KC)

advertisement sales representative. A member of an ADVERTISEMENT MANAGER'S sales team. Called a 'space salesman' until comparatively recently.   (KC)

advertiser. A person, firm or other organisation in the role of originator or sponsor of an advertisement or advertising campaign. Thus, 'Cadbury-Schweppes is a major British advertiser'. *See also* CLIENT.   (KC)

Advertiser's Annual. A professional directory, traditionally called 'the Blue Book' because of the colour of the cover, and now formally subtitled 'the blue handbook'. The 1997 edition's 2,250 pages provided, in three sections: (i) basic details of Britain's major national advertisers, general advertising agencies, specialist advertising agencies, public relations companies and sponsorship consultants, plus an index of major brand names and trade names; (ii) media data for national and local newspapers, business and consumer publications, independent television and radio stations, cinema, posters, transport advertising, 'sport advertising' and the major continental press titles, plus a listing of UK publishers and press cutting agencies; (iii) a gazette of providers of services to the advertising business, such as sales promotion agencies, creative consultancies, print services and exhibition organizers.   (KC)

advertising. This can mean several things: the craft or science of creating and disseminating ADVERTISEMENTS; the business or profession servicing the craft; a social institution affecting the daily lives of everyone; a force shaping popular culture; a factor in the economic theory of the firm; an element in the MARKETING COMMUNICATIONS MIX; a source of information about products, services and events. A narrow definition of the process rather than the concept might be: the placing of recognizable ADVERTISEMENTS

in definable ADVERTISING MEDIA at a published rate for the purchase of the space or time used.

An institutionalized advertising business has existed in Britain since about 1700, when newspapers began to feature advertising of a kind that present-day readers would recognize as such. Today, the business is characterized by five main organisational elements: (a) advertisers; (b) advertising agencies; (c) media owners; (d) various providers of ancillary services, such as market research agencies, design studios, typesetters, printers and so on; (e) trade bodies and professional associations.   (KC)

advertising agency. A service firm which exists to solve two basic problems for advertisers: the complexity of the MEDIA SELECTION decision and the intangibility of the skills required to formulate CREATIVE STRATEGY. Advertisers who choose to avail themselves of agency services thus buy a share in the media and creative expertise of the agency's staff, instead of having to recruit and retain costly experts themselves. The alternative, to set up an 'in-house advertising service', is today very uncommon except among small advertisers and retailers. It is estimated by the professional association representing advertising agencies, on the basis of returns from membership surveys, that about 80 per cent of total expenditure on DISPLAY advertising is channelled through their member-agencies, leaving less than a fifth paid to the media directly by advertisers not using agencies. There are just over a thousand advertising agencies all told in Britain, according to the most widely used directory (*see* BRADaal).

A typical advertising agency has five main functional divisions. (1) Client Service (or 'ACCOUNT handling') manages day-to-day liaison with the agency's clients, and is thus the logical equivalent of after-sales service in a conventional firm. It is of absolutely crucial importance in agencies, because clients tend to sever the working relationship as much on account of perceived shortcomings in account handling as for any other reason. (2) The Creative function is concerned with the conception and execution of advertising copy and graphics. It is normally staffed by pairs of COPYWRITERS and ART DIRECTORS, under the supervision of a Creative Director. Despite the glamorous aspects of such jobs, the function is conceptually equivalent to production in a conventional manufacturing firm, the creative department being actually the shopfloor of the agency, where the 'product' (as distinct from its service) is put together. Nevertheless, it too is of crucial importance, because clients tend to strike up a working relationship as much on the account of creative reputation as for any other reason. (3) The Media function attends to planning, selection and purchase of the means by which the product will be delivered, mainly advertising space and advertising time. MEDIA BUYERS negotiate rates and place orders with MEDIA OWNERS; they are the target market for ADVERTISEMENT SALES REPRESENTATIVES. Despite the obvious importance of buying the right media at the best price, industry surveys repeatedly show that clients are more influenced in practice by account handling and creative expertise. It is clearly tempting to relate media buying conceptually to the purchasing function in a conventional firm, but perhaps more helpful to think of it as management of the distribution chain. (4) The Traffic function controls and co-ordinates the variety of materials. The proliferation of documents and sheer number of separate operations involved in the execution of an advertising campaign involves a number of separate operations, a vital task if the end result is to appear on time in the right form. Unjustly, the staff of the Traffic Department are typically the unsung heroes of the agency world.

As well as these four operational functions, all but the smaller advertising agencies in Britain nowadays typically have one devolved planning function. (5) ACCOUNT PLANNING is an intellectual and strategic discipline involving acquisition, mastery and application of the body of knowledge concerned with the behaviour of target audiences as consumers in the marketplace, and with the theoretical underpinnings of effective communication. The corresponding department thus provides the planning input for creative strategy development, but is physically separate from the creative department. Despite the fact that media planning demands an equal degree of familiarity in depth with a large and often esoteric body of research data, that function typically remains within the media department. Account planning is the logical counterpart of the R&D and (to an extent) corporate planning functions in a conventional firm.

A significant activity in all advertising agencies is the one normally described as the 'new business' function. This is concerned with identifying potential new clients and working up appropriate presentations when one invites the agency to 'pitch for its account'. It is not included in our list of five main functions because it is typically executed by teams drawn on a project-by-project basis from the departments in which they routinely work. Larger agencies may have one director of new business, dedicated to the function full-time.

Paradoxically, advertising agencies are not paid for their work by their own clients directly, but by the media owners. See COMMISSION SYSTEM.

The best-known British advertising agency is SAATCHI & SAATCHI, which became a household name in the general elections of 1987 and 1989 by running the Conservative Party advertising campaigns. It rose to third position in the world league table of agencies before an internal crisis resulted in the separation of M&C Saatchi from Saatchi & Saatchi. Both were still in the British top ten in 1996. (KC)

advertising allocation. *See* ADVERTISING APPROPRIATION.

advertising appropriation. The amount of money an advertiser decides to spend on advertising in a fixed period, generally a year. 'Appropriation' is preferable to the alternative term 'budget', because the amount is in practice appropriated from the total funds available for marketing. Furthermore, although the everyday meaning of 'a budget' is indeed a sum of money to be used for a particular purpose, the true meaning is a form of plan, which describes future sources and uses of funds and sets standards for their cost-effective application to pre-determined objectives.

Textbooks identify a considerable number of techniques for deciding the amount to be spent on advertising, under a potentially confusing variety of names. In fact, they can be grouped into five distinct categories: executive judgement, internal ratios, external ratios, modelling & experimentation, and the 'objective-and-task' method. The application of executive judgement may sound an unacceptably vague approach to an important decision, but we shall see that the other options can be disturbingly illogical and highly inflexible. In that case, the accumulated wisdom and intuition of experienced practitioners may be as useful as any formal 'method'. Unfortunately, the usual descriptions hardly inspire confidence: 'AYCA' (All You Can Afford), 'notional sum', or the 'affordable' approach. The best known of the internal ratios is the 'A/S (Advertising-to-Sales) ratio', which entails setting the appropriation at a given percentage of either last year's sales or this year's forecast. It has the attraction of being a formula, but suffers the serious conceptual flaw that the ratio itself must be decided before the method can be used. In practice, that is normally done either by executive judgement all over again or by the adoption of industry norms (*see* ADVERTISING-TO-SALES RATIO), which may not be appropriate to the particular circumstances. Furthermore, it is potentially disastrous to apply this method when sales have been falling. If the assumption is that advertising can generate sales, then spending a constant ratio of a decreasing amount is hardly the way to go about remedying the situation. As the adage observes, numbers drive out reason. An altogether different internal ratio is 'historical parity': that is, spending the same as before, perhaps with adjustments for general media price inflation. The most familiar of the external ratios is 'competitive parity', which means setting the appropriation at around the same level as the competition does. A refinements uses the firm's market share to determine its share of total expenditure in the sector, with the aim of buying a fair 'share of voice' in the general advertising hubbub. A crucial assumption is that competitors are behaving rationally or that the collective wisdom is correct, or both. The more everyone follows everyone else, the less likely that is to be true. Furthermore, the method takes no account of the need for a new entrant to a market to take the risk of disproportionately heavy expenditure to gain a foothold. The many commercial and proprietary modelling and experimentation procedures are rather too complex to explain here. They are of course only as good as the formulae on which they are based, and the average practitioner lacks the mathematical sophistication to evaluate those. Using them is thus rather like buying a pig in a poke from a magician. The objective-and-task (sometimes simply 'task') method has won increasing support in recent years on the grounds that it is more 'logical' because it starts with an objective and computes the cost of the task of achieving it, rather than staring with a sum of money and then deciding what to do with it. However, two inconvenient problems arise in practice. First, advertisers notoriously find it diffcult to articulate precise and measurable objectives before the event (*see* ADVERTISING OBJECTIVES). Second, it does not follow that the means of achieving the objectives will be clear-cut and the costs therefore unequivocal. Nevertheless, this procedure does force decision makers to be more rigorous in their approach to a disturbingly vague science.

A collective weakness of all the common appropriation-setting methods is their focus on short-run profit maximization at the expense of long-term goals, as a result of which they can militate against continuity and stability in advertising campaigns. Indeed, the very convention of annual budgeting can encourage quite unnecessary change in CREATIVE STRATEGY, MEDIA STRATEGY, or both. It is also worth reflecting that advertising is likely in practice to compete with other marketing mix activities for a share of finite marketing funds, whereas the suggested methods for determining the appropriation are all open-ended calculations.

Historically, three procedures have dominated decision making. Amalgamating the findings of eight surveys of practice, published in Britain and America between 1970 and 1988, we find that 31 per cent of all respondents said they had used the A/S ratio, 28 per cent the objective-and-task method, and 27 per cent executive judgement by whatever name. No other choice was mentioned by more than one in five. These averages conceal the fact that objective-and-task had shown a steady increase in its generally low level of popularity over the years, to the point that it was narrowly second to executive judgement in the most recent British survey, almost exactly half a fully representative sample claiming to use it, and took first place ahead of the A/S ratio in a review of practice in Britain, Denmark, Finland, Germany and Sweden, published in 1989, accounting for more than half of all responses. This is interesting in the light of the comments just made about the pitfalls of applying it in practice. It is perhaps not surprising that this choice was twice as popular among respondents in companies with an annual turnover of more than £25 million as among those whose firms made less than £5 million a year. It is a sobering thought that such unsophisticated and inflexible 'methods' are routine in practice. Furthermore, the true significance of the composite picture is called into question by another set of findings from field surveys: that those with responsibility for spending the advertising appropriation very seldom have real authority to determine its size. Typically, they make the first estimate and are involved in subsequent negotiations, but the final amount is decided by board-level general management. The marketing manager of a food manufacturer summed up the situation vividly, in conversation: 'my budget is normally cut to half by the Financial Director, then a compromise is reached'. (KC)

Advertising Association (AA). The professional body representing all three main parties in the advertising business: ADVERTISERS, ADVERTISING AGENCIES and MEDIA OWNERS. Its origins were in a National Vigilance Committee formed following the 1924 annual conference of the Associated Advertising Clubs of the World, at Wembley, to monitor compliance with the general spirit of 'truth in advertising' and draw up a tentative code of ethics. The Advertising Association was established two years later. By 1948, this remit had resulted in the publication of a British Code of Standards in Relation to the to the Advertising of Medicines and Treatments, advertisements for which were still characterized by flagrantly dishonest and misleading claims, and the setting up of an Advertising Investigation Department to monitor advertising in general. In 1962, that self-regulatory aspect of the Advertising Association's work was handed over to the independent ADVERTISING STANDARDS AUTHORITY. Today, it concerns itself with the more general aims of (a) promoting public confidence in advertising; (b) safeguarding the common interest of the business; (c) encouraging the development of education for advertising and theoretical research into its effect; (d) maintaining professional standards and (e) fostering good relations with interested parties in business, the professions, the media and public service. It sponsors and co-publishes a considerable number of publications, ranging from textbooks to pamphlets, including the definitive Advertising Statistics Yearbook.
(KC)

advertising brief. A formal document passed to an ADVERTISING AGENCY by its client, containing the essential guidelines for the execution of an ADVERTISING CAMPAIGN. Structure and content vary in practice but might for example be: campaign objectives; budget; product, company and market profiles; strategy guidelines; timetable; implementation procedures, including authority and responsibilities; constraints set by other aspects of marketing strategy or by precedents; criteria for evaluation of effectiveness. Volume is also variable in practice: in the words of the INCORPORATED SOCIETY OF BRITISH ADVERTISERS, 'a good brief will be as short as possible but as long as necessary'.
(KC)

advertising budget. The sum of money earmarked for expenditure on advertising. See also ADVERTISING APPROPRIATION.
(MJB)

advertising campaign. A combination of advertisements appearing according to a predetermined schedule in a planned selection of advertising media, which logically constitutes one finite element in the advertiser's continuing advertising strategy. Campaigns vary considerably in duration. Some last only a matter of weeks or months; others, such as the famous series of surreal advertisements for Benson & Hedges Special Filter, ran for several years. Practitioners also distinguish sub-campaigns within a larger plan. The Benson & Hedges advertising, for instance, comprised: a 12-year 'OUTDOOR campaign' of several consecutive POSTERS, a 'PRESS campaign' of virtually identical graphic execution in a variety of magazines over the same period; and a 'CINEMA campaign' consisting of two mini-films in non-overlapping continuous schedules. The press and outdoor sub-campaigns have reappeared sporadically over the intervening years.
(KC)

advertising, case against. The case against advertising may be stated as follows. (a) Advertising leads to higher prices by conditioning demand and so leads to distortion of the productive machine, e.g. maize may cost only £0.01 per pound, but when converted into branded cornflakes it retails at about £1.40 per pound. (b) Advertising leads to non-price competition, e.g. the use of promotions. This creates diseconomies due to difficulties associated with the accurate measurement of demand, and results in a high proportion of product failures. (c) It is an unreliable guide to value and satisfaction. (d) It leads to oligopoly and monopoly. (e) It is a waste of national resources. See also ADVERTISING, CASE FOR.
(MJB)

advertising, case for. Proponents of advertising argue first, that advertised goods are cheaper because (a) advertising brings about economies in 'true' selling costs, e.g. by reducing the need for direct selling, encouraging the development of self-service, etc.; (b) it raises the scale of production, helps to stabilize output and promotes standardization; (c) competition ensures that the benefits of these economies will be passed on to the consumer. Secondly, they argue that advertised goods are better goods because (a) the identification of the product with the manufacturer through branding constitutes a guarantee of quality which must be maintained if the manufacturer is to secure repeat purchases from users; (b) to maintain market share manufacturers must constantly strive to improve their product to meet, or exceed, the claims of competing products. Thirdly, that branded and advertised goods create a freedom of consumer choice that was unknown when the same articles were sold from bulk. Fourthly, that advertising improves the standard of living by making new developments quickly available to the public and, by stimulating demand, creates investment, production and employment opportunities. *See also* ADVERTISING, CASE AGAINST.   (MJB)

advertising control. The British system of advertising control is tripartite, consisting of direct legislation, statutory regulation and self-regulation. In the United Kingdom, the first of these plays a much less significant role than in most other countries, because of the existence of the other two. Nevertheless, more than a hundred statutes and regulations can affect advertisers in some way, in England and Wales alone. Many of those apply also to Scotland and to Northern Ireland, both of which have their own relevant legislation in addition. The most significant laws controlling advertising in Britain are the Trade Descriptions Acts of 1968 and 1972 and the 1973 Fair Trading Act. The first empowered the government to decide what claims and descriptions made in advertisements or sales promotions can reasonably be assumed to mean, and to require the product or service to perform accordingly. The second set up the Consumer Protection Advisory Committee, with the statutory duty to investigate 'consumer trade practices', specifically including advertising and sales promotion, to see if they might 'adversely affect the economic interests of consumers'. It also established the Office of Fair Trading. The only valid defence an advertiser or advertising agency can offer to prosecution under either Act is 'innocent mistake' or the claim to have been relying on information supplied which could not reasonably have been verified. (*See also* CONSUMER PROTECTION.) Legislative control of advertising in Britain is thus a by-product of the general control of marketing.

'Statutory regulation' describes the special case of control over broadcast advertising. Regulation of television and radio advertising was the responsibility of a single Independent Broadcasting Authority until 1990, when general control of the two media was transferred to the INDEPENDENT TELEVISION COMMISSION (ITC) and the RADIO AUTHORITY, respectively. With respect to television advertising, Acts of Parliament charged the ITC and its predecessors with the

statutory duty to draw up a code of standards and devise a mechanism for enforcing it. The resultant Code of Advertising Standards and Practice states the General Principle that 'television advertising should be legal, decent, honest and truthful'. It is elaborated by 40 Rules spelling out more detailed Standards and by 5 Appendices dealing specifically with: Advertising and Children; Financial Advertising; Medicines, Treatments, Health Claims, Nutrition and Dietary Supplements; Charity Advertising; Religious Advertising. The ITC distributes its Code and many periodic advisory leaflets so widely throughout the industry that no advertiser or agency could credibly claim ignorance of its prohibitions or guidelines. The criteria of acceptability it sets out are enforced by mandatory pre-clearance of every commercial submitted to a television stations for broadcast. Except for a minority of cases in which this responsibility is devolved locally, clearance is given or withheld by a Copy Clearance Secretariat operated on behalf of the ITC by the Broadcast Advertising Clearance Centre (BACC). This office scrutinized 20,000 scripts for proposed television commercials during 1996. In practice, advertisers submit various other prototypes of the finished commercial for approval, step-by-step, because of the high cost of making any required changes to the finished product. Consequently, it is only when they or their agencies are determined to flout some aspect of the Code that eventual clearance will be refused altogether. This happens in fewer than 5 per cent of all cases, according to an informal statement by the BACC. When it does, the ruling is backed by the sanction of forbidding individual stations to air an uncleared commercial on pain of jeopardising their broadcasting franchise, awarded and reviewed by the ITC. In addition to this system of pre-clearance, a working party scrutinises new television commercials week-by-week, with a free remit to withdraw any for re-evaluation against the Code. Furthermore, the ITC has a statutory responsibility to invite and investigate complaints from the viewing public about commercials which have successfully cleared the system. In 1996, more than 5,000 were received concerning almost 2,000 commercials, and 98 upheld. It is questionable, however, that the public either recognizes its right to complain or knows how to do so, for the facts are publicized sporadically in the programme journals, in an information panel containing much else besides, and only very occasionally on the nation's television screens. It is a little difficult to know, on balance, how effective the ITC is in protecting viewers from being misled or offended by television advertising.

The rapid development of a European Single Market resulted in 1989 in the publication of Council Directive 89/552, generally called the Television Without Frontiers Directive, requiring member states to ensure that 'all advertisements shall be fair and honest ... shall not be misleading'. It was finally adopted two years later. Its three criteria together can be taken to have the same intent as the ITC Code's 'honest and truthful'. The 'legal' criterion can presumably be taken as read, but the Directive thus avoids the specific requirement in Britain that television commercials must be 'decent'. Several non-EU countries furthermore voluntarily subscribe to the terms of the European Convention on Transfrontier Television 1990, the content of which is virtually the same as the 1991 Directive.

Radio advertising had been jointly regulated with television advertising by the Independent Broadcasting Authority until 1990. Since then, the Broadcasting Acts of 1990 and 1996 have charged the new Radio Authority with the duty to draw up a separate code of standards and devise a mechanism for enforcing it. The resultant Advertising and Sponsorship Code states the same general principle as had previously applied to the two media together: that 'radio advertising should be legal, decent, honest and truthful', elaborated in 32 general Rules and seven Appendices relating to: the advertising of financial offers, alcoholic drinks, health products, charities and 'any body with objects wholly or mainly of a religious nature'; advertisements which make environmental claims; advertising addressed to 'listeners aged 15 and below'. It also requires that 'editorial control of sponsored programmes must remain with the licensee' (the station) and that 'all sponsor involvement must be declared so that the listener knows who is paying/contributing and why'. In contrast with the regulation of television advertising, radio commercials are mostly pre-cleared by the individual radio stations, which are explicitly held responsible for 'ensuring that any advertising and sponsorship they broadcast complies with this Code'. However, commercials to be aired nationally or regionally must be submitted to the Radio Advertising Clearance Centre, as must any in 16 'special categories'. If listeners subsequently complain about commercials which have survived local clearance, it is the station's responsibility to 'adopt appropriate procedures' and to refer any unresolved complaints to the Radio Authority. In 1996, 363 of these were received; 87 were ultimately upheld. In the same year, the Authority began to publish a quarterly report, commenting on general trends in complaining and providing details of every upheld case. It furthermore simultaneously implemented a policy of 'random spotlight monitoring' of stations' compliance with the Advertising and Sponsorship Code. Any station which falls foul of public complaint or in-house monitoring runs the risk of a fine, reduction of its licence period, or even total revocation of its franchise.

'Self-regulation' describes the form of control exercised over all non-broadcast advertising in the United Kingdom, including that on CD-rom and the Internet, by the ADVERTISING STANDARDS AUTHORITY. The ASA is financed by a 0.1% levy on the cost of every DISPLAY advertisement placed in all non-broadcast media, except those vehicles so minor as to operate outside the general system. Its criteria of acceptability are set out in the BRITISH CODES OF ADVERTISING AND SALES PROMOTION, a single document combining the two codes. The Advertising Code establishes the general Principle that 'all advertisements should be legal, decent, honest and truthful', precisely the same requirement as stated in the ITC Code. Its immediate predecessor, the British Code of Advertising Practice had been in use for so many years that no advertiser or agency could credibly claim to be ignorant of its general prohibitions. They are strongly advised to satisfy themselves that advertisements conform to the Code before placing them and, if in any doubt at all, to refer them to the ASA for pre-checking. There is no system of mandatory pre-clearance in the broadcast advertising manner (except in the special case of cinema commercials, explained later) for the understandable reason that some 30 million separate non-broadcast advertisements are estimated to appear each year. However, active publicizing and advertising of the ASA's existence and its remit have built up over the years a public awareness level of 72 per cent, according to a survey in 1996. The result is that just over 12,000 complaints were received in the same year about more than 7,000 advertisements, 1,750 of which the advertisers were asked to withdraw or modify. Details of the its judgements are issued in Monthly Reports to the news media and other interested parties. If these actions produce no response, the media (whose trade bodies are signatories to the Code) are asked to deny space to the advertiser in future and refuse COMMISSION to the advertising agency involved. In the rare event that the advertising nevertheless continues to run, perhaps in very minor media, the ASA has the final option of referring the whole case to the OFFICE OF FAIR TRADING, with the eventual possibility of prosecution under the terms of the Fair Trading Act.

Control of cinema advertising combines self-regulation with an element of statutory control. In general, cinema commercials are subject to the ASA's Advertising Code, but they must additionally be cleared by the CINEMA ADVERTISING ASSOCIATION's Copy Panel before prints are distributed to cinemas. As in the case of television commercials, and for the same reason, this process normally begins with submission of a script. Furthermore, all commercials of 30 seconds or longer must secure a certificate from the British Board of Film Classification.

The self-regulatory element of the British system of advertising control appears to work effectively. According to a survey carried out by the ASA in 1995, 98 per cent of posters and 96 per cent of press advertisements were 'found to be legal, decent, honest and truthful'.

The European Union has concerned itself with the harmonization of non-broadcast advertising regulation across national boundaries. The most significant EU measure to date has been the Misleading Advertising Directive of 1984, a 'framework law' setting out general principles which member states can implement by mechanisms appropriate to local culture and existing practices. In the case of the United Kingdom, the outcome was the Control of Misleading Advertisements Regulations 1988, which recognizes the Office of Fair Trading as the 'competent law enforcement agency' and the Advertising Standards Authority as one of the 'established means' of exercising control. In 1992, the EURO-PEAN ADVERTISING STANDARDS ALLIANCE was set up in Brussels to 'bring together advertising self regulatory bodies across Europe'. By 1997, it was represented in 19 European countries and Turkey, and had 'corresponding members' in South Africa and New Zealand.

Britain's particular tripartite system of advertising control is more often praised by commentators than criticised, at home and abroad, and is generally believed to work acceptably well. It is worth remembering that the advertisements of past times, especially the 1890s and 1920s, often far surpassed any present-day British campaigns in their transparently

dishonest claims. For instance, Coca-Cola was promoted as a 'brain tonic', the CARBOLIC SMOKE BALL promised to prevent influenza, 'Craven A' cigarettes were 'for your throat's sake', and Simpson's Iodine Impregnated Socks would cure an astonishing range of ailments unconnected with the feet, for instance. Unearned endorsements were rife, the Pope being only one of 'two infallible powers' and Prime Minister Gladstone apparently testifying to the ability of an 'electropathic belt' to cure, among more than a dozen other serious conditions, gout and epilepsy. (KC)

Advertising Council. The American (US) equivalent of the ADVERTISING ASSOCIATION.   (MJB)

advertising effectiveness. A vital measure of the outcome of an ADVERTISING CAMPAIGN. The INSTITUTE OF PRACTITIONERS IN ADVERTISING has sponsored the annual IPA Effectiveness Awards since 1980, and published twenty winning submissions as case studies every second year under the general title *Advertising Works. See* ADVERTISING TESTING.   (KC)

advertising expenditure. This can describe the amount spent on advertising by an individual firm or organization (*see* ADVERTISING APPROPRIATION), but is more usually taken to refer to the collective total of all advertising budgets within an industry group or a single country. Thus, total United Kingdom advertising expenditure in 1996 was £10.59 billion. This represents about £180 per capita and nearly £450 per household per annum; it is 1.4 per cent of the UK gross national product and 2.2 per cent of our total consumers' expenditure. As a proportion of GNP, it increased steadily after the recession of the late 1970s until 1989 and then fell for four consecutive years in this decade. A reversal of that trend over the last two years has returned the figure to its 1987 level, the fourth highest value it has ever reached. Internationally, UK total annual advertising expenditure is more than a billion ECUs above the average for 18 high-spending nations in a list compiled by the ADVERTISING ASSOCIATION. It accounts for 6.5 per cent of the collective total and ranks fourth, behind the USA, Japan and Germany. Britain is also fourth in terms of the proportion of GNP spent on advertising, this time behind Greece, Portugal and the USA. World expenditure is dominated by the United States, which accounts for almost half the total expenditure of the 18. Japan contributes almost a fifth, leaving 16 European countries to share the remaining third or so. Publications often contract 'advertising expenditure' to 'adspend'.   (KC)

advertising exposure. The presentation of an advertisement to an audience. Stimulus–response theory and HIERARCHY-OF-EFFECTS models regard exposure of an advertisement (a cue) as a necessary precondition of any subsequent action. It follows that a critical question for the advertiser must be 'how many exposures do I require to achieve the desired response?' *See also* OPPORTUNITIES TO SEE, RESPONSE FUNCTIONS.   (MJB)

advertising frequency. *See* ADVERTISING IMPACT.

advertising goals. *See* ADVERTISING OBJECTIVES.

advertising impact. One of three dimensions used in assessing ADVERTISING EXPOSURE and advertising response, the other two being reach and frequency. Impact is a qualitative concept and difficult to measure precisely whereas reach and frequency are objective and easier to quantify. Thus impact will vary according to the context in which the advertisement appears (which the advertiser may anticipate and seek to control) and the receiver's selective perception of both the advertisement and its context. Reach defines the number of receivers of an advertisement during a given time period, while frequency measures the number of times each receiver is exposed during the time period.   (MJB)

Advertising Investigation Department (AID). An antecedent of the ADVERTISING STANDARDS AUTHORITY (ASA). In 1948, the ADVERTISING ASSOCIATION published a 'British Code of Standards in Relation to the Advertising of Medicines and Treatments', seeking to control a product as characterized by flagrantly dishonest and misleading advertising, even 24 years after the self-regulation initiatives following the international convention at Wembley which provided the initial impetus for the formation of the Association. It simultaneously set up its own Advertising Investigation Department, to monitor advertisements for products other than patent medicines. Neither the Code nor the Department was backed by any kind of sanction against transgressors, however. Thirteen years later, a motion at the Advertising Association annual conference called for the establishment of an independent body to exercise self-regulatory control over advertising in non-broadcast media, the Independent Television Authority having

meanwhile devised a system for the control of television commercials. This was in effect a vote to formalize and extend the powers of the Advertising Investigation Department and resulted, in 1962, in the setting up of the ASA and the consequent demise of the AID.   (KC)

advertising manager. The generic job title of anyone with executive responsibility for ADVERTISING. However, the post does not exist in certain types of marketing company, particularly the FAST-MOVING CONSUMER GOODS manufacturers who tend to dominate the textbooks and everyday discussions about advertising. Here, BRAND MANAGERS (or their equivalents) normally assume responsibility for the advertising of their brand or brands. The distinction is that an advertising manager manages the advertising function for a whole company or division, typically including corporate and recruitment advertising as well as product advertising, but has no responsibility for other elements of the MARKETING MIX, whereas brand managers are responsible for the deployment of the whole marketing mix including advertising, but have no influence over advertising decisions relating to brands other than their own. The responsibility of one cuts vertically through the organization. that of the other spreads horizontally through it. It follows that the brand manager system requires some company-wide co-ordination of advertising at a more senior level. This responsibility is normally vested in managers or directors of 'marketing services', or perhaps just 'marketing'.

In practice, advertising managers usually deal with the whole MARKETING COMMUNICATIONS MIX: publicity. sales promotion. exhibitions and so on as well as advertising. But the traditional title tends to hang on, however inaccurate. To complicate the matter further, many business-to-business advertisers and several charities use the terms 'publicity department' and 'publicity manager' to describe what are in fact the advertising or marketing communications department and manager (*see* PUBLICITY). Advertising managers and publicity managers are the advertising agency ACCOUNT EXECUTIVE's contact on the client side of the agency–client relationship.   (KC)

advertising media. The means by which ADVERTISEMENTS are brought to the attention of a target audience. In Britain, the five 'major' advertising media are, in order of size, PRESS, TELEVISION, OUTDOOR, RADIO and CINEMA. 'Outdoor' is divided by media professionals into 'transport' and 'outdoor' or 'poster' categories. It is a point to remember when reading American marketing texts that cinema is not an advertising medium in the USA. 'Minor' advertising media is a large category including such opportunities for advertising messages as matchbooks, bus tickets, sports programmes, clothing or tethered balloons. 'Television' and 'radio' refer of course only to the independent services, since the BBC does not provide advertising opportunities.

Four of the five media are 'dual': they provide one product to the public (news, entertainment, and so on) and another to advertisers (the space or time in which to convey messages to a slice of that public). The press derives income from both sets of customers, via the COVER PRICE and the ADVERTISING RATES. Terrestrial television and radio, on the other hand, charge for only one of the two products, their revenue coming only from their ADVERTISING RATES and the sale of programme material to other broadcasters. They are thus 'free' to their listeners, subsidised by the advertisers, whereas newspapers and magazines are not – with the single exception of FREESHEETS – and neither is cinema. The poster medium is unique in being a non-dual medium, though one could argue intellectually that it provides the free public service of enlivening otherwise drab urban landscapes, if it is developed with restraint and a good design sense.

Advertising media are correctly subcategorised into MEDIA CLASSES, MEDIA VEHICLES AND MEDIA OPTIONS, but the term 'media' is often used to describe members of both of the first two categories. *See also*: MEDIA MIX, MEDIA SHARE. (KC)

advertising medium. The singular form of ADVERTISING MEDIA; the plural is not 'advertising mediums'. (KC)

advertising message. *See* MESSAGE EFFECT.

advertising objectives. These are called advertising 'goals' by some authors, but not the majority. In an ideal world, all ADVERTISING CAMPAIGNS should be underpinned by a set of sound and complete objectives. These should be (i) explicit; (ii) commonly agreed; (iii) unequivocal; (iv) specific advertising objectives; (v) calibrated; (vi) testable. The fact is, as surveys repeatedly show, that typical advertisers find it difficult to articulate objectives which meet these criteria. A real example will illustrate the problem. In a case history intended to demon-strate its skills and efficiency, an advertising agency explicitly stated five objectives for an advertising campaign. The list read: increase consumer awareness; rebuild trade confidence in the brand; motivate and support the trade; increase brand sales; increase market share. These were explicit, at least. Whether they had been commonly agreed before the campaign or whether the decision was a post-hoc rationalisation for the purposes of the case history must remain an open question. Four of the five do not relate specifically to advertising because they require the interaction of other elements of the MARKETING MIX. Those remaining are not calibrated. 'Increase awareness' is perhaps the most commonly encountered of all advertising objectives, but it fails to specify: of what, among which target audience, by how much, compared with when, and within what time period. It is furthermore untestable because it does not specify how the increase in awareness will be measured. Whether or not this list of objectives satisfies the last remaining criterion, being unequivocal, is more a subjective judgement than objective, but the point is in any case already made.

It is disturbing that this carelessness with objectives persists 35 years after Russell H. COLLEY'S celebrated treatise was reprinted in the *Harvard Business Review*. People remember his DAGMAR model of advertising effect but forget what the acronym stood for, which was the title of the treatise: 'Defining Advertising Goals for Measured Advertising Results'. The point is, of course, that meaningful measurement of effectiveness (see ADVERTISING TESTING) is impossible unless satisfactory objectives have first been specified. Colley himself listed 52 advertising 'goals' which might be relevant in practice, and they are an object lesson to practitioners in satisfying the criteria of usefulness offered above. (KC)

advertising penetration. A measure of ADVERTISING EFFECTIVENESS that indicates the proportion of the target market who can remember a significant part of the advertising message. (MJB)

advertising platform. *See* COPY PLATFORM.

advertising rates. MEDIA OWNERS' unit charges for ADVERTISING SPACE or ADVERTISING TIME. They are published in the media owners' own RATE CARDS and, except in the case of TELEVISION and

RADIO, in BRAD (q.v.). Standard rates are modified by both surcharges and discounts. The former are levied for the privilege of 'fixing' the time of COMMERCIALS or securing SPECIAL POSITIONS in newspapers and magazines, and for special print processes such as BLEED. The latter are for volume, series bookings or accepting a package deal. In addition, sophisticated or powerful advertising agency MEDIA BUYERS may be able to haggle successfully for further discounts in favourable circumstances.   (KC)

advertising research. Often taken to be synonymous with ADVERTISING TESTING, this term in fact embraces a wider variety of activities which might be summarized as: formative research; developmental research; concept testing; pre-evaluation; post-testing. Formative research is that carried out before 'concept generation' even begins, to establish the necessary background knowledge about – for instance – the beliefs of potential target audiences about the whole system of behaviour into which consumption of an advertised product fits. Developmental research, as the name clearly enough implies, relates to the progressive development of the advertising concept after it has been born out of the formative investigations. At the end of the 'concept development' stage, there will typically be a number of contenders for eventual translation into the main campaign concept; 'concept testing' procedures sort out the winners from the losers. Pre-evaluation and post-evaluation are described under ADVERTISING, TESTING. 'Advertising research' is not generally taken to include MEDIA RESEARCH.   (KC)

advertising schedule. A formal document setting out the timing of individual ADVERTISEMENTS in an ADVERTISING CAMPAIGN. Often called the 'campaign schedule' and more or less synonymous with MEDIA SCHEDULE.   (KC)

advertising space. That part of the total page-space in newspapers and magazines which is allocated by the MEDIA OWNERS to advertising rather than editorial matter. Sale of this commodity contributes to total revenue alongside income from the COVER PRICE. Until recently, the cinema industry also used the term, rather than the more logical ADVERTISING TIME. *See also*: ADVERTISING-TO-EDITORIAL RATIO.   (KC)

Advertising Standards Authority (ASA). A British self-regulatory body established in 1962, to devise a code of practice and a means for securing compliance with it, which aims to 'ensure that its system of self-regulation works effectively in the public interest'. Its origins lie in 1948, when the ADVERTISING ASSOCIATION published a British Code of Standards in Relation to the Advertising of Medicines and Treatments, advertisements for which were still characterized by flagrantly dishonest and misleading claims even 24 years after earlier self-regulatory initiatives, and simultaneously set up an Advertising Investigation Department to monitor advertising in general. In 1961, a motion was passed at the Advertising Association's annual conference which effectively formalised and extended that 13-year-old Department's powers, calling for the establishment of a fully independent body to regulate the content of all non-broadcast advertising and thereby complement the system for regulation of television advertising that had made its appearance in the interim. The outcome, a year later, was the ASA.

Though set up by the advertising business, it maintains a scrupulous independence from media owners, advertising agencies or advertisers. Its operation is financed by a surcharge on display advertising: *see* ADVERTISING STANDARDS BOARD OF FINANCE. A chairman who has no previous connection with the business appoints 12 council members, two-thirds of whom must be 'independent of any advertising interest' and all of whom must 'serve as individuals, not as representatives of any other body or section of the public'. The ASA publishes the BRITISH CODES OF ADVERTISING AND SALES PROMOTION (until 1995, separate Codes of Advertising Practice and Sales Promotion Practice) which set out criteria of acceptability. Its main function is to investigate complaints about non-broadcast advertising, mostly originating from the general public: *see* ADVERTISING CONTROL. Details of subsequent judgements are issued in Monthly Reports to the news media and other interested parties. In the case of upheld complaints, the ASA appeals to the advertiser to withdraw or modify the advertisement. If this produces no response, it directs the media owners involved, whose trade associations are all signatories to the Codes, to deny space to the advertiser in future and refuse COMMISSION to the advertising agency. The ASA has the final sanction option of referring the whole case to the OFFICE OF FAIR TRADING.   (KC)

Advertising Standards Board of Finance (ASBOF). Set up in 1974 by the ADVERTISING STANDARDS AUTHORITY to finance its own operations, ASBOF collects via the MEDIA OWNERS a

0.1 per cent levy on the price paid by British advertisers for all ADVERTISING SPACE except that occupied by CLASSIFIED ADVERTISING. Its remit does not extend to broadcast advertising, which is controlled by the INDEPENDENT BROADCASTING AUTHORITY. ASBOF revenue has been applied in particular to the task of informing the public that the ASA control mechanism exists, via advertising and publicity. As a result, the number of complaints processed jumped sharply from 300 in 1974 to more than 1,300 in 1976. The figure had shown signs of stabilising during the 1980s at between 7,000 and 8,000 per year, but has since risen again to reach its highest level so far in 1995, at 12,800 complaints about 7,700 advertisements.   (KC)

advertising testing. The process of measuring the effectiveness of an advertisement or an advertising campaign. Measurements can be carried out before the advertising finally runs (PRE-TEST) or after the campaign has started (POST-TEST), on a sample of the eventual target audience. Many of the established testing techniques are applicable to both situations; some are specific to one or the other.

Ideally, measurement of effectiveness should be a straightforward matter of comparing actual performance with specific criteria derived from predetermined objectives. Practice is seldom ideal, however, because practitioners – both ADVERTISING AGENCIES and ADVERTISERS – fail to articulate objectives which are usable for the purpose: see ADVERTISING OBJECTIVES. The vacuum left is filled by ready-made, general-purpose test methods. There is no doubt about the range and sophistication of advertising testing procedures available, but it should be understood that they are not as a rule 'bespoke' tests, specific to the peculiar circumstances of a given advertising campaign. Furthermore, it is not always easy to recognize the surrogate criterion they are actually measuring.

It can be argued that the standard procedures are in fact implicitly based on a HIERARCHY-OF-EFFECTS model of how advertising works, widely used as the conceptual framework for the literature of advertising in general. The six 'levels' or steps of this hierarchy provide the substitute objectives and hence the criteria of effectiveness. The result is that an advertisement is required to 'pass a test', rather than to demonstrate its effectiveness by satisfying specific criteria derived from specific objectives. The relationship of such a test to real effectiveness may be no stronger than

that of the standard driving test to driving ability: it measures only what it measures. Space does not permit one-by-one description of the substantial number of advertising tests available today. Instead, the most commonly encountered are separately described in their alphabetical turn, each time explicitly related to the relevant level in the hierarchy-of-effects. *See especially* ATTITUDE MEASUREMENT, LABORATORY TESTS, READING-AND-NOTING, RECALL testing.

Authors have remarked on a surprising tendency among practitioners not to test advertising campaigns at all, which is not what the interested but non-expert outsider would expect. Possible reasons are: the cost of making any modifications which a pre-test might indicate; reluctance on the part of advertising agencies to risk an unflattering pre-evaluation; the over-and-done-with syndrome, where post-testing is concerned; reluctance on the part of clients to discover an unwelcome truth; and vested interest in general. However, it would be improper to close without reiterating that no one doubts the skill and sophistication of British advertising researchers, whose reputation is high in the world, nor the breadth of their techniques. It is the conceptual underpinning of the tests which is questionable.   (KC)

advertising time. That part of total radio and television broadcasting time which is allocated by the MEDIA OWNERS to advertising rather than programmes, also called AIRTIME. Sale of this commodity in SPOTS contributes the majority of their revenue, increasingly supplemented by SPONSORSHIP arrangements with advertisers. (KC)

advertising-to-editorial ratio. The proportion of ADVERTISING SPACE relative to editorial matter in newspapers and magazines. The equivalent term with respect to ADVERTISING TIME is 'MINUTAGE'. The concept of such a ratio cannot really be applied to the OUTDOOR medium, unless in terms of the greater or lesser degree of 'visual clutter' created by a given number of poster sites in an urban landscape. Whereas television advertising minutage is statutorily regulated, advertising-to-editorial ratios reflect managerial balancing of the need for advertising revenue against the risk of losing readers, and vary considerably among the many thousand newspapers and magazines published in Britain. They are generally very high in the FREESHEETS, up to two-thirds in magazines and the up-market Sunday papers, and as low as one-third in the popular tabloids. Despite the fact that these ratios are far higher than broadcast advertising minutage, critics of advertising are less likely to comment on the interruption of newspaper or magazine stories by advertisements than on the intrusion of commercials into television programmes. (KC)

advertising-to-sales ratio (A/S ratio). (1) The ratio of total advertising expenditure in an industry sector to its total sales revenue. The UK figures are published annually by the ADVERTISING ASSOCIATION, in its *Advertising Statistics Yearbook*. In 1996, for example, brewers spent 0.5 per cent of sales on advertising whereas the double-glazing companies collectively allocated an extraordinary 77 per cent to the advertising effort. In between these extremes are, in round figures: soft drinks at 1.5 per cent, cars at 2, books at 3, petfood at 4, garden tools at 5, toys and games at 7, breakfast cereals at 9, detergents at 11, and indigestion remedies at 20 per cent of sales.

(2) One of the three most popular ways to set the size of the ADVERTISING APPROPRIATION. (KC)

advertising wearout. *See* WEAROUT.

advertorial. The colloquial description of editorial mention given in a newspaper or magazine to an organization, its products or its services because it has bought advertising in the publication. The most common example is 'advertisement features' in newspapers, which actually operate the other way round: companies are sold advertising on the grounds that they will be simultaneously mentioned in a review of fitted kitchens or whatever. It is also common in CONTROLLED-CIRCULATION BUSINESS-TO-BUSINESS magazines. The rationale is that readers are sceptical about what they are told by advertisers but believe what they read in the editorial columns. This is a dubious proposition, given the high standards of ADVERTISING CONTROL and frequently low standards of tabloid journalism in contemporary Britain. The practice is in any case tolerated only in very specific circumstances, British publishers otherwise observing the editorial/advertising distinction very carefully. 'Advertorial' is not the same thing as editorial mention in response to a PRESS RELEASE. The key difference is the involvement of paid-for advertising in the transaction. (KC)

affect. *See* ATTITUDE.

affective component. In a FACTOR ANALYSIS (one form of which is called component analysis) this is a factor which shows the communality between all affective attributions. (SKT)

affordable method. Determination of a budget, particularly for advertising, at a level which management thinks it can afford. *See* ADVERTISING APPROPRIATION. (MJB)

age groups. *See* SOCIO-ECONOMIC CLASSIFICATION.

agent. A third party or intermediary who acts on behalf of his principal in negotiations with customers. (MJB)

aggressive types. *See* INTERPERSONAL RESPONSE TRAITS.

AID. *See* ADVERTISING INVESTIGATION DEPARTMENT and AUTOMATIC INTERACTION DETECTOR.

AIDA. An acronym for Attention, Interest, Desire and Action, a HIERARCHY-OF-EFFECTS model first proposed by Strong in 1924. *See* ATTITUDE. (MJB)

aided recall. *See* RECALL TESTING.

AIRC. *See* ASSOCIATION OF INDEPENDENT RADIO CONTRACTORS.

airtime. That part of total broadcasting time on commercial television and radio which is allocated by the MEDIA OWNERS to advertising rather than programme material. Sale of this commodity accounts for almost all of their total revenue. *See also*: ADVERTISING-TO-EDITORIAL RATIO; COMMERCIAL BREAK; SPOT. (KC)

aisle. The passageway between display stands in a SUPERMARKET. (MDP)

à la carte. A term used to describe, by analogy with ordering from a menu, a situation in which advertisers buy in advertising services from individual suppliers as and when needed, rather than retaining the services of an advertising agency, media independent or creative shop. Several of the services may in fact be provided by some or all of these three kinds of service organization; the essential point of difference is that *à la carte* services are bought on an *ad hoc* basis, whereas advertising agencies and the two variants are normally retained on longer-term contracts. (KC)

allocation. The process of breaking a homogeneous supply down into smaller lots, commonly performed by wholesalers who 'break bulk' by purchasing full truck loads but selling case quantities.   (AJB)

allowance. A sum of money offered by a seller either as an incentive to a prospective customer to buy or as compensation for damage or inferior performance by a product. Allowances are frequently offered to encourage a customer to trade-in a durable product such as a car, washing machine or piece of industrial equipment in exchange for a new one. Allowances are also offered to retailers to encourage them to carry a product or to give it more shelf space at the point of sale.   (MJB)

alternative forms reliability. In psychological testing or ATTITUDE scale construction, this is the assessment of reliability by having two alternative forms of the test or scale. The alternative forms reliability is calculated by the PEARSON CORRELATION COEFFICIENT between scores on the alternative forms.   (SKT)

AMA. See AMERICAN MARKETING ASSOCIATION.

American Marketing Association (AMA). Formed in 1937, the AMA has long been respected as the leading US association for professionals involved in the broad spectrum of marketing careers. As a non-profit educational organization, AMA is led by a volunteer board of directors responsible for policy decisions and general management of the Association's activities. Elected officers are supported by a professional staff headquartered in Chicago. The Association, which has about 35,000 members, serves as a vehicle for interchange between its primary membership components, namely practitioners, educators and students and its publications include the biweekly *Marketing News,* and the quarterly *Journal of Marketing* and *Journal of Marketing Research.*   (GA)

AMSAC. See ATTWOOD MULTI-SEGMENTED ANALYSIS OF CONSUMERS.

analysis. That stage in the research process when data are examined for relationships among observed variables. For example, if a relationship between occupation and income is hypothesized, the data would be examined or analysed to confirm or refute that hypothesis. Analysis can be quantitative or qualitative, depending upon what type of data is collected.   (KAB)

analysis of covariance (ANCOVA). A statistical procedure for the ANALYSIS OF VARIANCE on a residualized variable. A residualized variable is adjusted for the effects of a covariate or covariates by using the residual after a regression model is fitted. It is of most value when there is a high correlation between the dependent variable and the covariates. For example, if you want to test the effect of alternative ADVERTISEMENTS on reading achievement, it is wise to adjust for the effects of reading ability, which will be highly correlated with reading achievement. A residualized version of reading achievement will present analysis of variance with a variable that has those parts of it that can be predicted from reading ability removed. The residual parts of reading achievement may well include some that are influenced by alternative advertisements.   (SKT)

analysis of variance (ANOVA). A statistical procedure for assessing the influence of a categorical variable (or variables) on the variance of a dependent variable. The key concept of the procedure is a comparison of variation between groups (how much each subgroup MEAN differs from the overall mean) and the variation within groups (how much each observation differs from the subgroup mean). If there is more variation attributable to between-groups differences, one may interpret some influence of the categorical variable (or factor) over the dependent variable. The F-test is used to decide whether there is more between group variation than within group variation: adjustments for the size of groups and numbers of subjects are made through DEGREES OF FREEDOM.   (SKT)

anchor label. In comparative judgements, the label against which other stimuli are compared.   (SKT)

anchor stores. A term used to describe major retailers who will act as a focal point in a retail development and so attract other more specialized or less well known outlets to take up space in the development. In the UK firms such as Marks & Spencer, Sainsbury or John Lewis would be considered anchor stores.   (MJB)

ANCOVA. See ANALYSIS OF COVARIANCE.

animatic. An approximation to the final form of a television COMMERCIAL, typically made by an advertising agency to secure its clients approval in principle before significant sums of money are committed to studio or location production. It may also be useful during the process of compulsory pre-clearance for airing: *see* ADVERTISING CONTROL. Until recently, animatics were in effect STORYBOARDS, shot under a static television camera and enlivened in the editing suite by a repertoire of cuts, zooms, pulls, pans, rotations and dissolves. Today, widespread access to Macintosh computer-graphics software permits agencies to produce an altogether more sophisticated end result from the same initial sketches that would formerly have been the individual frames of the storyboard. Furthermore, the availability of even more affordable, good-quality VHS recording and editing means that animatics are in practice often replaced, in the case of what will eventually be a conventional live-action commercial, by video 'prototypes' that lack only such costly elements as the actual locations and actors. (KC)

animation. In television and cinema production, a range of techniques for creating the illusion of live action by optical means in an animation studio. The most familiar form of animation is the animated cartoon, which is executed by producing a very large number of separate drawings, each presenting the scene a moment in time on from the last, photographing each one and finally joining them together as consecutive frames in a length of movie film. It is in widespread use for the production of television and cinema commercials, usually on its own but sometimes in combination with live action. Three-dimensional models may be used instead of drawings, for a particular effect. Recently, the increasing availability of computer graphics via the system for the electronic editing of video recordings has brought a new dimension of sophistication to animation. (KC)

Annual Abstract of Statistics. A comprehensive collection of statistics covering the UK. It contains data on population, manufacturing, social services, justice, finance, education, transport and defence. (MJB)

annual plan. A short-term operational plan covering a year's operations. Such plans are usually very detailed and disaggregated into a series of budgets which are monitored closely on a weekly and monthly basis for departures or variances between planned and actual performance so that corrective action may be taken as necessary. The

annual plan is itself derived from the firm's long-term plan. (MJB)

ANOVA. *See* ANALYSIS OF VARIANCE.

antecedent questions. *See* OPEN-ENDED QUESTIONS.

antedate. Date earlier than arranged. (GM)

antitrust. US antitrust legislation aims at curtailing monopolistic practices by private business and ensuring competition. Antitrust legislation developed in the USA in response to the numerous monopolies that arose because of the growth of big business and lack of government controls in the second half of the nineteenth century. By 1900 half the nation's railways were controlled by six financial groups which could manipulate rates. J.D. Rockefeller's Standard Oil Trust controlled most of American oil refining, US Steel controlled most steel production. Similar powerful trusts existed in meat-packing, sugar, lead and tobacco industries.

Although the first US antitrust laws were enacted in Kansas in 1889, the first Federal Law was the Sherman Antitrust Act of 1890. This made it illegal to monopolize trade or conspire to restrain trade or inhibit competition. However, these terms were not clearly defined. Consequently it was unclear as to what amounted to a violation of the Act.

In 1914 the Federal Trade Commission Act of 26 September created the Federal Trade Commission, empowering it to police competition by preventing persons, partnerships and corporations from using unfair methods of competition. In October of the same year (1914), the Clayton Antitrust Act tried to define illegal behaviour more specifically, and outlawed price discrimination.

Further strengthening of legislation has included the 1936 Robinson-Patman Act, which amended the Clayton Act in relation to price discrimination by prohibiting excessive quantity discounts to large buyers and 'unreasonable' low retail prices, and the Celler Antimerger Act of 1950, aimed at preventing stock acquisition which might hinder competition.

In reality, the effectiveness of all antitrust regulation has depended upon how the courts have interpreted it and the willingness of the US Department of Justice's Antitrust Division to investigate and prosecute alleged violations of the law. Some administrations have been more firm in their approach than others. Furthermore, it is often a difficult task to prevent a firm from acquiring too much market power and maintain the incentive to grow larger than its competitors. Large firms are often more efficient than smaller ones and it has been claimed that antitrust legislation can penalize them for this. Not surprisingly, the impact of antitrust legislation has not been clear-cut or consistent.   (JK)

anxiety. In strict psychological terms, a state of neurotic fear about some future or anticipated event (as distinct from normal fear, which is a direct response to a present threat). In a marketing context anxiety may be used in both a negative and positive way. In a negative mode, FEAR APPEALS seek to discourage particular behaviour such as smoking by drawing attention to the link between smoking and lung cancer. Conversely, by playing upon a person's fear of being ostracized or excluded because of bad breath or body odour one may encourage increased consumption of personal toiletries.

Fear-inducing advertising which plays upon people's emotions and stimulates anxiety as a drive to modify behaviour has been subject to much criticism. Further, in some areas such as health advertising, playing upon the audience's fears and anxieties has been found to be counter-productive as it creates DISSONANCE and is suppressed or screened out by the receiver.(MJB)

appeals. *See* MESSAGE EFFECTS.

arbitrage. An attempt to profit from price differences in different markets by buying in one and selling in the other simultaneously.   (MJB)

arbitrary approach. A term used to describe the setting of a budget or appropriation (usually for advertising or promotion) where a senior manager decides upon a sum of money without apparent reference to any objective facts. *See also* ADVERTISING APPROPRIATION.   (MJB)

area sampling. (1) A statistical SAMPLING procedure which involves clusters that are spatial areas. The areas (enumeration districts, POSTCODE sectors) serve as the primary sampling units. The POPULATION is divided exhaustively into a series of such areas and a random sample of the areas is selected.

(2) In the MARKET RESEARCH context, that type of sampling which is not necessarily followed by enumeration or RANDOM SAMPLING of the selected

areas, rather by QUOTA SAMPLING. Sampling of areas using AUTOMATIC INTERACTION DETECTOR (AID).   (SKT)

art director. The job title of those working on the GRAPHICS side in the creative department of an ADVERTISING AGENCY. 'Director' is used here in the same sense as in the film industry, defining their role in 'art direction' of advertisements, and does not imply a seat on the board. An art director normally works in tandem with a COPYWRITER on the translation of advertising strategy into advertisements. The board-level post is Creative Director, with responsibility for all the agency's teams of art directors and copywriters (or at least a substantial cohort of them, in very large agencies).   (KC)

article numbering. The development of a merchandise classification system which allocates numbers to stock-keeping units has been achieved in the grocery supplier industry and by some of the larger firms of retailers, manufacturers and business machine producers. The numbers allocated to the article or product are reproduced on the article label in a machine-readable form; the number is recorded at the point of sale to permit the capture of sales data using number reading equipment linked directly or indirectly to a computer. *See also* BAR CODE, UNIVERSAL PRODUCT CODE.   (AJB)

artwork. The raw material of a press advertisement, poster or print item, produced by the creative department of an ADVERTISING AGENCY, a design consultancy or the advertiser's own advertising department. Until recently, the development of artwork began with hand-drawn 'roughs' or 'scamps' produced in response to a 'creative brief' by a 'visualiser', usually passed through a number of modifications and re-workings, and ended with high-quality 'finished art' produced by a 'finished artist'. That would be married with the result of 'photo-typesetting' the accompanying text, by a 'paste-up artist', to produce 'camera-ready artwork', in the necessary condition for use as a master in the printing process. Today, Macintosh technology has largely replaced the traditional hardware: magic markers, Letraset, scalpels, spray-mount adhesive, Bristol board and the rest. The generic terms 'Mac operator' and, less disparagingly, 'Mac artist' have taken over in advertising agency creative departments and at design houses. The new artwork-production process generally still begins with a hand-drawn scamp, though a remarkable range of basic visual elements can now be taken from proprietary Macintosh software or obtained on CD from specialist suppliers, and manipulated on-screen as many times as necessary to arrive at a version approved for development into a finished advertisement. Thereafter, program suites with such self-explanatory names as 'freehand', 'illustrator' and 'photoshop' are used to compose the graphic elements, and computer-generated typefaces to set the text. The resulting output on disk can then be transferred digitally to an 'image setter', which will transform it via an integral output-processor into the 'bromide' photo-transparency required as the master for conventional printing processes. This last stage in the process is now being overtaken by technology, as the publications in which the advertisements appear and the printers who produce brochures and the like acquire the facility to work direct from disks, or to download digital information from the originating computer via the ISDN data-transmission network. As an advertisement for a 'digital imaging service' put it: 'no film, no plates, no hassle ... digital printing direct from disk'. The traditional art-studio skills are not totally redundant, however, for agencies still present material for client approval during the process in the form of artwork pasted-up on boards or made up into dummies of printed pieces. It is more practical to hand such material round the participants in a meeting than to have them look at a computer screen, and easier for most people to visualize the finished product. (KC)

ASA. *See* ADVERTISING STANDARDS AUTHORITY.

ASBOF. *See* ADVERTISING STANDARDS BOARD OF FINANCE.

aspirational group. A group to which an individual aspires (wishes) to belong. (MJB)

A/S ratio. Stands for 'advertising-to-sales ratio'. *See* ADVERTISING APPROPRIATION. (KC)

assets. Resources of the company which have the following properties: (a) legally belong to the company, (b) have real or perceived future benefits, (c) the benefits must be exclusive to the time or service (d) the item must have been acquired as a result of a transaction of the firm. Assets can be classed as fixed or current. Fixed assets refer to such items as buildings, machinery and fix-

tures and fittings. Current assets refer to such items as cash, STOCK and debtors. (GM)

asset turnover. The ratio of sales to net operating assets. It is a measure of how efficiently the company is using its operating assets. As with all ratios, percentages and yields, they are of little use if viewed in isolation. (GM)

Association of Independent Radio Contractors (AIRC). A non-profit trade body set up in 1973 to represent the new independent local radio (ILR) stations in Britain, which changed its name in 1996 to COMMERCIAL RADIO COMPANIES ASSOCIATION. (KC)

assorting. Building up an assortment of items for use in association with each other. The assortment may be sought by industrial buyers or consumer buyers. The provision of an assortment allows all types of buyers to make their purchases with a minimum of searching time. (AJB)

assortment strategies. Retail assortments may be varied according to two major characteristics: width and depth. The width of the assortment (or range) describes the number of different product categories which are represented in the assortment while the depth refers to the number of varieties, colours, or sizes represented in each category. The depth and width are determined by the marketing strategy being used by the retailer. (AJB)

attention. One possible result of exposure to advertisements, which is therefore an ADVERTISING OBJECTIVE and a criterion of advertising effectiveness. *See* HIERARCHY OF EFFECTS and ADVERTISING TESTING.

In television audience measurement, the definition of attention is problematical. 'When mention is now made of attention research it is usually a reference to numerous studies conducted by the major advertising agencies in the 1960s. These adopted a negative definition of attention: not doing something else that intuitively would distract from watching television. Reading a book was for example classified as non-attentive behaviour while drinking tea was attentive. Typical findings were that about three-quarters of the present housewife audience was defined as attentive at peak and later evening times.' (*Admap*, February 1980) Attention research was aimed at the goal of systematically discounting BARB viewing figures to account for the sporadic nature of attention. *See also* PRESENCE. (KC)

attitude. One of the most frequently invoked behavioural science concepts in marketing. While its relationship to behaviour is not entirely clear, the frequent association between attitude and likely future action has resulted in extensive use of attitude surveys in the area of new-product development and in the design and execution of many promotional campaigns. Similarly, public opinion (belief or attitudes) is playing an increasing role in shaping and modifying corporate policy in areas such as consumer protection. It follows that a basic understanding of the current state of knowledge of attitude theory is vital to the student of marketing.

Just as there is no single agreed definition of marketing, so there is a multiplicity of definitions of 'attitude'. In broad terms most of these definitions fall into one of two categories which reflect two basic models in current use, which may be defined as the cognitive-affective-conative (CAC) and expectancy-value (EV) models. The cognitive-affective-conative model has been traced back to Plato's elements of the human soul – reasonable, spirited, appetitive – which in more modern terms may be defined as the realms of thought, emotions and motives, or knowing, feeling and acting. Marketers have developed a number of variants of their own of the CAC model and some of the better known examples are contained in Figure 4 under the general heading of hierarchy-of-effects models. In all the marketing versions, starting with Strong's AIDA (1924) and progressing through Lavidge and Steiner (1961), Rogers (1962) to Engel, Kollat and Blackwell (1968), it is assumed that one proceeds from awareness (cognitive) to preference (affective) to action (conative) – an assumption of the direction of cause and effect for which there is little empirical support. In fact it is widely recognized that frequently one or more stages occur simultaneously, e.g. awareness and evaluation, while impulse purchases suggest that the cognitive and conative may occur together and that the affective may, or may not, follow. Despite these deficiencies the CAC model enjoys wide support, and the effectiveness of marketing strategy is often measured in terms of its ability to move consumers up the hierarchy of effects, i.e. from unawareness to awareness, from desire to action – in other words, attitude is seen as a predisposition to act. The expectancy-value model views attitude as comprising two components – beliefs and values – which are broadly equivalent to the cognitive and affective dimensions of the CAC model. It follows that the EV model is lacking a behavioural or action element and so is much more limited in its application.

The EV model is particularly associated with the work of Martin Fishbein, who built upon the work of Rosenberg, which in turn was developed from Fritz Heider's consistency model. In essence Fishbein argues that an attitude comprises two components – beliefs about the attributes of an object and the values ascribed to these beliefs. In order to maintain consistency (or balance, or congruity, as it is sometimes called) consumers need to act in accordance with their beliefs and the values associated with them. Thus, while EV models do not seek to establish a link between attitude and behaviour the association between expressed beliefs and action is strong where action occurs, i.e. beliefs experienced about different brands have been found to

	Strong *(AIDA)*	*Lavidge and* *Steiner*	*Rogers*	*Engel, Kollat* *and Blackwell*
CONATIVE (motive)	ACTION	PURCHASE CONVICTION	ADOPTION TRIAL	PURCHASE PROCESSES
AFFECTIVE (emotion)	DESIRE INTEREST	PREFERENCE LIKING	EVALUATION INTEREST	EVALUATION & SEARCH
COGNITIVE (thought)	AWARENESS	KNOWLEDGE AWARENESS	AWARENESS	PROBLEM RECOGNITION
		UNAWARENESS		

Figure 4: **Hierarchy-of-effects models**

be good predictors of actual brand preference, where the person expressing a belief about a brand actually consumes an item from that product category. However, there is a world of difference between holding a neutral or positive belief about a product and a willingness to buy it, e.g. 'I believe Romeo and Juliet cigars are of the highest quality, but I would never buy them, because I do not smoke.'

This latter caveat is particularly important and explains why the EV model is theoretically more acceptable than the CAC model, which extends the link between an attitude as a predisposition to act into behaviour without specifying the catalyst which makes action necessary. From a practical point of view this missing link is of crucial importance in converting the results of attitude surveys into realistic sales forecasts.   (MJB)

attitude balance theory. *See* ATTITUDE.

attitude clusters. The tripartite (C-A-C) model of ATTITUDE maintains that attitudes are unlikely to exist in complete isolation. Robertson *et al.* (T. S. Robertson, J. Zielinski and S. Ward, *Consumer Behaviour,* Glenview: Scott Foresman, 1984) propose the view that 'an individual's COGNITIONS about music, for example, may tend to relate to cognitions about entertainment or relaxation'. Therefore attitudes as a whole are thought to form CLUSTERS with consonant attitudes within the individual's attitudinal system – a person believing staunchly in the policies of the Conservative Party would therefore not be expected to favour the leader of the Labour Party as the next Prime Minister.   (GKP)

attitude dimension. Any factor, positive or negative, on which an attitude is based. The more intense and/or the more complex the factors on which an attitude is based the more difficult it is to change the attitude. *See* ATTITUDE MEASUREMENT, SCALING TECHNIQUES.   (MJB)

attitude measurement. The assignment to each individual of a numerical score indicating where he falls on the particular ATTITUDE DIMENSION on the basis of inferences drawn from the responses of the individual to statements directly related to that object or idiom that is the locus of the study (i.e. the attitude-object); measurement therefore is an open and direct reaction to the statements included within the ATTITUDE SCALE giving a numerical score of the strength of beliefs, feelings and inclination to take action in a given situation such as towards a product range, a brand name, a marketing practice etc.   (JLD)

attitude research. MARKET RESEARCH undertaken to analyse the behaviour and MOTIVATIONS of people as CONSUMERS. Most research of this type is undertaken using qualitative methods as a result of the great complexity of human behaviour. *See* QUALITATIVE RESEARCH.   (AMW)

attitude scale. One of the most widely used devices for measuring attitudes, consisting of a set of statements or items to which the individual responds.   (JLD)

attitude survey. Adapting ATTITUDE SCALE techniques to personal interviewing of large systematic samples of defined populations.   (JLD)

attribution theory. *See* SELF-PERCEPTION THEORY.

Attwood Consumer Panel. A long-established PANEL which monitors and reports trends in CONSUMER buying/consumption behaviour on a regular basis. *See also* PANEL RESEARCH.   (MJB)

Attwood Multi-Segmented Analysis of Consumers (AMSAC). In addition to their household CONSUMER PANEL, Attwood operates an individual panel of 15,000 members which is based on the cooperation of the individuals in the main panel homes. AMSAC is designed to measure those PRODUCT categories where a purchase decision is more likely to be made by an individual member of the household rather than by the housewife, e.g. cigarettes, records and tapes, toiletries and cosmetics.   (GKP)

audience measurement. The process of computing audience numbers exposed to advertising on television, radio, posters and in the cinema. *See* ABC, BARB, CAVIAR, JICPAR, JICREG, NRS, OSCAR, POSTAR, VFD.   (KC)

audience profile. A demographic and perhaps sociographic description of a television, radio or cinema audience. As vital a media planning variable as all the measures of quantity put together. *See also* READERSHIP PROFILE.   (KC)

audience research. Though it is generally taken to mean much the same thing as AUDIENCE MEASUREMENT, this broader term carries the implication that the audience may be measured demographically and psychographically (that is, in terms of behaviour patterns), rather than simply being counted. (KC)

audimeter. A device for monitoring television usage over a 24-hour cycle and recording any change lasting longer than 30 seconds. Nielsen television ratings in the USA are based upon a sample of 1,200 homes equipped with audimeters. A similar device is used in the UK for measuring audience size. *See* BARB. (MJB)

Audit Bureau of Circulations (ABC). Organizations in the UK and the USA which fulfil the same function under the same name but are otherwise unrelated. In Britain, it is a limited company founded in 1931, which is independent of media owners, advertising agencies or advertisers but has board members representing all three. Its function is to certify a net per-issue sale figure for newspapers and magazines, averaged over the six-month periods to the end of June and to the end of December each year. 'Sale' is defined as a copy bought by an individual and not received in any other way; bulk sales to companies or organizations and free copies are specifically excluded. The certified figure is described as the 'ABC circulation' of the publication in question, and is published in BRAD (q.v.). It is available for over 3,000 British and international newspapers, consumer magazines and business periodicals. *See also* CIRCULATION. (KC)

audit, distribution. The control tools of physical distribution systems are the regular auditing of inventory, freight costs, warehouse costs and order-processing times. In the past, these audits were often conducted separately but in the 1970s a form of output budgeting, the total function audit, became increasingly popular. These were conducted at intervals of five years and served as a basis for replanning the logistical system. (AJB)

audit, marketing. A set of techniques and activities designed to reveal and analyse the strengths and weaknesses of the marketing functions of a business organization. The marketing audit may frequently be an important element in the review of a business whose total activities are under scrutiny by external consultants. More routinely, the marketing audit is the initiating procedure in the compilation of annual marketing plans. (JRB)

audit, technique. *See* CONSUMER PANELS.

augmented product. The complete bundle of attributes perceived by or offered to an individual buyer. The bundle incorporates: (a) the properties of the CORE PRODUCT; (b) the specific properties differentiating the offering of one supplier by contrast with another; (c) the attendant elements of CUSTOMER SERVICE (whether pre-/during/post-transaction), which when added to the core and differentiated product features influence the customer's tastes and preferences. Many products that are indistinguishable physically become the preferred products of consumers because of these added features. (KNB, GA)

automatic checkout machine (ACM). A scanning device which allows shoppers to record their purchases by reading their barcodes. Payment may be made at the checkout or by using an authorised credit card. (MJB)

automatic interaction detector (AID). A statistical technique designed to produce distinct subgroups on the basis of one dependent variable and a series of categorical variables. Originally due to Sonquist and Morgan (J.A. Sonquist and J.N. Morgan, *The Detection of Interaction Effects,* Institute of Social Research Monograph no. 35, Chicago: University of Michigan, 1964), it involves the setting of criteria for separation of subgroups. Some believe it is unwisely named, for it is not automatic, and neither does it detect interaction (at least not in the same way as ANALYSIS OF VARIANCE). (SKT)

automatic reorder. The ordering of replacement stock when inventory levels fall to a predetermined threshold. The approach is widely adopted for staple items which fall into the category of STRAIGHT REBUY where the buyer does not need to re-evaluate the purchase decision. Such orders may be placed manually but, increasingly, are part of a computer-based system linking buyer and seller automatically without human intervention. (MJB)

automatic vending. The sale and delivery of products through automatic vending machines. The machine is operated by coin (or occasionally by currency note) and has been used in the sale of confectionery, beverages, cigarettes, petrol, snacks and a few non-food products. Servicing costs are high compared to the product unit value. (AJB)

autonomic decision making. Decision making within a family group in which partners assume individual responsibility for certain categories of decisions. For example, males tend to assume responsibility for decisions related to car equipment like tyres and batteries whereas females assume responsibility for most categories of household goods, over-the-counter medicines etc. *See* SYNCRATIC DECISION MAKING. (MJB)

auxiliary equipment. *See* INDUSTRIAL GOODS.

availability. A necessary but not sufficient condition for purchase. The more frequently a product is purchased and the less thought that is given to each individual purchase, the greater the importance of having products available in stock. This is particularly true of fast-moving convenience goods where display at the point of sale frequently acts as a prompt to purchase. The need for availability should not be confused with Says Law, which states that demand is a function of supply. This law has now been widely discredited. (MJB)

available market. A measure of the total market available to sellers of a particular product or service defined as all those persons with an interest in the product, access to supplies and discretionary purchasing power i.e. they can afford to buy the product if they desire to do so. (MJB)

average. A simple number that is representative of a set of numbers, showing a middle value around which the numbers are grouped. There are several types of average:

(1) The arithmetic mean (*m*);

$$m = \frac{X_1 + X_2 + X_3 + X_4, \dots, X_n}{n}$$

This is the most common type of average used, but it can be misleading when there are extreme values in a set.

(2) The MEDIAN; that number of a set which has the same number of values beneath it as there are above it. It is the middle number. Often used when the mean is inappropriate.

(3) The MODE; the value of a set of numbers that occurs most frequently. Often it is useful to know, for example, which number of consumers making purchases of a product occurs most frequently in a market. (MS)

average cost. The total cost of production of a given set or group of products, divided by the number of products comprising the set or group. Also referred to as unit cost, it is possible to distinguish between long-run and short-run average costs. (MJB)

average cost pricing. A method of setting the price of a product based on the average cost of producing and marketing that type of product. This method of pricing is comparatively simple to calculate and has the advantage of ensuring that total revenue will cover total costs if the assumed target of sales is achieved. (MS)

average fixed cost. The number of items produced divided into the total fixed costs (total costs less variable costs) of producing all items. Fixed costs do not vary with output or production rate and must be incurred whether production takes place or not. (MS)

average revenue. The total revenue divided by the number of products sold to yield that revenue. In a range of items each selling at the same price average revenue will equal price. Where the range of products is selling at different prices the average revenue will represent the average price. (MS, MJB)

average stock. *See* STOCK.

average variable cost. The number of items produced divided into the total variable costs (total cost less fixed cost). Variable costs change directly with the rate of output; for example, raw materials, fuel, labour costs. Although the variable costs are likely to be different at different rates of output, the average figure represents the average variable cost per unit. Variable costs may also be referred to as operating costs, on costs or direct costs. *See also* FIXED COSTS. (MS)

awareness. One possible result of exposure to advertisements, which is therefore an ADVERTISING OBJECTIVE and a criterion of advertising effectiveness. *See* HIERARCHY OF EFFECTS AND ADVERTISING TESTING. (KC)

awareness measurement. The process of measuring advertising effectiveness in terms of viewers' or readers' AWARENESS of the advertisement(s). *See* READING-AND-NOTING, RECALL TESTING. (KC)

AYCA. Stands for 'all you can afford'. *See* ADVERTISING APPROPRIATION. (KC)

Ayer, N.W. In 1869, F. Wayland Ayer founded the Philadelphia advertising agency of N.W. Ayer & Son by persuading his father to lend him $250 and give permission to use his name so that prospective clients would not be deterred by the 20-year-old son's lack of experience in the business. The ploy was successful, for the agency quickly became America's largest and remained in top place for many years until deposed by J. Walter THOMPSON.

Ayer made three significant contributions to advertising history. First, in the 1880s, he began to offer services to advertisers, rather than simply acting as an intermediary in the buying and selling of advertising space, as the traditional SPACE BROKERS had done until then in Britain and the United States. These services were COPY-WRITING, the design of their advertisements, and advice on MEDIA SELECTION. It seems that Ayer met the cost by a combination of the broker's traditional COMMISSION paid by the publishers, and a fee. In the process, he abandoned the entrepreneurial space-broker practice of never disclosing the buying price, so that space could be sold at whatever price the advertiser would pay, in favour of what he called the 'open' charging system: he disclosed the price he had paid for the space, acknowledged the commission received, and specified an additional fee for services. In this way, he cultivated a continuing client relationship with advertisers and was thereby the first FULL-SERVICE ADVERTISING AGENCY of the modern type.

Ayer's second significant contribution to advertising history was that he took the lead among individual advertising agents in campaigning, during the 1890s, for the rate of media commission paid to agencies to be standardized at 15 per cent. In 1917 the American newspaper owners finally agreed on the figure, which had first been set by Volney B. PALMER's negotiations with their predecessors some 70 years earlier. (In Britain, there was no standard rate until 1921, when it was set at 10 per cent; the present-day 15 per cent norm was finally established in the late 1930s.)

The third of Ayer's contributions to good advertising practice concerned the contemporary publishers' practice of varying their supposedly standard advertising rates according to the amount of money an advertiser was willing to spend. The *Los Angeles Times* was discovered to be applying a differential as large as 60 per cent between large and small buyers of space, in the 1890s. The N.W. Ayer agency was again in the forefront of a crusade for a system of 'open rates' – that is, the published media RATE CARDS we take for granted today. In truth, the companies stood to earn more in commission by not interfering. But Ayer was clearly the kind of man ready to take a long-term, professional view rather than the essentially short-term approach of less responsible advertising middlemen who attracted such epithets as 'huckster' and 'fast-buck merchant' to the practitioners of the day.

In 1924, more than 50 years after opening for business, the N.W. Ayer agency produced the first-ever advertiser-sponsored network radio programme, The Every Ready Hour. It is still a major force in the American advertising business, its total BILLINGS of $523 million in 1996 placing it 35th in the league table there, but has largely disappeared from the world-wide scene. By a nice coincidence, its London office merged in the 1980s with an agency founded by an equally influential figure in the history of British advertising, Charles BARKER. Although Ayer Barker became the thirtieth largest agency in Britain, it was soon after sold off along with the rest of the European network when its American parent suffered financial troubles. The name lived on for a year or two in the composite trading names so characteristic of advertising agencies, but by 1996 was no longer to be found anywhere except in the country of its birth.   (KC)

B

baby boomer. A person born between the end of the Second World War (1945), and the early 1960s when there was a significant increase in the birth rate or 'baby boom'. (MJB)

BACC. Acronym for the Broadcast Advertising Clearance Centre, a key player in the British system of ADVERTISING CONTROL. On behalf of the INDEPENDENT TELEVISION COMMISSION (ITC), the BACC operates a Copy Clearance Secretariat from which permission must be obtained before any television advertising can be aired. (KC)

backward channels. A description applied to the linkage of establishments engaged in the accumulation and sorting of waste products destined for recycling. Only waste products whose selling price exceeds the cost of accumulation and sorting attract establishments to engage in the process, e.g. scrap metal aluminium containers etc. Other waste products are disposed of by the responsible local authority which makes use of resaleable or reusable material to reduce costs. (AJB)

backward integration. Adding to the number of processes in which a firm is involved by bringing more industrial activities further back in the chain under the same control. For example, a steel manufacturer might acquire iron ore supplies. (JK)

bait advertising. The practice of advertising a product or service solely in order to attract customers to the point of sale, where they can then be persuaded to buy something else. The Advertising Code that is part of the BRITISH CODES OF ADVERTISING AND SALES PROMOTION says: 'Advertisers must not use the technique of switch selling ... criticise the advertised product or suggest that it is not available and recommend the purchase of a more expensive alternative ... place obstacles in the way of purchasing the product or delivering it promptly'. The ITC CODE OF ADVERTISING STANDARDS AND PRACTICE warns, in a rule relating specifically to mail order and direct response advertising: 'It will be taken as *prima facie* evidence of misleading and unacceptable bait advertising for the purpose of switch selling if an advertiser's sales representatives disparage or belittle any cheaper article advertised or report unreasonable delays in obtaining delivery or otherwise put difficulties in the way of its purchase.' The RADIO AUTHORITY ADVERTISING AND SPONSORSHIP CODE makes no specific mention of bait advertising or switch selling. (KC)

bait pricing. The practice of luring a customer into a store with an offer of an inexpensive item and then attempting to persuade the customer to purchase a higher-priced item by pointing out the disadvantages of the lower-priced item. (AJB)

balance of payments. A systematic record of all economic transactions during a given period between residents of a given country and residents of other countries. It can be likened to a company's profit and loss statement. It involves a variety of international accounts which show the types of payments and receipts. There are four main types:

(1) Visible imports and exports. These are all the recorded transactions between residents of Britain and non-residents which involve the exchange of merchandise. Visible exports are receipts from sales to people in other countries of goods produced in, or re-exported from Britain.

Visible imports are payments to people in other countries for the goods exported to Britain.

Until the discovery and export of North Sea oil, Britain did not manage to export sufficiently to pay for its imports. This situation was common throughout the nineteenth century and the period up to 1945. After the Second World War the trade gap narrowed, earnings from exports paying more of the import bill. By the mid-1980s oil exports were creating a surplus on current account, but, by the end of the decade, Britain's balance of trade in manufactured goods had deteriorated significantly. This was partly due to the depletion/running down of oil reserves which had been evident since 1985.

(2) Invisible imports and exports, often referred to as the 'invisibles'. These involve payments between residents and non-residents for transactions where there is no exchange of physical goods. Major categories of transactions include government expenditures (overseas military and political expenditure), transport (shipping, freight earnings, civil aviation), travel (tourism), other services (e.g. banking, insurance) and interest, profits and dividends. These above two categories ('visibles' and 'invisibles') together form the current account transaction. Debits and credits need not balance either individually or as a total. The general balance of invisible trade is an excess of invisible export earnings, over invisible expenditure.

The current account may have a surplus or a deficit. If it has a surplus a country is seen to be 'paying its way'. Developing countries may have deficits for longer periods if they have to import significantly before exports rise. However, for a mature economy like Britain's a persistent deficit would tend to suggest the economy was not fully competitive.

(3) A movement of capital for other motives than paying for imports and exports. Referred to as the capital account (or the finance and investment account), it includes (a) loans between Britain and other governments, and (b) long-term and short-term private investment by British citizens in other countries and by them in the UK. This account, too, may not balance. Some countries tend to be net exporters of capital, thus incurring a debt, others are net importers of capital, incurring a credit. Britain tends to export capital. If there is a credit on the current account, this can be used on the capital account to balance out the debit created by its surplus exporting of capital. Britain's requirements on the capital account are relatively heavy.

(4) Transfer of gold and convertible currency, called 'accommodating movements'. Because the balance of payments must technically balance (like any balance sheet) and because totals of the current and capital accounts do not equal each other even when taken together, monetary movements become essential.

However, surpluses or deficits on the total balance of payments cannot continue indefinitely for no country has infinitely large reserves. Eventually a country in deficit must take action to stop the outflow of its reserves. This may be done through devaluation of the exchange rate, which tends to stimulate exports and reduce imports. This is a successful method if the domestic economy can produce enough exports and substitute for imports without causing inflation. Another method which is often attempted is internal deflation.   (JK)

balance sheet. A statement of the financial position of a company at a particular time, normally at the end of a financial year. It shows the total value of the assets of a company balanced by the sum of the company's total liabilities and the value of the owner's equity. The conventional balance sheet consists of two vertical columns. In the UK liabilities are set out on the left-hand column and assets on the right. (In the USA the positions are reversed.)   (GA)

banded offers. This type of promotion takes two forms: (a) the use of an existing and well-known brand to 'carry' a free sample of another non-competing product. Both products may be produced by the same firm, for example soap and toothpaste, which has the dual advantage of increasing sales of the carrying brand while securing trial of the carried brand, or they may be complementary products of different producers, for example instant coffee and sugar. (b) Two-for-the-price-of-one: the practice of offering two related products for a price which is lower than each of them purchased separately.   (MJB, AJB)

Bank of England. The Bank of England was established in 1694 by Act of Parliament and Royal Charter as a corporate body; the entire capital stock was acquired by the Government under the Bank of England Act 1946. The Bank acts as banker to the Government, holding its main accounts, managing Britain's reserves of gold and foreign exchange, arranging new government borrowing and managing the stock of its existing debt. The Bank's main objectives are to:

ensure the soundness of the financial system through the direct supervision of banks and specialized City institutions;

promote the efficiency and effectiveness of the financial system, especially in the domestic and international payment and settlement systems; and

maintain the value of the nation's money, mainly through policies and market operations agreed with government.

The Banking Act 1987 assigns the Bank of England the overriding objective of protecting depositors. To this end institutions intending to take deposits from the public must gain authorisation from the Bank and submit to its continued supervision. Under the Financial Services Act1986, the Bank is also responsible for overseeing money market institutions. The Bank's supervision is 'prudential' – it sets minimum standards for authorized institutions but offers no guarantee that those institutions will not fail or that investors or depositors will be compensated in full.The Banking Act established the Deposit Protection Fund financed by contributions levied on the banking system; this entitles depositors to limited compensation if an authorized bank fails. In order to be and remain authorized an institution has to satisfy the Bank that it has:

adequate capital and liquidity;

a realistic business plan;

adequate systems and controls;

adequate provision for bad and doubtful debts; and

that its business is carried out with integrity and skill, and in a prudent manner.

As agent for the Government, the Bank is responsible for managing the National Debt, which involves arranging government borrowing and repayment of debt. It also maintains the register of holdings of government securities on behalf of the Treasury, and manages the Exchange Equalisation Account (EEA) holding Britain's official reserves of gold, foreign exchange, Special Drawing Rights (SDRs – claims on the International Monetary Fund) and European Currency Units (ECUs). The Bank may intervene in the foreign exchange markets on behalf of the Government using the resources of the EEA, to check undue fluctuations in the exchange value of sterling.

The Bank is able to influence money market conditions through its dealings with the discount houses which developed in the nineteenth century as bill brokers for industrialists. Discount houses hold mainly Treasury, local authority and commercial bills, and negotiable certificates of deposit financed by short-term loans from the banks. If on a particular day there is a shortage of cash in the banking system as a result, for example, of large tax payments, the Bank relieves the shortage either by buying bills from the discount houses or by lending directly to them. This permits banks to replenish their cash balances at the Bank by recalling some of their short-term loans to the discount houses. The Bank's dealings with the discount houses give it powerful influence over short-term interest rates.

The Bank of England has the sole right to issue banknotes in England and Wales. The note issue is no longer backed by gold but by government and other securities. Three Scottish and four Northern Ireland banks also issue notes. These issues, apart from a small amount specified by legislation for each bank must be covered fully by holdings of Bank of England notes and coinage. Responsibility for the provision of coin lies with the Royal Mint, a government trading fund which became an executive agency in 1990.

The Bank of England seeks to ensure that Britain's financial markets are efficient and competitive. To this end it runs two securities settlement systems with in-built payment arrangements – the Central Gilts Office and the Central Moneymarket Office. A permanent body of market and legal practitioners – the Financial Law Panel – hass been established by the Bank to help find practical solutions to problems of legal uncertainty in the wholesale financial markets.

(HMSO)

BARB. Acronym, pronounced as a word, for BROADCASTERS' AUDIENCE RESEARCH BOARD, the body which has commissioned and supervised research into the UK television audience since 1981. Its management committee comprise representatives of BBC-TV, the ITVA, Channel 4, BSkyB and the IPA. There are two continuous-research programmes: 'audience measurement' and 'audience appreciation'. The first, operated by Audits of Great Britain (AGB) and RSMB Television Research Ltd, surveys a national panel of approximately 4,500 households, made up of area samples ranging in size from 100 to 350. Their representativeness is ensured by systematic selection from an 'establishment survey' among a random sample of 43,000. This is also the source of replacements for households which become unrepresentative with the passage of time, or drop out for whatever reason. Electronic meters are wired to TV sets and video recorders in panel households and every member is provided with a personally-numbered, remote-control encoding device. There is a facility for guest viewers to enter their age and gender. Each individual uses the device to record the beginning and end of each continuous viewing session. An alarm signal flashes on the set meter if the set is on but it has received no input. The VCR meter imprints an electronic code on video tape being used to record off-air, and reads the code back whenever the tape is replayed. The data collected in this way are automatically downloaded every night to a central computer, which combines them with the schedules of programmes and commercial breaks and calculates estimates of audience numbers. BARB estimates that the panel response rate is between 98 and 99 per cent. Subscribers have access to the raw data or the computed audience statistics, which provide a reliable indication of audience PRESENCE but not necessarily of attention to what was on the screen at the time. Specialist reports are issued on live and time-shift recorded viewing of the terrestrial commercial channels, the BBC network, and Astra channels received by satellite dish and cable. The 'audience appreciation' research, carried out by the market research agency RSL, investigates reactions to programmes but not to commercials. A national panel of 3,000 adults complete weekly viewing diaries, in which they rate each one viewed on a scale from zero to ten. Their ratings are aggregated to produce an Appreciation Index for each. An additional booklet contains questions about aspects of particular programmes, and more general ones about series and serials. The data collected in that phase of the research are confidential to the broadcasters who specified the questions.   (KC)

bar code. A series of identical length lines, of varying widths used to identify PRODUCTS. By convention, the first two lines identify the country of origin, the next five identify the manufacturer, the next five the product and the last line is a check digit assigned by a computer. The country of origin digits are internationally agreed, the manufacturer numbers are allocated by the Article Numbering Association (ANA) and the product code is allocated by the manufacturer. Read by an optical scanner at a checkout desk, they provide data for internal records and produce till receipts. Bar codes are referred to as

Universal Product Coding in the USA. *See* ELECTRONIC POINT OF SALE.   (KRD)

Barker, Charles (1791–1859). Setting himself up in the famous year of 1812 as an 'advertising agent', having previously prospered by delivering military intelligence from Europe to the Duke of Wellington, Charles Barker bought blocks of ADVERTISING SPACE from newspaper and magazine proprietors and resold it in smaller units at a marked-up price to individual advertisers. He thus performed the classic functions of entrepreneurial intermediary and professional service provider, in combination. The media owners enjoyed the advantage of dealing with one selling agent instead of many separate buyers; the advertisers could consult and instruct one expert intermediary instead of dealing with the many different sellers of advertising space. The important and enduring concept of the ADVERTISING AGENCY was thus invented and established. Fragmentary historical records show that there had been advertising intermediaries 30 years before, but they seem to have charged a fee for their services to the advertiser, who paid the media bills direct, rather than making their living by marking up the media owners' wholesale prices. They were 'advertising agents', whereas Charles Barker – despite his own description – was really a 'space broker'.

During the twentieth century, his company developed into three distinct divisions, providing professional expertise in advertising, public relations and 'human resources'. The Charles Barker advertising agency built up a significant specialization in the financial sector. By a nice coincidence, it merged in the 1980s with the London office of one founded by an equally significant figure in the history of American advertising, F.W. AYER. Although Ayer Barker became the thirtieth largest agency in Britain, it was soon after sold off along with the rest of the European advertising network when the American holding company ran into financial troubles. This seminal name was not thereby consigned to the dustbin of history altogether, however. The new owners preserved the surname, at least, in the Barkers recruitment-advertising agency, with headquarters in London and local offices throughout the UK, and in the Barkers Regional Communications network in Birmingham, Edinburgh, Glasgow and Aberdeen. Meanwhile, in the public relations field, the Charles Barker agency negotiated a successful management buy-out from its ailing parent and remains a force in British PR, now without any ownership links to the advertising wing of the old firm. In short, the name of the man who invented the advertising agency has lived on in one form or another for 185 years as this dictionary goes to print. (KC)

barriers to competition. Forces which limit market competition, normally economic or technological conditions which make the entry of more firms to a market more difficult, thus providing a barrier to competition. Examples of potential barriers include a high degree of product differentiation, high ECONOMIES OF SCALE, and a high RESEARCH AND DEVELOPMENT threshold. (JK)

barriers to entry. Freedom of entry to an industry is widely regarded as a key indicator of an industry's competitiveness, such that in the case of a monopoly, by definition, no other firm can enter, while in perfect competition there are no barriers to entry. From the firm's viewpoint, the greater the barriers to entry the less the threat from new competitors, and the more secure its own position. Among the major barriers to entry may be noted: (a) ECONOMIES OF SCALE; (b) product differentiation; (c) capital requirement; (d) switching costs; (e) access to distribution channels; (f) cost disadvantages independent of scale; (g) government policy. (MJB)

barter. The most basic form of transaction, in which the parties exchange goods and/or services with one another without recourse to a common unit of account or medium of exchange such as money. Although generally associated with primitive economies lacking a medium of exchange, barter deals still continue between economies where currencies are not freely convertible in the world's money markets. *See* COUNTERTRADING and EXPORTS. (MJB)

basal skin resistance (bsr). The norm from which changes in emotional response to stimuli such as advertising messages are recorded by means of a PSYCHO-GALVANOMETER. (MJB)

basement store. A department within a DEPART-MENT STORE, usually in the basement, selling merchandise at bargain prices. Goods offered may be ends of ranges, out of season stock, seconds as well as specially purchased lines to be sold at discounted prices. One of the best known examples is Filene's in Boston (USA)

which discounts goods progressively until they are sold. (MJB)

base-point pricing. A form of pricing in which all competitors are required to quote their price for a common basing point. The benefit to the buyer is that it enables him to distinguish between the real price of the goods on offer from different suppliers, including any transportation costs to the basing point. Thus the delivered price is the basing point price plus the delivery costs to the buyer's location which will be constant for all sellers. In regulated MARKETS, the base-point price may be fixed, which offers some protection for local suppliers as those distant from the base-point will have to absorb the extra delivery charges. (MJB)

basic list price. The price of any commodity or service that is the maximum the seller expects to obtain from a buyer. The basic list price usually serves as the start point for sales negotiation or bargaining. It is also used by the seller as the base from which he will calculate special promotional discounts. (JRB)

batch. In the context of production, a series of units of output of identical specification made at one time or as part of one production run. Typically, although not always, 'batches' are standardized PRODUCTS, where repeat orders are probable and may be made for STOCK. As such, they represent the converse of production on a 'jobbing' basis. (KNB)

Bayesian theory. A name applied generically to STATISTICAL DECISION THEORY, even where the methods employed do not depend upon the theory proposed by Thomas Bayes during the eighteenth century. Enis and Broome (*Marketing Decisions: A Bayesian Approach,* 1971) summarize the Bayesian approach as consisting of five elements, namely: (a) The decision-maker is involved in a situation in which there are at least two alternative ways of reaching a specific objective(s), and he has the power to decide among the alternatives. (b) The decision-maker is uncertain as to which decision alternative to select, because he does not know the set of environmental conditions (state of nature) which will actually prevail at the time the decision is implemented. (c) The decision-maker has some knowledge of the situation, e.g. relative pay-offs of alternatives, and the likelihood of the occurrence of various events or states of nature which affect these pay-offs. (d) The decision-maker is willing to use expected value as his decision criterion. (e) The decision-maker may be able to obtain additional information (at some cost) which might change his assessment of the situation. Thus three concepts are central to the Bayesian methodology: (i) the identification of alternatives; (ii) the assignment of probabilistic expectations to the alternatives: and (iii) the use of expected value as the decision criterion.   (MJB)

behaviour. Physical acts performed or undertaken by individuals as opposed to attitudes, beliefs or opinions which constitute a state of mind towards a concept or object and may not lead to physical action.   (MJB)

behavioural intention. A decision to behave in a particular way based on beliefs about the consequences of such behaviour. Intentions to buy stated in response to market research are notoriously unreliable and should be treated with caution.   (MJB)

behaviourism. *See* STIMULUS RESPONSE.

behaviour segmentation. *See* MARKET SEGMENTATION.

beliefs. Defined by Engel *et al.* (J.F. Engel, R.D. Blackwell, and P.W. Miniard, *Consumer Behaviour,* 5th edn, Illinois: Dryden Press, 1986) as 'perceptions of an alternative's performance on important evaluative criteria' to which they add the opinion of Krech and Crutchfield as 'a generic term that encompasses Knowledge, Opinion and Faith – an enduring organization of perceptions and cognition about some aspect of the individual's world'. Beliefs are considered to be neutral and comprise one of the two components of an ATTITUDE, which is not.   (MJB)

below-the-line. Defines ADVERTISING MEDIA which do not pay MEDIA COMMISSION to advertising agencies buying space or time from them. The 'line' is a purely imaginary boundary between those which do and do not, a distinction generally believed to have been first made by Procter & Gamble in the 1950s. The commission-paying media above the line are newspapers, magazines, television, radio, posters and cinema. Since the distinction is historically between two sets of advertising vehicles, one would expect the below-the-line category to contain such minor media as directories, yearbooks, matchbooks and

(for the present) the Internet, none of which offers the commission discount. In practice, however, a 'below-the-line campaign' turns out to have deployed the non-advertising ingredients of the MARKETING COMMUNICATIONS MIX, particularly sales promotion and direct mail. The ADVERTISER'S ANNUAL confuses the issue further; by implying that two other ingredients, public relations and sponsorship, belong with advertising while separating sales promotion as an external service to the advertising business. It is not at all unusual to read reports of a 'below-the-line advertising campaign', strictly speaking a contradiction in terms. A clearer definition and more precise usage would be welcome. *See also* ABOVE-THE-LINE.   (KC)

benchmarking. The evaluation of competitors' products to determine their construction and performance compared with one's own. Benchmarking has become an essential element of competitor analysis in order to establish sources of competitive advantage and oppportunities for improving the performance of one's own products.   (MJB)

benefit segmentation. An approach to market segmentation popularized by Russell Haley ('Benefit Segmentation: A Decision-Oriented Research Tool', *Journal of Marketing,* July 1968) which seeks to describe market segments in terms of the benefits sought by prospective buyers. While sophisticated multivariate techniques and an extensive data base are usually necessary to define the segments, the end result can be a very powerful guide to the major market segments and the MARKETING MIX best suited to reach them. This is readily apparent from Haley's example of the toothpaste market. *See* Figure 5.   (MJB)

Bernbach, William (1911–82). One of the half dozen most celebrated modern American advertising men, co-founder of the Doyle Dane Bernbach advertising agency. His name lives on today only in the last initial of the London agency BMP DDB, fourth largest in Britain in 1996.

Bill Bernbach was especially known for his views about CREATIVITY. Though originally a writer himself, he became convinced that people look before they read, and therefore gave the artists and designers at Doyle Dane Bernbach standing equal to that enjoyed by the writers. In the great majority of advertising agencies, the creative function is headed by a COPYWRITER, not an ART DIRECTOR; this is presumably a legacy from the early days, when all advertising was verbal rather than pictorial. Bernbach was therefore an iconoclast. His agency's most famous advertising was for Volkswagen in the 1960s and 1970s. The VW Beetle, a car in the most marked possible contrast to the American norm, was propelled to almost cult status by (among other factors, no doubt) a series of advertising campaigns that were highly original both visually and verbally. Best known of these abroad was a press advertisement with the headline 'Think small' above a straightforward photograph of the car – a decidedly different approach, given the lush and exaggerated 'artist's impressions' in the domestic manufacturers' advertising. The BODY COPY below the illustration contained several hundred words of reasoned argument. The campaign was voted 'greatest advertising and marketing success of the past fifty years' by a panel of American judges in 1980. Bill Bernbach also expressed a robust scepticism about the value of much ADVERTISING TESTING, having reportedly said: 'The client wants some research, so cut him a yard of it.'   (KC)

Berne Union. An international organization of Export Credit Insurers, whether government- or commercially-sponsored, which attempts to lay down conditions to be observed by member nations in extending credit insurance. Current recommendations vary between a minimum of six months and a maximum of five years, depending on the nature of the goods which are being bought on credit.   (JML)

best-before date. The date stamped onto PRODUCTS, mainly food, to indicate the product should be consumed on or before that date. The date is determined by manufacturers after conducting trials to establish the product's SHELF LIFE. The term is being replaced by 'USE-BY DATE' as CONSUMER confusion with the term 'best-before' has been highlighted.   (SD)

beta error. *See* TYPE II ERROR.

bias. (1) Those errors in a sample survey which would persist even if every unit in the specified population supplied information in the same way as in the sample. *Contrast* SAMPLING ERROR.
(JAB)
(2) In consumer INFORMATION PROCESSING, bias occurs as a result of preferential processing of information which confirms existing BELIEFS.
(GKP)

bidding. Competitive bidding is a feature of the industrial market which occurs where a number

TOOTHPASTE MARKET SEGMENT DESCRIPTION

Segment Name	The Sensory Segment	The Sociables	The Worriers	The independent Segment
Principal benefit sought:	Flavour, product appearance	Brightness of teeth	Decay prevention	Price
Demographic strengths:	Children	Teen, young people	Large families	Men
Special behavioural characteristics:	Users of spearmint flavoured toothpaste	Smokers	Heavy users	Heavy users
Brands disproportionately favoured:	Colgate, Stripe	Macleans, Plus White, Ultra Brite	Crest	Brands on sale
Personality characteristics:	High self-involvement	High sociability	High hypochondriasis	High autonomy
Life-style characteristics:	Hedonistic	Active	Conservative	Value-oriented

Source: 'Benefit Segmentation: A Decision-oriented Research Tool', *Journal of Marketing*, July 1968, p. 33.

Figure 5: **Benefit segmentation**

of potential suppliers are invited to submit a written bid for a contract. Bidding may be restricted to an approved list of suppliers (closed bidding) or open to any supplier willing to apply (open bidding).   (STP)

bid pricing. Occurs when the supplier fixes a price for the goods or services to be provided which will cover all the costs incurred and make a predetermined contribution to profit.   (STP)

bill. In a MARKETING context 'bill' can have several meanings including the following.

(1) An ACCOUNT of money owed for goods or services. Instead of asking for an invoice, equivalent expression would be 'to ask for the bill'. As an account to pay 'a bill' should not be confused with a receipt, which is issued once an account is paid as proof of payment. In some situations, however, where simple transactions are being undertaken, as in a restaurant or café, a 'bill' and receipt can become interchangeable pieces of paper. The 'bill' serves as a receipt once the payment is made.

(2) A draft of a proposed law. While proposed legislation is under discussion in both Houses of Parliament it is a 'Bill'. Once it has passed all the prescribed stages a 'Bill' becomes an Act of Parliament. At the discussion stage it is termed a Parliamentary Bill.

(3) A placard or ADVERTISEMENT. Hence the use of the expression 'BILLBOARD' as a description of a POSTER SITE. This expression has an American influence, however, and more correctly in English a 'billboard' would be called a 'hoarding' (though the term is perhaps slightly outdated). In English it could be said that: 'The new poster was to be fixed to the hoarding.' Alternatively the same idea would be conveyed by the Americanized expression: 'The new bill was to be fixed to the billboard.' A small advertisement, a single page, handed out by someone in the street to passers-by can be called a 'hand-bill'.

(4) A BILL OF EXCHANGE.

(5) A BILL OF LADING.

(6) A bill of fare – a menu.   (BRM)

billboard. The generic term in America for an advertising POSTER, technically defining the 'board' on which a 'bill' is posted. Popular use of this description in Britain is probably absorbed from American literature, television and (another transatlantic borrowing) movies. Whereas a British 'billboard' is technically constructed

specifically for a 30-inch by 20-inch 'double crown' poster, colloquial usage implies a much larger size: *see* POSTER SITE.   (KC)

billing. The standard but indirect measure of an ADVERTISING AGENCY'S financial turnover. The term is often used in the plural. It comprises: (i) the total sum of money paid to MEDIA OWNERS on behalf of all its CLIENTS (ii) fees received direct from its clients for non-media services (iii) agreed on-costs associated with the production of campaign material. The first ingredient earns the agency MEDIA COMMISSION, the second is conventionally marked-up at a rate equivalent to the commission discount, and the third is a direct charge. It is assumed that the figure is annual, if unspecified. Billings are the usual yardstick for absolute and comparative evaluation of an advertising agency's size and success, despite periodic pressure in the business to find an alternative that is closer to general practice elsewhere. In 1996, one in Britain had total annual billings greater than £300 million and four more surpassed £200 million. A billing of £100 million would have placed an agency in eighteenth place, £25 million corresponded to 45th place; and so on. Worldwide, the billings of the leading agencies in the largest advertising economies were: Japan $11.7 billion; USA $3.1 billion; France $2.0 billion; Germany $1.0 billion; UK $1.0 billion; Italy $0.6 billion; Netherlands $0.5 billion.   (KC)

bill of exchange. A written order from one person (the drawer) to another (the recipient) desiring the latter to pay to a named person a sum of money on a certain future date.   (BRM)

bill of lading. A paper signed by the master of a ship which makes him responsible for the safe delivery of the goods listed in it.   (BRM)

bin. An open-topped (or otherwise easily accessible) receptacle. Organizations customarily have the items they hold in STOCK stored in 'bins'. Thus a 'bin' can be of very variable size. A bin for small sizes of screws and washers may be no larger than a shoe box, while a bin for flywheels or other foundry produced items may have many cubic feet of capacity. 'Bins' can be nondescript and featureless when used in manufacturing plants, or other positions behind the scenes, or else can be colourful and attractively designed if used in SUPERMARKETS to display merchandise for sale. In this latter context they act not only as storage receptacles but also as sales dispensers, hence 'dumpbins'.   (BRM)

bingo card. *See* READER SERVICE CARD.

biogenic needs. The biogenic (or primary) group of human NEEDS are defined by P.M. Chisnall (*Marketing: A Behavioural Analysis,* London: McGraw-Hill, 1975) as those referring 'to the basic physiological needs which are related to the bodily functions such as hunger, thirst, sex, sleep, and exercise'. The other general category of human needs is stated by Chisnall, citing Bayton, as being PSYCHOGENIC NEEDS – those needs which are psychological or emotional. A more complex categorization (or HIERARCHY) of human needs and attendant theory of their sequential development was proposed by MASLOW. *See also* MOTIVATION.   (GKP)

bipolar. Having two distinct end points. Scales used in measuring attitudes and opinions offer the respondent a range of alternatives between but inclusive of the end points which may be defined in words: e.g. hard ... easy; strongly agree ... strongly disagree; or in numbers: e. g. 1 ... 10.
                                              (MJB)

bivariate analysis. Literally a statistical ANALYSIS involving two variables. Bivariate analysis can refer to contingency table analysis, chi-squares or regression.   (SKT)

black box approach. Recognition of the invisibility of major influences on patterns of behaviour: a process of inference regarding the unobservable variables intervening between observable stimulus inputs and observable response outputs. Observation of associations between stimulus inputs and behavioural responses enables judgements to be made regarding the nature of the intervening variables – the contents of the black box. The concept originated in electrical engineering. *See also* STIMULUS RESPONSE.   (JLD)

bleed. A printing operation which results in the printed matter running off the cut edge of a newspaper or magazine page, so that there is no white margin around it. Full-page and double-page colour advertisements in the Sunday colour magazines usually 'bleed off the page' (or are 'bled to the margin'), while those in the *Radio Times* or *TV Times* more often do not. To ensure there is no accidental small white margin at any edge if the paper is not trimmed perfectly, the actual print area has to be significantly larger than the page dimensions. There is normally a surcharge for bleed, expressed as a percentage to be added to the RATE CARD charge for the space; it will be included in the details provided by BRAD (q.v.). The picturesque phrase 'bleeding into the gutter" describes the requirement for an illustration spread across two facing pages to be continuous across the dividing 'gutter', without any visible interruption.   (KC)

blind testing. Consumer evaluations of intrinsic product qualities undertaken in controlled test conditions with all brand identification features, such as packaging style, labels, prices and so on removed. A range of brands from a product field is presented in this homogeneous way, for purposes of comparison and recognition of known brands.   (JLD)

blister pack. An additional item, which may be the same PRODUCT or a complementary product, wrapped with the original purchase as part of a promotional campaign. An example of the first type would be a second free tube of toothpaste. A free packet of oatcakes attached to a block of cheese would be an example of the second type. A blister pack can also be known as a bubble pack.   (SD)

blocking factor. In perceptual testing, a technical term for a method for using only a subset of complete combinations in comparative judgements. The blocking factor describes what proportion of the number of complete judgements are removed. It can also be applied in SAMPLING techniques, and the design of experiments.
                                              (SKT)

body copy. The main text of an advertisement, as distinct from the headline, the signature line or any VISUALS. *See* COPY.   (KC)

body language. Non-verbal signals such as facial expressions and gestures which indicate a person's emotional state.   (MJB)

bonded warehouses. Warehouses which have been designated by the Department of Customs and Excise for the storage of products on which tax is due to be paid. They may be imported or home-manufactured products (e.g. tobacco or whisky). In the case of whisky the Customs officer is also a key-holder. In the case of some imported products the control method may simply be a stock accounting procedure. In some cases additional processing may be done while the product is in bond. (AJB)

bonus pack. A promotion which offers extra quantity of the PRODUCT, typically between 12 and 33 per cent, at no extra cost. It can be an effective promotional tool, but products can often be copied by competitors. The danger with such a promotion is that CONSUMERS can quickly come to expect the extra quantity, and it therefore becomes the norm for the product. (GM)

bonus payment. A reward paid for achievement of a set target. It is often used as an incentive for a sales force. (GM)

Boston box. See PRODUCT PORTFOLIO.

BOTB. See BRITISH OVERSEAS TRADE BOARD.

boundary spanning. Actions which go beyond a manager's normal area of responsibility especially at the interface between one task area and another. (MJB)

boutique. Specifically, a shop specializing in a particular range of mechandise. Generally, an organisation such as an advertising agency which specializes in a limited range of activities. (MJB)

BRAD. Acronym, pronounced as a word, which the publishers of British Rate and Data now use exclusively in place of the full title. It is a monthly index of current ADVERTISING RATES and MECHANICAL DATA for virtually every separate MEDIA VEHICLE available to advertisers in Britain, and indispensable reference source for advertising agency MEDIA BUYERS. In the case of press vehicles, entries also normally include figures for ABC or VFD (q.v.) CIRCULATION and NRS or JICREG (q.v.) READERSHIP, or independently audited alternatives. The on-line 'BRADbase Media Selector' has largely supplanted the paper original in the IT-rich environment of modern agency media departments. BRAD's American counterpart is *Standard Rate and Data.*

BRADaal. A quarterly index, from the publishers of BRAD (q.v.) which lists company names, addresses and contact names for a large proportion of all national advertisers and for most advertising agencies in Britain. It is cross-referenced so that the user can find out the agency retained by a particular advertiser or the clients of a particular agency. It thus duplicates part of the content of the ADVERTISER'S ANNUAL. (KC)

BRADbase. Shorthand for BRADbase Media Selector, the on-line version of BRAD. (KC)

brain hemisphere lateralization. The human brain consists of right and left hemispheres, linked by the corpus callosum. Each hemisphere appears to be responsible for different kinds of COGNITIVE activity, with the left brain responsible for logical thought processes, and the right brain for creative thought processes. To the extent that one set of thought processes dominates the other, it is possible to identify 'lateralization'. (*See* Fleming Hanson, 'Hemispheral Lateralisation: Implications for Understanding Consumer Behaviour', in *Journal of Consumer Research.* vol. 8 (June 1981). pp. 23–36). (MJB)

brainstorming. An activity designed to provide maximum opportunity for the emergence of new and creative ideas. approaches and solutions to particular problems; usually through group meetings of three to eight participants. The purpose of a brainstorming session is the emergence of ideas, not their evaluation, which should take place at a subsequent meeting. In a brainstorming session all ideas should be considered, no contribution should be discouraged, no idea is trivial or irrelevant. The technique is used, for example, in searching for new product concepts. (JRB)

brand. A product – a good or service – with a set of characteristics which clearly and readily differentiates it from all other products. Branding is a technique basic to marketing practice as an attempt to differentiate a product in the market place. Branding policy may call for emphasis on the 'house' name (Cadbury, Hoover, Ford, Kelloggs for example) as well as on the brand name, or each brand may be expected to stand on its own (the policy of Procter & Gamble, Lever Brothers, Beecham for example). For a consumer goods company, a brand – whether by name, packaging, 'image' or price – may do the job the salesman does for an industrial goods company, communicating directly with the end-user. See BRAND CHOICE, BRAND EXTENSION STRATEGY, BRAND IMAGE, BRAND LOYALTY etc.

(JRB)

brand awareness. A measure of the number of CONSUMERS able to recall or identify a BRAND, with or without assistance. AWARENESS is invariably much higher than purchase behaviour, but is a useful measure for assessing the effectiveness of ADVERTISING and promotional activity through, before and after studies.   (MJB)

brand choice. The decision to select a particular brand of product from the array of all brands with similar composition and cost/performance characteristics capable of satisfying the consumers' felt need. *See* BRAND PREFERENCE.   (MJB)

branded goods. PRODUCTS or services which are identified with a brand name, enabling CONSUMERS to recognize the good and, hopefully, develop a preference for it so that they will always ask for it by name.   (MJB)

brand equity. The value imputed to a brand which recognizes its worth as an asset. This value reflects the market share held by the brand, the degree of loyalty and recognition it enjoys, its perceived quality and any other attributes which distinguish it positively from competitive offerings e.g. patent protection, trademark etc. There is considerable debate as to whether brand equity should be included in a firm's BALANCE SHEET in the way in which 'goodwill' may be included. Those who argue that it should, point to the difference between the acquisition value of a company and its balance sheet value without brand equity as an indicator that the brand equity may be well in excess of all the firm's other assets. For example Nestle paid five times the balance sheet value of Rowntree Mackintosh in order to secure ownership of its brands such as Kit-Kat, Yorkie etc.   (MJB)

brand extension strategy. That policy which seeks to take advantage of the successful establishment in the market of one brand, by allying to it variants of that product, or products in other markets that can be related to it. Where the brand name has been developed without the help of a 'house name' (*see* BRAND) for example Fairy household toilet soap, then an extension policy (Fairy Toilet Soap, Fairy Liquid) may maximize the goodwill created by the original product.
(JRB)

brand image. The overall impression created in the market place by any one BRAND. All characteristics of that brand, real or imaginary, belong to the brand image. Usually each brand has a multiplicity of images, as different segments of the population have different, even contradictory, perceptions of such a brand. Creating an acceptable image for a product is an important part of marketing skill, but it can only be effective if such a creation lies within the boundaries of consumers' need and credibility.   (JRB)

branding. The practice of creating a unique name for a product and giving marketing support to that name. Such a name may or may not be supported by the company's name. Many companies use both these routes to market success, for example, Rowntree's Fruit Pastilles and Yorkie.   (JRB)

brand leader. The BRAND with the largest share of the MARKET in which it competes.   (MJB)

brand loyalty. For any one BRAND, the extent to which users of that brand re-purchase it, and, in any one market, the extent of loyalty that obtains across the spread of brands. Certain markets have relatively high levels of brand loyalty, for example after-shave lotion, while others have notoriously low levels of loyalty, for example petrol. Brand loyalty may be measured by a CONSUMER PANEL, and it is often claimed to represent the power of the BRAND IMAGE. It has been argued by Ehrenberg that in practice the proportion of 'solus' or loyal buyers is usually a simple function of brand share. It is generally considered that brand loyalty in a market is reduced by price and promotional competition.   (JRB, JAB)

brand management. An organizational structure in which a designated manager is made responsible for the MARKETING of a BRAND. Believed to have been adopted first by Procter & Gamble, the main weakness of the system is that the BRAND MANAGER usually has no line of authority over the management of production, selling, promotion or distribution, and so has to depend upon his negotiating ability to develop and implement his brand MARKETING PLAN. It is contended that this experience is excellent training for future general management.   (MJB)

brand manager. The individual responsible for the MARKETING of a specific BRAND or cluster or related brands.   (MJB)

brand mark. *See* BRANDING.

brand name. *See* BRANDING.

brand positioning. The policy used to ensure that the BRAND has a distinctive position in the market place, identifiable by the consuming public. As the business scene becomes increasingly competitive, the need for brand positioning to ensure the brand a distinct niche in the market becomes more important. Quality, performance, price, styling, value and so on, may be used to position a product in a segment of the market place to maximize profit opportunities and minimize competitive confrontation.   (JRB)

brand preference. The consumer's inclination to select or choose a specific BRAND of product in preference to any other having a similar composition and cost/performance characteristics. The strength of brand preference is implicit in the classification of convenience, shopping and specialty goods which are broadly equivalent to weak, moderate and strong brand preference and may usefully be thought of as the degree to which the consumer is prepared to accept substitutes for his original preference. The creation and maintenance of brand preference is central to the whole area of consumer marketing particularly in oligopolistic markets where a few major suppliers are competing directly with one another with largely undifferentiated physical products.
(MJB)

brand recognition. Ability to identify a brand and one or more of its salient characteristics in response to an appropriate cue.   (MJB)

brand share. The proportion of all sales for the PRODUCT category – washing-up liquid, chocolate bars, baked beans etc. – held by any given BRAND. Collectively, the brand shares account for 100 per cent of total sales of the product.   (MJB)

brand space map. *See* PERCEPTUAL MAP.

brand switching. The act of discontinuing the purchase of one BRAND in favour of another or others. The aim of sellers is to develop BRAND LOYALTY – the incidence of brand switching is a measure of their success in achieving this. By analysing the characteristics of brand-loyal and brand-switching customers, the marketer can devise SEGMENTATION strategies designed to encourage switching to their brand and develop loyalty to it.   (MJB)

break. Shorthand for COMMERCIAL BREAK, as in 'the centre break in News at Ten'.   (KC)

break-down. Division of sample survey results into subgroups, usually defined by independent variable or CLASSIFICATION VARIABLE. *See* SURVEY ANALYSIS.   (JAB)

break-down opportunities. The existence of convenient divisions within a database which enable the researcher to subdivide it into classes or categories for further analysis e.g. a population may be broken down in terms of its demographics, psychographics, usage etc. *See* MARKET SEGMENTATION.   (MJB)

break-even analysis. A technique of financial analysis for investigating the functional relationships between the rate of activity and costs, revenue and profits. Specifically, break-even analysis focuses attention on anticipated profit behaviour in response to changes in underlying conditions by predicting the profit consequences of changes in selling prices, product costs, rate of output and sales volume. It usually results in a break-even chart which presents diagrammatically significant cost–volume–profit relationships and determines the BREAK-EVEN POINT.   (GA)

break-even point. The volume level at which the company's revenue exactly covers total fixed and variable costs given a specific price situation, i.e. the volume at which neither profit nor loss is made. The break-even point is found by dividing total fixed cost by the excess of price over variable cost.   (GA)

break-even pricing. An ambiguous term which is used when discussing PRICING OBJECTIVES. Some writers use it to describe the setting of a price which will recover the manufacturing and marketing costs but *not* include a profit while others use it as being synonymous with *target profit pricing* which includes the costs of manufacturing and marketing *plus* a profit margin.   (MJB)

British Code of Advertising Practice. The predecessor of the Advertising Code contained within the BRITISH CODES OF ADVERTISING AND SALES PROMOTION.   (KC)

British Code of Sales Promotion Practice. The predecessor to the Sales Promotion Code contained within the BRITISH CODES OF ADVERTISING AND SALES PROMOTION   (KC)

British Codes of Advertising and Sales Promotion. A single document, despite the title, which sets out the criteria of acceptability applied to non-broadcast advertising in the UK by the ADVERTISING STANDARDS AUTHORITY. The Advertising Code establishes the general principles that 'all advertisements should be legal, decent, honest and truthful ... should be prepared with a sense of responsibility to consumers and society ... should respect the principles of fair competition generally accepted in business'. These are elaborated in 21 clauses dealing with specific aspects of the four criteria and with particular kinds of advertising, and in 6 Appendices containing Specific Rules relating to: Alcoholic Drinks; Children; Motoring; Environmental Claims; Health & Beauty Products and Therapies; Slimming; Employment and Business Opportunities; Financial Services and Products. There is also a separate Cigarette Code, which is 'exceptional in that it is the outcome of discussions between the UK Department of Health ... the Tobacco Manufacturers Association and the Imported Tobacco Products Advisory Council ... and the ASA'. A Committee of Advertising Practice, its membership drawn from 22 trade associations, is responsible for keeping the Code up to date and for ensuring the widest possible awareness of its content.   (KC)

British Export Houses Association. Established in 1961, having evolved from the National General Export Merchants Group (formed 1940). Its objective is to introduce potential UK suppliers and overseas customers and suppliers to members of the Association (which numbers 200 companies). The Association publishes *The Export Enquiry Circular* which appears at six-weekly intervals and consists of advertisements placed by UK manufacturers and suppliers looking for suitable export houses. *The Overseas Enquiry Circular* is another publication. This contains trade enquiries received from abroad. A third publication is the *Directory of British Export Houses,* a guide to the trading activities of members and services they provide. The Association also liaises with such bodies as the Export Credit Guarantee Department and acts as a pressure group by taking up members' matters of concern with such bodies as the Department of Trade.

Export houses themselves operate in three different ways: (a) as export merchants, buying and selling on their own account, as principals; (b) as UK firms' export departments or agents; (c) as agents for overseas buyers (i.e. buying and acting as a confirming house).

Having specialist knowledge of international trade in terms of packing, shipping, insurance, inspection requirements, buyers' credit and overseas markets, they are of most value to the smaller or medium-sized manufacturer who may wish to enter new markets or start exporting for the first time.   (JK)

British Market Research Bureau Ltd (BMRB). BMRB is one of the largest research agencies in Britain, providing a wide range of services including (a) consumer – ad hoc and social surveys; (b) advertising pre-testing and post-testing; (c) industrial, commercial, financial and corporate image surveys; (d) media surveys; (e) international services through the European Market Research Bureau; (f) other services, including the Holiday Booking Index, omnibus research and purchases by individuals of records, tapes and hi-fi equipment.

BMRB is a wholly-owned subsidiary of MRB International, a British-based market research group providing full-service marketing research and consultancy throughout the world.   (MDP)

British Overseas Trade Board (BOTB). A Government organization consisting of businessmen (from public and private sectors of industry and the City) and representatives from the Association of British Chambers of Commerce, the CONFEDERATION OF BRITISH INDUSTRY (CBI), the TRADES UNION CONGRESS and government departments involved in export promotion.

Liaising between government and exporters, it (a) advises government on strategy for overseas trade; (b) directs and develops government export promotion services on behalf of the President of the Board of Trade; (c) encourages and supports industry and commerce in overseas trade with the aid of appropriate governmental and non-governmental organizations at home and overseas; and (d) contributes to the exchange of views between government and industry and commerce in the field of overseas trade.

Its ten regional offices at London, Newcastle, Leeds, Birmingham, Manchester, Nottingham, Bristol, Cardiff, Glasgow and Belfast promote exporting through the provision of information, advice and help to exporters. Free services include (a) worldwide counselling for exporters based on expert knowledge and feedback from British Embassies, High Commissions and

Consulates-General overseas; (b) a data bank on overseas tariffs and import regulations; (c) overseas market assessment; (d) the provision of background information of overseas markets; (e) an export intelligence service highlighting specific export opportunities; (f) details on overseas regulations affecting manufacturing under licence; (g) an export marketing research scheme providing advice on undertaking marketing research; and (h) a Statistics and Market Intelligence Library at Export House, London, which has 1,000 volumes of books containing trade and economic data of foreign countries together with telephone numbers and directions likely to be of interest to exporters.

For a small fee the BOTB can arrange detailed enquiries into the prospects of selling a specific product in an overseas market; provide lists of business contacts and information on the standing of overseas firms; offer space at trade fairs and exhibitions, and allow British firms to exhibit products at the British Export Marketing Centre in Tokyo.

The BOTB also provides financial assistance for participants in overseas seminars and symposia, retailers marketing promotions of British goods overseas, group visits to overseas markets which are sponsored by a Chamber of Commerce, trade association or other non-profit-making body, and groups of British firms inviting overseas businessmen to Britain. Underwriting assistance in approved cases for certain costs which may be incurred in a new venture in overseas markets (the Market Entry Guarantee Scheme) is also available.   (JK)

British Rate and Data. *See* BRAD.

British Standards Institution (BSI). Prepares and publishes standards which specify dimensions. performance and safety criteria, testing methods and codes of practice for a large range of products and processes in most fields of production. It is a voluntary non-profit-making body, funded by sales of standards. subscriptions and government grant. Voluntary acceptance of the standards by manufacturers, buyers and sellers reduces unnecessary variety and simplifies the specification of requirements. The board of BSI includes representatives of the main organizations of employers and workers, professional institutions, consumers and the larger government departments.   (HMSO)

British Technology Group. This association is the result of a merger between the National Research Development Corporation and the National Enterprise Board in 1981. The British Technology Group (BTG) is among the world's leading technology transfer companies. It promotes the profitable commercialization of technology by:

developing and protecting technology arising from research carried out by individuals, universities and other research organisations which BTG considers will be commercially viable;
licensing the resulting intellectual property rights to companies throughout the world; and assessing the commercial potential of companies' proprietary technology and licensing this technology to other companies worldwide.
BTG administers over 9,000 patents covering more than 1,500 technologies. In 1992–1993 the Group's total revenue exceeded £26 million. Annual sales values of products currently licensed by BTG amounts to more than £1,500 million. The company is owned by a consortium consisting of BTG management, employees and financial institutions. (HMSO)

Broadcasters' Audience Research Board. *See* BARB.

broad (segment) spot. A MEDIA BUYER'S instruction, booking television advertising time in a specified TIME SEGMENT but allowing the CONTRACTING COMPANY to decide in which COMMERCIAL BREAK it will actually be aired. In practice, it is more usual for the specific break to be negotiated.   (KC)

broadsheet. The larger of the two page sizes common to almost all British newspapers. The 'heavyweight' papers, such as the *Guardian* or the *Financial Times*, are broadsheet format. The great majority of 'popular' papers, and the regional and local titles, are TABLOID. The 'type area' of a broadsheet page varies somewhat, but is generally either 560 or 540 mm deep (22 or 21 inches) and between 340 and 350 mm wide (13 or 14 inches). There are always 8 columns per page in the main sections. Precise dimensions for each title are given in BRAD (q.v.), under 'production specifications'.   (KC)

brochure. A pamphlet. Often an attractively designed and printed description of a PRODUCT or SERVICE. Brochures can be simple or elaborate in terms of design and colours used, quality of paper used and the extent of sketches or photographs incorporated. Brochures can vary from a few pages in length, or sometimes just one page, to dozens of pages. Brochures are customarily left with prospective customers by salespeople after a sales presentation to support and reinforce their verbal messages, or they can be posted to prospective customers in response to enquiries or on a speculative basis. Similarly, brochures are distributed from exhibition stands to prospective customers. Brochures are designed to represent the product or service accurately, but often do so in an idealized, or glamorous manner. Care has to be taken to make them factually accurate especially where product dimensions or characteristics are described. Typically, brochures combine pictorial and textual descriptions of the products and services they relate to, but the balance can vary from the extreme of all text and no pictures to the other way. Certain MARKETING situations call for the extensive use of brochures, e.g. where the products are large or heavy and cannot easily be physically displayed (as is the case with capital plant and hotels). Alternatively many CONSUMER GOODS marketing situations do not use brochures (e.g. confectionery), whereas others (e.g. bicycle manufacturers) have supporting brochures to assist their marketing activities.   (BRM)

broker. A person or organization which acts as an INTERMEDIARY or middleman between buyer or seller. Unlike an agent, the broker does not assume title to the goods, nor take physical possession of them, e.g. a stock-broker.   (MJB)

brown goods. A classification used to cover particular types of CONSUMER DURABLES, specifically those not covered in the WHITE GOODS category, e.g. televisions, videos, hi-fi equipment.   (MDP)

Brussels tariff nomenclature. A system of classifying goods for tariff purposes, accepted as standard by the United Kingdom and many other governments. The principles of valuation of imports are intended to provide a rational and relatively simple standard treatment of imports. Originally the system was confined to members of the European Customs Union, but is now widely used elsewhere.   (JML)

BSI. *See* BRITISH STANDARDS INSTITUTION.

bubble pack. *See* BLISTER PACK.

bucket shop. A slang term for a travel agency which deals in discounted airline tickets.   (MJB)

Bucklin, Louis P. (1928–). American marketing theorist. Graduated Harvard MBA, North Western PhD (1960). His first publication, *A Theory of Distribution Channel Structure* (1966), was followed by at least eight more publications, together with contributions to another twelve by 1981. His current work is in the area of productivity in retailing and in the development of improved management science techniques in retail management. Work also continues on the improvement of the exchange process based on the indigenous organizations in developing countries.   (AJB)

budgetary control. The processes by which an organization ensures that a close watch is kept on the organization's progress towards achieving its annual budget – its revenue and profit goals. This usually requires, at minimum, a monthly review in order to diagnose problems and seize opportunities.   (JRB)

budgeting. The financial practice of forward planning of revenues, costs and profits on an annual basis. Virtually all companies operate an annual budget which is the essential blueprint against which the financial progress of the company is measured as the year progresses. As marketing has the responsibility of achieving the input (revenue) of the budget, and additionally accounts for a considerable percentage of company expenditure, its interest in budgeting is pervasive.   (JRB)

built-in obsolescence. The design and construction of a PRODUCT such that it will automatically fail or otherwise become obsolete within a given period of time. The implication by consumerists such as Vance Packard is that producers deliberately manufacture goods with this characteristic so that users will have to replace them regularly. While it is known that many products have a finite life span (e.g. light bulbs, switches etc.) it is considered that most producers manufacture to a specification which results in value for money rather than deliberately designing products with built-in obsolescence.   (MJB)

bundling. Linking complementary products and/or services together to form a package deal with a lower price/higher value than would be available if the items were purchased separately.

(MJB)

Burke testing. *See* RECALL.

burst. *See* CONTINUITY.

business analysis. An important step in the strategic planning process whose purpose is to evaluate the company's current performance and identify realities upon which the strategic plan must be based. Its major components include: (a) current market analysis, the purpose of which is to identify the company's market share in all consumption and distribution markets by each product category; (b) distinctive-competence analysis, to identify the strengths and weaknesses and problems of the company and its major competitors; and (c) environmental analysis to forecast the extreme as well as the most probable economic, technological, political, legal, regulatory, and life-style conditions for the planning period. (GA)

business analysis (new product development). A stage of the new product development process where a new product idea surviving the screening stage is subjected to a more sophisticated and detailed analysis. Because new product development costs accelerate sharply thereafter, it is imperative to eliminate inappropriate ideas at this stage. Usually, sales potentials are forecast, cost estimates are made, BREAK-EVEN POINTS are calculated, and in some cases more comprehensive decision procedures such as BAYESIAN ANALYSIS are used. (GA)

business and professional press. The collective term for magazines directed mainly at the readership defined by the description, as used in the ADVERTISING ASSOCIATION'S *Advertising Statistics Yearbook*. BRAD (q v.) now describes the category simply as 'business press'. The implied alternative is the magazines of the 'consumer press', the separate 'trade and technical' category being no longer used by either BRAD or the *Advertising Statistics Yearbook*. (KC)

business cycles. In an attempt to predict future economic activity considerable effort has been devoted to the analysis of past trends to determine if there are sufficiently well-defined regularities to permit extrapolation into the future. At least four different types of cycle have been distinguished covering different lengths of time: (a) the Kitchin or inventory cycle with a length of 3–5 years – such cycles are frequently referred to as 'business cycles'; (b) the Juglar cycle with a length of 7–11 years, sometimes termed the 'investment cycle' in that it reflects the normal life of capital equipment; (c) the Kuznets cycle of 15–25 years duration, which is often referred to as the 'building cycle' in that most investors would regard buildings as assets to be depreciated over a period of 15–25 years; (d) the Kondratieff cycle of 45–60 years duration, referred to as the 'long wave'. Views differ as to whether the four cycles are dependent or independent of each other. It is tempting but very simplistic to propose that by juggling with the lengths of the various cycles we can come up with an equation which might state 1 Kondratieff = 3 Kuznets = 6 Juglars = 12 Kitchins. Although it is unlikely that the relationship will ever be so neat, especially now that governments seek to manage their economies, it is equally unlikely that there is no interdependence at all. Certainly there is a common thread in the normal life expectancy of the four basic types of investment (inventory, plant and equipment, buildings), and major infrastructural investments such as railways, motorways, airports, and so on. (MJB)

business definition. In strategic planning the first step in defining the needs to be served. Broad definitions of the kind suggested by Levitt in *Marketing Myopia* – the railroads are in the transportation business – lack sufficient focus to be useful for operational planning purposes and need to be extended by specifying which customers are to be served with which technology.

(MJB)

Business Monitors (UK) The UK Business Statistics Office, aided by industry and commerce, provides the statistical data required by Government for monitoring the economy. Business Monitors are a series of publications containing statistical information compiled from inquiry forms sent out regularly by the BSO to selected firms asking detailed questions about production, sales, employment and investment. Business Monitors are the primary, or in many cases the only, source of the information they contain.

Publications in the Business Monitor series can help monitor business trends, identify products where sales are increasing, identify new market opportunities, pinpoint seasonal factors in trading operations and assess efficiency by comparing a firm's performance with that of the industry as a whole. (MDP)

business portfolio. A set of business entities (divisions, product-lines, products or items) of a business organization. The concept of a 'business portfolio' was popularized by the Boston Consulting Group, which proposed that individual business entities have very different financial characteristics and face different strategic options depending on how they are placed in terms of growth and relative competitive position. Business entities can basically fall into any one of four broad strategic categories, as depicted schematically in the growth–share matrix, each having different implications for strategy development in the typical multi-business organization. (GA)

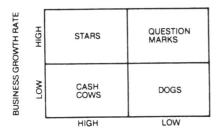

Figure 6: **Business portfolio**

business reply service. A service offered by the Post Office which allows a preprinted reply card or envelope (First or Second Class Post) to be used by customers, to reply free of charge to the company. The service costs £20.00 per year for a licence and an additional charge of half a penny per reply over and above the first or second class postage rate. The increase in response rates associated with both business reply and FREEPOST make the service very attractive. *See also* FREEPOST. (GM)

business strength. A self evident but vague term used widely in the strategic planning literature. Business strengths comprise one of the four dimensions of the SWOT ANALYSIS and may be any aspect of the firm's activities where it believes it enjoys a competitive advantage. (MJB)

business-to-business advertising. Advertising directed at purchasing officers, other business decision makers or professional users, rather than at ordinary consumers. The term is slowly replacing the less accurate and more circumscribing 'industrial advertising'. The implied alternative is 'consumer advertising'. (KC)

business-to-business marketing. Conceptually very similar to ORGANIZATIONAL MARKETING and INDUSTRIAL MARKETING, business-to-business marketing is concerned with all MARKETING activities and requirements existing between businesses of all types. It is therefore probably the most accurate descriptor of this macro segment of marketing, although the alternative terms persist in common use. (KNB)

bus side. An ADVERTISING SPACE on the side of a bus, between the two decks of a double-decker or under the windows of a single-decker. *See also* T-SHAPE. (KC)

buy-back allowance. An agreed sum offered by the seller if the buyer returns (resells) the PRODUCT to him. The buy-back allowance may only be forthcoming against a replacement purchase, and so can be used to encourage buyer loyalty. (MJB)

buy classes. Robinson and Faris identify three different types of organizational buying decision or buy classes. They suggest that the complexity of the decision-making process will depend on the buying decision facing the organizational buyer. The straight rebuy is defined as a repeat purchase of the same item from the same supplier, where the major responsibility for purchase is likely to remain with the purchasing department. The modified rebuy is defined as a purchasing situation where some degree of change has occurred either in product or supplier. More members of the organization are likely to be involved in different stages in the process for this type of decision than for the straight rebuy. The new buy situation involves the greatest degree of change in product and/or supplier and there is likely to be greatest involvement of management throughout the company for this type of decision. (STP)

buyer. The person who actually makes the purchase. This person may be buying on their own behalf or as an agent for another person or organisation. (MJB)

buyer behaviour. *See* CONSUMER BEHAVIOUR and ORGANIZATIONAL BUYER BEHAVIOUR.

buyer readiness stages. The stages an individual goes through in purchasing a product, normally assumed to be a hierarchy from cognitive, affective to conative stage. *See* ATTITUDES.   (KF)

buyer roles. The role is a pattern of behaviour expected of an individual in a specific social position. Family roles are carried out by one or more family members during the buying process, and consist of six key consumption roles – influencers, gatekeepers, deciders, buyers, preparers, and users. Roles vary over time and from product to product.   (KF)

buyer's market. A MARKET where there is excess supply. Buyers are relatively scarce and are therefore in a strong negotiating position as sellers compete with one another.   (MDP)

buy flow. *See* INDUSTRIAL BUYING PROCESS.

buy grid framework. An analytical framework which views organizational buying decisions as a problem-solving activity. The buy grid identifies eight BUY PHASES and three different types of buying decision, or BUY CLASSES (Robinson and Faris, 1967).   (STP)

buying centre. Those persons within an organization responsible for its purchasing decisions. While there may be a formal buying centre or purchasing department, research indicates that the informal buying centre may involve a number of persons who will influence the final decision without actually being responsible for it. Clearly it is important that the seller should identify both the formal and informal members of the buying centre so that he can communicate relevant information to them in appropriate ways.   (MJB)

buying intention survey. A form of ATTITUDE measurement designed to improve the prediction of behaviour from a knowledge of attitudes when the aim is to predict a specific behaviour, such as whether a consumer will purchase a given product. In this case consumer attitude to the (object) product is less appropriate than consumer attitude to the act of purchase of the given product, that is, the consumer's attitude towards performing a particular act in a given situation with respect to a given object.   (JLD)

buying motives. The factors which precipitate the buyer's need and guide their final selection of the PRODUCT perceived as best satisfying that need. While the context and perception of the buyer will mediate the information used and the interpretation put on it, all purchase decisions incorporate a mix of economic (price), technological (performance), and social and psychological (personal and emotional) factors. While one motive may dominate others, the availability of choice in the MARKET place means that buyers will often be faced with two or more acceptable solutions to their purchase need, and so may appear to behave 'irrationally' in making their final selection, e.g. cite a minor feature 'I like the blue colour' as the basis for a major purchase like a motor car. Identifying and understanding buying motives is a key factor in the development of effective MARKETING STRATEGIES.   (MJB)

buying power. A measure of an individual or organisations' resources and likely scale of purchase.   (MJB)

buying power index. An index number calculated from population, disposable income and retail sales data which is a measure of an area's buying power. Frequently used to describe markets in the USA, the higher the number the greater the buying power.   (MJB)

buy phases. Robinson and Faris identified eight phases/stages in the industrial buying process. In ascending order these are: (a) anticipation of/recognition of a problem/ need; (b) determination of characteristics/ quantity of needed item; (c) description of characteristics/quantity of needed item; (d) search for and qualification of potential suppliers; (e) acquisition and analysis of proposals; (f) evaluation and analysis of proposals and choice; (g) selection of order routine; (h) performance feedback and evaluation.   (STP)

buy-response. A method of pre-testing CONSUMER perceptions of what represents an acceptable price for a PRODUCT. It works on the premise that price is an indicator of quality – with too low a price being seen as 'too good to be true' and too high a price 'not worth the money'. As Margaret Crimp states in *The Market Research Process* (2nd edn, Englewood Cliffs, NJ: Prentice-Hall, 1985), the buy-response curve illustrates 'the limits within which a selling price would not be a barrier to acceptance, while the shape of the curve shows the limits where the

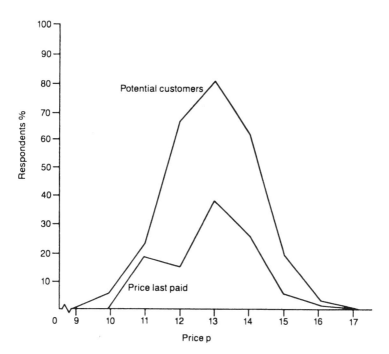

Figure 7: **'Buy-Response' and 'Price Last Paid' curves**

Source: André Gabor, *Pricing: Principles and Practices* (London: Heinemann. 1977)

most generally acceptable price is likely to fall'.
See Figure 7.   (GKP)

by-line. The name of the author responsible for a
report or article, i.e. 'By' John Smith.   (MJB)

by-product. A secondary PRODUCT created as a
consequence of the manufacture of the main or
primary product, e.g. producer gas is a by-
product of the manufacture of coke for use in
blast furnaces.   (MJB)

C

C1,C2. *See* SOCIO-ECONOMIC CLASSIFICATION.

CAA. *See* CINEMA ADVERTISING ASSOCIATION.

cable television. The distribution of television signals by means of a fibre-optic or co-axial cable to subscribers who have paid a fee for the service. The cable can be used for transmitting other data including telephone services. (MJB)

CAC (cognitive-affective-conative). One of two basic attitude models. *See* ATTITUDE. (MJB)

CAD. *See* COMPUTER-AIDED DESIGN.

California Personality Inventory (California Psychological Inventory). A personality test, most notably used by T.S. Robertson and J.A. Myers ('Personality Correlates of Opinion Leadership and Innovative Buying Behaviour', in *Journal of Marketing Research,* vol. 6, May 1969) to measure the links between personality, innovative buying behaviour and OPINION LEADERSHIP. The CPI's major function is to determine the personality characteristics of RESPONDENTS, using 18 major divisions: dominance; responsibility; capacity for status; SOCIALIZATION (i.e. degree of social maturity); sociability; self-control; social presence; tolerance; self-acceptance; good impression; sense of well-being; communality; intellectual efficiency; achievement via conformance; femininity; psychological mindedness; flexibility; achievement via independence. (GKP)

call bird. The use of low prices on items not normally purchased in large quantities, as a feature in advertising or window exhibits, The purpose is to increase STORE TRAFFIC in the hope of selling regularly priced merchandise. (AJB)

call frequency. *See* CALLING CYCLE.

calling cycle. The frequency with which a salesman will call upon an ACCOUNT. Usually dictated by the size and importance of the account to the seller. (MJB)

call plan. A formal plan setting out the ACCOUNTS to be visited by a salesman and the frequency of the visits over the planning period. (MJB)

call report. A source of objective data required by sales management giving details of each visit, the progress made and the outcome. (WD)

CAM. *See* COMPUTER-AIDED MANUFACTURING.

camera-ready copy (CRC). A printing term for finished ARTWORK or typeset material which is in a final form, from which plates can be made. (GM)

Campaign. The weekly news magazine of the advertising business. (KC)

campaign. *See* ADVERTISING CAMPAIGN.

campaign planning. An essential preliminary to the execution of an ADVERTISING CAMPAIGN. In practice, individual advertisers' and advertising agencies' approaches to campaign planning vary considerably, but the process should ideally comprise some or all of the following actions: product-market analysis, evaluation of competitive position, client brief, objective setting, budgeting, selection of target audiences, formulation of creative and media strategies, creative execution, media buying and scheduling, production, implementation, measurement of effectiveness. *See also* ADVERTISING APPROPRIATION, ACCOUNT PLANNING, ADVERTISING OBJECTIVES, ADVERTISING TESTING, MEDIA BUYING, MEDIA PLANNING, MEDIA SCHEDULE. (KC)

cannibalization. In marketing terms, any new activity undertaken by an organization which adversely affects existing business is said to cannibalize it. The launch of a new product into a market in which the organization already has an existing product will, almost inevitably, have some adverse affect on the existing brand. Such effect must be taken into account in forecasting the profitability of such new activity. An international aspect of cannibalization may be seen in the effect on national subsidiaries of a multinational company where there are 'cross-exports'; for example if a British car-maker sells his car at greater profit in Britain than in Belgium, he loses business through cannibalization every time a British buyer goes to Belgium to buy one of his cars: overall planned company profits decline. (JRB)

canonical correlation. A correlation coefficient between two sets of variables. Canonical correlation analysis can be loosely described as doing FACTOR ANALYSIS on each set of variables to produce factors (weighted combinations), subject to the constraint of maximizing the canonical correlation. (SKT)

canvass. Colloquially, to seek or solicit views on a subject. In MARKETING RESEARCH it is used with two different and distinct meanings: (a) to conduct a CENSUS of a defined POPULATION; (b) to identify respondents possessing a particular characteristic from a larger population and so FILTER them out. (MJB)

CAP Committee. The former name of the COMMITTEE OF ADVERTISING PRACTICE. (KC)

capital. The wealth employed in a firm or available for use. The capital account represents the claim of the owner against the firm's business assets. The term 'capital' is commonly used in three specific senses: capital invested, capital employed and working capital. Capital invested is the amount of money introduced into the business by the owner, and represents their

investment in the business. Capital employed is the amount of money being used in the firm, i.e. the total amount of fixed and current ASSETS at the disposal of the business. Working capital is the excess of the total current assets over the total current liabilities of the firm. Note that it is not only the cash available. (GM)

capital employed. *See* CAPITAL.

capital expenditure. Money spent on fixed ASSETS and long-term projects. *See* REVENUE EXPENDITURE. (GM)

capital goods. Goods which are used in the production process itself in order to produce other products. In marketing terms. capital goods represent industrial products, purchased by enterprises and include items such as plant, machinery, buildings and so on. (MS)

capital invested. *See* CAPITAL.

caption. A brief heading or description accompanying an illustration. Often worded to attract attention. Used colloquially in advertising for COPY-LINE. (DL)

captive audience/captive market. A group of potential customers who cannot avoid exposure to a MARKETING message or do not have ready access to an alternative source of supply. (MJB)

caravan tests. A mobile version of a HALL TEST, used to test CONSUMER ATTITUDES towards new PRODUCTS or new packaging. Unlike a hall test, which is located in one central location, the caravan or trailer can be taken around a number of testing sites enabling a wider SAMPLE of RESPONDENTS to be surveyed. This is particularly useful for undertaking RESEARCH in OUT-OF-TOWN SHOPPING CENTRES, entertainment centres or industrial estates. (AMW)

Carbolic Smoke Ball. A product which became the subject of a famous legal case in 1892, established the principle that words and claims could sometimes mean exactly what they said: very vexatious to hyperbole merchants, of whom there were many at the time, such as 'Professor' Thomas HOLLOWAY. On 13 November 1891, the Carbolic Smoke Ball Company advertised in the *Pall Mall Gazette* that '£100 reward will be paid ... to any person who contracts the increasing epidemic, influenza, colds, or any diseases caused by taking cold, after having used the ball three times daily for two weeks according to the printed directions supplied'. They further announced that '£1000 is deposited with the Alliance Bank, Regent Street, showing our sincerity in the matter'. A Mrs Carlill bought a Carbolic Smoke Ball, used it as directed, but nevertheless contracted influenza. Once recovered, she asked the manufacturers for £100; they refused, and she took them to court. The defendants' counsel made pleas on several grounds that there was no binding contract, including the argument that 'The advertisement was a mere representation of what the advertisers intended to do in a certain event ... (they) did not, by issuing it, mean to impose upon themselves any obligation enforceable by law'. Mr Justice Hawkins, on the contrary, ruled that an advertiser 'must not be surprised if occasionally he is held to his promise', adding that advertisements of this type exploited the 'credulous and weak portions of the community', even if they perhaps had no effect on the 'wise and thoughtful'. The Carbolic Smoke Ball Company appealed, but the Court of Appeal held that their promise had been 'as plain as words could make it', particularly in the matter of the £1000 deposited as evidence of good faith. Mrs Carlill eventually got her £100 – and many advertising copywriters got cold feet, though dubious claims would remain all too common for another half-century at least. *See also* ADVERTISING CONTROL.   (KC)

cardinal scales. *See* SCALING METHODS (INTERVAL SCALES).

carload. American expression to describe the use of a full railway freight car with the objective of reducing the carriage charges.   (MJB)

carry-over effects. Literally, those effects which are a carry-over from a prior period of analysis into a current or future period of analysis and therefore not directly attributable to present or future marketing actions. This effect is particularly noticeable in the case of advertising where there is often a significant lag between the publication of an advertisement and consumer reaction to it, with the result that expenditure may be incurred within one accounting period with no apparent return on that expenditure. However, the effects of this advertising will have a carry-over effect into succeeding accounting periods and forecasters and planners should seek to estimate these and incorporate them into their projections.

Recognition of carry-over effects has led many marketers to argue that marketing expenditure should be treated as a capital rather than an expense item as the benefits are only recouped over time and usually beyond the boundaries of conventional accounting periods.   (MJB)

cartel. An agreement between a group of companies in an industry for the purpose of regulating prices, output etc., with the aim of minimizing COMPETITION. A cartel is a formal system of collaboration with rules set down in a legally enforceable document. Cartels are not legal in the UK because they are held to restrict trade and create MONOPOLY conditions.   (MDP)

cartoon. A projective technique used in MARKET RESEARCH in which the RESPONDENT is invited to fill in what a character in a cartoon might be thinking or saying in the situation represented by the cartoon.   (MJB)

cash-and-carry retailer. Retail outlets offering discounted goods and limited or no service. Particularly popular with small businesses such as cafes, restaurants and boarding houses. (MJB)

cash-and-carry wholesalers. A wholesaling function which, by not providing a delivery service or a billing/credit facility to its customers, incurs lower operating costs and can then charge lower prices than a standard wholesaling operation. It necessitates their customers – retailers – having to pay cash, and to carry home the produce. In order to 'protect' the retail profession, cash and carry wholesalers attempt to keep out members of the general public from shopping in their warehouses.   (JRB)

cash cow. A term used to describe a product which is capable of generating considerably more revenue than the costs (production and marketing) of maintaining its share of the market. Hence the product can be 'milked'. *See* BOSTON BOX.
                             (MS)

cash discounts. Reductions in the cash price of goods. The term exists because not all discounts are cash: discounts may also be given in the form of free products: for example, to the consumer a free food mixer with every refrigerator, or to a distributor one case free with every ten.   (JRB)

cash flow. The identification of the movement of ASSETS, liabilities and capital during a period of time, and the resultant effect on cash. The ACCOUNTING for receipts and expenditures. The physical flow of money in and out of the organization. Cash flow is as important to a company as profitability, especially in periods of rapid expansion or high rates of inflation. In a rapidly growing company, the company may make good profits, but have a poor cash flow position because the profits generated are insufficient to cover the even larger increase in STOCK, debtors and capital expenditure caused by the rapid expansion resulting in the firm over-trading and getting into liquidity problems (lack of cash to pay immediate bills). In periods of high inflation the cash generated by a company is absorbed in the repurchase of higher-priced stock. For example, a wine merchant buys stock at 6 ecu and sells it for 9 ecu giving a profit of 50 per cent. However, in periods of high inflation, to repurchase the stock, the merchant has to pay 9 ecu, thus the cash generated by the profit is absorbed by the higher price of stock and the cash flow position is under threat. (GM)

cash on delivery. Payment for goods as they are delivered. It provides a safeguard to sellers and often buyers; sellers reduce debtors, while customers can avoid sending money in advance. (GM)

cash refund offers. A discount or rebate offered to persons providing a 'proof of purchase'. Used by manufacturers to build brand loyalty as application has to be to the manufacturer. (MJB)

catalogue. A BROCHURE or book containing the description of merchandise offered for sale. (MJB)

catalogue retailing. The sale of goods to the general public through the medium of a catalogue. The range of merchandise may be wide (e.g. Littlewoods) or focused on a specific category of goods such as car accessories. Catalogue retailers usually operate through MAIL ORDER and offer extended credit terms. (MJB)

catalogue showroom. A retail outlet selling durable products and other high mark-up merchandise from a catalogue. BUYERS choose items from the catalogue and complete an order form which is then processed in-store i.e. the store carries stock of most portable items. Argos is one of the best-known UK outlets. (MJB)

category killers. Name applied to aggressive retailers who offer deep discounts on specific categories of branded goods such as OTC (over-the-counter) medicines, cosmetics, perfumery etc. which traditionally have carried very high mark-ups. By doing so it is claimed that they will 'kill' the category and discourage manufacturers from maintaining the promotional support on which the original exclusivity/high price depended. (MJB)

category manager. A manager responsible for the management of a specific category of goods such as soups, frozen vegetables etc. comprising a number of different brands. The role of the category manager is similar to that of the product manager. See PRODUCT MANAGEMENT. (MJB)

CATI. See COMPUTER ASSISTED TELEPHONE INTERVIEWING.

causal path analysis. A method of analysis involving the decomposition and interpretation of linear relationships among a set of variables. It is assumed that there is some cause and effect relationship between a set of independent and dependent variables. The magnitude of the relationship is called the 'path' and this describes whether the assumption of cause and effect between two variables is justified. (KAB)

causal research. See EXPERIMENTAL RESEARCH.

caveat emptor. Let the buyer beware. This was, and still is in some instances, the legal judgement between buyer and seller. However as a result of the consumerist movement, CONSUMER PROTECTION legislation and more businesses adopting a more socially responsible attitude, the emphasis has changed more to let the seller beware! (GM)

CAVIAR. Acronym for CINEMA AND VIDEO INDUSTRY AUDIENCE RESEARCH, a continuous research programme to provide MEDIA PLANNERS with reliable audience profiles, commissioned by the CINEMA ADVERTISING ASSOCIATION and funded by a consortium of subscribers. For the 14th annual study, carried out in late 1996, one of Britain's best-known market research companies conducted in-home face-to-face interviews with a UK-wide sample of 2,800 cinemagoers from the age of seven upwards. (KC)

CBD. An abbreviation for Central Business District which is the area within an urban concentration where the majority of businesses are located. Also the hub for most public transportation services.   (MJB)

CBI. *See* CONFEDERATION OF BRITISH INDUSTRY.

CCTV. *See* CLOSED CIRCUIT TELEVISION.

Ceefax. BBC's teletext service. No ADVERTISE-MENTS are currently carried on this particular medium. *See also* TELETEXT and ORACLE.   (GM)

census. An examination of the entire POPULATION of a country or a MARKET. Unless the total population is quite small (e.g. in some specialized MARKET RESEARCH) this approach is rarely used in commercial research. Most censuses are directed by governments (e.g. the UK government undertake a national census every ten years) and are designed to provide vital information on trends in population, trade and industry.   (AMW)

centralized organization. An organization in which power and decision-making authority are concentrated or centralized in the hands of a small number of senior managers and only limited authority and power is delegated to subordinates.   (MJB)

central limit theorem. In the limit (loosely – if you do things again and again) whatever the distribution of a single SAMPLE, the total of the sets of samples will be distributed with the normal distribution. For example, if you want a BASIC program to give you a normal distribution, add the results of taking 12 numbers from the given uniform distribution. Often used as a justification for assuming the applicability of the normal distribution if the sample size is large.   (SKT)

central location test. Survey research in which respondents are invited with or without prior notice to some place (often a public hall or empty shop) where research may be more conveniently carried out. This is often so when respondents are to be asked to try products (*see* PRODUCT TEST) requiring preparation, or be exposed to advertising films.   (JAB)

central place theory. A theory of the distribution of market functions among market centres so that six of the smallest centres are served by a larger supply market. Six of those larger centres are served by a higher level with the pattern continuing until all the centres within the political boundaries are served by the six largest centres.

The number six is derived from the hexagon shape formed by equal sized circles being overlapped to use up all available space (as in a honeycomb). The circle's origins are determined by the distance a person is willing to walk to market, returning the same day. At each level the volume and type of demand has an effect on the function performed and the merchandise offered for sale.   (AJB)

central tendency measures. An obfuscating phrase to describe the set of single measures of the central value of a batch of numbers: MEAN, MEDIAN and MODE are the classic central tendency measures.   (SKT)

centre spread. The centre pages of newspapers and unbound periodicals. These publications open easily to the reader at this point and provide an unbroken surface for the printing of an advertisement, and as such, prove particularly attractive to advertisers. Called the 'centerfold' in the USA.   (JAB)

chain store. Multiple retail units, under common ownership, that use central buying and control systems. The UK Central Statistical Office now refers to those with ten or more branches as large multiple retailers.   (AJB)

change agent. A person or persons with particular responsibility for bringing about change in existing practices. Doctors, missionaries, agricultural advisers etc. all act as change agents in DEVELOPING COUNTRIES by introducing new practices and methods. In the business context, management consultants are frequently employed as change agents since they tend to be perceived as more objective and so more credible than change agents working within a company. Similarly, salesmen act as change agents when they persuade customers to try new products.   (MJB)

channel. (1) A television channel, such as Channel 4, BBC2 or Sky Gold. There will be an enormous expansion in the number available to UK advertisers from 1998, as DIGITAL TELEVISION becomes established. 'Return-path' capability is likely to result in a sudden increase in home shopping, video-on-demand and other interactive services. MEDIA BUYERS of the twenty-first century will be faced by such an enlarged choice that they will surely have to treat 'television' as more than one medium.

(2) In communication theory, the 'channel' is defined as the path along which a message moves from sender to receiver. The most obvious analogue in the marketing communications context is the MEDIA VEHICLE in which an ADVERTISEMENT or the outcome of a PUBLICITY initiative appear, though DIRECT MARKETING communications reach their audience via the telephone and postal systems. Other techniques in the MARKETING COMMUNICATIONS MIX communicate more or less directly. The significance of the communication channel lies in the modulating influence it can exert on the message: *see* CHANNEL EFFECT. (KC)

channel behaviour – conflict. The maintenance of harmony in a CHANNEL depends upon each member enjoying a comparative advantage in terms of the function or functions which they perform but using it to the mutual benefit of all the channel members, Where a member seeks to exploit its position this will lead to conflict and to CHANNEL CHANGE as other members seek to change their position too. *See also* CHANNEL CONTROL. (MJB)

channel behaviour – cooperation. The development of cooperation between two organizations is necessary if each is to achieve its goals in supplying products to the market. This is the first kind of behaviour in forming a CHANNEL OF DISTRIBUTION. (AJB)

channel behaviour – leadership. Within the relationship of a CHANNEL, one member may be observed to exercise some form of power which has been acquired through the control of resources. Leadership is then exercised to increase that member's control of resources. (AJB)

channel captain. The member of the distribution channel who exercises influence and/or power over the other CHANNEL members, and ensures that it provides an effective link between producer and CONSUMER. In recent years the channel captaincy has tended to gravitate to the organization in closest contact with the ultimate user. Thus in CONSUMER GOODS, RETAILERS have displaced manufacturers as the channel captain, and for many industrial goods, stockholders and distributors have assumed the leadership role. Other sources of power besides direct contact with the user include financial strength, legal requirements and trade practice. (MJB)

channel change. The relationship between members of a CHANNEL OF DISTRIBUTION is subject to conflict from time to time. When the conflict is dysfunctional then the relationship is severed and a new set of organizations develops. The change is explained as creative destruction by Schumpeter and by other more detailed models of explanation as cycle theories, the CORE-FRINGE MODEL, the crisis change model, and the dialectical model. (AJB)

channel control. A function of the firm's competitive strength *vis-à-vis* other members of a CHANNEL OF DISTRIBUTION. In general the dominant members are either producers or user/consumers, but there are situations where the channel intermediary may be dominant and so condition the structure and operation of the channel. The latter situation is most likely to occur where both producers and users are small and the market is geographically dispersed, and is equally true of retailers/wholesalers in the consumer goods market as it is of the industrial goods wholesaler. Overall, dominance or control is determined by a number of factors which may be summarized as: buyer/seller concentration ratios in terms of production/consumption, and spatial relationships. Technical complexity: in the case of technically complex products, dominance will be conditioned by the relative sophistication of the producer *vis-à-vis* the intermediary and/or user. Thus, a small firm may exercise a considerable influence over much larger users or intermediaries. Service requirements: the more complex these are the more likely it is that the producer will exercise control. In the final analysis, however, the determining factor is economic advantage, i.e. which channel member can perform the necessary channel functions at the lowest cost consistent with the required degree of efficiency. At a given point in time the structure of a trade channel serves as a rough and ready guide as to the relative efficiency of its members, but it is clear that over time environmental changes may predicate the adoption of an alternative structure to meet better the needs of users/consumers. Similarly, lack of control may persuade a channel member to modify his policies in order to protect his position – a tendency which is implicit in Galbraith's concept of COUNTERVAILING POWER. (MJB)

channel effect. The effect that the channel through which a MARKETING COMMUNICATIONS message is transmitted has upon the target audience's perceptions of it and their reactions to it, along with SOURCE EFFECT, MESSAGE EFFECT and the time effects created by the MEDIA SCHEDULE. The most obvious such channel is the MEDIA VEHICLE in which an ADVERTISEMENT or the outcome of a PUBLICITY initiative appear, though DIRECT MARKETING communications reach their audience via the the telephone and postal systems. No satisfactory theoretical explanation of channel effect is to be found in the literature of marketing communications, and the general social communication textbooks concentrate on direct transmission of messages from individuals to individuals without the modulating effect of an intervening channel. We are therefore obliged to infer the ingredients of channel effect from studies of source effect, postulating that audiences will treat the channel vehicle to some extent as a second source. In that case, they are 'credibility' (perceived objectivity and expertise), 'attractiveness' (familiarity and perceived congruence with the audience's own values) and 'power' (authority and prestige). These attributes, if positive, will potentiate 'internalization' of the message, 'identification' with the source and 'compliance' with the call to action in the message. There is experimental evidence only for the 'credibility' dimension. Despite this shortage of theoretical support for the phenomenon, MEDIA PLANNERS demonstrate implicit acceptance of a channel effect when they use such terms as 'relaxed', 'urgent' or 'chatty' to describe types of newspaper, or discuss 'media values' and 'rub-off effect' in their professional journals.   (KC)

channel flicking. *See* ZAPPING.

channel (of distribution). 'The structure of intra-company organization units and extra-company agents and dealers, wholesale and retail, through which a commodity, product or service is marketed' (American Marketing Association definition). In other words, a channel consists of all those stages and organizations through which a product must pass between its point of production and consumption. At its simplest, this may be a single, direct transaction between producers and consumer, e.g. DIRECT MAIL SELLING, or the sale of produce at the farm gate. On the other hand, where production is highly concentrated and consumers are widely diffused, a number of different channels may develop and coexist with a variety of agents, distributors, wholesalers, retailers and other intermediaries acting as the channel through

which goods will flow from producer to consumer.

At the macro level in the economy, a channel of distribution may be described as a sub-system that serves manufacturers and consumers in bridging the gap between production and consumption. At the micro level the channel is a set of enterprises who have formed a symbiotic relationship in economic and social agreements as a means of increasing their social assets, and making products and services available for consumption. *See also* DISTRIBUTION CHANNEL, FUNCTIONS OF.   (AJB, MJB)

channel leadership. *See* CHANNEL CAPTAIN.

channel performance. The output of CHANNELS OF DISTRIBUTION can be measured and compared with the inputs over a period of time at both micro and macro levels. Making the comparison in space (between firms, industries, countries or economies) has generally proved impossible. At the macro level the main measure has been the productivity of labour and capital although many more specific measures have also been attempted. At the micro level the main tools to measure the performance of the firm's channel(s) have been profitability analysis, the strategic profit model, and a wide range of operating measures which examine market penetration, effectiveness, and efficiency at many levels.

(AJB)

channel power. *See* CHANNEL CAPTAIN.

channel zapping. *See* ZAPPING.

checklist. A list of factors or actions which should be considered or implemented in performing a predefined task such as launching a new product.   (MJB)

cherry picking. The selection of only one or a few items from an assortment of goods.   (MJB)

chi-square. A statistical test of the existence (not the strength) of association between two or more variables, which may be only nominally scaled, strictly in random samples. The repeated use of the test on a body of data gives rise to the fallacy known as 'hunting'. *See* RANDOM SAMPLING.

(JAB)

chi-square contingency test. A statistical test (the CHI-SQUARE GOODNESS-OF-FIT TEST) applied a contingency table (a statistical medium). *See* phrase for a TWO-WAY TABLE. The test can be used to prevent over-interpretation of differences in percentages; by only interpreting those tables with significant CHI-SQUARE CONTINGENCY TESTS. It is still important to be cautious as the test's significance only indicates that the table as a whole has its differences in percentages that are unlikely to happen by mere chance.   (SKT)

chi-square goodness-of-fit test. The statistical test based on the chi-square distribution. Not only used for contingency tables but also for the fit of Maximum Likelihood Factor Analysis; in that case when the test is significant, it suggests that there is too much unexplained (residual) variation to be able to be confident in the FACTOR ANALYSIS results.   (SKT)

choice. Specifically, the decision either to buy or not to buy an object. More generally it refers to the alternatives available to an intending buyer consisting of products which are seen as close substitutes for one another. Such products comprise the buyer's EVOKED SET.   (MJB)

CIF. *See* COST, INSURANCE, FREIGHT.

cinema. One of the five 'major' ADVERTISING MEDIA in Britain. Over 90 per cent of all cinemas in the UK show COMMERCIALS, as distinct from film trailers, once in each complete 'showing'. Surprisingly, the medium is not available to advertisers in either Japan or the USA. It is the third-oldest in Britain, the first cinema in the country having opened in the Mohawk's Hall in Islington in 1901, but ranks last in terms of its share of total ADVERTISING EXPENDITURE. After its heyday in the 1930s and 1940s, when 19 million Britons 'went to the pictures' every week, cinema suffered steadily declining audiences in the face of changing lifestyles and the arrival of television as a rival mass-entertainment medium. Advertisers deserted the medium as the deliverable target audience shrank, and its media share fell from a high of 3.8 per cent in 1948 to a low of 0.4 per cent in every year between 1984 and 1989. Nevertheless, the profile of the audience that did remain loyal was unique among advertising media and potentially interesting to a variety of brand advertisers: penetration of the 18- to 25-year-old age group was around 80 per cent, almost half of them attended at least once a month, and the typical audience was exactly half male and half female. As an influential media

planner commented to a Marketing magazine reporter when cinema's fortunes were at their lowest ebb: 'a highly flexible medium positioned against a young audience cannot be all bad'. The industry at last responded constructively to the marketing challenge by making qualitative improvements in both programmes and accommodation, and starting to build the now familiar MULTIPLEXES. Annual attendance figures duly started to rise for the first time since the 1940s, reaching 70 million in 1985, breaking the 100 million barrier in 1993 (still less than a quarter of pre-war annual totals) and reaching 123 million in 1996. The number of screens available to advertisers has increased steadily since 1988, standing at 2,166 at the end of 1996. Advertisers started to return to the transformed medium in 1990: total expenditure has increased slowly but steadily in every year since, and the media share has risen from 0.5 to 0.7 per cent. CINEMA ADVERTISING ASSOCIATION (CAA) data for 1996 show that the contemporary audience is considerably more upmarket than the population as a whole (68 per cent ABC1 versus 49 per cent) and contains very nearly twice as many young adults (60 per cent in the 18–34 bracket versus 31 per cent). Unsurprisingly, the highest-spending advertisers are three brewers, two distillers, Levi's, Elida Gibbs, Kelloggs, Nestle and DeBeers. In 1997, the CAA commissioned a DAY-AFTER RECALL test to compare the effectiveness of a Virgin Atlantic cinema commercial against a simultaneous TV screening; the respective figures were 50 per cent against 4 per cent. Five years earlier, the same post-test of a DeBeers commercial had yielded recall figures of 53 per cent and 11 per cent. Cinema may be the smallest advertising medium in Britain, but it occupies a well protected niche. Advertising time is sold by two authorized contractors: Pearl & Dean, who control more than 80 per cent of the available options, and Cinema Media. It can be bought 'screen-by-screen' or in 'film packages'; campaigns can be co-ordinated by location, type of film, type of cinema, and certificate. Cinema is the most minor of the major media in every European country in which it is available, its media share exceeding one per cent only in Belgium.   (KC)

Cinema Advertising Association (CAA). The body representing authorized cinema advertising contractors, of which there were two in 1997: Pearl & Dean, who control more than 80 per cent of the available options, and Cinema Media. Its principal aims are to promote cinema as an advertising medium, to support it by the provision of reliable research data, and to maintain standards with respect to cinema commercials. The recent history of cinema advertising (*see* CINEMA) suggests that it is doing the first job well. It tackles the second aim by commissioning a continuous research programme (*see* CAVIAR) and carrying out periodic comparative POST-TESTS of cinema commercials against simultaneously broadcast television commercials for the same product. The third is addressed by a system of pre-clearance of commercials longer than 30 seconds (*see* ADVERTISING CONTROL) and the fact that cinema advertising is subject to the ADVERTISING STANDARDS AUTHORITY'S Advertising Code.   (KC)

circulation. In the case of PAID-FOR TITLES, this is the number of copies bought across the counter, delivered by a newsagent, received on subscription or otherwise paid for in any way. The figure specifically excludes complimentary copies or distributed copies returned unsold. In the case of FREESHEETS and CONTROLLED CIRCULATION PUBLICATIONS, the equivalent is the number of copies successfully delivered to an identifiable address. MEDIA BUYERS can find 'average net circulation' figures for about 3,000 paid-for newspapers and magazines, audited quarterly by the AUDIT BUREAU OF CIRCULATIONS ('ABC'), in BRAD (q.v.). For example, the 'ABC circulations' for the first half of 1996 for the *News of the World*, the *Hexham Courant*, *Good Housekeeping* and *The Economist* were respectively 4,607,189, 18,775, 488,243 and 318,255. Likewise, BRAD publishes 'average net distribution' figures for about 850 freesheets, audited quarterly by VERIFIED FREE DISTRIBUTION (VFD), a wholly owned subsidiary of ABC. For instance, the 'VFD circulation' of the *Lakeland Echo* was 17,554 in 1996. Alternative measures are an 'independent audit' conducted by a body other than the ABC or VFD, a 'publisher's statement' or a 'certificate of posting'. MEDIA BUYERS will normally want to know not only audited or verified circulation but also a reliable estimate of READERSHIP, the number of people who read an issue of a given publication as distinct from the number who actually buy it. That information is also published in BRAD.   (KC)

CKD (completely knocked down). The supply of products in an unassembled state usually to economize on storage and transportation costs arising from the shape or bulk of the article. More recently CKD products have been used to offer price reductions to persons willing to assemble the products themselves, for example furniture from MFI.   (MJB)

classical conditioning. *See* PAVLOVIAN LEARNING MODEL.

classification variables. Sample survey data may be analysed by tabulation to show the effect, and presumably the causality, of various independent and explanatory variables. Traditionally certain variables such as age, sex, socio-economic classification, area of residence, are used as well as direct classification relating to attitudes and usage in the product field.

Age is conventionally classified by groupings, or combinations of groupings based on: 16–24, 25–34, 35–44, 45–54, 55–64, and 65 and over.

Sex is noted, and may be combined with household studies. Housewives are however defined as persons responsible for buying food and so on, for a household, and may thus be male or female. *See* SOCIO-ECONOMIC CLASSIFICATIONS.

Area of residence is conventionally defined by the Gwerrin Economic Planning Regions, or the INCORPORATED SOCIETY OF BRITISH ADVERTISERS defined Independent Television reception areas.

Marital status, occupation, economic activity, income, terminal education age, size and composition of household, and tenure of accommodation are also frequently used.   (JAB)

classified advertising. The generic term for 'small ads', bought on a line-by-line basis. They include no graphics whatever, are not more than one column wide, are grouped under classifications in one section of a newspaper or magazine, and are mostly inserted by individuals rather than 'advertisers'. The implied contrast is with DISPLAY ADVERTISING.   (KC)

classified directory. A book listing individuals and/or organizations in terms of one or more classification variables, such as PRODUCT MIX, location etc.   (MJB)

client. What an ADVERTISING AGENCY calls a firm whose advertising it handles. Agencies also speak of an ACCOUNT, meaning a distinct 'chunk' of business handled. Thus, a single client may constitute more than one account, each being some grouping of its products or services. Furthermore, a single advertiser may distribute its advertising among several agencies and thus be a client of all of them, with different accounts in each. The vocabulary is thus 'Lever Brothers is a client of ours; we have the Persil account'. 'Client' is invariably used rather than 'account' in such phrases as 'I'm calling on the client to discuss the new product launch' or 'Client wants the schedule changed'. (KC)

client brief. Advertising agency terminology for the ADVERTISING BRIEF. (KC)

client list. A list of the CLIENTS belonging to a particular ADVERTISING AGENCY. (KC)

client service executive. A more precise and self-explanatory, but less common, version of ACCOUNT EXECUTIVE. (KC)

closed circuit television (CCTV). A television broadcasting system restricted to subscribers and not available to the general public. Frequently used for televising major sporting events in real time. (MJB)

closed question. A question calling for responses which are strictly limited. The RESPONDENT is offered a choice of alternative replies from which he is expected to select an answer appropriate to his own situation. Such questions can either take the form of a dichotomous question which has only two choices of response (e.g. yes or no) or of a multiple choice question where a range of possible answers is available. (AMW)

closure. The process whereby individuals will complete or close a stimulus which is incomplete. This tendency is intrinsic to the Gestalt school of psychology which argues that there is a basic human drive to see things as a whole so that missing information will be supplied by the respondent in order to make the stimulus complete and meaningful.

Closure is widely used in ADVERTISING both to involve the subject in the advertisement which encourages learning and retention and as a means of reminding/reinforcing earlier more complete expositions of the message. (MJB)

CLS. *See* CONSUMER LOCATION SYSTEM.

cluster analysis. Generic term applied to a variety of methods whereby a SAMPLE of objects or individuals may be classified into groups on the basis of factors which differentiate between them. The need for such a scheme of classification and grouping is to be found in most fields of research and enquiry, and has led to the development of varied nomenclature to describe essentially the same process: cluster analysis, Q analysis, typology, grouping, clumping, classification, numerical taxonomy, and unsupervised pattern recognition.

Ideally clusters should be self-evident and capable of identification simply by reviewing a set of data and distinguishing natural groupings within it, for example, classifying people as male or female. However, for most purposes, decision makers require a much finer discrimination than is possible using two or three dimensions, which is the maximum most of us can conceptualize simultaneously. Because of this need for greater sophistication there has been a proliferation of techniques such as discriminant analysis and FACTOR ANALYSIS designed to cope with larger numbers of factors simultaneously. (MJB)

clustering techniques. A generic term embracing a range of different methods and techniques for combining data into groups or clusters with a high degree of internal consistency and homogeneity which may be distinguished from another cluster or clusters in terms of the criteria used to define the cluster. Such methods are widely used in marketing for purposes of CLUSTER SAMPLING and MARKET SEGMENTATION. (MJB)

cluster sampling. The process of sampling on the basis of clearly defined groups or units within a POPULATION. Where the population is clearly defined and known, e.g. all households in an area, then cluster sampling may be used to reduce the costs of contacting RESPONDENTS compared with those which would be incurred if no clustering took place and the sample was drawn at random. Clustering is also appropriate where there is no satisfactory sampling frame, i.e. we cannot identify the members of the population, so that one has to define the groups or clusters to be sampled on the basis of a suitable clustering factor, e.g. convenience, accessibility etc. The obvious disadvantage of such a non-probabilistic approach to sampling is that it can lead to ERROR and BIAS by comparison with a truly random approach. *See* SAMPLING. (MJB)

clutter. The condition which exists when too many advertisements are competing for the viewer, listener or reader's attention at the same time with the result that none are likely to trigger awareness. (MJB)

code. Any symbol used for classifying data so that it can be processed or analysed in a more convenient way, e.g. for transferring data from a questionnaire to a punched card when the column and row number would be used. (MJB)

code of ethics. A CODE OF PRACTICE setting out the ethical standards adopted by an organisation and expected of its employees. (MJB)

code of practice. A collection of rules or guidelines relating to the proper conduct, or best practice of a service. In the marketing context, they relate especially to ADVERTISING but also to the other forms of MARKETING COMMUNICATIONS and to MARKET RESEARCH. They exert a self-regulatory influence upon practitioners who are not bound by professional codes of conduct or legislation, as is the case with the medical profession or the police. The conditions cannot be directly enforced by legislation (except in the case of television advertising), but their breach causes peer group displeasure and consequent damage to business. Members of associations are thus always encouraged to conduct themselves in accordance with the established 'code of practice' and thereby enhance their reputation with their clients and with their peers. For instance, a code of practice relating to the collection of MARKET RESEARCH information will provide guidelines for researchers to follow. These could include always carrying adequate means of identification, treating the information confidentially and being courteous to the public. Other codes have been developed by various associations in an attempt to overcome the problems caused by the bogus activities and fraudulent conduct of unscrupulous operators. The most familiar general codes of practice are: THE BRITISH CODES OF ADVERTISING AND SALES PROMOTION, the DIRECT MARKETING ASSOCIATION'S Code of Practice, the ITC CODE OF ADVERTISING STANDARDS AND PRACTICE, the INSTITUTE OF PRACTITIONERS IN ADVERTISING Bye-Laws, the Institute of Public Relations Code of Conduct, the MARKET RESEARCH SOCIETY Code of Conduct and the RADIO AUTHORITY ADVERTISING AND SPONSORSHIP CODE. (KC)

coding. A general term used to describe the procedure for classifying objects in terms of some predetermined principle. In MARKET RESEARCH, it refers to the classifying of DATA to make it amenable to subsequent ANALYSIS. In the case of

producers, the BAR CODE is a unique number which identifies a PRODUCT so that it can be processed by EPOS equipment. (MJB)

coefficient of determination (R^2). The square of the correlation coefficient. The percentage of variation explained by a REGRESSION ANALYSIS and used typically as a GOODNESS-OF-FIT measure; probably better to use the standard error of estimate which gives the size of residuals. (SKT)

coefficient of multiple determination. The coefficient of determination in a MULTIPLE REGRESSION ANALYSIS: a REGRESSION ANALYSIS with more than one predictor variable. (SKT)

coefficient of variation. A figure used to compare the size of distributions, calculated as the ratio of the standard deviation to the MEAN as a percentage. (SKT)

cognition. An individual's understanding of an object or CONCEPT derived from his PERCEPTIONS, ATTITUDES, BELIEFS, learned behaviour and NEEDS (conscious and subconscious). (MJB)

cognitive consistency theory. A theory first proposed by Heider's Balance Theory and developed in Osgood and Tannenbaum's Congruity Theory and Festinger's Cognitive Consistency Theory. It states that individuals strive to achieve consistency between their PERCEPTIONS, ATTITUDES, VALUES, and their BEHAVIOUR. (MJB)

cognitive dissonance. Theory developed in 1957 by Leon Festinger to describe a psychological state which results from the perception of incompatibility between two pieces of information held in the cognitive system, both of which are believed to be true. The inconsistency produces tension which acts to motivate the individual to restore harmony within the system.

Relating to the consumer world, cognitive dissonance arises after a choice decision has been made and the consumer is committed to a particular choice from a product field, leading the consumer to dissonance reduction behaviour. (JLD)

cohort. Term used to describe a group of individuals who share the same characteristic e.g. age, pattern of behaviour etc. (MJB)

cold call, calling. A visit to a prospect by a salesperson uninvited, without warning, in the hope of securing an interview. (WD)

Colley, Russell H. An American management consultant, noted for his formulation, in 1961, of one of the HIERARCHY-OF-EFFECTS descriptions of how advertising works. This is universally known by the acronym DAGMAR, actually derived from the title of the paper in which the hierarchical explanation was first proposed: Defining Advertising Goals for Measured Advertising Results. It is ironic that Colley should be remembered for a conceptually flawed model of advertising effect instead of for the very important point made in the title of the paper and developed at much more length than the description of the model. The point is that testing ADVERTISING EFFECTIVENESS is legitimate exercise only if specific criteria of effectiveness have been derived from explicit and measurable ADVERTISING OBJECTIVES. Despite the re-publication of his paper as an article in the *Harvard Business Review* in 1962 and its subsequent dissemination in several books of readings, this vital lesson seems to have been depressingly widely ignored throughout the three decades since.   (KC)

column-centimetres. The standard way to describe DISPLAY ADVERTISING space in a newspaper: its depth in centimetres by its width as a number of columns. Notice that this is the opposite of what the term implies. The basic unit of measurement and charge is the SINGLE COLUMN CENTIMETRE. Larger spaces are described as '20-centimetre double column', '40 centimetres across three columns' and so on, often in contracted forms, except for the quarter-page and half-page options. Magazines do not use the column-centimetre convention, but fractions of a page, even for the smallest display spaces on offer. Both types of publication sell CLASSIFIED ADVERTISING SPACE by the line.   (KC)

comb binding. A form of MECHANICAL BINDING where pages and cover are punched with a series of holes on the binding edge. A comb coil in the form of wire, strip metal or plastic is mechanically inserted into the holes to keep the pages together.   (MDP)

commando salesman. A person specifically designated to intensive selling in new markets, often with new products, to augment the existing salesforce. Commando salesmen are hired only temporarily, in many cases from an outside sales specialist agency.   (WD)

commercial. The correct term for an individual television, radio or cinema advertisement. It is presumably a contraction of 'commercial message'. The time slots made available by the television and radio MEDIA OWNERS are in multiples of 10 seconds, normally up to one minute. The most common length of a television commercial is 40 seconds, and of a radio commercial 30 seconds. In the case of cinema, the basic units are the same, cinema advertisers in practice often adapting their television commercials for the purpose. Typical cinema commercials tend to be either 30 or 60 seconds in length, but longer durations are not uncommon. Individual commercials occupy SPOTS, which are combined into COMMERCIAL BREAKS.   (KC)

commercial break. A period of time allocated to COMMERCIALS during television and radio programmes or between them. In the case of terrestrial television channels 3, 4 and 5, the INDEPENDENT TELEVISION COMMISSION statutorily controls the frequency of advertising as well as the total amount (see also ADVERTISING CONTROL). The rather complicated rules require that commercials should fill 'natural breaks' in programmes, and that the gap between consecutive breaks must normally be at least 20 minutes. Further, a programme of between 21 and 45 minutes' duration may contain one 3-minute break, a programme of between 46 and 65 minutes is permitted either one three-and-a-half-minute break or two of 3 minutes, and a programme longer than 65 minutes may add an extra three and a half minutes of advertising per 30 minutes. However, if the format of a particular programme prevents a station from offering the full number of breaks, the continuous action of sports broadcasts being a familiar case in point in Britain, it is permitted to transfer the lost 'minutage' to subsequent breaks. Before 1991, the amount and frequency of both television and radio advertising had been regulated by a single body, but the newly devolved RADIO AUTHORITY announced its intention to exercise 'a lighter touch' in regard to all formal controls. Since then, the frequency of breaks has been a decision to be made by individual station controllers, who must decide whether listeners are more likely to desert the station because of frequent brief interruptions than because of less frequent long ones, or vice versa. Radio experts are understandably reluctant to suggest a 'typical' outcome among the 160 commercial stations on air in 1997. In the case of cinema, total advertising time available comes in one commercial break during each 'house'. *See also* AIRTIME; ADVERTISING-TO-EDITORIAL RATIO.   (KC)

commercialization. The final phase in the NEW PRODUCT DEVELOPMENT process when the product is launched into the marketplace, thus initiating its life cycle. Commercialization increases the firm's financial commitment by several orders of magnitude. Capacity must be installed to cater for the anticipated demand, inventory must be built up to ensure that supplies can be made available to the distribution channel, intensive selling-in must take place to ensure widespread availability at the point of sale or to canvass orders from prospective buyers, maintenance and servicing facilities may be necessary and a large promotional investment will be needed to create awareness of the new product's existence. (MJB)

commercial radio. The network of 158 local, 5 regional and 4 national radio stations in the UK. that are supported by advertising revenue and collectively constitute the second smallest of Britain's five MAJOR MEDIA. It complements BBC Radio, financed by the licence fee and carrying no advertising. *See also* INDEPENDENT LOCAL RADIO, INDEPENDENT NATIONAL RADIO, RADIO.
(KC)

Commercial Radio Companies Association. Colloquially called 'Cracker', on account of its initials, the CRCA is the successor, since 1996, to the Association of Independent Radio Contractors (AIRC). Funded by the subscriptions of its member CONTRACTING COMPANIES, its remit is mainly to be an industry forum, to represent the medium in negotiations with the government and the RADIO AUTHORITY, and to be the authoritative source of all information about commercial radio in the UK (not including offshore stations broadcasting in English, such as Manx Radio, Radio Luxembourg or RTE in the Republic of Ireland). It is joint owner with the BBC of the RAJAR audience research service and is closely involved in the implementation of the RADIO AUTHORITY ADVERTISING AND SPONSORSHIP CODE. (KC)

commercial television. The network of terrestrial, cable and satellite television channels in Britain that are supported entirely by advertising revenue and programme sales. It complements the BBC-TV network, which is financed by the licence fee and programme sales. *See* INDEPENDENT TELEVISION. (KC)

commission. (1) A payment for the provision of a service, usually directly proportional to the revenue, turnover or other such sum involved. Commission payments, for example, are frequently given to salesmen; such a commission may be a percentage of the revenue the sales have generated, or a set payment for achievements above a pre-set sales target.
(2) *See* MEDIA COMMISSION.

commission rebating. Most ADVERTISING AGENCIES earn most of their income from MEDIA COMMISSION on the value of the space or time they buy from MEDIA OWNERS, rather than being paid a fee by their clients. The price is fixed by the standard scales of charges published in the media owners' RATE CARDS and in BRAD (q.v.). It follows that agencies can compete with one another for business only on the quality of their expertise or their client service, two qualities notoriously susceptible to subjective judgement rather than objective measurement, unless they are willing to share their commission with their clients: the practice of 'commission rebating'. It is often described in the trade press as the 'returning' or 'handing back' some of the standard 15 per cent commission. That is inaccurate, on two counts. First, it is the media owners who award the commission, not the advertisers to whom it is supposedly given back. Second, commission is not a payment, but a privilege discount on a published list price, so there is no actual sum of money to be shared between agency and client. The actual mechanism is that the agency charges the client less for advertising space and time pre-bought on its behalf than the published list price it is entitled to recover. Its own initial discount is of course eroded by this second discount. It is tempting to assume that a 2 or 3 per cent 'rebate', fairly typical figures in practice, will reduce the agency's total commission in direct proportion. In fact, the effect is much more severe, because the rebate percentages are applied to a figure which is also a percentage: the 15 per cent commission. Thus, a 2 per cent rebate will cut earnings by 13.3 per cent, and a 3 per cent rebate by 16.7 per cent. Given that advertising agencies' net profits are typically less than 5 per cent, it should be no surprise that so many have landed themselves in a serious financial predicament by practising rebating. On the other hand, it has to be conceded that others have suffered equally by losing clients as a result of refusing to do so.

Controversy about commission rebating was one of the factors in the formation of the forerunner of the INSTITUTE OF PRACTITIONERS IN ADVERTISING (IPA), in 1917, and it became a contentious issue again in the late 1970s, as economic recession obliged agencies to be competitive on more fronts in trying to win new business or retain existing clients. In 1982, the sixth-ranked advertising agency in Britain took a three-page advertisement in *Campaign,* the advertising trade journal, to put the case against commission rebating. The main thrust of its argument was that the usual 15 per cent commission rate was yielding no more that 2 per cent net profit after tax for the typical advertising agency, according to a survey conducted for the IPA the year before, and that the erosion of that margin by rebating was bound to lead to commensurate hidden cuts in the quality of service delivered to the client. The advertisement was adamant that the agency would refuse point blank to work for any advertisers who expected a rebate. Almost exactly a year later, it parted company with a client spending £3.5 million for that very reason. Extending its argument, one can surmise that smaller advertisers will suffer most when rebating is widespread. If a large client puts pressure on an agency to rebate, standards will be maintained on that account at the expense of the less significant ones in the agency's portfolio. Ten years after the three-page anti-rebating manifesto, the practice was again making headlines in the trade press.

The anti-rebaters clearly have a logical argument, but there is a case to be made on the client side. The crux is the amount an advertiser spends on buying space and time. The creative and administrative effort an agency must put into a £10 million national television campaign is not a hundred times greater than that required for a £100,000 poster campaign, let alone a thousand times more than would be demanded by £10,000-worth of advertising in local newspapers. Yet the corresponding commission amounts are £1.5 million, £15,000 and £1,500. It therefore seems not unreasonable for the higher spending advertiser to expect a reduction in the service charge. In the circumstances, the only way that can be arranged is by 'rebating'. The debate is likely to continue. (KC)

commission system. Shorthand for 'the system of remunerating advertising agencies by commission from media owners'. The implied alternative is 'fee system'. A combination is usual in practice, but periodic industry-wide surveys show that commission accounts for at least two thirds of a typical agency's total earnings. *See* MEDIA COMMISSION. (KC)

Committee of Advertising Practice. The body which devises and enforces the BRITISH CODES OF ADVERTISING AND SALES PROMOTION. Its members represent 22 organizations directly involved in the advertising and sales promotions businesses, including the Royal Mail. (KC)

commodity. A basic product which is capable of little or no differentiation and so generally sold purely on the basis of price in accordance with the theory of perfect COMPETITION. Farm produce, raw materials and a number of fabricated products such as steel qualify as commodities and call for the addition of value adding services if the supplier is to avoid straight price competition. (MJB)

common carrier. An organization offering to transport goods for anyone willing to accept its terms of trade. (MJB)

common thread. A term used by Ansoff (*Corporate Strategy,* 1965) to define the element linking the strategies of MARKET PENETRATION, MARKET DEVELOPMENT AND PRODUCT DEVELOPMENT proposed in his growth vectors matrix to the firm's current position and strategy. According to Ansoff, the common thread is based upon three factors: (a) the product/market scope which specifies the particular industries to which the company confines its product/market position; (b) the growth vector which indicates the direction in which the company is moving with respect to its current product/market position; and (c) the competitive advantage which seeks to identify particular properties of individual product/markets that will give the company a strong competitive position. *See also* DIVERSIFICATION. (MJB)

Commonwealth preference. A system of discriminatory TARIFFS intended to give mutual tariff concessions to members of the Commonwealth. Developed as Imperial Preference in the 1930s, it was important in the immediate post-war years, when most of the nations practising the system also cooperated in currency controls. Commonwealth preference declined rapidly in the 1950s and 1960s and was virtually ended by the accession of the United Kingdom to the EUROPEAN ECONOMIC COMMUNITY. (JML)

communality. A quantity in FACTOR ANALYSIS that indicates the proportion of the variance of a variable that is explained by the ANALYSIS. A high communality means that the variable is well explained by the factor analysis, a low figure means that the variable is not and probably has little to do with the other variables. A factor analysis requires communality estimates to tell the algorithm in advance how much of each variable is to be explained. One figure used is the square of the multiple correlation (coefficient of multiple determination) that you would get if you did a MULTIPLE REGRESSION to predict each variable from all the other variables.   (SKT)

communication brief. A formal document, delivered to a design consultancy by its client, fulfilling the same general function as an ADVERTISING BRIEF but relating to the achievement of MARKETING objectives by means of design strategy.   (KC)

communication channel. *See* CHANNEL (2).

communications effects. A generic term to describe the effects of communications on the intended audience's ATTITUDES, INTENTIONS AND BEHAVIOUR.   (MJB)

company mission. A broad statement of the organization's direction. It represents its overall justification for its existence.   (SD)

comparative advantage. A concept described first by David Ricardo in his *Theory of Comparative Advantage* in the early nineteenth century. To illustrate his theory Ricardo considered the case of two countries – England and Portugal. In England it required 120 hours of labour to produce 1 gallon of wine and 100 hours to produce a yard of cloth. In Portugal the respective times were 80 and 90 hours indicating that Portugal enjoyed an absolute advantage over England in the manufacture of both goods. But, Ricardo pointed out that if Portugal specialized in accordance with the theory of comparative advantage then she would cease to produce cloth and concentrate solely on the production of wine as she could produce 1.125 gallons of wine in 90 hours which she could exchange for 1,125 yards of cloth, an improvement of 12.5 per cent on what she could have produced domestically. England gains too for, despite her absolute inferiority she can translate the 120 hours required to produce 1 gallon of wine into the production of 1.20 yards of cloth which can be converted into 1.20 gallons of wine, an increase of 20 per cent in productivity.

Nowadays, modern theory has established that the only necessary condition for the possibility of gains from trade is that price ratios should differ between countries. The essential concept remains the same – by specialization and through trade countries improve their overall standard of living.   (MJB)

comparative advertising. A tactic in which the text of an advertisement makes direct comparison with competing products or services. It is disparagingly called 'knocking copy' by many commentators, and achieved notoriety during the CONSUMER PROTECTION boom of the 1960s and 1970s, particularly in America. The alternative view is that properly controlled comparative advertising is helpful to audiences and welcomed by them. In Britain, the BRITISH CODES OF ADVERTISING AND SALES PROMOTION expressly permit direct comparison 'in the interests of vigorous competition and public information', provided that the advertisements or sales promotions in question 'respect the principles of fair competition generally accepted in business' and, specifically, that the comparisons are 'clear and fair' and are not 'selected in any way that gives the advertisers an artificial advantage'. The ITC CODE OF ADVERTISING STANDARDS AND PRACTICE and RADIO AUTHORITY Advertising and Sponsorship Code both permit comparative advertising for the same reason, state the same general requirement that comparisons are fair, and add that the details must be based on facts which can be substantiated.   (KC)

comparative marketing. The organized study of marketing systems in many countries. Often used as an approach to study INTERNATIONAL MARKETING, it examines the similarities, differences and reasons for this. The study of comparative marketing is often considered a useful approach to broaden one's understanding, to help develop general theories of marketing and to help classify aspects of marketing.   (JK)

comparative rating scale. The use of the rating scale for comparative judgements. Rather than judging PRODUCTS in isolation one would use a scale to judge the differences between pairs of products.   (SKT)

comparative shopping. The process of 'shopping around', that is, visiting a number of retail outlets in order to get the best value when buying a particular PRODUCT. Comparative shopping may not only be undertaken by the CONSUMER to find the lowest price (generally in the case of large consumer durables), but perhaps for the best credit terms or the best service facilities.   (GKP)

comparative testing. *See* PRODUCT TESTING.

comparison advertising. Advertising in which direct and indirect comparisons are made between the advertiser's product and those of their immediate competitors. Where these are particularly negative the practice is known as 'knocking copy' and is a practice which is banned in some countries e.g. Australia. *See* COMPARATIVE ADVERTISING.   (MJB)

compatibility. One of the five characteristics of an INNOVATION specified by Everett M. Rogers (*Diffusion of Innovations,* 3rd edn, New York: The Free Press) which defines the degree or extent to which something new is compatible with the current way of doing things or with the object which it seeks to displace.   (MJB)

compensatory consumption. A term coined to describe the phenomenon whereby individuals who feel frustrated in achieving personal goals may compensate for this through their consumption BEHAVIOUR. It applies particularly to individuals with low incomes/ occupational mobility.   (MJB)

competition. 'Outside the economic sphere, the word "competition" means a type of activity that involves contestants who are pitted against each other, some common goal sought by them, efforts on the part of each to achieve superiority in attaining the goal, some methods of judging superiority in attaining the goal, judges or judging mechanism to do the judging, the selection of one or perhaps several of the contestants, and rejection of others.' (L. Abbott, *Quality in Competition,* Columbia University Press, 1955).

Most economists write about competition without defining it, presumably because they believe its meaning is self-evident. As Frank Knight has said, 'the critical reader of general economic literature must be struck by the absence of any attempt accurately to define that competition which is the principal subject in a discussion' (*Ethics of Competition,* 1936). Even when an attempt is made at a definition, what is defined is not competition, but a particular kind of competition, such as 'pure' or 'perfect' (*see* COMPETITION, PERFECT). Such definitions are usually of the sort that does not tell us what competition is, but simply describes the conditions under which it exists, or its consequences. Nevertheless, the work of a number of modern economists to define the kind of competition or the accompanying conditions needed to ensure desirable results is a valuable source of ideas about competition itself. One significant idea advanced by J.M. Clark, Corwin D. Edwards and others is that competition means the availability of alternatives. The word 'availability' implies two things. First, that the alternatives exist and second that the participants have the power to choose freely amongst them. Clark, for instance (*Towards a Concept of Workable Competition,* 1940), defines competition in price between business units as rivalry in selling goods under conditions such that the price or prices each seller can charge are effectively limited by the free option of the buyer to buy from a rival seller or sellers. This definition focuses attention on a crucial point which is sometimes neglected, namely the nature of the option actually open to the buyer. Edwards characterizes the competition that prevails in actual competitive markets as consisting of access by buyers and sellers to a substantial number of alternatives, and their ability to reject those which are relatively unsatisfactory. Suppliers and customers do not need to be so numerous that each trader is entirely without individual influence, but their number must be great enough that persons on the other side of the market may readily turn away from any particular trader, and may find a variety of alternatives.

A second and closely related idea is that the alternatives need not be identical in quality. Edwards states that 'competition implies that there are alternatives available in the market in business policies, whether towards prices, production, or the kind of goods and services which are furnished ... in markets where all producers are united ... in a common policy towards the term of sale or towards the characteristics of their products, effective option by the buyer is destroyed' (Corwin D. Edwards, *Maintaining Competition: Requisites of Governmental Policy,* 1949). Schumpeter (*Capitalism Socialism and Democracy,* 2nd edn, 1947) points out that in capitalist reality, as distinguished from its textbook picture, competition in price amongst sellers of the same commodity, produced by the same methods, is far less effective and less powerful than competition that arises when qualitatively different alternatives are pitted against each other.

A third idea is that competition is more than the mere existence of a situation in which rival, dissimilar alternatives are available. It is a type of action induced by such a situation, the action being of the nature that alters the relationship between rival participants. It is a dynamic process, its central element offering the other party a bargain good enough to induce him to deal with you in the face of his free option of dealing with others. It is the effort of each producer to get, or to keep, patronage which might go to another. These efforts take the form of striving to make the offer more attractive to the buyers than the offers of competitors. This improved attractiveness of the offer may be a lower price, or may be improved quality, a more attractive design, a more useful or attractive package, greater convenience of location of the point of sale, an assurance of dependability that comes from a long-established record, improved after-sales service, such as repairs or adjustment and many other features (Abbott, op. cit.).

M.A. Adelman ('Effective Competition and the Antitrust Laws', 1948) likewise describes competition as 'the pursuit of business advantage in a competitive market, and takes the form of reduction in price, improvement in quality, and constant search for cost reduction and innovation.' Hayek views competition in this light. He points out that competition is by its nature a dynamic process, whose essential characteristics are assumed away by the assumption underlying static analysis. It withers away when perfect knowledge and equilibrium are attained. Perfect competition means indeed the absence of all competitive activities.

Abbott views economic competition as 'a contest, or more usually a succession of contests, in which independent sellers enter products of their own choosing, at prices of their own choosing for appraisal and purchase by independent buyers, the products being substitutes for each other in the sense of being alternative means for the attainment of some activity or experience, the buyer being free to select or reject any bargain offered, and to make their own offer of terms, and all participants are guided in their decisions by their conceptions of their best interest'.

From the above comments two main points emerge: first, the essence of competition is rivalry between business units to get customer patronage, thereby increasing sales and consequently security, growth and profits. Second, a complete understanding of competitive markets involves an understanding of the price adjust-ment aspects, the product adjustment aspects, and sales effort aspects, and requires a framework of analysis comprehensive enough to embrace them all. In other words, competition can no longer be confined to the price facet of competitive strategy, it must go beyond that to embrace all the elements of the MARKETING MIX which should be manipulated together to accomplish the firm's objective. This contradicts the classical approach to competition, which only considers price as a factor which affects the demand for products.

(MJB)

competition, barriers to. *See* BARRIERS TO COMPETITION.

competition, monopoly. A market where one firm markets all the products that are sold. Often the term 'monopoly' is also applied where one firm controls a very high share of the market. This results in a very low level of competition. *See also* MONOPOLISTIC COMPETITION.   (MS)

competition, oligopoly. A market where a small number of firms represent a large proportion of sales. This can still result in a high degree of competition amongst the leading firms, although nowadays this often takes the form of competition in product differentiation and innovation as opposed to price competition.   (MS)

competition, perfect. Although there are some differences in definition, there is a general consensus that a perfectly competitive market is one in which four conditions are met. The first is that there should be a homogeneous product which cannot be differentiated. In that case, every firm in the market produces and sells output that is a perfect substitute for the output of every other producer, and it is impossible for any producer to gain a competitive advantage over any other producer. The second condition is that there should be such large numbers of both buyers and sellers, each so small relative to the total market that no one buyer or seller can by his own actions alone affect the market price. That being the case, everyone in the market will be a price taker, and the prevailing prices are determined by aggregate forces of supply and demand. These prices are free to fluctuate both upwards and downwards, reflecting market changes, and they perform the essential task of rationing resources between alternative goods, and goods among customers.

The third condition in perfect competition is perfect resource mobility to ensure that quantity adjustment can be made to allow increases or decreases in output as notional prices fluctuate. The fourth condition is that there should be perfect knowledge about market conditions with regard to production, techniques, resource supplies and prices. Under such circumstances a firm has no need for a price policy; it sells at a price over which it has no control. The market itself fixes prices that equate quantities sellers are willing to sell with quantities buyers are willing to buy. The only decision required by a firm is whether to produce at all and, if so, in what quantities. The firm would maximize its profit by equating its marginal revenue and marginal cost, and would earn normal profit, while its cost will be at a minimum. Normal profit is defined as an element of the cost to a firm, and is synonymous with the term 'OPPORTUNITY COST'. It is a payment necessarily provided to factors of production in order to prevent them choosing to be employed elsewhere, and is equal to the value of the factors in its most profitable alternative usage. The model of perfect competition has been subject to many criticisms, especially the difficulty of finding markets to which it applies in more than a very approximate way. (MJB)

competition, price. Market conditions where firms compete with one another by undercutting others prices, rather than other forms of competition such as product quality, product differentiation and advertising. (MS)

competitions. A form of PROMOTION. (MJB)

competitive advantage/edge. A source of differentiation between a firm and its competitors which confers an advantage on it. Such advantages may arise from product features, price, availability, image or reputation which offer higher value to intending buyers. As a result of technological change it is becoming increasingly difficult for firms to secure a SUSTAINABLE COMPETITIVE ADVANTAGE from objective differences arising from product differentiation or cost leadership apart from certain markets such as pharmaceuticals where intellectual property rights are still protected by patents. For most markets sustainable competitive advantage is more likely to arise from the less tangible and more subjective factors such as service levels, BRAND IMAGE and the like. (MJB)

competitive analysis. An integral element of the SWOT ANALYSIS through which a firm seeks to identify the strengths and weaknesses of rival firms. This includes all elements of the competitors marketing mix and goes well beyond direct comparison of financial performance indicators. (MJB)

competitive bidding. A system under which competing suppliers are invited to submit bids to the intending buyer with the expectation that the order will be given to the supplier putting in the most competitive quotation. Such bids are usually sealed and submitted by a deadline. Bidding of this kind is commonplace in the sourcing of public sector requirements. (MJB)

competitive intelligence. The gathering of information about one's competitors as part of a COMPETITIVE ANALYSIS. (MJB)

competitive-parity method. A method of setting the ADVERTISING APPROPRIATION in which the firm commits a budget which is proportionate to that of its major competitors using sales volume or market share as the basis for comparison. (MJB)

competitor analysis. An integral part of the MARKETING AUDIT or SWOT analysis in which the firm seeks to BENCHMARK all aspects of its immediate competitors' performance. Based on this and the other elements of its STRATEGIC ANALYSIS the firm will decide how, where and with whom it will compete. (MJB)

complementary goods. Two or more PRODUCTS are said to be complementary when an increase in the price of one is generally associated with a decrease in demand for the other. The complementarity results from the way such products are consumed together or from a technical reason which makes one necessary to the other. Examples are cars and petrol, electricity and electric cookers, razors and shaving foam. (MDP)

completely randomized design (CRD). In the statistical design of experiments, procedures where treatments are assigned to RESPONDENTS at random, without any preclassification. (SKT)

completely structured question. See CLOSED QUESTION.

completely unstructured question. See OPEN-ENDED QUESTION.

complex buying behaviour. The kind of behaviour encountered in situations where there is high involvement and perceived risk such that the intending buyer engages in EXTENDED PROBLEM SOLVING. Such situations are usually encountered when the purchase is a NEWBUY or MODIFIED REBUY.   (MJB)

complexity. One of the five characteristics of an INNOVATION specified by Everett M. Rogers (*Diffusion of Innovations,* 3rd edn, New York: The Free Press) which defines the degree to which a new object or IDEA is perceived as difficult to use or understand, particularly by comparison to the object or idea it seeks to displace.   (MJB)

compliant types. *See* INTERPERSONAL RESPONSE TRAITS.

comprehension. The stage following AWARENESS and INTEREST in the individual's information processing behaviour at which they recognize and understand the potential benefits/limitations associated with the object/IDEA which has attracted their ATTENTION.   (MJB)

computer-aided design (CAD). The use of computer technology to assist in the design process. The draughtsman uses the VDU as a board; various application packages to allow him/her to draw on the screen. Mathematical tests and formulae facilitate tolerance analysis etc.   (KRD)

computer-aided manufacturing (CAM). A computer-based system that links invoicing, production, INVENTORY, manpower scheduling and raw material/component flows to control and monitor the production of goods.   (KRD)

computer-assisted telephone interview (CATI). Computer packages, of which there are a number, that are designed specifically to help in telephone interviewing. The interviewer sits at a monitor while conducting the interview and appropriate prompts and questions appear on the screen. Routing is automatic and dependent on the result which is (interactively) keyed in. Advantages include instant data entry (and therefore reduced data transfer errors), rapid ANALYSIS of the DATA and validation checks which can be incorporated.   (KRD)

computer card. An obsolete medium for communicating information to computing machinery. Classically, SURVEY ANALYSIS involved the use of counter sorter and decks of cards, each card representing a RESPONDENT. Techniques such as

multi-punching were developed to allow more than 80 variables to be coded using the 80 columns of twelve rows of punching positions.   (SKT)

computer conferencing. Where a computer is used to store, analyse and relay information between participants in a group exercise who are usually based at widely separated locations. The participants in the conference use a network of computer terminals to communicate with individual users or groups of users. Opinions may be exchanged and information retrieved at the convenience of the participants.   (DB)

computer graphics. A technology which, during the 1990s, revolutionized the production of advertising ARTWORK and the creation of special effects in television or cinema COMMERCIALS.   (KC)

computerized search. The use of ON-LINE DATABASES to assist in the search for secondary data. The remote databases are accessed via an acoustic coupler or modem. There is a connect charge as well as a variable charge for the information received. Depending on the nature of your search, you may not require information that is up to the minute. Under these circumstances, the emerging optical disc (CD-ROM) technology may be more appropriate. The OPTICAL DISCS are held by the user and are updated at appropriate time intervals by the supplying company (usually monthly or quarterly).   (KRD)

concentrated marketing strategy. One of three basic marketing strategies (the other two being UNDIFFERENTIATED and DIFFERENTIATED). In the case of a concentrated marketing strategy the producer deliberately selects one of the major market segments (see MARKET SEGMENTATION) and concentrates all his efforts upon it. It should be noted that this approach is different from user self selection, which amounts to an undifferentiated strategy. In the latter case, the subsets of the market are not clear – the supplier does not possess profiles of different market groupings or segments – and so he cannot devise a targeted or concentrated strategy for matching his output to the needs of one segment. By contrast, in the case of a concentrated strategy the supplier has been able to define highly specific market segments but has chosen to concentrate his efforts on only one of them. Such a strategy is particularly appropriate to the small producer that is unable to develop a range of differentiated products suited to the needs of the different segments which comprise the total market.   (MJB)

concentration. The degree to which the market is oligopolistic or monopolistic. A market is more highly concentrated if a small number of firms represent a still larger proportion of total sales or if even fewer firms retain control of some large share of the market. *See* COMPETITION, MONOPOLY and COMPETITION, OLIGOPOLY.   (MS)

concentration ratio. A numerical measure of the degree of concentration of a market. Various measures exist, including the Herfindahl Index: where:

$$H = \sum_{i=1}^{n} \left(\frac{x^1}{x} \right)^2$$

So, when $H = 1$ market concentration is at its highest, and when $H = 0$ market concentration is at its lowest.   (MS)

concentric zone theory. According to this theory urban settlements develop in a series of concentric zones. The first of these is the CENTRAL BUSINESS DISTRICT next to which is a zone in transition, workers' homes, residential suburbs and the commuter belt. As cities grow zones expand into the adjacent zone.   (MJB)

concept. An idea or thought created by abstracting a particular quality from the general state in which it occurs with other qualities and identifying it with a specific name or description e.g. difficulty, simplicity, hardness, softness, fear, happiness are all concepts. In marketing the term is used to denote situations where producers seek feed-back on a proposed course of action – usually new product development – by providing information and descriptions of the product without actually having produced it.   (MJB)

concept testing. (1) Trying out alternative treatments of an advertising theme on a sample of the eventual target audience. Advertisers and advertising agencies quite often dispute its value and claim not to bother with concept tests themselves. However, they will often admit to 'creative development research', as a guide to decisions about the right way to put the concept over in the advertisements. This is semantic juggling. Acceptance of concept testing is most likely in practice among advertisers whose product or service is particularly abstract: for instance,

health charities whose message may be the proposition that the audience should *not* buy and use something. In such cases it is clear that the way the concept is presented can be as critical as the concept itself. Otherwise, avoidance can perhaps be traced to an influential article by the respected planner and researcher, Stephen King of the J. Walter THOMPSON advertising agency, in 1965. He questioned its validity, let alone value, on the grounds that the material shown to the respondents in the test would be either so stripped down that they could not react to it as advertising, or so dressed up that their reactions to the varied elements could not be distinguished from those to the execution as a whole. The argument was elegantly put, but it seems illogical to assume that a middle ground between these extremes cannot be found in practice.   (KC)
(2)   Market research techniques designed to measure the acceptability, among target users, of new marketing elements, new products, new advertising campaigns, new consumer promotions, before incurring expenditures by actually producing these items. While it is hazardous to generalize, such techniques are better used to detect potential disasters than to attempt to establish certain winners as a high level of acceptance of the concept does not guarantee success in the market place.   (JRB)

concomitant variation. A phrase used in CAUSAL RESEARCH to describe observed association between variables predicted by your model: this contrasts with spurious variation which is not accounted for by the model.   (SKT)

concurrent validity. Methods for assessing the validity of an assessment that involve a measure that is taken at the same time as the assessment.   (SKT)

conditional association. A looser term for partial correlation: an association between variables where the effect of control variables has been somehow removed.   (SKT)

conditional probability. The probability of an event, when it is known that some other event has occurred. It would be useful, for example, to compare the effects on probability of purchase of a set of different predetermining events.   (SKT)

Confederation of British Industry (CBI). UK employer's organization formed in 1965 by the amalgamation of the Federation of British Industries (FBI), The British Employers'

Confederation (BEC) and the National Association of British Manufacturers (NABM), which had all previously represented industrial interests.

The CBI is an independent body financed by its membership, which is entirely corporate and represents about 250,000 companies from all sectors employing over 60 per cent of Britain's workforce. Membership ranges from the smallest to the largest companies, private sector and nationalized, and includes companies in manufacturing, agriculture, construction, distribution, mining, finance, retailing, and insurance. Most national employer's organizations, trade associations and some chambers of commerce are members.

The CBI's major objective is to represent, promote and protect its members' interests both nationally and internationally. Politically neutral itself, the CBI advises and consults with government and nominates representatives to various governmental and public bodies. It both disseminates information about economic policies and legislation and provides British industry with a channel by which its views regarding development and implementation of economic and industrial policies can be relayed back. In addition to this liaison and lobbying function, it provides advice and assistance to its members on any aspect of running their business with the objective of making them more efficient and competitive and thus enhancing the contribution of British industry to the national economy.

The CBI has a permanent staff of about 350 headed by a Director General. Responsibility for the activities of the CBI are vested in a council which consists of nominated representatives from trade associations and individual firms. Thirty-four standing committees have been established to formulate policy in particular subject areas.

One of the CBI's major publications is its quarterly industrial trend survey (dating from 1958) which provides much immediate information on trends in manufacturing industry along with business perceptions of short-term expectations. Since 1975 the CBI has also conducted a short monthly trends enquiry. It has 12 regional offices and an office in Brussels.   (MJB/JK)

confidence interval. See STATISTICAL HYPOTHESIS TESTING.

confidence levels. An obfuscating phrase used to denote the effect of different distributional tail sizes on CONFIDENCE INTERVALS. *See also* STATISTICAL HYPOTHESIS TESTING.   (SKT)

confounding variable. A variable whose effect in a MULTIPLE REGRESSION is to obscure the effect of another predicting variable; can be caused by having correlations between predictor variables.   (SKT)

confrontation technique. When using OPEN-ENDED questioning, confrontation is a technique used to improve the quality of earlier responses – by asking questions to underline earlier inconsistency in a RESPONDENT'S answers. P.M. Chisnall in *Marketing Research: Measurement and Analysis* (Maidenhead: McGraw-Hill, 1981) notes that when seemingly inconsistent replies occur, it may be possible to 'discover something' by confronting respondents with their apparent inconsistencies.   (GKP)

confusion matrix. A table where each cell indicates the chances that the row element is confused as the column element. Used in perceptual judgements for MULTIDIMENSIONAL SCALING and also in assessing the performance of discriminant analysis.   (SKT)

conglomerate. A firm operating in a number of distinct INDUSTRIES/MARKETS through a variety of distinct and separate operating units, usually pieced together through a series of mergers and acquisitions.   (MJB)

conglo merchant. A multi-unit retailer, or retail holding company, which has developed or acquired different, non-competing store groups in their store portfolio, in order to cover many different segments of the market.   (AJB)

conjoint analysis. A scaling technique which estimates the best values for each row and column of a table to fit the observed values. Typically, conjoint analysis is used to impute the utilities of PRODUCT ATTRIBUTES from preferences between hypothetical PRODUCTS with combinations of these attributes.   (SKT)

conjoint measurement. A way of measuring utilities or evaluations through combinations of attributes. Decompose the set of stimuli into levels of attributes; comparisons of the stimuli can be used to impute utilities for attribute levels, which are then used to predict evaluation of new stimuli with different levels of attributes.   (SKT)

conjunctive rule. A decision-making rule in which the intending buyer sets minimum values for a number of factors and rejects any offering which does not meet the minimum value on all of the factors i.e. a superior performance on one factor cannot compensate for underperformance on another (a compensatory rule). (MJB)

conscious parallelism. A situation in which firms emulate each others' strategy. Most frequently observed in the case of pricing qv. ADMINISTERED PRICING. (MJB)

consistency. The degree to which various product lines enjoy similar end uses and MARKETING MIXES. (MJB)

consistency theory. A theory which states that individuals will seek to maintain consistency between values, attitudes and behaviour. *See* COGNITIVE CONSISTENCY THEORY. (MJB)

consistent estimator. A statistical term to indicate a formula that produces an optimal statistic irrespective of a range of deviations from the conditions. (SKT)

consonance. The achievement of a consistent self-image. Self-image is the way we see ourselves and consonance represents our effort to behave in a manner consistent with this perception of ourself. As a result it has a significant impact on our behaviour as we strive to avoid the opposite state of DISSONANCE. (MJB)

conspicuous consumption. Conspicuous consumption relates to the theory that CONSUMERS will use the purchase of a PRODUCT in order to communicate something about themselves (CONSUMER SELF-ENHANCEMENT). Robertson *et al.* (T.S. Robertson, J. Zielinski, and S. Ward, *Consumer Behaviour,* Glenview: Scott Foresman, 1984) quote Veblen's 'Theory of the Leisure Class' to illustrate: 'In order to gain and hold the esteem of men, it is not sufficient merely to possess wealth or power. The wealth and power must be in evidence, for esteem is awarded only on evidence.'

Bourne is reported by Engel *et al.* (J.F. Engel, R.D. Blackwell, and P.W. Miniard, *Consumer Behaviour,* 5th edn, Illinois: Dryden Press, 1986) as proposing two components of conspicuousness. First, the product must have good visibility, in the sense that it can be seen by others, and secondly, that it stands out or is conspicuous in some way. Further, they state that the results of the study on 'product conspicuousness as a determinant of social influence' by Bearden and Edzel found that subjects reported that normative social influences were more relevant for decisions involving products that other people would be aware the subject possesses, as opposed to products only the subject and perhaps their immediate family would be aware of. Engel *et al.* also state that conspicuousness is not a fixed characteristic of the product, but depends on how the product is used. (GKP)

constant sum scale. A comparative rating scale format where the RESPONDENT is asked to divide a particular sum among a series of alternatives. For example, respondents might be asked to compare possible PRODUCT improvements by 'spending' £1,000 and varying the amount spent according to their idea of the importance of the improvement. Differing subjects' ratings should then sum to the given constant. (SKT)

construct validity. A method of validating a measure through examining the construct that the measure is 'actually' measuring. Rather a loose theoretical approach compared with criterion and concurrent validity assessment. If a measure has construct validity one can know that it is actually measuring something! (SKT)

consumer. Ultimate user of economic goods and services. (JLD)

Consumer Advice Centre/Bureau. Local authority funded and staffed centre for individual consumer pre- and post-purchase counselling. Centres were established in 1974 by the Department of Prices and Consumer Protection under the auspices of the consumer protection divisions of local authority Trading Standards Departments. (JLD)

consumer behaviour. Observable activities chosen to maximize satisfaction through the attainment of economic goods and services, such as choice of retail outlet, preference for particular brands and so on. (JLD)

consumer cooperative. Any retail establishment characterized by consumer ownership. Ownership is achieved by investing capital which receives a fixed rate of interest while profits are distributed according to purchases. The shareholders elect directors who appoint a chief executive officer. (AJB)

consumer durable. Consumer durables are PRODUCTS (e.g. TV sets, washing machines, motor cars) which are used over a period of time, and not used up at the moment of consumption.

(MDP)

consumer focus group. A group of actual or potential users of a product, usually six to eight in number, formed to discuss a topic under the guidance of a moderator. This QUALITATIVE RESEARCH technique is widely used in NEW PRODUCT DEVELOPMENT. (MJB)

consumer goods. Goods manufactured for individual use by members of the general public, as against INDUSTRIAL GOODS which sell primarily to organizations. Consumer goods are generally divided into three subcategories according to the method by which they are purchased – CONVE-NIENCE GOODS, SHOPPING GOODS and SPECIALTY GOODS. (MJB)

consumerism. The modern consumer movement launched in the mid-1960s by the concerns triggered indirectly by Rachel Carson in *Silent Spring* (1962) and directly by Ralph Nader's automobile safety investigation (*Unsafe at Any Speed,* Pocket Books, New York, 1966) and by President Kennedy's efforts to establish the rights of consumers to safety, to be informed, to choose and to be heard. It encompasses the set of activities of government, business, independent organizations and concerned consumers that are designed to protect the rights of the consumer. Consumerism is concerned with protecting consumers from all organizations with which there is an exchange relationship. *See* CONSUMER RIGHTS.

(JLD)

consumer jury. A group of actual or prospective CONSUMERS of a PRODUCT invited to evaluate its performance as a basis for informing future MAR-KETING decisions. (MJB)

Consumer Location System (CLS). Launched early in 1983, this comprises a composite of the TARGET GROUP INDEX (TGI) and ACORN with the aim of achieving a significant increase in the use of direct mail to reach highly specific target markets. The system itself is based upon a reduction of the 563 product categories covered by TGI into 153 for which direct mail appears to offer a particularly strong advantage over alternative media. These product categories are then corre-lated with the ACORN classification to permit precise identification of which out of more than 18 million households are potential customers for the particular product or service in question. *See* POSTCODE. (MJB)

consumer market. The market comprising ulti-mate consumers who purchase goods and services for their own consumption or those of other ultimate consumers. i.e. they do not buy for resale or profit. (MJB)

consumer movement. A group of activists and their supporters who promote the rights of con-sumers with government, manufacturers, retailers etc. (MJB)

consumer panel. A research method designed to provide behavioural information on a continuous basis, thus tracing movements over a period of time: panel members are selected on the princi-ple of RANDOM SAMPLING with the aim of achieving a representative membership. The two major methods of collecting data through the consumer panel are the HOME AUDIT and the diary. Home audits involve research staff visiting panel members' homes and making physical checks of product usage. The diary method involves panel members in noting purchase and usage of specific products on a regular basis. (JLD)

consumer price index (CPI). A summary statis-tic published by the US government which tracks the price of a standardized shopping basket.

(MJB)

consumer protection. The Fair Trading Act 1973 provides machinery (headed by the Director General of Fair Trading) for the continuous review of consumers' affairs, for action to deal with trading practices which unfairly affect con-sumer' interests and with persistent offenders under existing law, and for the negotiation of self-regulatory codes of practice to raise trading standards. The Director General is also responsi-ble for the working of legislation which regulates consumer credit and hire business and estate agency work.

The consumers' interests with regard to the purity of foods, the description and performance of goods, and pricing information are safe-guarded by the Food and Drugs Acts 1955 and 1956, the Medicines Act 1968, the TRADES DESCRIPTIONS ACTS 1968 AND 1972, the Prices Act 1974, the Unfair Contract Terms Act 1977, the Sale of Goods Act 1979, and the Food Safety Act

1990. The marking and accuracy of quantities are regulated by the Weights and Measures Acts 1963 and 1979, the latter introducing a system of average weights for certain pre-packed goods. The Consumer Protection Acts 1961 and 1971 and the Consumer Safety Act 1978 empower the Government to control the supply of any goods in the interests of safety.

The European Community's consumer programme covers a number of important activities, such as health and safety, protection of the consumer's economic interests, promotion of consumer education and strengthening the representation of consumers. The views of British consumer organizations on Community matters are represented by the Consumers in the European Community Group (UK). British consumer bodies are also represented on the European consumer 'watchdog' body, the Bureau Europeen des Unions de Consommateurs. *See also* ADVERTISING CONTROL. (HMSO)

consumer research. The systematic gathering, recording and analysing of data about consumers as initiators of purchase decisions, buyers of economic goods and services, or users of such goods and services. (JLD)

consumer rights. Following President Kennedy's 1962 first consumer address to Congress these are generally accepted as: (a) the right to safety – to be protected against the marketing of goods which are hazardous to health or life; (b) the right to be informed – to be protected against fraudulent, deceitful or grossly misleading information, advertising, labelling or other practices, and to be given the facts needed to make an informed choice; (c) the right to choose – to be assured, wherever possible, access to a variety of products and services at competitive prices and in those industries in which government regulations are substituted, an assurance of satisfactory quality and service at fair prices; (d) the right to be heard – to be assured that consumer interests will receive full and sympathetic consideration in the formulation of government policy and fair expeditious treatment in its administrative tribunals. (MJB)

Consumers' Association. An independent non-profit-making consumer testing and advisory agency with membership by subscription. It publishes *WHICH?* consumer magazine, available only to members, to set out details of comparative technical user tests of a wide range of CONSUMER GOODS, large-scale membership surveys of issues

of general consumer interest, and value-for-money buying advice. (JLD)

consumer self-enhancement. *See* CONSPICUOUS CONSUMPTION.

consumer socialization. *See* SOCIALIZATION.

consumer sovereignty. A fundamental CONCEPT which underpins MARKETING as both a business philosophy and a business activity. Given that the purpose of economic and social activity is to maximize satisfaction through the consumption of scarce resources, it is regarded as self-evident that the satisfaction to be maximized is the aggregate of the satisfaction of individual CONSUMERS who, in a free MARKET, exercise their sovereignty by casting their money votes in favour of those goods and services which best serve their NEEDS. (MJB)

consumption function. Expresses the relationship between total consumption, expenditure and income. Three broad theories have been proposed to explain variations in aggregate consumption functions, namely the ABSOLUTE INCOME HYPOTHESIS, the RELATIVE INCOME HYPOTHESIS and the PERMANENT INCOME HYPOTHESIS. (MJB)

containerization. Term used to cover the tendency in recent years to pack exports in returnable standard-sized metal containers which can be rented from container companies. The advantages are speed of movement, cheapness and security in that, ideally, a container loaded in the exporter's premises is not unloaded until its final delivery to the buyer. Containers can be carried on specially designed road vehicles, rail wagons and ships. Containerization requires special loading and unloading facilities at either end of the sea journey and container ports have been developed rapidly throughout the United Kingdom and most other nations. (JML)

content analysis. A method of analysis used to identify the main themes contained within a body of data – usually unstructured qualitative interviews (*See* GROUNDED THEORY) – or in written or broadcast material. The latter approach was used by Naisbeth in developing his book *Megatrends*. (MJB)

content validity. A method of validating a measure through examining whether the measure adequately covers all salient attributes of the construct. Sometimes called 'face validity', it suggests that the measure at least appears to cover what is commonly believed to be the important characteristics of the construct.   (SKT)

contingency coefficient. A statistic used to indicate the association between the rows and columns of a contingency table. In other words, a correlation coefficient between two nominal variables.   (SKT)

contingency planning. The development of an alternative plan or plans to allow for changes in the assumptions on which the original and operational plan is based. *See* SCENARIO PLANNING.
                    (MJB)

contingency table. A table that displays at least the frequency of occurrence of the co-occurrence of each category of two nominal variables. Also referred to as a 'cross-tabulation', contingency tables are often associated with statistical analysis by chi-square or log-linear models.   (SKT)

continuity. A strategic option open to MEDIA PLANNERS: the question of when individual insertions or spots should be scheduled to occur. Two broad strategies are possible: 'burst', which implies peaks of intense advertising exposure with troughs of comparative inactivity between; 'drip', which implies a regular pattern of exposure at a more or less steady level.   (KC)

continuous innovation. A term coined by Robertson *et al.* (T. S. Robertson, J. Zielinski and S. Ward, *Consumer Behaviour,* Glenview: Scott Foresman, 1984) to describe PRODUCTS which represent a marginal, incremental development of an existing product or service. Such INNOVATION is readily acceptable to CONSUMERS as it is highly COMPATIBLE with their existing BEHAVIOUR, low in COMPLEXITY and offers additional benefits or RELATIVE ADVANTAGE.   (MJB)

continuous research. Regularly repeated research to assess particular trends. Often SYNDICATED RESEARCH.   (JAB)

contracting company. The technically correct name for an INDEPENDENT TELEVISION or INDEPENDENT RADIO station, in its capacity as a seller of ADVERTISING TIME, deriving from the fact that advertisers or (more usually) their agencies make a contract with them to buy the time. Television

stations may also be 'programme companies', if they are producers of programmes for the Independent Television network.   (KC)

contract manufacturing. The manufacture under contract on behalf of another company. Often encountered in foreign markets particularly where the foreign market imposes restrictions or tariffs on imported goods. In the latter case the agreement may take the form of a JOINT VENTURE.
                    (MJB)

contract purchasing. Occurs when an organizational buyer enters into an agreement to purchase a specified quantity of a product within a predetermined time period, under price and delivery conditions which are agreed at the start of the contract.   (STP)

contribution analysis. Analytical financial technique which, recognizing the difficulty in allocating overhead (fixed) costs to individual products, concentrates instead on analysing the contribution such products make to profits, after all direct/variable costs have been allowed for. Contribution may be defined in various ways, but usually consists of the difference between revenue and direct costs. Companies may also include some marketing costs; advertising, trade and consumer promotions and so on, as direct costs, and then refer to the residual as 'contribution-after-marketing'.   (JRB)

control. Any activity designed to ensure that actual results are consistent with those budgeted or planned. Quality control and cost control are obvious examples of situations where the planner will set down clear objectives and standards and then monitor performance to ensure that it is satisfactory. Control also implies that if results are not satisfactory then remedial action will be taken or else the plan revised to reflect a new set of conditions.   (MJB)

control group. In experimental design the group of subjects who do not get the treatment, but are measured, so that a COMPARISON can be made. If subjects are randomly assigned to control and experimental groups differences can be attributed to the treatment.   (SKT)

controlled circulation publications. Newspapers or magazines distributed to a mailing list, and usually unsolicited. The recipients do not pay a cover price, the total production and distribution cost being borne by the advertisers, who pay for the chance to reach a highly specific readership. Controlled circulation magazines typically contain a high proportion of DIRECT RESPONSE ADVERTISING. They are listed separately from paid-for titles in BRAD (q.v.). FREESHEETS may be thought of as a special case of the controlled-circulation principle. (KC)

convenience goods. Those CONSUMER GOODS which the customer usually purchases frequently, immediately and with the minimum of effort. This category encompasses a wide range of household products of low unit value. It is implicit that products in this category have low brand loyalty, as the user is not prepared to go to any effort to secure a supply and will accept a substitute. From this it follows that the producer must secure the widest possible availability if he is to maximize sales. (MJB)

convenience sample. A form of non-probabilistic or purposive SAMPLE drawn on a purely opportunistic basis from a readily accessible subgroup of the POPULATION. e.g. travellers at an airport, shoppers in a shopping mall. (MJB)

convenience store. A retail outlet whose appeal is based upon convenience primarily in terms of location, but also in terms of opening hours and STOCK assortment – usually frequently purchased CONSUMER GOODS, such as bread, milk, canned foods, beverages etc. (MJB)

convergent validity. A method of determining the validity of a measure by showing high correlations with other measures of the same construct. Often used in conjunction with discriminant validity which checks a measure does not correlate too highly with measures of unrelated constructs. (SKT)

convertibility. This term, used in respect of currencies such as sterling, has had a variety of meanings, but as understood at present, it means the freedom of the holder of one currency to change it to another. Many monetary authorities permit currency convertibility, i.e. a foreigner who sells goods will be allowed to convert his earnings into his own or another currency; and a resident in the country will be allowed to import goods etc. freely from overseas, converting his own currency to pay. But the authorities will not necessarily allow capital convertibility, i.e. the right to transfer capital funds abroad without control. This is, by and large, the present state of convertibility of sterling. (JML)

cooperative. A form of organization in which suppliers or buyers agree to join forces to increase their bargaining power. (MJB)

cooperative advertising. Procedure for sharing the cost of advertising between advertisers and the retailers who stock their products or promote their services. The advertiser produces standardized press advertisements or television commercials, and permits exclusive agents or main dealers to run them in local media under their own names and LOGOTYPES. The advertiser thereby retains some control over the way in which the retailer presents his product. The dealer benefits by running an advertisement which will bring customers into the premises, who can be sold more products or services, for less than it would otherwise cost. The most usual sharing of cost between advertiser and retailer in co-operative advertising deals is 50/50. (KC)

Co-operative Retail Society. A UK consumer cooperative which has been registered under the Industrial and Provident Societies Act, including branches of the Co-operative Wholesale Society. (AJB)

copy. The words in an ADVERTISEMENT as distinct from the VISUALS. The term is borrowed from journalism, where it is still used to describe editorial text: '200 words of copy on freak weather conditions in the North Atlantic', for example. (KC)

copy brief. A document presented to the ADVERTISER by the ADVERTISING AGENCY, in response to an ADVERTISING BRIEF received, explaining the rationale for the copy proposed and setting out a COPY PLATFORM for approval. It could also describe the element of the ADVERTISING brief itself that relates to the copy platform. *See also* CREATIVE BRIEF, MEDIA BRIEF. (KC)

copy clearance. *See* ADVERTISING STANDARDS AUTHORITY.

copy date. The date by which all elements of the ADVERTISEMENT or COMMERCIAL have to be delivered to the publishers, contracting companies, cinema advertising contractors or outdoor advertising contractors. In this sense, 'copy' refers not just to the text of an advertisement (see copy) but to its verbal and visual elements.   (KC)

copy platform. A summary statement of the themes and propositions to be developed by the COPY in an advertisement.   (KC)

copyright. Legal exclusive right to print or publish a book, article, written material, or a work of art, protected by a copyright statement.   (MDP)

copy testing. Measuring the effectiveness of the copy in a print advertisement or a commercial, independently of the other elements. Many standard tests have been developed for this purpose over the years. *See* ADVERTISEMENT TESTING on the subject of standardized versus *ad hoc* testing procedures.   (KC)

copywriter. A writer of COPY for advertisements. Most copywriters work as a team with an ART DIRECTOR in the creative departments of ADVERTISING AGENCIES. Some are employed by advertisers themselves, but generally to write the company's product literature and promotional material, rather than the media advertisements. There is also a tradition of freelancing. Real copywriting talent commands a very high price in London or New York, which is why most advertisers buy a share in the expertise on tap at an advertising agency rather than hiring it themselves. Many top advertising people are former copywriters; *see* BERNBACH, WILLIAM and OGILVY, DAVID.   (KC)

core competence. The primary source of an organization's COMPETITIVE ADVANTAGE.   (MJB)

core-fringe model. A model recognizing that business institutions supply a core market which forms their main source of profit and a fringe market into which they attempt to expand as they develop expertise. If faced with competition from a stronger competitor, the institution withdraws to seek another area of its fringe market.   (AJB)

core product. This is the most fundamental level of a PRODUCT. It is what the buyer is actually getting for his/her money. Thus the buyer purchases photographs, rather than a camera or music, rather than a compact disc. *See also* AUGMENTED PRODUCT and PHYSICAL PRODUCT.   (KRD)

core strategy. The identification of the MARKET SEGMENT to be served and the POSITIONING to be used by the firm to exploit its COMPETITIVE ADVANTAGE.   (MJB)

corner shop. Term applied to any small shop serving a localized neighbourhood. Such stores are usually owner-managed and carry a mixed assortment of CONVENIENCE goods although some may be more specialised in CTN (confectionery–tobacco–newsagent). Often open for long hours.   (MJB)

corporate advertising. The usual description of advertising which promotes a firm or organization in general, rather than its products or services in particular.   (KC)

corporate brand strategy. Name applied to the strategy where the firm uses its name as an UMBRELLA name or brand for all of its products.   (MJB)

corporate culture. The shared VALUES, BELIEFS, norms and traditions within an organization which influence and shape the BEHAVIOUR of the individuals comprising it – 'The way we do things around here.'   (MJB)

corporate identity. A system of symbols, signs, decor, colour schemes and so on by means of which companies and organizations signal to the world outside the way that they wish to be perceived. They often state their aim to create thereby a CORPORATE IMAGE, but the reality is that corporate identity is only one of many factors which influence the image of the company or organization. It is, so to speak, a person's clothes and household decor rather than the personality perceived by others.   (KC)

corporate image. The composite public perception of a company or organization, the corporate equivalent of an individual's image or persona. Various methods have been developed for 'profiling' companies and organizations in such a way that their corporate image may be compared with a target, an ideal or the images of competitors. Corporate managements often mistakenly believe that they can 'change' or 'create' a corporate image by cosmetic adjustments to the CORPORATE IDENTITY or by means of a CORPORATE ADVERTISING campaign. The reality is that images 'belong' to the observers, not to the observed; real changes of corporate behaviour and policy are almost certainly necessary before the corporate image will actually change.   (KC)

corporate mission. Two broad definitions of mission prevail. For some organizations, mission is conceived of primarily as an intellectual discipline and a strategic tool which is fundamental to strategic management and addresses the key question 'What is our business, and what should it be ? 'For others, mission is regarded 'as the cultural "glue" which enables them to function as a collective unity.' Both definitions see it as a fundamental expression of the beliefs and values which underlie the purpose of the organization to which its members subscribe. It follows that changing an organization's mission requires a major cultural change and is usually only possible if faced with a major threat to survival. Under such circumstances a new leader is often needed to articulate a new vision and mission for the organization.   (MJB)

corporate plan. Usually a formal written statement of the organization's mission, objectives and the means of achieving them by prescribed actions within an agreed time frame.   (MJB)

corporate strategy. The decisions made and the activities undertaken by an organization to achieve its broad long-term goals. An organization's definition of its purpose and of its broad goals in the area in which it operates will serve as the foundation of its strategy, on which can be built the tactical, shorter-term activities to ensure that the purposes and the goals are fulfilled. As with marketing, there is a wide diversity of opinion as to the precise nature of corporate strategy. There is also a widespread tendency to use the word interchangeably with 'policy'. A policy is a statement of how the organization is to respond under given circumstances, and such policies will influence both the formulation and implementation of corporate strategy. In turn, corporate strategy may be thought of as a statement of the organization's objective or purpose, together with the policies and plans necessary for achieving it.   (MJB, JRB)

correlation. A measure of the relationship between two sets of data, e.g. age and tea drinking, expressed as a coefficient with a value ranging between 1.0 and −1.0. A value of 1.0 represents perfect agreement, while a value of −1.0 indicates perfect disagreement, and a value of 0.0 no relationship at all.

In the natural sciences very high levels of correlation are required to establish the existence of a relationship between two factors particularly if

this is to be used for predictive purposes. In the social sciences it is much more difficult to achieve a controlled experiment where the intervention of other variables may be suppressed or controlled so that where a chemist might look for correlations of 0.95 or better, a marketer would probably be delighted to establish a correlation of 0.70 between, say, a change in advertising and consumer recall of his product.   (MJB)

cost centre. Any organizational grouping of people and/or equipment used for the purpose of estimating and allocating costs.   (MJB)

cost, insurance, freight (CIF). A term used in foreign trade contracts where the price quoted by the exporter includes all charges incurred up to the point of delivery. The exporter arranges all shipping details, obtains BILLS OF LADING together with the insurance policy or certificate, and provides INVOICES. He packs the goods, arranges shipment, pays freight charges and marine insurance.   (CNW)

cost, marginal. The exact rate of change of total cost as output changes.   (MJB)

cost of goods sold. The total or net cost of the products or services sold by the firm.   (MJB)

cost of living index. An alternative and commonly used description of the Government's RETAIL PRICE INDEX. The index is a single number computed by measuring the relative prices of a wide range of goods and services consumed by the 'average' household on a regular basis. The prices are weighted to reflect their relative importance in terms of total expenditure as indicated by SURVEYS of household expenditure. Changes in the index are frequently used as a surrogate for the rate of inflation and may be heavily skewed if a significant element (e.g. mortgage repayments) is subject to a major rise.   (MJB)

cost-oriented pricing. See COST-PLUS PRICING.

cost per inquiry. The amount of money spent on a promotional activity divided by the number of enquiries received as a direct result.   (GM)

cost per thousand. Generally shortened to 'CPT' in the UK or 'CPM' (from the Latin, M = 1,000) in the USA, this is a crude yardstick for assessing the cost-effectiveness of advertising, which takes no account of qualitative considerations. It is calculated by the formula: cost per unit of advertising space or time, multiplied by a thousand, divided by the CIRCULATION or the audience reached. Multiplication of the numerator by 1,000 has the effect of dividing the denominator by 1,000 so that the result is indeed a unit cost per thousand. Notice that this does not necessarily mean per thousand actual readers, viewers or listeners (*see* READERSHIP; BARB; OSCAR; RAJAR). Media sales departments normally calculate CPT figures which express the cost to the advertiser of reaching a thousand people in various broad demographic categories. Users need to beware of considerable variation in the basis on which the separate figures in the formula may have been computed, meaning that separately derived CPTs may not actually be comparable. Despite its conceptual limitations, the cost per thousand criterion is a powerful determinant of MEDIA SELECTION choices.   (KC)

cost-plus pricing. Embraces all methods of setting prices with exclusive reference to cost. It is the practice of adding to an estimated product cost an amount of money to arrive at a selling price. This added money is considered the profit expectation if the sale is made on the basis of adding this anticipated profit to total or full costs. However, not all cost-plus methods use full cost as the mark-up base: some methods use only a portion of the total product costs, in which case the margin serves to cover the balance of non-estimated cost plus the expected profit. Whatever the segment of cost marked-up, the nature of the cost is subject to some variation from company to company. In some instances actual or present costs are used; in other cases expected or future costs are used, and in some cases standard costs are used. The magnitude of the mark-up also varies: some mark-ups are calculated by the certain return on sales; others to give a desired rate of return on invested capital; others to provide a fair profit. In some methods different elements of the product cost are marked up at different rates to reflect the differences in invested capital in those elements. In some cases the mark-ups are rigid and in other cases they are flexible.

Cost-plus pricing has been criticized on the following grounds: (a) it ignores demand; (b) it fails to reflect competition adequately; (c) it overplays the precision of allocated costs; (d) it is based upon a concept of cost that is frequently not relevant for the price decision; (e) the avoidable costs of any job represented in the variable cost of production depends on the firm's degree of commitment at the time in question; (f) it includes circular reasoning in some degree if current forecast is used as the base; (g) the concept of profit as an addition to unit costs is quite false – profits are not necessarily increased by adding a bigger profit margin to unit costs and raising prices to allow this bigger margin; this may often be the surest way to make a loss; (h) it assumes that all products should absorb the fixed expenses of the business at the same rate, therefore it allocates the fixed expenses common to any group of products on a uniform basis; (i) instead of pricing being fixed in relation to the competitive requirements of a particular market, and the overhead structure of the business being attuned to these requirements, the reverse procedure is adopted and prices are adjusted to the existing overhead structure by including in each unit cost a share of fixed expense; (j) it is particularly inappropriate during a period of cost inflation, for strict adherence of this approach by a manufacturer leads to a steady increase in his selling prices; (k) the system often becomes too mechanical and decisions are made at too low a management level and often lead to friction between sales and manufacturing divisions; (l) this method takes no account of the capital backing of different lines, and hence the more expensive facilities will tend to be very active, while the less expensive facilities will be underutilized.   (MJB)

countertrading. A more sophisticated form of exchange than BARTER, as it may involve multiple exchange agreements between two or more organizations (or countries) and also involve cash and/or credit for part of the transaction.   (MJB)

countervailing power. A state proposed by John K. Galbraith in *American Capitalism: The Concept of Countervailing Power* (Boston: Houghton Mifflin, 1956), in which the MARKET POWER of buyers and sellers cancel each other out, and so encourages an equitable equilibrium within the MARKET.   (MJB)

country of origin effect. Any effect on a person's perception arising from stereotypes or associations with a product's country of origin. For example, certain countries are regarded as offering superior performance for certain categories of goods – French wines, German engineering, Swiss watches. Conversely, negative associations may exist for some countries, e.g. high technology products like cars produced in less developed countries. As multinationals source manufacturing in low-cost locations around the world it has become necessary to distinguish the country of origin (COO) from the country of manufacture (COM). There is an extensive and growing body of literature dealing with this phenomenon. Advocates of globalization tend to play down its importance while those who point to nationalistic trends see it as an issue of growing importance.   (MJB)

coupon. A SALES PROMOTION device which offers an incentive, usually a price reduction, to buy a product. Coupons are often incorporated into PRINT MEDIA advertisements but may be distributed door-to-door or included with a product to encourage repeat purchase.   (MJB)

coupon research. The use of coupons returned by consumers to analyse or compare the effect of promotions or advertisements in connection with where the coupons were distributed or published.
                                                    (JAB)

coupon response. *See* DIRECT RESPONSE ADVERTISING.

coverage. Generically and at its most basic, this term describes any statement of how well a MEDIA VEHICLE can reach a particular market segment, expressed as a percentage. Specifically, it is used in practice to define that particular aspect of effectiveness by MEDIA OWNERS in their sales pitches to MEDIA BUYERS. BRAD (q.v.) defines broadcast media coverage as 'the percentage of a target audience receiving at least one opportunity to see a commercial', or to hear it in the case of radio, but uses 'weekly REACH' as the practical measure. Thus, *The Scotsman* achieves 9.8 per cent coverage of ABC1s in Scotland, which is effectively its PENETRATION of a particular market deliverable on a statistically average day to an advertiser including the title in its MEDIA SCHEDULE. Similarly, Classic FM achieves a weekly reach of 18 per cent of all men aged 55 or over in the UK, its penetration of that target audience deliverable to an advertiser who airs a typical pattern of commercials during an average broadcasting week. However, 'coverage' can mean much more than this. The Media Research Group suggested in an article in the professional journal of media planning, in 1979: 'the most widely used (and most probably misunderstood) use of the word coverage is the description of the performance of an advertising schedule. To try to

put it simply, the net coverage ... of a schedule is the proportion of a target group who will have at least one opportunity of seeing the advertisement. Thus, if a press campaign is said to achieve 70 per cent net coverage amongst all adults, 70 per cent of the adult population will have at least one chance of seeing the advertisement.' (*See* OPPORTUNITIES TO SEE.) The MRG strongly emphasizes the significance of this coverage figure to media planners: 'Coverage is a vitally important concept ... probably the most important concept in the planning of media'. In media planning practice, the concept of cover is qualified in several ways. First, '**gross cover**' is differentiated from '**net cover**'. For instance, the gross figure for a television campaign would be a count of the total number of TVRs (television ratings) achieved by individual SPOTS occupied, making no allowance for viewers seeing the same COMMERCIAL in more than one spot: if three spots individually score 15, 25 and 30 TVRs, the 'gross cover' is 70 TVRs. 'Net cover', on the other hand, takes account of the fact that, as a campaign continues, each new spot can be expected to contribute proportionately less to total coverage, until some add no new viewers at all. '4+ cover' measures the percentage of a target audience exposed at least four times as the television schedule proceeds. The figure four reflects the hypothesis that a television commercial should be fully familiar after the fourth exposure and that subsequent re-exposures will make little extra contribution to effectiveness. Though the general principle is unarguable, this practical rule ignores the time scale within which the re-exposures take place and the fact that advertising campaigns do not normally consist of repetitions of exactly the same material. It seems likely that it derives from unduly literal interpretation of learning theory. The 'cumulative cover' figure for a newspaper or magazine adjusts gross cover to take account of the fact that, although the number of people reading the average issue of a publication remains constant, there is a cumulative build-up of total readership because the individual readers of each successive issue are not entirely the same people.

Coverage data for all five media are nowadays garnered from substantial programmes of continuous market research: *see* BARB, CAVIAR, JICREG, JICPAR, NRS, OSCAR, RAJAR.   (KC)

cover price. The price to be paid for a copy of a 'paid-for' newspaper or magazine. CONTROLLED

CIRCULATION PUBLICATIONS and FREESHEETS carry no cover price at all.   (KC)

CPA. *See* CRITICAL PATH ANALYSIS.

CPM. *See* COST PER THOUSAND.

CPT. *See* COST PER THOUSAND.

Cramer's V-statistic. A statistic that transforms chi-square (for a CONTINGENCY TABLE larger than two rows by two columns) to a range of zero to one, where unity indicates complete agreement between two nominal variables.   (SKT)

CRC. *See* CAMERA-READY COPY.

CRD. *See* COMPLETELY RANDOMIZED DESIGN.

creative. A term much overworked in the advertising business. Creative expertise is one of the two prime services an ADVERTISING AGENCY can offer a prospective client, the other being MEDIA SELECTION skills. Creativity is consequently a highly valued commodity among advertising agency people, and agency Creative Departments are subject to considerable mystification. In reality, they are the equivalent of the manufacturing company's shop-floor, where the product is actually made. ART DIRECTORS and COPYWRITERS tend to look markedly different from production workers in other businesses, however, and the mystique is thereby preserved. Creative strategists are seldom required to defend their proposed 'creative solutions' but permitted to take refuge in 'creativity'. Rigorous questioning would be difficult, indeed, since the process of 'creative concept generation' is not fully understood even by academic theorists. Consequently, creativity sometimes runs riot at the more glamorous end of the business, resulting in advertising for fast-moving consumer goods or consumer durables which is visually stunning and verbally cunning, but quite possibly irrelevant or ineffective. A remarkable transformation in the visual aspect of the creative process has been wrought in recent years by the virtual replacement of magic markers, drawing pens, airbrushes, scalpels and spray mount by keyboard, mouse and software: see ARTWORK.   (KC)

creative brief. A document presented to an ADVERTISER by an ADVERTISING AGENCY, in response to an ADVERTISING BRIEF received, explaining the rationale for the creative elements of the proposed campaign. The term could also describe the part of the advertising brief itself that relates to creative strategy. *See also* MEDIA BRIEF, COPY BRIEF.   (KC)

creative department. The section of an ADVERTISING AGENCY responsible for translating the relevant parts of the ADVERTISING BRIEF into 'concepts' and ultimately into finished advertisements (though the more mechanistic operations in the final stages are likely to be delegated to a Production Department or subcontracted). It is normal nowadays for creative departments to be structured into 'creative groups' or 'creative teams', made up of COPYWRITERS and ART DIRECTORS, under the overall leadership of a Creative Director.   (KC)

creative shop. So called 'hot shops' or 'creative boutiques' began to appear in the advertising business in the 1960s, offering clients the option to buy solutions to their creative needs direct from a specialist service instead of depending on the creative department of a FULL-SERVICE ADVERTISING AGENCY. 'Shop' is a colloquial synonym for an advertising agency, especially in the USA. The impetus for their development was a belief that many advertisers suspected a jack of all trades could be master of none. The new creative shops provided no media buying or other kinds of client service, only design and writing. Not having access to media COMMISSION, they were paid by fee for their services, unlike the great majority of conventional agencies. After making news for a decade or so, they have since had a much lower profile. Many simply got bigger and slowly metamorphosed into full-service advertising agencies, SAATCHI & SAATCHI being the classic example. Their lasting contribution to the advertising business was a challenge to the complacency of the big, undifferentiated agencies of the 1950s. *See also* MEDIA INDEPENDENT.
                                                        (KC)

creative strategy. One of the two halves which make up a complete advertising strategy, the other being MEDIA STRATEGY. There is often debate as to which of these two is more 'important' than the other. This seems a sterile argument. On the one hand, it is certainly true that a creative strategy cannot possibly achieve its aims unless the advertisements are placed where they can work to best effect. On the other hand, it is equally true that the most skilful media strategy will be to no avail if the creative execution is ineffective. It is only possible to conclude that creative and media strategies are wholly interdependent, both crucial, and that it would be wrong to think of one or the other as a first priority or as more important. (KC)

credence qualities. Qualities of services which consumers have to take for granted as they are unable to assess them in any meaningful way even after consumption e.g. dental or medical treatment. (MJB)

credentials presentation. A relatively informal presentation by an ADVERTISING AGENCY (or other kind of MARKETING COMMUNICATIONS intermediary) to a firm which it hopes will in due course become its client. A series of credentials presentations from a number of agencies is the basis for the PITCH LIST of those to be included in the final phase of the agency selection procedure. (KC)

credit. The provision of goods or services in exchange for a promise to pay at some future time. Credit is an important element of customer service, particularly in encouraging the purchase of 'big ticket' CONSUMER GOODS like cars, WHITE GOODS etc., and CAPITAL GOODS and equipment in INDUSTRIAL MARKETS. For the seller, the granting of credit and its control are of vital importance. While it may help secure orders, over-generous credit can erode profit margins, while delays in payment may create grave cash-flow problems. (MJB)

credit account. One element of the TERMS OF TRADE between supplier and customer, whereby payment (or settlement) is deferred for an agreed period of time after the date of supply. Goods thus supplied 'on credit' may be resold or consumed before payment becomes due.

Control of a company's credit ACCOUNTS (often described as accounts receivable) is commonly regarded as one of the major duties of accounts departments, whose responsibilities may also include establishment of credit limits for individual customers, the monitoring of the amount of money owed to the company and the extent to which customers comply with the agreed trading terms.

Credit accounts are generally taken to be the norm in ORGANIZATIONAL MARKETING contexts; the opposite being cash accounts or proforma accounts, which many companies operate until customers have provided acceptable evidence of creditworthiness. (KNB)

credit card. (1) A card issued by a bank or finance house, enabling the holder to obtain goods and services from businesses accepting the card, without payment of cash. The issuer provides an extended credit facility enabling the card holder to delay payment. Examples are Mastercard and Visa.

(2) A card issued by a WHOLESALER or RETAILER, enabling the holder to obtain goods or services from their outlets without immediate payment. An example of this is the Marks & Spencer Chargecard. (AMW)

crisis management. Generally, the actions adopted by management to deal with a crisis and often used in a negative sense to imply that such actions could have been avoided with better advanced planning. More specifically, the recognition that crises are bound to occur and the development of a contingency plan to deal with these e.g. the withdrawal of a defective product from the market. (MJB)

criterion variable. *See* DEPENDENT VARIABLE.

critical path analysis (CPA). A technique used in the planning and scheduling of interrelated and often complex events. As a first step, a special type of chart – a network – consisting of arrows and circles is drawn. This depicts the entire process with an event being represented by a circle and an activity being represented by an arrow. The circles are connected by the arrows. Logically, an event cannot take place until all the activities leading up to it have been completed. Estimated 'time to completion' values are then placed on each activity. The critical path of the network is determined by considering each event in turn, and calculating the earliest possible time that it can occur. Clearly, if an event is dependent on two or more activities, the earliest time is determined by the longest activity. The critical path is the resultant sequence of interconnected events and activities which will require the longest time to accomplish. Summing all the times on the critical path will give the shortest time for the project to be completed.

The technique is used in areas such as production planning and NEW PRODUCT DEVELOPMENT, and provides managers with an analytical tool for controlling the process and identifying problem areas. Computer packages exist which allow the user to enter their network and examine various 'what if?' scenarios. (KRD)

critical success factors (CSF). Those factors considered critical to success in a competitive market. Perhaps the best known set of critical success factors were those set out *In Search of Excellence* by Peters and Waterman (1983). However, while managers will continue to search for such formulae for success, experience indicates that in a dynamic market the nature of critical success factors is highly situation specific i.e. it varies from situation to situation.   (MJB)

cross elasticity of demand. *See* DEMAND, PRICE ELASTICITY OF.

cross-impact analysis. A means of analysing the likely impact that predicted developments (technological, social, political, economic) have on each other. The cross-impact matrix provides the structure for accomplishing the analysis. It lists specific future developments along both the horizontal and vertical axes. The impact (frequently expressed as a probability) that two specific developments will have on each other is noted in the appropriate cell of the matrix.   (DB)

cross-sectional design. A survey design that involves taking a sample or a series of samples at one point in time. *Contrast* LONGITUDINAL DESIGNS.   (SKT)

cross-sectional sample. A SAMPLE SURVEY involved in a cross-sectional design. RESPONDENTS are sampled at one point in time for one survey only; to contrast with panels and other samples involved in LONGITUDINAL DESIGNS.   (SKT)

cross-sectional study. Research that simply involves a sample taken at one point in time.   (SKT)

cross-tabulation. The process of producing a cross-tabulation or CONTINGENCY TABLE. In counter-sorter days (*see* COMPUTER CARD) this involved tabulating one variable and then tabulating each deck of cards from each category separately on a second variable.   (SKT)

cross-tabulation table. A table expressing the number of cases found to have each combination of values from two variables; also known as CONTINGENCY TABLE.   (SKT)

cues. Weak stimuli not strong enough to arouse consumer action but capable of providing direction to motivated activity. Cues in the shopping environment would include such things as promotions, product colouring, distinctive packaging, and so on. Consumers can use these cues to make the choice between response options in a learning situation.   (JLD)

cultural universals. Cultural factors which are common to most if not all cultures e.g. belief in a superior being, concepts of right and wrong etc.   (MJB)

culture. A man-made system consisting of three interdependent elements: (a) an ideological system, or mental component that encompasses the ideas, beliefs, values and ways of reasoning that members of the culture learn to accept in defining what is desirable or undesirable; (b) a technological system, made up of skills, crafts and arts that enable members to produce material goods derived from the natural environment; (c) an organizational system, such as the family and social class, that makes possible the effective coordination of individual member's behaviour with the actions of others.   (JLD)

cumulative brand penetration. *See* BRAND SHARE PREDICTION MODEL.

customary pricing. Such prices are fixed by custom where there is an expectation that the object will be priced at a particular point e.g. 50p. The use of such prices assumes a kink in the demand curve but this assumption appears to have lost support with the abolition of resale price maintenance and the growth of inflation. However, 'psychological prices' ending in 99p or cents still prevail. With the disappearance of 1cent coins in many countries this 'custom' seems likely to disappear too.   (MJB)

custom-built. Made to order. A unique PRODUCT or service designed to a customer's requirement. The term is usually used in the context of ships or tanks or other items of heavy capital equipment, rather than 'handmade' clothes. Custom-built products are the opposite of mass-produced and mass-marketed standardized products. A pump for use at a reservoir's pumping station may have to be 'custom-built' or 'purpose-made' to a unique specification in terms of size, pumping capability and speed variability. Similarly computers may be 'custom-built' for a bank's requirements. Some manufacturers, with a standard range of products, will permit or encourage clients to introduce minor modifications to give their product unique features. In this way individual characteristics are provided to a standard product – but this is a cosmetic marketing ploy designed to give 'custom-built' characteristics or uniqueness to an otherwise standard product. In such situations both parties do benefit – the supplier through being able to meet the customer's wishes for an individual product and the customer by obtaining the price benefit of a nearly standardized product.   (BRM)

customer. The actual or intended purchaser of goods and/or services.   (MJB)

customer characteristics. Any distinctive, singular, typical or special feature or features which may be used to distinguish a customer or group of customers from any other customer or group of customers. The basis for MARKET SEGMENTATION.   (MJB)

customer delivered value. The benefit enjoyed by the customer which represents the difference between the cost to them and the actual value received – i.e. the 'profit to the customer' as perceived by them.   (MJB)

customer lifetime value. A measure of the total value to be earned from a customer over the lifetime of the relationship. Given the frequently used rule-of-thumb that it costs five times as much to create a customer as to keep one, this concept is particularly important in guiding the firm as to how much it can afford to invest to create a customer, given its expectations that it will continue to benefit from that customer's patronage into the future. This approach is fundamental to the whole concept of RELATIONSHIP MARKETING and distinguishes it from TRANSACTIONAL MARKETING where marketing expenses are regarded as direct costs, rather than investments, and so have to be recovered from the transaction. This may well result in the CUSTOMER DELIVERED VALUE falling below expectations so that the customer will not repeat purchase and so not enter into a continuing relationship.   (MJB)

customer orientation. An essential and (some would argue) the distinguishing feature of the MARKETING CONCEPT, as it reflects an ATTITUDE of mind and approach to business which places the customer at the beginning and the end of the production–consumption cycle.   (MJB)

customer research. Any investigation or inquiry into the ATTITUDES, OPINIONS or BEHAVIOUR of customers as a basis for responding to and/or predicting their future needs.   (MJB)

customer satisfaction. A measure of the degree to which an object meets the customers' expectations. The challenge to be met by suppliers is that if you raise customers' expectations too high and fail to meet them they will be dissatisfied and likely to switch to an alternative supplier. Conversely, if customer expectations are low and you exceed them they are likely to repeat purchase and recommend your product to others. The paradox to be solved is the level at which to pitch the initial appeal in order to encourage trial.   (MJB)

customer service level. The standards set by any establishment which it seeks to achieve in the physical distribution of goods to its customers. The main standard is the time taken from receipt of order to delivery, but may also involve accuracy of order filling, dependability in meeting delivery quotation or ease and flexibility of order placement.   (AJB)

customer switching costs. The costs incurred when one changes or 'switches' suppliers. Some of these costs are real e.g. setting up new administrative procedures, but most are psychic and related to the perceived risk and uncertainty associated with moving from a known source of supply to one which is untried. It is claimed that buyers are reluctant to switch from existing suppliers to new ones without an incentive equivalent to a 10 per cent price reduction.   (MJB)

cut-price. Any PRICE which purports to offer a DISCOUNT from the recommended or prevailing MARKET price.   (MJB)

cut-throat competition. COMPETITION based upon PREDATORY PRICING under which one competitor will seek to eliminate another or others by cutting PRICES well below normal levels and often to less than the actual cost of production.   (MJB)

Cuttings. *See* PRESS CUTTINGS.

cycle models. Cyclical change models have been used to explain changes in retail institutions since 1958 when McNair first proposed the 'wheel of retailing'. This is a four-stage cycle of: (a) innovation; (b) accelerated development; (c) maturity; (d) decline. Another cycle of change has concentrated on store types which evolved from specialist to generalist and then back to specialist.   (AJB)

D

DAB. Digital audio broadcasting, called simply DIGITAL RADIO since 1997. (KC)

DADA. *See* DESIGNERS' & ART DIRECTORS' ASSOCIATION.

DAGMAR. *See* COLLEY, RUSSELL H.

data. Any observation(s) or element(s) which may be facts, numbers, characters or symbols. The term is usually used as a collective noun and accompanied by a singular verb. It should not be confused with information, which, by contrast, is the result of data manipulation. (KRD)

data accuracy. The extent to which recorded information represents the phenomena from which it derives. Data inaccuracies come principally from errors of measurement and errors of transcription. (SKT)

database. A file of DATA, so structured that programs (analytical, presentation, update, etc.) may draw on the file but in no way inhibit the content or design. (KRD)

database management system (DBMS). Software designed specifically for the organization and manipulation of DATA. The term is rather loose, as a DBMS associated with a mainframe has features and capabilities not found on a Personal Computer version, though the gap is narrowing. Mainframe DBMSs allow the user to build complex data structures and provide a high level of language interface. MARKET LEADERS in the PC market are Ashton Tate (dBASE IV) and Microrim (Rbase 5000). (KRD)

database marketing. The use of databases containing personal information for the purpose of identifying actual and potential customers with a view to establishing contact and building a relationship with them. (MJB)

data collection. The process of obtaining and recording information. (SKT)

data deck. A historical term from counter-sorter practice (*see* COMPUTER CARD) when data was recorded on a deck of cards. (SKT)

data error. An inaccuracy in recorded information. Some, but not all, data errors can be found by wild-code checking (e.g. sex coded as 3!) or contingency checks (sex – male with three pregnancies!). (SKT)

data file. *See* DATA SET.

data matrix. A view of information as a table (*see* RELATIONAL DATABASES) consisting of rows of cases, each with a value (possibly missing) in the column of each variable. (SKT)

data processing. The steps involved in transforming recorded information, typically by computer. A traditional term for all computer use in business (DP departments) but more restrictively applied to the production of cross-tabulations after DATA COLLECTION. (SKT)

Data Protection Act. The Data Protection Act of 1984 is concerned with any personal information on individuals which is held in a computer system, with those individuals who process such data and the individuals to whom the data relates.

It does not relate to data held in any other format, nor to information relating only to corporate bodies or computers used for personal, family or household affairs, or recreational purposes. The Act gives individuals the right of access to personal data held in many computer files. They can ask for, and receive a copy of any such personal data held. If the data is false or wrongly disclosed and causes the individual to suffer damage as a result, claims for compensation are accepted. The Act requires those who hold or process computer data on individuals to register with the Data Protection Registrar (Springfield House, Water Lane, Wilmslow SK9 5AX). Failure to do so is a criminal offence. The Act embodies several principles which must be observed: for example, data should be obtained and processed fairly and lawfully, be accurate, secure, be no more than is required for the stated purpose, and be up to date.

(GM)

data set. A collection of data RECORDS. (KRD)

date coding. *See* BEST-BEFORE DATE.

day-after recall (DAR). A standard technique for evaluating ADVERTISING EFFECTIVENESS by testing recall of an advertisement among its target audience 24 hours after their first exposure to it. *See also* RECALL. (KC)

DBMS. *See* DATABASE MANAGEMENT SYSTEM.

dc. Stands for 'double column'. Hence '25 cm dc' means a newspaper advertisement occupying a space 25 cm deep and two columns wide. It is equally likely to be described in everyday conversation as a '25 centimetre double'. (KC)

DC. Stands for 'double crown'; a small POSTER SITE. (KC)

DE. *See* SOCIO-ECONOMIC CLASSIFICATIONS.

dealer. Literally anyone who deals (buys or sells) in a MARKET. More specifically used to describe RETAILERS – hence DEALER LOADER. (MJB)

dealer listing. The listing of dealers in an advertisement for a product indicating where it may be purchased. (MJB)

dealer loader. Some form of incentive offered to a DEALER to encourage him to give or increase STOCKS or display of the supplier's goods. (MJB)

dealership. An agreement under which a distributor or RETAILER is given exclusive selling rights for the manufacturer's PRODUCTS within a defined MARKET area. (MJB)

debit card. A card issued by a bank or finance house, enabling the holder to obtain goods and services from businesses accepting the card, without payment of cash. On presenting the card, money is debited directly from the holder's bank account. This transaction is often undertaken instantaneously by electronic fund transfer. *See* ELECTRONIC FUND TRANSFER AT POINT OF SALE.

(AMW)

decay. The gradual forgetting of an ADVERTISING MESSAGE over time. However, AWARENESS/recognition may be readily re-established by further ADVERTISING, suggesting that decay is of the conscious rather than subconscious memory. (MJB)

decentralized organization. An organization in which decision-making power and authority are devolved to the operating units. (MJB)

decentralization. The devolution of decision-making authority from the centre or top of an organization to its operating managers. In large and complex organizations, decentralization is considered as essential to enhancing effectiveness by ensuring that decisions are made in the context of the local environment in which they are to be implemented. (MJB)

deceptive advertising. Advertising intended to mislead consumers by making false claims or suppressing information which might influence the consumer's decision. (MJB)

deceptive pricing. Pricing tactics intended to deceive the consumer into thinking that the price has been discounted or reduced when it has not e.g. publishing a higher price than intended and then offering a saving on this. (MJB)

decider. The member of the decision-making unit who actually makes the purchasing decision. *See* BUYER ROLES. (MJB)

decision criteria. Although a number of possible decision criteria are available, theorists are unanimous in recommending that one should seek to maximize the expected utility (MEU) flowing from a decision. In turn, it is usual to express maximum expected utility in monetary terms so that EXPECTED VALUE becomes the appropriate decision criterion.   (MJB)

decision making under uncertainty. The making of decisions under conditions where the decision maker has little or no prior experience and so cannot assign objective probabilities to the possible outcomes identified by his analysis and incorporated in his DECISION TREE. To address problems of this kind, a new school of decision theorists has emerged since the late 1950s (led by Raiffa and Schlaifer at the Harvard Business School) which emphasizes the role of probability in decision making and the use of Bayes Theorem as a means of combining prior estimates with new information to generate a set of revised or posterior probabilities.   (MJB)

decision-making unit (DMU). A key element Within the CONCEPT of ORGANIZATIONAL BUYING BEHAVIOUR, embodying the involvement of a number of people or groups in the decision-making process. Conventionally the DMU is taken to comprise four potential role players: gatekeepers, influencers, deciders and buyers. It is therefore seen as being a prime function of marketers in organizations to identify the structure and members of the DMU, to serve as foci for the communications effort.   (KNB)

decision support system (DSS). More advanced than a standard information system, a DSS consists of a set of functional modules which allow the user considerable flexibility in the selection of data, analyses and presentation format. G. Anthony Gorry and Michael S. Scott-Morton ('A Framework for Management Information Systems', in *Sloan Management Review,* Fall 1971, pp. 55–70) characterized such systems as 'supportive, functional in problem areas that are not well structured, and interactive'.   (KRD)

decision tree. A methodology for exploring the existence and relative merits of alternative courses of action available to the decision maker in solving a problem. As explained in Michael J. Baker, *Marketing Management and Strategy* (London: Macmillan, 1992), one of the clearest explanations of the use of the decision tree is to be found in John F. Magee's 'Decision Trees for Decision Making' (in *Harvard Business Review,* July–August 1964, pp. 126–38). Magee starts with a simple example to illustrate the salient characteristics of the decision-tree approach by posing the problem of what to do on an overcast

Saturday afternoon when 75 people are coming round for cocktails. This he describes as follows:

You and your wife feel it is time you returned some hospitality by holding a party. You have a pleasant garden and your house is not too large; so if the weather permits, you would like to set up refreshments in the garden and have the party there. It would be more pleasant, and your guests would be more comfortable. On the other hand, if you set up the party for the garden and after all the guests are assembled it begins to rain, the refreshments will be ruined, your guests will be damp and you will heartily wish you had decided to have the party in the house ... What should you do? This particular decision can be represented in the form of a 'pay-off' table:

	Rain	No Rain
Outdoors	Disaster	Real comfort
Indoors	Mild discomfort, but happy	Mild discomfort, but regrets

In turn the information in the pay-off table can be represented pictorially by means of a decision tree (Figure 8).

As Magee comments:

The tree is made up of a series of nodes and branches. At the first node on the left, the host has the choice of having the party inside or outside. Each branch represents an alternative course of action or decision. At the end of each branch or alternative course is another mode representing a chance effect – whether or not it will rain. Each subsequent alternative course to the right represents an alternative outcome of this chance event. Associated with each complete alternative course through the tree is a pay-off, shown at the end of the rightmost or terminal branch of the course.

From this description, it is clear that a decision tree will always combine action choices with different possible events or outcomes which are subject to some degree or other to chance (distinguished by different symbols for emphasis).

In the case of the relatively simple decision discussed so far, one probably needs neither a pay-off table nor a decision tree to help one come to a decision. But given more complex decisions where several alternatives are available, it is easy to understand how the content of a pay-off table could confuse rather than illuminate while a decision tree would help disaggregate the problem in a clear and meaningful way. Magee presents such a tree when he analyses the familiar MARKETING problem of whether or not to invest in PRODUCT DEVELOPMENT. (MJB)

decline stage of product life cycle. *See* PRODUCT LIFE CYCLE.

decoding. The act of interpreting incoming communications and placing meaning on them. (MJB)

deferred gratification. The foregoing of current consumption opportunities, particularly impulse purchases, in the expectation of some greater future satisfaction. Saving, investment and the avoidance of credit purchases are all manifestations of deferred gratification, as is giving up smoking or other habits which are likely to affect one's future health. (MJB)

deferred rebate. *See* SHIPPING CONFERENCE.

degrees of freedom. A statistical term that indicates the number of free parameters involved in calculating a statistic. For example, the degrees of freedom associated with the MEAN of a series of numbers is the number of cases minus one: once the mean is known you only need all the cases bar one to be able to know the values of all the cases. (SKT)

Delphi conferencing. The use of COMPUTER CONFERENCING to conduct a Delphi forecast. The participants (experts) are polled for their opinion about future developments by means of a network of computer terminals. The inter-round analysis of forecasting data and its feedback to participants is part of a pre-programmed routine: this being so it is effectively conducted in real-time. *See also* DELPHI TECHNIQUE. (DB)

Delphi technique. A method of soliciting and aggregating the opinions of a group of experts to derive a consensus view concerning the time-scale during which speculated future developments may occur (or the probability that they will have occurred by a particular date). The technique minimizes socio-psychological influences by keeping individual responses anonymous. It proceeds by means of a programmed sequence of

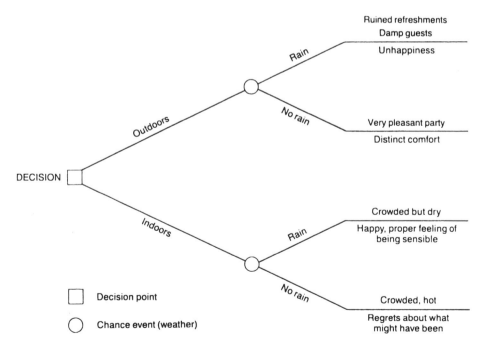

Source: Michael J. Baker, *Marketing Strategy and Management* (London: Macmillan, 1992)

Figure 8: **Decision tree**

interrogations (conducted by questionnaire) interspersed with the feedback of information describing the consensus view.

(DB)

demand, cross elasticity. Cross elasticity of demand measures one of the most important demand relationships – the closeness of substitutes or the degree of complementarity of demand. A high cross elasticity means that the commodities are close substitutes. A cross elasticity of zero means that they are independent of each other in the market, and a negative cross elasticity means that the goods are complementary in the market in that one stimulates the sales of the others.   (MJB)

demand, industry. An industry demand schedule presents the relation of the price of the product to the quantity that will be bought from all firms. It has a clear meaning when the products of the various firms are close substitutes, when they differ from that of other industries, and when they have a well-defined price level. The concept of industry demand becomes nebulous when there is a considerable product differentiation within the industry and substitute competition with other industries.   (MJB)

demand, latent. A demand which the consumer is unable to satisfy, usually for lack of purchasing power. For example, many housewives may have a latent demand for automatic dishwashers but, related to their available disposable income, this want is less strong than their demand for other products and so remains unsatisfied. In other words, wants are ranked in order of preference and satisfied to the point where disposable income is exhausted. From the manufacturer's point of view the problem is to translate latent demand into effective demand by increasing the consumer's preference for his particular product *vis-à-vis* all other product offerings. Marketing is largely concerned with solving this problem.

Latent demand may also be thought of as a vague want in the sense that the consumer feels a need for a product, or service, to fill a particular function but is unable to locate anything suitable. If such a product exists, marketing's role is to bring it to his attention; if it does not exist, then marketing should seek to identify the unfilled need and develop new products to satisfy it.

Potential demand exists where the consumer possesses the necessary purchasing power, but is not currently buying the product under consider-ation. Thus, where a marketer has identified a latent demand and developed a new product to satisfy it, the potential demand consists of all those who can back up their latent want with pur-chasing power. In another context, potential demand may be thought of as that part of the total market (effective demand) for an existing product which a firm might anticipate securing through the introduction of a new, competitive brand.

(MJB)

demand, law of. Indicates an inverse relation-ship between price and quantity, assuming the other determinants of demand, income, consumer changes, and the prices of substitutes are held constant. This causes the demand curve to have a negative slope, implying that the higher the price the smaller the quantity demanded in a period of time, and the lower the price the greater the quan-tity demanded (*see* Figure 9).   (MJB)

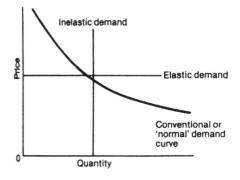

Figure 9: **Demand curves**

demand, price elasticity of. Elasticity of demand is a common device describing the shape of a demand function. It measures the sensitivity of sales to changes in a particular causal factor. More precisely, elasticity is the ratio of relative change in a dependent variable to the relative change in an independent variable. Demand is said to be elastic when the relative change in the independent factor to the relative change in quan-tity is greater than 1 and inelastic when it is less than 1. Although originally the concept of elas-ticity referred only to price:sales ratios, it can be generalized to apply to each demand determinant, e.g. consumer income, advertising expenditures etc. The main interest in price elasticity arises from the fact that it provides information about the effects of price changes on revenues.

Depending on price elasticity, a given change in price will result in an increase in total revenue, a decrease, or no change. Total revenue increases with price reductions when demand is elastic, decreases when demand is inelastic, and is unaffected when unitary elasticity prevails.   (MJB)

demand schedule. This is a table which shows the quantities of a PRODUCT demanded at different prices (*see* Figure 10). From this information a demand curve can be drawn.   (MDP)

demand, short-run versus long-run. Short-run demand refers to existing demand, with its immediate reaction to price changes, income fluctuation etc., whereas long-run demand is that which will ultimately exist as a result of changes in pricing, promotion or product improvement, after enough time has elapsed to let the market adjust itself to the new situation. The distinction between short-run and long-run dictates competitive response. In the short run the question is whether competitors will meet the cut in price while in the long run the entry of potential competitors, exploration of substitutes, and other complex factors may affect the response.   (MJB)

demand, theory of. Deals with the relation between quantity demanded and the price of the commodity, and regards demand for a product as a function of its price, the price of substitutes and complements, consumer tastes and incomes. The relation between demand and price is central to price theory and demand schedules and demand curves are the techniques of describing demand–price relationships.   (MJB)

demarketing. A term coined by Philip Kotler and Sidney J. Levy ('Demarketing, Yes Demarketing', *Harvard Business Review,* Nov–Dec 1971) to describe means of reducing overfull demand. 'Demarketing deals with attempts to discourage customers in general or a certain class of customers in particular on either a temporary or permanent basis.' In other words demarketing seeks to modify demand through differential pricing or the reduction of promotion, quality, service etc.   (MJB)

demographics. Factual characteristics which define the composition of a POPULATION such as age, sex, marital status, family or household composition, income, education, occupation etc. In most countries such data are collected regularly by government agencies through censuses of the population. Demographics provides the foundation for most approaches to MARKET SEGMENTATION.   (MJB)

demographic segmentation. *See* MARKET SEGMENTATION.

demography. The study of human populations in terms of such characteristics as age, gender, marital status, education, occupation, location etc.   (MJB)

Department of Employment Gazette. Now known simply as the *Employment Gazette.* UK

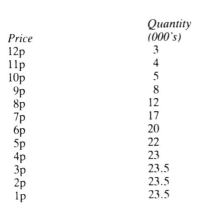

Price	Quantity (000's)
12p	3
11p	4
10p	5
9p	8
8p	12
7p	17
6p	20
5p	22
4p	23
3p	23.5
2p	23.5
1p	23.5

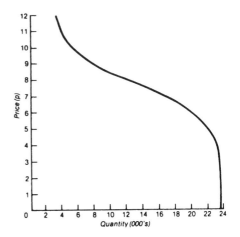

Figure 10: **Demand curves and schedule**

government publication including articles, tables and charts on manpower, employment, unemployment, hours worked, earnings, labour costs, retail prices, stoppages due to disputes etc. *See* LABOUR MARKET TRENDS.   (MJB)

Department of Trade and Industry (DTI). UK government department, formerly known as the Board of Trade, responsible for all aspects of competition and industry policy.   (MJB)

department stores. Large general stores on multi-levels, selling a wide variety of merchandise including clothing and soft furnishings. To qualify for the title of department store, the shop must employ at least 25 staff and sell a wide range of products. The merchandise is usually organized into different departments, each often regarded as a 'shop within a shop'. There can also be leased departments within the store which are operated by suppliers; British examples include Jaeger, Revlon, Dior. The store receives a rent from the lessees. British examples of department stores include Harrods, the John Lewis shops and the Debenham Group.   (MDP)

dependent variable (criterion variable). The dependent variable is the measure of the construct whose values we expect to be influenced by the predictor variables (also called the independent variables). The term is used in REGRESSION ANALYSIS, ANALYSIS OF VARIANCE and other techniques to describe the variable whose outcome we are attempting to attribute either to some experimental manipulation or to the values of some predictor variables.   (SKT)

depression. The stage in the BUSINESS CYCLE where there is high unemployment, low wages and low disposable incomes. Persons in employment lack confidence and so save rather than spend thus increasing the recessionary trend.   (MJB)

depth. Measures the number of distinct products within a product line.   (MJB)

depth interviews. Face-to-face unstructured, informal interaction between INTERVIEWER and RESPONDENT. Starting with general QUESTIONS the interview develops into more specific question areas probing for NEEDS, desires, motives and emotions of the CONSUMER. It can also be a non-directive interview in which the respondent is encouraged to talk about the subject.   (JLD)

derived demand. That demand created by and arising from the consumption of a finished good or service, e.g. the demand for car tyres and batteries is derived from the consumption of cars and in turn influences the demand for rubber, lead, acid etc. used in the manufacture of those products.   (MJB)

descriptive research. Research undertaken to describe a problem or issue and so provide background or context for persons unfamiliar with a situation. Often provided at the beginning of a research report or a research brief as the basis for more detailed analysis using quantitative data.   (MJB)

design. A crucial factor in maintaining and improving the quality and competitiveness of manufactured goods. It receives continuous attention from industry and assistance is available from the UK government-sponsored Design Council, while the Computer-Aided Design Centre also provides assistance to individual firms. The Design Council has centres in London, Cardiff and Glasgow, and its services include advice on design matters, the organization of product displays and overseas trade fairs, conferences and seminars on design and help for design education.   (HMSO)

Designers' & Art Directors' Association (DADA). Professional body representing the specialists on the CREATIVE side of the advertising business. It runs one of the most important annual competitions for creative excellence in British advertising, the D&AD Awards, and publishes *Direction* monthly in association with the publishers of CAMPAIGN.   (KC)

design factor. The ratio of the SAMPLING ERROR of a complex sample to a simple sample. The complicated calculations required to estimate the sampling error (*see* ERROR) in a complex sample are often calculated for one or two QUESTIONS in a SURVEY, and the design factor thus derived applied to estimate roughly the sampling error in other questions, or other surveys. A typical value of the factor is two.   (JAB)

desk research. A study of SECONDARY DATA, such as official statistics, or published studies. This is very important in industrial research, and in the study of any unfamiliar market.   (JAB)

detached types. *See* INTERPERSONAL RESPONSE TRAITS.

detailing. Selling to members of the medical professions. (MJB)

developed countries. Those countries whose economies are industrial rather than agricultural or raw material producers, with a high and rising standard of living. They are both rich and technologically developed, and can readily absorb and adapt new industries wherever in the world they originate. They have the opposite characteristics to those found in DEVELOPING COUNTRIES and include North America, most of Western Europe, Australia, New Zealand and Japan. (JK)

developing countries. A description of the poorer nations which came into current usage in the 1960s and began to replace more perjorative terms like 'underdeveloped countries', 'less developed countries', 'The Third World'. 'Developing countries' as a term is often now replaced by 'industrializing countries'. Each term tends to have certain connotations, some being more complimentary than others: 'underdeveloped' suggests countries capable of economic development, but which have failed to fulfil some unstated potential. 'Developing' sounds better but was an optimistic gloss, as in reality a country may not be developing. 'Less developed' is perhaps less objectionable than 'Third World' or 'underdeveloped', but implies that such countries should model themselves on those which are more developed. This may prove a very dangerous guide to strategy. 'Industrializing', like 'developing', was an optimistic gloss. Another term which avoids the above controversy but does little to clarify the issue is to talk about the 'South'. The Brandt Report (1980) made the distinction between the 'North' (or technically-advanced nations) and the 'South' (all other countries incorporating a range from half-industrialized countries like Brazil to extremely poor countries like Chad).

'Developing', or whatever term one chooses to use, means basically poverty. However this is extremely difficult to define and measure absolutely. There are hundreds of millions of people who are illiterate and inadequately sheltered, clothed and nourished. Relatively, poverty can be measured by countries' per capita income. Thus an attempt to quantify 'developing' has been made. A country is considered to be developing if income per head falls below a more or less arbitrarily stated level, usually one-fifth of the per capita income in the United States.

However, to say that any country with a per capita income below one-fifth of the US is 'developing' and all other countries are 'developed' is not satisfactory. Using such a criterion, some countries like the oil-producing Middle East states would become advanced. But when one considers other factors like income distribution, level of available services etc., this is clearly not the case. Consequently, other non-monetary indicators such as number of telephones, energy consumption, number of vehicles, life expectancy, illiteracy and unemployment levels have been used. No single indicator has proved to be satisfactory or universally acceptable. The World Bank subdivides developing countries into low income economies, middle income economies (subdivided into oil exporters and oil importers) and least developed countries.

Closely related to the problem is the controversy surrounding what is economic development. The meaning of this has ranged from 'economic growth' to 'modernization' to 'distributive justice' to 'socio-economic transformation'. In the early post-Second World War years, development meant a rapid and sustained rise in real income per head, together with shifts in economic, technical and demographic characteristics. Since the total volume of output rather than the individual was all-important, a country could become 'developed' almost overnight if it could generate foreign exchange rapidly.

Then development or 'modernization' emerged, stressing social, psychological, political and educational changes. From the late 1960s economic development has been envisaged more as 'distributive justice' since it was realized that the benefits of growth were not reaching the poorest sections of the community.

Today, economic development is regarded as a socio-economic transformation. Economic growth and industrialization are essential but if no attention is paid to the quality of growth, and to social changes, one cannot speak of economic development. Consequently, per capita income is increasingly considered inadequate as a measure of development but must be taken together with other social indicators such as life expectancy, percentage employed in agriculture, consumption of proteins, levels of education etc. Developing countries tend to be characterized by a high percentage of the population employed in agriculture, rapid population growth with high birth rates and high but falling death rates, low levels of savings per head, low net investment, low public health and poor sanitation, poor technology, high illiteracy and heavy dependence on exports in a small number of often primary products as well as low per capita incomes. The result is that their peoples have a much lower standard of living than that enjoyed in the more economically advanced nations.   (JK)

deviation. Departure from the normal. (1) In the behavioural sciences deviant behaviour is that which differs from the norms of the deviant's culture or subculture.

(2) In statistics the term has a precise technical meaning in that deviation measures the spread of data around the MEAN or average value of the data as a whole. Based upon the parameters of the NORMAL DISTRIBUTION it is known that 99 per cent of all observations will be within plus or minus 3 standard deviations of the mean. Thus if we know the mean and standard deviation of a POPULATION we can draw informed conclusions as to the actual distribution of that population as a whole. *See* ERROR, SAMPLING.   (MJB)

diadic. *See* PRODUCT TEST.

diary. *See* CONSUMER PANEL.

Dichotomous questions. *See* CLOSED QUESTIONS.

differential advantage. A property or attribute possessed by a PRODUCT, service or organization which differentiates it from all other competing products or organizations in the same generic grouping or MARKET.   (MJB)

differential sampling. The practice of setting QUOTAS for certain subgroups within a POPULATION out of proportion to their representation within that population e.g. a RANDOM SAMPLE would contain say, 12 per cent over 65 years old but the needs of this segment might be important to the researcher who would set a higher quota for persons in this age group. *See* SAMPLING.   (MJB)

differential scale. *See* SCALING TECHNIQUES.

differential threshold. The smallest change in a stimulus that can be noticed. *See* JUST NOTICEABLE DIFFERENCE.   (MJB)

differentiated marketing strategy. One of three basic marketing strategies (the other two being UNDIFFERENTIATED and CONCENTRATED). A differ-

entiated strategy exists where the supplier seeks to supply a modified version of the basic product to each of the major subgroups which comprise the basic markets. In doing so he will develop a different MARKETING MIX in terms of the PRODUCT CHARACTERISTICS, its PRICE, PROMOTION and DISTRIBUTION, although attempts will often be made to standardize on one or more of these factors in the interests of scale economies (usually distribution, e.g. car dealerships, consumer durables etc.). Such differentiation is only possible for very large firms which can achieve a sufficient volume in each of the SEGMENTS to remain competitive.   (MJB)

diffusion curve. *See* ADOPTION CURVE.

diffusion process. The characteristics of the diffusion process may be summed up as: (a) acceptance (b) over time (c) of some specific item (d) by adopting units – individuals or groups – (e) linked by communication channels (f) to a social structure (g) to a given system of values. In this context acceptance is probably best defined as 'continued use'. Thus, while purchase of a durable good would count as acceptance or adoption, first purchase of a low price consumable item might only amount to a trial such that adopting would only be assumed given repeated purchase of the item.   (MJB)

Digest of UK Energy Statistics. Contains tables and charts of UK energy production and consumption. Separate sections deal with production and consumption of individual fuels, oil and gas reserves, fuel prices and foreign trade in fuels.
                    (MJB)

digital radio. A developing system of digitally encoded radio broadcasting, complementing the existing analogue technology. At the end of 1996, the RADIO AUTHORITY had awarded 18 'restricted service licences', all on an 'experimental' basis, to the operators of 4 MULTIPLEXES. Applications for the first 'permanent' licences were to be invited in the Spring of 1998. *See also* RADIO.
                    (KC)

digital television. Developing system of digitally encoded television broadcasting, complementing the existing analogue technology. By mid-1997, licences had been awarded for the operation of: six terrestrial MULTIPLEXES sharing 15 channels, one satellite multiplex offering 150 channels and between 100 and 200 new cable channels, to be operated by the existing providers. The terrestrial licences were held by the BBC, ITV, Channel 4, Channel 5 and British Digital Broadcasting (BDB). The satellite licence was held by British Interactive Broadcasting (BIB), owned jointly by BSkyB, BT, Midland Bank and Matsushita. Digital television was expected to offer interactive communication from the start, via 'return paths' provided by BT, permitting an explosion of home shopping by television. The new cable network would also be interactive, using the operators' own return-path technology. It was expected that the digital system would be launched during 1998. It will deliver better clarity of picture and more convenient channel selection, but viewers will have to buy 'set-top boxes' and pay subscriptions. *See also* TELEVISION.   (KC)

diminishing returns. *See* LAW OF DIMINISHING RETURNS.

direct costing. American term for marginal costing. *See* MARGINAL COST PRICING.   (GM)

direct costs. Any charge which can be directly allocated to a cost centre or cost per unit. For example, sales COMMISSION given for the sale or negotiation of a contract can be allocated to that sale or contract, and therefore is a direct cost.
(GM)

direct investment. The decision to enter or consolidate in a foreign market by investing in assembly, manufacturing, service or other facilities.   (MJB)

direct mail. Considered by some authors to be an advertising medium but by others to be a quite separate element of the MARKETING COMMUNICA-TIONS MIX, direct mail defines itself by its use of the postal service to disseminate promotional material. Each initiative is called a 'mail shot', 'mailing shot' or simply 'mailing'. It may comprise anything from a single 'mailer' to a whole series of separate items under one cover. The best known regular users of the direct mail technique in Britain today are probably Reader's Digest, the Automobile Association and the numerous 'direct merchants'. Considerable impetus has been given to its development in Britain by a combination of the POSTCODE mail sorting system and the recent proliferation of CONSUMER LOCA-TION SYSTEM databases. It is estimated that British companies spent about £1.4 billion on distributing direct mail in 1996, for a return of £16 billion

in sales revenue. If the object of a direct mailing is to persuade recipients to order the product or service by return post, it should be called a MAIL ORDER initiative or (if direct mail is considered a form of advertising rather than an alternative to it) DIRECT RESPONSE ADVERTISING. There has been a tendency in recent years to describe direct mail as DIRECT MARKETING, but it is in fact only one of several direct marketing communications techniques. The process of direct mailing is regulated by: the DIRECT MARKETING ASSOCIATION'S Code of Practice; 'specific rules' in THE BRITISH CODES OF ADVERTISING AND SALES PROMOTION relating to 'distance selling' and 'list and database practice'; the Advertising Association's Code of Practice on the Use of Personal Data for Advertising and Direct Marketing Purposes; the Mail Order Protection Scheme (MOPS), which safeguards the interests of consumers sending cash with off-the-page orders; the Mailing Preference Service, which allows individuals to stop 'cold mailings' from companies they have had no contact with; and the Data Protecion Act, which requires all direct mail advertising to include an 'opt-out box' to be ticked by those who wish to receive no further offers from the same source. Members of the Direct Marketing Association are required by their Code to subscribe to the Video Standards Council, if they use that means of communication with a target audience. Recipients of direct mail shots can and do make complaints to the ADVER-TISING STANDARDS AUTHORITY, which investigates such cases for compliance with the 'specific rules' in The British Codes of Advertising and Sales Promotion relating to 'distance selling' and 'list and database practice'. Despite this variety of controls, many commentators believe that direct mail shots are almost universally unwelcome and mistrusted, and disparage them as 'junk mail'.   (KC)

direct marketing. Defined by the DIRECT MAR-KETING ASSOCIATION (DMA) as a form of marketing involving 'the creation and maintenance of a database of information to record names of customers, actual and potential, and to provide the means for continuing direct communication with the customer'. A key feature in practice is that it 'seeks to generate a direct and measurable response to advertising which offers goods and services or information about them', with the important proviso that 'advertising' is here used as shorthand for 'all forms of selling communication, written, visual, electronic or oral'. Variations on the theme abound, but all have in common the criteria of direct response and immediately measurable results. Direct marketing practice is subject to a considerable number of controls: the DMA's Code of Practice; 'specific rules' in the BRITISH CODES OF ADVERTISING AND SALES PROMOTION relating to 'distance selling' and 'list and database practice'; the Advertising Association's Code of Practice on the Use of Personal Data for Advertising and Direct Marketing Purposes; the Mail Order Protection Scheme (MOPS), which safeguards the interests of consumers sending cash with off-the-page orders; the Mailing Preference Service and Telephone Preference Service, which allow individuals to stop 'cold mailings' and 'cold calls' from companies they have had no contact with; the ICSTIS Code of Practice, which requires companies using premium-rate telephone numbers to specify the cost of a call; and the Data Protecion Act, which requires all direct mail advertising to include an 'opt-out box' to be ticked by those who wish to receive no further offers from the same source. Members of the DMA are furthermore required by their Code to subscribe to the Direct Selling Association if that is the form of direct marketing they are using, and to Video Standards Council if they communicate with a target audience by that means. Despite all this, direct marketing is widely regarded as more intrusive and manipulative than any other ingredient of the MARKETING COMMUNICATIONS MIX. *See also* DIRECT MAIL, DIRECT RESPONSE ADVERTISING AND MAIL ORDER.   (KC)

Direct   Marketing   Association   (DMA). Established in 1993 as successor to the British Direct Mail Advertising Association, this professional association representing UK practitioners of DIRECT MARKETING 'has as one of its primary objectives to establish, maintain and support a credible and effective system of self-regulation that will meet the reasonable expectation of consumers and businesses'. Accordingly its Members must undertake to abide by the letter and spirit of the DMA Code of Practice, and also the BRITISH CODES OF ADVERTISING AND SALES PROMOTION. The DMA sponsors the annual Direct Marketing Awards.   (KC)

Direct Marketing Authority. Established by the DIRECT MARKETING ASSOCIATION but comprising six or more wholly independent members, this body monitors compliance with the DMA Code of Practice and 'adjudicates and conciliates' when a complaint against a member under the

terms of the Code cannot be satisfactorily resolved. If it finds that there has been a breach of the Code, it can seek an undertaking that the cause will not recur, 'issue a formal admonition which would normally be made public', or suspend or terminate the perpetrator's membership of the DMA. It is funded by a Mailing Standards Levy on direct mail postage invoices.
(KC)

direct marketing channel. A distribution channel without intermediaries in which the seller is in direct contact with the buyer.   (MJB)

direct observation. The monitoring/observation of an event or activity in real time by the researcher, as contrasted with indirect observation, where the researcher may use audio-visual methods to record the event for subsequent ANALYSIS. *See also* OBSERVATION TECHNIQUE.
(MJB)

Director General of Fair Trading. A political appointee reporting to the President of the BOARD OF TRADE who has the authority to inquire into and report on any practice or act which restricts, distorts or prevents competition or results in unfair trading conditions.   (MJB)

directory. A reference book published annually or more frequently which sets out a complete list of individuals, members of a profession, companies, PRODUCTS and services in a particular field, e.g. the ADVERTISER'S ANNUAL or Sell's Directory.
(MDP)

direct response advertising. Describes an advertising strategy in which special techniques are used to invoke an immediate response (not necessarily instantaneous) rather than a delayed one. The most familiar instance is the coupon-response press advertisement in which a return coupon is provided, by means of which the reader may order the advertised product or service, request further information or a sales call. Other variants involve incentives to visit the retail outlet immediately, such as special preview invitations, money-off coupons and so forth. Direct response is problematical in other media, because viewers and listeners do not normally keep pencil and paper to hand, but imminent developments in DIGITAL TELEVISION are specifically intended to facilitate 'interactive' advertising. This category of advertising is regulated by the ADVERTISING STANDARDS AUTHORITY, which investigates complaints about empty claims or unfulfilled offers against 'specific rules' in the BRITISH CODES OF ADVERTISING AND SALES PROMOTION relating to 'distance selling'. *See also* MAIL ORDER.   (KC)

direct selling. A form of selling without retail outlets, distributors, wholesalers or any type of middlemen. Traditional UK methods of direct selling to the consumer include the milkman and the creamboy. This form of selling is also used by various publishing houses especially to sell encyclopaedias. More sophisticated versions of direct selling are used by companies such as Avon Cosmetics and Tupperware who organize in-home demonstrations of their goods. *See also* DOOR-TO-DOOR SELLING.   (MDP)

discontinuity. A trend line plots the rate and direction of the change that has occurred in a variable (e.g. price indices, GNP, exchange rates) over a period of time. Where the underlying forces that drive the trend are in equilibrium the rate and direction of change will be constant. If events cause these forces to be in disequilibrium sudden and unexpected sharp changes in the nature of the trend may occur. Where this is so the trend line will exhibit a discontinuity. The discontinuity may herald a fundamental shift in the rate and direction of change, or it may represent a temporary or intermittent sharp fluctuation in the trend. Prior to the events that precipitated the Middle-East crisis of October 1973, there was great debate as to whether the price of oil would ever rise above two dollars per barrel. However history reveals that in the periods 1973–4 and again in 1979–80 the price of oil rose suddenly and unexpectedly by almost 400 per cent. These unprecedented increases in price represent sources of discontinuous change that have had a sudden and far-reaching impact on many previously stable economic trends.   (DB)

discontinuous innovations. PRODUCTS, the purchase of which would be perceived by CONSUMERS as involving a revolutionary (or at least, major) change to their accepted purchase habits. For example, purchases involving new technology may be considered as discontinuous innovations – the purchase of a microwave oven rather than a conventional gas or electric cooker, or a compact disc player, rather than a record player. *See also* CONTINUOUS INNOVATIONS. (GKP)

discount. A reduction in the price of a product or service. Discounts may be given to intermedi-

aries by manufacturers with the difference between the recommended retail price and the discounted price representing the retailer's margin. Discounts may also be offered by retailers to their customers as an incentive to purchase and/or as an *ad hoc* SALES PROMOTION.   (MJB)

discounted cash-flow. Accounting/management method for evaluating investment projects involving the calculation of a present value. Because money in the hand is worth more than that earned at a future date the method is used to calculate the present value of earnings of specified future times (by discounting the flow of expected earnings at chosen rates) and comparing it with capital investment required to obtain such earnings.   (GA)

discount store. A retail outlet which features discounted prices as a means of differentiating itself from other, usually full-service, RETAILERS.(MJB)

discretionary income. Money available for expenditure after paying taxes and purchasing the necessities of life – food, shelter, clothing, transportation etc. *See also* DISPOSABLE INCOME.(MJB)

discriminant analysis. A multivariate statistical procedure for finding the weighted combination of variables that in some defined sense best discriminates between two or more groups.   (SKT)

discriminant validity. The assessment of validity of a measure by showing it does not correlate with measures of other CONCEPTS. Often used in combination with CONVERGENT VALIDITY.   (SKT)

discrimination test. A form of PRODUCT TEST in which the objective is to discover whether one product is perceived to be different from another. It may be carried out by expert panels to monitor production quality, or formulation changes. A common form is the triangle test, in which the judges are presented with three samples, two of which are the same. They are required to identify the one that differs.   (JAB)

diseconomies of scale. Additional costs or disbenefits which may be incurred if the organization exceeds the prevailing ECONOMIES OF SCALE. For example, beyond a certain size, problems of organization and logistics may result in inefficiencies which offset actual economies in production, MARKETING and distribution costs.   (MJB)

displacement. An ego defence mechanism whereby the individual directs energies aimed at one object onto another; e.g. low performers will blame others for their inadequacies rather than accept that these are due to their own BEHAVIOUR. (MJB)

display. The presentation of product, promotional material or advertising directed to attract the attention of the potential purchaser. The term is used constantly by the distributive (retail and wholesale) trades in respect of the presentation of the product 'on-shelf'. The term 'display' advertising is also used to differentiate between advertising for products and classified financial advertising. (JRB)

display advertising. The generic description of advertising in which some combination of design, typography, illustration, colour and size is used to enhance the presentation of the message. The implied contrast is with CLASSIFIED ADVERTISING. 'Semi-display' advertisements are a compromise between the two. They are more than one column wide, use typography and layout to achieve visual impact, and can incorporate limited graphic elements, usually the advertiser's LOGOTYPE. The ADVERTISING RATE for semi-display space is higher than that for classified advertising but less than the full display charge for the same space. (KC)

disposable income. That proportion of an individual's income available for consumption or investment after meeting prior charges such as income tax. (MJB)

disproportionate stratified random sampling. SAMPLING designs where strata are not sampled with the same sampling fraction. Sometimes sampling is 'proportional to size'; sometimes over-sampling of small strata is required to obtain sufficient cases for accurate estimation. (SKT)

dissatisfaction. The opposite of SATISFACTION. The state experienced when the perceived benefits are less than expected. (MJB)

dissonance. *See* COGNITIVE DISSONANCE.

dissonance-reduction strategies. BEHAVIOUR designed to reduce COGNITIVE DISSONANCE following purchase. Common strategies include telling others about the purchase and the acquisition of more information by reading

ADVERTISEMENTS, BROCHURES, consumer reports etc. (MJB)

distinctive competence. An attribute which is particular to a given firm and the source of its COMPETITIVE ADVANTAGE. (MJB)

distribution. (1) In the marketing sense, the proportion of outlets stocking or dealing in a designated product.

(2) A general term which includes every function concerned with the transference of goods from the point of origin until they come into the possession of the final buyer. It includes transportation, storage. merchandising, promotion, selling and packaging. (JAB, AJB)

distribution centre. A centrally located warehouse, usually highly automated, which acts as a focal point for the output of various suppliers where bulk can be broken and orders collated and filled for onward delivery to customers within the catchment area served by the centre. (MJB)

distribution channel, functions of. The primary function of a CHANNEL OF DISTRIBUTION is to provide a link between production and consumption by filling any gap or discontinuity which exists between them. Discontinuities between producers and consumers may arise from a number of causes, including the following: (a) geographical separation; (b) time (production and consumption rarely occur simultaneously, with the exception of personal services, and channels of distribution help even out fluctuations in supply and demand by holding stocks and through the provision of credit); (c) information; (d) ownership (in addition to making goods physically available (possession) channels also provide the mechanism whereby transfer of the legal title to ownership may be accomplished); (e) sorting. (MJB)

distribution check. An enquiry among retail outlets to establish the proportion having stock of various products. Often repeated in the same outlets, which thus compose a PANEL. (JAB)

diversification. The process of introducing new products (which may or may not be related to the company's present products) into existing or new markets. It may be the result of a deliberate attempt by management to hedge against the company's future being tied too closely to a small number of products/markets and is accomplished either by new investment or through mergers and acquisitions. Diversification is the fourth of Igor Ansoff's basic strategies under which the company seeks increased sales by developing new products for new markets. *See also* MARKET PENETRATION, MARKET DEVELOPMENT and PRODUCT DEVELOPMENT.   (MJB, GA)

division of labour. The next step in the process of economic development after the emergence of task specialization. This stage of economic development is usually exemplified by Adam SMITH'S account of the pin-making industry, where an enormous increase in output followed job simplification with the same input of factors of production, excluding raw materials. Smith noted that where men were engaged on all processes involved in the manufacture of pins, their average output was 20 pins per day; when the manufacture of pins was broken down into separate processes output for the group rose to 4,000 pins per man per day. Two points are of particular significance in this step forward. First, organization is required to bring together the men, provide a place of work and a supply of raw materials. Second, the enormous increase in output reduces the price of the commodity, necessitates the development of channels of distribution to make the article available to those with a demand for it, and leads to the exploitation of a much larger market.   (MJB)

DMA. *See* DIRECT MARKETING ASSOCIATION.

DMU. *See* DECISION-MAKING UNIT.

dogs. *See* PRODUCT PORTFOLIO.

door-to-door selling. A form of DIRECT SELLING where goods are sold to a consumer on his/her doorstep. The advantages to the seller are that the company has complete control over the sales of the product and it is also an effective method of selling goods and services where demonstrations or complex explanation is necessary (for example vacuum cleaners, insurance policies). The disadvantages are that unsolicited calls can be viewed with suspicion, the high costs involved (usually offset by paying low basic salary with high commission), and that it can be difficult to recruit and retain suitable salesman owing to the unattractive working conditions. Examples of this type of selling include Avon Cosmetics, Tupperware, various publishing houses.   (MDP)

double-barrelled question. A question that on examination contains two concepts, and could lead to two different replies.   (SKT)

double-page spread (DPS). Two pages of a newspaper or magazine, facing one another, used for the reproduction of a single advertisement. A CENTRE SPREAD ('centrefold' in America) is the two facing pages at the very centre of the publication, the only case in which the right and left halves of the advertisement are actually printed on one piece of paper. Booking the centre spread minimizes the risk of mismatching between the two halves in the trimming and collating of the newspaper or magazine after printing. There is normally a surcharge for specifying it, however. 'Double page spread' is usually contracted to DPS in media orders. An alternative description is 'two facing pages'.   (KC)

Dow Jones Index (US). An index compiled from the average stock prices for 30 leading industrial stocks, 20 leading railroad stocks, and 15 public utilities. The US equivalent of the *Financial Times* Index in the UK or the Hang-Seng Index in Hong Kong.   (MJB)

downsizing. The reduction in a firm's size by removing units, levels of management, or individuals.   (MJB)

DPS. *See* DOUBLE PAGE SPREAD.

drawback. The repayment of tariff duties on goods and raw materials which are subsequently used for exports. The main problem of such schemes is to avoid an accusation of export subsidies in contravention of the GENERAL AGREEMENT ON TARRIFS AND TRADE (GATT). *See also* EXPORT REBATE.   (JML)

drip. *See* CONTINUITY.

drive. In marketing, a special planned effort to increase sales: sales drive, export drive.   (JRB)

drives. *See* MOTIVATION.

drop-error. A decision to drop a PRODUCT from the line, or to discontinue development of a new product which subsequently proves to have been a premature decision, in light of successes achieved by competitors with similar developments. The converse of GO-ERROR.   (KNB)

Drucker, Peter F. (1909–). Economist and management consultant. He was born in Vienna and educated in Austria and England. From 1929 he was a newspaper correspondent and an economist for an international bank in London. Since 1937 he has been in the United States of America, first as an economist and later as a management consultant in several of the country's largest companies as well as to leading companies abroad. From 1942 to 1949 he was Professor of Philosophy and Politics at Bennington College. From 1950 to 1971 he was Professor of Management at New York University's Graduate School of Business. Since 1971 he has been Clarke Professor of Social Science at Claremont Graduate School, California. His books include *The Practice of Management, The Effective Executive, Managing For Results, The Age of Discontinuity, Managing Discontinuity, The Manager and the Organisation, Managing For Tomorrow, The Concept of the Corporation.*

(MJB)

DSS. *See* DECISION SUPPORT SYSTEM.

dual distribution. Term used to describe the situation where a seller uses two distinct channels of distribution e.g. direct to major customers and via intermediaries for smaller ones.   (MJB)

dualism. A concept most commonly found in the context of the industrialization process. It holds that, since development starts from an initial node of activity, its benefits diffuse unevenly, giving rise to segments of the POPULATION which become more developed and more wealthy than others – and hence more attractive as targets for further MARKETING attention. Dualism is commonly characterized as differentiating between relatively sophisticated urban communities and unsophisticated rural communities. Conceptually, the definition may be extended to show differentiation based on educational levels, and on social/religious/ racial levels as well as being defined by purely economic criteria. It may be considered that dualism is not only an inevitable consequence of the development process, but also, once established, a permanent feature of modern society.   (KNB)

dubbing. Adding a soundtrack or VOICE-OVER to the film or videotape of a television COMMERCIAL.

(KC)

dummy. An imitation or mock-up of reality; as in the dummy pack used by designers of packaging to show what the packaging will look like, or dummy magazines used by market researchers to establish measures of advertising effectiveness

without incurring the cost of actually placing the advertising in a circulated magazine.   (JRB)

dummy variable. A variable that represents the presence or absence of single values of a multivalued nominal question. For example, from a single variable which records the RESPONDENT'S favourite BRAND, one can derive a dummy variable for each brand that records whether or not that subject had it as their favourite. A dummy variable has only two values, and thus can be entered into procedures that typically require variables with extensive quantitative properties.

(SKT)

dummy variable multiple regression. A MULTIPLE REGRESSION that includes dummy variables. Beware of the degrees of freedom problem; if you produce as many dummy variables as values from a simple nominal variable, it is possible to predict the values of the last variable from all the others; this will produce insurmountable problems for the multiple regression procedure.(SKT)

dump display. Merchandise is 'dumped' into a tub-like container for self-selection in a retail outlet. Used for a variety of merchandise, for example tins, packets, bread rolls. This type of display is often used to attract attention to special price or other promotional offers.   (MDP)

dumping. In general, selling below costs in the export market. Unfortunately it is very difficult to define when this occurs, although as a rule the sale of goods in the export market below the price in the home market (after allowing for taxes) could constitute a *prima facie* case of dumping. Most nations have anti-dumping provisions which can be invoked when a charge of dumping can be substantiated.   (JML)

durable goods. Goods which may be used time and time again. Technically CONSUMER GOODS which have a life expectancy of more than three years are classified as durable, while those with a life expectancy of between six months and three years are classified as semi-durable. It follows that consumer goods with a life of less than six months are regarded as non-durable.   (MJB)

dustbin check. *See* CONSUMER PANELS.

dyadic relationship. A relationship between two parties in which both have the power to influence the other. A common characteristic of ORGANIZATIONAL MARKETING.   (MJB)

E

early adopters. *See* ADOPTER CATEGORIES.

early majority. *See* ADOPTER CATEGORIES.

EASA. *See* EUROPEAN ADVERTISING STANDARDS ALLIANCE.

Ebbinghaus, Hermann. German psychologist, author of *Grundzuge der Psychologie* (Leipzig, 1902) in which he reported one of the first empirical investigations of the relationship between retention, repetition and the elapsed time since exposure/learning. His main findings, which have been confirmed by subsequent and more rigorous research were that: (a) repetition is subject to diminishing returns; (b) spaced exposure is more effective in achieving retention than massing the same number of experiences into a concentrated time period; (c) forgetting is an exponential function; (d) the more complex/extensive the information to be communicated the greater the number of repetitions necessary to achieve a given level of learning/recall.   (MJB)

EBQ. *See* ECONOMIC BATCH QUANTITY.

ECGD. *See* EXPORT CREDIT GUARANTEE DEPARTMENT.

ecology. The study of living things and their relationship with their environment. In the marketing domain ecological concerns have given rise to the GREEN MARKETING MOVEMENT. *See* ENVIRONMENTALISM.   (MJB)

econometrics. The statistical approach to testing economic hypotheses and models and the estimation of economic parameters.   (MJB)

economic batch quantity (EBQ). An application of the generic ECONOMIC ORDER QUANTITY principle into the field of production scheduling. The same standard formula is applicable, and the same general limitations are operative.   (KNB)

economic environment. The prevailing economic climate in which the firm has to compete usually defined in terms of the state of the BUSINESS CYCLE and market structure, conduct and performance.   (MJB)

economic forces. Those forces which determine the ECONOMIC ENVIRONMENT and so influence POTENTIAL DEMAND.   (MJB)

economic growth. Generally taken to mean an increase in national income or in the total volume of capacity to produce and volume of production of goods and services of a country. However, there are many ways of defining and measuring economic growth. Each is problematic in relation to income; it may be done firstly by examining total real income over a long period of time. But even though this allows for changes in the value of money and cyclical swings in output, it may be that increase in real income is accompanied by even faster growth in population so that the average standard of living is reduced. The second method – dividing increase in national income by increase in population giving increase in income per head – avoids this problem but takes no account of distribution of wealth. To take this into consideration a third measure, income per head supplemented by information on the distribution of income can be used.

In relation to production, economic growth is often measured by the annual increase in a nation's gross national product, as adjusted for price changes. A better measure is increase in real gross national product per capita, but as with income, yearly gains in output may be surpassed by gains in population leaving the average person with a lower standard of living. Even when population changes are taken into account growth rates do not always accurately measure changes in the standard of living.

Comparative growth rates must also be treated with care. Because of business fluctuations, output rarely rises smoothly and evenly from one year to the next. By careful selection of beginning and terminal years, it is possible to make economic growth in one period good or bad in relation to another. The comparison of international economic growth rates is even more complicated due to differences in definitions and accounting methods.

The rate of economic growth, despite the difficulties of measurement, is used as an indicator of the increase in the real standard of living of a people. *See* DEVELOPING COUNTRIES.   (JK)

economic man. A model of buyer behaviour which assumes that buying decisions are the result of rational and conscious economic calculations designed to maximise the buyer's satisfaction. *See* MARSHALLIAN ECONOMIC MODEL.
                                                       (MJB)

economic order quantity (EOQ). A mathematical means of determining the optimum order size for items or materials in regular use, based on the equation of INVENTORY holding costs with the costs of ordering – and hence their collective minimization. The basic formula may be expressed thus:

$$EOQ = \sqrt{\left(\frac{2AS}{CI}\right)}$$

where: A is the total demand for the standard time period (usually taken as one year); S is the cost of ordering (or set up costs); C is the unit cost (or price) of the item; I is the cost of holding inventory, as a percentage of the unit cost.

The main limitations of the technique are that it is based on the following presumptions: that opening and closing STOCK levels should be the same; that there is a regular and constant usage pattern of the item; that there are no changes in price or lead time; that suppliers are able to

deliver in precise quantities; and that there is an absence of deterioration and obsolescence.

Several refinements of the formula exist to take into account price variations (quantity discounts) and phased or partial deliveries. Use of EOQ-based routines is generally limited to class A, and perhaps class B categories of inventory. *See also* ABC ANALYSIS.   (KNB)

economies of scale. This basically means the benefits of reduction of average costs resulting from larger-scale production. Gains in output and/or costs may be achieved from increasing the size of plant, the size of firm or the size of industry. For example, costs per unit output are likely to decrease if lower prices of inputs are possible through bulk buying. Also technological methods which may be impractical at lower levels of production may become economically beneficial at higher levels. Equally, if by-products are produced in larger quantities and more continuously, they may become saleable commodities for a ready market.

Economies of scale may be internal or external. Internal economies of scale result from the imperfect divisibility of the factors of production. They will influence the size and number of firms in the market, the ease of entry into a market and the potential as well as the actual competition in it. If the most economic scale of production is large, firms will tend to be relatively few and large, capital requirements for starting up will be high, protecting existing competition, and any new entrants to the market are likely to be established firms wishing to use their resources to diversify. Such economies of scale can lead to OLIGOPOLY or MONOPOLY and are typical of such industries as electricity generating, needing large generating units, or steel-making, when large blast furnaces and rolling mills are integrated. External economies of scale result from expansion of the industry as a whole.

Economies of scale, or scale effects, were identified in the PROFIT IMPACT OF MARKETING STRATEGY study as a major factor giving rise to the association between market share and profitability. The relationship between increased size and lower cost is well illustrated in process industries in which capital costs increase by 6/10ths power of capacity. Thus a 90-million-ton oil refinery costs 90/45 x 0.6 = 1.5 times as much as a 45 million-ton refinery, or, put another way, doubling unit size reduced unit cost by 25 per cent reinforced by lower depreciation costs. Similarly, large plants require less labour proportionately and can make more effective use of control systems etc. Nowadays, the greatest economies of scale probably accrue to RESEARCH AND DEVELOPMENT and MARKETING, for example. Further, in the short run (of which the long run is made up) marketing efficiency/dominance is the best way to ensure full capacity utilization and justify the larger initial capital investment. *See* EXPERIENCE CURVE.   (MJB, JK)

ECU. *See* EUROPEAN CURRENCY UNIT.

edge of town. Sites on the periphery of urban centres which have seen rapid growth of retail establishments in recent years mainly due to the lower cost of land for parking facilities and access to roads and residential suburbs.   (MJB)

editing. Sample survey data after collection should be inspected for completeness, consistency, and uniformity to sampling requirements. This editing is usually done initially by hand, and later by computer to check logical consistency. Errors may be treated by return of the data to the field, by discarding, or by arbitrary alteration. This last may be done by computer, and is described as a 'forced edit'. Editing is an important process in maintaining data quality, but the quality of editing is hard to judge subsequently.   (JAB)

education. The process of acquiring knowledge, often involving specific training or instruction. May be generic, for example higher education, or specific, for example health education, consumer education.   (DL)

EEC. *See* EUROPEAN ECONOMIC COMMUNITY.

effective demand. Demand backed by purchasing power. *See* DEMAND, LATENT.   (MJB)

efficiency, in marketing. Efficiency must be distinguished from effectiveness in that the former consists of 'doing things right' while effectiveness means 'doing the right things'. It follows, therefore, that one should be able to assess the efficiency of any marketing action or technique by reference to the extent that it succeeds in achieving the objectives appropriate to it. For example, in the case of a DIRECT MAIL shot soliciting a particular action how many actually respond, in the case of a POSTER SITE how many people actually have the opportunity to see it etc. However, efficiency in these terms does not nec-

essarily mean that the most effective marketing tactic was to seek action through a direct mail shot or to communicate using posters. It follows, therefore, that one should seek to develop the most effective MARKETING MIX and then seek to monitor and measure its efficiency in execution through appropriate tests and controls.   (MJB)

efficient estimator. In the statistics of SAMPLING, a method for estimating a POPULATION parameter is more efficient if the variance of its sampling distribution is smaller than that of another method.   (SKT)

EFTA. *See* EUROPEAN FREE TRADE ASSOCIATION.

EFTPOS. *See* ELECTRONIC FUNDS TRANSFER AT POINT OF SALE.

ego. One of the three dimensions of an individual's psyche distinguished by Sigmund FREUD – the others being the ID and the super ego. According to Freud, the ego is the individual's conscious planning centre through which he seeks to find outlets for the instinctual urges and drives which reside in the id while the super ego seeks to control the ego by directing these instinctive drives into socially acceptable behaviour. In marketing, the concepts are of importance as an explanation of buying behaviour and are central to the practice of MOTIVATION RESEARCH.   (MJB)

ego-involvement. Defined by Robertson *et al.* (T.S. Robertson, J. Zielinski and S. Ward, *Consumer Behaviour,* Glenview: Scott Foresman, 1984) as 'the proximity of a persuasive attempt (such as an ADVERTISEMENT) to attitudes which define a person's status or give him some relative role with respect to other individuals, groups or institutions'.

As part of SHERIF'S THEORY OF SOCIAL JUDGEMENT, reported by Robertson *et al.,* it is suggested that there are three possible outcomes of a persuasive attempt. It may fall within the *latitude of acceptance* (usually when it advocates an opinion consistent with the individual's existing beliefs) resulting in assimilation, positive evaluation and consequently positive attitude change; it may fall within the *latitude of rejection* (ADVERTISING counter to the individual's beliefs in this case) being resisted, or evaluated as biased, producing attitude change opposite in the direction to the intentions of the ADVERTISER; or, it may fall within the *latitude of non-commitment, when the* advertising is not relevant to any existing beliefs, and involvement is low.

Social judgement theory also states that an individual in a highly ego-involved purchase situation will have a narrow latitude of acceptance. Robertson *et al.* give the example of a person whose ego is involved in the purchase and ownership of a car will tend to reject competing ADVERTISEMENTS, whereas a less involved person will be likely to be less resistant.   (GKP)

eigenvalue. In FACTOR ANALYSIS, the size of each extracted factor, on such a scale that 1 represents the size of an unanalysed variable. A common answer to the problem of how many factors to extract is to only deal with those whose eigenvalues are greater than one.   (SKT)

Eighty-Twenty Rule. *See* PARETO ANALYSIS.

Elastic Demand. *See* DEMAND, PRICE ELASTICITY OF.

electroencephalograph. A piece of equipment used (in the area of MARKETING) to measure brain-wave activity in response to ADVERTISING (both print and televisual) – and most especially in research relating to the study of BRAIN HEMI-SPHERE LATERALIZATION occurring during the processing of information from MARKETING COMMUNICATIONS.   (GKP)

electronic funds transfer at point of sale (EFTPOS). Defined by Michael J. Thomas (*Pocket Guide to Marketing,* London: Basil Blackwell, 1986) as 'a technological development which enables the CONSUMER to pay for goods at the retail store checkout points with a plastic card which directly debits his bank account, eliminating the need to produce cash or write cheques'. Recently Barclaycard have met with resistance from the retail business in response to their bid to introduce a version of EFTPOS to British stores – with large retail groups such as Storehouse (Habitat, Mothercare, BHS) stating their reluctance to pay what they consider to be an excessive percentage COMMISSION (similar to that charged on credit cards) in return for the privilege of operating the system.   (GKP)

electronic point of sale (EPOS). A scanning system, increasingly used by retail stores, to read a PRODUCT code. All goods are marked with a unique thirteen-digit BAR CODE. A He:Ne laser beam is used to read the bar code as the product is passed over it at the checkout. The code is then converted by computer to provide the shopper with a product description and price, and to provide the store with an INVENTORY update to facilitate STOCK ordering and product purchase pattern ANALYSIS.   (KRD)

embargo. Stoppage by authority of the physical movement of trade, originally specific to ships, but now used in a much broader economic sense. Embargo is also used in the MARKETING context as a ban, particularly with regard to the release of information until a specified time and date. Information released by organizations for public interest to the MEDIA may have an 'embargo' placed upon it. Issuing information in advance of the time when it may be widely distributed allows time for the receiving organization to assess and comment upon the information. The organization receiving the information is expected to honour the request not to divulge the information before the stipulated time and date. For example, press releases about a company's annual reports or a chairman's statements may be made available on the understanding that the information they contain will not be available to the public until the time and date authorized. Exceptions have occurred where there is a breach of trust, but in most cases 'embargoes' are respected. News disseminators who respect the requests benefit as they continue to be supplied with information. Where information is divulged prematurely the errant organization often finds it is not subsequently favoured with information.   (BRM)

emotional appeals. *See* MESSAGE EFFECT.

encoding. The act of CODING.   (MJB)

endorsement advertising. Describes an advertising strategy that uses endorsers as a device to increase the perceived credibility of the message. These may be celebrities, experts, typical users or wholly anonymous third parties; what they have in common is that they endorse the advertised product or service, explicitly or implicitly, by their presence. The term 'presenter' is used to distinguish performers who are obviously selling on behalf of the advertiser rather than speaking for themselves. They tend to say 'We at Megalo believe that we've ... ' instead of 'I'm Humphrey Rossiter and I'd like to talk to you about ...' *See* SOURCE EFFECT.   (KC)

Engel's law. Generalizations about consumer spending patterns in relation to income, made in 1857 by the German statistician Engel. These have been tested in a number of national and city level circumstances, and shown to be generally true. The best known law is 'as income increases the proportion of income spent on food decreases'. (AJB)

entrepreneur. The name given in economic theory to the owner-manager of the firm. The entrepreneur organizes resources or the factors of production (land, labour and capital) within their firm with the aim of building up a successful profit-making company. The entrepreneur is the risk-taker in business, the risk lies in the fact that their resources have to be committed to the enterprise. 'Entrepreneur' is a French word which means 'the one who undertakes tasks'. (MDP)

envelope curve. Broadly speaking, a curve that summarizes a number of subsidiary curves is known as an envelope curve. As an analytical tool it has found wide application in the study of the path of technological progress. In this context an envelope curve is an S-curve that envelops a series of subsidiary S-curves which plot the historical development of a performance parameter, functional capability or some other attribute of an advancing technology. An envelope curve will describe the pattern of development of a specific technology: the series of S-curves contained within the envelope will represent the emergence of substitute developments and new applications of the technology. As an example, Figure 11 shows the envelope curve which follows the historical development of illumination technology. It plots the progressive improvements made to the parameter lighting efficiency (lumens/watt) as a result of the development of two specific illumination devices – each the product of successive technical advances. The envelope curve is the line that is drawn tangential to the subsidiary S-curves. (DB)

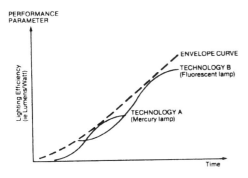

Figure 11: **Envelope curve**

environment. Forces external to the firm which influence the courses of action available to it. Usually seen as comprising the Macro-environment and the Micro-environment. The Macro-environment is concerned with the major forces which are beyond the control of the individual firm which act as the ultimate determinant of its freedom of action. These forces, which are common to all organizations, are often summarized by the acronym PEST standing for Political, Economic, Socio-Cultural and Technological. The Micro-environment defines the industry/market within which firms compete with one another and is usually seen to embrace competitors, customers and suppliers. See EN-VIRONMENTAL ANALYSIS. (MJB)

environmental analysis. The compilation and examination of data related to the environment in order to identify key trends and developments as a basis for anticipating their likely effect upon the organization. External environmental factors which must be taken into account when formulating a marketing strategy may be classified into five major categories: demographic, social and cultural, political, economic and technological. (MJB)

environmental impact analysis. Evaluation of the likely impact of a course of action on the physical environment especially in ecological terms. (MJB)

environmentalism. A concern for the preservation of the natural environment popularly referred to as the Green movement. During 1988 the movement began to gather considerable momentum following gains in the European elections and the public recognition of the damage caused by acid rain, the greenhouse effect, etc. In the post-industrial society it is anticipated that growing affluence and a concern for the quality of life will lend even greater importance to the phenomenon. (MJB)

Environmental Protection Agency. A Federal agency in the United States which prescribes the acceptable levels for the emission of pollutants. (MJB)

environmental scanning. Term developed by Francis Aguilar of the Harvard Business School (1967) to describe the activities of managers in monitoring their external environment. (MJB)

EOQ. See ECONOMIC ORDER QUANTITY.

EPOS. *See* ELECTRONIC POINT OF SALE.

equipment. Those industrial goods which do not become part of the physical product and which are exhausted only after repeated use, such as major installations or installations equipment, and auxiliary accessories or auxiliary equipment. (AMA)

error. In sampling surveys, error is defined as being of two kinds. (1) Statistical error (or sampling error) is the difference between the result actually achieved and that which would be achieved had data been collected from the entire survey population by the same methods as that used for the sample. Such error may be statistically estimated, and diminishes as sample size increases.

(2) Non-statistical error (or BIAS) arises from many causes, such as failure to understand questions, failure to contact the correct sample, or to record the correct data. Error is often of great importance, but owing to the difficulty of measuring it by statistical methods, its effects are often neglected. Indeed, error is often assumed to be only statistical. (JAB)

escalator cards. ADVERTISING cards or posters displayed next to escalators, especially on the London Underground. (MJB)

escalator clause. A clause in an agreement which specifies how prices will be adjusted to reflect increased costs. They are particularly prevalent in wage bargaining agreements when automatic wage increases will be triggered by rises in some specified index, e.g. the COST OF LIVING INDEX. (MJB)

ESOMAR. The European Society for Opinion and Marketing Research. An international body founded in 1948 representing established MARKETING and MARKET RESEARCH specialists. It stands for the highest possible standards – both professionally and technically. (MJB)

esteem needs. *See* MOTIVATION.

ethical pricing. The pricing of a professional service with an inelastic demand where the seller has an obligation not to overcharge the buyer. (MJB)

ethics. The study of the right and the good. The subject as it is allied to business and marketing practice has become of increasing importance to society, and a factor of increasing importance in the making of marketing decisions. (JRB)

ethnocentricity. The BELIEF that one's own CULTURE and way of life are superior to that of others. (MJB)

European Advertising Standards Alliance (EASA). A non-profit organization established in Brussels in 1992 to 'bring together advertising self-regulatory bodies across Europe ... to promote and support advertising self-regulation ... to co-ordinate the handling of cross-border complaints, and to provide information and research on advertising self-regulation'. By May 1997, when it published its *EASA Guide to Self-Regulation*, the Alliance had 25 'members' in Austria, Belgium, the Czech Republic, Denmark, Finland, France, Germany, Greece, Ireland, Italy, Luxembourg, the Netherlands, Portugal, the Slovak Republic, Slovenia, Spain, Switzerland, the UK and one non-European country, Turkey. There were 'corresponding members' in South Africa and New Zealand. (KC)

European Currency Unit (ECU). The ECU is a currency unit used in the European Community whose value is based on the weighted average of the value of the currencies of the member states. As a weighted average its value fluctuates less than the value of the individual countries' currencies. (MJB)

European Economic Community (EEC, Common Market). Customs union consisting of twelve member states: Belgium, France, West Germany, Italy, Luxembourg, the Netherlands, the United Kingdom, the Republic of Ireland, Denmark, Greece, Spain and Portugal.

Established in 1958 under the Treaty of Rome (1957), it aimed at the economic integration of six countries: Belgium, France, Germany, Italy, Luxembourg and the Netherlands. However, the creation of a political unit in Europe also stemmed from a desire to preserve peace in a traditionally bellicose part of the world. The preamble of the Treaty of Rome states the objective as to 'lay the foundation of an even closer union among the people of Europe and by pooling resources is to preserve and strengthen peace and liberty'.

In 1945 the urgency of preserving peace had become especially apparent as a result of the physical devastation, human loss and vulnerability exposed through World War II and Western governments' mistrust of Russian policy in Europe. In 1946 Winston Churchill had suggested creating 'some kind of United States of Europe'. But progress was slow. Despite various initiatives, e.g. Marshall Aid in 1947, the establishment of the Organisation for European Economic Co-operation (later integrated into the Organisation of Economic Co-operation and Development), the Brussels Treaty of 1948, a pact of mutual assistance between the UK, France and the Benelux Countries, the North Atlantic Treaty of 1949 and the Establishment of the Council of Europe 1949, little integration had been achieved.

The first concrete development was the European Coal and Steel Community (ECSC), established in 1950. This aimed at pooling all coal and steel industries of the area, reaping the benefits of a unified market, appealing to many interests and making it impossible for members (initially France and Germany, but joined by Belgium, the Netherlands, Luxembourg and Italy under the Paris Treaty of 1951) to go to war with each other. The same six members formulated the European Defence Community in 1954 after the outbreak of the Korean war and in 1955 the Foreign Ministers of the Six met at Messina to discuss the possibility of general economic integration and the peaceful development of atomic energy. The result was two 1957 Rome Treaties which launched the European Economic Community (EEC) and the European Atomic Energy Community (EURATOM). Both of these became effective in 1958 for a period of unlimited duration.

The common institutions of the three communities (ECSC, EEC, EURATOM) were established by a treaty signed in Brussels in April 1965 (effective 1967) and became recognized as the European Community. (MJB)

European Free Trade Association (EFTA). This free trade area was established in 1960, following the ratification of the Stockholm Convention signed in November 1959. EFTA originally comprised seven members: Austria, Denmark, Norway, Portugal, Sweden, Switzerland and the UK with Finland joining on 27 March 1961 as an associate member. The association was formed following the breakdown of negotiations for a wider European Free Trade Area embracing the EEC, the UK and the other members of the Organisation for European Economic Co-operation (OEEC).

Typical of any free trade area, the seven undertook to abolish all tariffs, quotas and other restrictions on products which originated or were produced within member countries over a ten-year period (subsequently reduced to six years). On the other hand, unlike the EEC's external tariff they maintained their own tariffs against imports from non-member countries. As a result a system of 'declaration of origin' became essential to discriminate EFTA goods from non-EFTA goods in order to prevent the deflection of trade.

EFTA's composition, however, has changed. Iceland joined on 1 March 1970, the UK and Denmark left EFTA on 31 December 1972 and Portugal left on 31 December 1985. Austria, Finland and Sweden acceded to the EUROPEAN UNION in 1994 leaving Iceland, Lichtenstein, Norway and Switzerland as members. With the exception of Switzerland these countries are linked to the EU through the European Economic Area.

EFTA has a number of free trade agreements with non-EU countries including Turkey (1991), Israel, Poland and Romania (1992), Bulgaria, Hungary, Czech Republic and Slovakia (1993).
(MJB)

European Investment Bank (ETB). Established under the Treaty of Rome in 1958. The Bank's aims are to help to stimulate development in less favoured regions, to modernize or convert industries, to help to create new activities and to offset structural difficulties affecting certain states. The Bank also serves projects of common interest to several member states or the European Union as a whole.

The members of the ETB are the 15 member states of the European Union who have all subscribed to its capital. In 1994 its financing amounted to almost 20,000 million ECU with most of its funds being raised in the international capital markets. As it is a non profit organization its rates closely parallel those of the world capital market. (HMSO)

European Union (EU). On 11 December 1991 the Maastricht Treaty was negotiated where a new Treaty of Economic Union comprising an Economic and Monetary Union (EMU) and a Political Union were agreed between the members of the ECONOMIC COMMUNITY. The Treaty came into effect on 1 November 1993 and established the European Union (EU) which incorporated the existing European Community (EC) together with the new EMU and European Political co-operation Framework with a common European Citizenship and the principle of subsidiarity (decisions to be made at the most appropriate level) among its major features.

(MJB)

evaluator. One of the BUYER ROLES involved in decision making. (MJB)

even pricing. A form of PSYCHOLOGICAL PRICING where even rather than odd numbers are used e.g. £10.00. (MJB)

evoked set. Those BRANDS in a multi-brand MARKET which a CONSUMER is aware of, has positively evaluated and consequently would actually consider purchasing. (MJB)

exchange. An action of transferring ownership of a product or service to another in return for another object deemed to be equivalent in value by the recipient. Although both parties will only agree to exchange on the basis of equivalent value, they both believe they will increase the value of their assets. (AJB)

exchange controls. Controls imposed by government on exchange rates and the quantities of currency which may be exchanged. (MJB)

exchange rate. The rate at which one currency can be exchanged for another. Under a fixed rate of exchange, for example the Gold Standard, the exchange rate will vary only between very narrow limits. If a currency has no parity then it is described as having a floating exchange rate which will vary from day to day. (JK)

exclusion clause. A clause in an agreement which specifies circumstances or situations in which the supplier will not accept responsibility for their execution of the agreement, e.g. a WARRANTY or guarantee may be rendered void if misuse or wilful damage can be shown; delivery of goods may be made the responsibility of the buyer so that the seller will not accept responsibility for damage in transit etc. (MJB)

exclusive dealing. A requirement by the seller or lessor that customers sell or lease only the supplier's products or no other directly competitive products. The buyer benefits in some way, such as the exclusive right to deal with that supplier's products in a stated territory. The freedom of suppliers to enforce such agreements is restricted in the EEC by the Treaty of Rome, and in the UK by the Fair Trading Act. (AJB)

exclusive distribution. Restriction of the distribution of a good to a limited number of outlets thereby conferring a degree of exclusivity on those outlets. (MJB)

ex div. Without next dividend.

executive judgement. Any decision where the decision maker uses judgement rather than facts. Often used for SALES FORECASTING and setting ADVERTISING APPROPRIATIONS. (MJB)

exhibition. An organized display of goods, equipment etc. by manufacturers. There is usually a common thread, e.g. computer equipment and supplies, medical diagnostic equipment, chilled foods or toys. Participating selling companies are invited by the organizing company or association to rent floor space and display their merchandise. Potential customers are either given a complimentary pass or are required to purchase a ticket. Such events are normally advertised in the appropriate TRADE PRESS. (KRD)

ex int. Without next interest.

ex officio. By virtue of office.

expectancy value (EV). One of two basic attitude models. *See* ATTITUDE. (MJB)

expectations. Benefits or satisfactions which the consumer hopes to receive through consumption of particular goods or services. Failure of a product to live up to the consumer's expectations will invariably lead to its commercial failure.

(MJB)

expected value. Sometimes referred to as the expected monetary value or EMV, this is a monetary value placed upon the outcome of a decision. The expected value can also be defined in terms of the value of perfect information – hence EVPI – in which case it is a measure of the maximum amount one would be willing to pay in order to achieve complete certainty about the outcome of a decision. For example, if one is considering modifying a PRODUCT to reduce its cost, it may be that some customers will notice the difference and switch to a competing BRAND. Suppose current profits are £15 million, the saving is £5 million and the expected level of switching is 15 per cent, then we can construct a decision pay-off table as follows:

Actual outcome	Estimated possibility	Make change	Do not make change
Difference detected	15%	-£15m	£0m
Difference not detected	85%	£5m	£0m
Expected monetary value		£2m	£0m

Here the EMV is the sum of the probabilities of losing 15 per cent of current profits of £15m (–£2.25m) against the gain of 85 per cent of £5m of savings (£4.25m). The EVPI is the value of information which confirms that customers will not notice any difference which is £5m x our current expectations that only 85 per cent would not notice the change, i.e. £5m x 0.85 = £4.25m.

(MJB)

experience curve. A diagrammatic representation of the inverse relationship between the total value-added costs of a product and a firm's experience in manufacturing and marketing it. Experience in this context is measured by the cumulative number of units produced to date. The experience curve for a product depicts the way in which total unit costs will decline due to the combined impact of: ECONOMIES OF SCALE in production, purchasing, sales, distribution, marketing, administration, and research and development, and the so-called experience effect, whereby total value-added costs decline by a fixed percentage (usually 10 per cent to 30 per cent) each time the cumulative number of units produced (experience) is doubled.

The experience curve generalizes the learning effects that were originally observed in aircraft manufacture, where the number of direct labour hours required to assemble a plane was seen to decline as the total number of aircraft assembled increased. The work of the Boston Consulting Group has observed the operation of the experience effect in the manufacture and marketing of a wide range of products, including integrated circuits, cars, petrochemicals, synthetic fibres, steam turbines and earth moving machinery. The general form of the experience curve can be represented as follows:

$$Yn = a \cdot n^{-b}$$

where Yn is the cost of manufacturing, distribution, selling, etc., the nth item; n is the cumulative production; a is the cost of the first unit (i.e. where $n = 0$); and b is a parameter representing the learning rate. An 80 per cent learning rate means that each time experience doubles, costs per unit fall to 80 per cent of the original figure; or, in other words, costs per unit decrease by 20 per cent for each doubling of the cumulative production. As the experience curve below shows (*see* Figure 12) on linear axes the rate of cost decline is logarithmic (therefore using a log-log scale the decline would be linear).

(GA)

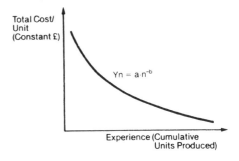

Figure 12: **Experience curve**

experience effects. The decline in costs with cumulative production arising from (a) labour efficiency; (b) work specialization and method improvement; (c) new production processes; (d) better performance of equipment; (e) changes in the resource mix; (f) product standardization; (g) product redesign. The combined effects of experience are usually described in terms of an EXPERIENCE CURVE. In simple terms experience curves record the decline in costs to be anticipated with cumulative increases in output and are usually reported as a percentage for each doubling in output, e.g. an 85 per cent experience curve means that every time output doubles costs decline to 85 per cent of the earlier rate, i.e. a 15 per cent decline for every doubling of output.

(MJB)

experiment. This implies the application of some treatment to experimental material and the observation of some effect. The classical method of experimentation is to maintain constant all other conditions than the chosen variable, so that a causal connection between the treatment and the effect may be deduced. In MARKETING, RESEARCH the material is usually people, and the numerous uncontrollable influences to which they are subject require the repetition of the experiment and statistical methods to estimate whether the results could have arisen by chance.

Much experimentation is done in marketing research, often of an informal kind in which only limited attempts are made to repeat the research among many people or occasions, and assumptions from previous experience are used instead to decide on the meaningfulness of the results. Test marketing is usually an experiment of this kind. A PRODUCT TEST is another type of experimentation extensively used.   (JAB)

experimental method. *See* EXPERIMENT.

experimental research (causal research). Research procedures which attempt to indicate the presence and/or extent of causal relationships, typically by random assignment of cases to experimental conditions.   (SKT)

expert system. A DATABASE of knowledge gleaned from experts in a particular field and freely available to non-experts. Rules and conditions in the software lead the inexperienced through a decision-making process.   (KRD)

exploratory studies. Preliminary research designed to clarify the nature of a problem and the issues to be addressed.   (MJB)

exponential growth (diffusion). Many new products or services exhibit a pattern of exponential growth when they are first introduced to the market. This is characterized by slow initial growth of sales accelerating as the product becomes better known by the market, then finally slowing down as the market becomes saturated and most purchases become a repeat or replacement decision. *See* DIFFUSION PROCESS.   (STP)

exponential smoothing. A forecasting technique which uses some fraction of the difference between the original forecast and actual performance to generate a new forecast.   (MJB)

export agent. A SELLING AGENT/AGENCY which specializes in representing its principals in foreign MARKETS.   (MJB)

Export Credit Guarantee Department (ECGD). UK Government department founded in 1919 to encourage exports by providing insurance for exporters against risks involved in overseas trade which may not be ordinarily insured on the commercial market. Having responsibility to the President of the Board of Trade, it provides medium- and long-term support for projects and capital goods exports sold on credit terms of two years or more. By guaranteeing credit, ECGD helps British exporters overcome many of the risks in selling overseas. In order to encourage investment in less developed countries ECGD also insures against the main political risks of such investments.

The cover available to exporters was extended in the 1992 Autumn Statement and spring 1993 Budget. Particular attention is being given to increasing cover for exports to countries like Hong Kong, China, Indonesia, South Africa and Malaysia. ECGD's Insurance Services Group, dealing with exports sold on credit terms of less than two years, was sold to the private sector in 1991.   (HMSO)

export rebate. System of repayment to exporters of certain taxes which have been charged on raw materials, fuel etc. used in the manufacture of exports. In practice it is impossible to assess rebates on individual products and the practice has been to fix a figure for goods falling into this category. Such schemes are liable to be criticized as being a concealed form of export subsidy contrary to the provisions of the GENERAL AGREEMENT ON TARIFFS AND TRADE. The original British export rebate scheme of 1965 was criticized, particularly by the US government, on these grounds.   (JML)

exports. The sales of a country's goods and services overseas. Exports may be 'visible' (goods) or 'invisible' (services): see BALANCE OF PAYMENTS. On an individual company basis, export is often considered the easiest form of overseas market development with the least financial risk attached compared to other methods of overseas marketing (e.g. setting up a subsidiary company). However, it may also be a sound and permanent way of operating internationally.

'Sales' can include the exchange of goods not only for money, but also for other goods, i.e. BARTER. Barter is one of the oldest forms of exporting, dating back to the Greek and Phoenician merchants. It is also increasingly important in today's economic climate as many countries, especially DEVELOPING COUNTRIES and Marxist regimes are short of foreign exchange. *See* COUNTERTRADING.   (JK)

extended credit. A period of time taken or offered between the supply of goods and settlement of the relevant ACCOUNT, in excess of normal trading terms. Extended credit may be offered by marketers as an inducement to customers either to purchase or take delivery of goods 'out of season' (e.g. toys in June) or to increase the value of orders being placed, usually without prejudice to normal credit limits. This device is commonly employed by suppliers to the retail trades in respect of slow-moving or high-value STOCKS, where variety is perceived to be a key influence on CONSUMERS' buying behaviour. The device is also frequently used as a means of differentiating amongst customers, at the behest of either supplier or customer.   (KNB)

extended interview. *See* INTERVIEW.

extended marketing mix. The extension of the traditional MARKETING MIX beyond the 4Ps of product, price, promotion, and place to include Process, People, and Physical Evidence, all of which are considered important when developing a mix for SERVICES.   (MJB)

extensive distribution. Making a product as widely available as possible. Usually associated with MARKET PENETRATION and the opposite of SELECTIVE DISTRIBUTION.   (MJB)

extensive problem solving. Occurs where the buyer is uncertain how to proceed or perceives a high risk because he is unclear as to what alternatives are available to meet his need and the appropriate criteria for selecting the most suitable alternative once he has identified these. To overcome these deficiencies the buyer will engage in extensive data collection and consultation to improve his understanding and reduce the risk he perceives.   (MJB)

external audit. That part of the MARKETING AUDIT concerned with establishing the threats and opportunities facing the firm for incorporation in a SWOT analysis.   (MJB)

external secondary data. Information that is available for MARKET RESEARCH requirements which has been compiled outside the organiza-tion for some purpose other than the current research investigations, and is available for purchase or can be accessed in libraries. Examples are government reports/statistics, newspaper/journal articles, computerized on-line data information services, published MARKET RESEARCH reports etc.   (AMW)

external stimulus. An external cue, prompt or stimulus perceived by the individual as opposed to an internal stimulus which comes from within the individual such as an emotion or feeling like hunger or thirst.   (MJB)

external validity. A measure of validity of a measurement that involves assessing the correlation of the measure with an independent measurement of the same concept.   (SKT)

extinction. The psychological term used to describe the act of forgetting when something which has been learned is unlearned or extinguished.   (MJB)

extraneous variable. Variables in a REGRESSION or FACTOR ANALYSIS that are superfluous to the model-building in progress.   (SKT)

extrapolation. Projecting into the future on the basis of past data or events.   (JRB)

eye-movement camera. *See* LABORATORY TESTS OF ADVERTISING EFFECT.

e-zine. A site on the World Wide Web which carries paid-for advertising. Some are entirely new, such as *Camden Lock*. Others are electronic versions of single or multiple magazines or newspapers already existing in print. For instance, *Guardian Online* is what its name suggests, while the *Construction* web site is compiled from three professional journals. BRAD listed 194 such web sites under 29 subject headings, at the end of 1996, providing: 'site profiles'; size of site and frequency of update; 'media available' (text, graphics, audio, video); visitor charges (the equivalent of COVER PRICE); 'visitor counts' (the approximate equivalent of CIRCULATION); ADVERTISING RATES.   (KC)

F

fabricated materials. Those industrial goods which become a part of the finished product and which have undergone processing beyond that required for raw materials but not so much as finished parts e.g. steel, plastics, processed chemicals. (MJB)

facets. A side of a many-sided object; an aspect of a subject. Thus a listing of the facets of MARKETING would include pricing, promotion, distribution, product policy etc. No general agreement exists on how many 'facets' there are of marketing, as many aspects of the subject are further subdivided into specialist areas. Distribution, for example, has aspects of physical distribution and marketing channels of distribution. These in turn could be labelled 'facets' of distribution strategy. (BRM)

facing matter. A MEDIA BUYER'S booking instruction, often contracted to 'fm', requesting a SPECIAL POSITION for a booked ADVERTISEMENT opposite specified editorial material. *See also* NEXT MATTER. (KC)

fact book. A book kept by BRAND MANAGERS or ADVERTISING AGENCY ACCOUNT EXECUTIVES in which all the available facts about a PRODUCT, its MARKETING and performance are recorded. (MJB)

factor. An agent who buys accounts receivable at a discount and takes responsibility for collecting the amount owed by the debtor. (MJB)

factor analysis. A group of methods of MULTIVARIATE ANALYSIS used to examine the inter-relationships of a set of measured data, typically a number of ATTITUDE SCALES applied to a number of people. The technique seeks by one of a number of factor methods employing various criteria to deduce the existence of certain underlying factors which contribute to the scores achieved by individuals for the various scales according to the strength for the individual of these factors. The method has been attacked on the grounds that the results are arbitrary, since they are determined by a series of arbitrary decisions on methods, and that a better understanding of the data may be obtained by an examination of the correlations between scores for the various scales. Such an examination should certainly precede factor analysis. (JAB)

factorial design. An experimental design used to study the effects of two or more variables: the values of the variables are called levels of factors, and observations are taken on designed combinations of levels of factors. A complete factorial design involves all possible combinations of levels of factors. Factorially designed experiments are typically processed by ANALYSIS OF VARIANCE. (SKT)

factoring. Similar to INVOICE DISCOUNTING, but in this instant, the factor takes on responsibility for credit control, debt collection and credit risk. Fees for such a SERVICE are naturally higher than for INVOICE DISCOUNTING. INVOICES are handed over to the factor, who pays sums of money at regular intervals to the client, or when finance is included in the contract, a percentage of the invoice value on invoice presentation. The exact percentage will vary from industry to industry and from firm to firm. (GM)

factor loading. A statistic in FACTOR ANALYSIS that indicates the relationship between each observed variable and the hypothetical (underlying) factor: standardized to the same range as a correlation coefficient. (SKT)

factor method. *See* FACTOR ANALYSIS

factor score. A score that estimates what a case's score would have been on the underlying factor. The central indeterminacy of FACTOR ANALYSIS loosely means that factor scores can only be estimates. (SKT)

factory outlet. Stores owned and operated by manufacturers through which they sell branded merchandise at a discount. In addition to surpluses on normal manufacturing runs they are also used for disposing of discontinued lines and seconds. (MJB)

fad. A fad product is one which has a special appeal to a particular MARKET SEGMENT and appears to diffuse almost instantaneously following its introduction. However, fads or 'crazes' are notoriously short lived and likely to be dropped as quickly as they were taken up in favour of something new, e.g. hula hoops, platform shoes, flared trousers, Sinclair C5s. (MJB)

Fair Trading. *See* CONSUMER PROTECTION, OFFICE OF FAIR TRADING.

family brand. A BRAND NAME/identity used for two or more PRODUCTS usually produced by same manufacturer, e.g. Ford, Heinz, Philips. However, family brands are also associated with major RETAILERS such as Sears, Marks & Spencer and C&A etc. (MJB)

family buying. As a group the family exhibits all the aspects of any organization: the differences among families that affect their consumer behaviour lies in how they are organized. Every family must have someone who is responsible for acting as the purchasing agent for the group as a whole, with considerable interpersonal communication and influence about products regardless of who buys or who, on the surface, appears to make the decision about what to buy. (JLD)

family life-cycle. A sociological CONCEPT first proposed in the early 1930s which posits that families change over time and that these changes are accompanied by significant changes in their CONSUMPTION BEHAVIOUR. Engel *et al.* (J.F. Engel, R.D. Blackwell, and P.W. Miniard, *Consumer*

Behaviour, 5th edn, Illinois: Dryden Press, 1986), summarize the nine stages in the family life-cycle as: Single Stage, Newly Married Couples, Full Nest I, Full Nest II, Full Nest III, Empty Nest I, Empty Nest II, The Solitary Survivor, The Retired Solitary Survivor. This classification offers more divisions than the Full and Empty Nest stages that were traditionally recognized, and reflects the marketer's desire to define MARKET SEGMENTS with increased precision. This trend has been further updated by Patrick E. Murphy and William A. Staples ('A Modernised Family Life Cycle', in *Journal of Consumer Research,* vol. 6, June 1979, pp. 12–22) to recognize the impact of divorce, single-parent families, later family formations etc. (MJB)

fashion cycle. A variation of the PRODUCT LIFE CYCLE which reflects the sales history of the prevailing style of consumer articles such as clothing, soft goods, interior decoration, car design etc. Styles may be very short lived, in which case they may be termed 'FADS' or last for many years. Either way, a fashion cycle is seen as comprising three stages defined as distinctiveness, primary emulation and secondary or economic emulation. Take up of a new fashion by INNOVATORS seeking distinctiveness who will then be emulated by EARLY ADOPTERS who wish to copy them. In turn, if the fashion appears to be attractive to the mass market, manufacturers will rapidly bring out large quantities of similar articles at much lower prices – Spice Girl look-alikes, designer jeans – with the result that the innovator may well look elsewhere to regain distinctiveness thereby initiating a new cycle. (MJB)

fast moving consumer goods (FMCG). *See* CONVENIENCE GOODS.

fear appeals. Appeals used in communication strategy to persuade. A strong fear appeal is less effective than mild fear appeals, except where SOURCE CREDIBILITY is high or the audience has high self-esteem. *See also* ANXIETY. (KF)

feasibility study. In a MARKETING context, feasibility studies are often undertaken at an early stage in the development of a new PRODUCT. An inventor may have an idea but wants the idea justified as being practicable. This was just the case recently when the inventor of a new heavy vehicle tyre pressure equalization gauge commissioned a feasibility study of his idea. The practicability of the product idea was vigorously assessed by a university specialist before detailed and expensive PRODUCT DEVELOPMENT, MARKET testing and COMMERCIALIZATION of the product took place. Undertaking a feasibility study is thus a safeguard against an organization wasting its scarce managerial and financial resources on impractical projects.   (BRM)

Federal Trade Commission (FTC). US equivalent of the UK OFFICE OF FAIR TRADING. A government body set up to encourage competition and protect consumers from anti-competitive practices.   (MJB)

Federal Trade Commission Act (1914). The Act which created the Federal Trade Commission.
                    (MJB)

feedback. Figure 13 illustrates this concept.
                    (JRB)

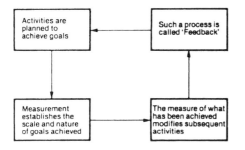

Figure 13: **Feedback**

field edit. *See* PRELIMINARY EDIT.

field experiment. An experiment that is not done in the laboratory, but typically somewhere a little more realistic. 'Field' is here used in the survey methodology sense, and not the agricultural one!
                    (SKT)

field research. The collection of primary data by FIELDWORK.   (IAB)

field salesforce. The personnel assigned by the sales manager to assist and/or persuade prospective customers to buy a product or service. Such people are concerned with some or all of the elements in the sales process and operate away from the company's own premises.   (WD)

field sales manager. The first-line supervisor of the salesforce who is responsible for research, planning and implementing sales policies in the field.   (WD)

field selling. This is an expression which has come to be applied to the activities of an organization's salespeople who work outside their organization's offices, usually, but not always, in a specified territory. Field selling is thus the activity of calling upon customers and prospective customers away from day-today control of a manager, but probably making daily reports by telephone or mail to their offices. Whereas the term may originally have been applied to rural SALES TERRITORIES, it is now used for both rural and urban sales territories. Field salespeople usually work alone and in this sense they are pioneers, attempting to win new customers for their organizations and to retain existing business. They do not carry STOCK of their PRODUCTS, as would a van salesman, but possibly carry samples. Field selling activities are undertaken by both CONSUMER GOODS and industrial goods producers.   (BRM)

fieldwork. The organization and execution of the collection of PRIMARY DATA in MARKETING RESEARCH from outside sources. Data may be either QUALITATIVE or QUANTITATIVE, CENSUS or SAMPLE and yielded by individuals, organizations or objects.   (JAB)

FIFO. Literally, 'First In, First Out'. A policy for rotating STOCK to ensure that the oldest stock is always consumed first.   (MJB)

fighting brand. A brand used to protect an established brand from lower-priced competition. The fighting brand will usually be of lower quality than the premier brand and may be withdrawn if it succeeds in deterring the low-price competitor.
                    (MJB)

filler spot. A SPOT needed to fill a COMMERCIAL BREAK which has not yet been bought. Such spots may be offered by the MEDIA OWNER as a last-minute deal at a substantial discount.   (KC)

filter. In survey research a question designed to isolate a sub-group to which further questions will exclusively be directed. Similarly in survey analysis, a selection of a sub-sample for tabulation, equivalent to a controlling variable in multivariable tabulation.   (JAB)

financial intermediaries. Any organization which helps finance commercial transactions or provides insurance against financial loss.   (MJB)

Financial Services Act 1986. UK legislation designed to protect investors.   (MJB)

financial year. The 12-month period used by an organization to serve as a fixed time span in which to meet its operational goals – revenue, profits etc. Frequently not the same as the calendar year: many organizations choose, for example, to operate a financial year which keeps in step with the government's fiscal year (e.g. mid-March/early April in the UK). (JRB)

first-mover advantage. Sometimes referred to as a 'pioneering advantage' these are the additional benefits thought to accrue to the first firm to enter a market. Most of the literature on this subject deals with innovation or new product development where advantages are seen to come from pre-empting competition, setting industry standards etc. There is evidence to suggest that first mover advantages may be illusory, particularly where the innovation is radical when followers may move in with improved versions of the innovation as the market enters the early stage of the growth cycle and displace the pioneer. The latter was certainly true of the launch of established brands into East European markets (a market development strategy). Pioneer brands enjoyed buoyant sales initially but their novelty value was lower than their high prices and repeat purchase did not occur. Followers learned from this experience and formed partnerships with domestic firms with lower costs and established distribution channels. (MJB)

Fishbein attitude model. *See* ATTITUDE.

fixed break. A MEDIA BUYER's booking instruction to a television or radio CONTRACTING COMPANY to book time in a specified COMMERCIAL BREAK on a particular day. This privilege will always carry a surcharge, if it is available at all. (KC)

fixed costs. Those costs which cannot be altered in the short or medium term and which exist irrespective of the volume of output. Depreciation, insurance, rent and rates are all fixed costs. (MJB)

fixed effects model. Statistical approaches in the general linear model (ANALYSIS OF VARIANCE and MULTIPLE REGRESSION) where the levels (values) of variables are taken as fixed, rather than (as with random effects) as samples of a population range of values. *Contrast* RANDOM EFFECTS MODEL. (SKT)

fixed spot. A MEDIA BUYER's booking instruction to a television or radio CONTRACTING COMPANY to book a specified SPOT on a particular day. This privilege will always carry a surcharge, if it is available at all. (KC)

flagship. The most important and best-known PRODUCT or BRAND in a firm's range; the object on which its reputation depends. (MJB)

flagship stores. Stores belonging to firms which are leaders in their category such as Marks and Spencer and Lewis's. Such firms are considered vital to ensure the success of new shopping developments. The term is also applied to the main branch of a store with multiple outlets, e.g. Marks & Spencer's Marble Arch outlet. (MJB)

flanker. A LINE EXTENSION to an existing brand intended to protect the primary brand's flanks from competition. (MJB)

flanking strategy. *See* LIMITED STRATEGIC ALTERNATIVES.

flexible price policy. A PRICING STRATEGY sometimes referred to as 'charging what the market will bear' in which the seller offers the same product at different prices according to the bargaining power of the customers and their perceived ability to pay. (MJB)

flexible pricing. Selling at different prices to different customers or 'charging what the market will bear'. *See* PRICING STRATEGIES. (MJB)

flow chart. A diagrammatic representation of a sequence of activities showing inter-relationships and sequential linkages. Typically decision processes, documentary inputs and outputs and physical activities are denoted by distinctive symbols. Specialized types of flow chart are CRITICAL PATH ANALYSES and PERT CHARTS. (KNB)

fly poster. An illicit poster placed on an ADVERTISING hoarding, often on top of the existing poster, although rarely of the same size. (BRM)

fm. *See* FACING MATTER.

FMCG. *See* FAST MOVING CONSUMER GOODS.

FOB. *See* FREE ON BOARD.

focus. Term used by Michael Porter to describe a generic strategy which is equivalent to a CONCENTRATED MARKETING STRATEGY. (MJB)

focus group. *See* GROUP DISCUSSION.

follower advantage. The opposite of FIRST MOVER ADVANTAGE. Given that market leaders tend to have a vested interest in maintaining the status quo, most radical innovations are introduced by small entrepreneurial firms. Once it becomes clear that the new technology is likely to displace the old the established firms are likely to enter the market with improved versions of the pioneer's new product. Given their size and market position such firms following the 'strategy of the fast second' will often displace the pioneer and so benefit from follower advantages.
(MJB)

Food and Drug Administration (FDA). The American (US) agency responsible for setting standards for all foods, drugs and cosmetic products. All new products must be submitted to the FDA for approval with full evidence that they are effective and will not cause harm to consumers.
(MJB)

food court. An area within a shopping centre served by a variety of different food outlets but usually sharing the same eating area.   (MJB)

forced-choice scale. A scale on which the RESPONDENT is required or 'forced' to express an order of preference for the activities or attributes listed, e.g. 'Please rank the following television programmes in your order of preference assigning the number 1 to your most preferred programme, 2 to the second and so on: Brookside, Coronation Street, EastEnders, Neighbours.' Such scales are ordinal. *See also* SCALING TECHNIQUES.
(MJB)

forecast. An estimate or prediction about a future state of affairs. Most forecasting is based upon extrapolative techniques which extend forward past and current trends as a basis for setting targets and budgets for future levels of activity. Given the rapidity of change it has become increasingly difficult to make long-term forecasts and many organizations now make use of much more broadly based scenario-planning in their decision making on future courses of action.
(MJB)

forecasting. The prediction of future outcomes. In marketing demand and sales are particularly important areas for forecasting with such forecasts providing the basis for most SHORT-TERM MARKETING PLANNING. TREND ANALYSIS and EXTRAPOLATION are frequently used for developing forecasts. However, given the accelerating pace of technological change and the dynamic nature of competition, it is becoming increasingly difficult to use traditional forecasting methods with the result that many organizations have turned to alternative techniques such as SCENARIO PLANNING.
(MJB)

foreign trade organization. Most Communist countries conduct overseas trade through such organizations under the general control of a Foreign Trade Ministry. They are responsible for both exports and imports in a particular industry. Generally these are the organizations with whom British exporters will have to deal initially in Communist markets; one problem they may create is that the FTO's interests may not be exactly the same as the prospective buyer's, and they may therefore, for purposes of their own, attempt to link a sale with some extraneous conditions such as payment in part or full by BARTER.
(JML)

formal group. *See* REFERENCE GROUPS.

formula selling. A structured sales presentation designed to move the prospective buyer through the stages of Attention, Interest, Desire and Action (AIDA). *See* HIERARCHY-OF-EFFECTS.
(MJB)

forward buying. Buying quantities in excess of current needs to ensure continuity of supply and/or volume discounts.   (MJB)

forward integration. The acquisition by a member of a DISTRIBUTION CHANNEL, of a facility or establishment, closer to the market. The acquisition allows the exercise of more control over the distribution of the product.   (AJB)

fragmented industry. One in which there are many small players and good opportunities for NICHE MARKETING.   (MJB)

frame of reference. The standard or framework which serves as a reference against which the properties of a particular object are judged. A way of referring to the influence of a cognitive system upon its component cognitions.   (JLD)

franchising. A form of marketing and distribution by which one company grants to another the right to use any tangible or intangible possession it owns, for the purpose of trade, in return for some benefit. The possession may be a patent, recipe, trademark, business method, architecture, design, or any other possession which clearly cannot be easily obtained without legal action. For the grantor of the franchise the benefit it yields is expansion for a very low investment, and the receipt of fees, royalties, or profits.(AJB)

freebie. A slang term used to describe any free promotional item given to the trade or an agent. Examples are pens, diaries and notepads. (GM)

Freefone. A British Telecom service which allows a caller to contact a company free of charge via the telephone operator from anywhere in the UK, by asking for the appropriate Freefone number or name. (GM)

free on board (FOB). Term used in foreign trade contracts where the price quoted by the exporter for goods includes all charges up to the point of embarkation. It is compared with COST, INSURANCE, FREIGHT (CIF), where the price quoted includes all charges up to the point of delivery. (MDP)

Freepost. A Post Office service which allows an organization to quote a Freepost address on ADVERTISEMENTS which permits prospects to respond using their own stationery, but without the expense of using a stamp. The fees for such a service are a £20.00 licence fee and a surcharge over and above the normal first or second class rate of half a penny per item received. *See* BUSINESS REPLY SERVICE. (GM)

free samples. Of all the promotions this method offers the greatest chance of getting a consumer actually to try the product. At the same time it is the most expensive, and its usage is invariably restricted to brands with potential annual sales of several million pounds. (On a door-to-door basis the cost could well be in the region of £100 per 1,000 households!) A number of companies seek to reduce sampling cost by cooperating in a joint promotion of non-competing products on similar lines to the gift pack given to mothers of first babies. (MJB)

freesheet. A regional or local weekly or monthly newspaper distributed free of charge door-to-door in a defined geographical area, as opposed to a 'PAID-FOR TITLE'. For some years after their first appearance in numbers in the early 1980s, freesheets contained almost nothing but CLASSIFIED ADVERTISING placed by individuals and 'semi-display' advertisements (*see* DISPLAY ADVERTISING) placed by local trades and services. Printing and distribution costs could thereby be met in full by advertising revenue. Although the fact that freesheets arrived on the mat unsolicited and cost nothing earned them the epithet 'local rag', they provided a strong challenge on many counts to the less than thriving local paid-for newspapers of the time. ADVERTISING-TO-EDITORIAL RATIOS fell steadily as titles became economically viable and journalists could be hired, though they remain dominantly a vehicle for local advertising. When the first edition of this dictionary appeared, in 1984, 300 freesheets were up and running across Britain; by the second edition, six years later, the number had tripled; another six years later, there were 672 free titles nationwide. (KC)

free trade. 'A policy of non-intervention by the state in trade between nations, where trade takes place according to the international division of labour and the theory of comparative advantage. Such a policy would lead to the most efficient allocation of resources on a world scale and to the maximization of world INCOME. Despite its strong theoretical backing, free trade has rarely, if ever, been practised by one country let alone by the community of all countries. Governments may intervene in international trade for non-economic reasons, e.g. for national defence or for social reasons such as the maintenance of a particular class like the peasantry or for economic reasons. The latter include the protection of established industries under threat from imports, the protection of infant industries, the terms of trade (or optimum tariff) argument and the pauper labour argument' (D.W. Pearce, *Macmillan Dictionary of Modern Economics,* London: Macmillan, 1981).

free word association. *See* WORD ASSOCIATION.

freight absorption. A PRICING STRATEGY whereby the seller charges the same freight costs as those levied by local competitors. A form of geographic pricing. (MJB)

freight absorption pricing. The setting of prices which include the cost of transportation to the buyer's premises. (MJB)

freight forwarders. Organizations specializing in assisting manufacturers of goods to export their products to overseas markets. 'Freight forwarders' have specialist knowledge of distribution services available in various parts of the world. They are familiar with the customs and excise requirements of the importing countries and handle all the documentation to assist in the export/import procedures. They do not take title of the goods they are dealing with but provide a useful service in a specialist area. (BRM)

frequency. A measure of the number of times an individual reader, viewer or listener sees or hears a given ADVERTISEMENT or COMMERCIAL in an advertising CAMPAIGN. Average frequency is computed as gross cover divided by net cover (*see* COVERAGE) and is usually expressed in terms of OPPORTUNITIES-TO-SEE ('OTS'), even in the case of radio listening. (KC)

frequent shopper programme, The offering of an incentive to customers to encourage loyalty and repeat purchase, e.g. Airmiles, BAA Bonus Points etc. (MJB)

Freudian psychoanalytical model. One of four basic models of buyer behaviour proposed by Kotler (*Marketing Management,* 1972). This model is concerned with the subconscious motivations which direct and condition behaviour. (MJB)

Freud, Sigmund (1856–1939). Born in Czechoslovakia, studied at Vienna as a medical student but developed an interest in the study of the human mind. He was the founding father of psycho-analytic techniques. He showed the importance of unconscious motivations and desires in understanding behaviour and introduced the concepts of EGO, ID and super-ego. He was forced to leave Vienna in 1938 to escape anti-semitic Nazi persecution and died a year later aged 83. (KF)

full cost approach. Also known as absorption costing, a full cost approach to price-setting for a product looks to cover all costs, both direct (or variable) and indirect (overheads), to which is then added the required profit margin for profits. This approach fails to take into account the fact that a price which fails to cover all such costs may yet make a contribution to the organizations' profitability, as long as its price is greater than direct (variable) costs. (JRB)

full-service advertising agency. One which offers its CLIENTS a range of services over and above the creative and media expertise which were the historical rationale for the existence of advertising agents. These might include planning (as distinct from simply executing creative treatments or media schedules to a brief from the client), MARKET RESEARCH, product-name testing, marketing advice, PROMOTIONS, EXHIBITIONS, corporate identity, PUBLICITY, PUBLIC RELATIONS, annual reports, house journals, a 'house style' for stationery, and so on. The full-service agency tends to be the norm today (or, at least, most agencies aspire to be full-service) despite the alternatives offered to advertisers over the last two decades by CREATIVE SHOPS, MEDIA INDEPENDENTS, the À LA CARTE option and THROUGH-THE-LINE agencies. (KC)

full-service retailer. Retailers providing a full range services to customers. (MJB)

full-service wholesalers. Wholesalers providing a full range of services to their customers. (MJB)

functional organization. An organization in which specialists in different functions are grouped together in departments each of which is headed by a director or manger who reports to the chief executive. The benefit of such a structure is that specialization leads to greater efficiency and productivity. The disbenefit is that it can lead to competition between functions instead of collaboration and so reduce effectiveness. It may also lead to one function dominating the others and so influence the overall orientation of the business. *See* MARKETING ORIENTATION. (MJB)

functional spin-off. When a market channel relationship has been established, one of the results is that each member has agreed to fulfil particular functions based on expected cost structures. If these costs are increased, the functionary may decide to sub-contract that function, or delegate it to the buyer using power or persuasion to do so. *See* CHANNEL BEHAVIOUR – CONFLICT and CHANNEL CONTROL. (AJB)

fundamental scientific research. Also known as fundamental research. This is research which will contribute to the aggregate level of available scientific resources (knowledge). It involves the investigation of natural phenomena and the development of the framework of natural laws, principles and theories which guide understanding. Scientific endeavour of this kind is broadly concerned with the empirical postulations of emerging and existing scientific theories. (DB)

fundamental technological research. Research which is oriented to the development of the potential of existing technology. It involves making wide use of the available scientific and technological resource base to advance the evolution of a technological capability. The synergistic cross-fertilization of knowledge and ideas has a pivotal role to play in the success of the research venture. (DB)

funnelling technique. A technique used in MARKET RESEARCH whereby the RESPONDENT is taken from the general to the particular through a series of increasingly focused questions. (MJB)

futures. One of a number of terms to denote the study of the future (also futuristics, futurology and futurics). It encompasses a broad area of activity which attempts to identify, analyse and evaluate possible future developments in human life. The use of the plural term emphasizes that there is an element of choice concerning what the future will hold. The area of study is based on three important premises:
– the future is not predictable
– the future is not predetermined
– future outcomes can be influenced by individual choices.
As an emerging disciplined area of study it is concerned to develop an integrative framework for study and research, which although based on a rational approach to the future also accepts that some contributions will have irrational origins. However, although some ideas about the future are very important for decision making, as a scientific area of activity in the conventional sense, futures is thought to be limited in its potential for development. Futures research attempts to describe possible future technological, political or social developments. It assigns probabilities to these developments and also assesses their impact on society. The study of the future then has three basic goals to attain: first, to form perceptions of the future, i.e. the possible; secondly, to establish the probabilities of events and trends occurring, i.e. the probable; thirdly, to express preferences for particular futures as a way of guiding action, i.e. the preferable. Proponents of the futures movement (futurists) take the view that thinking seriously about and planning for the future provides an organizing principle that will enable mankind to better manage human endeavour (futurism). (DB)

futures trading. The futures market is concerned with contracts for sale and delivery at some future, and usually specified, time.

In fact, the futures contract is not a contract to buy or sell at all, but is an option to buy at an agreed price, at a stated time. From the buyer's point of view an option ensures the future availability of supplies at a fixed, maximum price. If, when the option matures, the market price is less than that negotiated, the option is not taken up, for the commodity can be obtained for less in the open market. Conversely, if the price in the market is higher, the option will be exercised and the seller will have to bear the loss. Naturally, the dealer's success depends on his being able to predict accurately the future level of supply, and setting a price which will be attractive to the potential purchaser while exposing the dealer to the minimum of risk. To achieve this the dealer must secure a continuous supply of accurate market data as the basis for forecasting future price levels. Although some dealing in futures is purely speculative, the majority of dealers depend on it for their livelihood and so base their forecasts on facts rather than hunches. In doing so they perform a valuable service, for they reduce uncertainty concerning both demand and supply in the markets in which they operate.

(MJB)

futurism. The philosophy or mood that emphasizes the importance of seriously thinking about and planning for the future. *See* FUTURES. (DB)

G

galley (galley proof). Printing term used to mean first impressions of typesetting to be corrected before make-up of pages. (MDP)

Gallup. Originally started in the USA by Dr G.H. Gallup, there are now independent Gallup companies all over the world. They come together as Gallup International, with its secretariat based in the British Gallup. Gallup is a full-service research company offering a complete range of research facilities including its own field force of over 450 interviewers. Gallup is a founder member of Gallup International Research Institutes, a worldwide association of independent market research companies. Gallup is a household name, and was one of the first independent market research companies in Britain, founded in 1937. Gallup's operations cover a wide range, the main services are as follows: ADVERTISING and communication, publishing periodicals and media research, OMNIBUS RESEARCH, social, ethical and religious studies, computer analysis, *ad hoc* services, QUALITATIVE RESEARCH and the Gallup Poll. The Gallup political opinion poll represents the most well-known of the Gallup research services as far as the general public is concerned. (MDP)

galvanic skin response. *See* BASAL SKIN RESISTANCE.

game theory. A theory developed out of the pioneering work of Von Neumann and Morgenstern contained in their *The Theory of Games and Economic Behaviour* (1944). The theory seeks to extend the conventional micro-economic analysis in which decisions are made under conditions of certainty into situations where the decision maker is operating under conditions of risk or uncertainty and having to interact with other decision makers, often in a competitive situation. In very general terms games may be divided into zero sum situations, where the gain of one participant represents the loss of another participant, and non-zero sum games, where it is possible for all participants to gain. (MJB)

gap analysis. *See* STRATEGIC GAP ANALYSIS.

gatefold. A special option in the page format of a magazine, consisting of a left or right page which is printed on paper twice the usual width and then folded in half so that the reader can open it out, as though opening a gate. Presuming that readers do in fact bother to do this, the ADVERTISEMENT printed on the resulting 'gatefold' is thought to have special impact. The arrangement has the additional advantage of allowing a creative team to exploit the unusual LANDSCAPE space, rather similar to the shape of a poster in miniature. The gatefold format is sometimes applied to DOUBLE-PAGE SPREADS as well as single pages. It adds a significant surcharge to the cost of the space. (KC)

gatekeepers. Persons involved in the decision-making process who control the flow of information. While the gatekeeper (e.g. the purchasing agent) in a firm may not be directly responsible for the buying decision he or she can exercise considerable influence over it by admitting or excluding information from the decision-making unit. (MJB)

gender segmentation. The segmentation of a market on the basis of gender. (MJB)

General Agreement on Tariffs and Trade (GATT). A multilateral trade agreement, negotiated at Geneva in 1947 and operational since January 1948. It both sets out the rules of conduct for international trade relations and provides a forum for multilateral negotiations.

The objective of GATT is to liberalize world trade through the key commercial principles of non-discrimination, reciprocity, and the gradual elimination of tariffs and other barriers to trade. With the exception of customs unions and free trade areas, all contracting parties are generally bound by the MOST FAVOURED NATION clause. GATT also provides a framework for the settlement of grievances of members who believe that other members have violated the agreement.

Tariff reductions as a result of seven major trade negotiations conducted under the auspices of GATT have been significant. The Kennedy Round of negotiations held in Geneva 1964–7 marked the first time tariff reductions were negotiated on whole groups of goods rather than individual items. The Tokyo Round (1973–9) addressed the problem of non-tariff as well as tariff barriers.

GATT has also given some attention to trade problems of DEVELOPING COUNTRIES. In 1964 it established an International Trade Centre (operated jointly with UNCTAS since 1968) to provide information on export markets and assistance with the formulation and administration of export promotion programmes. In 1965 the General Agreement was amended to include a section on Trade and Development. This permits developing countries to trade with DEVELOPED COUNTRIES on a non-reciprocal basis and allows a system of generalized trade preferences by developed for developing countries, thereby waiving the Most Favoured Nation clause. *See* WORLD TRADE ORGANISATION. (JK)

general line wholesalers. Wholesalers who carry inventory and provide a full range of services, such as delivery and credit. *See also* CASH AND CARRY. (AJB)

generic brands. Products distinguished by the name of the product itself, e.g. washing-up liquid, but without any other name or identity such as the manufacturer's or retailer's name. See also GENERIC NAME. (MJB)

generic competitive strategies. Phrase coined by Michael Porter (*Competitive Strategy,* 1980) to describe three broad strategic approaches which offer the potential of success, namely: (a) overall cost leadership; (b) differentiation; (c) focus. These approaches correspond closely to undifferentiated, differentiated and concentrated marketing strategies respectively. *See* UNDIFFERENTIATED MARKETING STRATEGY, DIFFERENTIATED MARKETING STRATEGY AND CONCENTRATED MARKETING STRATEGY. (MJB)

generic name. (1) The name given to a class of product, for example washing powder, as against PRODUCT/BRAND NAME within the product field – Daz, Ariel.

(2) In marketing, a term frequently used to denote a product/brand name which has come to stand for the product category, for example people may refer to 'a Hoover', or 'a Biro', where the generic terms are vacuum-cleaner and ball-point pen. (JRB)

generic products. Grocery ranges introduced by major SUPERMARKET and HYPER-MARKET operators in recent years. Although the term 'generics' is now emerging as the most usual descriptive term, these ranges have also been described as brand-free, no-names and unbranded products. Such ranges have in common a deliberate austerity in PACKAGING. The product description is normally in black, stencil-like lettering and the pack carries only the required label information. Prices are normally significantly below those of comparable brands. The concept of generic products initiated in France in 1976 and rapidly spread to many parts of the world including the USA and UK from 1977. Fine Fare's Yellow Packs are a typical example of generic products in the UK. (CA)

geodemographics. The study and analysis of population in terms of geographical location. Popularized by the development of programmes such as ACORN and the growth of DATABASE MARKETING. (MJB)

geographical concentration. The extent to which a TARGET MARKET is, or is not, geographically dispersed. In the marketing of many industrial goods, high geographical concentration may be found, e.g. in the UK, the textile industry used to be heavily concentrated in the North of England, car manufacture in the Midlands etc. Concentration is a factor of great marketing importance where, for example, transportation costs are very high, e.g. bulk animal feeds. (JRB)

geographic organization. The organization of a firm based on geographical locations in order that production units may be close to the customer. This is important where the product is highly perishable, e.g. bakery products, or the unit value is low in relation to transport costs, e.g. cement, aggregates, hire plant and equipment. Each unit will normally have responsibility for both production and sales.   (MJB)

geographic pricing. The fixing of prices on the basis of location or geography (e.g. petrol prices in the UK), usually by reference to the point of production or manufacture.   (MJB)

geographic segmentation. SEGMENTATION of a market on the basis of location or geography.
                                                       (MJB)

gestalt psychology. The branch of psychology which holds that individuals are conscious of a perceptual field as a whole rather than the individual perceptual stimuli which comprise it. Thus we have a tendency to expect stimuli to occur together – a 'set' – and when one or more stimuli are missing from a perceptual field we fill the gap through CLOSURE. This tendency to perceive what we expect to see leads to, as well as being a consequence of, SELECTIVE PERCEPTION and distortion. *See also* LEARNING.   (MJB)

Giffen good. A PRODUCT which does not seem to obey the 'law of demand', as more is bought as the price rises and vice versa. This special case is named after the Victorian economist Sir Robert Giffen, who is attributed with noting an actual example. He noted that, among the British labouring classes of the nineteenth century, when the price of bread (their staple diet) rose, their consumption of bread also rose. When the price of bread fell, consumption fell. This was contrary to the normal concept of demand varying inversely with price. The reason for this is as follows. When a CONSUMER'S expenditure on any product takes up a significant part of his or her INCOME, then any increase in the price of the product will have a resultant effect of reducing consumers' real income (and vice versa). If that product is an inferior good, a fall in income will cause a rise in demand. Sir Robert Giffen observed that when bread became costlier, the poorer people were left with less of their income to spend on other more expensive foodstuffs and so they actually bought more bread.   (MDP)

GIGO syndrome. An acronym for 'Garbage In, Garbage Out', which emphasizes that the output of a system or ANALYSIS is directly dependent upon the quality of the inputs to that system or analysis.   (MJB)

global firm. A firm which regards the world as its marketplace and locates its functions in different countries in order to secure competitive advantages unavailable to the domestic firm.
                                                       (MJB)

global industry. An industry such as car manufacturing where the strategies and competitive standing of the competing firms are determined by their global positions.   (MJB)

globalization. *See* GLOBAL MARKETING.

global marketing. The MARKETING of PRODUCTS or services world-wide using the same MARKETING MIX in every country and region. While global marketing or 'globalization' received a great deal of attention in the early and middle 1980s it is now generally accepted that it is appropriate to only a small range of global BRANDS. These may be luxury goods such as perfumes, fashion clothing and shoes, jewellery, personal accessories etc. (e.g. Chanel No. 5, Burberry, Gucci, Rolex, Dunhill) or FMCG with strong BRAND IMAGES, such as Marlboro cigarettes or the ubiquitous Coca-Cola. Essentially, global marketing is a form of UNDIFFERENTIATED MARKETING STRATEGY and most marketers take the view that cultural, social and language differences require some modification to the MARKETING MIX if goods and services are to be marketed effectively in a number of international MARKETS.   (MJB)

global products. *See* GLOBAL MARKETING.

glocalization. The pursuit of a strategy which requires one to 'think global but act local' in recognition of the fact that while there are economies of scope and scale to be gained from global operations the differences between different national cultures often call for modification of the marketing strategy to meet local requirements.   (MJB)

go-error. A decision to persevere with the development (and commonly, the launch) of a new PRODUCT which proves to be unsuccessful. The process of IDEA SCREENING is designed to minimize such an occurrence, but go-errors are perceived to persist, in part, as a result of management pressure and/or the unjustified efforts of PRODUCT CHAMPIONS. Premature investment in the early stages of a new product, without adequate marketing information or RESEARCH, may tempt companies to continue to launch, solely to recoup some of the development costs – this is to risk pouring good money after bad.   (KNB)

going-rate pricing. Setting prices at the 'going-rate' prevailing in the market without direct reference to the firm's costs.   (MJB)

Gompertz function. Named after the English actuary and mathematician, Benjamin Gompertz (1779–1865) and used to describe growth process (e.g. trends in time-series) where the rate of growth is small at first, increases over a period and then slows down as a limit is approached. It is expressed in the following form:

$$Y = Ka^{bx}$$

where a, b and K are constants and where $0<a<1$, $0<b<1$. The symbol K is the upper limit of the function and b is the dampening factor. It results in an S-type growth curve which resembles the PRODUCT LIFE CYCLE and as such it is usually reserved for long-run sales forecasts of new and existing products.   (GA)

gondola. An upright, illuminated, shelved, refrigerated unit used to display fresh, chilled foods effectively, conveniently and safely.   (SD)

goods. A term used in economics to describe any objects desired in the market.   (AJB)

goodwill. A term which comes to MARKETING from the accountancy profession. 'Goodwill' is an intangible asset of a company and which is therefore of value to it. It cannot, however, be divided from the business and sold separately as can items of equipment or machinery. 'Goodwill' can be recorded in the ACCOUNTS of a company. 'Goodwill' is important when selling the company as the price asked can be enhanced by the 'goodwill' element. Customer lists, introductions to key customers and BRAND NAMES are all examples of 'goodwill'.   (BRM)

government markets. Those markets in which government, central or local, is the primary customer e.g. defence, education, health, roads etc.   (MJB)

grand strategy. The long-term, broadly-based statement of objectives and the means of achieving them within which the medium-term strategies and short-term tactics will be developed.   (MJB)

graphic rating scale. A rating scale where RESPONDENTS show the intensity and direction of their response to a scale by making a mark on a line drawn between two labelled extremes. (SKT)

green marketing. The marketing of goods which are seen to be environmentally 'friendly' and promoted as such e.g. refrigerators and aerosols without CFC which destroys the ozone in the atmosphere, wood and paper products made from renewable forests, recycled materials etc.   (MJB)

green movement. A social movement akin to CONSUMERISM which is concerned about the impact of consumption on the natural environment and particularly the use or destruction of non-renewable resources. Pollution and waste disposal/recycling are high on the 'green' agenda. In some countries like Germany the green activists have formed a political party and have a significant impact on government policy.   (MJB)

Green, Paul E. S.S. Kresge Professor of Marketing at the Wharton School, University of Pennsylvania. A member of the editorial boards of both the *Journal of Marketing and the Journal of Marketing Research,* he has published several books and many articles in the field of marketing research. Over the years, his research interests have included areas such as BAYESIAN decision theory, multidimensional scaling and CONJOINT ANALYSIS.   (KAB)

green products. PRODUCTS which will not cause damage to the environment in either manufacture or use, e.g. recycled paper, the elimination of CFCs from aerosol products etc. *See also* ENVIRONMENTALISM.   (MJB)

gross domestic product (GDP). The total output of the domestic economy in a year.   (MJB)

gross margin. Allowing for the very great looseness in the use of accountancy/financial terms, this term in practice usually refers to the contribution towards profits left after direct (variable) costs have been deducted from sales revenue. Also called gross profit or net contribution. *See* CONTRIBUTION ANALYSIS.   (JRB)

gross national product (GNP). The total value of a country's output of goods and services within a defined time period (usually a year) prior to the deduction of depreciation and capital consumption.   (MJB)

gross profit. *See* GROSS MARGIN.

gross sales. The nominal value of sales, before allowing for special (not standard) discounts which will affect the cash revenue. Net sales, then, equals 'cash' and is the actual money paid by purchasers after the discounts have been allowed. Where the discounts have a real element of discretion to them (i.e. are not absolutely essential to achieving the sale) they must be considered as part of the marketing budget: hence the necessity to account for such expenditure and the value of gross sales.   (JRB)

grounded theory. A research methodology popularized by Glaser and Strauss in which the researcher collects data about a subject without any preconceived ideas concerning its content or structure. The data set is then content analysed to identify common themes or constructs which are then used to develop generalizations about their meaning and relationship to one another (theory). Thus the theory is 'grounded' in the data rather than the data having been collected to test a preexisting theory, a procedure which it is held is likely to bias the data used.   (MJB)

group discussion. Research technique designed to study the interaction of group membership on individual behaviour, with a free exchange of ideas, beliefs and emotions helping to form a general opinion about the subject.   (JLD)

group interview. *See* GROUP DISCUSSION.

growth share matrix. *See* PRODUCT PORTFOLIO.

growth stage. The phase in the PRODUCT LIFE CYCLE when sales begin to accelerate and grow rapidly.   (MJB)

Product Mission	Present	New
Present	Market penetration	Product development
New	Market development	Diversification

Figure 14: **Growth vector matrix**

growth vector matrix. A simple two-by-two matrix proposed by Igor Ansoff in 1965. The two dimensions are defined as product and mission, each of which is defined in terms of the present position and the new position resulting in four basic strategies, namely MARKET PENETRATION, MARKET DEVELOPMENT, PRODUCT DEVELOPMENT and DIVERSIFICATION.   (MJB)

GRP. *See* GROSS RATING POINTS.

guarantee. A promise to make good a defect in an article or be responsible for a wrongful act. The term has a strict interpretation in law and any major text on commercial law will provide details on the legal meaning of the term.   (MJB)

guaranteed homes impressions (GHI). 'Home' is used in practice as often as the technically correct 'homes'. An advertising package deal offered by the ITV CONTRACTING COMPANIES. A package of SPOTS is guaranteed to achieve a specified number of 'impressions', measured in terms of TV RATINGS, monitored by continuous syndicated audience-surveys. Either spots are added to the schedule until the target is achieved or the cost is adjusted downwards if it is not reached within a specified period. The timing of the spots is at the contracting company's discretion, which means that the package could achieve the promised number of ratings but in fact deliver only viewers of minority-interest programmes broadcast at times when there is least demand for advertising time.   (KC)

guaranteed homes ratings (GHR). A term more or less exactly interchangeable with GUARANTEED HOMES IMPRESSIONS. Television RATE CARDS may in practice describe both as 'guaranteed home(s) packages'.   (KC)

Guide to Official Statistics. A comprehensive reference tool for anyone who uses official statistics. It provides help for all users of statistics with brief descriptions of data and their availability. It is compiled by the Office of National Statistics and comprises 16 chapters. Chapter 1 provides an overview of the government statistical service, sources available, details of classification systems etc. The remaining 15 chapters consist of two sections each. The first presents the main data sets and series available within the subject area while the second lists sources in alphabetical order. The subject areas are: Population; Education; Labour Market; Health and Social Care; Income; Living Standards; Crime and Justice; Housing; Environment; Transport; Social Statistics; The Economy; Agriculture, Fisheries, Food and Forestry; Production and Manufacturing; Distribution and Other Services; Public Services.

(MJB)

gutter. The junction between right-hand and left-hand pages in a newspaper or magazine. *See* BLEED. (KC)

Guttman scales. A method of deriving ATTITUDE SCALES so that a series of statements represent successively stronger attitudes. The number of agreements is thus a measure of the strength of the attitude. It is difficult to generate a series of statements so that all of a sample of people agree with the whole of the series up to a certain point but agree with none of the statements after. However, procedures, some computerized, exist for selecting a series of statements that achieve this as nearly as possible. Guttman scales are little used in marketing research, being mainly a tool of social researchers. (JAB)

H

habit. A consistent pattern of behaviour that is performed without considered thought. Many purchasing situations are habitual and the consumers will not change their behaviour without a major stimulus to do so. (KF)

haggle. To bargain or wrangle over something, to negotiate price, terms, etc. (MDP)

half-tone. A printing process which can produce any shade of grey between solid black and solid white, or natural gradations of tone in colours, for the reproduction of illustrations in print advertisements. The alternative is 'line engraving' a solid colour. The material to be reproduced is photographed through a mesh screen, which converts the image into a series of dots of differing diameter but with equidistant centres. During printing, an agglomeration of large dots produces a dark shade, one of small dots a pale shade. Examine any newspaper photograph under a magnifying glass to see the outcome. Half-tone reproduction is important because some vehicles in the print media are not as amenable to realistic gradation of tones as others. Individual half-tone illustrations are often simply described as 'half-tones'. *See* SCREEN. (KC)

hall test. *See* CENTRAL LOCATION TEST.

halo effect. The tendency of respondents to supply good attributes to every aspect of an organization or product to which they have a generally favourable attitude. (JAB)

handout. An official news item given to the press for publication. In addition to this strict definition a 'handout' has come to be used in common usage in the following two ways. (1) Any documents handed out to students in educational establishments or other training institutes that relate to or give a summary of the lecture. (2) Free brochures or pamphlets, or even product examples, given away at an exhibition stand or trade show stand, which provide information about the products on display, or elsewhere. (BRM)

hard goods. Goods such as furniture, washing machines, TVs etc. as opposed to soft goods which have a textile base. (MJB)

hard sell. *See* SOFT SELL.

harvesting strategy. A strategic management decision to reduce the investment in a business entity (division, product line, product or item) in the hope of cutting costs and/or improving cash flow. Harvesting strategy has been popularized by the Boston Consulting Group in its application to what is termed 'dogs' (*see* BUSINESS PORTFOLIO). Generally, this strategy is advisable when (a) the business entity is in a stable or declining market; (b) the business entity has a small market share and building it would be too costly; (c) jobs would not decline too rapidly as a result of reduced investment; and (d) the business entity is not a major component of the company's business portfolio. (GA)

headhunting. A term used to describe the process of poaching staff from one company and placing them with another. (GM)

heavy half phenomenon. This occurs where a limited number of users constitute the major part of the demand for a product or service, with the balance fragmented among a large number of small or irregular users. *See* PARETO PRINCIPLE.

(MDP)

heavy users. Among any group of those who consume/use a product/service, there are those whose usage accounts for a disproportionately large share of the total. The existence of such 'heavy users' in nearly all markets makes them valuable and important targets for the attention of marketers. *See* PRODUCT USAGE SEGMENTATION.

(JRB)

hedging. A means of reducing risk by entering into a future contract to buy or sell an object at a fixed price. See FUTURES. (MJB)

heterogeneity. One of the characteristics associated with the creation of services which distinguishes them from products which are usually homogeneous being the output of a standardized manufacturing process. (MJB)

heterogeneous shopping goods. Products for which the purchaser is willing to expend effort seeking the best buy, and which are regarded as having different qualities, style, or durability. Demand for such products is less likely to be responsive to price changes. *See* HOMOGENEOUS SHOPPING GOODS. (AJB)

heuristic programming. A simulation method which seeks to understand the process of solving problems, especially the mental operations typically useful in this process. In essence, this term is used to describe the efforts involved in developing and computerizing the 'rules of thumb' an individual relies upon to solve complex, ill-structured problems. (GA)

hierarchical organization. An organization in which power and responsibility are clearly specified and allocated to individuals according to their standing or position in the hierarchy. Military formations are the classic example of such organizations where decisions are made by the leader and passed down through the levels of the hierarchy for implementation in conformity with a strict chain of command. Such organizations were defined as 'mechanistic' by Burns and Stalker. While suited to routine and clearly specified tasks they leave little room for flexibility or initiative. Given the increasing importance of interaction and service in business relationships it is unsurprising that few business firms adopt this form of organization. More 'organic' structures with fewer levels of management and more flexible stuctures are widely preferred. (MJB)

hierarchy-of-effects. A term summing up the proposition that ADVERTISEMENTS exert their influence on the audience by a simple hierarchical progression of effects. First postulated 70 years ago, it continues to dominate the conceptual frameworks of textbook authors and advertising practitioners alike, despite severe criticism on theoretical and experimental grounds over the years. It is a clearly detectable implicit assumption in much if not most of what is written on both advertising effect and the measurement of ADVERTISING EFFECTIVENESS today. Over the intervening seven decades, a considerable number of 'verbal models' of the hierarchy-of-effects have been published in the academic and practitioner literature – each different, but all clearly closely related. The most familiar four are: (1) Daniel STARCH, 1923: 'To be effective, an advertisement must be ... seen – read – believed – remembered – acted upon' (2) E.K. STRONG, 1925: 'AIDA': attention – interest – desire – action (3) Robert C. Lavidge and G.A. Steiner, 1961: 'Hierarchy of Effects': awareness – knowledge – liking – preference – conviction – action. (5) Russell H. COLLEY, 1961: 'DAGMAR': unawareness – awareness – comprehension – conviction – action. Psychologists would recognize these as a specific example of the generic 'cognitive-affective-conative' or 'C-A-C' pattern of response to stimuli other than advertisements. Cognitive responses are the outcome of thinking about what is happening, affective responses result from an emotional reaction to the stimulus, and conative responses involve consequent actions. Colloquially, the C-A-C model is summed up by the vividly explanatory 'think–feel–do'.

Though Lavidge and Steiner coined the phrase 'hierarchy of effects' it is nowadays used as a generic term. Strong's AIDA is the most widely quoted of all, despite the antiquity which is seldom made explicit. Very similar models were proposed by E.M. ROGERS in 1962, to explain the adoption of innovations and William J. McGuire in 1969, to explain 'information processing'. To facilitate discussion, let us combine these variants into the consolidated model of advertising effect below. The levels of response have been arranged in a vertical hierarchy and assigned labels mostly taken from the established versions.

The two sets of labels take different perspectives on the process by describing respectively what the advertisment 'should achieve' and how the audience 'should respond'. For example, it should communicate and the audience should comprehend. These two modes have historically been mixed together in a single model. The third column relates the new scheme to the generic C-A-C model in its colloquial form.

Performance characteristic:	Expected response:	C-A-C equivalent
Motivation	Action	Do
Persuasion	Conviction	Feel
Empathy	Sympathy	Feel
Communication	Comprehension	Think
Involvement	Interest	Think
Impact	Attention	Think

Figure 15: **Hierarchy-of-effects**

What the hierarchy-of-effects hypothesis does not do is explain how the audience is propelled, or voluntarily progresses, through the levels of the hierarchy of effects. More specific criticisms have also been made by academic theorists over the last 30 years. Most influential among the objectors is KRISTIAN S. PALDA, who published a widely reported evaluation of Lavidge and Steiner's model. The first of his fundamental objections, based on *a priori* reasoning, is that progression from one rung of a hierarchical ladder to the next does not mean that the probability of eventual action has necessarily been increased. His second is that in particular circumstances, such as impulse-buying, the deliberate step-by-step progression implied by the hierarchical models may actually be highly telescoped. The third is that he could find no conclusive evidence in the literature to show that 'affective' change (conviction, sympathy) necessarily preceded behaviour change, rather than resulting from it. This calls into question the very sequence of the hierarchical levels, and is certainly the most important of the three. Furthermore, Professor A.S.C. Ehrenberg and his colleagues at the London Business School (and latterly at South Bank University, London) have, over a period of more than 20 years, published the findings of meticulous empirical research studies and theoretical analysis supporting Palda's proposition that attitude change may follow new behaviour rather than causing it. Their view is that, once the decision to try a new product has been arrived at, probably somewhat

arbitrarily, and provided that the first trial is not an unsatisfactory experience, a stable pattern of subsequent re-selection develops. The user then deliberately pays attention to advertising for the product, which in turn reinforces the choice. In other words, 'do' responses trigger 'think' responses and precipitate 'feel' responses aimed at rationalization of a choice already made. This is certainly not the sequence of the orthodox hierarchies.

In 1973, Michael L. Ray suggested that three arrangements of the hierarchy were possible. 'Learning' corresponds to the conventional hierarchies: think–feel–do. 'Dissonance attribution' postulates an exactly reversed sequence, which he believes will apply when the decision is an 'involving' one and differences among the brands available are small. The eventual choice (do) is made on a relatively trivial factor, attitudes are rearranged (feel) in order to reduce post-decision dissonance and only finally is close attention paid to the advertising (think) in search of a rationalization for the choice. A 'low involvement' hierarchy, think–do–feel, applies when the audience is casual about the whole business. Perceptual defences are lowered, permitting awareness and recall to be achieved by sheer weight of advertising, brand choice is then made on the basis of what is best remembered, and attitudes are thereafter steadily rearranged in order to confirm the choice. In 1965, the highly influential theorist Herbert Krugman had argued that a low-involvement hierarchy best described the circumstances of television advertising.

Despite the serious shortcomings of the conventional hierarchy-of-effects models, we have to recognize and accept that they are still the implicit conceptual underpinning of present-day advertising practice, in the great majority of cases. In particular, this means that the measurement of ADVERTISING EFFECTIVENESS is implicitly based on a learning hierarchy. This must remain the case, of course, until marketing academics are able to produce a better model which practitioners can understand and are willing to use.   (KC)

hierarchy of needs. *See* MOTIVATION.

high-involvement products. Goods which possess a particularly high salience for the individual as they are perceived as being important in expressing the individual's personality and in helping them achieve personal goals.   (MJB)

hire purchase. A form of purchase by installment payments in which title does not pass to the purchaser until the final payment is made. The UK conditions of a contract of hire purchase are regulated by Acts of Parliament.   (AJB)

histogram. A chart in which data are recorded in columns or bars (hence 'BAR CHART').   (MJB)

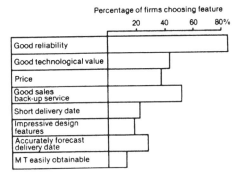

Figure 16: **Histogram**

historical trend. The pattern revealed (e.g. of sales, MARKET growth) through the ANALYSIS of past or historical data. Such data are declining in importance as a basis for developing FORECASTS of future outcomes.   (MJB)

hoarding. The traditional name for a POSTER SITE, little heard nowadays. Technically, it is the wooden framework on which posters are posted, more often called a 'panel' by contemporary media professionals.   (KC)

Holloway, Thomas (1800–1883). British entrepreneur. The 'Age of Bold Enterprise' in the nineteenth century produced many colourful characters, among whom Holloway was particularly daring and successful. In 1855 he launched 'Professor' Thomas Holloway's ointment and Universal Pill with a press advertising campaign costing £30,000, a very large budget indeed for that time. The wild claims and general hyperbole characterizing Holloway's advertising were by no means uncommon then, seeking to exploit a populace that was newly literate, as a consequence of the 1870 Education Act, but still credulous and therefore gullible. *Punch* commented that Holloway's ointment 'will mend the legs of men and tables equally well and will be found an excellent article for frying fish in'. Huge profit margins sustained the massive advertising expenditure, a charge still levelled today at some of our more visible advertisers.

In the last decade of the century, it became clear that Thomas Holloway had been a harbinger of things to come, at least in the scale of his investment in advertising. Both Lever Brothers and Pears' spent annual budgets of more than £100,000 at turn-of-the-century values of the pound; Coca-Cola, launched as a 'brain tonic' in the USA, in 1886 was being supported by an advertising budget of $120,000 by 1902; Beechams were spending £120,000 a year in 1895.

Holloway had opened an American branch office as early as the 1850s. It prospered to the extent that George P. ROWELL commented: 'Millions who have never heard of Napoleon ... have heard of Holloway, the most general advertiser of today.' Later in his career, he quietly dropped the spurious title of Professor and began to spend his wealth on worthy projects, perhaps a private penance for his earlier opportunism. He built a sanatorium for 'the mentally afflicted of the lower middle classes' in Surrey and endowed, in memory of his wife, a seat of learning which was eventually to become London University's Royal Holloway College, also in Surrey. Thomas Holloway died at his house in Berkshire, valued by a *Times* leader writer 'without exaggeration at more than five million sterling' in 1883.   (KC)

home audit. A means of establishing consumption patterns in a product field by the recruitment of a SAMPLE of homes, representative of the TARGET MARKET, in order regularly and systematically to measure product purchase and usage. Recruited households may be asked to keep a DIARY of purchases and/or be asked to retain the PACKAGING of all products bought for counting by the visiting home auditor. Because of the considerable expense involved in setting up and running such audit operations, they are usually syndicated by market research operators independent of manufacturers. Principally useful in the field of FAST-MOVING CONSUMER GOODS bought frequently by the average household.
                                                           (JRB)

homeostasis. A state of balance achieved when physiological needs are satisfied.   (MJB)

homogeneous shopping goods. Product for which the consumer is willing to expend effort seeking the best buy, but which products are seen to be similar in terms of quality, style, durability. Demand is likely to be responsive to price changes.   (AJB)

Hopkins, Claude (1886–1932). One of the great advertising COPYWRITERS of the past. In a short textbook, *Scientific Advertising*, first published in 1923 and reprinted in 1966 with a foreword by David OGILVY, he set out his philosophy of writing copy that would sell. He had decided as a young man that people liked to buy products and services; all they needed was a reason. So he pioneered the 'reason-why' style of copywriting, as he called it – often long, but always written in simple and direct language. Hopkins was also a believer in market research, once sending a team of interviewers from door to door to find out how people baked their own beans before writing an advertisement for canned beans with the memorable introduction: 'We have no secrets madam. We are going to tell how you – if you had the facilities – could bake pork and beans exactly as good as Van Camp's.' Similarly, he discovered 'film on your teeth', to the lasting benefit of Pepsodent, and made Schlitz America's best-selling brand by advertising that the bottles were 'cleaned by live steam'. Ogilvy considers that he invented TEST MARKETING, product sampling, COPY TESTING, brand imagery, and the tactic of 'pre-empting the truth'. In 1908, when Hopkins was 41, he was lured from the client side for an annual salary of $185,000, which is close to a million at present-day values. He died in 1932, with a string of all-American successes behind him and a permanent place in advertising folklore.   (KC)

horizontal diversification. The process of adding new products which broaden the mix of products offered to existing customers and which may or may not be related in technological requirements to the existing product mix.   (GA)

horizontal integration. Involves bringing together industrial activities under unified control through expansion in one process. It may involve the amalgamation of firms making the same product, but can also be achieved by the diffusion of additional production facilities all making the same product or parts for a product. Many multinational companies integrate horizontally, producing the same product or product range in many different markets, building up sales on reputation or knowledge (technical or marketing). A good example of this is the major car manufacturers like Ford, which have production capacity in many parts of the world all orientated to the same basic models.   (JK)

horizontal marketing systems. The system developed when two or more companies cooperate, or form a new company by combining assets, which will provide greater benefits than by acting alone. The purpose of cooperation is to offer a better service to the market on a national rather than local level.   (AJB)

horizontal publication. One directed at readers who have one main characteristic in common but who are located in a variety of organizations or locations, e.g. *The Director*. The implied alternative is a VERTICAL PUBLICATION.   (KC)

house agency. An in-house advertising service, operated by a relatively small number of ADVERTISERS as an alternative to or in addition to buying-in the services of an ADVERTISING AGENCY or contracting for separate advertising services on an À LA CARTE basis. The option is most characteristically chosen by retailers. Otherwise, the argument seems to hold sway generally that it is less expensive to buy a time-share in the expertise of expensive talents who are permanently on another company's payroll than to try recruiting, reimbursing and retaining them oneself. The most celebrated 'house agency' was maintained for some years by Lever Brothers; but it eventually became independent of the parent company, as Lintas Ltd (Lever Internal Advertising Service). The name has lived on through subsequent mergers, and Ammirati Puris Lintas was Britain's 12th-ranked agency in 1996 with BILLINGS of £147.7 million.   (KC)

house brand. *See* OWN LABEL.

house journals. Publications organized by private organizations primarily for the benefit of their employees. They are frequently important vehicles for marketing the company to the company.   (JRB)

house style. A printing term used to describe a particular style of layout and typeface used by a company for their printed outputs, e.g. brochures, letter headings, corporate logos.   (MDP)

hype. A slang term used to describe exaggerated and/or excessive publicity for a PRODUCT or event. The implication is that one should be particularly careful in evaluating 'hyped' products.   (MJB)

hypermarket. A store of 50,000 square feet or more, generally at one level, with an inventory of food and non-food merchandise, which may include domestic and garden appliances, furniture, camping equipment, convenience products and clothing. All sales are completed by self-service and transported by the purchaser. Car parking facilities require the store to be free-standing in a low-cost location close to a motorway or dual carriageway, since the catchment area extends a considerable distance.

(AJB)

hypodermic needle model. Early models of communication regarded both impersonal sources (the mass media) and personal sources as establishing direct contact with an audience – the so-called hypodermic needle effect. Belief in this model lead to speculation concerning the influence of the mass media upon voting behaviour and resulted in one of the most celebrated pieces of communication research reported in P.F. Lazarsfeld *et al., The People's Choice* (1944). Lazarsfeld and his colleagues set out to study the influence of mass media on individual voting behaviour in the 1940 presidential election in the United States. Contrary to expectations, it was found that influence did not flow directly from a medium (press, radio etc.) to an audience, but was channelled through an intermediary who was designated the OPINION LEADER. It was this finding which gave rise to the two-step model. However, it must be emphasized that the two-step model does not exclude the possibility of a direct flow (one step) and its main contribution is in introducing the mediating effect of personal influence on impersonal communications. (MJB)

hypothesis. A statement or an assumption which may be accepted or rejected on the basis of reasoning or research. In marketing research based on sample surveys, such acceptance or rejection may be based only on a level of confidence or PROBABILITY. Acceptance and rejection are to be distinguished from proof and disproof.   (JAB)

I

IBA. Independent Broadcasting Authority, replaced in 1990 by the INDEPENDENT TELEVISION COMMISSION and the RADIO AUTHORITY. (KC)

id. The id is made up of the basic untamed desires which demand immediate gratification. The id is regulated by the EGO and the super ego (*see* FREUD, SIGMUND). In marketing, the concepts are important in explaining buying behaviour and are central to MOTIVATION RESEARCH. (KF)

idea generation. Literally, the process of producing a new idea; taken in MARKETING terms, it relates to new PRODUCT ideas. The idea generation process is conventionally regarded as a substage of the NEW PRODUCT DEVELOPMENT process, which occurs before the IDEA SCREENING stage. The postulation of idea generation as a discrete management activity is one of the principal differences between the 1965 and 1980 versions of the Booz, Allen and Hamilton NEW PRODUCT DEVELOPMENT (NPD) model, and is taken to be one of the key factors in the sharp apparent fall in the drop-out rate of new product ideas between screening and COMMERCIALIZATION. The 1965 version of the model suggested a survival rate of 1:57; the 1980 version showed an improvement to 1:7. One change detected in management practice over the fifteen-year interval was the growth in the number of companies which not only actively sought new product ideas, but which devoted resources to the search for ideas in response to specific product problems or perceived MARKET OPPORTUNITIES. Idea generation is thus a proactive element of a company's product (or new product) strategy. (KNB)

idea screening. *See* SCREENING and PRODUCT IDEA SCREENING DEVICES; *see also* IDEA GENERATION and NEW PRODUCT DEVELOPMENT.

ILR. *See* INDEPENDENT LOCAL RADIO.

image. Consumer PERCEPTION of a BRAND, company, retail outlet, etc. Made up of two separable but interacting components, one consisting of the attributes of the object, the other consisting of the characteristics of the user. *See also* BRAND IMAGE. (JLD)

imitative strategy. A strategy of copying or imitating one's competitors. This may involve both the product or service as well as the marketing mix used. Because of the difficulty involved in preventing imitation firms rely increasingly on BRANDING in order to differentiate themselves from their competitors. (MJB)

impact. (1) The lowest level of the HIERARCHY-OF-EFFECTS and, by extension, a criterion of ADVERTISING EFFECTIVENESS.

(2) A MEDIA BUYER'S term for a single exposure to an advertisement or commercial, also called an 'impression'.

(3) Used in a general sense as a universally desirable characteristic of any advertising – unless it happens to have the aim of being subtle. (KC)

imperfect competition. Literally any form of competition which does not conform with the definition of PERFECT COMPETITION. Specifically, it is used to describe competition between many (as opposed to a few – OLIGOPOLY) suppliers where the emphasis is on differentiation and non-price competition. (MJB)

implementation. The act of translating plans into action. (MJB)

implied warranty. A promise, enforceable in law, that an object is fit for the purpose for which it is sold even though no express statement to this effect has been given by the seller.   (MJB)

imports. Goods and services purchased by a country and brought in by commerce. Imports may be 'visible' (goods) or 'invisible' (services) (see BALANCE OF PAYMENTS). Historically imports have been subject to the imposition of various forms of control, all governments preferring to export and earn foreign exchange rather than spend it. However, the GENERAL AGREEMENT ON TARIFFS AND TRADE (GATT) has done much to reduce import controls and increase international trade. As with exporting, 'purchases' can include the exchange of goods for goods, i.e. barter, attractive to countries short of foreign exchange (*see* EXPORTS).   (JK)

impression. A MEDIA BUYER'S term for a single exposure to an advertisement or commercial, also called an 'impact'.   (KC)

impression formation consumption. *See* CONSPICUOUS CONSUMPTION.

impulse goods. Any goods which are purchased on impulse, that is after a very brief planning period. This kind of product is usually characterized by a low unit value but the income level of the purchaser has an influence. *See* IMPULSE PURCHASE.   (JLD)

impulse purchase. An unplanned purchase, a novelty or escape purchase that breaks a normal buying pattern.   (JLD)

incentive. In the specific marketing sense, incentives to motivate salesmen to sell, distributors to stock and users to buy form an important part of the marketing tactics to sell products.   (JRB)

incentive marketing. A growing activity which encourages employers and sellers to offer incentives for above AVERAGE performance. While many incentives are small 'give-aways', like pens and T-shirts, the nature and value at the top end is exhibiting considerable ingenuity, with hospitality and travel assuming increasing importance as incentives.   (MJB)

income. Payment in money or in kind in exchange for goods or services rendered within a defined period of time.   (MJB)

income effect. The effect of changing levels of income on consumers' purchasing patterns. *See* ENGEL'S LAWS.   (MJB)

income segmentation. The SEGMENTATION of a market based on income.   (MJB)

Incorporated Society of British Advertisers (ISBA). The professional body representing ADVERTISERS and, specifically, ADVERTISING MANAGERS. It describes itself as 'The Voice of British Advertisers' and sums up its mission as 'Action for Advertisers'. ISBA's origins are in the Advertisers' Protection Society, formed in 1900 to lobby for the provision of reliably verifiable CIRCULATION figures by the newspaper publishers of the day. Frustrated by lack of results, the Society forced the issue by publishing its own estimates. The *Observer* took them to court for estimating 5,000 when the actual figure was 80,000 but the Society won the action on the grounds that there was no means of making more accurate estimates. Thereafter, the newspaper publishers began to provide statements of audited circulation, starting with the *Daily Mail* and the *Daily Mirror.* The culmination of the Society's initiative was the establishment of the AUDIT BUREAU OF CIRCULATIONS in 1931. Meanwhile, it changed its name to the present form in 1920, and concentrated its attentions on pioneering the first independent readership surveys to describe demographic characteristics as well as counting heads.

Today, ISBA provides a wide range of membership services, runs training workshops and publishes a wide range of guides and reference booklets. Its key publications set out guidelines for such important advertising management tasks as writing an ADVERTISING BRIEF, managing a PITCH for the account, understanding how MEDIA BUYERS make their choices, managing the business relationship with an ADVERTISING AGENCY and, specifically, evaluating an incumbent agency's performance. The whole list ranges beyond the narrow interests of 'advertisers', with titles relating to sales promotion, direct marketing, sponsorship, exhibitions, public relations and market research on such aspects of practice as the selection, briefing and remuneration of advertising agencies.   (KC)

incrementalism. A view that organizations are reactive rather than proactive such that their strategy consists of a series of adjustments to changing market conditions rather than a deliberate attempt to take charge of their future. While such an approach may seem logical (hence 'logical incrementalism) the cumulative effect of numerous small changes may result in the organization losing contact with its market and losing competitiveness.   (MJB)

Independent Broadcasting Authority. A statutory body responsible between 1973 and 1990 for the licensing of commercially-funded television and radio stations in the United Kingdom, and for regulating both programme and advertising content. It replaced the Independent Television Authority, there having previously been no legal on-shore commercial radio in Britain, and was in turn replaced by a separate INDEPENDENT TELEVISION COMMISSION and RADIO AUTHORITY.   (KC)

Independent Local Radio (ILR). The major part of the COMMERCIAL RADIO network in the UK, consisting of stations awarded a franchise by the RADIO AUTHORITY to broadcast to a local reception area. In 1997, there were 159 local and 4 regional ILR stations in England, 23 local and 1 regional in Scotland, 8 local in Wales and 6 local in Northern Ireland, 21 more in total than had been on air a year before. The remainder of the commercial radio network comprises 3 INDEPENDENT NATIONAL RADIO stations and one other, operating outside the RADIO AUTHORITY franchising system. *See also* RADIO.   (KC)

Independent National Radio (INR). A recent addition to the COMMERCIAL RADIO network in the UK, set up by the RADIO AUTHORITY in 1992. Though its 3 constituent stations are numerically swamped by the 163 comprising the INDEPENDENT LOCAL RADIO network, each of them offers a different, strategically interesting audience profile to MEDIA PLANNERS. In 1997, they were Classic FM, Virgin 1215 and Talk Radio UK, the present holders of the 'INR1', 'INR2' and 'INR3' franchises. The Radio Authority has meanwhile published a consultation document examining the feasibility of introducing 'INR4' on a long-wave frequency. There are in fact already four non-local commercial radio stations in the UK. Atlantic 252, which started broadcasting to a reception area covering more than half the British Isles exactly three years before Classic FM, operates under an ILR 'incremental' licence. *See also* RADIO.   (KC)

independent retailer. Defined in the UK Census of Distribution as single establishment traders, and multiples having less than ten branches. They were later renamed single outlet retailers, and small multiple branches.   (AJB)

Independent Television (ITV). Part of Britain's second-largest ADVERTISING MEDIUM. The term defines the commercially-funded regional sta-tions broadcasting on terrestrial channel 3. The remainder of the TELEVISION advertising medium mainly comprises national Channel 4 and Channel 5, morning-only national GMTV, 6 of the 26 cable channels and 33 of the 56 satellite channels originating in the UK.   (KC)

Independent Television Association (ITVA). The body representing INDEPENDENT TELEVISION stations in the United Kingdom, which operates in practice as the ITV Network Centre. It is one of the organizations concerned with awarding the designation 'RECOGNIZED ADVERTISING AGENCY'. Until quite recently, it also played a key role in the ADVERTISING CONTROL system, its Copy Clearance Secretariat pre-vetting television commercials against the ITC CODE OF ADVERTISING STANDARDS AND PRACTICE. However, it had become obvious by mid-1993 that the need to perform that function for the new satellite and cable services which were not members of the ITV network would require separation of the Secretariat from the ITVA's other activities, and the BROADCAST ADVERTISING CLEARANCE CENTRE was duly established.   (KC)

Independent Television Commission. The statutory body responsible since 1990 for the licensing of commercially-funded television stations in the United Kingdom (*see* INDEPENDENT TELEVISION) and for regulating both programme and advertising content (*see* ADVERTISING CONTROL). Its history begins with the 1954 Television Act, which sanctioned the development of television financed by advertising revenue and hence 'independent' of the government support characterizing the existing BBC service. An Independent Television Authority (ITA) was established, with the statutory duty to oversee creation and regulation of the new system. Within a year, a nation-wide network of regional television stations was on air. Each was set up as both 'programme company' and 'contracting company'. In the first of those capacities, they could make programmes, broadcast them, sell them to one another and schedule their own output. In the second, more specifically relevant here, they could make sales contracts for the supply of advertising time with advertisers or ADVERTISING AGENCIES. However, ITA set a uniform limit on the amount of time any station was allowed to sell, and on the number of minutes of advertising permitted in any hour of broadcasting: *see* MINUTAGE and COMMERCIAL BREAK. The Television Act had also charged the

ITA with a statutory duty to devise and implement a system for regulating the content of the COMMERCIALS which occupied those breaks. In 1955, in collaboration with the INSTITUTE OF PRACTITIONERS IN ADVERTISING and INCORPORATED SOCIETY OF BRITISH ADVERTISERS, the ITA produced 'Principles for Television Advertising'. The title gives a clue that compliance was at that stage voluntary rather than compulsory, but the Authority did hold a trump card: it could refuse to renew the franchise of any contracting company which persistently failed to exercise proper control. In 1964, a second Television Act required the ITA to draw up a mandatory code of standards and devise a control mechanism to enforce it. Later that year, a Code of Advertising Standards and Practice duly replaced the Principles, and a system was set up for the compulsory pre-vetting of all commercials by a 'Copy Clearance Secretariat' as the trade body representing the independent television companies collectively. For an account of how the code and control system evolved into those operated by the Independent Television Commission today, *see* ADVERTISING CONTROL. In 1972, the Sound Broadcasting Act amended the second Television Act, changing the ITA into the Independent Broadcasting Authority (IBA) and extending its remit to the general licensing and regulation of both independent television and the newly established independent radio. The following year, an Independent Broadcasting Authority Act further charged the IBA with the statutory duty to devise and implement a television-style system of controls over radio advertising. After another 17 years, it was decided to devolve the administration of the two media to separate statutory bodies. The 1990 Broadcasting Act created the Independent Television Commission, almost reverting to its original name, and the RADIO AUTHORITY.   (KC)

independent variable. A predictor variable in single or MULTIPLE REGRESSION. The independent variable(s) are examined for the extent to which they predict the dependent (or criterion) variable.   (SKT)

in-depth interview. An extended interview, usually on a one-to-one basis, in which the interviewer explores a topic in considerable depth. The interviewer may follow an unstructured approach using an *aide-memoire* to remind him of the salient issues to be covered, or a semi-structured approach with a more detailed checklist of questions.   (MJB)

index. A summary statistic which condenses a large amount of data into a single readily understandable number which can be compared over time and related to the original base number, e.g. RETAIL PRICE INDEX, DOW JONES INDEX.   (MJB)

indirect costs. Costs not directly attributable to a PRODUCT under manufacture but which are necessary for its production, e.g. lubricating oil for machine tools, quality inspections etc.   (BRM)

indirect observation. *See* DIRECT OBSERVATION.

individual branding. The use of separate names for each product in the portfolio.   (MJB)

industrial advertising. *See* BUSINESS-TO-BUSINESS ADVERTISING.

industrial buying process. Organizational buying decisions can be seen in terms of a problem-solving activity with identifiable decision stages. In Robinson and Faris's model the process begins with recognition of a need which may be satisfied by purchase, continues with the search for and evaluation of alternatives and finishes with choice and establishment of a purchasing routine. *See* BUY PHASES.   (STP)

industrial distributor. A distributor of PRODUCTS serving industrial or organizational MARKETS, e.g. steel stockholders and heavy duty battery distributors. Manufacturers of industrial products may have a national or international network of industrial distributors to assist them in reaching their ultimate customers. Industrial distributors provide a valuable range of services depending upon their size, resources and proficiency. Services offered can include breaking bulk, making up mixed consignments of goods, holding STOCKS, local deliveries, local ADVERTISING, providing credit to customers. Industrial distributors can be independent organizations or form part of the distribution activity of large companies.   (BRM)

industrial goods. Goods destined for use in producing other goods or rendering services, as contrasted with goods destined to be sold to ultimate consumers. Certain goods which fall into this category may also be classified as consumer goods, e.g. paper, typewriters, chairs, fuel oil etc.

Where such an overlap exists, the purpose for which the product is bought determines its classification. Industrial goods fall into four main categories: (a) Raw materials: those industrial materials which in part or in whole become a portion of the physical product but which have undergone no more processing than is required for convenience, protection, economy in storage, transportation or handling. Threshed grain, natural rubber and crushed ore fall into this category. (b) Equipment: those industrial goods which do not become part of the physical product and which are exhausted only after repeated use, such as major installations or installations equipment, and auxiliary accessories or auxiliary equipment. Installations equipment includes such items as boilers, presses, power lathes, bank vaults etc., while auxiliary equipment includes trucks, office furniture, hand tools and the like. (c) Fabricated materials: those industrial goods which become a part of the finished product and which have undergone processing beyond that required for raw materials but not so much as finished parts. Steel, plastic moulding powders, cement and flour fit this description. (d) Supplies: those industrial goods which do not become a part of the physical product or which are continually exhausted in facilitating the operation of an enterprise. Examples of supplies include fuel, stationery and cleaning materials.   (MJB)

industrial market. Nowadays often referred to as BUSINESS-TO-BUSINESS markets as the products and services exchanged are used in the creation of other goods and services for sale into ultimate consumption.   (MJB)

industrial marketing The marketing of INDUSTRIAL GOODS. Although basic marketing principles are believed to apply equally to all categories of goods and services it is usual to recognize differences in emphasis according to the specific type of product/service. In the case of industrial goods these may be summarized as: (a) Derived demand: the demand for industrial goods, and raw materials, is derived from the demand for consumer goods in the sense that any expansion or contraction in the latter will be reflected by a corresponding shift in the former. The more distant the manufacturer is from the production of a specific consumption good, the less direct will be the impact of a change in demand for that good. (b) Rational buying motives dominate the industrial market. This is frequently misinterpreted in one of two ways: (i)

there is an absence of emotional motives in the industrial purchasing situation, or, (ii) consumer purchasing behaviour is irrational. Neither of the above statements is correct: consumers are rational and industrial buyers are influenced by emotional factors, but there is a difference in degree, i.e. the industrial buyer will emphasize objective criteria to a greater degree than the average consumer. (c) Concentration of buyers: the number of potential buyers for an industrial good is generally far smaller than is the case with consumer goods. Further, industrial buyers tend to be concentrated geographically, e.g. the cotton and woollen industries. One must be careful not to overstate the importance of this distinction for its validity clearly depends upon the precise nature of the product. For example, the market for office supplies is both large and dispersed, whereas the market for some consumer goods may be both small and concentrated, e.g. specialty goods produced on a purely local basis. It is also important to remember that although a national brand may have millions of users, the producer may concentrate his direct sales and distribution efforts upon a limited number of major buyers, e.g. wholesalers and grocery chains. (d) The scale of industrial purchasing is greater. In absolute money terms this is generally, but not always, true. In a proportionate sense, i.e. size of purchase, *vis-à-vis* disposable assets, the reverse may often be true. (e) Industrial products are technically more complex. Again this is true absolutely but not relatively. The purchaser of a car or television set is faced with a similar degree of technical complexity as the buyer of a computer: in both instances the buyer evaluates performance rather than construction, and is dependent upon the seller for both advice and service. (f) Industrial buying is a group process. The same might also be said of the household as a decision-making unit for consumer purchases. It is unlikely that the latter will have formalized evaluation and decision procedures, however, both of which are common in the industrial buying context. (g) The role of service is greater. Again this depends upon the nature of the product and the type of service. Immediate availability is a prerequisite for sale of a CONVENIENCE GOOD – this is rarely the case with even the most common of industrial goods – and CONSUMER DURABLES need after-sales service just as much as many industrial goods. (h) Leasing, renting, and the extension of credit are important. This is increasingly true of consumer goods. *See also*

BUSINESS-TO-BUSINESS MARKETING and ORGANI-
ZATIONAL MARKETING. (MJB)

industrial marketing research. Literally the research of industrial MARKETS. The term now embraces all aspects of BUSINESS-TO-BUSINESS MARKETING. (MJB)

industrial product. Any good (or service) sold in an industrial market which will be used directly or indirectly to produce goods for final consumption. (MJB)

industrial service. Any service sold in an industrial market which will be used directly or indirectly to support the activities of a business. (MJB)

industry. The collection of firms which are engaged in producing goods or services which are close substitutes for one another, e.g. the car industry, the electronics industry etc. (MJB)

inelastic demand. See DEMAND, PRICE ELASTICITY OF.

inept set. Those BRANDS in a multi-brand MARKET, which a CONSUMER is aware of (see AWARENESS SET), but have a negative evaluation and, consequently, will not be purchased. The negative evaluation may be based on past experience, rejection of promotional claims, etc. See also UNAWARENESS SET, INERT SET, EVOKED SET. (GKP)

inertia selling. The delivery (sale) of goods to past customers who are required to take positive action to discontinue the continuing supply or to return the unwanted products. Book clubs and direct debit agreements often depend on inertia as the basis for a substantial proportion of their sales. (MJB)

inert set. Those BRANDS, in a multi-brand MARKET which the CONSUMER is aware of (see AWARENESS SET), but will not purchase due to the brands being neither positively nor negatively evaluated. This situation may arise through insufficient information or lack of perceived brand differentiation. See also INEPT SET, EVOKED SET, UNAWARENESS SET. (GKP)

inferential statistics. Statistics used to make decisions, rather than descriptive statistics, which merely describe. (SKT)

inferior goods. A PRODUCT for which demand falls as INCOME rises. Normally it would be expected that a rise in income would lead to a rise in the amount of a good being consumed; an inferior good is an exception. An inferior good is one which is a cheap but inferior substitute for some other product, and when incomes rise CONSUMERS can afford to buy the superior product and so demand for the inferior one drops. Examples of this type of product could be: public transport with a switch to private cars, margarine for butter, lumpfish roe for caviar, instant coffee for ground coffee. (MDP)

inflation. A situation in which prices rise faster than incomes resulting in a decline in purchasing power. (MJB)

influencer. Person who helps to shape another person's evaluation of a product and the ultimate decision to buy the product. (JLD)

infomercial. Advertising presented in the form of a programme usually seeking a direct response from the listener/viewer. (MJB)

informal group. See REFERENCE GROUPS.

informant. See RESPONDENT.

information inputs. Strictly speaking the sensations received and interpreted by the human sensory organs. More generally used to describe any kind of data selected for analysis and processing. (MJB)

information processing. The acquisition, storage and interpretation of information usually with respect to making decisions on specific issues or topics. (MJB)

information search. The stage following ATTENTION AND INTEREST in HIERARCHY-OF-EFFECTS MODELS in which the decision-maker decides to search for additional information concerning the object in which they are interested. (MJB)

informative advertising. Advertising with a high information content designed to explain the features of a product or service and stimulate primary demand for it. (MJB)

informative label. A label containing specific information about the preparation, use or care of a product rather than one designed to identify or promote the product.   (MJB)

in-home retailing. Personal selling to potential buyers in their own homes, e.g. double glazing, household cleaning materials, etc.   (MJB)

in-house advertising service. *See* HOUSE AGENCY.

in-house marketing research. That RESEARCH conducted by the organization on its own behalf as distinguished from research commissioned or bought in from independent MARKET RESEARCH agencies external to the firm.   (MJB)

initiator. The individual who first recognizes a felt need and initiates the buying process.   (MJB)

inner-directed. A personality trait of social character, ranging on a continuum from inner-directedness to other-directedness. Available evidence indicates that inner-directed consumers tend to rely on their own 'inner' values or standards in evaluating new products and are more likely to be consumer-innovators.   (KF)

innovation. The commercial exploitation of an invention. Often used loosely to describe any object or idea which is perceived as new by the observer. In a marketing context inextricably linked with NEW PRODUCT DEVELOPMENT.   (MJB)

innovators. *See* ADOPTER CATEGORIES.

in pack. *See* ON PACK.

input-output data. Data used in industry analysis in which the output of one industry is seen as the input of another in the VALUE CHAIN.   (MJB)

INR. *See* INDEPENDENT NATIONAL RADIO.

inseparability. One of the features used in distinguishing services from products. The concept of inseparability recognizes that the consumer and provider of a service are directly and personally involved in the creation and consumption of a service.   (MJB)

insert. A separately prepared piece of promotional material inserted into a newspaper or magazine. It can be loose, gummed or bound-in. Sometimes called 'insets'. *See also* LOOSE INSERT, PROMOTIONS.   (KC)

insertion. A single occurrence of a press advertisement, as in: 'They booked 10 insertions in *Homes & Gardens* through 1997.'   (KC)

inset. *See* INSERT.

installed base. Generally, the total number of units of a durable good that are in use which is equivalent to current market size, e.g. washing machines, lathes, looms etc. Specifically, in an industrial context, it refers to the number of items held by a given user. The size and age of the installed base is an important indicator of market opportunity.   (MJB)

instant gratification. The converse of DEFERRED GRATIFICATION. A term ascribed to CONSUMER BEHAVIOUR associated with 'free spending' and the philosophy of 'buy now, pay later'.   (GKP)

Institute of Direct Marketing. The professional body representing the interests of UK practitioners in DIRECT MARKETING, it is also an examining and awarding body, a training provider and a research centre.   (KC)

Institute of Export. Non-profit-making company established in 1935, limited by guarantee and registered as an educational charity. Governed by an elected council, it seeks to provide a forum for the exchange of experience between those presently, potentially, directly and indirectly engaged in exporting. It also promotes relevant education and training aimed at improving the standards of export management. To this end the Institute issues a Certificate in Export Office Practice and sets professional examinations. The Institute also sponsors and approves courses, workshops, and seminars on export management and practice. With a head office in London and 15 branches covering the whole of the UK it publishes a journal *Export* and various books on export marketing.   (JK)

Institute of Practitioners in Advertising (IPA). Body representing BRITISH ADVERTISING AGENCIES. In mid-1997, just over 200 were incorporated members of the IPA and were thus entitled to call themselves 'Incorporated Practitioners in Advertising' (notice that it is not 'of advertising'). The shorthand description is 'IPA member agency', or simply 'IPA agency'. This total is less than a fifth of the 1,100 throughout the United Kingdom, listed in the standard reference book, but includes 48 of the 50 largest. The IPA provides specialist services to members, is represented on most industry-wide committees and working parties, commissions research surveys, produces handbooks and occasional papers, publishes reports on aspects of the advertising business and runs biennial Advertising Effectiveness Awards. It was originally founded as the Association of British Advertising Agents in 1917. (KC)

institutional advertising. Advertising which promotes the interests and objectives of an institution as opposed to a product or service. (MJB)

institutional market. Demand emanating from institutions such as hospitals, schools, universities etc. which often exhibit quite different buying behaviour from business organizations. (MJB)

in-store promotion. The use of special display material and/or the use of demonstration at the point-of-sale designed to encourage increased purchase of the promoted goods. Usually tied in with other promotional activities, such as ADVERTISING, couponing, and leaflet drops etc., which are 'out-of-store'. (MJB)

in supplier. The supplier currently enjoying the buyer's patronage. (MJB)

intangibility. One of the features used in distinguishing services from products, the concept of intangibility recognizes that services cannot be physically touched or possessed. (MJB)

integrated software. A suite of application software packages that fully supports the easy transfer of data between them. Typically this would comprise a DATABASE, a word processor, a SPREADSHEET and a graphics package. Thus, data held in a sales DATABASE may be transferred to a SPREADSHEET package for statistical manipulation to produce a FORECAST. The results could then be transferred to a word processor for inclusion in a report and simultaneously transferred to a graphics module to be plotted and subsequently printed out. (KRD)

intellectual property. Intangible forms of property such as patents, trademarks, copyright etc. Intellectual property rights are becoming increasingly important due to the difficulty in preventing the imitation of tangible or objective product advantages. (MJB)

intensive distribution. The strategy used by a company when it attempts to sell its products through as wide a range of wholesalers and retailers as will accept the product. (AJB)

intensive interview. *See* INTERVIEW.

interaction effect. In ANALYSIS OF VARIANCE, effects on the dependent variable that involve more than one factor – in contrast to main effects. In regression, effects in the model that represent the interaction of two variables. (SKT)

interactive MIS. A computer-based marketing information system which may be accessed and interrogated on an interactive basis. (MJB)

interdependence technique. A MULTIVARIATE ANALYSIS procedure which has no dependent variable. FACTOR ANALYSIS of correlation matrices is an interdependence technique. (SKT)

intermedia comparison. Making comparisons among MEDIA CLASSES in terms of their potential for inclusion in an advertising schedule. *See* MEDIA SELECTION. (KC)

intermediary. Any establishment which buys from a producer, and sells to another, without changing the form of the product. The intermediary's customer may be another producer, the final customer or yet another intermediary. (AJB)

internal marketing. The notion that in addition to developing strategies for interacting with its external publics, management must also ensure that all employees understand the implications of the marketing concept and regard one another as internal customers with whom they should develop mutually satisfying exchange relationships. (MJB)

internal secondary data. Information that is available for MARKET RESEARCH purposes, which has been compiled inside the organization for some purpose other than the current research investigations. Examples are SALES REPORTS, data held on competitors, MARKET conditions, ADVERTISING/promotional expenditure, data held on the organization's MARKETING INFORMATION SYSTEM. (AMW)

internal validity. Assessments of the validity of a measurement or an experiment that depend on information collected by the investigator at the time of the experiment. Typically based on the component parts of the measurement overall. Checks that the variability in the measurement was the result of the treatment. (SKT)

International Advertising Association (IAA).
Founded in 1938, the IAA comprises mainly
executives from advertisers, the media, advertising
agencies and related services concerned with
marketing communication at an international
level. The IAA advises its members of current
trends and developments affecting their business
interests, and provides a forum for the exchange
of ideas and information. The Association sponsors
a Diploma in International Advertising,
holds biennial conferences and publishes a
number of books and reports.   (CNW)

international marketing. Defined as the performance
of business activities that direct the flow
of a company's goods and services to consumers
or users in more than one nation. Basically the
same principles and process are involved as in
domestic marketing. The marketer's task is still
to establish what is required, who is buying,
where and why, and how to supply the product at
a profit. However, because in international marketing
more than one country is involved, the
complexity and diversity involved is much
greater, and the uncertainty much worse.

Despite this, there is increasing interest in
international marketing because of the changing
competitive structures and shifts in demand characteristics
in markets throughout the world.
Domestic markets no longer have limitless
expansion, nor are they safe from attack from
overseas. There is therefore a need to go international
not only to increase marginal earnings but
more importantly for long-term security in the
home market (as well as overseas) by widening a
company's marketing beyond the vagaries of a
single national economy. There are different
levels of commitment in international marketing
ranging from EXPORTING to LICENSING to JOINT
VENTURING to manufacturing in a wholly owned
subsidiary overseas.

There is a distinction made between export
marketing, which puts the emphasis on the successful
marketing of goods and services
produced in one or more countries in overseas
markets, and international marketing, which
gives more weight to the development of a business
in a number of countries, within a
framework capable of incorporating the establishment
of local manufacturing distribution and
marketing systems. Whilst not a neat distinction,
an exporter can be differentiated from the international
marketer by the foreign nature of his
products in the overseas market. The international
marketer is more capable of avoiding or
eliminating such 'foreignness' in many circumstances.
(JK)

international trade. The exchange of goods and
services between nations. International trade
theory suggests nations trade because they can
buy goods elsewhere more cheaply than they can
produce them themselves. (Adam SMITH
explained 'the wealth of nations' by such specialization
and division of labour.)

The reason that this is possible is that countries
have different COMPARATIVE ADVANTAGES.
Countries differ in their endowment of both
natural and acquired resources (e.g. climate,
human skills) and they will tend to have a comparative
advantage in the production of goods
which require resources of which they have a relatively
plentiful supply. Thus a country will tend
to produce and export goods wherever it has the
greatest comparative advantage in return for
goods whose production require resources which
are relatively scarce and therefore more expensive
to their countries. For example, even though
it is possible to grow pineapples or bananas in
Britain under artificial conditions, the cost would
be such that it is more productive to import from
other countries with warmer climates and pay for
the imports with the exports of products which
the UK can produce more cheaply than they can.
(JK)

interpersonal response traits. A system of classifying
individuals according to their
predominant trait, evident when reacting to
others, first proposed by the leading non-Freudian
psychoanalyst Karen Horney. Her
tripartite model reads as follows: (a) *compliant
types* – those who move towards people; (*b*)
aggressive types – those who move against
people; (c) *detached types* – those who move
away from people. P.M. Chisnall, in *Marketing:
A Behavioural Analysis* (London: McGraw-Hill,
1975), reports Horney as summarizing her paradigm
thus:

Where the compliant type looks at his fellow
men with the silent question 'Will he like me?'
– and the aggressive type wants to know 'How
strong an adversary is he?' or 'Can he be
useful to me?' – the detached person's concern
is 'Will he interfere with me? Will he want to
influence me or leave me alone?'

J.B. Cohen ('An Interpersonal Orientation to the
Study of Consumer Behaviour', *Journal of*

Marketing Research, vol. 4 (1967), pp. 270–78) carried this research on into the area of CONSUMER BEHAVIOUR using Horney's three basic interpersonal configurations to help to explain a person's perception of his social environment and his action tendencies towards the objects in his life space when making a purchase. Kassarjian *et al.* (H.H. Kassarjian and T.S. Robertson, *Perspectives in Consumer Behaviour,* Glenview: Scott Foresman, 1968) describe Cohen's findings as being that 'compliant types prefer BRAND NAMES and use more mouthwash and toilet soaps; aggressive types tend to use a razor rather than an electric shaver, use more cologne and aftershave lotion, and buy Old Spice deodorant and Van Heusen shirts; and detached types seem to be least aware of brands'. Ibis leads the authors to the conclusion that 'CONSUMER decision making and MARKET behaviour seem in part to be a response to significant others – who are either physically or referentially present at the time.' *See also* OPINION LEADERS, (GKP)

interpolation. Statistical method of estimating a value between two known values. (DL)

interval scale. A measurement which assigns numbers to some phenomena in such a way that the differences between scale positions are comparable. (SKT)

interview. The process of eliciting information from a RESPONDENT or group in a CENSUS or SURVEY either face-to-face or by telephone. The interview may be more, or less, structured. The fully structured interview is used in QUANTITATIVE RESEARCH, and consists of questions read out verbatim by the interviewer to respondents. In qualitative research semi-structured interviews in which the interviewer guides discussion through a number of predetermined topics is used. These are usually with individuals, and may be termed extended or depth depending on the type of discussion which the skill of the interview is meant to generate. Unstructured and little-structured interviews are often with groups, and known as GROUP DISCUSSIONS or group interviews. In these group discussions the interaction between respondents it is hoped largely replaces the interviewer as a stimulus. (JAB)

interviewer. In the UK most interviewers conducting quantitative consumer research are part-time female workers associated with specialist fieldwork companies or fieldwork departments of other organizations. The recruitment, training and supervision of many of them is monitored by the Market Research Society Interviewer Card Scheme.

Quantitative and qualitative research among organizations, that is, industrial market research, is carried out by more specialized interviewers, often with knowledge of the field of the enquiry. Individual interviews are usual.

Qualitative research among consumers, often by group interviews, is carried out by a variety of specialists, often called group moderators. They may have psychological training, thought particularly appropriate if 'depth' or 'motivational' areas are to be explored. *See* GROUP DISCUSSIONS.
(JAB)

in toto. In total.

intramedia comparison. Making comparisons among MEDIA VEHICLES within a media class, in terms of their potential for inclusion in an advertising schedule. *See* MEDIA SELECTION. (KC)

intrapreneurship. Literally internal entrepreneurship. An approach adopted by some large companies to simulate the flexible and innovative behaviour of individual entrepreneurs particularly in the development of new products. (MJB)

introduction stage. The stage in the PRODUCT LIFE CYCLE when the new product is first introduced into the market. (MJB)

introductory offer. A 'special' offer associated with the launch of a PRODUCT or service to encourage buyers to try the product and, hopefully, adopt it. The implication is that prices will be increased and/or any other inducements will be dropped on the expiry of the introductory offer. (MJB)

intuition. An insight or expectation concerning a future outcome which may be followed by a decision maker under conditions of uncertainty. Intuition is often the product of knowledge or past experience which the decision maker does not link explicitly with the problem to be solved. (MJB)

invention. A new idea or way of doing things which has not been tested in practice. (MJB)

inventory. List of units of goods kept for trade by a merchant or the value of such goods. The valuation may be used in financial accounting and planning of the stock units. Of Latin origin, this term is more widely used in the USA; the UK term is 'stocktaking'.   (AJB)

Inventory Audit of Retail Sales. Also called the 'Nielsen index'. Once the manufacturer's products leave his factory there is invariably a time-lag before they are purchased and consumed. The longer this time-lag, the more difficult it becomes for the producer to exercise control over supply to meet variations in demand and modify his production to maximize profit. The Inventory Audit helps reduce these uncertainties by monitoring both sales and stock levels for three major product groups – food, drugs and pharmaceuticals. The actual audit is made in a representative sample of outlets, carefully selected from the population of all retail outlets stocking the three product groups. Each outlet enters into an agreement with NIELSEN under which all invoices are retained for inspection and auditors are permitted to take physical stock on the premises. By the simple process of adding goods invoiced to opening stock and deducting closing stock, sales of each item may be determined. These data are then circulated to subscribers, together with information covering the number of outlets stocking given brands, prices, average order sizes, merchandising schemes etc.   (MJB)

invisible assets. A major source of competitive advantage in that such assets largely reside in the skills of individuals and other intangible factors like reputation, image, corporate culture etc. Because they are invisible they are difficult to benchmark and even more difficult to replicate.
                                                    (MJB)

invisible trade. Refers to current transactions which involve payments between residents of a country and non-residents for transactions, where there is no exchange of physical goods. Major categories of transactions include: (a) the provision of services, e.g. shipping, civil aviation, tourism; (b) interest, profits, dividend payments on past investment (invisible imports) and repatriated profits from subsidiaries or British firms overseas (invisible exports); and (c) payments arising from governmental activities. In this final category outgoings (or invisible imports) include maintaining embassies and similar establishments in other countries, military expenditure abroad and official aid to DEVELOPING COUNTRIES.

Incomings (invisible exports) involve payments to UK residents which arise from similar activities of foreign governments in this country. *See* BALANCE OF PAYMENTS.   (JK)

invoice. A list sent to the purchaser giving details of quantities, descriptions and prices of the goods, together with any discounts or additional charges, such as transport or postage. The date on the invoice is used to signify the tax point, i.e. VAT is claimed on the invoice and not when the actual payment is received.   (GM)

invoice discounting. A method of obtaining cash on the security of book debt. A company with too many debtors may sell these debts to a finance company. The finance company agrees to pay a percentage advance of the outstanding debt to the client. The borrower acts as agent in collecting the debt and repaying the finance company, plus interest. The borrower is responsible for any bad debts. *See* FACTORING.   (GM)

involvement. An indicator of the importance attached to an object by an individual. High involvement objects receive more attention from actual or intending users. They receive more thorough and careful attention and evaluation prior to purchase and are usually the outcome of extensive problem solving leading to the formation of strong ATTITUDES. By contrast low involvement objects are often acquired without much prior thought or the formation of attitudes towards them prior to purchase.   (MJB)

IPA. *See* INSTITUTE OF PRACTITIONERS IN ADVERTISING.

ISBA. *See* INCORPORATED SOCIETY OF BRITISH ADVERTISERS.

island displays. Free-standing merchandising units containing the products for sale in a self-service distributive outlet.   (JRB)

ITCA. *See* INDEPENDENT TELEVISION COMPANIES ASSOCIATION.

ITC Code of Advertising Standards and Practice. The document in which the INDEPENDENT TELEVISION COMMISSION sets out its criteria for judging the acceptability of television advertising, which must be pre-cleared for broadcast. For details of its content, *see* ADVERTISING CONTROL. It was first drawn up as the Independent Television Authority (ITA) Code of Advertising Standards and Practice in 1964, as successor to the more advisory Principles for Television Advertising, established when commercial television was established in Britain ten years earlier. The Sound Broadcasting Act of 1972 extended the ITA's remit to radio advertising, and renamed it the Independent Broadcasting Authority (IBA), with the result that the ITA Code became the IBA Code. Its present title dates from 1991, when the Radio Authority was set up to regulate commercial radio separately and the IBA became the ITC, almost reverting to its original name.   (KC)

itemised rating scale. A type of scale used in measuring individual attitudes or opinions towards an object in which the respondent has to select from a predetermined set of alternatives. *See* SCALING TECHNIQUES.   (MJB)

item nonresponse error. Error associated with surveys that comes from RESPONDENTS refusing or being unable to answer specific questions.
                                                       (SKT)

ITVA. *See* INDEPENDENT TELEVISION ASSOCIATION.

ITV homes. Describes UK households with at least one television set capable of receiving the signal from an ITV transmitter. The number of ITV homes defines the total UNIVERSE available to advertisers buying time on the Independent Television network, which was 97 per cent of all households in 1996. *See* NET HOMES.   (KC)

ITV region. A geographical area 'belonging to' one CONTRACTING COMPANY rather than another, defined by drawing a line around all local government areas in which not less than 15 per cent of ITV HOMES could receive that station's signal if their aerials were aligned appropriately. In some parts of the country, two or even three stations can claim 15 per cent penetration of given districts, but such 'overlaps' represent only about 1 in 20 of all ITV HOMES. The two or three contracting companies involved always claim every such home as part of their own 'universe' (gross potential audience), but MEDIA PLANNERS generally calculate net audiences or net homes by arbitrarily allocating the overlap homes equally to the overlapping regions.

A contracting company's share of network is the ratio of its ITV homes to the total UK figure. Share discounts and share dealing have been causing controversy in the advertising press recently. Each station always hopes to receive a share of an advertiser's total television expenditure in proportion to its share of network, but many are habitually denied the logical allocation. To encourage advertisers, the contracting companies offer a variety of incentive schemes and discounts for matching or exceeding parity of shares. The controversy arises because some have been more aggressive than others in promoting the concept.   (KC)

J

JICNARS. Acronym, pronounced as a word, for Joint Industry Committee for National Readership Surveys. Established in 1968 to commission and co-ordinate research into the readership of British newspapers and magazines, it took over the existing NATIONAL READERSHIP SURVEY, established by the INSTITUTE OF PRACTITIONERS IN ADVERTISING in 1954. It was superseded in this role in 1992 by National Readership Surveys Ltd. (KC)

JICPAS. Acronym, pronounced as a word, for Joint Industry Committee for Poster Audience Surveys. Established in 1967 and wound up in 1989, this was the first of a series of JICs which comprised representatives of the ADVERTISING MEDIA, ADVERTISING AGENCIES and ADVERTISERS and were set up to commission and co-ordinate programmes of audience and readership research for the four largest media. It began its work by carrying out meticulous surveys of audience flows in specimen geographical areas, and duly produced a general formula for the COVERAGE of a given outdoor advertising campaign, measured in OPPORTUNITIES-TO-SEE. This 'poster audience model' was based on pioneering research a decade earlier, and took the form: $100\ AS/AS + b$, where A was one of a set of figures to be published periodically by JICPAS, S was the number of posters comprising the campaign in the area in question, and b was a constant, then set at 3.6 but susceptible to variation. If a value for A was not yet published, it could be calculated by applying another formula: $\log A = 0.6813\ \log P + 1.3304$, in which P was the population in thousands of the area where the campaign would run. Not surprisingly, application of the poster model to campaign planning was never truly widespread in practice. MEDIA BUYERS were more likely to take on trust the various package deals offered by the MEDIA OWNERS. Eventually, poster audience measurement was revolutionized by the establishment of an entirely new research programme (*see* OSCAR), and JICPAS was shortly thereafter replaced by JICPAR, q.v. (KC)

JICRAR. Acronym, pronounced as a word, for Joint Industry Committee for Radio Audience Research. Established in 1974 to commission and co-ordinate research into the audience for INDEPENDENT RADIO, then a new advertising medium in Britain, and superseded in 1992 by Radio Joint Audience Research: *see* RAJAR. (KC)

JICREG. Acronym, pronounced as a word, for Joint Industry Committee for Regional Press Readership Research. Set up in 1990 and comprising representatives of ADVERTISERS, ADVERTISING AGENCIES and MEDIA OWNERS, its general remit was to do for the REGIONAL PRESS what the NATIONAL READERSHIP SURVEY had been doing for the NATIONAL PRESS since 1954. Specifically, its objectives were to establish common research standards, build up quantitative and qualitative research databases, and persuade the media owners to adopt the JICREG standard. By 1996, 98 per cent of the titles with CIRCULATION figures audited by ABC or VFD had become subscribers, and brad (q.v.) was routinely including a 'readership' heading in the entries in its Regional Press section. Research data are collected twice yearly by in-home interviews with a representative sample of readers, who are asked which of a series of publications, identified by their mastheads, they have 'read or looked at for at least two minutes yesterday', for dailies, or 'within the last seven days', for weeklies.

Aggregated answers provide the estimated 'average issue readership' figure. Other information gathered in the surveys is used to model general readership profiles and typical reading behaviour. MEDIA PLANNERS can obtain 'newspaper summary reports', 'location reports' or 'area reports', which provide 18 categories of READERSHIP and COVERAGE data. They are available in hard copy, on floppy disk, as 'JIC in a Box' software for Windows, or via Mediatel. JICREG hopes that this new level of planning information will halt the more or less steady decline the regional press has suffered since 1980.   (KC)

JICTAR. *See* JOINT INDUSTRY COMMITTEE FOR TELEVISION ADVERTISING RESEARCH.

jingle. A short piece of music, composed or adapted specifically to form part of a television or radio COMMERCIAL, the name of the advertiser or the product featuring prominently in the lyrics. A classic example from the British archives is 'Murraymint, Murraymint, the too-good-to-hurry mint'. The description is normally used pejoratively, to imply that the melody is trite and the lyrics banal, but a Coca-Cola jingle reached number one in the UK charts as 'I'd Like to Teach the World to Sing'. More recently, the traditional purpose-written jingle has largely given way to borrowed classical themes and rock classics, acting as mood-establishing background music. As a result, Bach and Holst have become irrevocably associated with small cigars and sliced bread. In such cases, the music is used more as a 'signature tune' than as a sales pitch set to music. One commentator has called well-chosen examples 'sonic logos', in contrast to mere 'jingles'.
    (KC)

JIT. *See* JUST-IN-TIME.

jobber. A type of intermediary who performs a selling function between a supplier and other dealers. He may specialize in buying or finding buyers for surplus production or imports. One type – a rack jobber – specializes in providing a servicing function for non-food products sold on a consignment basis to supermarket operators.
    (AJB)

job specification. The description of the role and duties that are attached to a particular post or job in an organization.   (JRB)

joint demand. Goods whose consumption creates a demand for other goods closely associ-

ated with them, such that the level of demand for one tends to parallel the other, e.g. eggs and bacon, bread and butter, cars and petrol, machine tools and lubricating oil.   (MJB)

joint probability. The likelihood of two (or more) events occurring together, computed by multiplying together their separate probabilities of occurrence, i.e. if there is a 0.5 probability of A occurring and a 0.3 probability of B occurring under a given set of circumstances, then the joint probability of their both occurring is $0.5 \times 0.3 = 0.15$.   (MJB)

joint venturing. The formation of a partnership by two or more (but generally not more than three) individuals or organizations who choose to collaborate in a business activity. The partners share the costs and profits in agreed proportions. In INTERNATIONAL MARKETING, joint venturing is a form of greater participation in an overseas market than EXPORTING or LICENSING. The foreign partner normally supplies technology and knowhow (often marketing). The local partner usually has knowledge of the market and often useful political contacts or access to the local distribution system. Joint ventures are cheaper than wholly-owned subsidiaries and the political risk is reduced because of the partnership. They are potentially more profitable than merely exporting and offer quick access on a knowledgeable basis to the local market. They are, furthermore, more acceptable to many developing countries than wholly-owned subsidiaries and their numbers here are increasing. If a company lacks capital or personnel capabilities to expand its international activities, a joint venture may be very attractive.

However, advantages tend to be short term. Often the local partner, having acquired the technology will want to buy out the foreign partner. Another problem lies in the potential clash of interests between the partners. This is especially apparent when a MULTINATIONAL CORPORATION with a global perspective clashes with its joint venture partner who is likely to have local interest more at heart. The multinational's freedom of action is likely to be curtailed. In addition to two private sector partners, joint ventures may also be between private sector companies and (a) the public sector (either with a nationalized industry or a parallel organization like the National Enterprise Board or Scottish Enterprise); or (b) another holding organization like a bank, common in many developing countries where there is no alternative source of raising finance like a stock exchange.   (JK)

journey mapping. One element in the process of estimating audiences for OUTDOOR advertising in the UK. Since the establishment of POSTAR, the term itself is comparatively little used in practice, but the technique remains firmly in use as one input into the research methodology which replaced OSCAR during 1996. Details of 'recent journeys' were collected by the market research company NOP from a random sample of 7,000 individuals, at two different times of the year. The results were transferred to maps and cross-indexed to the locations of poster sites. Appropriately weighted data were then used to construct a mathematical model for the prediction of 'one-day cover' from gross OPPORTUNITY-TO-SEE figures for a given campaign. Certain anomalies had not been fully resolved by early 1997, and development of the model continues.
(KC)

journey planning. The activity involved in determining the most cost-effective sequence of calls on a delivery route or in a SALES TERRITORY.
(MJB)

judgement forecasting. The use of judgement in forecasting sales of both present and potential products. Three methods of making judgement forecasts of sales are (a) aggregate of individual sales representative forecasts; (b) expert consensus; and (c) the DELPHI TECHNIQUE.
(GA)

judgement sample. A form of non-probability or purposive sample in which the researcher selects potential RESPONDENTS on the basis that they conform with some basic criterion specified as relevant to the POPULATION to be sampled, e.g. age, ownership of an article, activity etc., judgement samples are selected on the basis of what some expert thinks particular sampling units or elements will contribute to answering the particular research question or problem in hand. For example, in test marketing, a judgement is made as to which cities would constitute the best ones for testing the marketability of a new product. In judgement sampling the degree and direction of the SAMPLING ERROR are unknown and definitive statements are not meaningful.
(MJB)

junk mail. A colloquial expression used to categorize items of unsolicited mail such as unsolicited letters, pamphlets, special offer brochures, catalogues and questionnaires, which may or may not be addressed to named individuals, but which are mailed out by organizations in an attempt to get people to try, or buy, their products or service. The expression has been coined in recent years with the increasing use of direct mail as a sales method with its associated computer generated and printed addressed labels. The occurrence of direct mailing has increased considerably in recent years. Some members of the public are offended by the growth in volume of 'junk mail' and have sought to have themselves excluded from mailing lists. Although not extensively researched, it is thought that much 'junk mail' is disposed of unopened or after only a cursory glance by recipients. However, direct mail continues to be used extensively by organizations (e.g. *Reader's Digest*) which regard it as a cost-effective means of promoting their products or services.
(BRM)

jury of executive opinion. The role of forecasting is central to marketing competence. One means of improving forecasting is to recruit, on an *ad hoc* or systematic basis, a jury of executives – experienced in the relevant market – to provide a multiple input to forecasting, rather than to rely on the guesswork of one or two marketing executives.
(JRB)

just-in-time (JIT). A fashionable title for the harmonization of supply with demand, conceptually idealized as stockless production, or STOCKLESS PURCHASING. The practice may be seen as the practical apotheosis of MARKETING, although in reality it is somewhat limited in applicability, at least in its ultimate form. The key requirements for the operation of the concept are generally regarded as being the availability of accurate demand forecasts, the existence of dependable suppliers and the willingness of suppliers to treat the customer on a preferential basis. Apart from the benefit of materials INVENTORY reduction or elimination, the adoption of the concept also entails reduction of work-in-progress inventories, reduction in the numbers of suppliers, involvement of suppliers in quality improvement programmes and the encouragement of long-term working relationships with suppliers. Risks to the customer are increased in the event of supply failure, and also in the event of suppliers or customers lapsing into a state of competitive inertia.
(KNB)

just noticeable difference (JND). The minimal difference that can be detected between two stimuli. The minimal level at which a stimulus is first detected is the differential threshold. *See* WEBER'S LAW.
(KF)

K

keiretsu. Japanese term to describe an alliance between a number of businesses. (MJB)

Kelly repertory grid. *See* REPERTORY GRID.

key account. A customer (account) that represents a significant proportion of the seller's business and so is likely to receive special treatment. (MJB)

keyed advertisement. In DIRECT RESPONSE ADVERTISING, a reply coupon may be 'keyed' to the publication in which it appears by means of code letters or numbers, for the purpose of measuring that MEDIA VEHICLE's effectiveness in generating response. (KC)

Keynes, John Maynard (1883–1946). British economist. Fellow and lecturer at King's College, Cambridge, from 1909 and during the First World War he worked at the Treasury, of which he was the principal representative at the negotiations preparatory to the Treaty of Versailles. Having shown, by his resignation, disapproval of the financial proposals, especially those relating to reparations, he predicted trenchantly in *The Economic Consequences of the Peace* (1919), the results of imposing obligations which a defeated Germany would be unable to meet. The book made Keynes the centre of immediate controversy and ensured his fame when his worst fears were realized. He was equally critical of Britain's return to the gold standard (1925) and predicted the rapid increase in unemployment that would arise from its deflationary effects. The direction in which his mind was working was shown by the proposals he made for dealing with unemployment in the 1929 election manifesto of the Liberal party (to which he belonged), a large programme of public works being among the chief recommendations. His matured ideas for regulating the economy as well as his new conclusions on monetary theory were elaborated with great skill and persuasive power in *The General Theory of Employment, Interest, and Money* (1936). The general acceptance of its main tenets in many countries after the Second World War constituted what is known as the Keynesian revolution. It marked the end of the classical economists' belief in the self-regulating economy: aggregate demand was to be adjusted to available supply, consciously using such financial techniques as enlarging or reducing the credit base or varying the rates of interest; government expenditure, too, should be adjusted as necessary so as either to stimulate or to discourage public demand. Keynes himself modified some of his prescriptions in later years: it is clear from the 'stop–go' tactics enforced upon governments in Britain and elsewhere that the full answers have not been found; but the great overall post-war rise in prosperity in the developed countries and the absence of catastrophic unemployment is largely due to Keynes.

He was one of the few theoretical economists who had the opportunity or skill to bring his ideas into practice. In the Second World War he was adviser to the Chancellor of the Exchequer having become (1940) a peer and a member of the Court of the Bank of England. The years from 1943 on were mainly spent on financial missions to America. He was the chief British delegate at the Bretton Woods Conference (1944) and it was his plan, welded with similar American proposals, that became the basis of discussion and agreement there on the foundation of the

International Monetary Fund and the World Bank. Keynes was a lover and patron of several arts and built and endowed the Cambridge Arts Theatre; he married (1925) the Russian ballerina, Lydia Lopokova.   (MJB)

key prospect. Those potential customers whose profile matches most closely the profile of the persons or organizations perceived as having the strongest need for a good or service.   (MJB)

key success factors. Sometimes referred to as critical success factors. These are factors which are essential to the organization's success. While they are *necessary* they are not always *sufficient* in the sense that once the key success factors are known it is likely that all the firms competing in the market will apply them with the result that they become the minimum necessary to attract the intending buyer's attention. To stand out one needs a JUST NOTICEABLE DIFFERENCE.   (MJB)

kickback. A payment made to a buyer in return for their order. Unlike a DISCOUNT which is a reduction in the selling price a kickback is a payment to the individual and so may be regarded as a bribe and an unethical practice.   (MJB)

knocking copy. An ADVERTISEMENT for a PRODUCT where the text compares its competitors disparagingly. Examples are commonly found in lawn-mower, antiperspirant, beer and lager, and car advertisements. *See also* COMPARATIVE ADVERTISING.   (MDP)

knowledge. The first stage of an innovation decision process. The knowledge stage begins when a consumer receives physical or social stimuli that gives exposure and attention to the innovation's existence and some understanding of how it functions.   (KF)

Kolmogorov-Smirnov test. A non-parametric inferential statistical procedure employed with ordinal scale data. One version tests whether the sample conforms to a POPULATION pattern, another compares two independent samples.   (SKT)

L

labelling. The identification of a product and the provision of information concerning its composition and use. In response to consumer pressure and legislation producers are now required to provide full information on all their products.

(MJB)

laboratory experiment. In contrast with a FIELD EXPERIMENT, an experiment done in a situation where the experimenters can manipulate conditions and control for extraneous influences that might confound a more realistic inquiry. (SKT)

laboratory tests of advertising effect. Advertising researchers sometimes borrow the hardware of experimental psychology to measure the effect of advertisements or package designs on test subjects under laboratory conditions. The research companies often take potential users of their services to 'a perception laboratory where they can peer into boxes, have electrodes stuck to them, twiddle dials, press knobs and generally enjoy themselves' according to Lovell and Potter in *Assessing the Effectiveness of Advertising,* 1975, now out of print but still the only British textbook devoted entirely to the subject. Five laboratory tests use physiological indicators of arousal as a surrogate for interest or involvement as a criterion of effectiveness. The psychogalvanometer measures sweating in the palms, the pupilometer records dilation and contraction of the pupil, the blink-rate meter is self-explanatory, the electroencephalograph measures brain-wave patterns, and the polygraph (popularly called the 'lie detector') simultaneously records heart-rate, respiration and sweating. Three more measure perceptual activity or acuity. The eye camera (or eye-movement camera) records the amount of time spent looking at various elements of an advertisement. The tachistoscope (or T-scope) and variometer measure a threshold level of response, the first by exposing the stimulus for increasingly larger fractions of a second until elements are recognized, the second by slowly improving very low light levels until recognition occurs. In all three cases it could be argued that nothing more than attention, a low-level response, is being proved (see HIERARCHY-OF-EFFECTS). Finally, a small handful of proprietary devices provides direct measurement of interest and involvement by having the test subjects indicate it in various ways themselves. The physiological tests are cheat-proof, a point in their favour. Respondents may react atypically under laboratory conditions, but can hardly produce a particular reaction at will. However, neither these nor the perceptual tests were purpose-made for the testing of advertisements or packaging, and they suffer in practice from the serious difficulty of knowing how to interpret the observations. The perceptual and direct-reaction tests may be susceptible to distortion by 'reactivity' on the part of the test subject. All procedures are costly, because of the need for trained experts to supervise them. In the light of these many drawbacks, it is perhaps as well that British advertising practitioners seem mostly sceptical about the value of laboratory tests for measuring effectiveness, despite the obvious enthusiasm of general advertising textbooks for describing them in detail.

(KC)

labour. One of the three basic factors of production – the others being land and capital. It comprises all persons within an economy available to participate in the production of goods and services. (MJB)

Labour Market Trends. Incorporates EMPLOYMENT GAZETTE. A monthly magazine presenting a wide range of information relating to the labour market. (MJB)

laddering. A PROJECTION TECHNIQUE used to help establish the underlying motivation behind consumer behaviour by establishing the perceived benefits derived from specific product attributes. (MJB)

LAFTA. Latin American Free Trade Association. *See* LATIN AMERICAN INTEGRATION ASSOCIATION.

laggards. *See* ADOPTER CATEGORIES.

LAIA. *See* LATIN AMERICAN INTEGRATION ASSOCIATION.

landscape. An ADVERTISING SPACE wider than it is tall, in contrast to PORTRAIT or upright format, e.g. '8 x 10 cm landscape'. (KC)

late majority. Those ADOPTERS who only buy a new product some time after its introduction and often because of difficulties in sourcing the original product for which it is a substitute. (MJB)

lateral integration. Alternative term for horizontal integration. The linking together of formerly independent units engaged at the same stage or level of production, distribution or marketing. (MJB)

lateral thinking. Concept developed by the Cambridge mathematician Edward de Bono which is of particular relevance to the idea generation stage of NEW PRODUCT DEVELOPMENT. According to de Bono, lateral thinking is a way of using the mind, a deliberate process, a general attitude which may make use of certain techniques on occasion. The most basic principle of lateral thinking is that any particular way of looking at things is only one form among many other possible ways. Lateral thinking is concerned with exploring other ways by restructuring and rearranging the information that is available. As the word 'lateral' suggests, the movement is sideways, to generate alternative patterns, instead of moving straight ahead with the development of one particular pattern. (MJB)

Latin American Integration Association (LAIA). A free trade association which replaced

the Latin American Free Trade Association (LAFTA) on 1 January 1981. Members comprise Argentina, Bolivia, Chile, Columbia, Ecuador, Mexico, Paraguay, Peru, Uruguay and Venezuela. (MCC)

latin square technique. A type of experimental design in which two experimental treatments each at several levels are administered in various combinations to experimental material. On the assumption of additivity of their effects and other simplifying assumptions, estimates of the importance of each treatment may be made. The name derives from the appearance of a diagram showing which treatment is applied to each combination of levels of treatments. Each treatment appears once only in each column and each square, in the manner of a medieval word charm. (JAB)

latitude of acceptance. *See* EGO-INVOLVEMENT.

latitude of non-commitment. *See* EGO-INVOLVEMENT.

latitude of rejection. *See* EGO-INVOLVEMENT.

law of demand. *See* DEMAND, LAW OF.

law of diminishing marginal utility. The situation which arises when the consumption of an additional unit adds less satisfaction for the consumer than that obtained from the immediately preceding unit. (MJB)

law of diminishing returns. As increments of a variable factor are added to or combined with a fixed factor then, beyond a certain point, the returns on the variable factor will decline or diminish. (MJB)

law of effect. A law which holds that learning is based on the consequences or *effect* of a given act. If the effect is positive the behaviour is likely to be reinforced and repeated if a similar occasion arises in the future – the basis of BRAND PREFERENCE. Conversely, if the effect is negative then the situation will be avoided in future. (MJB)

law of inertia of large numbers. Sampling is based on two fundamental principles of statistical theory which are usually termed the LAW OF STATISTICAL REGULARITY and the law of inertia of large numbers. The latter law holds that large groups are more stable than small groups owing to the compensating effect of deviation in opposite directions. *See* SAMPLING. (MJB)

law of statistical regularity. Sampling is based on two fundamental principles of statistical theory which are usually termed the LAW OF INERTIA OF LARGE NUMBERS and the law of statistical regularity. The latter holds that any group of objects taken from a larger group will tend to possess the same characteristics as the larger group. (MJB)

layout. The draft of a print advertisement for approval by the client. (MJB)

leading indicator. A product whose sales pattern anticipates or 'leads' those of another e.g. bricks and house building. (MJB)

leading question. A question which is constructed in such a way that it suggests the 'right' or desired answer to the respondent. Answers to such questions are of doubtful VALIDITY and so introduces BIAS into the DATA collected, e.g. 'Don't you agree ...?' (MJB)

leading series. These are certain economic time series which have been observed to move in the same direction as other major measures of economic activity, but at an earlier date. They are thus often used to forecast economic activity. (JAB)

leads and lags. A phenomenon which occurs when a currency is under pressure and threatened with devaluation. The crisis may be increased by a change in the pattern of payments for exports and imports. Any importer in the country who is due to make a payment in another currency may prefer to do so ahead of the due date lest he should incur extra costs by delay if his own currency is devalued: conversely any overseas buyer who is due to pay an account in the threatened currency will delay payment as long as possible, hoping that a devaluation will reduce the expenditure in his own currency. (JML)

lead time. The time required from the decision to do something and its achievement, e.g. the time taken from the receipt of an order to its delivery. (MJB)

lead users. Individuals or organizations for whom the benefits of early adoption of an innovation are seen as more significant than they are for others who will hold off buying until there is more evidence of the new product's superiority. Clearly, if the innovator can identify lead users they will be able to concentrate their early selling efforts on them and so accelerate the take up of the innovation. Unfortunately, this is not an easy task as firms and individuals who are early adopters on some occasions may not be equally receptive to the next round of innovation. (MJB)

lean thinking. An approach to operations and manufacturing management popularized by the work of Womack and his collaborators based upon Japanese practices particularly in the automobile industry. The lean thinking model may be summarized in five key principles:

1 The definition of VALUE from the perspective of the customer.
2 The identification of VALUE STREAMS for each product and the elimination of MUDA (WASTE) in the entire supply chain.
3 Organizing value creating activities around FLOW rather than 'batch and queue' approaches.
4 Responding to the PULL of product through the supply chain by customers to eliminate stocks.
5 The pursuit of PERFECTION.

Firms applying these principles may be thought of as 'lean enterprises'. (MJB)

learning. Learning may have a number of meanings, depending upon the context in which it is used, and Sperling (in *Psychology,* 1967) comments that 'the process of learning can consist of all, or some, or one of three steps: inventing an original solution to a problem. or thinking: committing a solution to memory, or memorizing: becoming efficient at applying the solution to a problem, or forming a habit.'

In essence there are two schools of thought concerning what is learned – the stimulus–response (S–R) school, and the cognitive school. Although there are some divisions within the S–R camp, the basic theory is that we learn to associate given responses to specific stimuli and these become habitual. One group of S–R theorists subscribes to the view that learning occurs only when there are rewards or punishments to reinforce the correct response, while others believe that learning is the result of an association between a stimulus and response occuring together, i.e. they are contiguous, and that reinforcement is not necessary. In contrast to the S–R theorists, the cognitive school argues that we learn cognitive structures, i.e. more broadly based interpretations of the association between stimuli and alternative courses of action.

In a marketing context there would seem to be support for both theories, in that some consumption behaviour is routinized and habitual (S–R school), while other purchasing decisions are subject to extensive problem-solving generalizing from past experience (cognitive school). The division of opinion about what we learn also exists in the case of how we learn. S–R theorists maintain that learning occurs through a process of trial and error – a view based on extensive experimental evidence using animals. However, some leading members of the cognitive school (notably Wolfgang Kohler) developed what is termed the GESTALT explanation of learning as being based on insight. While it seems likely that the truth is a combination of both schools of thought, in which some actions are learned through direct personal experience based upon trial and error, while others are the product of reasoning, that in seeking solutions through symbolic reasoning, the S–R explanations tend to dominate consumer-behaviour research in marketing. In turn the most sophisticated statement of S–R theory which underlies much of this consumer-behaviour research is that developed by Clark Hull in *Principles of Behaviour: An Introduction to Behaviour Theory* (1943), whose basic model is as follows:

$$E = D \times K \times H \times V$$

where E = behaviour and is a multiplicative function of D = drive, K = incentive potential, H = habit strength, and where V = intensity of the cue.

Drives are discussed at greater length under MOTIVATION, where a distinction is made between a drive which is viewed as the initial stimulus and a motive which is a tendency to activity. It is not felt that this distinction is important in the context of Hull's model. The remaining terms are essentially self-explanatory, and it is clear that in a marketing situation two of the variables – the incentive potential, or satisfaction offered by the product, and the intensity of the cue – are controllable to a considerable degree by the seller. It should also be noted that as the equation is multiplicative no reaction will occur if any of the variable has a zero value. At first sight this would seem to suggest that consumers would never try new products, for if they have not consumed them before, then H (or habit) would be expected to have a zero value.

However, this possibility is negated by the principle of generalization, whereby we extrapolate from past experience to a new situation. This potentiality is exploited by companies with generic brand names, where satisfactory experiences with one product group create a favourable predisposition towards new product groups. Of course generalization is only potential, and past experience soon teaches us that it is not always true that all the products introduced by a company will automatically yield the same level of satisfaction as the one which we originally approved of. In other words we learn to discriminate between very similar cues or stimuli.

Before leaving this brief overview of some learning-theory concepts which have been incorporated into studies of consumer behaviour, it should be noted that Howard and Sheth's *Theory of Buyer Behaviour* (1969) is essentially a learning model. It should also be noted that two important areas of research in marketing draw heavily upon learning theory for their conceptual framework – namely, the study of ADVERTISING EFFECTIVENESS and of BRAND LOYALTY.   (MJB)

learning curve. A source of study among experimental psychologists as long ago as the beginning of this century, the learning curve is a graphic depiction of the acquisition of a skill. It has important applications to manufacturing processes as calls for changes in production schedules and processes reduce efficiency because such change involves some learning/relearning. For similar reasons the cost characteristics of new products tend to improve with time as machine speeds, labour efficiency and material usage levels increase as the learning curve affects them.   (JRB)

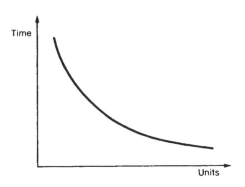

Figure 17: **Learning curve**

leased department. An area within a DEPARTMENT STORE leased to an individual or organization specializing in the sale of a particular product or service e.g. cosmetics, instant shoe repairs etc. (MJB)

leasing. The hire of an asset from its owner under the terms of a formal contract, e.g. car hire. (MJB)

least squares. This is a method of determining an equation of 'best-fit' to a set of data to enable the prediction of one variable from others. That equation is chosen which minimizes the total of the differences (after squaring them) between each data point and the corresponding mathematical properties, but equations derived from it have no validity beyond the arbitrary choice of the criterion. (JAB)

less developed countries. A term used for DEVELOPING COUNTRIES. It is now used infrequently in favour of less pejorative terms. (JK)

letter of credit. Financial document issued by one bank generally to a correspondent bank instructing it to pay money to a third person, e.g. to an exporter who has shipped goods and has documents which he can present to the bank to prove it. (JML)

level of confidence. In inferential testing, the size of TYPE I error; the chances of rejecting the null hypothesis when it is true: *See also* SIGNIFICANCE. (SKT)

level of service. The degree of satisfaction offered by a company to its customers over a period of time. Level of service is notionally quantifiable as the percentage of orders (or volume of goods) which can be supplied on time to meet the customers' demands, whether from STOCK or from current production. It is the degree to which STOCKOUTS do not affect customers. Level of service may thus be the focus of a business strategic objective. (KNB)

leverage. An additional benefit which accrues to an individual or organization by virtue of their position or relationship, e.g. ownership of a raw material in scarce supply, entitlement to landing times at an international airport etc. (MJB)

levering. Practice mostly used by meat departments of SUPERMARKETS in arranging prices for different cuts of meat so that normally high-priced cuts are less expensive, This has the effect of increasing the attractiveness of the store. (AJB)

Lewin, Kurt. The originator of field theory in psychology, which is itself a derivative of GESTALT psychology, which contradicts the prediction of dissonance theory that subjects exposed to information which contradicts an earlier decision would seek to reduce the dissonance by convincing themselves of the correctness of the original decision. According to Lewin, subjects will use the new information to review the earlier decision and may well change their mind. (MJB)

lexicographic model. When faced with the problem of choosing one alternative from among many, this model makes use of a list of criteria by order of importance. If one alternative surpasses all others on the most important criterion then it is selected, otherwise the process continues to the next criterion. Used to select an alternative from a number of sites or suppliers. (AJB)

licensing. Method of controlling, restricting or recording the number of suppliers of a product or service and/or the amount produced or sold. Its economic effect varies depending on how restrictive it is. If used simply to record, it has little effect on supply and price. At the other extreme it may be used to replace the market mechanism.

In INTERNATIONAL MARKETING licensing involves a company with marketable technology, in the form of general know-how, patents or even a trademark or brand name, exporting this intangible (rather than the product) for the payment of royalties. The company is really licensing a foreign manufacturer to produce a firm's products rather than exporting them. A company may choose this alternative to licensing if capital is scarce since in theory licensing avoids the necessity of expenditure in terms of money or effort overseas, or if the company lacks market knowledge. Alternatively, it may be necessary to license rather than lose a market where exporting or local manufacture is not possible, due to import restrictions or sensitivity to foreign ownership, as in overtly Marxist or intensely nationalistic countries or where strategic goods are involved.

Licensing appears attractive on the surface. Royalties are paid for no investment and limited expenses. There is no immediate risk involved. However such advantages tend to be short term, in addition to greater potential returns from other forms of international marketing being precluded.   (JIC)

life cycle. *See* FAMILY LIFE CYCLE, PRODUCT LIFE CYCLE.

life-style. Distinctive or characteristic ways of living adopted by communities or sections of communities, relating to general attitudes and behaviour towards the allocation of time, money and effort in the pursuit of objectives considered desirable.   (JLD)

life-style analysis. Development of market profiles from life-style measurements based on demographic information as well as ratings of consumers' activities, interests and opinions, to give a broader, more three-dimensional view of customers.   (JLD)

light pen. A computer input device that permits the direct drawing of lines on a special screen.
                                                  (SKT)

Likert scales. Differ from THURSTONE SCALES in that respondents are presented with a series of statements and asked to indicate their degree of agreement/disagreement with each. Respondents are usually offered five categories – strongly agree, agree, uncertain, disagree, strongly disagree, though three or seven divisions are used by some researchers – and are asked to select the position corresponding most closely with their opinion. By scoring a series of statements on a given subject, e.g., qualities of a BRAND, content of an ADVERTISEMENT, it is possible to construct a generalized ATTITUDE towards the object with an indication of the intensity with which the attitude is held.   (MJB)

limited decision making. Describes situations in which the decision maker seeks only limited information to supplement that already held.
                                                  (MJB)

limited function wholesaler. A stock-holding wholesaler who provides only some wholesaling functions. Typical of these are the CASH AND CARRY WHOLESALER, the drop shipper (takes title of the goods, but does not handle or deliver) or the broker (brings buyers and sellers together).
                                                  (AJB)

limited liability. A form of business organization under which the liability of the shareholders is restricted to the full nominal value of the shares which they own.   (MJB)

limited problem solving. The second stage of learning to buy a brand of product. The buyer is confronted with a new brand in a product class with which he/she is already familiar (i.e. evaluative criteria are formed and other alternatives are known). Limited search is likely to follow. (KF)

limited-service retailer/wholesaler. Those retailers/wholesalers who only provide limited services to their customers by contrast with those offering FULL SERVICE.   (MJB)

limited strategic alternatives. A concept proposed by Baker (*Marketing New Industrial Products, 1975*) based upon a military analogy, which argues that in competitive situation firms have only a very limited choice of broad strategic options open to them.

In a war situation it is usual to assume that the basic purpose of the contestants is to overcome their opponent. Further, it is also assumed that in overcoming the enemy one will also occupy their territory, which in business terms may be likened to competitive actions designed to increase one's MARKET SHARE. If we consider two armies facing each other it is clear that only a few basic choices exist. First, one may attack the enemy head-on. In a business context the frontal assault may be likened to PRICE COMPETITION between undifferentiated products. This is a very crude form of competition for ultimately it must resolve itself into a war of attrition in which the party with the greater resources must eventually win. Because of the waste implicit in such a crude strategy a preferred alternative to the frontal assault is the flanking attack. Simplistically, the theory of the flanking attack is that one identifies a weakness in an opponent's defences and then concentrates the mass of one's own efforts against this weakness. In reality, of course, opponents are equally as sensitive to the potential of a flanking attack as are their adversaries and consequently they devote considerable effort to avoiding the development of weak points in their defences. For this reason it is frequently necessary for one party to have to make a diversionary manoeuvre or feint attack in an attempt to persuade the other party to concentrate an excessive amount of their resources at one point to the detriment of some other point.

In a commercial context, the flanking attack or strategy may be likened to a policy of indirect competition based upon the creation and PROMO-TION of product differences. Clearly such a strategy places considerable emphasis upon product development and may result in a strategy of PRODUCT DIFFERENTIATION which reflects a product orientation, or a strategy of MARKET SEG-MENTATION which reflects a MARKETING ORIENTATION.

Essentially, the difference between the two approaches is that product differentiation tends to be an intuitive response of the producer faced with direct competition from an identical product. To avoid the inevitable price competition associated with a homogeneous supply the manufacturer seeks to differentiate his product in some way, although not necessarily with any clear idea of how the market will react to the differentiating factor. Therefore the emphasis tends to be on 'selling what we can make' in contrast to a policy of market segmentation which stresses 'making what we can sell'. Thus the firm pursuing a segmentation strategy starts from the premise that demand for a product is not the homogeneous entity it is frequently purported to be but rather an aggregation of lesser demands for a spectrum of different features with a common basis.

Accordingly, one sets out to measure the nature and strength of demand for variants of the basic product in order to determine whether any segment of the market is of sufficient size to warrant the development and production of a differentiated good or service.

As the history of the Second World War shows, frontal assaults and/or attempts to outflank the enemy frequently result in a stalemate between evenly matched opponents. Given such a situation a third alternative open to both parties is to lapse into a state of coexistence in which both cease to compete actively with one another so long as they feel that their territory (or market share) is not threatened by any activity of the other. Recognizing that such a strategy is essentially negative in character the military or business strategist may prefer to withdraw from a particular arena of operations. It must be emphasized that in the case of a withdrawal strategy one has control over the situation and therefore gets out with a minimum loss and on one's own terms. This is quite different from a retreat in which one is forced to retire as best one can and usually at the mercy of one's adversary.

A final strategy, and one which has most frequently led to a decisive outcome in both military and business struggles, is a strategy of INNOVA-TION. In simple terms the result of innovation is

so to change the competitive situation that one party is vested with complete superiority. Thus the invention of mechanical extensions to a man's reach, such as the long-bow, conveyed an enormous superiority upon the innovator, as did the invention of gunpowder and the concept of the Blitzkrieg based on mechanized armoured divisions. In the business context technological innovation results in the creation of a product so different from anything which has preceded it that it automatically creates a new market and endows the innovator with a monopoly of the supply to that market. Recent classic examples of this are provided by the Polaroid camera and the process of xerography. (MJB)

lineage. The standard way to describe CLASSIFIED ADVERTISING space in a newspaper or magazine: a count of the number of column-wide lines an advertisement occupies. DISPLAY ADVERTISING is sold by the COLUMN-CENTIMETRE or by fractions and multiples of a page. (KC)

linear programming. A technique developed in 1949 by G. Danzig (USA) for setting out the mathematical relationships between a complicated set of conditions and making calculations to find the ideal or optimum solution to the problem. It is usually used to solve allocation problems and it is the relationship between objectives, activities and constraints expressed in 'straight line' (linear) algebraic form. Any linear programing problem can be expressed in the following form:

$$\text{Maximize} \sum_{j=1}^{n} C_j X_j$$

$$\text{Subject to} \sum_{j=1}^{n} A_{ij} X_j \leq b_{ij} \quad \text{for} \quad C = 1, 2, ..., m$$

and $X_j >= 0$ for $j = 1, 2, ..., n$ where $X_1, ... X_n$ are the decision variables and $\sum_{j=1}^{n} C_j X_j$ is the objective function and the two sets of inequalities are the constraints. (GA)

line chart. A two-dimensional chart usually recording successive observations of a variable over time e.g. cumulative sales, prices. See HISTOGRAM. (MJB)

line extension. The addition of a new variety to an existing product line using the same brand name e.g. the Kellogg's family of breakfast cereals. *See* BRAND EXTENSION.   (MJB)

liner conference. *See* SHIPPING CONFERENCE.

Linkline. A service provided by British Telecom. Telephone numbers starting with the numbers 0345 or 0800 allow a customer, prospect, supplier or staff to call the user from anywhere in the UK at local call rates or free.   (GM)

liquidity. Ability to produce cash; especially a company's ability to produce cash or its equivalent to pay its financial obligations (debts). Such ability may be identified through two balance-sheet ratios namely current ratio and liquid ratio. Current ratio is the ratio of the total value of the current assets of a company to its total current liabilities. Liquid ratio is the ratio of current assets minus stocks to current liabilities. The liquid ratio is a safer yardstick of a company's liquidity than the current ratio because it does not involve reliance on stocks which at the critical time may not be readily saleable.   (GA)

liquidity ratio. *See* ACID TEST.

list price. In the USA the price that users are normally asked to pay for products, or the price that a manufacturer has established for the products in his range and which can be varied by add-on or discounting percentages.   (AJB)

literature search. The study of SECONDARY DATA to determine what is known about a topic under investigation. *See* DESK RESEARCH.   (MJB)

livery. In the marketing context, such elements of CORPORATE IDENTITY as corporate colour schemes, symbols, uniforms and so on.   (KC)

Lloyds. Incorporated society of private insurers in London, established in the seventeenth century. Although its activities were originally confined to the conduct of marine insurance business, a very considerable world-wide market for the transaction of other classes of insurance business in non-marine, aviation and motor markets has been built up. Lloyds is regulated by a series of special Acts of Parliament, dating from 1871 to 1982.

Lloyds is not a company but a market for insurance administered by the Committee of Lloyds, where business is transacted by individ-

ual underwriters for their own account and risk and in competition with each other and with insurance companies. Lloyds does not accept insurance itself: insurance may only be placed through Lloyd's brokers who negotiate with Lloyd's underwriters on behalf of the insured. Only elected underwriting members of Lloyd's, who must transact insurance with unlimited liability and who have met the most stringent financial regulations laid down by the Committee, are permitted to transact business at Lloyd's; these safeguards give security to the Lloyd's policy.

There are over 20,000 underwriting members of Lloyd's grouped into about 430 syndicates and represented at Lloyd's by underwriting agents who accept risks on behalf of the members of their syndicates.   (HMSO)

loaded question. A less obvious variant of the LEADING QUESTION in that the words or phrase which points the RESPONDENT to a given answer is disguised or more subtle, e.g. 'Should the wearing of rear seat belts be made compulsory to save lives?' By including a reason 'to save lives', it becomes less likely that respondents will disagree than might have been the case if the 'save lives' proposition had been left out.   (MJB)

lobbying. An attempt to influence those with the power to make decisions in favour of the individual or organization likely to be affected by the decision.   (MJB)

local advertising. Advertising carried in a local media vehicle, as against a national media vehicle: local press, local radio station etc.
          (JRB)

local press. The collective description for newspapers and, less often, magazines that circulate only in a local area, e.g. the *Saffron Walden Reporter* or *Cotswold Life*. Boundaries are often blurred in practice between this designation and REGIONAL PRESS; the implied contrast is with the NATIONAL PRESS.   (KC)

location decisions. The location of a manufacturing plant, a warehouse, or a retail store requires a decision which balances the attractiveness features such as benefits of large scale, with the deterrence features such as the cost of reaching the market, or the centre. Many of the features may be quantified and evaluated making possible the construction of a model to guide the decision.   (AJB)

logistics. The strategic management of the movement and storage of material into production and thence, as finished goods into the distribution channels to the final purchaser.   (AJB)

logo. *See* LOGOTYPE.

logotype. Commonly referred to as 'logo'. This is used on company packaging, the term given to the BRAND NAME/COMPANY name which visually identifies a particular product or service by its typography and design characteristics. Most companies take care to register their product logos to provide some protection against counterfeiting, in recognition of the value of the logo in the market place.   (JRB)

longitudinal design. In contrast with cross-sectional designs, SAMPLING designs where more than one time point is involved.   (SKT)

longitudinal study. In contrast with cross-sectional studies, a study where information is collected at more than one point in time.   (SKT)

long-range plan. Any plan which covers a period beyond that normally used for budgeting and control purposes, usually more than one year. While some commentators recommend a minimum of 3–5 years, and some even 5–10 years, experience shows that the period must be realistic in terms of the rate of change in technology and the MARKET place. Thus in very volatile markets or for companies which are

experiencing difficulties, short-term horizons may be much more appropriate.   (MJB)

long run. *See* DEMAND, LONG RUN.

loose insert. An INSERT that is not bound into the spine of a magazine. Newspaper inserts are by definition 'loose', except in magazine sections.   (KC)

loss leader. A product or service whose price is deliberately cut to a point below its cost in the hope of attracting additional customers willing to buy profitable items. Supermarket grocers traditionally offer a limited number of goods at deep price cuts in the hope of enticing customers into their shops.   (JRB)

love needs. *See* MOTIVATION.

lower class, lower-lower class, lower-middle class, lower-upper class. *See* SOCIO-ECONOMIC CLASSIFICATIONS.

low involvement goods. Goods which are bought routinely by the consumer without much thought, search or purchase time.   (AJB)

loyalty, brand. *See* BRAND LOYALTY.

luxury goods. Certain commodities are called luxuries, which are PRODUCTS that are not considered essential or necessary to everyday life, but are expensive pleasures or comforts, e.g. hand-made chocolates, limousines, designer clothes.   (MDP)

M

machine-readable code. Printed material that can be directly read in by a computer peripheral, and designed primarily for that purpose: BAR CODES and special magnetic ink systems are examples of machine readable codes.   (SKT)

macro environment. The external environment as determined by the major environmental forces – demographic, economic, legal, political, social etc.– which is common to all organizations and which largely controls the MICRO ENVIRONMENT within which firms compete with one another.
    (MJB)

macro marketing. The area of study of the nation's exchange process, within its own borders, in which political, cultural, social and economic interactions are examined.   (AJB)

macrosegmentation. The subdivision of industrial or business-to-business markets into segments according to the type of buying organization.   (MJB)

Madison Avenue. Between Park Avenue and Fifth Avenue in New York City, this used to be the address of most major American advertising agencies. It is therefore used figuratively to stand for the whole American advertising business, as 'Wall Street' is for its financial institutions. (KC)

mailing lists. A comprehensive listing of the title, names and addresses of the members of clubs, societies, associations, companies, colleges or other groupings who share a common interest. Mailing lists are of value as they constitute target MARKETS or segments of people with interests, or purchasing characteristics, in common. Mail order companies jealously guard their mailing lists as they are central to their business. Often mailing lists are the result of self-selected groups which present attractive target audiences for the promotion of goods and services. Travel agents specializing in winter sports holidays, for example, use the mailing lists of the membership details of ski clubs to circulate details of forthcoming holidays at the appropriate times of the year. Similarly, hotels build up mailing lists of people who have used their facilities and who can become prime targets, if used selectively for concessionary or promotional offers. Access to mailing lists can be sold, although organizations making their list available do not usually actually pass over the details to the interested user. Rather they prefer to arrange for the mailing of the circulars, brochures or promotional material to their members which have been supplied by the promoters. In this way the organization retains the exclusivity and confidentiality of its mailing list and can obtain repeat fees should the promoter wish to use the list on future occasions. Once divulged, mailing lists can be copied and sold to other users and the list originator loses control of it.   (BRM)

mail interview. A survey method which uses the mail to circulate a structured self-completion questionnaire to the chosen respondents. Its main advantage is low cost. Its main disadvantage is low response rates – usually around 20 per cent. These may be significantly improved through careful sample selection.   (MJB)

mail order. A method of selling in which the product or service is promoted by either media advertising or DIRECT MAIL and the prospective buyer is invited to order by post. The product is then usually delivered through the mail, though larger items will be delivered by carrier. If the promotional vehicle is media advertising, the alternative term is DIRECT RESPONSE ADVERTISING.

(KC)

mail order retailing. The selling of products using the postal service for delivery to the customer. Purchases may be selected from a mail order catalogue or be placed in direct response to an advertisement. (MJB)

mail order wholesaler. A wholesaler that services its customers by filling orders from a catalogue issued by it. (MJB)

mail questionnaire. *See* MAIL SURVEY.

mail shot. A colloquial expression used to describe a sales promotional letter and/or brochure sent by post to a named individual (or family) at his or her home or place of work. It is a direct mail sales approach to a preselected target group of recipients thought to be existing, or potential, users of the promoted goods or service. (BRM)

mail survey. MARKET RESEARCH questions sent to potential RESPONDENTS who are encouraged to answer and return them. This survey method is particularly valuable where the POPULATION of target respondents is large, and perhaps widely dispersed. Although the initial overall costs of a mail survey may appear very attractive, the true costs depend on effective response rates, and these can vary significantly. Techniques used to enhance response rates include: (a) using a QUESTIONNAIRE package that is personalized, (b) enclosing a covering letter detailing the benefits of filling out the questionnaire; (c) offering a free gift or monetary incentive; (d) sending reminder letters to non-respondents (e) enclosing a stamped self-addressed envelope. See MAIL INTERVIEW. (AMW)

major media. The five principal ADVERTISING MEDIA: press, television, outdoor, radio and cinema. Some might argue that the last two are not major on the grounds that they shared just 3.9 per cent of total media advertising expenditure between them in 1996, but the description is entrenched. The description corresponds to ABOVE-THE-LINE, but has a quite different origin.

(KC)

Mallen, Bruce E. Professor of Marketing at Concordia University, Canada from 1964; consultant and adviser to industry, commerce and governments. His studies have centred on channels of distribution. He has contributed to several guides, textbooks and journals in Canada, USA and the UK. His publications include *Principles of Marketing Channel Management* (1977).

(AJB)

mall intercept. A research method in which prospective respondents are intercepted in a shopping mall and asked if they will participate in a survey, product test etc. *See* SAMPLING.(MJB)

management-by-walking about (MBWA). One of the attributes of excellent companies described by Thomas J. Peters and R.H. Waterman in *In Search of Excellence* (New York: Harper & Row, 1982). (MJB)

management contracting. A contract, often a joint venture, under which one firm provides management expertise to another which provides the capital. Often encountered in international markets. (MJB)

management information system (MIS). Like the MARKETING INFORMATION SYSTEM a formal method for collecting all kinds of information relevant to the management of an organization and making it available to appropriate decision makers. The marketing information system is a subset of the larger management information system. (MJB)

manufacturer's agent. A salesman who represents one or more non-competing manufacturers for commission on sales. He performs no other function than selling. (AJB)

manufacturer's brand. A brand created by a manufacturer and promoted by them direct to the public. Sometimes referred to as a 'national brand'. *See* OWN LABEL. (MJB)

margin. The difference between the cost and the selling price. (MJB)

marginal analysis. A method of analysis developed by neo-classical economists such as J.M. Clark, MARSHALL and Pareto, founded upon the concepts of marginal utility and marginal productivity. The essence of the approach is that attention is focused upon the effect of changes in the value of one variable arising from the addition of one more (marginal) unit to another variable. According to the theory one should continue to incur costs to the point when marginal revenue is exactly equivalent to the marginal cost necessary to create that revenue, at which point profits will be maximized. Marginal analysis of this kind is often referred to as a contribution approach on the grounds that so long as marginal revenue exceeds marginal cost then the surplus is a contribution to fixed costs (which exist anyway) and profit. *See* CONTRIBUTION ANALYSIS.

(MJB)

marginal cost pricing. According to this method, marginal costing often means variable or direct costing, which is the economists' marginal cost averaged over a large block of output units. Economists generally use the term 'marginal cost' to describe the increase in total costs, starting from a given level of output, that results from an additional unit of output without expanding the firm's production and distribution facilities, and while marginal costs and variable costs per unit may be the same at a given level of output, the economist clearly distinguishes between marginal and variable cost per unit. This approach is not exactly equivalent to the economists's approach of equating marginal cost and revenue, but it is a practical application of the principle which takes into account the cost of costing, time available for making calculations, the degree of accuracy required, and the multidimensional features of the modern firm.

The philosophy underlying this approach to costing is that fixed costs are unavoidable, and that what matters is to cover variable cost and make some CONTRIBUTION to fixed cost. Whether or not to accept an order depends on what contribution will be made to fixed costs after variable costs are covered. The approach is an attempt to take account of the fact that it is difficult to allocate fixed overhead cost to production on a basis varying with the level of output and the recognition that the resources available for meeting the fixed expenses of a business depend directly on the contribution, which is the difference between sales revenue and variable costs, and a firm should seek to fix its prices so as to maximize its total contribution. In deciding prices according to this approach, fixed cost must be omitted from unit cost and the price determined on the basis of marginal cost.

Marginal cost pricing is generally seen as being superior to full cost pricing for some or all

of the following reasons: (a) it is more effective in the short run than full costing because of the virtual impossibility of calculating the total cost of different products in a product portfolio and because the optimal relationship between cost and prices will vary substantially both among different products and between different markets. Further, the emphasis upon innovation and the rate of change means that long-run situations are often highly unpredictable so that one should aim at maximizing contribution in the short run. (b) It lends a marketing rather than a costing orientation to pricing policy; prices are fixed in relation to market conditions so as to take advantage of the elasticity of demand (*see* DEMAND, PRICE ELASTICITY OF). (c) Marginal cost is more relevant to pricing decisions than absorption cost as it reflects future as distinct from present cost levels and cost relationships. (d) Marginal cost pricing permits a manufacturer to develop a policy to make prices more differentiated and more flexible through time which leads to higher sales and possibly reduced marginal costs through increased marginal physical productivity and lower input factor prices. (e) It gives a much clearer indication of profit potential and so enables decision makers to decide better which products they should sell in what markets. (MJB)

marginal propensity to consume. The proportion of each additional unit of income which one is willing to spend on increased consumption.

(MJB)

marginal propensity to save. The proportion of each additional unit of income which one is willing to save. (MJB)

marginal revenue. The additional revenue generated by selling one more unit of output.

(MJB)

mark-down. A reduction in the price asked usually expressed as a percentage of the recommended sale price. (MJB)

market. Strictly speaking, a physical location where buyers and sellers come together in order to exchange products or services with one another. Over time this concept became extended to include places where buyers and sellers met to exchange a title to goods, particularly in the case of commodities and commodity exchanges. Given improvement in communications, the concept of a market has now come to refer to any situation where buyers and sellers are in communication with one another without the need for any specific physical location designated as a market, e.g. the market for money or shares. In a marketing context the term is also used to designate the demand for a specific product or a specific physical area such as the American market or the Japanese market.   (MJB)

market aggregation. The use of an UNDIFFEREN-TIATED MARKETING STRATEGY which treats all the potential customers in exactly the same way.
(MJB)

market atomization. The opposite of MARKET AGGREGATION i.e. a marketing strategy which treats every individual customer as a unique market segment.   (MJB)

market attractiveness. A summary measure of the perceived profitability of a market or market segment used in making MARKET ENTRY DECI-SIONS. *See* AUDIT, MARKETING.   (MJB)

market build-up method. A method of estimating the market potential of a new or existing product. It calls for identifying all the potential buyers for the product in each market (segment) and adding up the estimated potential purchasers for each. Because it requires a list of all potential buyers and a good estimate of what each will buy, it is usually used by industrial goods companies operating in OLIGOPOLISTIC MARKETS.   (GA)

market challenger strategy. One of four basic competitive marketing strategies identified by Philip Kotler (*Marketing Management,* 4th edn, 1980) the others being MARKET LEADER, MARKET FOLLOWER and MARKET NICHE.
  Market challengers are seen as those firms in an industry/market which are next, in terms of market share, to the leaders and are actively challenging the leaders for their dominant position. In essence the challenger has three strategic alternatives open to him: (a) direct or head-on attack using cost/price/value for money as the key strategic variable; (b) an indirect or flanking approach using product differentiation or promotional activities as a means for winning consumer preference and loyalty; and (c) a by-pass strategy based upon radical innovation through which the challenger seeks to change existing purchasing behaviour in favour of a new solution to basic consumer needs. *See* LIMITED STRATEGIC ALTER-NATIVES.   (MJB)

market concentration. *See* CONCENTRATION.

market coverage. A measure which indicates the degree of market exposure achieved. It is the total product sales of all the producer's retail customers expressed as a percentage of all retail sales for the product group or classification. May be calculated by value or volume. Used by suppliers of groceries, and other convenience goods.
(AJB)

market coverage strategy. A definition of strategy in terms of product types and market segments, with selection of suitable combinations being made using a grid of options. (AJB)

market demand. Strictly speaking the total demand for a good arrived at by adding together the individual demand of all potential consumers of the product. By aggregating the quantity demanded by all consumers at any given price one is able to construct a demand curve for the market as a whole.   (MJB)

market development. One of the four generic strategies identified in Ansoff's GROWTH VECTOR MATRIX. It involves introducing present products into new geographical markets.   (MJB)

market-driven economy. A form of economic organization in which the forces of supply and demand determine price and, thereby, what goods and services will be produced for whom. Often referred to as a 'free market economy'.   (MJB)

market entry strategy. The strategy selected for entering a market for the first time. The basic choice is between a PENETRATION and SKIMMING approach when one uses a low price, extensive distribution and mass advertising or high price, selective distribution and targeted advertising respectively.   (MJB)

market follower. A firm which takes its lead from other more dominant firms in the market qv. MARKET LEADER.   (MJB)

market follower strategy. One of four basic competitive marketing strategies identified by Philip Kotler (*Marketing Management,* 4th edn, 1980) others being MARKET CHALLENGER, MARKET LEADER and MARKET NICHE. Market followers tend to constitute the majority of firms in a market albeit that their collective share may only account for 20–30 per cent of total sales. While

no market follower is likely to challenge the leader or its immediate competitors this is not to say that they do not indulge in very active competition between themselves. Denied the ECONOMIES OF SCALE which accrue to the larger firms the followers have to be particularly efficient in their marketing and service policies if they are to survive and many of them choose to develop a concentrated or market niche strategy.
(MJB)

marketing. There is no single, universally agreed definition of marketing and a selection of those in common currency underlines the diversity of perspectives adopted by different authors, viz.:

(1) Marketing is the process of determining consumer demand for a product or service, motivating its sale and distributing it into ultimate consumption at a profit (E.F.L. Brech, *Principles of Management*, 1953).

(2) Marketing is selling goods that don't come back to people who do.

(3) Marketing is not only much broader than selling, it is not a specialized activity at all. It encompasses the entire business. It is the whole business seen from the point of view of its final result, that is, from the customer's point of view. Concern and responsibility for marketing must therefore permeate all areas of the enterprise (Peter F. Drucker, *The Practice of Management*, 1954).

(4) Marketing is the distinguishing, the unique function of the business (ibid.).

(5) Marketing – the performance of business activities that direct the flow of goods and services from producer to consumer or user.

Marketing is the creation of time, place and possession utilities.

Marketing moves goods from place to place, stores them, and effects changes in ownership by buying and selling them.

Marketing consists of the activities of buying, selling, transporting and storing goods.

Marketing includes those business activities involved in the flow of goods and services between producers and consumers (Converse, Huegy and Mitchell, *Elements of Marketing*, 7th edn, 1965).

(6) Marketing is the set of human activities directed at facilitating and consummating exchanges (Kotler, *Marketing Management*, 2nd edn, 1972).

(7) The delivery of a standard of living.

(8) Marketing is the process whereby society, to supply its consumption needs, evolves distributive systems composed of participants, who, interacting under constraints – technical (economic) and ethical (social) – create the transactions or flows which resolve market separations and result in exchange and consumption (Robert Bartels, 'The General Theory of Marketing', *Journal of Marketing*, XXXII (Jan 1968) pp. 29–33).

(9) The function of marketing is the establishment of contact (Paul T. Cherington, *The Elements of Marketing*, 1920).

The proliferation of definitions was the subject of an article entitled 'What Exactly is Marketing' (*Quarterly Review of Marketing*, Winter 1975) in which Keith Crosier reviewed over fifty definitions and classified them into three major groups:

(a) Definitions which conceive of marketing as a process 'enacted via the marketing channel connecting the producing company with its market', e.g. 'The primary management function which organizes and directs the aggregate of business activites involved in converting customer purchasing power into effective demand for a specific product or service and in moving the product or service to the final customer or user, so as to achieve company-set profit or other objectives' (L.W. Rodger, *Marketing in a Competitive Economy*, 3rd revised edn, 1971).

(b) Definitions which see marketing as a concept or philosophy of business – 'the idea that marketing is a social exchange process involving willing consumers and producers', e.g. 'Selling is preoccupied with the seller's need to convert his product into cash; marketing with the idea of satisfying the needs of the customer by means of the product and the whole cluster of things associated with creating, delivering and finally consuming it' (T. Levitt, 'Marketing Myopia', *Harvard Business Review*, 1960).

(c) Definitions which emphasize marketing as an orientation – 'present to some degree in both consumers and producers: the phenomenon which makes the concept and the process possible'. Only one example is cited by Crosier (from the philosopher Erich Fromm) and is felt to be an unconvincing argument in favour of a third category beyond the view of marketing as a function or as a concept. However, one cannot argue with Crosier's final group of definitions, which seem agreed only on the point that marketing is a complex and confusing phenomenon that combines both the philosophy of business and its practice.

There is a general consensus in these definitions but there is no single definition. An explanation of this is to be found in M. Halbert, *The Meaning and Sources of Marketing Theory* (1965): 'Marketing, however, has no recognized central theoretical basis such as exists for many other disciplines, notably the physical sciences and, in some cases, the behavioural sciences.' Despite the absence of a central theoretical core there are clear indications that marketing, like medicine and engineering before it, is emerging as a practical, synthetic and applied discipline in its own right. (MJB)

marketing audit. *See* AUDIT, MARKETING.

marketing budget. A term generally applied to that sum of expenditure agreed to be spent on sales promotion, advertising, trade promotions/discounts, consumer promotions and allied expenditures. A term which normally excludes the cost of running the salesforce and often (but not always) excludes the cost of market research. (JRB)

marketing channels. The sets of firms who have cooperated in the production, marketing, wholesaling, physical distribution and retailing of the product or service of a particular producer, in order to place the product in the possession of the end user. (AJB)

marketing communications. The process of using communication techniques for a marketing purpose. In the familiar 'four Ps' version of the MARKETING MIX, 'promotion' has the same meaning. (KC)

marketing communications mix. A subset of the MARKETING MIX that is available to be deployed in the pursuit of communication objectives, this mix-within-a-mix takes the form of a 'menu' of familiar and less familiar techniques. Authors differ as to its scope and the terminology of its ingredients, but it is not unduly controversial to suggest that it comprises ADVERTISING, PUBLICITY, DIRECT MARKETING, SALES PROMOTION, PACKAGING, SPONSORSHIP and PERSONAL SELLING. Though the last of these is routinely included in published definitions, its distinctive characteristics – particularly the direct and unmediated person-to-person communication involved – should probably place it in a category by itself. The alternative term 'promotional mix' is equally common, following the familiar 'four Ps' version of the marketing mix, but risks terminological confusion with 'PROMOTIONS' and SALES PROMOTION. (KC)

marketing communications plan. A formal, written-down framework for planning MARKETING COMMUNICATIONS campaigns. There are surprisingly few templates for its construction in the standard textbooks, and structures vary considerably in practice. The proposal which follows is more complete than most, and empahises that this in an action plan by its use of questions to be answered.

1 RAW MATERIALS
What and whom is this plan about?

1.1 *Product or Service Profile*
Specification: what can it do?
Benefits: what can it offer?
1.2 *Company or Organization Profile*
Specification: what do we do?
Identity: how do we present ourselves?
Image: how are we seen?
1.3 *Audience Profile*
Socio-demographics: who are they, and where?
Psychographics: what do they want?
1.4 *Market Profile*
Structure: what does it look like?
Competition: who is there with us?
Dynamics: what's in the future?

2 CONSTRAINTS
What externalities need to be taken into account?
2.1 *Marketing Mix*
Product policy: what effect on communication strategy?
Pricing policy: what effect on communication strategy?
'Place' policy: what effect on communication strategy?
2.2 *Givens*
Precedents: what is traditional?
Mandatories: what is compulsory?
2.3 *Budget*
Appropriation: what funds are available?
Allocations: how and where are they to be spent?
Control: how will cost-effectiveness be monitored?

3 OBJECTIVES
What is this plan meant to achieve?

3.1 *Goals:* what are our overall, long-term aims?

3.2 *Targets:*	what are the intermediate aims of this plan?
3.3 *Criteria:*	how will communication effectiveness be measured?

4 STRATEGY
How will this plan meet its objectives?

4.1 *Message:*	what do we want to tell the audience?
4.2 *Creative:*	how do we want to tell them?
4.3 *Vehicle:*	what means will we use to do so?

5 TIMETABLE
How will the strategies become a campaign?

5.1 *Timescale:*	how soon must the objectives be met?
5.2 *Schedule:*	what needs to happen when?

6 IMPLEMENTATION
How will the campaign be managed?

6.1 *Authority:*	who can say yes or no?
6.2 *Responsibility:*	who will co-ordinate it?
6.3 *Delegation:*	what will be sub-contracted?
6.4 *Procedures:*	how will we keep track of progress?
6.5 *Evaluation:*	how will we measure results?

(KC)

marketing concept. Like marketing, the marketing concept has been the subject of numerous attempts at definition. Essentially, it would seem to consist of three basic elements: (a) a consumer orientation by which is meant the belief that the consumer should be the centre of all the organization's thinking and activities; (b) an orientation which seeks to coordinate and integrate all the organization's efforts towards common goals; (c) a profit orientation by which the company seeks to achieve its goals through maximizing consumer satisfaction rather than by maximizing sales. However, despite these three common features the marketing concept is sometimes conceived of as a philosophy which directs the company's thinking and sometimes as an operating policy for solving its problems.

In recent years, there has been some concern that the original marketing concept is inadequate to ensure the social responsibility of the organization. To reflect this the modern marketing concept is also based on three elements: consumer satisfaction, company profits, and community welfare (the three Cs).   (MJB)

marketing databank. A file of marketing data compiled from both internal and external sources.   (MJB)

marketing decision support system. *See* DECISION SUPPORT SYSTEM.

marketing effort. The total amount of company resources invested into the marketing mix (price, promotion, place, product) for the purpose of generating sales.   (GA)

marketing environment. The MACRO ENVIRONMENT and MICRO ENVIRONMENT within which firms compete with one another.   (MJB)

marketing expense to sales ratio. The ratio (more often a percentage figure) of marketing expenditure (*see* MARKETING BUDGET) to sales revenue/gross sales revenue. Such a ratio is typically one of a number of financial criteria to judge the competence of the control over profitability demanded by an organization from its marketing function. The organization's financial strategy may strictly constrain this ratio as a means of controlling profitability.   (JRB)

marketing flows. Activities which must be undertaken within the marketing channel to result in the transfer of ownership. Definitions of the activities vary but may include negotiation, ordering, financing, information, service, and security flows.   (AJB)

marketing information systems (MkIS). The systematic organization of all marketing data required by a business organization to provide a reliable, illuminating and timely flow of information to marketing and general management. *See* MANAGEMENT INFORMATION SYSTEMS.   (JRB)

marketing information system subsystems. The individual subunits or modules that make up the MkIS. In a well developed, sophisticated system, there are eight modules: sales, forecasting, PRODUCT planning, MARKET RESEARCH, distribution, pricing, promotion and NEW PRODUCT DEVELOPMENT. Data flows freely between the subsystems and externally to the Production Information System, Financial

Information System etc. which collectively make up the MANAGEMENT INFORMATION SYSTEM (MIS). (KRD)

Marketing Initiative. One element of a multi-stream attempt sponsored by the UK Department of Trade and Industry to improve the technical and managerial skills of small and medium-sized companies, by the provision of subsidized consultancy services. The Marketing Initiative, launched in 1988, was administered by the Chartered Institute of Marketing and replaced a number of previous schemes with a similar intention (e.g. Support for Marketing, Better Business Services). The DTI paid half the cost of between five and fifteen man-days of consultancy. In Assisted Areas and Urban Programme Areas the DTI paid two-thirds of the cost and the client paid for the remainder. (KNB)

marketing intelligence systems. A basic component of the MARKETING INFORMATION SYSTEMS, providing marketing executives with current information about developments and changing conditions in the macro and task environments (competitors, customers, suppliers etc.). The efficiency of such systems can be augmented by improved training of sales people in their intelligence responsibilities, the development of a marketing-intelligence centre, and the purchase of information when appropriate from specialized intelligence services. (GA)

marketing intermediary. *See* INTERMEDIARY.

marketing management. The act of managing the marketing function. Given the lack of any agreed definition of what MARKETING is, it is not surprising that the term is used very loosely to embrace individuals with very narrow and specific responsibilities as well as persons responsible for coordinating and controlling the marketing activities of major MULTI-NATIONAL CORPORATIONS. (MJB)

marketing manager. The person responsible for the management of the marketing function. (MJB)

marketing mix. The idea of a mix of marketing functions was conceived by Professor Neil Borden of the Harvard Business School as 'a schematic plan to guide analysis of marketing problems through utilization of: (a) a list of the important forces emanating from the market which bear upon the marketing operations of an enterprise; (b) a list of the elements (procedures and policies) of marketing programmes' (*Science in Marketing,* 1965). The marketing mix refers to the apportionment of effort, the combination, the design, and the integration of the elements of marketing into a programme or mix which, on the basis of appraisal of the market forces, will best achieve the objectives of an enterprise at a given time.

A search of the available literature concerned with marketing mix components reveals that there is a wide diversity of opinion among marketers on what elements compose the marketing mix. Of these alternatives, perhaps the best known is that proposed by McCarthy which comprises four elements described as the four Ps, namely product, price, place and promotion.

The longest list is that proposed by Borden himself which contains twelve subdivisions as follows: (a) merchandising-product planning; (b) pricing; (c) branding; (d) channels of distribution; (e) personal selling; (f) advertising; (g) promotion; (h) packaging; (i) display; (j) servicing; (k) physical handling; (l) fact finding and analysis, marketing research. (MJB)

marketing mix equation. The application in the market of a package of marketing activities – made up of the four Ps; product, price, promotion and place – calculated to result in a desired level of revenue and income to the organization may be loosely described as an equation. All marketing planning is logically based on the assumption that such an equation exists. (JRB)

marketing mix modification. The activity of changing the balance in the package of four Ps. *See* MARKETING MIX EQUATION. (JRB)

marketing mix optimization. The concept that for any one product at any one time there is a unique blend of marketing activity which will maximize the chances of achieving the organization's desired objectives for that product. An attractive and logically impeccable idea, frequently impractical in its realization. (JRB)

marketing objective. The goal or result to be achieved through marketing activities. (MJB)

marketing orientation. In the conduct of business, at least five distinct business functions are involved, namely Research and Development, Production, Sales, Finance and MARKETING. One or other of these functions is likely to dominate the others so that the whole business is orientated in terms of the key attributes of that function. In the case of a marketing orientation, it has been suggested by Edward S. McKay (*The Marketing Mystique,* New York: American Management Association, 1972), that these key features are as follows. (a) The focus is on the MARKET place – customers, competitors and distributors. (b) A commercial intelligence system monitors the market. (c) It requires recognition that change is inevitable, but manageable in the business arena. (d) The business is committed to strategic business and MARKETING PLANNING and to creative PRODUCT planning. (e) The emphasis is on profit – not just volume – with growth and profit kept in balance.

It goes without saying that marketers believe that all organizations should be marketing orientated – a view which has attracted growing support from top management and largely accounts for the current attention given to the MARKETING CONCEPT (orientation) and the marketing function.   (MJB)

marketing plan. A plan which focuses on a particular PRODUCT/MARKET and details the resources, strategies and programmes for achieving the products objectives in that market. Most plans contain eight sections: executive summary, current MARKETING situation, opportunity and issue ANALYSIS, objectives, MARKETING STRATEGY, action programmes, projected profit and loss statement and controls.   (KRD)

marketing research. *See* MARKET RESEARCH.

marketing strategy. The establishment of the goal or purpose of a STRATEGIC BUSINESS UNIT and the means by which it is to be achieved through management of the marketing function. *See* STRATEGIC MARKETING PLANNING.   (MJB)

market leader. A dominant firm which has the largest market share and which tends to set the terms for competition within the market particularly in terms of the marketing mix to be used.
                                                        (MJB)

market leader strategy. One of four basic competitive marketing strategies identified by Philip Kotler (*Marketing Management,* 4th edn, 1980) the others being MARKET challenger, market follower and MARKET NICHE. By definition there can only be one market leader in a given industry/market and its dominant position may have arisen from any one or combination of several factors. Frequently, the market leader was first to market and has maintained its lead as other rival firms have attempted to emulate it. In many cases, the innovator has had patent protection and this has enabled him to develop a dominant position before direct competition has become possible, e.g. Polaroid in instant photography, Xerox in dry-copying. In other situations, the dominant firm was not first to market but, due to its greater efficiency in either production and/or marketing it has been able to secure the leading share of the market.

Market leader strategies are often defensive in character, particularly where the firm controls a market share which might be construed as enabling it to exercise MONOPOLY power (25 per cent or more in the UK). In such situations growth may be easier to achieve by expanding the total market size through stimulating primary demand or by diversifying into a completely new market. In stimulating primary demand the basic options available are: (a) find new users; (b) find new uses; (c) encourage greater usage.   (MJB)

market logistics. A view of the design of a LOGISTICS system which starts at the customer with package design and then structures carton design and handling equipment suited to each stage of the movement and storage process.   (AJB)

market managers. Managers responsible for some or all of the marketing activities in one, usually of a number, of the markets in which the organization operates. This system of marketing management is used where the differences between markets dominate marketing options and hence where it makes sense to 'manage' markets (as against PRODUCT MANAGEMENT).
                                                        (JRB)

market map. A depiction of brand relationship by plotting on axes representing consumer perceptions arrived at by SCALING TECHNIQUES in a product space. Consumers may also be plotted in a similar or the same ('joint') space, to indicate combinations of product attributes represented or not by products. The methods are elegant, but their contribution is more in illustrating relationships already known than in discovering unsuspected new product opportunities.   (JAB)

market measurement. Usually applied to fundamental measurement of market volume, value, brand shares and the trends of all of these. Data for these may be collected from secondary sources, from special censuses or surveys, or from syndicated research such as CONSUMER PANELS. The definition of the market to be measured is often difficult, and depends on the marketing or corporate objectives involved.

(JAB)

market niche strategy. One of four basic competitive marketing strategies identified by Philip Kotler (*Marketing Management,* 4th edn, 1980) the others being MARKET CHALLENGER, MARKET FOLLOWER and MARKET LEADER. A market niche strategy coincides with a concentrated marketing strategy in that the firm realizes that it lacks the resources to compete directly with bigger firms in the industry and so seeks to identify a particular niche or segment of the market upon which it can concentrate all its energies. The key to success in developing such a strategy is to define a viable MARKET SEGMENT and then develop an offering which is perceived as differentiated from the competition by the users comprising the segments thereby by conferring a temporary MONOPOLY upon the supplier. (MJB)

market opportunity analysis. A formal and preferably structured attempt to identify future situations which may be exploited to the advantage of the organization. Market opportunity analysis is one of the four basic elements of the strategic or STRENGTH, WEAKNESSES, OPPORTUNITIES, THREATS (SWOT) analysis in which the firm seeks to identify threats and opportunities in the environment as a basis for maximizing its strengths and avoiding or rectifying its weaknesses. A wide variety of techniques from simple extrapolation through to technological forecasting may be employed in seeking to identify and define market opportunities. (MJB)

market opportunity index. A rank ordering of market opportunities identified through market opportunity analysis in terms of the criteria considered most relevant to the firm in terms of its present and future strengths and weaknesses.

(MJB)

market penetration. One of four basic strategies proposed by Igor Ansoff whereby the company seeks increased sales for its present products in its present markets through more aggressive promotion and distribution. The other three strategies are MARKET DEVELOPMENT, PRODUCT DEVELOPMENT and DIVERSIFICATION. (MJB)

market positioning. The development of a marketing strategy utilizing any or all of the elements of the MARKETING MIX which enables one to distinguish and occupy a niche or segment of the market in which one enjoys a competitive advantage over one's rivals. (MJB)

market potential. An estimate of effective demand, i.e. demand backed up by purchasing power, for a specific product or service during a defined period of time in the future. In common usage, the potential market for a product is considered to be synonymous with the total effective demand. *See* DEMAND. (MJB)

market profile. The description of a market in terms of salient characteristics which must be taken into account when developing an effective MARKETING PLAN. Such a profile may be based upon any of the key MARKET SEGMENTATION variables but is usually a composite of demographic, behavioural and psychographic factors. (MJB)

market research. A branch of social science which uses scientific methods to collect information about all those factors which impinge upon the marketing of goods and services, and so includes the measurement and analysis of markets, the study of advertising effectiveness, distributive channels, competitive products and marketing policies and the whole field of consumer behaviour. In his *Principles of Management,* 2nd edn, E.F.L. Brech defines the objective of undertaking research as 'To reduce the areas of uncertainty surrounding business decisions'. The British Institute of Management defines marketing research as 'The objective gathering, recording and analysing of all facts about problems relating to the transfer and sale of goods and services from producer to consumer or user.' The last word in this definition emphasizes that marketing research is equally concerned with industrial goods, a point which is frequently overlooked in definitions which refer solely to consumers. (MJB)

market sales potential. An estimate of the total sales achievable within a market given the adoption of a given marketing mix. (MJB)

market segment. Buyers who have broadly similar needs and wants which differ in some relevant way from those of other customers in the same market. (MJB)

market segmentation. In essence, the concept of market segmentation rests upon recognition of a differentiated demand for a product, while its use as a marketing tool depends upon identification of the most appropriate variable or variables with which to subdivide total demand into economically viable segments. 'Economically viable segment' may be understood as 'being of sufficient size to enable a marketer to earn an adequate profit by catering to the specific needs of its members'.

In a survey, 'Issues and Advances in Segmentation Research' (*Journal of Marketing Research,* August 1978). Yoram Wind identifies four basic procedures or methods for segmenting markets, namely *a priori,* clustering, flexible and componential. In general, *a priori* segmentation models have as the dependent variable (the basis for segmentation) either product specific variables such as product usage or loyalty, or general customer characteristics, e.g. demographic factors. The typical research design for an *a priori* segmentation model involves seven stages: (a) selection of the *a priori* basis for segmentation; (b) selection of a set of segment descriptors (including hypotheses on the possible link between these descriptors and the basis for segmentation); (c) sample design – mostly stratified – and occasionally a quota sample according to the various classes of the dependent variable; (d) data collection; (e) formation of the segments on a sorting of respondents into categories; (f) establishment of the (conditional) profile of the segments using multiple discriminant analysis, MULTIPLE REGRESSION ANALYSIS, or some other appropriate analytical procedure; (g) translation of the findings about the segments' estimated size and profile into specific marketing strategies, including the selection of target segments and the design or modification of specific marketing strategies.

In the case of CLUSTERING or post-hoc segmentation, the only significant difference is that the segments are determined after the data has been collected on the basis of perceived groupings or clusters within the data. Frequently such clusters will be determined through the use of FACTOR ANALYSIS whereby variables will be grouped on the basis of their correlation with each other (and their lack of correlation with variables included in other factors) and the amount of variance in the dependent variable which they are able to 'explain'.

Flexible segmentation is a dynamic procedure in which CONJOINT ANALYSIS is combined with a simulation model to allow managers to explore the large number of alternative approaches to segmenting a particular market.

The componential procedure is an extension of conjoint analysis and shifts the emphasis of the segmentation model from the partitioning of a market to a prediction of which person type (described by a particular set of demographic and other psychographic attribute levels) will be most responsive to what type of product feature.

(MJB)

market share. The ratio of a company's sales of a product (either the number of units sold or the value of sales) during a period in a specified market to the total sales (industry sales) of that type of product during the same period in that market.

(GA)

market size. A quantified statement of the total demand for a given product in terms of the volume and/or value of that demand.

(MJB)

market specialization strategy. *See* CONCENTRATION and MARKET POSITIONING.

market structure. A loose term, generally referring to essential parameters of a market: size, value, distribution, major operators, level of competitiveness and so on.

(JRB)

market targeting. The selection of the MARKET SEGMENT or segments which appears to offer the greatest opportunity to the firm.

(MJB)

market termination stage. A stage of a product's life cycle (also known as the decline stage), characterized by declining sales and profits and resulting in the product's withdrawal from the market. *See* PRODUCT LIFE CYCLE.

(GA)

market test. Offering a (new) product for sale on a limited basis within a sub-market believed to be representative of the intended market using, insofar as possible, the same marketing mix as to be used in the whole market. *See also* TEST MARKETING.

(MJB)

Markov model. A model widely used to explain BRAND SWITCHING behaviour developed from the Markov process which relates current values (e.g.

BRAND SHARE) to previous values with the inclusion of a random error term. (MJB)

mark-up. The amount added to the cost of goods to determine the selling price. *See* MARGIN. (MJB)

mark-up pricing. The practice of arriving at the selling price by adding a sum of money to the cost. The determination of the amount is calculated as a percentage of the cost price, or of the desired selling price. Generally practised by retailers who require to price thousands of items using a standard method. (AJB)

Marshall, Alfred (1842–1924). English economist. From the time he became an undergraduate at Cambridge his whole life was spent in academic circles. After resigning (1881) for health reasons as principal of the new University College at Bristol he returned to Cambridge as professor of political economy (1885–1908). He is the last of the line of the great classical economists and his *Principles of Economics* (1890) became a standard work used by many generations of students; and though some of its conclusions are now disputed or outmoded it remains a basic work. He also wrote *Industry and Trade* (1919) and *Money, Credit and Commerce* (1923). (MJB)

Marshallian economic model. One of four basic models of buyer behaviour proposed by Philip Kotler (*Marketing Management*, 4th edn) which is based upon neo-classical economic theory and postulates that buying decisions are the results of rational and conscious economic calculations designed to maximize the buyer's utility or satisfaction. Industrial buying behaviour is usually believed to be of this type. (MJB)

Maslow, Abraham. *See* MOTIVATION.

mass marketing strategy. Adopting an approach to marketing (a product/service) usually associated with manufacturers of mass market products i.e. FAST MOVING CONSUMER GOODS. By implication such an approach tends towards heavy advertising and other promotional activity, wide and rapid distribution and an aggressive attitude in seeking market success. (JRB)

mass media. Means of communication reaching the majority of the public; newspapers, television and the radio collectively are mass media. (MDP)

mass merchandiser. A retailer who offers a very wide assortment of product lines using massive displays of merchandise. The assortment is mostly in clothing, hardware, toiletries, entertainment equipment, toys and any product line in popular demand. A supermarket service style is used in selling. (AJB)

master sample. A number of marketing research survey organizations maintain a fixed sample of primary sampling units, often parliamentary constituencies, from which many further samples can be taken. This enables field facilities to be concentrated economically. (JAB)

matched sample. Following the principles of experimentation, researchers often seek to exclude the effects on experimental or observational results of differences between samples by selecting them to be of identical composition in aspects such as age or region considered influential. A similar effect can be produced by WEIGHTING. The procedure is often disappointing, since the control variables may be in fact little related to the variable being measured. It is used, for example, in product testing. (JAB)

materials handling. The physical management and handling of materials. (MJB)

materials management. A coordinated approach to supply-side management, entailing the unification of control of PURCHASING INVENTORY and production scheduling. Benefits derived are many, including the elimination of buck-passing/responsibility evasion and of duplication of organization and documentation; manpower-saving; a coordinated approach to suppliers and the improvement of bargaining strength; the reduction of inventories; the improvement of production resource utilization and of information flow to marketers and customers. Materials management is frequently regarded as a symptom of the adoption and application of a corporate MARKETING ORIENTATION. *See also* PRODUCTION CONTROL. (KNB)

matrix organization. A type of organizational structure in which teams of people are formed to carry out specific tasks or projects e.g. new product development. (MJB)

maturity stage of product life cycle. *See* PRODUCT LIFE CYCLE.

maximum distribution. A statistic contained in retail audit data which defines the number (percentage) of outlets which have stocked the product at any time since the previous audit. By itself the statistic may be highly misleading as an outlet holding one item of the product may have sold it immediately after the preceding audit and have been out of stock for almost the whole of the next audit period.   (MJB)

MBWA. *See* MANAGEMENT-BY-WALKING ABOUT.

McLuhan, Marshall. Canadian Professor of English who coined the celebrated phrase '[The]Medium is the Message' as a chapter title in *Understanding Media: the Extensions of Man* (1964). His original argument is very detailed and conceptually difficult; in the marketing communications context, it is usually taken as a reminder that audience reaction to a message may be significantly affected by their evaluation of the medium through which it is transmitted. Thus the choice of advertising medium mediates response to an advertisement, or a sales representative's appearance influences the reaction to the sales pitch. In practice, MEDIA PLANNERS demonstrate implicit acceptance of McLuhan's hypothesis when they use such terms as 'relaxed', 'urgent' or 'chatty' to describe types of newspaper, or discuss 'media values' and 'rub-off effect' in their professional journals. *See* CHANNEL EFFECT. (KC)

MEAL *See* AC NIELSEN. MEAL.

mean. The mean (or average) of a set of numbers is equal to the sum of observations divided by the number of observations; for example, the mean of 12, 10, 8, 14, 9, 7 is

$$12 + 10 + 8 + 14 + 9 + 7/6 = 60/6 = 10$$

The mathematical symbol for the mean of a sample is x~.   (KAB)

means-ends chains. The link between product attributes, perceived benefits and higher order consumer values. *See* LADDERING.   (MJB)

measurability. One of the requirements of a viable MARKET SEGMENT i.e. that one should be able to define it in objective terms.   (MJB)

measures of dispersion. In contrast to measures of central tendency, measures of dispersion indicate the size of the spread of a distribution; standard deviation, variance, range, and interquartile range are all measures of dispersion.   (SKT)

mechanical binding. A term used in printing. The need for a flat opening type of binding, with or without loose leaf, stimulated the development of mechanical binding. The covers and pages are first punched with a series of round or oblong holes on the binding edge and then a coil of wire, strip metal or plastic is mechanically inserted into the holes to keep the pages together.   (MDP)

mechanical data. Page-size, column-width, printing requirements and other related characteristics of newspapers and magazines. Published in BRAD (q.v.).   (KC)

mechanical observation devices. Any machine or device used to observe and/or record consumer behaviour.   (MJB)

media. In the marketing context, this means ADVERTISING MEDIA, not 'news media' or 'mass media'. The singular is medium, not 'a media'. *See* MEDIA MIX, MEDIA SHARE.   (KC)

media brief. A formal document presented to the ADVERTISER by the ADVERTISING AGENCY, in response to an ADVERTISING BRIEF received, explaining the rationale for the MEDIA SELECTION proposed and setting out a MEDIA SCHEDULE for approval. The term could also describe the element of the advertising brief itself that relates to MEDIA choice. *See also* COPY BRIEF, CREATIVE BRIEF.   (KC)

media buyer. An employee of an ADVERTISING AGENCY or MEDIA INDEPENDENT whose job is to place orders for ADVERTISING SPACE or ADVERTISING TIME with MEDIA OWNERS.   (KC)

media class. The largest subdivision of the ADVERTISING MEDIA. For example: national newspapers, consumer magazines, local radio or cinema.   (KC)

media commission. In the advertising context, often called simply 'commission' or sometimes 'agency commission'. This is the discount which an ADVERTISING AGENCY receives from the ABOVE-THE-LINE media, subject to 'recognition' by the trade bodies representing the five major media (see RECOGNIZED ADVERTISING AGENCY). It accounts for about 70 per cent of the total revenue of a typical FULL-SERVICE ADVERTISING AGENCY, according to the INSTITUTE OF PRACTITIONERS IN ADVERTISING. The media commission convention was established in the middle of the nineteenth century by George P. ROWELL. The figure of 15 per cent is universally cited as the 'standard', but is not in fact universal. In Britain, it does apply to television, radio, cinema, national newspapers, the major consumer and business magazines, and the larger categories within the 'outdoor' medium, but 10 per cent is normal in the case of regional and local newspapers, most other magazines and the lesser 'outdoor' media. These percentages became standard quite late in the history of media commission. The figure of 15 per cent had been first set by Volney B. PALMER, an American contemporary of Rowell's, but did not become universal there until 1917, after vigorous lobbying by N.W. AYER. In Britain, an Incorporated Society of Advertising Agents was formed in 1904 to campaign for a standard rate, but disbanded five years later without having achieved its goal. At that time, 10 per cent and 12.5 per cent were common, and 15 was unheard of. In 1921, the *'Times* Agreement' between 56 members of the Association of British Advertising Agents and several publishers established that 'registered advertising agencies' would receive an invariable 10 per cent, plus a further 2.5 per cent for 'new' advertising. However, a steady increase in the number of American-owned agencies in Britain in the 1930s precipitated an inexorable change from the British standard to the American 15 per cent. It is generally thought that *The Times* was the last national newspaper to change to the new rate in 1942, having been the first to agree to standardization 20 years earlier.

The arithmetic of remuneration-by-commission is simple enough but widely misunderstood. Suppose the 'rate-card cost' or 'standard rate' for a 20-second slot of television time is £1,000. The agency invoices the advertiser at this published rate, but the television company charges the agency £1,000 less 15 per cent of £1,000 = £850. By invoicing its client the full rate-card cost, as published in BRITISH RATE AND DATA and therefore readily verifiable, the agency in effect 'earns' £150. Notice that it is the MEDIA OWNERS who 'pay' the agency, not its own CLIENTS.

Ever since agencies began to offer creative services to their clients it has been obvious that the conventional 15 per cent media commission could not cover all the production costs of a professionally executed advertising campaign. The norm has therefore been established that all production charges and certain creative costs are invoiced direct to the advertiser by the agency. Furthermore, FULL-SERVICE ADVERTISING AGENCIES offer their clients services over and above the planning and executing of media and creative strategies, and a second norm has emerged that the agency is entitled to mark up the real cost of such items by the equivalent of 15 per cent on the list price. Suppose the agency contracts on the client's behalf for a market research survey or the use of a mailing list. The question is, what percentage mark-up must be added to the supplier's actual charge to be the equivalent of the 15 per cent discount subtracted from the rate-card cost in the case of media time and space? Suppose that the supplier's charge for the market research is £850; the necessary calculation is:

£850 plus *n* per cent of £850 = £1000
To solve:
$$850 + (n/100 \times 850) = 1000$$
$$850 + 8.5n = 1000$$
$$n = (1000 - 850)/8.5$$
$$= 17.65$$

Thus the required rate appears to be 17.65 per cent. If this is correct, the following equation must balance:

$$£850 + 17.65\% \text{ of } £850 = £1000$$

Checking:

$$850 + (17.65 \times 850)/100 = 1000$$
$$850 + 150.03 = 1000.03$$

which is quite close enough.

Although media commission has been the norm for 150 years, the advertising business has debated two other modes of remuneration more or less continuously over the last century. The first would require the media to negotiate commission percentages with the agencies; the second would replace commission with a service fee negotiated between agency and advertiser. Variable commission rates were common at the turn of the century, but have generally been resisted because of their potential effect on competition in the advertising agency marketplace. It is argued that the practice would create barriers against the entry of entrepreneurial newcomers. The fee system has the obvious attraction that it reflects the pragmatic realities of the 'agency–client' relationship rather than the legal reality that the agency is in fact a principal in a contractual relationship with the media. And yet remuneration by fee has never become widespread in practice. The main reason is almost certainly inertia. The commission system has four strong characteristics in its favour: (a) historical precedent; (b) it is a standard practice; (c) it is generally understood in the business; (d) it is easily put into practice. Furthermore, advertisers may have a vested interest in retaining the commission system, suspecting that any fee arrived at by a calculation of overheads, production costs and profit margins would come to more than 15 per cent of media bills plus chargeable extras. And agencies may be unwilling to contemplate the paperwork involved in calculating a realistic fee. The whole commission system was declared a restrictive practice by the OFFICE OF FAIR TRADING as long ago as December 1978, but the ruling has yet to have any noticeable impact on practice. The media continue to offer commission to recognized advertising agencies and the agencies continue to depend on it as the major component of their remuneration.   (KC)

media cost. *See* RATE-CARD COST.

media data form (MDF). The Audit Bureau of Circulation will provide one of these for almost all newspapers and most magazines published in the UK. It gives: the AUDIT BUREAU OF CIRCULATION net CIRCULATION figure; READERSHIP figure and READERSHIP PROFILE, if available; geographical distribution; publisher's statement of editorial policy; the standard ADVERTISING RATES; other general information of interest to advertisers and advertising agencies.   (KC)

Media Expenditure Analysis Ltd (MEAL). A firm that monitors UK total advertising expenditure in the MAJOR MEDIA except posters and cinema. Its quarterly digests and annual reports cross-index the raw data by generic and specific product groups and by medium. The acronym is used as an adjective in practice, as in 'the Meal figures for mineral waters'. *See also* MEDIA REGISTER.   (KC)

media impact. An estimate, usually qualitative, of the likely or actual effect of a given message in a particular MEDIUM.   (MJB)

media independent. A service provider that offers ADVERTISERS an alternative to the services of a traditional FULL-SERVICE ADVERTISING AGENCY, as far as the planning and buying of ADVERTISING MEDIA are concerned. Media independents first appeared in Britain in the 1970s. The impetus seems to have been entrepreneurial, some MEDIA PLANNERS perceiving a business opportunity in the setting up of an independent service which could lay claim to highly specialized, highly developed expertise in an especially complex area of advertising strategy. They offered no other services at all. Their subsequent success was no doubt sustained by a suspicion on the part of more sophisticated advertisers that the full-service advertising agencies might be jack-of-all-trades but master of none. Media independents ask no fee for their services because they are eligible for MEDIA COMMISSION. They are, in effect, a modern-day reincarnation of nineteenth-century SPACE BROKERS. Having lower overheads than full-service agencies and no extra servicing costs, they can afford to discount the price of their service by COMMISSION REBATING; this adds a second dimension to the competitiveness of their offering against that of the conventional agencies. After the initial burst of openings, some of the smaller entrepreneurs proved unable to survive on margins severely eroded by commission rebating, but there remains a core of large and successful survivors. In 1996, the biggest of them, Zenith, had total BILLINGS of £554 million. That compares with the £306 million earned by the largest full-service advertising agency. Media independents are often called 'media shops', 'shop' being the colloquial synonym for an advertising agency, especially in the USA.   (KC)

media mix. (1) The combination of ADVERTISING MEDIA deployed in a campaign schedule.

(2) The relative proportions of national total advertising expenditure accounted for by the MAJOR MEDIA available. The UK media mix is described under MEDIA SHARE.   (KC)

median. If a set of numbers is arranged from smallest to largest, the median is the middle observation if the number of observations is odd, or the number halfway between the two middle observations if the number is even. For example, the median of 22, 25, 27, 30, 42 is 27.   (KNB)

media option. A purchasable unit of ADVERTISING SPACE or ADVERTISING TIME, such as a peak-time spot on London Weekend Television, a full-page advertisement in the *Draper's Record* or a 6-sheet poster site at London Heathrow Terminal 4. (KC)

media owners. Organizations which have the right to sell ADVERTISING SPACE or ADVERTISING TIME, principally: newspapers and magazine publishers; independent television and radio CONTRACTING COMPANIES; outdoor advertising contractors and cinema advertising contractors. They do not literally own the advertising media in question, only the selling rights. (KC)

media planner. An employee of an ADVERTISING AGENCY or MEDIA INDEPENDENT whose work is concerned with the formulation of media strategy rather than its execution, which is the task of the MEDIA BUYER. Media planners keep in touch with developments in MEDIA RESEARCH and maintain considerable banks of data relevant to MEDIA SELECTION, most of them now available on-line. It is only in the largest advertising agencies and media shops that the media planning and media buying functions are clearly separate in practice. (KC)

media planning. The selection of a medium or media and the distribution of the advertising appropriation over time within those media in order to achieve the specified marketing and advertising objectives set by the advertiser. *See* MEDIA SELECTION. (MJB)

Media Planning Group. The professional common-interest group for those working in the MEDIA PLANNING function in ADVERTISING AGENCIES. (KC)

Media Register. *See* AC NIELSEN. MEAL.

media research. The collective term for an extremely diverse range of investigations into the size, specification and behaviour of ADVERTISING MEDIA readers, viewers, listeners and audiences. Media research is today a sophisticated, highly quantitative and somewhat esoteric discipline, pursued by MEDIA PLANNERS. Some research relates specifically to the performance characteristics of individual MEDIA VEHICLES, while some is aimed at improving general understanding of how people consume and use media. (KC)

media schedule. A formal document setting out the choice of MEDIA VEHICLES and timing of MEDIA OPTIONS comprising an ADVERTISING CAM-PAIGN: that is, describing where and when the advertising will appear. (KC)

media selection. The process of choosing MEDIA VEHICLES for an ADVERTISING CAMPAIGN; the culmination of the MEDIA PLANNER'S work. An evaluation of an advertising medium requires consideration of four major factors: (1) its character; (2) its atmosphere; (3) the coverage of the medium; (4) its cost. Two further factors which should be taken into account are the size and position of the advertisement.

The character of a medium may be largely determined on an objective and factual basis through consideration of the following: (a) the geographical coverage of the medium, e.g. national, regional, local; (b) the socio-economic composition of the audience; (c) composition of the audience by age and sex groupings; (d) the medium's physical characteristics – visual, oral, standard of reproduction, availability of colour, possibility of movement etc.; (e) frequency of publication. Allied to this is the duration of interest in the medium – most daily papers are thrown away the same day, while magazines may be kept for several weeks and read by a number of people. The frequency of publication also has a direct effect on the booking of time or space, i.e. the timing of the appearance of an advertisement. (f) The power to reach special groups – this is closely related to (b) and (c) above, e.g. *Private Eye* or the *Financial Times, Vogue* etc., preselect a particular type of audience and so are especially suited to selling to this segment of the population. Further, the association of a product with a medium may give that product favourable connotations by transferring confidence in the publication to items advertised therein.

The atmosphere of a medium is difficult to define in that it is based on a subjective evaluation of its content, presentation etc. A broad distinction may be drawn between acceptable and intrusive media, in that the latter create IMPACT through intrusion and irrelevance to context, e.g. television commercials, whereas many magazines are purchased as much for their advertisements as their other content. The concept will become clearer when related to individual media. The essential criterion on which coverage is judged is the actual number of persons exposed to the medium, in the sense of being made aware of its content. For example, the number of people who actually see a poster is considerably less than the number that have the opportunity to see it; on the other hand, the readership of a magazine may well exceed ten times its actual circulation.

For purposes of comparison the cost of publishing an advertisement is usually expressed in terms of COST PER THOUSAND, which is arrived at by dividing the cost of publication by the audience in thousands. The difficulty in ensuring comparability in the measurement of audience size in terms of coverage, as defined above, makes this a rough measure at best, and media planners are actively seeking more sophisticated measures of cost effectiveness.

The effect of increased size or duration of an advertisement is to increase effective coverage, but on a progressively diminishing scale. Larger advertisements enable the advertiser to make more selling points, or to create greater impact when properly used. It is also contended that 'bigness', of itself, creates confidence and prestige.

Detailed studies of the positioning of advertisements within a medium have shown that certain 'slots' consistently achieve greater coverage than other positions. Further, certain positions can be very useful in isolating a particular segment of the general audience. (Timing has the same effect for broadcast messages on radio and television.) *See also* VEHICLE EFFECT.

(MJB, KC)

media share. The proportion of national total advertising expenditure held by each of the MAJOR MEDIA available. In the UK in 1996, they shared the pie as follows, in rank order: press 60.6 per cent; television 31.5 per cent; outdoor 3.6 per cent; radio 3.2 per cent; cinema 0.7 per cent. It is clear that three of the 'major' media are comparatively not major at all, accounting collectively for substantially less than ten per cent of the total. The share breakdown among the three largest has remained stable over the last two decades. Radio and cinema have both increased their share significantly during the 1990s, but are still very small media in absolute terms. (KC)

media shop. An informal description of a MEDIA INDEPENDENT. 'Shop' is a colloquial synonym for an advertising agency, especially in the USA.

(KC)

media strategy. One of the two halves which make up a complete advertising strategy, the other being CREATIVE STRATEGY. There is often debate as to which of these two is more 'important' than the other. This seems a sterile argument. On the one hand, it is certainly true that the most skilful media strategy will be to no avail if the creative execution is ineffective. On the other hand, it is equally true that a creative strategy cannot possibly achieve its aims unless the advertisements are placed where they can work to best effect. It is only possible to conclude that media and creative and strategies are wholly interdependent, both crucial, and that it would be wrong to think of one or the other as a first priority or as more important. (KC)

media vehicle. An individual member of a MEDIA CLASS. For example, London Weekend Television, the *Draper's Record* or 'roadside posters'.

(KC)

media weights. 'Weighting' is the process of modifying the numbers in a set of numerical data to reflect variables not taken into account in the original calculation or manipulation. MEDIA PLANNERS weight quantitative counts of readers, listeners or viewers to allow for qualitative factors such as trends over time, editorial stance, programme environment, image, print quality and so on. (KC)

medium. In the marketing context, this means an ADVERTISING MEDIUM, not a 'news medium' or a 'mass medium'. The plural is media, not 'mediums'. *See* MEDIA MIX, MEDIA SHARE. (KC)

merchandise allowance. An incentive given to retailers by manufacturers to encourage the retailer to display the manufacturer's products in a given way. (MJB)

merchandising. (1) The activity of ensuring that a product is widely available and prominently visible. An organization may employ teams of merchandisers, whose sole task is to ensure these objectives are met.

(2) The action of pre-packaging a product into a display unit – also called a merchandiser – to improve product display among distributors.

(JRB)

merchant. An individual or organization which takes title to goods and then resells them. (MJB)

merchant banks. Traditionally, merchant banks have been primarily concerned with acceptances (the term is derived from the method of financing trade by which commercial bills are 'accepted' or guaranteed by a merchant bank against documents, after which they may be discounted for cash by a discount house or other intermediary) and with the sponsoring of capital issues on behalf of their customers. Today they have a widely diversified and complex range of activities with an important role in international finance and the short-term capital markets, the provision of expert advice and financial services to British industrial companies, especially where mergers, takeovers and other forms of corporate reorganization are involved, and in the management of investment holdings, including trusts, pensions and other funds. The sector is split between independent houses and those which are part of larger banking groups.   (HMSO)

merger. The act of two or more organizations of usually roughly equal size and standing choosing to join into a single entity.   (JRB)

message. Information to be communicated by the sender to the receiver in a COMMUNICATION CHANNEL.   (MJB)

message effect. The effect that the innate characteristics of a MARKETING COMMUNICATIONS message has upon the target audience's perceptions of it and their reactions to it. At first sight, this may seem the only such effect of any significance. On the contrary, the theoretical literature is equally concerned with SOURCE EFFECT and CHANNEL EFFECT; there is also the question of time effects created by the MEDIA SCHEDULE.

The ingredients of message effect are: codes, appeals and structure. Two classes of message code are recognized. 'Verbal' relates to the objective 'denotative' and subjective 'connotative' meaning of the vocabulary used: that is, what the chosen words denote and connote. 'Non-verbal' (or 'paralinguistic') relates to modulation of the overt message by tone of voice, cadence, speed of delivery and 'body language'. A third class of code, manifestly absent from the literature and therefore lacking an accepted name, exercises a further modulating influence through the choice of colour, sound, setting and typography. Similarly, the texts discuss two classes of message appeal: humour and fear. There is an extensive literature on both, but it is inconclusive on the question of how such appeals can in practice be used productively rather than counterproductively. Furthermore, one is bound to wonder why there is no discussion of other categories, such as (most obviously) sex appeal and snob appeal. Lastly, message structure is discussed under three headings. 'Polarity' concerns the choice to make the main proposition either one-sided or two-sided, 'order' the decision to place strong arguments nearer the beginning or the end of the message, and 'completion' the question of whether to close an argument or leave it open. Translation of this theory into practice is hindered by the fact that it is based on experiments in social communication. Typical marketing communications messages do not generally put 'arguments' to the audience, nor do they have the formal structure of the lectures and articles which the experimenters' test subjects were asked to evaluate.   (KC)

metric data. A term from psychological scaling that indicates measurements which are at least at interval level. The contrast is with non-metric data, where only ordinal level properties are appropriate.   (SKT)

micro environment. The immediate environment within which the firm competes defined by the industry, market(s), channels, customers and competitors with which it interacts. *See* MACRO ENVIRONMENT.   (MJB)

micro-marketing. A term used to mean MARKETING at the level of the individual firm as opposed to macro-marketing which encompasses marketing on a much broader, national or international level. Micro-marketing focuses narrowly on the activities of a business which are directed towards satisfying CONSUMER needs at a profit.   (MDP)

microsegmentation. The subdivision of industrial or business-to-business markets on the basis of the characteristics of the buying centre and the individual members of it. *See* MACROSEGMENTATION.   (MJB)

middleman. *See* INTERMEDIARY. Any of the traders who stands between the producer and the consumer of the product. The main function is to facilitate the exchange process.   (AJB)

minimum order. The minimum order size acceptable to the seller.   (MJB)

minority sample. One of the most difficult tasks of the survey researcher is to obtain at a reasonable cost a representative SAMPLE of a group of users of a small brand of whom there are relatively few in the general population. The first step is to sift through a large sample of the general public to find members of the minority group. This is often done by means of an OMNIBUS SURVEY ('piggy-backing') The second is to find some specialized list containing a higher proportion of the group. Dealer lists are an example, however these may not be completely representative. A third method, often informally used in the field, when a 'difficult' QUOTA has been set involving such a group is to use those RESPONDENTS found to give information about acquaintances or neighbours in the desired group. This is a very arbitrary procedure. The problem is very important to many firms operating on a small or medium scale.   (JAB)

minor media. A diverse collection of often transient ADVERTISING MEDIA other than the MAJOR MEDIA, for example: matchbooks, sports programmes, bus tickets, clothing or tethered balloons. The description overlaps considerably with BELOW-THE-LINE, but has a quite different origin.   (KC)

minutage. The proportion of total broadcasting time, or the total duration of one cinema 'showing' programme, given over to advertising. The equivalent in the non-broadcast media is the ADVERTISING-TO-EDITORIAL RATIO. Minutage is restricted by the INDEPENDENT TELEVISION COMMISSION to: 10 per cent of total broadcasting time on Channels 3, 4 and 5, averaged over the day, 9 minutes in any clock hour (15 per cent) of satellite and cable broadcasting originating in the UK; 12 minutes per hour (20 per cent) in the special case of UK home-shopping channels. Complicated regulations further govern the length and frequency of COMMERCIAL BREAKS within each clock hour. In 1989, Article 18 of the EU Council Directive 89/552, generally called the Television Without Frontiers' Directive, permitted member states' television stations up to twice as high a minutage ratio as in the UK, although it restricted the daily average to a 15 per cent ratio.

The ITC has so far elected to maintain the 10 per cent daily average, which has been in place since commercial television broadcasting began in Britain in 1955. Total terrestrial television minutage on all CHANNELS is 2,076 per week (34.6 hours), according to Cable & Satellite Yearbook 1996. When the RADIO AUTHORITY was devolved from the Independent Broadcasting Association in 1991, it announced its intention to exercise 'a lighter touch' with regard to the amount of time allocated to advertising, and duly removed the previous statutory restriction to nine minutes per hour: a 15 per cent ratio. No formal monitoring has taken place since, but figures extracted from available research data seem to suggest that the existing ratio has been generally taken as a sensible norm. Individual station controllers may well decide to offer proportionately more minutage for sale in general or periodically, but equally cannot afford to allow a weight of advertising that could irritate listeners so much that they would turn off or re-tune elsewhere. It is well known that Classic FM has a strict policy of restricting both total advertising time and the number of breaks in a given period, for that reason, and that they aim to make good any consequent loss in earnings by asking a premium price for an uncluttered listening environment and attracting programme sponsorship. The CINEMA ADVERTISING ASSOCIATION estimates that the main cinema chains offer advertisers between 6 and 14 minutes of advertising per complete programme: a ratio of from 4 to 9 per cent. Despite the fact that television minutage is far lower than press advertising-to-editorial ratios, critics of advertising are more likely to comment on the intrusion of commercials into television programmes than on the interruption of newspaper or magazine stories by advertisements. (KC)

misleading prices. Prices which are set or presented in such a way that they are likely to confuse and mislead intending buyers.   (MJB)

missing value category. In the CODING of a QUESTIONNAIRE response or observational category, the missing value is the one given for reasons such as 'Not Asked', 'No Response' or 'Refused'. Most DATA analysis systems allow missing value categories so that missing data only removes a case from analyses which involve that variable.   (SKT)

missionary selling. Approaching potential new customers/distributors with a view to increasing sales by expanding the number of sales accounts. Also known as 'cold calling', 'cold canvassing' and 'prospecting'.   (JRB)

mission statement. A formal statement publicized by an organization which is intended to communicate its purpose and aspirations. (MJB)

mixed economy. An economy in which the operation of the free MARKET is tempered by an element of central control. This central control will involve regulation through monetary and fiscal policy, individual and corporate taxation and may also involve ownership and operation of certain industries, such as transportation, energy supply etc. Most advanced industrial economies are mixed economies. (MJB)

mode. That observation in a SAMPLE which occurs most frequently. However, if each OBSERVATION occurs the same number of times there is no mode. If two observations occur the same number of times, but more frequently than any of the other observations, the sample is 'bimodal'. (KAB)

moderator. A person responsible for leading FOCUS GROUP DISCUSSIONS. (MJB)

modified rebuy. One of three types of buyer behaviour defined by Robinson, Faris and Wind. The salient characteristics of a modified rebuy situation are that: (a), a regular requirement for the type of product exists; (b) the buying alternatives are known, but sufficient changes have occurred to require some alteration to the normal supply procedure; (c) change may be stimulated by external events, e.g. inputs from supplying companies; (d) change may be stimulated by internal events, e.g. new buying influences, value analysis, reorganization. (MJB)

monadic. See PRODUCT TESTING.

monadic testing. See PRODUCT TESTING.

money-back guarantee. A promise that the purchase price will be refunded if the goods are returned within a specified time to the seller. Frequently found in the case of mail order selling, where the buyer does not have the opportunity to inspect the goods before delivery. (MJB)

money-off pack. See OFF-PRICE LABELS.

Monopolies and Mergers Commission (MMC). A governmental agency in the UK to which the DTI or DIRECTOR OF FAIR TRADING may refer a firm for investigation if it is seen as using anti-competitive behaviour and/or if its share of the total market exceeds 25 per cent. (MJB)

monopolistic competition. The theory of monopolistic competition developed by Edwin Chamberlin to describe the type of market structure (*Theory of Monopolistic Competition*, 1933), which combines the characteristics of both perfect competition and monopoly. It retains many of the assumptions of the model of PERFECT

COMPETITION, but differs from it in one major respect. Whereas the industry is assumed to consist of a large number of firms, each of which is run by the entrepreneur, who pursues the goal of PROFIT MAXIMIZATION using marginal analysis under conditions of perfect knowledge, and whereas there is a freedom of entry into and exit out of the industry, each firm can no longer be treated as a price taker. This stems from the fact that firms are selling products which are close, but not perfect, substitutes for each other, which is due to PRODUCT DIFFERENTIATION.

According to Chamberlin, a general class of product is differentiated if any significant basis exists for distinguishing the goods (or services) of one seller from another. Such a basis may be real or fancied, so long as it is of any importance whatever to buyers, and leads to a preference for one variety of the product over another. Differentiation may be based upon certain characteristics of the product itself, such as exclusive patented features; trademarks; trade names; peculiarities of the package or container, if any; or singularity in quality, design, colour or style. It may also exist with respect to the condition surrounding its sale.

In monopolistic competition the action of a firm has no perceptible effect upon the other sellers because of the large number of firms where no individual producer is in a position to supply more than an insignificant share of the total market, and the offering of one firm is not identical to others because of product differentiation. The demand curve faced by the monopolistic firm is not perfectly elastic but, instead, slopes downward to the right; it does not have a very steep slope because of competition from close substitutes (*see* DEMAND, LAW OF). The elasticity of demand for the firm's product depends on the degree of differentiation of its products. In the short run the monopolistic firm may earn supernormal profit. In the long run the firm earns normal profit only because, in the absence of BARRIERS TO ENTRY, excess profits attract new firms to enter the industry over time and hence expand total supplies. This results in a cut of the MARKET SHARE held by any individual firm. Also new firms extend the range of product differentiation, and this weakens the preference of customers for any single producer's goods. A major criticism of monopolistic competition is the difficulty of defining the group of firms which are in monopolistic competition. Chamberlin referred to the group of competing firms as follows: 'the group contemplated is one which would ordinarily be regarded as composing one imperfectly competitive market: a number of automobile manufacturers, of producers of pots and pans, of magazine publishers, or of retail shoe dealers. From our point of view, each producer within the group is a monopolist, yet his market is interwoven with those of his competitors, and he is no longer to be isolated from them.' (MJB)

monopoly. The case of a single seller, enjoying absence of COMPETITION of any kind, with complete control over the supply of the product, including control over entry into the industry. In making decisions on prices, the monopolist is independent, and does not have to allow for the price policies of other sellers, or take other prices into account because they, as always, help to determine the demand for the product. The position of the monopolist's demand curve is steady, given the buyer's tastes and incomes, and given the prices of the not so close substitutes, because raising or lowering price does not provoke any change in price policy by rivals, a change that would shift the monopolist demand curve. The monopolist has no existing competitors, and is protected by BARRIERS TO ENTRY from the encroachment into its market of potential competitors. Barriers to entry are the foundation of all monopolies. Some of them are set by government, such as granting patents, imposing TARIFFS, issuing exclusive FRANCHISES, and some arise from superior technology and management, ECONOMIES OF SCALE, and the enormous investment that few industries have to have.

The monopolist demand curve (*see* DEMAND, LAW OF) is equivalent to the demand curve of the entire industry, and slopes downward to the right, which means that as he lowers the price he will be able to sell more and vice versa. The monopolist looks for a combination of a price–output that provides him with the greatest total difference between cost and revenue. He can maximize his profit in both long and short run by equating marginal revenue and marginal cost. He is a price maker, and can earn supernormal profit.

The major criticism of the model is that pure monopoly is a kind of market structure which does not exist in the real world. Underlying that is the belief that there is no such thing as a non-competing product, because everything has some kind of substitute, no matter how imperfect. (MJB)

monopsony. A market in which there is only one buyer, or monopsonist. (MJB)

monostasy. A fundamental drive in the individual which creates a desire to be independent, to stand alone. When for example the drive for monostasy is dominant in a member of a distribution channel, the probability of conflict between channel members increases. (AJB)

moral appeals. The use of messages which are designed to appeal to the audiences' view of morally acceptable behaviour, e.g. advertising that cosmetic products have not been tested on animals. (MJB)

mores. The most strongly held norms held by members of a society which govern its organization and conduct. Mores are often codified and incorporated in formal laws by contrast with *folkways* which are less strongly held norms governing acceptable behaviour. Thus breach of the mores will usually result in legal sanctions to enforce conformity whereas breach of folkways may result in disapproval by members of groups holding to them but no formal punishment.(MJB)

morphological analysis. Broadly speaking morphology is the study of form. Morphological analysis is a collective term for techniques which share a common approach to problem (form) analysis based on the systematic identification of all possible means of achieving a given end. The approach has been used widely in technological forecasting. In this context the morphological analysis will systematically explore the structure of a technological system to identify its basic parameters and all the known alternative means of fulfilling them. A matrix can then be constructed (*see* figure 18 below) which relates the key parameters to the different means by which each is achieved. The combinations represented in the cells of the matrix will not only identify known technological configurations, some will also suggest previously untried configurations which may point to the way ahead. (DB)

mortality effect. In longitudinal studies, the problem of RESPONDENTS from an early wave of interviewing not being available for subsequent interviews. Death is one cause, but moving away is a more common reason. More specifically referred to as 'panel mortality'. (SKT)

mosaic systems. A geodemographic database available from the credit reference agency CCN. It offers detailed demographic ANALYSIS for any chosen catchment, MEDIA or postal area. For use by MARKETING managers interested in identifying the unique characteristics of an area, and then

Morphological Matrix for Domestic Timepieces

Key Parameters	Alternatives 2	3	4	5	6	7	8	9	10
A Energy input source	Manual wind	Vibration or movement	Expansion winding	Pressure fluctuation	Temperature fluctuation	Hydraulic energy	Galvanic reaction	Light rays	External power supply (electric)
B Energy storage	Weight Store	Spring Store	Bimetallic coil	Pressure container	Electric accumulator or battery	Volume container	Expansion bar	Solar cell	No store
C Motor or power transmission	Spring	Electric	Pneumatic	Hydraulic	None				
D Regulator	Balance wheel	Pendulum	Armature	Centrifugal governor	Tuning fork with contact	Inching pendulum	Constant Electric mains frequency	Crystal resonance (quartz crystal)	Capacitor-phasing circuit
E Information transmission	Pinion gear drive	Chain drive	Worm gear drive	Magnetic coupling	Lever system	Fluid coupling	Counter/ decoder		
F Indicator device	Hands and dial	Plates and marks	Roller and window	Slide and marks	Digital display (mechanical)	Moving figures	Light-emitting diodes	Liquid crystal display	Sound effects

Source: H. Blohm &. K. Steinbuch. eds., *Technological Forecasting in Practice* (London: Saxon House. 1973)

Figure 18: **Morphological analysis**

examining its suitability for a given PRODUCT or service. Data is held on customers, outlets, prospects and media. Associated application software displays the results in report and map format. It is available both on-line and as a PC version. (KRD)

Most Favoured Nation. A system whereby any TARIFF or similar concession made by one nation to another is automatically extended to another nation which has a 'Most Favoured Nation' clause in a commercial treaty with the first nation. GENERAL AGREEMENT ON TARIFFS AND TRADE (GATT) is an example of the generalized application of this principle. (JML)

motivation. An inner state that activates or moves people towards goals, resulting in purposive means/ends behaviour. Reference was made under LEARNING to the distinction between a drive as an initial stimulus, and motive as a tendency to act, though the terms tend to be used interchangeably in everyday speech. However, perhaps a clearer distinction is apparent if one defines drives as physiological stimuli to action, while motives constitute the intervening variable between the stimulus and response. For example, I have a strong drive to smoke a cigarette but my doctor has told me it is bad for my health and will shorten my life. I wish to live to a ripe old age and am strongly motivated to avoid anything which prejudices that goal – result, I stop smoking and resist drive. Drives and motives are also often called 'needs' and one of the most enduring and widely used classifications of needs is that proposed by Abraham Maslow ('A Theory of Human Motivation', *Psychological Review,* vol. 50, 1943). According to Maslow's basic theory we possess five basic needs which can be placed in a hierarchy such that as lower-order needs are satisfied we lose interest in them and concentrate upon satisfying needs at the next higher level which have become the most pressing. The five steps in the hierarchy in ascending order are: (1) physiological needs; (2) safety needs; (3) love needs; (4) esteem needs; (5) self-actualization needs.

Physiological needs or basic drives arise mainly from internal stimuli such as hunger or thirst, though some arise from external sources which threaten the individual with pain, injury or death. It is generally believed that satisfaction of these needs is dominant and overrides all other considerations. It is significant that a marketing function as it has developed in advanced economies in the past 50–60 years is irrelevant in countries where basic needs are not satisfied.

Safety needs come next in importance and can themselves be ranked into a rough hierarchy: physical security, stable and routine pattern of living, i.e. avoid the risk of the unknown, acquire protection against an uncertain future (religion, insurance).

Love needs include the need for affection and the feeling of belonging to a group: family, social group, work group etc. Much marketing activity seeks to cater for these needs and includes some approaches most criticized by anti-marketers, e.g. advertising which suggests that failure to use a product (toothpaste, shampoo etc.) will lead to ostracism or exclusion from a group which a person aspires to join.

Esteem needs include such things as recognition, status, prestige, reputation etc. In affluent societies achievement of these needs is often reinforced and made public through the acquisition of physical objects which are felt to be appropriate to a person's position in life. (Consider the Sunday colour supplements or *Country Life* for a sample of such objects.)

Self-actualization represents the highest level of need to 'do one's own thing'. Relatively few people would seem to achieve this level and when they do they are unlikely to be much influenced by or interested in the market-place!

Maslow's hierarchy of motives constitutes a general statement of behaviour at the macro level; to understand the behaviour of the individual we need a more comprehensive classificatory scheme such as that provided by the concept of personality.   (MJB, JLD)

motivation research. That branch of MARKETING RESEARCH concerned to establish the 'real' reasons, motives, that stimulate sales/favourable responses to market offerings. Fully structured questionnaire techniques rarely make possible any detailed probing of attitudes and emotional responses among consumers in the market. Motivation techniques tend to succeed more by being less rigid, more subtle, more informal and more open-ended. GROUP DISCUSSIONS, depth interview and other techniques may be used and the qualitative data that emerges may be interpreted psychoanalytically and/or in the light of the body of knowledge of clinical/social psychology, to provide indications of important motivational factors underlying purchasing and usage behaviour.   (JRB)

motive. An inner drive which predisposes an individual to act in a particular way.   (MJB)

moving average. An average calculated to allow for seasonal variations. In the case of an annual moving average for sales with monthly data the initial calculation would be the simple average arrived at by dividing the annual sales by 12. Thereafter as each new sales figure is reported the contribution of month 1 is discarded and the new month added and the total divided by 12, giving a clear indication of how sales are moving allowing for seasonality.   (MJB)

MRO items. Items to be used in maintenance, repairing or operating plant and equipment. Sometimes termed operating supplies.   (MJB)

multi-attribute attitude models. Models which combine measurements of a range of PRODUCT ATTRIBUTES or features in order to predict ATTITUDES towards the objects possessing those attributes.   (MJB)

multi-brand strategy. The product strategy based on the belief that a company which markets two brands in the same market will, all other things being equal, hold a greater brand share than one brand can attain on its own, and, in the right circumstances, three brands may also achieve greater share than two, and so on. (JRB)

multi-channel marketing system. A supplier's system which makes use of two or more channels to reach consumers with his product(s). It may create conflict between the supplier and his middlemen when inter-channel competition to sell the same product intensifies. When the channels are used for different products there are few problems.   (AJB)

multi-client survey. A survey undertaken by a MARKET RESEARCH agency which is sponsored by a number of clients, the findings of which are either available exclusively to the sponsoring clients, or the findings may be available for purchase by any interested party. (AMW)

multicollinearity. A problem in MULTIPLE REGRESSION caused by correlations between the predictor variables. (SKT)

multidimensional scaling. The basic characteristic of multidimensional scaling is that respondents are asked to make judgements concerning the degree of similarity/distance between pairs of stimuli using a scale which may be either metric (interval or ratio scale) or non-metric (ordinal scale). A particularly attractive feature of non-metric multidimensional scaling is that it converts an ordinal input into an interval scale or metric output. Thus as long as the respondent can rank order all the stimulus pairs it is possible to convert such 'greater than', 'less than' statements into absolute statements concerning the status of all the objects. (MJB)

multinational corporation. There is no universally accepted definition, but a multinational corporation is generally considered to be a very large company with production units in several countries, and a turnover often as large as the national income of some small countries like Switzerland or the Netherlands. Vernon's precise but arbitrary definition of a multinational, being a company with a turnover of over $100 million and production units in six or more countries, has been adopted by the United Nations. A multinational corporation is also considered to be world-orientated, linking markets and resources of the world on a profitable basis, reaping the advantages of vertical and horizontal economies of scale.

However the dimensions of multinationality are many and varied. A company may be considered multinational if it markets in many countries, manufactures in many countries, is multinationally financed, owned, managed or organized, or has multinational research and development.

There has also been much discussion on the difference between 'international', 'multinational', 'transnational' and 'supranational'. An international enterprise could be seen as one which operates on an international scale other than merely exporting, but still makes a distinction between domestic and foreign markets. It might become 'multinational' once the distinction between domestic and foreign markets begins to disappear and 'transnational' when the earlier stages have reached the point where the original nationality of the enterprise no longer matters. 'Supranational' would imply the enterprise's legal incorporation was not within a nation state but with a supranational authority. In reality the latter does not exist; international and multinational are often used synonymously, while the United Nations refers to all multinationals as transnationals.

Whatever the semantic confusion, the number of multinational corporations has increased significantly since the 1950s. Four waves of development can be traced. The first was the establishment of US companies pulled to Europe (which was short of foreign exchange after the Second World War) to pay for imports. The second was the establishment of assembly or manufacturing subsidiaries by British companies in former traditional export markets (generally the Commonwealth) which had created their own infant industries in the war and were protecting them. European companies then began to exploit a continental-sized market partly in reaction to US success in Europe. The most recent wave of development is the internationalization of Japanese companies, just as the other waves reached or passed their peaks. (JK)

multinational marketing. The process of focusing resources and the objectives of an organization on global market opportunities. It is an extension of simply exporting products, involving the crossing of national frontiers not only physically (through the movement of exports or the building of production plant overseas) but also in the less tangible movement of financial transactions: in capital investment abroad, payment of royalties, licence fees etc.

Before the Second World War there was little multinational marketing, the basic pattern being a few countries producing the world's industrial and consumer goods and exporting these to the numerous raw-material producing economies. Although there was some overseas investment in the form of extractive industry it is only since the 1950s that there has been a dramatic explosion of multinational marketing with the result that there have been profound economic and political changes on a world scale. *See* MULTINATIONAL CORPORATIONS. (JK)

multiple category question. A question where there are more than two available categories of answer. (SKT)

multiple correlation coefficient. The correlation coefficient calculated between a set of variables, represented by a weighted sum, and one dependent variable. (SKT)

multiple discriminant analysis. Like REGRESSION ANALYSIS, this technique uses a set of independent variables to predict one or more dependent variables. The technique is particularly useful in marketing as a means of discriminating between market segments in terms of member characteristics. CONJOINT MEASUREMENT seeks to identify the relative importance of each product attribute in creating an overall desirability for the product, i.e. you ask respondents to rank order a product in terms of each of the attributes which you consider might be important to potential buyers, such as price, ease of use, taste etc. (MJB)

multiple-item scale. An attitude scale formed from more than one simple item or question. (SKT)

multiple regression analysis. Seeks to develop a model of the relationship between a dependent variable such as sales and two or more interdependent variables, such as price, promotional expenditure etc., so that variations in the former may be explained and predicted in terms of changes in the latter. It is a statistical technique for investigating the relationship between one variable (dependent) and several other (independent) variables. Multiple regression calculates the linear relationship that exists between variables and may be used to predict the change in one (dependent) that will occur from altering one or more of the remaining (independent) variables. (MJB, GA)

multiple retailers. *See* CHAIN STORE.

multiplex. (1) A group of channels in the DIGITAL TELEVISION network, or group of frequencies in the DIGITAL RADIO network.

(2) A cinema complex characterized by several salons under one roof, all operating simultaneously and each showing a different programme. In Britain, the precursors of modern multiplexes appeared in the 1970s, when some large traditional cinemas were subdivided internally so that two or three more screens could be installed. The 1980s have seen a wave of completely new, purpose-built cinemas with as many as a dozen separate screens, plus a family restaurant and

sometimes a creche. Multiplexing worked as a marketing strategy, cinema audiences starting to increase steadily and significantly after a history of sustained decline since the 1950s. By 1996, 83 sites had collectively added 732 screens to the national total, a rounded-off average of nine each. Five operators accounted for 80 per cent of multiplexes and almost 95 per cent of the screens within them. In order of size, they are UCI, Showcase, MGM/Cannon/Virgin, Warner and Odeon. The CINEMA ADVERTISING ASSOCIATION says that 'the multiplex boom ... shows no sign of abating, with a further 50 sites set to open by 1998'. These continuing developments are having a significant but time-lagged effect on the performance of cinema as an ADVERTISING MEDIUM: *see* CINEMA. (KC)

multiplexity. *See* ATTITUDE MULTIPLEXITY.

multiplier. (1) A ratio which measures the change in national income in response to a change in investment. The concept is closely linked with the marginal propensity to save (which is the reciprocal of the multiplier) and the marginal propensity to consume. The operation of the multiplier is the result of the rise in income which follows an increase in investment, part of which will be spent or consumed and part of which will be saved. The proportion which is spent will represent income to others who, in turn, will spend/save their increased income thus stimulating further consumption/production and saving/ investment.

(2) If the READERSHIP of a newspaper or magazine is not known, it can be estimated by applying conventional multipliers to the CIRCULATION thus: daily and evening newspapers x3.0, Sunday newspapers x2.8, general weekly magazines, including Sunday supplements x3.6, general monthly magazines x7.8, women's weekly magazines x2.9, women's monthly magazines x5.5. (KC)

multi-stage sampling. RANDOM SAMPLING conducted in a series of distinct steps or stages by using subgroups or strata within the POPULATION to be surveyed. The procedure is sequential in that one first draws a random sample based upon a given criterion, e.g. 10 polling districts, then draws a random sample from within these subsamples, e.g. every 10th street, and possibly a third random sample, e.g. every 10th household. The key factor to bear in mind is that if, for example, one is sampling households, that those selected by the multi-stage method should have had an equal chance of being chosen by a truly random sample of the population as a whole. To achieve this, great care has to be taken in defining the sub-samples or strata. (MJB)

multivariate analysis. An approach widely used in marketing research due to the complexity of most marketing problems, where several factors are operating together, when one wishes to estimate the influence of each of the variables on the end result, e.g. in monitoring a test market, devising a media schedule etc. Discriminant analysis and FACTOR ANALYSIS are the two best known and widely used multivariate techniques. (MJB)

multivariate data. *See* DATA CLASSIFICATION.

MVO. *See* VOICE-OVER.

N

NAFTA (North American Free Trade Association). A free trade agreement between Canada, Mexico and the United States.   (MJB)

national brand. A brand available nationally as distinct from a regional or test-market brand.
(JRB)

National Consumer Council. Official UK consumer agency located in London, with autonomous subsidiary agencies located in Scotland, Wales and Northern Ireland. Responsible for representing the interests of consumers in exchange relationships with all organizations, including business, state services, local authorities, and so on. Takes particular responsibility for the consumer disadvantaged by low income or any other way.   (JLD)

national income. The sum of the earnings from all factors of production in current use in an economy i.e. producing goods and services, and excluding any transfer incomes i.e. any income which accrues other than in payment for current services to production.   (MJB)

nationalization. The assumption of control over an industry or business by the government. The opposite of PRIVATIZATION.   (MJB)

national press. The collective description of newspapers and magazines that circulate nationwide, rather than only in one part of a country, e.g. the *Financial Times, Newsweek, Der Spiegel, Le Figaro.* The implied contrast is with the LOCAL PRESS and REGIONAL PRESS.   (KC)

National Readership Survey (NRS). A programme of quantitative and qualitative research into readership of the NATIONAL PRESS in Britain, established in 1954. It was first commissioned and co-ordinated by the INSTITUTE OF PRACTITIONERS IN ADVERTISING, then by JICNARS (q.v.) and since 1992 by NATIONAL READERSHIP SURVEYS LTD. The market research agency RSL collects the input data twice a year, by Computer Assisted Personal Interviewing of around 37,500 readers of national newspapers and magazines. Respondents are asked when they 'last looked at, no matter where' a series of publications identified by their mastheads. The number who answer 'yesterday' or 'today' for a daily, 'within the last seven days' for a weekly or 'within the last four weeks' for a monthly are aggregated into the estimated 'average issue readership' for each title. Their composite socio-demographic make-up defines its 'readership profile', and their reading behaviour is similarly aggregated into a general description. MEDIA PLANNERS can obtain data for titles individually, by area or by category, extensively broken down into sub-categories. The most basic details for each title covered by the NRS research are reported in BRAD (q.v.).
(KC)

near pack. *See* ON PACK.

necessity good. A PRODUCT which is considered essential or necessary to everyday life, e.g. bread, vegetables, tables, chairs, shoes.   (MDP)

need. Any physical or emotional body requirement, a lack of something useful required, or a desire for any reason. A need is something fundamental to the maintenance of life, such as food, drink, shelter and clothing. Needs are largely physiological in the sense that they are basic and instinctive drives with which we are born. It is clear, however, that a need may be satisfied by any one of a large number of alternatives, for example thirst may be assuaged by water, tea, coffee, beer, wine, and so on. The availability of alternative means of satisfying a need constitutes choice, provision of which is central to the practice of marketing. In the absence of substitute, or alternative, goods there can be no choice, and needs and wants become synonymous. Where there is more than one way of satisfying a basic need, physiological drives will be modified by economic, sociological and psychological factors. Variations in these factors will predispose individuals to prefer a specific alternative and this preference constitutes a want. *See* MOTIVATION. (MJB)

need hierarchy. Preference order in which innate NEEDS are satisfied. *See* MOTIVATION. (JLD)

need recognition. The first stage in the buying process. (MJB)

negotiated pricing. The agreement of a price based on negotiation. (MJB)

negotiation. The process by which buying and selling organizations resolve differences in terms of price, delivery or product specification. (STP)

net cover. A quantified measure of how well a MEDIA VEHICLE can reach a particular audience. *See* COVERAGE. (KC)

net effective distribution. A measure of the intensity of distribution achieved. *See* MARKET COVERAGE. (AJB)

net homes. A notional figure for the total number of ITV HOMES in an ITV REGION. It is smaller than its gross UNIVERSE because the geographical boundaries of Regions are set by including every local government administrative unit in which a STATION's signal is receivable by at least 15 per cent of all households. Since the ITV network as a whole reaches 97 per cent of households in the country, it follows that there is considerable overlap of reception at the boundaries. Though it is normal for neighbouring stations to claim every household in an overlap area as part of their universe, 'dual-channel' households are correctly split 50/50 between the two Regions involved and 'triple-channel' households, common enough in the South East of England, allocated by thirds.

The result is a net figure for the potential total audience in each Region, as distinct from the gross figure which is its 'universe'. (KC)

net national product. GROSS NATIONAL PRODUCT less deduction for depreciation and capital consumption. (MJB)

net present value (NPV). The current value of an investment after discounting the future cash flows arising from the investment at an agreed rate (usually the best estimate of future inflation) over the life of an investment. (MJB)

net price. The selling price less any discounts or special offers. (MJB)

net profit. The profit that remains after all deductions have been made – all direct and indirect costs, taxation, etc. Also referred to as the 'income' of the organization. (JRB)

net sales. The actual revenue (cash) that accrues to an organization as a result of the sale of its products or services after allowance for standard and special discount which may affect the price invoiced. *See* GROSS SALES. (JRB)

new product committee. A committee established usually but not always on an *ad hoc* basis to evaluate specific product development proposals. Members with relevant expertise will be drawn from the various functional areas of the firm and their brief will usually be to reach conclusions on proposed courses of action and then ensure that action is coordinated and integrated between the departments involved. Such an arrangement may well be adequate for firms with small PRODUCT PORTFOLIOS operating in markets where change is slow and life cycles are prolonged. Where the rate of change is faster and/or the product line is bigger, then such a committee may be established on a standing basis. This arrangement may also suit a multidivisional firm where the top management requires advice on the comparative merits of proposals from divisions in radically different markets. (MJB)

new product departments. Usually found only in large organizations with big product lines subject to frequent change. The advantages of setting up a department with sole responsibilities for developing new products right up to the commercialization phase when they can be handed over to the operating divisions are obvious.

However, the efficiencies which may be expected to accompany task specialization may well be diluted or completely negated unless communication between the partners is first-class. Where it is not, an 'us and them' mentality may well arise and there is considerable evidence to suggest that new products succeed best where they are the responsibility of a single 'product champion' who will see them through all the way from conceptualization to commercialization and beyond.   (MJB)

new product development (NPD). The development of a new product is seen as a sequential process normally containing six distinct phases. While some models contain additional sub-phases and may employ slightly different terminology, the most widely accepted sequence proposed by Booz-Allen & Hamilton Inc, based on their experience with several hundred companies, is: exploration, screening, business analysis, development, testing, commercialization. Like the PRODUCT LIFE CYCLE CONCEPT, the new product development model is of greatest value when regarded as a framework or structure to guide one's own approach. Clearly no single, simple process model can allow for all the complications and problems likely to be encountered by the firm which sets out to manage new product development, nor is such a model appropriate to many radical innovations or to situations where technology 'push' is dominant. That said, however, all phases are recommended and are usually found to be present in case histories of NPD. Hence a brief review of each will be helpful.

The exploration phase, sometimes termed 'idea generation', may be structured or serendipitous. A structured procedure for new product ideas may rest upon continuous market research into consumer reactions both to one's own product and to those of one's competitors in order to give early warning of failing interest or dissatisfaction or, more positively, to suggest areas for improvement which will enhance the product's standing with its target audience.

Monitoring competitive activity has assumed increasing importance in recent years with the growing popularity of what is termed 'the strategy of the fast second' whereby firms depend more on their ability to copy or improve upon a new product and cash in on the market as it moves into the growth phase than on being the first to market with a new product. The Japanese are past masters of this strategy, and are imitative innovators of the first order across almost all classes of goods, depending upon an enhanced product, competitive prices and excellent distribution and after-sales service to ensure a dominant position in almost all the world's growth markets. Significantly, the Japanese have been responsible for no major technological innovations themselves.

Unstructured idea generation tends to be more typical of firms with a single product or small range of products experiencing a decline in their current profitability – that is, the firm does not have a formal new product development function but operates on an *ad hoc* basis. Brainstorming is a frequently used technique in these circumstances in which the second phase of screening or sifting the ideas assumes particular importance. An unstructured approach is also often associated with serendipity when an idea for a new product occurs by chance – as a by-product of research into something else, for example, or as the result of an approach by a prospective user asking if you could make something to meet a specific need. Once the firm has generated a portfolio of ideas for new product, it is essential that these be 'screened' to ensure that only the most promising are subjected to thorough analysis, if for no other reason than that the further one proceeds with any given idea the greater the expense involved, as shown in Figure 19.

Screening is an essentially subjective procedure in which managers use their knowledge and experience to weed out the obvious non-starters. Beyond doubt, managers are most confident when applying their knowledge of internal constraints and will eliminate many ideas as being inconsistent with the firm's product policies and objectives, with the existing skills and resources and so on. In the same way, ideas which are incompatible with the firm's existing markets and its knowledge of its current users and customers are likely to be screened out at this phase as the firm seeks to build upon its existing strengths.

Given a short-list of 'possible' ideas, the next step is to subject these to a more formal analysis – a task which will be greatly improved if an explicit check-list is developed, setting out the criteria and their relative importance one to another. In general, this evaluation should assess each of the ideas in terms of its technology and its 'fit' with the production system, its marketability and its competitiveness, and finally in terms of the financial implications of proceeding with it further.

Assuming that evaluation indicates that development of the product appears feasible, that forecasted sales and budgeted costs promise a satisfactory return on investment, and that the company is satisfied it can gain access to the target market, then the next phase in the process is technical development. At this juncture, the objective is to establish if it is physically possible to produce an object with the desired performance characteristics within the cost constraints indicated by the forecast demand schedule. Usually this phase is the longest in the whole process, and it is vitally important that, throughout development, the innovator should continue critically to observe events and changes in the proposed target markets. In addition to updating the product concept to reflect changes in the market, the development phase should also provide for testing the product under real world usage conditions to ensure that it will deliver the promised satisfactions. The more complex the product and·the more radical the behavioural change required of the end user, the more important this phase becomes. Indeed, with many capital, material and consumer durable innovations, the development phase frequently continues well into the market launch stage on the grounds that deficiencies and defects in the final product will only become apparent once it is exposed to a broad spectrum of usage situations.

With complex products, the development phase may well proceed in parallel with physical and market testing, but in other cases, the test phase may be a discrete activity in its own right. Obviously testing is a risk reduction strategy as the firm's commitment is limited and a final go/no-go decision can be deferred pending the test results. With a major and complex new product, marketing on a small scale to iron out the bugs has much to commend it, but, with less sophisticated products, test marketing can give the game away to one's competitors and allow them to counter your full-scale launch with a strong competitive reaction. Indeed, with many consumer goods, test marketing can be a complete waste of effort as competitors create abnormal trading conditions in the test area so that little or no reliance can be placed on the results.

The final phase of the NPD process is commercialization when the product is launched in the market, thus initiating its life cycle. As can be seen from Figure 19, commercialization increases the firm's financial commitment by several orders of magnitude. Capacity must be installed to cater for the anticipated demand; inventory must be built up to ensure that supplies can be made available to the distribution channel; intensive selling in must take place to ensure widespread availability at the point of sale or to

Percentage of total evolution expenditures (cumulative)
(expense items plus capital expenditures)

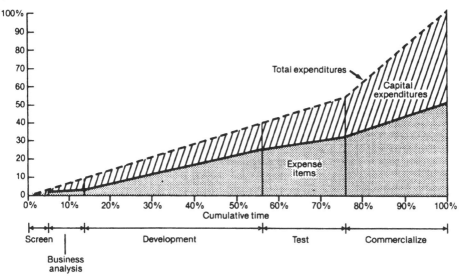

Figure 19: **New product development costs**

canvass orders from prospective buyers; maintenance and servicing facilities may be necessary and a large promotional investment will be needed to create awareness of the new product's existence. Given the importance of this phase, one might reasonably expect discussions of it to dominate texts dealing with the subject, but it only requires a cursory examination to reveal that this stage rarely receives equal treatment with the preceding phases and attracts comparatively little attention. (MJB)

Newspaper Publishers' Association (NPA). The body representing the publishers of UK national daily newspapers and the one London evening paper. Founded in 1906, in addition to the usual range of activities of a trade association, it acts on behalf of the dailies in wage negotiations and industrial disputes, and is one of the bodies involved in the awarding of 'recognition' to RECOGNIZED ADVERTISING AGENCIES. (KC)

newspapers. A major print medium published daily or weekly on a national or regional basis. Newspapers are bought largely for their news value and are particularly appropriate for announcing new products or new developments of existing products. Because of their frequency of publication they are also well suited to opportunity markets (cotton dresses in a heatwave) and for regular features and advertising which reflect habitual behaviour, e.g. advertising grocery products on Thursday and Friday as most of these products are bought on Friday and Saturday.

Conventionally, newspapers are divided into three groups: national, regional and Sunday, each of which possesses different characteristics in terms of character, atmosphere and coverage. Although the importance of newspapers has declined since the advent of commercial broadcasting they still constitute an important medium, with a central role to play in most advertising campaigns and dominance in the field of classified advertising. (MJB)

Newspaper Society (NS). The body representing the publishers of UK regional daily and weekly newspapers, founded in 1836. In addition to the usual range of activities of a trade association, it acts on their behalf in wage negotiations and industrial disputes, and is one of the bodies involved in the awarding of 'recognition' to RECOGNIZED ADVERTISING AGENCIES. (KC)

news release. A more precise but less common term for a PRESS RELEASE. (KC)

new task. One of three types of buying behaviour proposed by Robinson, Faris and Wind (*Industrial Buying and Creative Marketing*, 1967). The salient characteristics of a new task buying situation are: (a) the need for the product has not arisen previously; (b) little or no past buying experience is available to assist in the purchasing decision; (c) members of the buying unit require a great deal of information; (d) alternative ways of meeting the need are likely to be under review; (e) the situation occurs infrequently, but the decisions taken may set a pattern for more routine purchases subsequently, (f) opportunities exist at an early stage in the decision process for external (marketing) inputs to have an influence on the final decision made. (MJB)

next matter. A MEDIA BUYER'S booking instruction, requesting a SPECIAL POSITION for the booked ADVERTISEMENT on the same page as specified editorial material. *See also* FACING MATTER. (KC)

niche strategy. A CONCENTRATED marketing strategy followed by small firms which are unable to compete directly with larger firms with COST LEADERSHIP advantages. Involves the selection of a segment or segments which are sufficiently large to be profitable and developing highly differentiated products to meet their needs. (MJB)

Nielsen. Nielsen is the global authority in providing marketing and decision support solutions to the fast-moving consumer goods industry. As a strategic partner with the world's top companies Nielsen has been the primary supplier of information-based systems and analysis for over 70 years and now has coverage in 88 countries worldwide. Nielsen is currently a company of the Dun and Bradstreet Corporation. (MJB)

Nielsen Retail Index. A.C. Nielsen Co. Ltd operates its Retail Index services in over 27 countries. These services consist of undertaking RETAIL AUDITS (in grocers, confectioners, pharmacies etc.) every two months to provide information to subscribers on purchases, STOCKS, SALES PROMOTIONS and price levels over a range of CONSUMER PRODUCTS. The data produced can provide information on MARKET SIZE, MARKET SHARES and effectiveness of pricing and promotional methods to subscribing manufacturers. (AMW)

noise. A term from communication theory to describe interference in a communication channel which distorts the signal and so renders the message difficult or impossible to interpret. *See* COMMUNICATION.   (MJB)

nominal scales. *See* SCALING TECHNIQUES.

non-business marketing. The application of MARKETING theory and practices to non-profit organizations such as schools, universities, hospitals, councils etc. A classic article on the subject was written by Philip Kotler and Sidney Levy ('Broadening the Concept of Marketing', in *Journal of Marketing,* vol. 33, January 1969) and concluded that the question facing non-business organizations was not whether to MARKET or not (because no organization could avoid marketing), but rather whether to do it well or poorly. *See also* NON-PROFIT ORGANIZATIONS.   (GM)

non-durable goods. *See* DURABLE GOODS.

non-parametric statistical tests. Either not relying on any assumptions about the statistical distribution of the parent population, or not dependent on the data being in metric form.
                                             (JAB)

non-price competition. The use of factors other than price to differentiate the firm's output, e.g. quality, differentiation, branding, service levels etc. *See* COMPETITION.   (MJB)

non-probability sampling. Methods of SAMPLING which do not involve a non-zero probability for each member of the POPULATION. Some stage of selection usually involves judgement, rather than random selection. QUOTA SAMPLING is a non-probability sampling method.
                                             (SKT)

non-profit organization (NPO). No precise definition exists as the distinction between public and private organizations and/profit/non-profit are blurred. Michael J. Thomas ('Marketing: Not for Profit', in Michael J. Baker (ed.), *Marketing in Adversity,* 1976) suggests that '... in general parlance, it is a term used to refer to organizations that are not considered business, i.e. organizations that operate in the non-business sector or environment. Their products and services tend to be public goods and services, as opposed to private goods and services, a definition which encompasses cultural activities, public safety, health care services, education and politics.'

Interest in NPOs has grown markedly since the late 1960s as an element of the SOCIAL MARKETING concept and the general argument that marketing is a universal activity which is applicable to all kinds of social institutions irrespective of their profit orientation.   (MJB)

non-representative sample bias. BIAS in SURVEY SAMPLING which is due to the particular sample obtained being non-representative. Simple random sampling procedures have no safeguards to ensure representative coverage of important subgroups, and thus can on occasion (not in general) generate non-representative sample bias.
                                             (SKT)

non-response. The act of not taking part in a market research survey: refusing to be interviewed, failing to return a completed mail questionnaire. It is an important factor in assessing the validity and reliability of survey data: a non-response rate in excess of 25 per cent of the target sample must raise some doubt as to the value of the survey information.   (JRB)

non-sampling error. Errors that are not due to SAMPLING: these can include errors of question design, coding, statistics and interpretation of the results, and also errors from interviewers. (SKT)

non-store retailing. Any form of retailing e.g. DIRECT MAIL, where the buyer purchases without visiting a store.   (MJB)

non tariff trade barriers. Barriers to trade of a non monetary kind.   (MJB)

non-traceable common costs. Those costs incurred in the production process which cannot be attributed directly to any specific activity and so can only be allocated on an arbitrary basis.
                                             (MJB)

normal distribution. A distribution in which the elements are distributed symmetrically about the mean with many small deviations and few large ones. The characteristics of normal distributions are known precisely and provide the basis of sampling theory. Thus it is known that in a normal distribution 68 per cent of all cases will fall within plus or minus 1 standard deviation of the MEAN, 95 per cent within plus or minus 2 standard deviations and 99 per cent with plus or minus 2.6 standard deviations. Accordingly if one knows that the distribution of a sample is approximately normal then one may use the parameters of the normal distribution to make statements about the population from which the sample was drawn with a given level of confidence. The normal distribution has many applications in marketing and underlies the concept of the PRODUCT LIFE CYCLE and the classification of adopters. *See* ADOPTER CATEGORIES. (MJB)

norms. Rules of behaviour adopted by a society which determine what is acceptable or unacceptable within that society. *See* MORES. (MJB)

NPA. *See* NEWSPAPER PUBLISHERS' ASSOCIATION.

NPV. *See* NET PRESENT VALUE.

NRS. *See* NATIONAL READERSHIP SURVEY.

NS. *See* NEWSPAPER SOCIETY.

nuclear family. The basic family unit of man, woman and children. (MJB)

null hypothesis. In inferential statistics, the null hypothesis is what the statistical test allows one to decide as being unlikely. One constructs a no-difference or no-effect null hypothesis and the test informs the researcher that the null hypothesis is extremely unlikely. The researcher then accepts the hypothesis that he is really interested in. (SKT)

nutritional labelling. Labels which provide detailed information of the contents (carbohydrates, fat, protein and calories etc.) of processed foods. (MJB)

O

objective. A desired outcome which is established to measure the effectiveness of a course of action intended to achieve some purpose or goal. Objectives should be quantifiable and capable of measurement so as to provide a benchmark against which to compare actual performance.

(MJB)

objective-and-task method. One of the three most popular ways to set the size of the ADVERTISING APPROPRIATION. (KC)

observation technique. Method involved in that area of MARKET RESEARCH which uses observation rather than questioning in order to obtain DATA. For example, valuable data on the use and misuse of CONSUMER DURABLES may be obtained by observing their use in the home, rather than questioning the user. (JRB)

obsolescence. The act of becoming obsolete or out of date. Many manufacturers are subject to criticism on the grounds that they deliberately pursue a policy of planned obsolescence and so accelerate the process of product replacement.

Planned obsolescence may occur in styling or design, in terms of the materials used or in the performance and functions of the product. While the issue is an emotive one most marketers would argue that CONSUMER SOVEREIGNTY is the best defence against deliberate exploitation through planned obsolescence. (MJB)

occasion segmentation. SEGMENTATION using the occasion prompting purchase or use as the basis for sub-dividing the market. (MJB)

odd–even pricing. The practice of setting prices to end in certain numbers in the belief that this will have a desirable persuasive effect. In some product ranges it is believed that the numbers five and nine indicate lower prices while in other product ranges even pricing is more popular, in order to avoid change-giving. (AJB)

Office of Fair Trading. A UK Government agency established by the Fair Trading Act 1973 to monitor trade and commerce, and ensure compliance with the legislation governing industrial and commercial behaviour, and to promote and protect the consumers' interests. (AJB)

off-peak. *See* PEAK TIME and PRIME TIME.

off-price labels. In terms of consumer acceptability the label featuring Xp off the regular price is the most popular promotion. It is also popular with retailers as it involves none of the diseconomies associated with coupon redemption and also provides the opportunity to feature a price reduction in their local advertising.

The actual extent of the price reduction is an important determinant of the level of sampling, and careful thought, and preferably testing, must be given to the selection of a discount. Some prices have the apparent effect of being perceived as less than they really are, and it is these which have the greatest impact on IMPULSE PURCHASES. Obviously, if sales volume can be increased sufficiently the firm may be able both to even out seasonal fluctuations and make a profit.

A price reduction is a short-term strategy, however, and the simplest for one's competitors to duplicate. For these reasons it is avoided by companies that are sensitive to a price war wherever possible, e.g. the petrol companies, until in the UK Jet and others pre-empted a sufficient market share through price cutting to make a general price reduction necessary on the part of the 'Big Five' to protect their market share.

(MJB)

Ogilvy, David (1911–). Market researcher, copywriter and founder of a famous ADVERTISING AGENCY. Born in London, schooled in Edinburgh and educated at Oxford, he went to the USA, worked for a large market research company and then set up an advertising agency in New York, on $6,000 capital and no clients at all. In 1996, Ogilvy & Mather ranked tenth in the USA and third in the UK. To the founder's chagrin, however, the company was bought in 1989 by Martin SORRELL's WPP Group, the largest advertising organization in the world. David Ogilvy is best known for a press advertising campaign in America in the 1960s which established Rolls-Royce as a serious competitor to Cadillac and Lincoln. The celebrated headline of one advertisement was 'At 60 miles an hour, the loudest noise in this new Rolls-Royce comes from the electric clock.' Ogilvy himself attributes the success of the campaign not only to that and other clever headlines but also to the long, detailed 'reason-why' arguments in the main text, as pioneered by Claude HOPKINS. Nevertheless, he once remarked that a good headline is 'eighty cents of your client's dollar'. An Ogilvy characteristic which many commentators have criticised is his predilection for devising 'rules' for successful advertising and enshrining them in publications. It is alleged that Ogilvy & Mather advertising regularly violated many of the more dogmatic injunctions, but he has responded that the original intent was often misinterpreted. Despite retiring to a chateau in France, he continued for many years to exercise control-by-memo over the agency's creative standards, and ceased his voluntary active involvement with the agency world-wide only when his health obliged him to at the age of 85. David Ogilvy's highly individual view of advertising can be sampled in *Ogilvy on Advertising* (1983), an updated re-issue of *Confessions of an Advertising Man* (1962). (KC)

oligopoly. Oligopolistic markets exist when there are so few sellers of a particular product or service that the market activities of the seller have an important effect on the other sellers.

Oligopolistic markets have many different structures; a small number of sellers is only one characteristic of an oligopolistic market. Other characteristics are homogeneity or differentiation of the product, the kind of CONCENTRATION in the industry, and the height of the BARRIERS TO ENTRY faced by new firms. In a pure or homogeneous oligopoly there is a small number of firms in the industry, and they sell a homogeneous product or service. All of them are compelled to ask the same price, since the purchase decision is predominantly influenced by price when homogeneous products are involved. Furthermore, because there are few sellers each seller must consider what effect his price will have on prices by competitors, and must expect retaliation if he reduces prices. In a differentiated oligopoly there is some real or imagined product differentiation. Hence, prices vary among firms in an oligopoly, and they vary in direct proportion to the differences in the degree of product differentiation among firms.

(MJB)

oligopsony. A market in which there are more than two (duopsony) but only a small number of buyers or oligopsonists.

(MJB)

omnibus survey. A form of syndicated commercial MARKET RESEARCH survey, much used by ADVERTISERS. It offers the opportunity to add a limited number of extra questions to a basic questionnaire at a particular time. It is thus possible to POST-TEST an ADVERTISING CAMPAIGN with respect to easily standardized and measured performance criteria, such as spontaneous awareness, recall of a slogan, or brand image. The cost is significantly lower than a purpose-designed one-off survey, but the scope for detailed findings is distinctly limited.

(KC)

One Minute Management. A technique of management introduced by Kenneth Blanchard and Spencer Johnson in their book *The One Minute Manager* (London: Fontana, 1983). The technique is based on setting a goal on one sheet of paper, which can be read in one minute. If the team achieves the goal, they are given one minute's praise, and if not, they are given a one minute reprimand. Follow-on books include *One Minute Selling* and *Putting the One Minute Manager to Work*.

(GM)

One Minute Selling. *See* ONE MINUTE MANAGEMENT.

one-sided question. A type of biased question design where only one of the two alternatives in a dichotomy is illustrated. For example: 'Do you think car engines should be prevented from destroying the atmosphere?' provides no information on the implied alternative.   (SKT)

one-stop shopping. The provision of a full range of foodstuffs, cleaning materials and other frequently purchased household goods within a single outlet, so that shoppers can satisfy all their regular purchasing needs without having to visit or stop at a variety of outlets.   (MJB)

one-tailed test. An inferential statistic test where the direction of effect is taken into account: in the contrasting TWO-TAILED TEST one asks whether a sample is different (either bigger or smaller) from the POPULATION; in a one-tailed test one asks whether the sample is bigger or smaller – but not both at the same time!   (SKT)

one-way table. A table listing the values for a single variable such as age, level of education etc.   (MJB)

on-line computer shopping. Buying and selling using on-line, interactive computer services.   (MJB)

on-line database. A popular and useful source of up to date MARKET data, scientific publications and new technology information. They are comprehensive databases covering surveys, journal articles, books etc. held by host companies which may be accessed at any time for a fee. Each host company may have databases in one or several areas, e.g. technical, chemical, medical or business. Examples include Datastar, Dialog and Info-line. Access is possible using an acoustic coupler or modem and a terminal. Searches are accomplished by keying in relevant keywords. For example, a manager interested in computer games may first type in the word 'computer'. The system would search for all records containing this word. If there were too many 'hits', a second keyword 'games' would narrow the subset. Time limits may also be applied, e.g. post-1987. The result is a comprehensive list of relevant articles, reports, books etc. A charge is made for the connect time, for database royalties and for printing out the search details.   (KRD)

on-line real time. The ability of field salespersons, amongst others, to access a centrally held database by means of a remote terminal. Telephone lines are used to make the connection, from anywhere in the world, by means of an acoustic coupler or modem. 'Real time' refers to the instant updating of central databases and the concomitant instant availability of all such new data to future users of the system.   (KRD)

on pack. The SALES PROMOTION term referring to the location of a premium or offer of a premium given with the PRODUCT. It is also known as 'in pack' or 'near pack'.   (GM)

open account. In this situation an exporter merely presents his accounts to the overseas buyer for payment at the agreed time, without any preliminary documentary proof that the terms of the export contract have been met. This is probably the simplest method of export finance, but it is advisable only where there is no danger of disagreement about whether the terms of the contract have been met.   (JML)

open dating. A method of publishing on the product in an uncoded form and so 'open' to the public the latest date by which it should be sold.   (AJB)

open-ended question. A type of question that has no suggested answers, as opposed to the case with a CLOSED QUESTION. The RESPONDENT is given the opportunity to phrase his answer in his own words. Interviewers are expected to record answers verbatim.   (AMW)

open markets. The traditional kind of market in which sellers rent stalls and sell a wide variety of foodstuffs and household goods, usually at competitive prices. While such markets are often held in the open air in some instances they are held in covered buildings and stall holders may rent space on a permanent basis.   (MJB)

open-to-buy (OTB). An indication of purchasing readiness. The term may be used (a) qualitatively, to denote willingness to purchase and the readiness of buyers to receive selling propositions; (b) quantitatively, to denote the volume of PRODUCT or material for which the buyer is soliciting offers.   (KNB)

operant conditioning. Seeking to change behaviour by altering the consequences of that behaviour e.g. giving an unpleasant taste to harmful substances or vice versa.   (MJB)

operating statement. Usually a progress report which is designed to show actual achievements versus forecast/budgeted goals, and which high-lights and explains variances between them.

(JRB)

operations planning. The planning undertaken to achieve short-term (say, from one month to two years) objectives, as against strategic planning undertaken to achieve longer-term objectives. (JRB)

opinion. The distinction between opinion and ATTITUDE is frequently blurred in marketing usage. Technically, opinions are seen as contributing to the formation of attitudes which are less subject to change and more likely to influence behaviour. It would seem therefore that while all attitudes might be classified as opinions the reverse is not the case. For all practical purposes, however, both attitude and opinion reflect an individual's view about a subject and the strength of this would be better quantified, e.g. using SCALING, rather than relying on an assumption that the semantic difference is understood.

(MJB)

opinion leaders (industrial). People who are referred to by members of their own organization (or members of other organizations) for opinions or advice prior to the purchase of an industrial product or service. (STP)

opinion leadership. Early models of communication regarded both impersonal sources (the mass media) and personal sources as establishing direct contact with an audience – the so-called 'hypodermic effect'. Belief in this model led to speculation concerning the influence of the mass media upon voting behaviour and the 1940 presidential election in the United States was the subject of one of the most celebrated pieces of communication research, reported in Paul F. Lazarsfeld *et al., The People's Choice* (1944). Contrary to expectations Lazarsfeld and his colleagues found that influence did not flow directly from a medium (press, radio, etc.) to an audience but was channelled through an intermediary who was designated the 'opinion leader'. In simple terms an opinion leader is one to whom others turn for information and advice. However, it must be emphasized that in the usual marketing context opinion leaders are not a distinct and easily classified group in the sense in which government ministers or managing directors of major companies are. More often than not opinion leaders are just ordinary people,

for if they are to be effective at a personal influence level they must be accessible, which implies that they are members of REFERENCE GROUPS with which people have contact. In fact most reference groups develop around shared interests and some members will be seen as more influential than others in the context of that interest. But people belong to many reference groups, leader and follower roles may be reversed, for example, the captain of the football team may well seek the first reserve's opinion on the merits of hi-fi systems. It is this tendency which makes the identification of opinion leaders difficult. (MJB)

opinion polls. A survey designed to measure opinions on the subject of the survey. While the opinions to be measured may relate to any topic, their use in connection with public opinion on political issues has resulted in most people regarding the term 'opinion poll' as synonymous with 'political opinion poll'. (MJB)

opportunities-to-see (OTS). 'Average OTS' is a measure of the number of chances an average member of the TARGET AUDIENCE will have of being exposed to an ADVERTISEMENT in an advertising campaign. 'Gross OTS' is computed by adding the average OTS figure for each advertisement in a campaign. The Media Research Group has cautioned that 'the definition of an opportunity to see is different for each medium and not directly comparable. An opportunity to see an advertisement on television is quite different from an opportunity to see a press advertisement, or a poster site, or a cinema or radio commercial' (*Admap,* August 1979). As a rule of thumb, a burst of television advertising would normally be planned to achieve a minimum OTS of 2.5, while a press campaign would be planned for a figure of 5 or more. (KC)

opportunity analysis. One of the four dimensions of the SWOT ANALYSIS, intended to identify and describe opportunities available to the firm in relation to its existing skills and resources or those which it could reasonably expect to acquire. (MJB)

opportunity and threat analysis. *See* SWOT ANALYSIS.

opportunity cost. The cost in terms of lost income or profit of the foregone alternative investment or course of action. Where management fails to take an opportunity or make a decision to commit funds in an alternative way that would have produced a better net return, the lost revenue is an opportunity cost. For example, the opportunity cost of a marginal product allowed to linger in the product-line is the profit contribution that a new product could produce if the effort and resources being devoted to the existing product were redirected to the new one. (GA)

optical character recognition (OCRA). Method used for interpreting BARCODES. (MJB)

optical disc. A five-inch plastic disc containing digital data. It is composed of thousands of concentric circles, each containing microscopic pits that are read by a laser. The information is passed to the computer CPU and transferred to ASCII format for manipulation by the appropriate system. Currently data may only be read from the disc and not written to it, though the technology to write to it interactively is being developed. Current storage capacity is 540 megabytes or the equivalent of 1500 floppy discs (or to a pile of A4 paper the height of an eight-storey building!), though the rate of technological change will probably have rendered that figure obsolete by the time you read this. (KRD)

option. A contract to buy or sell an object at a fixed price on or before an agreed future date. (MJB)

Oracle. ITV's TELETEXT service, which carries ADVERTISEMENTS. The cost of a national full-page advertisement per week is around £4,500. Viewing figures are estimated at around 5 million, and ads can be interleaved between pages of editorial. See TELETEXT. (GM)

ordinal scales. See SCALING TECHNIQUES.

organizational behaviour. The study of how and why people behave within organizations with a view to improving ORGANIZATIONAL STRUCTURES and performance. (MJB)

organizational buyer behaviour. Organization buying decisions can be seen in terms of a problem solving activity with identifiable decision stages. In Robinson and Faris's model the process begins with recognition of a need which may be satisfied by purchase, continues with the search for and evaluation of alternatives and fin-

ishes with choice and establishment of a purchasing routine. See BUY PHASES. (MJB)

organizational climate. The personality of an organization conditioned by its structure, technology and the people that work within the organization. (STP)

organizational learning. The acquisition of new skills and competencies by members of an organization which increase and enhance its ability to compete effectively. Widely regarded as a major source of SUSTAINABLE COMPETITIVE ADVANTAGE. (MJB)

organizational marketing. A development of the well-established term 'INDUSTRIAL MARKETING' to cover the MARKETING of all goods and services between one organization and another. The marketing approach is thus identifiably linked to the subsumed existence of ORGANIZATIONAL BUYER BEHAVIOUR.

The key CONCEPT is that the fundamental differentiating feature between types of marketing activity is not the nature of the goods being traded, but the nature of the demand. Whereas CONSUMERS are perceived as buying frequently (if not always) for immeasurable personal satisfaction, organizations are seen as buying deliberately, usually with quantifiable benefits in view. Marketers thus require to base their approaches accordingly – even if the PRODUCT being traded is for eventual personal consumption. See also BUSINESS-TO-BUSINESS MARKETING. (KNB)

organizational structure. The pattern of relationships between members of a group which define and describe their relationships with one another. Following the work of Burns and Stalker organizational structure is often distinguished as being Organic or Mechanistic, the former implying *flexibility,* the latter *rigidity.* (MJB)

Organization of Petroleum Exporting Countries (OPEC). An association of oil producing countries formed in 1960 to control supply for the benefit of its members. By raising prices in the early 1970s they precipitated the energy crisis which led to the development of many oil fields, including the North Sea, which previously had been uneconomic, as well as encouraging the development of energy saving devices, more efficient internal combustion engines etc. Members include: Algeria, Bahrain,

Brunei, Ecuador, Gabon, Indonesia, Iran, Iraq, Kuwait, Libya, Nigeria, Oman, Qatar, Saudi Arabia, Trinidad and Tobago, United Arab Emirates and Venezuela.   (MJB)

original equipment manufacturer (OEM). An industrial company which produces a complete product for sale to other industrial companies e.g. radios for installing in cars, or final sale to ultimate consumers.   (MJB)

OSCAR. Acronym, pronounced as a word, for Outdoor Site Classification and Audience Research. From 1989 until 1995, OSCAR provided MEDIA PLANNERS with COVERAGE and FREQUENCY figures for OUTDOOR advertising. Its data were at first based on a 30-year-old 'poster audience model' (*see* JICPAS), but a new programme of continuous field research greatly improved the quality of the inputs to the model and immediately rendered poster media buying a more 'user-friendly' process than at any time before. One technical refinement had the dramatic effect of reducing claimed POSTER SITE audiences by about a third. OSCAR was superseded at the end of 1995 by POSTAR, q.v.   (KC)

Osgood scales. Widely used semantic differential technique developed by Osgood *et al.* (*Method and Theory in Experimental Psychology,* 1952). It is much simpler to construct than many other scales, for example, THURSTONE SCALE, LIKERT SCALE or GUTTMANN SCALING, and yet yields a very high measure of agreement with these more elaborate measures. The method consists of a series of bipolar adjectives (strong–weak, good–bad etc.) separated usually by between five to nine points. The respondent is asked to checkmark the point which best indicates their attitude. Scale positions are sometimes qualified, for example: extremely good, very good, fairly good, neither good nor bad, fairly bad, extremely bad. However, such qualification tends to discourage selection of the extreme positions.   (MJB)

OTB. *See* OPEN-TO-BUY.

other-directed. A personality trait of social character defined by Riesman *et al.* (D. Riesman, N. Glazer, and R. Dinny, *The Lonely Crowd,* New Haven, Conn.: Yale University Press, 1950) which results in the individual adapting his or her VALUES, BELIEFS and BEHAVIOUR to those of the peer group with which he or she seeks to iden-

tify. Other-directed persons tend to conform by contrast with INNER-DIRECTED persons, who tend to innovate.   (MJB)

outdoor. The oldest of the five 'major' advertising media in Britain. Media professionals subdivide the medium into 'outdoor' and 'transport' categories, separating POSTER SITES seen mainly by motorists and public transport users from those not deliberately located to reach that particular target audience. In 1996, the non-transport outdoor category took 71 per cent of total expenditure on this medium. The distinction is made on the basis that the audience's relationship to the medium is markedly different in the two cases, but it must surely become blurred if one considers an 'outdoor' site next to a city-centre shopping precinct but facing a car park used by commuting motorists. Furthermore, there is considerable inconsistency in the use of the two terms. The ADVERTISING ASSOCIATION's Advertising Statistics Yearbook describes the combined medium as 'Outdoor & Transport'; BRAD (q.v.) calls it 'Posters & Outdoor'; the ADVERTISER'S ANNUAL distinguishes 'transport' from 'poster & outdoor'. The key characteristic of the medium is, of course, that the vehicle for the advertisement is generally a POSTER of some sort. Granted, the options available to advertisers at one time or another have included illuminated signs such as those in Piccadilly Circus and Times Square, electronic 'spectaculars', sandwich boards, milk bottles and a host of other spaces listed elsewhere in this entry, but those constitute only a very small part of the whole. Whatever we choose to call this diverse medium, it is today the third largest, accounting for exactly 4 per cent of total UK advertising expenditure in 1996. Its slice of the pie was around 8 per cent until the arrival of commercial television in 1955, after which it fell steadily to just under 4 per cent in 1966. The figure has since fluctuated within a narrow band between 4.3 per cent in 1979 and 3.4 per cent in 1989. Outdoor is a much less significant medium in the USA, taking just 1 per cent of total advertising expenditure in 1995, but much more important in France at 12 per cent and Japan at 14 per cent. MEDIA PLANNERS face a variety of MEDIA VEHICLES and a potentially daunting choice of MEDIA OPTIONS. The listings in BRAD distinguish four vehicles within the medium it calls 'posters and outdoor': 'roadside', 'transport', 'specialized' and 'venue' advertising. Options available in the first category comprise conventional posters in ten sizes, targeted geographically and demographically: for example, a 'roadside 48-sheet (*see* POSTER SIZES) Captains of Industry package'. The second consists of a considerable variety of available spaces in and on buses and taxis, in underground and 'overground' stations, and at airports, also targeted geographically and demographically: for example, 4-sheet posters at all 'Inner Commuter' railway stations in London. The 'specialized' category comprised, at the time of writing, spaces on hot-air balloons, airships, blimps, supermarket trolleys and fresh eggs, and aeroplane-towed banners. 'Venue' options included posters and signs at or in: hospitals; exhibition halls; sports and athletics stadia; motor racing circuits; golf courses; pub and restaurant washrooms. MEDIA BUYERS negotiate campaigns 'line by line' (that is, site by site individually) or in packages. Located between the precision of the first and the pig-in-a-poke risk of the second is the 'PSC' option, standing for Pre-Selected Campaign. Large advertisers can reserve prime locations indefinitely by placing a 'TC' (till countermanded) order. Outdoor advertising space is bought either direct from the MEDIA OWNERS, called 'contractors', or through 'poster buying specialists', intermediaries who are paid a booking fee by contractors. Roughly half the available media options are owned by a large number of small contractors, the remainder by three very large ones: Maiden Outdoor Advertising, Mills & Allen and More O'Ferrall Adshel. MEDIA PLANNERS have access to a range of audience data based on large-scale research surveys. Outdoor advertising in general is covered by the POSTAR continuous research programme, which replaced OSCAR at the end of 1995: *see* the respective specific entries. The audience for bus advertising in the London area has been measured since 1991. Initial research specified the services, timetables and advertising spaces available on every 'link' between 'nodes' in the 'bus network'. In-home interviews with 1,000 residents of Greater London and 150 hours of video recordings made by a survey car yielded a database that provides planners with COVERAGE and FREQUENCY figures, relating to both pedestrians and motorists, for every 'link' between 'nodes' in the 'bus network'. The audience for London Underground advertising was measured by the 'TRAC' survey (Tube Research & Audience Classification), in which 5,000 travellers recruited at a number of stations around the system kept travel diaries over 28 days in 1993. That database provides an average figure for 'number of exposures per person, per campaign,

per site and per panel size'. Some of the contractors offering more specialized options provide their own audience breakdowns: for instance, a demographic profile of travellers on the Tyne & Wear Metro, based on a field survey of the local market in 1994. The general audience for outdoor advertising obviously has pretty much the same profile as the population at large. In the case of bus advertising, it is significantly more upmarket than the population as a whole and somewhat younger, while London Underground users are very much more upmarket (perhaps unexpectedly), younger and more likely to be male than female. It should consequently come as no surprise that the top-spending outdoor advertisers in 1995 were Nestle, Vauxhall, Honda, International Distillers & Vintners, Royal Mail and BT. (KC)

Outdoor Advertising Council. Established in 1947, the Council was a major contributor to the framing of the Town and Country Planning (Control of Advertisements) Regulations one year later. The principal objective of the five representative bodies in membership, which are said to cover the great majority of the many firms and organizations involved in OUTDOOR advertising in the UK, is to exercise appropriate control over the use of the medium by fostering good working relationships among the MEDIA OWNERS, sign manufacturers and the firms whose advertising occupies POSTER SITES around the country. (KC)

over positioning. Specifying the brand or product too narrowly with the result that some of the target customers are not reached effectively.
(MJB)

overseas marketing research. The systematic gathering, recording and analysing of data to help reduce uncertainty and aid decision making in overseas markets. The tools and techniques, although perhaps receiving different emphasis, are the same as those used at home (*see* MARKET RESEARCH) but the environment overseas is likely to be more difficult and uncertain with greater cultural, economic, technological and political constraints. Consequently the problems encountered in domestic marketing research are likely to be exacerbated in overseas marketing research. For example the case of mechanically implementing marketing research is likely to be less as well as varying from country to country. The information required may well need different emphasis.

The scope of overseas marketing research is also likely to be broader. General information about the country area and/or market, like size of market, price and cost structure in the market, sources of competition, distribution systems, etc. in order to assess market opportunities will be required. More attention may need to be given to forecasting future market requirements than in domestic marketing where such factors are better known and understood. At the same time the specific information to solve marketing mix problems, on which marketing research tends to concentrate in the domestic market, will also be necessary for overseas markets.

Overseas marketing research tends to be more expensive and often the quality is lower especially in DEVELOPING COUNTRIES where market research agencies are fewer and less sophisticated than in DEVELOPED COUNTRIES. *See also* INTERNATIONAL MARKETING.   (JK)

Overseas Trade Analysed in Terms of Industries. Published in *Business Monitor* quarterly by

HMSO. This gives an analysis of commodities imported and exported, according to the industries of which they are principal products.
(MDP)

Overseas Trade Statistics of the United Kingdom. HMSO publication giving detailed statistics of exports and imports cumulated throughout the year. More detailed annual volumes are also produced.   (MDP)

own label. This is the practice of BRANDING PRODUCTS by a RETAILER using its own private brand label, as opposed to branding by a manufacturer or a distributor, e.g. Marks & Spencer, Boots the Chemist, Safeway. This practice is widely used by SUPERMARKETS and chain stores where their own label products are intended to enhance the store's image and encourage customer loyalty. Own label branding was taken a stage further by some supermarket retailers with the introduction of GENERIC PRODUCTS in the late 1970s.   (MDP)

P

packaging. Is the art of packing goods in efficient and attractive containers. The basic function of any pack is to protect its contents in transit, in storage and in use. To fulfil these functions packaging serves a number of different purposes as the PRODUCT moves through the channels of distribution from producer to the final CONSUMER. The criteria of appearance, protection, function, cost and disposability all have to be considered when developing a package, weighing up physical properties against suitability for promotional purposes, providing the user with a visual means of identification. While protection of the contents is probably the single most important aspect of pack design and construction the aspects of its use as a promotional tool – a visual cue at point-of-sale – and the issue of disposability of packing are receiving increasing attention. (MDP)

Packard, Vance (1914–1996). Author of the hugely influential *Hidden Persuaders*, first published in 1957, and periodically reprinted by Penguin ever since. The 1981 edition includes an Introduction and Epilogue by the author. A lifelong crusading journalist, Packard set out to expose what he saw as the undue influence that American advertisers of the time were capable of exercising over their audiences if they were advised by 'motivational researchers'. He was no witch-hunter, however, and his carefully articulated concerns are understandable in the context of the post-war and cold-war period during which the book was written. He is widely credited with having alerted the world to the manipulative potential of SUBLIMINAL ADVERTISING, which has been a subject of debate ever since, though it in fact occupies only two pages in the original text and another two in the 1981 Epilogue. The *Hidden Persuaders* is the one book about advertising with which total outsiders are likely to be familiar, almost always at second hand. It was followed by four more equally trenchant critiques of the consumer society: *The Status Seekers*, *The Waste Makers*, *The Pyramid Climbers* and *The Naked Society*. (KC)

page proofs. A term used in printing to describe an impression of typesetting in page form to be corrected before the printing production takes place. (MDP)

page traffic. A measure of the number of readers of a newspaper or magazine who actually look at a particular page, or more specifically at a particular ADVERTISEMENT. 'Page traffic scores' are obtained from READING-AND-NOTING research. (KC)

paid-for title. A newspaper or magazine for which there is a COVER PRICE to be paid, as distinct from a FREESHEET or CONTROLLED CIRCULATION PUBLICATION. (KC)

paired comparison. Evaluation of two objects by asking questions about their relative attributes. *See* PRODUCT TESTING. (JAB)

Palda, Kristian. Canadian academic who in 1966 voiced serious misgivings about the prevailing theory of advertising effect in a widely quoted and reprinted journal article (*see* HIERARCHY-OF-EFFECTS). Despite his cogently argued objections and those of several equally respectable theoreticians in the intervening thirty years, that model remains the dominant conceptual underpinning of advertising practice – usually implicitly rather than explicitly.   (KC)

palletization. System of transporting goods on a platform, on which the goods remain throughout the journey. The advantage of the platform (pallet) is that it can accommodate mechanical handling methods (e.g. forklift trucks, etc.) thus reducing handling costs. A pallet may be no more than two strips of wood separated by two blocks, but more sophisticated versions in cardboard, plastic, or metal which may be reusable, are also available.   (JML)

Palmer, Volney B. Generally identified as the first advertising agent in America, Palmer began his career as an 'advertisement solicitor' selling ADVERTISEMENT SPACE for newspapers as present-day 'advertisement sales representatives' do. In 1841, he set himself up in business in Philadelphia as an intermediary between MEDIA OWNERS and ADVERTISERS. Unlike SPACE BROKERS of the time, such as Charles BARKER and George P. ROWELL, he solicited advertising orders from advertisers who might otherwise have placed them direct, and asked a fee for giving advice on choices among rival newspapers and even writing the advertisements. After Rowell had established the alternative practice of taking MEDIA COMMISSION from publishers instead of fees from advertisers, Palmer negotiated a uniform standard commission discount to be paid to an 'advertising agent' on all orders of whatever size; his figure was 25 per cent. For that reason, he is often wrongly credited with invention of the media commission convention itself. By 1850, Palmer had opened branch offices in Boston and New York and was publishing *V.B. Palmer's Business-Men's Almanac*. His success attracted others to follow suit and, by the time of his death a few years later, competition had brought the normal discount down to 15 per cent. That figure was formally standardized in America in 1917 and in Britain in the 1930s, remaining ever since the normal discount routinely allowed to advertising agencies by major media owners around the world.   (KC)

palming off. A deceptive practice in which the seller claims a product has been made by another firm or in another country than the real one.   (MJB)

panel. Representative SAMPLE of sellers (retailers) or buyers who provide information on a regular basis. Thus RETAIL AUDITS are conducted by prior arrangement and over time by firms like Nielsen using a panel of outlets. Similarly, AUDIENCE RESEARCH is conducted with a panel whose TV or radio has been fitted with the appropriate meter for recording usage.   (MJB)

panel conditioning. The phenomenon whereby the consumption behaviour of PANEL members becomes influenced or 'conditioned' as a direct result of their involvement in the panel.   (MJB)

panel homes. Households which have agreed to participate as members of a PANEL.   (MJB)

panel research. Research in which the same RESPONDENTS give information on more than one occasion, usually regularly. The resulting data thus are not affected by changes in sample composition between readings, and give good trend measures. On the other hand any BIAS in the panel will persist throughout its life. *See* CONSUMER PANELS.   (JAB)

pantry check. Physical examination of goods possessed by RESPONDENTS. This enables more detailed and often more accurate identification of product detail, as for example, precise flavour name for food products, or model number of appliances.   (JAB)

parallel pricing. Pricing at the same level as one's competitors. *See* ADMINISTERED PRICES.   (MJB)

parameter. The value of the measure in the POPULATION. The parameter is what one tries to estimate with the sample statistic; SAMPLING ERROR gives an idea of the accuracy of such estimates.   (SKT)

parametric procedures. Procedures in statistics and scaling where variables are compared at at least the interval level of measurement.   (SKT)

Pareto analysis. Commonly referred to as the 80/20 rule, which states that 80 per cent of sales by value will come from 20 per cent of the customers.   (STP)

party selling. A method of direct selling where the salesperson uses a party as an opportunity to sell to the persons attending the party, e.g. Tupperware.   (MJB)

pass-on readership. Synonym for SECONDARY READERSHIP.   (KC)

patent. An exclusive right granted to an inventor for a period of 17 years to produce and sell the product, process or material described in the patent. The patentor may licence others to use the patent in return for a fee or royalties e.g. Pilkington's licenced most of the world's leading glass producers to use its process for making float glass. Because one has to describe the novel features on which the patent is based many firms choose not to patent original new products on the grounds that it will be easier for their competitors to imitate them and because of the difficulty of enforcing their rights under the patent. (MJB)

patronage motives. The motives which predispose a buyer to prefer and patronize a given seller or outlet. (MJB)

patronage rewards. A benefit given to customers as a reward for their (continuing) patronage. Frequent Flyer schemes are a good example. (MJB)

Pavlovian learning model. One of four basic models of buyer behaviour proposed by Kotler (*Marketing Management*, 1972) derived from Pavlov's learning model, which contains four central concepts: drive, cue, response and reinforcement. Drives may be inherited or learned – hunger is a basic physiological drive, for example, ambition is learned – but they are usually latent or passive until stimulated by a cue. In the case of hunger, this may be internal (being physiologically hungry) or external (the sight or smell of food), but either way response is called for. In the model proposed by Everett Rogers this response is trial, for only if the outcome is satisfactory will reinforcement occur and the new learned behaviour become habitual, or, as Pavlov would have termed it, a conditioned response. (MJB)

payback period. The time period that corresponds to a percentage return-on-investment (ROI). That is, a return on investment of 20 per cent would recover such an investment in five years: it could be said to have a five-year payback period. Widely used as a planning concept to justify effort and expenditure, and enable comparison between alternative projects. (JRB)

peak time. The period of the day when television and radio audiences are at their highest and the CONTRACTING COMPANIES can therefore charge the highest price for ADVERTISING TIME. TELEVISION peak time is from 17:15 to 23:29, split into 'early peak' until the surprisingly precise time of 19:24 and 'late peak' from then on. RADIO peak time is defined as 'morning drive time', which varies from station to station but is generally between 06:00 and 09:00. The American term is PRIME TIME. (KC)

Pearson correlation coefficient (Pearson product–moment correlation). A statistic to indicate the association between two interval or ratio variables. The basis of FACTOR ANALYSIS is a matrix of correlation coefficients. It is calculated as the cross-product (sum of the product of one score with the other over cases) of the standardized variables scaled by dividing by the product of the variances of the two variables, and ranges from -1 (perfect negative correlation) through zero to $+1$ (perfect positive correlation). Generally a higher positive correlation indicates an increasing tendency for increases in one variable to be associated with an increase in the other variable. (SKT)

peer group. Those persons whose VALUES, BELIEFS and BEHAVIOUR are salient to the individual and whose approval and acceptance are sought after. The peer group may be either formal – colleagues at work etc. – or informal – friends and members of other social groups of which the individual wishes to become/remain a member. (MJB)

penalty. A loss, disbenefit or forfeit imposed for failure to complete an exchange on the terms agreed between the parties. (MJB)

penetration. (1) The proportion of a target audience or audience segment which actively reads a given newspaper or magazine; the proportion of the general population, or a segment of it, which attends the cinema regularly. The equivalent term in radio and television usage is REACH. Changes over time measure cumulative penetration, and together with repurchase rate give an indication of potential. *See also* COVERAGE.

(2) Achievement level, infiltration, brand share, and the marketing activity which leads to such effects. Traditionally a low-profit, high-volume marketing strategy adopted with the launch of a new product is called a PENETRATION PRICING POLICY. (JAB, JRB, KC)

penetration pricing policy. Policy of launching a new product at a low price in order to capture quickly as large a share of the market as possible. (GA)

per capita income. The average level of income of each member comprising the POPULATION. Per capita income statistics are a crude measure of the standard of living enjoyed by a country.   (MJB)

perceived risk. The element of risk perceived by an intending buyer when faced with a purchase opportunity. As a subjective state it is specific to the individual and may well vary over time according to their changing circumstances. The lower the perceived risk the more likely one is to act positively and vice versa. *See* OPPORTUNITY COST.   (MJB)

perceived value pricing. Charging 'what the market will bear'.   (MJB)

percentage-of-sales method. A method of setting the ADVERTISING APPROPRIATION in which the amount to be spent is fixed as a percentage of the sales volume or the selling price.   (MJB)

perception. A complex process by which people select, organize and interpret sensory stimulation into a meaningful picture of the world. A fundamental aspect of perception is that it represents the receiver's effort to organize received stimuli into a meaningful structure. In doing so two major groups of factors are involved – stimulus factors and functional factors. Stimulus factors are neutral in the sense that they are intrinsic to the stimulus and so will be received in exactly the same way by all receivers with normal sensory capabilities. On receipt the brain organizes the incoming stimuli into patterns following four basic tendencies: similarity, proximity, continuity and context.

Figure 20: **Perception**

By similarity we understand the tendency of the receiver to group similar things together, while proximity results in the perception that things which are close to one another belong together. In marketing practice similarity is to be seen in the concept of segmentation, while prox-

imity is employed in the use of prominent people to endorse particular products, in the use of generic brands like Safeway, and so on. The need to impose a meaningful structure on stimuli is particularly noticeable in the case of continuity, which is closely associated with closure. The phenomenon of continuity is well illustrated by Sperling with the use of a simple diagram like that shown in Figure 20.

In this one sees the dots as straight lines rather than as separate dots, and as two continuous lines rather than four short ones. Closure occurs when one completes an otherwise incomplete diagram, picture, sentence etc.

Finally, context, or the setting in which a stimulus is received, will have a marked effect upon perception (see any basic book for illustrations of the context influencing perception). In this sense context can have a similar 'halo' influence to proximity and is frequently used by marketers when seeking to develop an image of a product by using media or a setting which conveys the overall impression they wish to create, e.g. use of the Sunday colour supplements to convey a feeling of quality allied to value for money, or young people in leisure situations for Coca-Cola.

As noted, stimulus factors are neutral and create sensations which are then interpreted in light of what are generically termed functional factors. Thus individuals have an ability to screen out stimuli which they do not understand or do not wish to recognize, just as they also have an ability to modify stimuli to make them acceptable to us – a phenomenon sometimes termed SELECTIVE PERCEPTION.

Another perceptual phenomenon of importance to the marketer is that of PREPARATORY SET, which, put simply, means that people tend to perceive objects in terms of their expectations (*see* CLOSURE). A well-known marketing manifestation of the influence of preparatory set is the use of branding and price labelling. Hence, while consumers are unable to distinguish between unbranded products they have no such difficulty when brand names are given. Similarly, Gabor and Grainger, Shapiro and others have clearly demonstrated that we use price as an indicator of quality and will select products with a higher price as 'better' when no differences exist with those carrying a lower price and even when the higher-priced items are objectively inferior.
   (MJB, JLD)

perceptual map. A representation of how consumers perceive comparative products along certain dimensions or attributes derived from the technique of non-metric MULTIDIMENSIONAL SCALING.   (JLD)

perfect competition. *See* COMPETITION, PERFECT.

performance standard. The level of output or achievement required of a PRODUCT or service. Performance standards may be set for an industry either by regulation (e.g. hygiene laws) or by mutual agreement (e.g. British Standards). They may, of course, be set independently by the buyer to reflect his own needs.   (MJB)

perimeter advertising. A collective term for the variety of posters, boards, signs and banners at sports grounds, arenas, racecourses, race tracks and so on. Their purpose is to achieve 'accidental' exposure to the television audience for the event rather than only to the spectators. BRAD (q.v.) classifies this MEDIA VEHICLE as the 'sports' sub-category of 'venue advertising' under the general heading 'outdoor and posters'.   (KC)

periodical. A MEDIA VEHICLE in the PRESS category that appears less frequently than once a week, normally at regular intervals. Periodicals can be newspapers, news magazines, glossy magazines, trade journals or annuals. Media professionals normally classify directories as a quite distinct form of occasional publication.
(KC)

Periodical Publishers' Association. Body representing the publishers of UK consumer, business and professional magazines, founded in 1913. In addition to a wide range of services and activities in the general interest of publishers of PERIODICALS, it acts on their behalf in legal matters and industry negotiations, and is one of the trade associations which award 'recognition' to RECOGNIZED ADVERTISING AGENCIES.   (KC)

perishability. One of the factors used to distinguish services from physical goods. Unlike physical products services cannot be stored for later sale so that a failure to sell at the time of creation results in a complete loss of the service e.g. seats at the theatre, in transport, or hotel rooms.
(MJB)

perishables. PRODUCTS which are particularly liable to damage or decay, e.g. fresh foods.
(MDP)

permanent income hypothesis. This holds that expenditures are based on average income expec-

tations over time. The hypothesis recognizes that consumption patterns are relatively stable over time, which suggests that consumers average out their expenditures, i.e. under inflation they anticipate that they will make good current dissaving, due to price increases, out of future wage increases.   (MJB)

personal communication channels. Any channel through which people communicate personally with one another.   (MJB)

personal disposable income. The money remaining after paying taxes and buying necessities required for survival.   (MJB)

personal factors. Those factors which are particular to individuals involved in the buying process. When it is difficult to distinguish between product offerings in terms of their objective features, personal factors assume a very important role in determining the final decision. Recognition of this is one of the factors which has prompted growing interest in RELATIONSHIP MARKETING.   (MJB)

personal influence. The influence exercised by one person over another especially in the context of consumer decision making.   (MJB)

personal interview. Questions asked by a trained interviewer in a face-to-face situation with the RESPONDENT. Rapport is gained through direct interaction and usually permits greater depth than is possible in TELEPHONE or MAIL SURVEYS. In addition, personal interviews can be longer, thus yielding more information. Personal interviews may be undertaken in the street or at the respondent's home for CONSUMER RESEARCH, and in the respondent's office for industrial research.
(AMW)

personality. A personal and unique way of responding to the environment; those characteristics that account for differences among people and that are predictive of their behaviour; behavioural traits which have become incorporated into the complete personality of the individual giving rise to stable dispositions to respond to certain situations in characteristic ways.
In his *Introduction to Psychology* (1967), Ernest Hilgard defines personality as 'the configuration of individual characteristics and ways of behaving which determine an individual's unique adjustment to his environment'. While

Hilgard is atypical in offering a definition, since most psychologists fail to do so, his definition reflects the consensus concept of personality as a consistent pattern of response. Because of this overall consistency in an individual's pattern of behaviour it is possible to categorize dominant traits and develop a classification of personality 'types'. In turn such classification provides a valuable working construct for marketers, as it enables them to use personality as a factor in developing marketing strategies and marketing mixes to suit them.   (MJB, JLD)

personality promotion. A somewhat misleading term for the type of promotion that (usually) features the product as a 'person'; teams of men or women are recruited and dressed up as, say, a bar of chocolate, calling on or meeting members of the buying public and giving away prizes and supplies of the promoted product. As with the door-to-door distribution of samples, this type of promotion is limited to the big brands with large advertising appropriations. The method employed is to offer a prize if the housewife has the advertised product in her home when the personality (Egg-chick, Ajax Superman etc.) calls, provided that she can answer a simple question. Including in-store displays, leaflet distribution etc., but excluding display advertising, this type of promotion can cost in excess of £200,000.
(JRB, MJB)

personal needs. *See* MOTIVATION, NEED.

personal selling. Oral presentation in a conversation with one or more purchasers for the purpose of making a sale. Its function is to provide specific inputs which ADVERTISING and non-personal selling cannot offer at the individual levels. It takes several forms, such as sales calls by a field representative, assistance by a sales clerk, and so on. It can be used for many purposes, such as creating product awareness, arousing interest, developing product preferences, negotiating prices and other terms, closing a sale, and providing post-transactional reinforcement.

Despite the importance of advertising and sales promotion in disseminating information and stimulating interest in products and services, there are many circumstances where personal contact is necessary to affect sales, as most advertising is generalized and cannot answer all the consumer's information needs. It is a complementary activity to advertising and most

appropriate to high price, technically complex products which are bought infrequently.   (MJB)

persuasion. The act of influencing a person or organization to act in a particular way in a selling situation.   (MJB)

PERT. *See* PROJECT EVALUATION AND REVIEW TECHNIQUE.

photomechanical transfer (PMT). A full-size photographic print of the finished ARTWORK for an ADVERTISEMENT, produced direct from a special camera on special paper, without the need for an intervening negative. The process is rather more akin to colour photocopying than conventional photography, but produces a higher-definition result, suitable for use by the publication in which the advertisement is to appear as the master for production of the printing plate. The artwork itself could be used for that purpose, but the existence of a PMT is a useful safeguard against the consequences of accidental damage during the process. Recent developments in computer graphics make it possible to compose the equivalent of artwork on the screen and send it electronically to the publisher (*see* ARTWORK), but production of a PMT is one aspect of the old technology still holding its own in many situations, at the time of writing at least.
(KC)

phototypesetting. Before the 1970s, the setting of COPY in type for incorporation into advertisements was accomplished by a variety of mechanical means, which ultimately printed it on special paper that could be manually cut up, rearranged and pasted into the 'artwork' that eventually became the 'master' delivered to the printer. Phototypesetting produced the same results by transferring images electronically from the keyboard via a glass disc to photographic paper. The new technology has since been overtaken by further developments which have refined the process from a form of basic word processing to 'digital imaging': *see* ARTWORK. Phototypesetting is nowadays restricted in practice to unsophisticated users and certain specialized applications.   (KC)

physical distribution. The tasks involved in planning and implementing the physical flows of materials and final goods from points of origin to points of use or consumption to meet consumer needs at a profit. *See* LOGISTICS.   (AJB)

physical product. Also referred to as the tangible PRODUCT. It is the product manager's job to turn a CORE PRODUCT into a physical product. They may possess up to five identifiable characteristics: a quality level, features, styling, a BRAND name and packaging. Frozen chickens, compact discs, Filofax and Margaret Thatcher are all physical/tangible products. *See* AUGMENTED PRODUCT and CORE PRODUCT. (KRD)

physiological needs. *See* NEEDS.

pictogram. A chart or figure on which symbols are used to represent the values of the items involved, e.g. barrels of oil, people, cars, etc. (MJB)

pie chart. An alternative to the histogram or line chart for presenting data pictorially. A circle or 'pie' is used to represent the subject of the chart and the size of the 'slices' indicates the importance of the subdivisions. (MJB)

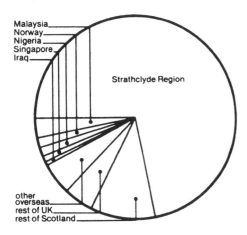

Home residence of students

Malaysia
Norway
Nigeria
Singapore
Iraq

Strathclyde Region

other overseas
rest of UK
rest of Scotland

Undergraduate entrants from Scottish Schools compared

Figure 21: **Pie chart**

piggyback service. The transportation of loaded trucks by rail. (MJB)

pilot marketing. Fulfils the same function for the marketer as the pilot plant does for the production engineer, i.e. it tests the feasibility of the proposed course of action. In many instances companies become so involved with the development of a new product that by the time successful product tests have been completed they feel irrevocably committed, and any course of action other than full-scale marketing is unthinkable. However, companies of this type are usually aware of the critical importance of a well-designed and coordinated marketing plan, and so test its feasibility in practice prior to full-scale operations. Pilot marketing on a regional basis may also serve to give the firm valuable marketing experience while commissioning new plant to meet the anticipated demands of a national market. *See* TEST MARKETING. (MJB)

pilot testing. The testing of a MARKET RESEARCH survey's methodology and QUESTIONNAIRE prior to the commencement of the full survey. This involves administering the questionnaire in conditions which reflect in miniature, the main survey. The arbitrary size of sample to be used for pilot testing varies, depending on time, cost and practicability, but would tend to be around 5–10 per cent of that of the main survey. Testing of this type may reveal possible difficulties in the methodology or RESPONDENT's misinterpretation of QUESTIONS prior to the main survey, which may then be corrected before administration of the full survey. (AMW)

PIMS. *See* PROFIT IMPACT OF MARKET STRATEGIES.

pioneering advantage. Benefits which accrue to the first organization to introduce a new product into a market or to develop a new market. While there is evidence for their existence there is also much other evidence to suggest that other organizations which monitor the pioneer's progress may subsequently outperform them as the market takes off. This approach is sometimes known as 'the strategy of the fast second.' (MJB)

pioneer salesman. A person specifically designated to obtaining new business by educating and training new prospective customers on the uses and benefits of the product or service. (WD)

pitch. The formal presentation that a firm invites from ADVERTISING AGENCIES (or other kinds of MARKETING COMMUNICATIONS intermediary) which it has placed on a 'pitch list' of those it considers qualified to handle its business, the term being derived from SALES PITCH. This shortlist will normally have been drawn from a wider pool of prospective collaborators who have already made 'credentials presentations'. In agency jargon, they are 'pitching for the ACCOUNT'. The pitch will typically be made by a small team representing each of the key functions in the agency to another team representing all those at the potential client company who have a stake in the decision. It is the final stage in a systematic procedure for selecting an agency.   (KC)

pitch list. *See* PITCH. Typical pitch lists comprise between four and six agencies.   (KC)

place. One of the four Ps, 'place' takes into account all those activities involved in making products available to customers i.e. distribution.   (MJB)

place marketing. Activities designed to encourage people to locate in or visit a particular physical place e.g. 'Glasgow's Miles Better'.   (MJB)

placement. *See* MEMORY CONTROL OF PROCESSES.

place utility. The added value created by making a good or service available to consumers with a need for it.   (MJB)

planned economy. In a planned economy the government decides what will be produced, by whom and in what quantities, by contrast with a market economy in which the forces of demand and supply determine how scarce resources will be allocated.   (MJB)

planned obsolescence. *See* OBSOLESCENCE.

planning. A pervasive human activity by which we seek to exercise some degree of control over the future. As a process it will vary enormously depending upon a number of variables, foremost among which will be the complexity of the activity and the degree of uncertainty concerning the future situation in which the activity will take place. Fundamentally, however, all planning seeks to arrive at a present decision concerning future action – the more complex the activity and the more uncertain the future, the greater the need for formal, systematic planning procedures.

It is important to distinguish clearly between the environmental constraints within which the firm must operate and those activities over which it can exercise control. It is also important to recognize that in the long run all fixed constraints are variable in some degree – thus in the short term management must accept the existing distributive network, in the long term it can modify

it through its own action, just as it can develop new markets and shape the nature of competition. However, in time the environment will change too owing to technological innovation and competitive activity, and the firm must seek to develop objectives which are sufficiently well defined to require commitment, yet flexible enough to permit a change in emphasis and direction as the situation evolves. 'Servicing the travelling public' is a good example of an overall long-term objective which meets these criteria. In the short term, the skill lies in developing strategies which make the best use of available resources in moving the firm from where it is to where it wants to be.

In essence a strategy is a broad statement of the means to be employed in achieving a given objective, while the actual methods used constitute the tactics.

At the risk of overstating the obvious, the success of a given strategy depends upon the coordination of the tactics into an integrated, complementary and cohesive whole. There is a finite number of alternative strategies open to the firm and, in a given market, it is usual to find several competing firms pursuing the same basic strategy simultaneously. If this is so, then observed variations in performance must arise out of the quality of the plan, or statement of tactics, and its execution. Factors such as motivation and morale have an important bearing on the execution of a plan, but also tend to be a function of the plan's quality and credibility.

Some guidelines are included on the analysis and presentation of a written marketing plan. There is little point in restating the descriptive content of a case as the objective of an appreciation is to define the central issue. This is probably best achieved by a systematic analysis of the available material in terms of: (a) What business is the company in and what are the salient features of this business? (b) What is the firm's goal, explicit or implied? (c) What resources has the company – productive – technical – financial – marketing? (d) What policies, explicit or otherwise, has it adopted in respect of these resources? (e) Is there a single strategic variable which dominates all others – if so, what is it? (f) Has the firm any special skill or distinctive competence?

In analysing the case (or problem, in real life), one should seek to isolate those areas which bear directly upon both the immediate problem and the more general problem of which it is symptomatic. Once these areas have been defined they should be ranked in some rough order of importance and analysed in detail. For example, if a major issue is the nature of the product itself, one should list all the advantages and disadvantages which one can think of to permit an overall conclusion to be drawn. Similarly with all other issues. The conclusions drawn from the separate analysis of the relevant issues should then be summarized and stated as the basis upon which the plan has been based. This statement should also make explicit any assumptions which have been made, together with the reasons which support their adoption.

The marketing plan must be realistic in the light of the analysis described in the appreciation, and should commence by stating the overall objective or aim. If it is felt that the company's stated aims are incapable of attainment it must be able to present a very convincing argument as to why, and how, they should be changed. Thus the statement of the long-term aim must be supported by an exposition of all those factors which will affect the company's ability to achieve its objective, paying particular attention to environmental changes and changing consumer needs.

Following the statement of the long-term aim, the plan should state the short-term objective and the specific policies to be adopted to achieve it. In the interests of both clarity and coverage of all salient factors, some form of outline should be used similar to that given below:

(a) Short-term aim, e.g. to increase market share by 5 per cent; (b) forecast of market conditions for the period of the plan; (c) statement of further marketing research to be undertaken to provide feedback on performance and to be used in the preparation of future marketing plans; (d) statement of product policy; (e) statement of pricing policy; (f) statement of packaging policy; (g) statement of distribution policy; (h) statement of advertising and sales promotion policy; (i) statement of sales policy; (j) budget statement with explanation of how it is to be used for control purposes; (k) outline of how plan is to be financed; (1) timing for implementation of various policies.

Clearly, the amount of detail will vary considerably depending upon the central issue identified in the appreciation, and the data available. It should be remembered, however, that the overall marketing plan cannot be expected to go into the same detail as would be expected of, say, the media plan, but it should provide the skeleton around which such plans can be prepared by the various functional specialists.

Finally, the impact of a marketing plan will be lost if it lacks clarity of expression, no matter how logical the sequence or how sophisticated the analysis. (MJB)

PLC. *See* PRODUCT LIFE CYCLE.

plus-one dialling. In telephone interviewing, a method of increasing the number of subscribers to be dialled is simply to add one to the numbers on an existing list. This runs into problems of unobtainable and off-frame numbers. (SKT)

PMT. *See* PHOTOMECHANICAL TRANSFER.

point-of-purchase display (POP). Any promotion placed near the product in its usual location which serves to inform and persuade the shopper. It may consist of signs, special offers, product features, and price information. (AJB)

point-of-sale display (POS). A display of merchandise located beside the cash point or cash register in order to serve as a reminder to the shopper before they pay for their purchases. Also referred to as the point-of-service display. (AJB)

political factors. An important aspect of the EXTERNAL ENVIRONMENT which needs to be taken into account when making a MARKETING AUDIT or developing a MARKETING STRATEGY. (MJB)

POP. *See* POINT-OF-PURCHASE DISPLAY.

population. (1) According to mid-1991 estimates, Britain's population is 57.8 million. It ranks seventeenth in the world in terms of population. The estimated home population in April 1981 was 55,676,000 compared with 38.2 million in 1901 and about 6.5 million at the end of the seventeenth century. Early figures are based on contemporary estimates, but from the beginning of the nineteenth century relatively plentiful and reliable information is available. Most of it comes from two main sources: the regular flow of statistical information based on compulsory registration of births, marriages and deaths, and the censuses taken regularly every ten years since 1801 (because of war there was no census in 1941). The most recent was in April 1991. In the period 1975–8 for the first year since records began (other than in war) the population fell slightly, reflecting a temporary decline in the birth rate. The upward trend was resumed in 1979. On the mid-1991-based projections, the population in Britain is forecast to rise to 59.7 million in 2001 and 61.1 million in 2011.

(HMSO)

(2) Technically the sum total of persons or things about which information is required. Sometimes termed the 'universe'. Definition of a POPULATION is an essential prerequisite of SAMPLING and SAMPLE SURVEYS. (MJB)

Porter's generic strategies. The three strategies identified by Michael Porter in his work on competitive advantage, namely COST LEADERSHIP, DIFFERENTIATION, FOCUS. Prior to Michael Porter's work these three strategies were generally identified as UNDIFFERENTIATED, DIFFERENTIATED and CONCENTRATED marketing.

(MJB)

portfolio analysis. Technique popularized by the BOSTON CONSULTING GROUP for analysing the products or businesses owned by the company.

(MJB)

portfolio, sales. A folder or other aids used by a salesperson to assist in the sales process. Such a portfolio may contain photographs, pricing examples and comparisons, research and technical data and customer endorsements to reinforce the sales message. (WD)

portrait. An ADVERTISING space taller than it is wide, in contrast to LANDSCAPE format, e.g. '8 x 10 cm portrait'. Also described as 'upright'.(KC)

POS. See POINT-OF-SALE DISPLAY.

position. (1) As a verb, this refers to the strategy of POSITIONING.

(2) As a noun, it defines the location of an ADVERTISEMENT in a publication or of a COMMERCIAL within a COMMERCIAL BREAK. See also SPECIAL POSITION. (KC)

positioning. This widely misused term has a simple meaning and a much more complicated one. Practitioners typically employ it to describe what is accurately called 'PRODUCT POSITIONING' – that is, defining the location of a PRODUCT (or service) relative to others in the same MARKET place and then promoting it in such a way as to reinforce or change its 'position'. This is easier said than done, however. The process of defining a 'position' requires dimensions, along which the competing products can be compared, and the resulting definition must be comparative if it is to be any use as the basis of a positioning strategy.

Typically, positioning strategies meet neither of these criteria. A famous chocolate manufacturer once stated its strategic objective, in print, as being 'to re-position brand as the ultimate'. This might give useful guidance to the ADVERTISING AGENCY in the development of a COPY PLATFORM and could even help the MEDIA PLANNER, but it clearly does not establish the product's position in the full sense just defined, and is therefore more a statement of aspiration than a framework for strategy development. The ADVERTISER in question should preferably have used MARKET RESEARCH findings to draw a PERCEPTUAL MAP of the market, which could then have formed the basis of a precise plan for re-positioning the brand.

However, a textbook written by two American advertising practitioners (A. Ries and J. Trout, *Positioning: the Battle for Your Mind,* McGraw-Hill, 1986) points out that even this more rigorous approach to 'positioning' contains a misleading implication. They argue that the position in question belongs to the audience, not to the advertiser. Therefore, 'positioning is not what you do to a product (but) what you do to the mind of the prospect'. This collective mind is likely, inconveniently, to be already made up on the subject of the relative position of products that already exist – a proposition supported by classic CONSUMER BEHAVIOUR theory. If the aim is to 're-position' (which is commonly the case, in practice), then it follows that the traditional advertising tactics of shouting louder or trying to look better run a significant risk of failure.

This fact, combined with the communication overload suffered by modern audiences, dictates a distinctly lateral approach to the implementation of a 'positioning' strategy. In essence, the advertiser must identify a new dimension for the audience to use in constructing its perceptual map, and should then use simple messages in suggesting it to them, rather than the sophisticated and complicated imagery that characterizes much contemporary advertising.

Trout & Ries present a case of the celebrated Avis car rental campaign ('We try harder') in sufficient detail to render its underpinning positioning logic suddenly clear and, in the process, show exactly how a true 're-positioning' strategy differs from the result of using the term in the normal, imprecise way. (KC)

postal research. Research carried out through the post, as against personal or telephone interviews. (JRB)

postal survey. *See* MAIL SURVEY.

POSTAR. Since 1995, the industry service providing MEDIA PLANNERS with COVERAGE and FREQUENCY figures for OUTDOOR advertising in the UK. Using data collected during an 18-month survey of typical journeys made by 7,400 adults and on 7,000 local-authority traffic counts, it estimates the number of people likely to take notice of each of 73,000 POSTER SITES, rather than simply to be within viewing range: that is, 'likelihood-to-see' instead of OPPORTUNITY-TO-SEE. Audience profiles for a given campaign can be broken down into 240 demographic subgroups. See also JOURNEY MAPPING, SITE PASSAGE, TRAFFIC COUNT, VISIBILITY ADJUSTED IMPACT.   (KC)

postcode. An alphanumeric code, with up to seven elements, which forms the last line of British postal addresses. Machine operators in the main sorting office of the area in which the letter was posted convert the postcode into phosphorescent dots on the envelope, which is thereafter electronically routed to the appropriate delivery office. A closely related system is in use in Canada, whereas all other countries employ a purely numeric code of up to five digits for the same purpose (*see* ZIP CODE). The combination of letters and numbers is preferred in Britain because: (a) it is a fact that such codes are easier to read and memorize than the same number of figures alone; (b) the use of a letter permits fifteen variations (eleven letters of the alphabet are easily confused with numbers and are therefore not used) instead of the nine offered by a numeric digit.

An example will illustrate these qualities: G14 9NZ. The Royal Mail calls G14 the 'outward code' and 9NZ the 'inward code'. The single or double letters in an outward code (except in some London addresses) define one of 120 'postcode areas' in the country. There is always some relationship to the name of the city or town through which the mail will first be routed, though local knowledge is needed to recognize some of the links. G is Glasgow. Figures between 1 and 99 define a 'postcode district', of which there are about 2,800. The 14th district of G2 comprises two inner suburbs, Whiteinch and Scotstoun, plus half of a third, Jordanhill. Turning to inward codes, a single digit defines a 'postcode sector', of which there are up to 10 per postcode district and about 9,000 in the country. In this case, Sector 9 is one of only two in G14, made up of four easily definable neighbourhoods: the Scotstoun and Victoria Park Conservation Areas, and South Jordanhill. A pair of letters following the digit narrow the destination down to a 'postcode unit', containing on average 15 addresses. About 1.8 million of these cover the 25 million separate 'delivery points' in the UK. In this case, NZ defines a street called Victoria Park Corner in which there are 16 houses. A full, machine-encodable 'delivery instruction' for the sixteenth is thus G14 9NZ No.16, though the names of streets and cities or towns are still used in all addresses in practice. There is one exception to this pattern. Outward codes in London are different from those in all other parts of the country, consisting of the pre-existing geographical suffixes (N, NE, E, EC, SE, SW, W, WC and NW) plus one or two digits and, in four of those areas, a final letter: for example, EC4N or W1X.

The flexibility and precision of the postcode system has significant practical benefits, particularly in relation to MARKET RESEARCH and DIRECT MARKETING. Anyone who has dealt with a telephone ordering system is very likely to have been asked for their postcode and told their address, except for the house number. Such CONSUMER LOCATION SYSTEMS as ACORN and MOSAIC furthermore use postcodes to construct their socio-demographic and 'lifestyle' market segmentation systems, on the basis that human equivalents of birds of a feather flock together in residential neighbourhoods. Returning to our case example, any demographer would immediately identify G14 9NZ as a professional enclave in an area containing both large tracts of council housing and street upon street of archetypal middle-class properties. ACORN captures the essence of this distinctive make-up in its taxonomic allocation of the postcode to one each of its 6 'categories', 17 'groups' and 54 'types': a 'mature, well-off suburban' street, inhabited by 'wealthy achievers' in a generally 'thriving' sector of society.   (KC)

poster. The advertising vehicle which characterizes the OUTDOOR medium. In practice, advertisers are equally likely to apply the term to the medium itself. Posters are generally called 'billboards' in America, a description that has recently become a common alternative in Britain. Both terms derive from the 'posting' of 'bills' on 'boards' or hoardings. Posters come in a variety of shapes and sizes, and are found in diverse locations, thereby reaching a number of distinct target audiences: motorists, train commuters, shoppers and so on. *See also* POSTER SITE.   (KC)

Poster Audit Bureau. Independent UK watchdog organization, whose inspectors collectively check every POSTER SITE in the country at least once every six weeks to verify that the right poster appeared on the right site at the right time and that damaged, defaced or weathered posters are replaced. Its existence has helped to alleviate concerns about 'site control' in the poster medium expressed by advertisers and advertising agencies in past years.   (KC)

posterior analysis. Second step DATA analyses: Having found that a factor is significant, a technique for working out which (if any) levels are significantly different from others. A posterior analysis should take into account previous steps in setting up distributions for decision making.
(SKT)

poster site. An OUTDOOR advertising site for one or more POSTERS. Newer poster sites often feature a small landscaped area, a visually attractive structure to receive the poster – the 'panel', or 'hoarding' – and special lighting. The smallest nationally-available site is the '4-sheet', a 60 inch by 40 inch PORTRAIT-format panel. (*See* SHEET for an explanation of poster sizes.) These are located in residential areas, shopping precincts and stations, and are aimed at a predominantly pedestrian audience. Once popular for national campaigns, its share of total outdoor 'sheetage' had fallen under 4 per cent in 1996 and it is nowadays generally bought site-by-site. The larger portrait-format 6-sheet site has become correspondingly more popular, with a 27 per cent share in 1996. It is typically incorporated into bus shelters and back-illuminated, but there are also free-standing sites of this size. The target audience is both pedestrian and vehicular. By far the most familiar poster site is the much bigger 48-sheet, a LANDSCAPE format which accounts for more than half of all sheetage in Britain. It targets a predominantly vehicular audience, except for those facing the platforms in London Underground stations, and can be bought either in 'pre-selected packages' or site-by-site. Any site larger than this is called a 'supersite', the only common example of which is the 40 foot by 10 foot landscape-format 96-sheet. Such very large panels are located where they can reach a vehicular audience and are generally bought in pre-selected packages. Poster sites come in four other sizes, available only in relatively small numbers: 16-sheet portrait format, and 12-sheet, 32-sheet and 64-sheet landscape. Notice that

'billboard' does not define any of these sites. It is simply the American word for an outdoor poster, imported into colloquial British usage but not into the technical vocabulary.   (KC)

post-industrial society. The stage of economic development following industrialization. The emphasis is on services and knowledge-based occupations.   (MJB)

postponement. One of three concepts proposed by Louis P. Bucklin ('Postponement, Speculation and the Structure of Distribution Channels', *Journal of Marketing Research,* vol. 2, February 1965) which affect the structure of distribution channels. The principle of postponement states that changes in form and inventory location are to be delayed to the latest possible moment.
(MJB)

post-production. Collective term for the stages in the production of a television or cinema COMMERCIAL after studio or location shooting has been completed, of which there are potentially many. Post-production editing is typically concerned with the enhancement of audio or video effects, but may even involve relatively radical modifications such as changing a sound-track.
(KC)

post-purchase anxiety. Anxiety, or DISSONANCE, caused by feelings of doubt after a purchase commitment. This dissonance can be resolved by various strategies, e.g. by discussing with friends, by reading/viewing advertisements for the product etc.   (KF)

post-test. A procedure for evaluating ADVERTISING EFFECTIVENESS, during or after an ADVERTISING CAMPAIGN. Because 'test' can imply a rather rough and ready approach to the task, 'post-testing' should preferably be called post-evaluation of effectiveness.   (KC)

post-testing. The evaluation of the effectiveness of a marketing action after its implementation, especially of advertising.   (MJB)

potential market. The total number of persons who might buy a product or service.   (MJB)

potential technological distance. This can be defined as the capability of a recipient to assimilate new technology from its source. This concept is often used in the context of international business and usually refers to the extent to which a LESS DEVELOPED COUNTRY can assimilate new technology from a DEVELOPED COUNTRY. (KAB)

power. With reference to marketing channels, the ability of one member of the channel to influence the trading behaviour of another. The corollary is that the member influenced is dependent in some way on the influencing member. However, in the total relationship the dependence is mutual and power therefore only exists as a potential force, depending on the perception of each party. *See* CHANNEL CONTROL. (AJB)

PPA. *See* PERIODICAL PUBLISHERS' ASSOCIATION.

pragmatic validity. The acceptance of a measure as being valid when it can predict consistently some other outcome. (MJB)

preceded question. *See* QUESTIONNAIRES.

precision level. In SAMPLING, a term used to indicate a desired level of precision. For example, with sampling formulae, it is possible to work out what size of SAMPLE is required to give a precision level of plus or minus 2 per cent on a variable category. (SKT)

predatory pricing. In a decision by the Office of Fair Trading (Highland Scottish Omnibuses Ltd, Local Bus Services in Inverness, 1989), predatory pricing was defined as:

behaviour of the sort (which) involves the deliberate acceptance of losses in the short run with the intention of eliminating COMPETITION, so that enhanced profits can be earned in the longer term by raising prices above the competition level. Several conditions are necessary if predatory behaviour is to be feasible. The predator must have market power and the ability to finance losses for the time necessary, whether through greater cash reserves, better financing or cross-subsidization from other markets or products. There must also be barriers to entry in the market so that once competition is eliminated, prices can be raised above the competitive level so as to more than compensate for the period of losses, without merely attracting new entrants.

The OFT uses three factors in assessing whether behaviour is, in fact, predatory: (a) whether the structure and characteristics of the market are such as to make prediction feasible; (b) the rela-

tionship between revenue and costs; (c) evidence on the motives and intentions of the firm, including relevant evidence from its behaviour in other markets.

The OFT states that pricing below short-run variable costs (SRVC) is clearly predatory in that it involves out-of-pocket losses. However, prices above SRVC may also be judged to be predatory if it represents a price below that necessary to contribute fully to overheads and the minimum return necessary to remunerate investment with the result that other firms in the industry, which are just as efficient, are forced out of business. In the latter case, the motives and intentions of the claimed predator are considered as important evidence. For examples of both evidence and judgement, the reports of the OFT are essential reading. (MJB)

predictive validity. The assessment of the validity of a measurement through predictions of some criterion measurement made at a later stage. A higher correlation between the measure and the criterion is associated with higher predictive validity. (SKT)

pre-empt structure, pre-emption. A somewhat controversial system of selling ADVERTISING TIME on terrestrial television stations. Although the CONTRACTING COMPANIES are statutorily required to publish in a formal RATE CARD their charges for every SPOT length available during every 'time segment' on offer, most in fact regard these as no more than the guideline prices in what is effectively an auction. MEDIA BUYERS book time at one price on a bewilderingly complex scale of premier and standard rates, and the contractors reserve the right to give priority to another buyer who subsequently offers a higher price. The losing buyer's booking has thus been 'pre-empted'. In times of high demand, this can happen literally minutes before transmission, but most contractors are willing to offer some security within the final 12 or 24 hours. The only way to be completely certain of avoiding pre-emption is of course to pay the highest rate. Otherwise, cost-effective media buying requires the considerable skill of being able to judge likely competitive demand for spots to be booked, and to guess the lowest price that will not be pre-empted. It is no wonder that television media buying is a very specialized business. (KC)

preference segmentation. Segmentation *a posteriori* once customer preferences have become known through usage. Such segmentation may be based upon usage patterns correlated with the perceived benefits of consuming the preferred brand. *See* MARKET SEGMENTATION, BENEFIT SEGMENTATION.   (MJB)

pre-industrial country. A country which has yet to industrialize. The main characteristics are: high dependence on agriculture; essentially rural population with low levels of literacy; absence of manufacturing and high dependence on more advanced countries for imports of manufactured goods, capital equipment etc.   (MJB)

preliminary edit (field edit). An initial scan and corrections of completed data collection schedules by a field supervisor. A field edit allows the most glaring omissions to be spotted quickly in order to allow quality control of interviewers and sometimes reinterview.   (SKT)

premium. The amount in cash above the average price for its classification that a product is able to obtain at the retail level. Often associated with superior quality or image.   (AJB)

premium offers. There are three main types of premium offer: (a) The free gift. This may be contained in the package, plastic animals in breakfast cereals, attached to it, a plastic rose, tea-towels; given out at the checkout to those purchasing the item carrying the offer, bowls, waste-paper baskets, and so on. In some instances the offer will be the pack itself, as is the case with instant coffee packed in storage jars. A common feature of these promotions is that they encourage a collecting habit and so achieve extended trial as the consumer builds up the collection.

(b) The free, send-away premium. This type of promotion offers a free gift in exchange for proof of purchase of the product. This approach has greater appeal to the retailer than those promotions which require him to stock 'giveaways', especially as the promotion usually involves point-of-sale material that builds store traffic and stimulates IMPULSE PURCHASES. From the promoter's angle an added advantage is that many people buy the product intending to send off for the premium but in fact never do.

(c) Self-liquidating premiums. These differ from the other types of premium in that the consumer has to send both money and proof of purchase to obtain the offer. The advantage to the consumer is that he secures merchandise, often carrying a leading brand name, at a significant discount on its normal retail price. The promoter

benefits in that as the name suggests, the offer pays for itself. If combined with a collecting habit, offers of this kind may run for years ensuring long-term usage, for example Kellogg's silverware offer.   (MJB)

pre-paid expenses. Charges for items which have been pre-paid, but have not yet been received. For example, insurance is paid at the beginning of a period but the benefit is consumed throughout the period. Any form of payment in advance. *See also* ACCRUALS and ACCRUAL ACCOUNTING.   (GM)

preparatory set. Perceptual phenomenon by which people tend to perceive objects in terms of their expectations. A well-known marketing manifestation of the influence of preparatory set is the use of branding and price labelling. Hence, while consumers are unable to distinguish between unbranded products they have no such difficulty when brand names are given. Similarly, as a number of researchers have clearly demonstrated, we use price as an indicator of quality and will select products with a higher price as 'better' when no objective differences exist with those carrying a lower price even in situations when the higher priced items are objectively inferior. *See* PERCEPTION.   (MJB)

presence. A term which distinguishes the number of people actually present during a COMMERCIAL BREAK from the potential audience measured by the BROADCASTERS' AUDIENCE RESEARCH BOARD (BARB). To count as 'audience' in the BARB data, viewers need to be within viewing range of a set for 8 minutes or more in any 15-minute period. However, people do not sit immobile in front of the TV set as long as it is on, let alone pay attention to what is on the screen. Legend has it that people seize the opportunity presented by commercial breaks to brew tea, put out the cat and relieve pressure on their bladders (no doubt due to so much tea drinking). Periodic surveys have shown that they also engage in a bewildering variety of other distracting activities. Therefore, researchers have tried to quantify the negative weighting which should be applied to convert 'exposure' into 'presence'.   (KC)

press. The second-oldest of the five 'major' ADVERTISING MEDIA in Britain, and the one which attracts the largest share of UK total annual ADVERTISING EXPENDITURE. It is a particularly diverse medium. The ADVERTISING ASSOCIATION'S

Advertising Statistics Yearbook distinguishes 5 sub-categories: national newspapers (see NATIONAL PRESS), regional newspapers (see LOCAL PRESS, REGIONAL PRESS), consumer magazines, business and professional magazines, and directories. Newspapers may be PAID-FOR TITLES or FREESHEETS. BRITISH RATE AND DATA further distinguishes 3 varieties of national and regional newspaper (daily, Sunday and weekly), categorizing the national dailies and Sundays as either 'quality' or 'popular'. Consumer magazines are classified into 9 main categories by subject matter and the business and professional press into 27. This already fragmented medium will present an even greater challenge to MEDIA PLANNERS of the twenty-first century, as on-line versions of existing titles proliferate and new 'E-ZINES' proliferate. Meanwhile, the *Daily Mail*, *Daily Express* and *Daily Telegraph* lead the newspaper rankings in terms of revenue from advertising sales, the *Radio Times*, *Good Housekeeping* and *Vogue* are the three highest-earning consumer magazines, and the revenue tables for the business and professional press are dominated by computer-related titles. Car makers dominate the list of the heaviest spenders on newspaper advertising. Media planners are generally well provided with reliable, independent data on CIRCULATION and READERSHIP, though data on the smaller titles in each sub-category are often harder to come by: *see* AUDIT BUREAU OF CIRCULATIONS, JICREG, NATIONAL READERSHIP SURVEY, VERIFIED FREE DISTRIBUTION.

Despite accounting for well over half of total national advertising expenditure in 1996, the medium as a whole has suffered a decline in its share in each of the previous seven years. Starting with just over three-quarters of the total during the period after the arrival of COMMERCIAL TELEVISION as a rival medium in 1955, it maintained share in a narrow band either side of 70 per cent throughout the Sixties and Seventies, but could not reach two-thirds in any year after 1980. The 1996 figure was the lowest so far recorded, at 61 per cent. Popular wisdom attributes this long-term trend to advertisers increasingly shifting their spending to television. Although the expenditure graphs for the two media were virtual mirror images until the mid-Eighties, the media share held by television has since stabilized at around 31 per cent, almost exactly half the figure for the press. The compensating upward trend has in fact been a steady and significant improvement, albeit from a very low base, in the proportion of total expenditure directed to the

OUTDOOR, RADIO and CINEMA media. Within the press, the large number of regional newspapers collectively take over a third of total advertising revenue, the national newspapers exactly a quarter, the equally large number of business and professional magazines 17 per cent, directories 12 per cent and, perhaps surprisingly in last place, consumer magazines only a tenth. Over the past decade, however, the regional press has been steadily losing share. This large and somewhat cumbersome medium faces an uncertain future beyond the millennium. (KC)

press cuttings. Editorial material relating to a firm and its PRODUCTS or services, clipped from the publications in which it appeared and kept in a 'cuttings book' as a record of the effectiveness of PUBLICITY initiatives, particularly PRESS RELEASES. (KC)

press date. The deadline for submission of an ADVERTISEMENT to the publication in which it is to run. *See also* COPY DATE. (KC)

press relations. The process of cultivating an information-exchange relationship with newspaper and magazine editorial offices, the long-term objective of which is to facilitate the PUBLICITY process. *See also* PUBLIC RELATIONS. (KC)

press release. An article written from a company's point of view by the company or its agent, having general news content which is both of interest and value, and which it is hoped the press will be willing to publish as editorial, and hence, free of charge. However, as much as 80 per cent of all press releases in the UK fail to be published. In the US, this figure is nearer 90 per cent. *See also* NEWS RELEASE. (GM)

Prestel. The British Telecom viewdata system which allows interactive access to a DATABASE consisting of over one million pages on 1,200 different subjects. The system involves two-way electronic communication and requires the use of a telephone line, a modem and a terminal. (GM)

prestige pricing. The pricing of a PRODUCT at above the going MARKET price on the basis that many buyers regard price as an indicator of quality and so will impute enhanced quality to products with higher than usual prices. Sellers are able to ask prestige prices for products which have distinctive BRAND NAMES and reputation, e.g. Estée Lauder cosmetics. (MJB)

pre-test. A procedure for evaluating probable ADVERTISING EFFECTIVENESS, before an ADVERTISING CAMPAIGN begins. Because 'test' can imply a rather rough and ready approach to the task, 'pre-testing' should preferably be called pre-evaluation of effectiveness.   (KC)

pre-testing (of questionnaires). Use of a questionnaire on a trial basis. Sometimes distinct from a pilot which trials not only the questionnaire but also other field operations.   (SKT)

price. The amount of money which is asked in consideration for the transfer of legal title to a product or service. By custom and practice 'price' may be used to define the value of other goods or services, as in a BARTER transaction, and so need not always be expressed in monetary terms.   (MJB)

price bundling. Offering two or more objects for a single price.   (MJB)

price competition. *See* COMPETITION, PRICE.

price controls. The regulation of prices by government order. In times of scarcity price controls may be used to slow down inflation but if there is a severe imbalance between supply and demand (e.g. in wartime) rationing may be necessary also.   (MJB)

price cutting. Reductions in price designed to undercut competitors and secure increases in MARKET SHARE. In the absence of significant cost advantages, the price cutter may not be able to sustain this tactic for long, particularly as other sellers are likely to reduce their prices too in the short term in order to protect their own market share.   (MJB)

price discrimination. This may take two forms. (a) The seller may charge different prices to different buyers; (b) the seller may charge different prices for supplies of the same PRODUCT, e.g. two-part tariff for gas, electricity, telephone usage etc. In both cases the seller needs to have a good understanding of the PRICE ELASTICITY OF DEMAND in order to set the price or prices which will optimize his returns.   (MJB)

price elasticity of demand. A CONCEPT from the economic theory of demand which is of particular use to practitioners is the concept of elasticity. As originally conceived the concept of elasticity refers only to price/sales ratios (price elasticity of demand), but it has now become generalized to apply to each demand determinant such as CONSUMER INCOME, ADVERTISING EXPENDITURES etc. Thus, in the abstract, elasticity is the ratio of the relative change in the dependent variable (demand) to the relative change in an independent variable (price, consumer income). Thus, demand is said to be elastic when the relative change in the independent factor is greater than the relative change in the quantity demanded, and inelastic when it is less than the relative change in the quantity demanded. Graphically these differences are reflected in the slope of the demand curve with totally inelastic demand being represented by a vertical line and infinitely elastic demand by a horizontal line. These differences are indicated in Figures 22 and 23 respectively, while 24 represents the type of demand curve typically found in which elasticity will vary according to price. As can be seen from Figure 22, a minority of users have a very strong demand for the PRODUCT and therefore price is inelastic for them. However, as price falls, more and more users will become willing to buy units of the product and demand becomes very elastic relative to price. This tendency continues until the MARKET approaches saturation, at which point even drastic reductions in price are unlikely to result in very much more demand so that the price elasticity once again is inelastic.

Another very important dimension of demand is known as 'cross-elasticity'. Cross-elasticity of demand measures one of the most important demand relationships – namely the closeness of substitutes or the degree of complementarity of demand. A high cross-elasticity means that the commodities are close substitutes for each other, while a zero cross-elasticity means that they are

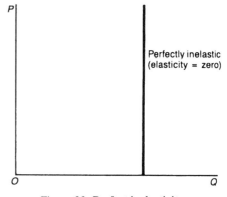

Figure 22: **Perfect inelasticity**

independent of each other in the market. Finally a negative cross-elasticity means that the goods are complementary in the market in that one stimulates the sales of another. (MJB)

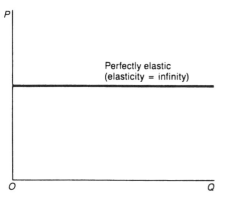

Figure 23: **Perfect elasticity**

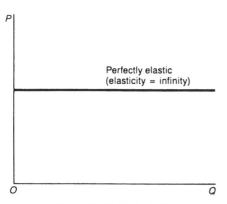

Figure 24: **Unit elasticity**

price fixing. An agreement between two or more producers to charge the same price. Such agreements are usually illegal if they are in restraint of trade. (MJB)

price leaders. Products sold at very competitive prices, sometimes at or below cost, in order to encourage sales of other products. (MJB)

price lining. The adoption of specific prices for certain types of merchandise by RETAILERS which is closely related to both customary and PSYCHOLOGICAL PRICING. (MJB)

price negotiation. Form of price fixing based on the premise that the buyer is a price-maker rather than a price-taker. Although a price list may be used as the starting point, it is likely to be modified on the basis of other considerations such as delivery and payment terms. (STP)

price packs. Products with special packaging specifying the selling price. (MJB)

price skimming. Charging the highest price customers are prepared to pay so restricting sales to those for whom it has the greatest salience and the necessary purchasing power. Usually only viable in NICHE markets or in the case of an INNOVATION where the seller can protect the exclusive nature of their product. (MJB)

price theory, limitations of. Price theory has a number of limitations in respect of business pricing. These may be summarized as (a) the theory usually rests on the assumption of profit maximization. In the real world, profit maximization is no doubt a primary objective, but research indicates that managers are motivated by other objectives such as target return on investment, stability of price and margin, target market share, and meeting or forestalling competition. (b) The theory does not distinguish clearly between long- and short-run effects of price changes. (c) The theory does not face the problem of uncertainty. It is assumed that entrepreneurs know their demand and cost functions but there are grave statistical problems in formulating these. (d) The theory fails to view the firm as an organization in which pricing decisions are influenced by a number of different people with varied objectives and motivations. (e) The theory assumes that the only significant group to consider in the pricing of a product is the firm's customers when in reality several parties have to be considered simultaneously, e.g. rivals, suppliers, distributors, governments etc. (f) The theory assumes that prices are businessmen's chief policy instrument while the emergence of a marketing orientation clearly indicates that other elements of the marketing mix tend to dominate. (g) The theory regards price solely as a device for attaining financial objectives which ignores the fact that price can be used as a communication device to communicate facts to the market participants about the firm, its products and its capabilities, in a manner that might increase sales, raise prices or reduce costs. (MJB)

pricing objectives. While many firms do not state explicit pricing objectives, there is substantial agreement with the findings of a survey conducted by Lanzillotti published in 1958 in which he states 'the most typical pricing objectives cited were: (a) pricing to achieve a target return on investment; (b) stabilization of pricing margin; (c) pricing to realize the target market share; and (d) pricing to meet or prevent competition.'

(MJB)

pricing strategies. Until recently only two broad strategic approaches to prices have been recognized, namely SKIMMING and PENETRATION. As the name suggests, skimming recognizes that in almost all markets there is a 'hard core' of demand for whom the product in question has a particular importance. Because of the strength of their perceived need such users tend to be relatively insensitive to price and this insensitivity can be exploited through a policy of setting a very high price and thus 'skimming the cream off the market'. By contrast, a penetration strategy is based on the assumption that if you can produce a similar product to your competitor and underprice him then you will take away some or all of his market share. As a result of ECONOMIES OF SCALE and the EXPERIENCE EFFECT, the strategist using a penetration policy hopes to reduce his initial cost structure to a point at which he can support the penetration price profitably. More recently, a number of authors have begun to suggest an alternative value-based strategy which is based on the belief that the appropriate concept is the perceived value held by the customer. This approach would seem to have much in common with what is popularly called 'charging what the market will bear', which a recent UK survey found to be the most widely used pricing strategy in manufacturing industry.   (MJB)

primary data. Original data collected by the researcher through observation, experimentation, or survey (primary research). This is in contrast with secondary data, which is data that has already been collected and recorded for some other purpose.   (MJB)

primary demand. The total demand for all products in a given category such as washing machines or vacuum cleaners.   (MJB)

primary readership. The number of people who buy a copy of a newspaper or magazine plus other members of their households. The figure specifically excludes anyone else who may also read the buyer's copy, defined as its SECONDARY READ-

ERSHIP. A primary readership figure would thus be expected to be higher than CIRCULATION but is bound to be lower than overall 'READERSHIP', normally taken to mean primary plus secondary.

(KC)

prime time. The period of the day at which the radio audience is largest and the CONTRACTING COMPANIES therefore charge the highest rate for ADVERTISING TIME. It is generally defined as six in the morning to nine in the morning, but a half-hour may be added or subtracted at the two ends on an individual station's RATE CARD. *See also* PEAK TIME.   (KC)

principal component analysis. A method usually loosely referred to as one of FACTOR ANALYSIS, in which the number of scales is derived by a method requiring no arbitrary assumptions. The first few factors usually account for the bulk of the variation in the data, and the others are neglected.   (JAB)

principle of massed reserves. The principle of reducing the size of the many inventories at the retail level while increasing the size of inventories carried by wholesalers, with the effect of reducing the total stock carried in the system.

(AJB)

principle of minimum total transactions. The principle applicable when the insertion of an intermediary between buyers and sellers results in a reduction in the total number of transactions.

(AJB)

principle of relative loss. The principle that failure by a producer to achieve sales to the retailer who has available retail shelf space, results in production capacity being unused, and therefore in unrealized profit opportunity, or relative loss.   (AJB)

print run. A term used in printing where a specified number of pages, books etc. is to be printed, e.g. a print run of 20,000. Quotations from printing companies usually give costings for different print runs or quantities printed, and the cost per unit usually drops with larger print runs.   (MDP)

prior analysis. DATA analyses which take into account probabilities known before the ANALYSIS. For example, discriminant analyses generate different best weighed combinations of variables to distinguish groups that differ in frequency of occurrence. Prior analysis is more deeply covered by BAYESIAN statistics. (SKT)

prior probability. The probability of some event (e.g. group membership) using information known before some statistical procedure. Associated with BAYESIAN THEORY. (SKT)

private brands. Any brand name whose copyright is owned by a party other than the producer of the product. Commonly the owner of the brand name is a retailer, or wholesaler, or other intermediary. (AJB)

private sector. All those organizations which are in private as opposed to public ownership usually with the objective of trading for profit. (MJB)

privatization. The return of nationalized industries into private ownership through the sale of shares in the company. The Conservative Government privatized a number of nationalized industries during the 1980s, such as British Airways, British Telecom and British Steel. (MJB)

PRO. *See* PUBLIC RELATIONS OFFICER.

probability. In simple terms, probability reflects the likelihood of an event expressed on a scale which runs from certain to impossible, to which, by convention, have been assigned the values 1.0 and 0.0 respectively. Intermediate points are assigned values which reflect the frequency with which they are expected to occur and the critical issue is the basis upon which the expectation is founded. For managerial purposes, three methods of assessing probability are important for managers, namely, *a priori,* relative frequency and subjective. An *a priori* probability expresses the frequency with which the event may occur in terms of the total number of possible outcomes so that the *a priori* probability of a head in coin tossing is half or 0.5, of a 6 on a single throw of dice 1/6 or 0.166, of the ace of spades on a single draw from a pack of cards 1/52 or 0.019, and so on. The *a priori* method of assigning probability is of little practical application other than in games of chance, but the relative frequency method is much more useful and is the technique used when defining risk. As the term suggests, probabilities of this kind are based upon knowledge concerning the frequency with which an event has occurred in the past, thus enabling one to express a view as to the likelihood of its recur-

rence in the future. This concept is central to the whole theory of SAMPLING which is a procedure used extensively in marketing research. In the absence of objective information concerning previous occurrences of events identical to the one which one is trying to predict, i.e. under conditions of uncertainty, the decision maker will have to depend upon his own skill and experience and use his subjective expectation of the occurrence of an event as the basis for an actual decision. (MJB)

probability-proportional-to-size. In MULTI-STAGE SAMPLING procedures, a system to allow the selection of primary sampling units (typically areas) to be more likely for larger units. This can then allow for a clustered interviewing schedule to achieve reasonably equal probability of selection for elements when the clusters (PSUs) are of varying size. A simple random sample of clusters followed by a constant sampling fraction at the second stage would lead to smaller clusters being more likely to be included, but that the number selected in a large cluster would be larger. Probability-proportional-to-size followed by a fixed number to be interviewed at each cluster makes for easier field-work. (SKT)

probability sampling. Sample selection schemes that involve no judgement on the part of the interviewer, with each member of the POPULATION having a known (or calculable) non-zero probability of selection before SAMPLING commences. (SKT)

probe. An additional question added on a topic in a QUESTIONNAIRE, at the discretion of the interviewer, such as 'exactly how long ago was that?' (JAB)

problem children. An alternative description for 'question marks' in the Boston Box PRODUCT PORTFOLIO analytical approach. (MJB)

problem definition. An essential prerequisite to the formulation of strategies, plans and tactics for its successful resolution. Problem definition is generally accepted as the most difficult and demanding aspect of problem solving and often requires a creative and novel approach in order to provide an original perspective. For example Alex Osborn (*Applied Imagination,* 3rd edn, 1963) suggests that in addressing the problem of product development one should consider putting to other uses, adaptation, modification, magnification, miniaturization, substitution, rearrangement, reversal or combination of the existing product features and/or consumer needs. Techniques like this and BRAINSTORMING are helpful in suggesting alternative approaches to problem definition but, ultimately, good diagnosis would seem to depend as much upon insight and experience as it does upon formal analysis. That said, 'judgement' should not be used as an excuse for ignoring the procedures set out in most books on problem solving.   (MJB)

problem recognition. The first step in the decision-making process.   (MJB)

procurement. While often regarded as synonymous with 'purchasing' procurement is now seen as a managerial function responsible for all aspects of the acquisition of goods and services from the identification of attributes and performance indicators through vendor selection, requisitioning and quality assurance both during and after use. This goes much beyond the purely clerical aspects commonly associated with purchasing and reflects the recognition that with 80% or more of the cost of goods sold accounted for by bought-in supplies, efficient and effective procurement is a KEY SUCCESS FACTOR.   (MJB)

producer cooperative. An agreement between growers/farmers to pool their output and market it together.   (MJB)

product. Experience suggests that it is possible to classify types of products in terms of the relative emphasis accorded to their objective and subjective characteristics and the manner in which they are bought. Such classification is both desirable and necessary to provide a useful basis for specifying the appropriate strategy to be used in the markets into which the different classes of goods are sold.

Perhaps the simplest and most obvious approach to product classification is the dichotomies between industrial and consumer goods, and durable and non-durable goods. These are essentially simplistic classificatory systems and greater sophistication is necessary to enable rational marketing strategy decisions to be made. This attempt to provide greater sophistication to be found in the three best-known systems described in the literature. First, there is Copeland's trichotomy of convenience goods, shopping goods, and specialty goods based upon consumer buying habits ('Relation of Consumer

Buying Habits to Marketing Methods', 1923). Although this scheme was developed in the context of consumer goods it may be generalized easily to include industrial goods as well. Aspinwall ('Characteristics of Goods Theory', 1962) offers an alternative product classification also based on a trichotomy: pure red goods (roughly parallel to convenience goods), pure yellow goods (roughly parallel to shopping goods), and orange goods lying between the red and yellow goods) based on such characteristics as the replacement rate, gross margin, adjustment (services applied to goods in order to meet the exact needs of the consumer), time of consumption (durability) and searching time (time and distance from source of supply).

Subsequently, Aspinwall's work was revised and extended by Miracle ('Product Characteristics and Marketing Strategy', 1965) who delineates five product groups instead of three by specifying nine product characteristics instead of five. Miracle's nine product positioning characteristics are: (a) unit value; (b) significance of each individual purchase to the customer; (c) time and effort spent purchasing by customers, (d) rate of technological change, including fashion change; (e) technical complexity; (f) customer need for service before, during and after the sale; (g) frequency of purchase; (h) rapidity of consumption, (i) extent of usage or variety of ways in which the product provides utility. By rating products against these characteristics on a range from very high to very low, certain combinations of rating occur together regularly for specific groups of products and lead Miracle to propose five basic product groups.

In sum, therefore, a product may be defined as a combination of objective (tangible) and subjective (intangible) properties designed or intended to provide need-satisfying experiences to consumers.   (MJB)

product assortment. All those items which are available for sale. Usually used to describe a reseller with the term PRODUCT MIX being used to describe the items made by a manufacturing firm.
          (MJB)

product attributes. *See* PRODUCT CHARACTERISTICS.

product champion. Someone, usually with authority and power, who takes on responsibility for promoting the development and marketing of a particular product. The existence of a product champion is strongly associated with the success of a product. (MJB)

product characteristics. Those factors or attributes which buyers and sellers typically take into account in determining the suitability of a product or service to satisfy a felt need.

Conventionally, product characteristics are classified as technical or economic, with the latter category being divided into non-price and price related factors. The summary table (*see* Figure 25) indicates the kind of factors which fall into these various categories. (MJB)

product deletion. A decision to discontinue the production and marketing of a given product within a company's activities. Such a decision may be the result of external pressures (e.g. government policies and regulations), technological obsolescence, the development of a new (replacement) product and/or the product's poor technical, financial or commercial performance. *See* PRODUCT ELIMINATION. (GA)

product design. The physical design and development of a product based on the feedback from the PRODUCT CONCEPT test. (MJB)

product design quality. The degree to which design specifications of a PRODUCT satisfy customer design requirements. (GM)

product development. *See* NEW PRODUCT DEVELOPMENT.

product differentiation. *See* DIFFERENTIATED MARKETING STRATEGY.

product elimination. The removal of products from the PRODUCT PORTFOLIO once they have reached the decline stage of the life cycle. Usually the choice rests between immediate withdrawal and phasing it out slowly. The latter approach is often referred to as killing, harvesting, run-out, or product petrification. (MJB)

product idea screening devices. Basically, idea screening calls for an explicit listing of criteria to be used in the judgement of new product proposals. It is in essence an information-seeking and appraisal process in which the information sought is not only on these relative to certain external factors. The object of the process is not to determine in absolute terms whether a proposed product should be added to a company's product-mix, rather it is to indicate whether further detailed investigation is justified.

It is generally agreed that a screening process should consist of a series of finer and finer meshes so that only those ideas which appear to have a reasonable chance of success are subjected to detailed evaluation. The selection of the criteria to be used and the weighting to be attached to them will depend upon the specific context in which the decision is to be taken and should be reviewed regularly to ensure they reflect the prevailing conditions.

While idea screening has many advantages it also possesses limitations, not least of which is that the method does not permit easy comparison between alternative projects, nor does it provide any indication of the likely absolute size of the pay-off. However, once recognized, alternative procedures may be employed to remedy these deficiencies. (MJB)

Technical	Economic	
	Non-Price	Price
Size	Servicing costs	List price
Shape	Availability of part and service	Sale price
Weight		Net price after trade-in allowance
	Running costs	
Consistency		
	Breakdown costs	
Material used in construction	Depreciation	Financing or leasing arrangements
Complexity	User training facilities	Discounts
Power source		
	Instructions	Sale or return
Power output		
	Delivery	Special offers
Speed/production rate		
Reliability		
Flexibility/Adaptability		
Ease of use		
Ease of maintenance		
Safety		
Appearance/Design features		
Smell		
Taste		

Sources: Roy Rothwell & P Gardiner in *Design and the Economy op. cit.* Joel R Evans & Barry Berman, *Marketing,* Macmillan Publishing Co Inc. New York, 1982.

Figure 25: **Product characteristics**

product image. The customer's perception of a product.   (MJB)

product innovation strategy. A deliberate decision by the firm that it will seek to compete through the development of new products rather than on a basis of price, promotion or distribution, i.e. the product is seen as the key strategic variable rather than one of the other elements of the marketing mix although these will be utilized in support of the core strategy.   (MJB)

production concept. The traditional view of the business in which management 'knows' what the customer wants and so can concentrate all their efforts on producing the best quality for a given cost in the most efficient and effective way. This orientation is often seen as antithetical to the MARKETING CONCEPT because of its inward looking internal focus. A more enlightened view would recognize that successful firms need to give equal attention to both production and marketing as they are inextricably linked to one another.   (MJB)

production control. A complex set of activities concerned with the determination of, and operation of, the production facilities of the firm. While the responsibility for production control does not normally rest with marketers, they have significant levels of input at several stages, and are vitally concerned with the physical and information output.

Production control is commonly subdivided into three subsets:

(a) Facilities control or specification: the determination of the plant and buildings required by the company, for which decision key elements include the long-range MARKET outlook and the strategic MARKETING PLANS for the firm.

(b) Methods control: the determination of production methods and systems. This aspect is of less direct concern to marketers in most cases, although in markets for specialized industrial products (especially where jobbing techniques are involved) MARKETING MANAGEMENT may have a significant role via their responsibility for specification definition and interpretation.

(c) Production scheduling: the determination of the actual production programme. Key MARKETING inputs include sales forecasts, analyses of orders received and in hand, indication of customer needs as regards timing, determination of market priorities, especially in circumstances where demand exceeds current supply capability.

Key marketing outputs include the product itself, and status reports of orders in hand and of future INVENTORY availability.

The scheduling techniques employed vary in part, according to the nature and frequency of demand, and also according to the type of production facilities required. Production scheduling as a function is commonly integrated as a key constituent of MATERIALS MANAGEMENT. *See also* ECONOMIC BATCH QUANTITY.   (KNB)

production orientation. A basic business orientation which dominates when demand exceeds supply. According to Edward S. McKay (*The Marketing Mystique*, New York: American Management Association, 1972), it may be identified by seven principal characteristics, namely: (a) The factory floor is considered to be the business. (b) The focus and emphasis are upon making PRODUCTS. (c) Little attention is given to MARKET RESEARCH and product planning. (d) There is a tendency to base prices on cost and cost alone, with value and competitive considerations largely ignored. (e) Cost reduction efforts may sacrifice quality, product performance, and customer service. (f) The role of the sales organization is to sell whatever the factory chooses to make. (g) If customers aren't happy, the salesmen are told to go out and get some new ones. *See also* MARKETING ORIENTATION.   (MJB)

productivity measurement. The application of the concept of efficiency to the institutions of marketing channels (mainly wholesalers and retailers) at both macro and micro level has resulted in measures of efficiency in the use of capital and labour using the strategic profit model, performance ratios such as sales per person, per square foot, stockturn rate, and the use of improved cost analysis techniques to estimate the profit contribution of different retailer types, salesmen, or territories.   (AJB)

product life cycle (PLC) concept. The paradox of the product life cycle (PLC) concept is that it is one of a very small number of original marketing ideas to enjoy a wide currency and yet is largely discredited in terms of practical application and relevance. That it should be discredited reflects a failing on the part of practitioners to understand the role and potential contribution of theory and concepts rather than any intrinsic deficiency in the concept itself – an assertion we will now seek to substantiate.

The analogy of a product life cycle is firmly founded in the biological sciences and the observation that living organisms pass through an inevitable cycle from conception through gestation to growth leading to maturity. In turn, the mature organism begins to decay progressively until its life is terminated in death. This progression is as familiar to us as life itself, and none would deny the inescapable sequence through which the normal organism will pass. That said, it would be a foolhardy bioscientist who would attempt to generalize about the expectations of a particular organism without first establishing its genus, species and sub-species, and even then they would only speculate about any distinct organism in terms of some form of probabilistic statement concerning expected future outcomes,

The validity of this assertion is easily demonstrated by reference to ourselves – human beings. An inspection of life expectancies quickly reveals major disparities between the inhabitants of advanced, affluent economies and their less fortunate brothers and sisters in the developing countries. Thus, while the average British male can look forward to a life span of 72 years, an Indian has a life expectancy of only 51 years. However, if we were to compare a Briton and an Indian aged 30 years, the discrepancy in their respective life expectancies would be relatively small. The problem is a familiar one in the field of descriptive statistics; means or averages are largely meaningless unless we also possess some measure of dispersion about the mean. In the case of Indians, infant mortality is very high and the age distribution at death is heavily skewed towards young persons. On the other hand, if you survive the dangers of childhood the probability of a reasonably long life is quite high. A broadly similar pattern also applies to Britons, in that infants and young children are more susceptible to disease and death by accident or genetic defect than are teenagers and adults. On the other hand, by enabling weak specimens to survive childhood one increases the probability of death in middle life, with the result that life expectancies for mature adults are very similar in advanced as well as in developing countries.

Actuaries understand this perfectly and base life insurance premiums upon average probabilities. The impression that your policy is written specifically for you is illusory, for no actuary would presume to predict your personal life expectancy. The irony is that while all of this is entirely commonplace and acceptable to us as insurance risks, as managers we expect analogous models to possess a level of predictive ability which cannot be achieved with very large populations of essentially homogeneous units.

The level of information we are likely to possess about a product group such as detergents or industrial fasteners is minuscule by comparison with the demographic data available upon people in general or particular nationalities. But, despite this, we try to make a generalized statement about the sales history of a successful (unspecified) product into a highly specific predictive device. In fact, PLCs can be used as forecasting tools, but only when one has a considerable amount of information about the product, or one analogous to it, and the market into which the product is to be introduced.

However, the real relevance of the PLC is that it is a constant reminder of the inevitability of change and does mirror the stages through which all successful products pass. These stages and the titles given to them are represented in Figure 26.

As can be observed, the conventional PLC is seen as comprising four basic stages when sales are plotted against elapsed time from introduction. First, there is a period of very slow growth when the new product or idea is introduced to prospective users. This phase is terminated by a transition to a period of very rapid growth which eventually levels off into a period of maturity followed by a decline culminating in termination of the life cycle. As noted, this is a conventional representation of a life cycle and must not be taken too literally, for depending upon the product type, the length of the various phases may vary considerably in just the same way as the average length of the mature phase of human beings has a strong correlation with socio-economic status. Similarly, overall life spans will

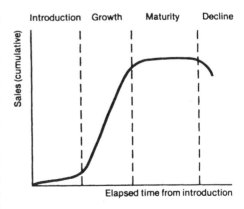

Figure 26: **Product life cycle**

vary enormously, so that fashion goods, like mayflies, are here today and gone tomorrow, while basic materials such as steel have very extended lives analogous to, say, elephants. But, given these caveats, the PLC does contain a number of important messages for us at both a strategic and a tactical level.   (MJB)

product line. Consists of a group of products with similar characteristics and/or similar end use applications, e.g. lubricating oils, lathes, detergents, cosmetics.   (MJB)

product-line analysis. Analysis of the PRODUCT LINE to determine the comparative strengths of the firm's individual products *vis-à-vis* each other and those of their competitors. Such an analysis is an essential input to PRODUCT PORTFOLIO analysis.   (MJB)

product-line filling. The addition of more items to a product line to fill it out and make it more complete.   (MJB)

product line pricing. As the term suggests, product line pricing presents a different set of problems from those associated with the pricing of individual products or a series of products which do not constitute a PRODUCT LINE. By definition, items in a product line have similar characteristics and/or end use applications from which it follows that they are likely to share costs (possibly of production, certainly of marketing) and may complement or compete with each other in the market place. In some instances, e.g. car models, it may be very difficult to distinguish the extent to which the individual L, HL, Ghia/Vanden Plas models compete with each other as compared with matching the offerings of the competitor. Under these circumstances, pricing becomes as much an art as a science and the problem is that the economist's concept of cross-elasticity of demand can probably only be determined through a process of trial and error (i.e. one can define cross-elasticity *post facto* but cannot use the concept to price the product line in any precise or definitive way).   (MJB)

product line relaunch. The re-positioning of a product to improve or extend its sales.   (MJB)

product-line stretching. See PRODUCT-LINE FILLING.   (MJB)

product management. A form of management found in many multi-product firms where full responsibility for the management of discrete products and products lines is delegated to a single product or brand manager. Such a manager will be responsible both for introducing new products and for managing them throughout their life cycle. There is a very large literature which deals with the advantages and disadvantages of the product manager system, particularly as compared with the alternative of organizing around markets as the common factor (market manager). From this literature it is clear that there are many different kinds of product management and considerable difference of opinion as to the merits and demerits of the system. Many of the problems are a direct consequence of the difficulty in assigning product managers sufficient authority commensurate with their responsibility. A great deal depends upon the calibre of the persons appointed to this position and many firms regard the product manager's job as a proving ground for aspirant general managers. This is hardly surprising given the seven roles which Luck and Ferrell suggest the product manager must play: (a) a coordinator of the various functions and department operations, so that they synchronize relative to the particular product(s) and programmes; (b) an entrepreneur or profit centre within the corporation, who develops and is responsible for an area of the business, the assigned product(s); (c) an expediter who sees that tasks get done, products are distributed, crises are met etc. relative to the product(s); (d) an expert information centre who is most knowledgeable about his or her products and their markets, serving as adviser and source of information about them; (e) a forecaster, who studies the markets, competition etc. and projects the likely effects of plans, expenditure, and demand changes on the product(s); (f) an innovator, who finds or creates new ideas regarding the product(s), their marketing etc.; (g) an integrater, who brings together the ideas, plans and viewpoints of others into a systematic product plan.

(MJB)

product manufacture quality. The degree to which the PRODUCT, after purchase and delivery, conforms to design specifications.   (GM)

product mix. Comprises all the product lines of an organization. With the emergence of the STRATEGIC BUSINESS UNIT (SBU) as the basic planning unit, definition of the product mix is usually confined to the SBU. The product mix is usually assessed in terms of three-dimensions – width, depth and consistency. Width is defined in terms of the number of different product lines. Depth measures the number of distinct products within a product line. Consistency reflects the degree to which the various product lines enjoy similar end uses and marketing mixes.   (MJB)

product portfolio. Also known as the BUSINESS PORTFOLIO or GROWTH-SHARE MATRIX. A concept developed by the Boston Consulting Group to diagnose a firm's strategic position. The purpose of the product portfolio is to classify individual products in terms of their life cycle (*see* PRODUCT LIFE CYCLE) reflected by their competitive position measured in terms of their market share relative to that of the largest competitor, and market growth rate. Using these criteria individual products can be assigned to one of four 'boxes' in a 2 x 2 matrix (hence 'Boston Box') as shown in Figure 27.

Question mark products are those at an early stage of their life cycle, when there is uncertainty as to their ability to penetrate a high growth market and secure a worthwhile share of it. Star products are those which have taken off and are exhibiting rapid growth, but where most if not all of their cash generation has to be ploughed back into the business to increase production and distribution and match competitors' marketing activity. Cash cows are established products in the mature phase of their life cycle where both the market and competition have stabilized so that cashflow is large and positive and can be used for new product development and bolstering the rising stars.

Dog products are those which have entered the decline stage of their life cycle. In this phase they can still make a useful contribution to profits but one must be careful that they do not become 'pets' which have outlived their usefulness and demanding more attention than they are worth. Dog products are a major contributor to PRODUCT PROLIFERATION and should be subject to rigorous PRODUCT ELIMINATION procedures.

While the Boston Box has been criticized by Wensley and others on the grounds that it stresses market leadership when there is considerable evidence that such a position does not automatically give rise to lower costs and higher profits, it

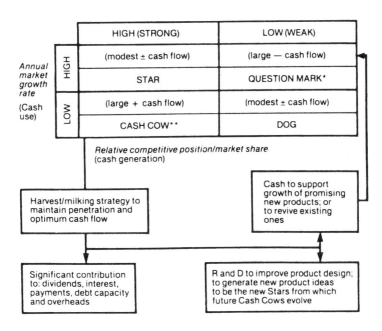

Figure 27: **Product portfolio**

enjoys wide acceptance with strategic planners as a useful device for clarifying the broad options available to the company.   (MJB)

product positioning. 'The differentiation of brands by studying the ways in which their consumers differ as well as how consumer perceptions of various brands differ ...' (Lewis Alpert and Ronald Gatty, 'Product Positioning by Behavioural Life Styles', *Journal of Marketing,* April 1969). In other words, product positioning consists of defining end consumer needs and then developing differentiated products and services which match precisely these pre-identified requirements so that the supplier is able to focus specifically upon selected market segments.

(MJB)

product proliferation. As a result of concentration upon product differentiation as a key competitive strategy, *see* DIFFERENTIATED MARKETING; STRATEGY, there has been a marked increase in new product development leading to a proliferation of products competing with one another in the same end use market. The trend is most noticeable in the consumer packaged goods industry, where most retailers have to exercise very strict control over the number of brands stocked to keep these to manageable proportions, e.g. the average supermarket is likely to have approximately 25,000 different items in stock.

From the individual company's point of view, product proliferation often results due to the unwillingness of management to eliminate products from the portfolio as they reach the decline stage and can lead to severe diseconomies and dilution of effort. *See* PRODUCT DELETION, PRODUCT ELIMINATION.   (MJB)

product quality. The degree to which the PRODUCT satisfies customer requirements. (GM)

product recall. The withdrawal and request for return of a product by the manufacturer or distributor in order to remedy or replace it due to the detection of a fault or faults which render it unfit for the purpose for which it was sold. Such recalls have become more common with the growth of consumerism and the enactment of legislation to protect CONSUMER RIGHTS. All companies should have a clear policy of how they will deal with product defects, whether due to design or faulty materials, particularly when the incidence of defects is high. In 1990, the worldwide withdrawal of contaminated Perrier water is estimated to have cost the company £76 million.   (MJB)

product reliability. The ability of the PRODUCT to function as, when, where and for the time period required.   (GM)

product system. Denotes either the development of a single product into a system by incorporating into the product functions formerly performed manually by the customer (single product system) or the development of an application integrated system where several discrete products and components are linked together to perform a specific function (application). Either of these systems seek to stimulate sales volume through increasing the utility of products to the customers (e.g. convenience, elimination of unpleasant tasks, time and cost savings).   (GA)

product test. A very common marketing research procedure for FAST MOVING CONSUMER GOODS intended to evaluate or compare similar physical forms of the product concerned. The procedure basically consists of giving one or more sample packs to a RESPONDENT to use and to evaluate under more or less realistic use conditions, and to ask evaluative questions. The respondents are drawn from the intended or actual market. The products are usually presented 'blind' in unidentified plain packs to attempt to remove the effect of brand image and other nonproduct variables. However, the appearance of the product and style of packaging often give unintended clues to the respondent as to these other variables. Alternatively the product may be presented in branded packages where it is desired to check the product differences in the brand context. A formulation change in an existing brand might be an example. It is difficult to carry out tests of this kind for services or for durable products where the preparation of small numbers of prototypes or the removal of brand identity may be impractical. Product concept testing may be used instead, or in addition.

Product tests may be monadic, or single, in which the respondent is invited to test one product and evaluate it absolutely or against a 'usual product'. Alternatively they may be dyadic, or double, in which comparisons or preferences are invited. Combinations of these approaches may be used, and numbers of different products evaluated in more complicated experiments using experimental design techniques.

Care has to be taken to obtain evaluation on dimensions relevant to consumer decisions, and to circumvent the effect of various kinds of BIAS, such as the gratitude effect – unrealistically high evaluation due to politeness – or the HALO EFFECT.
(JAB)

product usage segmentation. Also called volume segmentation, this attempts to identify the HEAVY USERS of a product category. The 80–20 or PARETO thesis is frequently put forward, where 20 per cent of customers in a market account for 80 per cent of sales, showing the importance of a small group of consumers to the health of a firm's product.
(JLD)

professional services. Services which are frequently regulated and usually require the provider to be highly skilled and qualified, e. g. accounting or legal services.
(AMW)

profile. In marketing research, an analysis of data showing the way in which all those with a particular attribute (e.g. using a named brand) are split between different demographic or other relevant groups. Such a set of profiles is obtained by percentaging a cross-tabulation sideways, instead of in the usual columns, assuming that, as is conventional, the independent or predictive groupings (such as demographic) have headings across the page. In attitude profiles, the profile is often similar to that of the user of a brand, and a set of average scores on various attitude scales displayed, to give a profile of the brand.
(JAB)

Profile. The *Financial Times* on-line information service, which gives access to over 70 international information sources, selected to provide a comprehensive and authoritative coverage of business information.
(GM)

profit centre. *See* COST CENTRE.

Profit Impact of Marketing Strategies (PIMS). One of the most significant research projects undertaken by the Marketing Science Institute at Cambridge, Mass. The basic aim was to provide information to management of the profit performance of different kinds of businesses under various competitive conditions. It was hoped to 'uncover the laws of marketplace' through a cross-sectional model of major factors influencing return on investment. Some findings from the PIMS study of 57 corporations, with 620 separate businesses, have been made public. In brief,

profit performance was found to be related to at least 37 factors including market share, product quality, research and development expenditures, marketing expenditures, investment intensity and corporate diversity. These factors included in a profit-level equation were reported to have explained close to 80 per cent of the variations in profitability among businesses in the PIMS data base. The PIMS program, first located at the Harvard Business School, in 1975 became an independent non-profit organization called the Strategic Planning Institute. The data base is under the custody of the University of Massachusetts at Amherst.
(GA)

profit maximization. The whole of the early theory of the firm, and even the bulk of its modern development, is founded on the hypothesis that firms seek to maximize profits. The principle of total profit maximization demands that price should be set at the level at which a small change in total cost would be just equal to the change in total revenue, i.e. the firm should seek to equate marginal cost with marginal revenue. According to economists such as Milton Friedman the competitive pursuit of maximum profits creates the greatest economic welfare, the question of how those profits should be distributed being a matter for political and social policy. Accordingly, it is argued that the formal purpose for which companies are established is to maximize the return on the assets employed and that such profit maximization provides management with a relatively unambiguous criterion for business decision making.

However, as Gabor and numerous other economists have argued, there are at least four ways of interpreting what is meant by maximizing profit. First, there is the absolute interpretation which means that capital would be poured into a firm until the increase in total profit due to the last increment was equal to the interest charge on that capital, irrespective of any more favourable investment opportunity. The second interpretation is that one maximizes the mark-up rate; the third, one maximizes the rate of return on that part of capital only which belongs to the owners of the firm, and, fourthly, that one maximizes the rate of return on the total assets of the firm irrespective of the origin of the funds. Pragmatically it would seem that many businessmen think of maximizing profits in terms of making profits larger in a relative rather than absolute sense. There is considerable empirical evidence to support this view and this has led to the emergence of an alternative thesis of profit-seeking behaviour which has been termed SATISFICING as opposed to maximizing.   (MJB)

profits. The excess of total revenues over total costs.   (MJB)

proforma. A specimen.

project. A clearly defined task assigned to a designated group of people. This form of organization is often found in NEW PRODUCT DEVELOPMENT but is becoming increasingly popular in other contexts in preference to more rigidly structured organizational forms.   (MJB)

project evaluation and review technique (PERT). Used in planning the events and activities which are required to accomplish a project. Normally used in large construction projects, it may also be applied to the substantial marketing projects often associated with new products.
                                                        (AJB)

projection. An ego defence mechanism through which one projects on to others one's subconscious needs, fears etc. It is the basis of PROJECTION TECHNIQUES in marketing research.
                                                        (MJB)

projection techniques. These are used in an interview to overcome some of the barriers to communication arising from the inability or unwillingness of respondents to state their 'real' feelings or actions. Respondents are invited to say what other people might feel or do. Techniques such as sentence completion or filling-in speech balloons in cartoon drawings may be used, or, more simply, a question such as 'what do you think most people think is the most important feature of this product?'   (JAB)

projective techniques. See PROJECTION TECHNIQUES.

promotion. One of the four Ps, promotion includes all activities involved in bringing the product to the attention of the intended customer and persuading them to buy it.   (MJB)

promotional allowance. A discount or payment to a dealer or retailer to reward them for participating in a promotional campaign.   (MJB)

promotional mix. An alternative term for the MARKETING COMMUNICATIONS MIX.   (KC)

promotional pricing. Offering discounted prices to encourage purchase as part of a promotional campaign.   (MJB)

promotions. Any device designed to increase consumer purchases. The more important promotions include FREE SAMPLES, OFF-PRICE LABELS, BANDED OFFERS, PREMIUM OFFERS, COMPETITIONS and PERSONALITY PROMOTIONS. See SALES PROMOTION.   (MJB)

promotools. Promotional tools, for example mailing shot, on-pack promotion, special sales drive.   (JRB)

prompted recall. See RECALL.

proof of purchase. A token or some element of a PRODUCT'S packaging which proves purchase for the purpose of participating in a COMPETITION, special offer or other promotional activity sponsored by the manufacturer or seller.   (MJB)

propaganda. Information intended to persuade people to adopt or subscribe to a doctrine or particular point of view.   (MJB)

proportionate stratified (random) sampling. A stratified sampling procedure which selects numbers proportional to size of strata.   (SKT)

proposal. A formal sales proposition which is presented to the customer to make the case for purchase. The typical proposal will attempt to analyse the problems of the customer and seek to show how the seller's product or service can meet the customer's needs effectively and better than the competition.   (STP)

proprietary drugs. Any non-prescription medicine or drug which can be purchased 'over the counter'.   (MJB)

prospect. A potential customer identified as having an EFFECTIVE DEMAND for a good or service.   (MJB)

prospecting. Identifying new customers.   (STP)

protectionism. A policy of protecting domestic industries from foreign competition by erecting trade barriers against imports.   (MJB)

prototype. The first model of a new product or full description of a new service which incorporates the features identified during concept testing during the NEW PRODUCT DEVELOPMENT process. The prototype is then subjected to testing to establish its performance characteristics and ensure it meets the specification. (MJB)

pruning, product line. Synonymous with simplification and variety reduction, the process of reducing the number of specific product types or versions, sizes and models of product types within a given product-line. The process of product-line pricing is designed to counteract the management's tendency to increase the variety of products manufactured to satisfy (at a high cost to the company) every conceivable shade of market requirements. Some studies of this problem date back to the 1920s. (GA)

Ps of marketing mix. An alliteration created to encapsulate the basic activities of the marketing discipline, the 'four Ps' are product, price, promotion and place. (JRB)

psychogalvanometer. *See* LABORATORY TESTS OF ADVERTISING EFFECT.

psychographic analysis. *See* LIFESTYLE ANALYSIS.

psychographics. The measurement of lifestyle is the subject of an area of research known as psychographics and is discussed at length in Engel *et al., Consumer Behavior* (1968). An excellent overview of the subject is to be found in an article by William D. Wells, 'Psychographics: A Critical Review' (*Journal of Marketing Research,* vol. 12, May 1975). In this article Wells proposes an operational definition of psychographic research as 'quantitative research intended to place consumers on psychological – as distinguished from demographic-dimensions', a definition which emphasizes the distinctive features of the area – it has a quantitative rather than a qualitative orientation and goes beyond demographics. (Engel *et al.* point out that 'psychographics' is often used interchangeably with the mnemonic AIO standing for Activities, Interests and Opinions as a research area.) (MJB)

psychological drives. Non-physiological drives learned through the process of SOCIALIZATION. They represent the higher order drives identified by MASLOW such as love (belongingness), esteem and self-actualization. (MJB)

psychological measurement. *See* PSYCHOMETRICS.

psychological pricing. The adoption of prices which appear significantly lower than other very similar prices and so appear to offer better value for money (e.g. prices ending in 99p) rather than prices in whole numbers, e.g. £7.99 versus £8.00. (MJB)

psychometrics. A group of techniques depending on the theory that particular psychological measurements can be used to divide consumers into groups each of which has sharply different purchasing behaviour in a number of product fields, and also in media usage. Several systems of psychological classification have been advocated. The application of these to respondents by applying attitude scales is usually lengthy enough to restrict their use to panels from which the brand and media information is obtained later. (JAB)

public. Any group of people of relevance or importance to the organization with whom it may wish to communicate. (MJB)

public domain. Intellectual property unprotected by copyright, or on which the copyright has expired, which may be freely used by anyone wishing to do so. (MJB)

publicity. Whereas advertising entails the placing of recognizable ADVERTISEMENTS in definable ADVERTISING MEDIA at a published rate for the purchase of ADVERTISING SPACE or ADVERTISING TIME, publicity is the delivery of information to the news media in the hope that it will be judged newsworthy and therefore mentioned editorially at no charge. This distinction is not always carefully observed in practice. Charities are particularly inclined to use 'publicity manager' to describe an executive with responsibility for advertising as well as publicity, perhaps because the term sounds less blatantly commercial, and the error is also common among business-to-business advertisers. It is wise to be alert to the possibility of confusion as a result.

Publicity and advertising are clearly distinguishable also in terms of cost and control. In the case of advertising, both are high. Advertisers pay a price for the right to fill a block of time or space with messages and images exactly to their own specification; the MEDIA OWNERS have a duty to make sure no variations or distortions occur. In the case of publicity, cost and control are both low. It costs very little to produce news releases, pay postage and make telephone calls, but the news media have a perfect right to ignore the information altogether or use it to suit their own editorial purpose rather than the originator's marketing objectives. Sceptics often assume that 'accurate' publicity can be bought – that is, control can be achieved for a price. This is not an argument that can be taken up here, for the outcome in practice depends on the ethics of individual editors, but one can safely say that there is no evidence of widespread corruption of this sort in the British press or broadcast media.　(KC)

public limited company. The larger of the two forms of joint stock company, the other being the limited liability company. Both have independent legal status, thus allowing limited liability of the shareholders and continuity to the business. They account for two-thirds of the capital employed by all companies. There are several differences between public and limited liability companies, such as cost of formation, size, methods of raising capital and transferability of shares. PLC formation is a very expensive business, in relation to the formation of a limited company. The PLC must have at least seven members; it must raise capital through public subscription, which can be involved and costly; shareholders may freely transfer their shares to other members of the public; all PLCs must file annually with the Registrar of Companies details of turnover, profits, assets, names of directors and any material changes to their structure or activities. (GM)

public market. A market owned and operated by a local authority in which the sellers rent space. They are particularly common for the sale of foodstuffs e.g. Smithfield for meat, Les Halles in Paris for fresh fruit and vegetables etc. While wholesale markets usually specialize, retail markets often offer a wide range of household goods and textiles in addition to foodstuffs.
(MJB)

public opinion. The majority view held by members of a given population concerning a particular topic. (MJB)

public policy. Guidelines set down by government concerning matters of public interest such as health, education and welfare which are usually incorporated into legislation spelling out how the policies are to be implemented. (MJB)

public relations. Defined by the INSTITUTE OF PUBLIC RELATIONS as 'the planned and sustained effort to establish and maintain goodwill and mutual understanding between an organization and its publics'. In everyday usage, the term is often used interchangeably with PUBLICITY. As the Institute's definition clearly shows, public relations has a broad and strategic focus whereas publicity is a narrowly-defined tactical operation that may be deployed in the service of a public relations initiative but also for many other purposes. Furthermore, a public relations campaign may well make use of more elements of the MARKETING COMMUNICATIONS MIX than publicity alone. (KC)

public relations consultant. A consultant specializing in the PUBLIC RELATIONS field. Firms vary in size, from one-man businesses to large international organizations. They are often used by organizations as a forerunner to the setting up of an internal public relations function and for specialist operations, where there is no internal expertise. (GM)

public relations officer (PRO). An employee of an organization who is charged with responsibility for PUBLIC RELATIONS. 'PRO' can have a pejorative connotation when used by those not themselves involved in the activity. (KC)

publics. Segments of the population identifiable as distinct in terms of marketing. A concept much used by public relations operators, who frequently have the task of reaching many 'publics' in the course of their work, for example consumers, legislators, media operators, distributors, local authorities, civil servants and so on. (JRB)

public sector. The sector of the economy which comprises the central government, local authorities, nationalized industries and public corporations. (MDP)

public service announcement. Any communication published or broadcast in an advertising medium without charge to the organization promoting the message. Such messages usually relate to charities or other types of non-profit organisation acting in the public service, e.g. Cancer Research. (MJB)

puff. A distinctly archaic term for advertisers' claims. It is often used pejoratively, especially in the version 'puffery'. The description is used more in the USA than the UK, probably because of the unintended *double entendre* in British colloquial usage. (KC)

pull strategy. Appropriate strategy where a market has a clearly defined need for a product so that the producer can appeal directly to ultimate consumers whose demand will then 'pull' that product through the channels of distribution. Pull strategies tend to dominate in the case of fast-moving branded goods where evidence of extensive promotion to ultimate consumers is often necessary to persuade retailers to stock the brand in question. Diametrically opposed to a PUSH STRATEGY. (MJB)

pulsing. Publishing advertising material in bursts. (MJB)

pulsing strategy. The use of concentrated bursts or 'pulses' of advertising in an ADVERTISING CAMPAIGN. (MJB)

pupilometer. A device for measuring the dilation and movement of a watcher's eye in order to discover what elements of a visual display have attracted their attention. (MJB)

purchase contracts. Legal agreements between buyer and seller to buy specified goods under agreed terms and conditions. (STP)

purchase decision. Final stage in the buying process which has culminated in the decision to buy a particular product/service from a particular supplier. (STP)

purchase distribution. The percentage of all retail outlets which have received a delivery of the product in question since the last audit, whether or not they were in stock then or at the current audit. (AJB)

purchase intention. A measure of the claimed level of future consumption of a PRODUCT or service by target customers who almost invariably overstate their subsequent purchase behaviour. (MJB)

purchase probability scale. This is a form of buyer evaluation conducted by suppliers whereby they assess the probability of being awarded the contract on the basis of their bid and the likely strategy of competitors. The probability of obtaining the award forms a continuum with various points on the scale representing the likelihood of being successful. For example:

Prob-	0.0	0.3	0.5	0.7	1.0
ability	No chance	Slight Possibility	Fair	Prob-able	Certain

Figure 28: **Purchase probability scale**

purchases. Those products or services which are bought in by an individual or an organization. (STP)

purchasing department. Functional grouping of individuals within an organization who are involved in the procurement of the company's bought-in components or services. (STP)

purchasing leverage. The impact of effective purchasing on profitability. In many organizations the value of goods and services acquired by the firm may account for up to 50 per cent of the value of sales. An increase of 5 per cent in the cost of bought in items adds to a company's direct costs, reducing profit by the same amount. If a company had been earning 10 per cent profit on sales, an increase in costs of 5 per cent would reduce profits by 25 per cent.

As firms have increasingly recognized the leverage which effective purchasing has on profit, so greater attention has been given to the way in which buying decisions are taken. This has had major repercussions on industrial marketing activity. The industrial customer has become more demanding of its suppliers and has increasingly begun to plan its purchasing carefully. (STP)

pure competition. *See* COMPETITION.

pure monopoly. *See* COMPETITION.

purposive research. *See* SAMPLING.

push money. Cash paid to salespeople as a bonus when they sell specific items of merchandise. It may be paid by the manufacturer or the retailer. (AJB)

push strategy. Appropriate strategy where the ultimate consumer is unfamiliar with the product or its properties and the producer needs to secure the cooperation of intermediaries in the channel of distribution in order to bring these to the attention of the ultimate consumer. Push strategies are also necessary in the case of the smaller producer who is unable to afford a sufficient investment in advertising and promotion to pull the product through the channels of distribution. Thus, push strategies are most appropriate for shopping goods, specialty goods and innovative products. *See* PULL STRATEGY.   (MJB)

pyramid selling. A multi-level selling structure in which the promotor sells the franchise for a sales level. Franchise operators at every level are required to obtain their merchandise from the next highest level, and in many cases to purchase a minimum quantity. The UK Fair Trading Act of 1973 requires that unsold stocks must be redeemed by the franchisor.   (AJB)

Q

Q-type analysis. A FACTOR or COMPONENT ANALYSIS based on correlations between variables (or questions). This is in contrast to an R-TYPE ANALYSIS where the correlations are between RESPONDENTS. (SKT)

qualitative research. Collection of data usually by semistructured or unstructured method from small samples in discursive verbal form. Analysis is by subjective summary, again in discursive form. Often GROUP DISCUSSIONS are used. Although this technique lacks the apparent essential of statistical reproducibility and is dependent on the collector and the analyser of the data, nevertheless it is widely used, not only on account of the relative speed and cheapness of data collection but also because of the relationships between all the variables which may be revealed. (JAB)

quality. The perceived ability of an object to meet the customer's requirements in terms of both physical performance characteristics ('fitness for purpose'), and associated subjective benefits. Quality tends to be judged against expectations which, in turn, are influenced by reputation, experience and price. Thus, while quality may be expressed in terms of objective criteria it is usually interpreted or inferred from the user's subjective experience. (MJB)

quality control. The monitoring of outputs (usually goods but the term also applies to service delivery) to ensure that they meet the standards necessary to deliver the satisfaction expected by the purchaser. Traditionally, quality control has been achieved by regular samples of individual units of output to determine that they meet the agreed standards for content and performance.

More recently it has been recognized that quality is something you build into a PRODUCT or service and not something which you seek to control after it has been produced. To encourage the development of attitudes and practices which maintain and improve quality, many firms now encourage the formation of quality circles which are informal groups of people concerned with the production process who are made responsible for both maintaining and improving quality. (MJB)

quality of life. The sense of wellbeing about one's life and life style, the objective indicators of which will vary by individuals and culture over time. (KF)

quantitative research. Collection of data usually from samples as numbers possessing attributes or particular values of variables. The information is thus reproducible within the limits of statistical error (*see* ERROR), but associations may be deduced only by analytical techniques. Non-statistical error may also reduce the value of quantitative information. Its objectivity is the major advantage. (JAB)

quantity discount. Price reduction given on the basis of the quantity bought; the greater the quantity bought, the cheaper the unit price to the buyer. Frequently the basis on which a manufacturer/distributor bases his 'scaled' price list. Also the logic that lies behind the economy pack sold to consumers, the bigger sizes being pro-rata cheaper than the smaller. (JRB)

quasi-experimental design. A research design which contains some of the controls and manipulations of experimental design, but usually lacks random assignment of subjects. A before–after study is an example of a quasi-experimental design.   (SKT)

Queen's Award to Industry for Technological Innovation. An award given annually to companies which have successfully developed and introduced significant innovation into the market place.   (STP)

question marks. *See* PRODUCT PORTFOLIO.

questionnaires. Question schedules for fully structured face-to-face, telephone or postal sample survey enquiries. The design of questions to minimize bias and non-response is an art in which experience is needed. Lengthy and repetitious questionnaires are particularly to be avoided. The poor quality of data produced by poor questionnaire design is seldom apparent at later stages, but nevertheless affects results greatly. Piloting, or small-scale trial of questionnaires by research executives is desirable.

The questions are set out in a sequence, which may be varied for individual respondents according to their responses to earlier questions by routing instructions to the interviewer. Questions may be open-ended, where verbatim responses are transcribed by the interviewer, to be classified later. They may he closed-ended, where the respondents are presented with a limited number of answers from which to choose, or pre-coded, where the range of answers can be foreseen. Closed-ended questions are easier for interviewers and analysis, but may lead to bias.

The questionnaire is usually set out to facilitate subsequent data capture for computer. The questionnaire may also be presented on a visual display unit screen for direct data entry by key depression.   (JAB)

questions. *See* QUESTIONNAIRES.

quick ratio. *See* ACID TEST.

quota. *See* SAMPLING.

quotas. System of limiting imports by fixing their permitted quantity or value in advance for a given period: quantities in excess will either be banned or have to pay a higher rate of duty. The main concern to the potential exporter is likely to be how the quota is administered – whether, for example, there is a historical national quota, a national quota fixed by other means, 'first come, first served' etc. since this will largely determine his marketing strategy to deal with the situation.   (JML)

quota sampling. *See* SAMPLING.

R

RAB. *See* RADIO ADVERTISING BUREAU.

rack jobber. *See* JOBBER.

radio. One of the five 'major' ADVERTISING MEDIA in Britain. Radio funded by revenue from advertisers came comparatively late to Britain. Before the Second World War, two foreign stations broadcasting in English and carrying advertising had attracted just over 3 per cent of total UK ADVERTISING EXPENDITURE. One, Radio Luxembourg, resumed broadcasting after the war and provided the only 'commercial radio' option for British advertisers for another two decades. Meanwhile, offshore 'pirate' stations such as Radio Caroline confirmed that there was indeed a large, young audience for a programme mix that was distinctly different from the BBC offering of the time. Eventually, the 1972 Sound Broadcasting Act sanctioned commercially funded local radio services alongside the BBC's national network. The first such station to go on air was Capital Radio in London, in November 1973, followed by Radio Clyde on, appropriately, New Year's Eve. Ten years later, there were 40 on air. From 1986 onwards, stations were permitted to broadcast different programmes to different audiences on their AM and FM frequencies, a development called 'split frequency' or 'narrowcasting'. In 1989, an 'incremental' licence was awarded to Atlantic 252, broadcasting to a reception area covering more than half the British Isles. A year later, the 1990 Broadcasting Act sanctioned the establishment of national commercial stations in competition with the BBC, and Classic FM came on air in 1992. In 1997, the UK commercial radio network consisted of 196 local stations, 5 regional and 4 national: *see* INDE-PENDENT LOCAL RADIO, INDEPENDENT NATIONAL RADIO.

Radio's share of UK total ADVERTISING EXPENDITURE reached 2.4 per cent by 1979, but remained stubbornly on a plateau around 2 per cent for the next 13 years, despite the number of commercial stations having risen above 100. It earned itself the nickname 'the two per cent medium' and signally failed to engage the interest of national advertisers. Three events in 1992 marked a sea-change in its fortunes: the setting up of the Independent National Radio network, the RADIO ADVERTISING BUREAU and the RAJAR audience measurement system. The following year, its 'media share' returned to 2.4 per cent, and then rose in successive years to reach 3.2 per cent in 1996. It shared the radio listening audience exactly 50:50 with the BBC network, but took more than 60 per cent in every age group up to the mid-forties; 78 per cent of all adults listened to a commercial radio station at least once in any four-week period. Not surprisingly, national advertisers have been won over: the five highest spenders on radio in 1996 were the Central Office of Information, Dixons, Coca Cola, McDonalds and Carphone Warehouse. The great majority of radio AIRTIME is sold to such advertisers by five SALES HOUSES. Despite a prolonged adolescence, radio is now the fastest-growing of the five MAJOR MEDIA in Britain. (KC)

Radio Advertising Bureau (RAB). Established in 1992, as successor to the moribund Radio Marketing Bureau which had been set up 10 years earlier, the RAB's remit is to promote the UK commercial radio network as an advertising medium, especially to the large number of national advertisers who still do not include it in their advertising schedules more than 25 years after the first of the British commercial stations went on air. The RAB publishes a considerable array of research data, case histories and general marketing information, and is generally given the credit for radio's MEDIA SHARE moving significantly above the persistently low level which had earned it the tag, 'the two per cent medium'.

(KC)

Radio Authority. The statutory body responsible since 1990 for the licensing of commercially-funded radio stations in the United Kingdom (*see* INDEPENDENT RADIO) and for regulating both programme and advertising content (*see* ADVERTISING CONTROL). Its history begins in 1972, when the popularity of offshore 'pirate stations' such as Radio Caroline persuaded the Government to sanction commercial competition with the BBC in Britain. The Sound Broadcasting Act changed the Independent Television Authority into the Independent Broadcasting Authority and extended its existing remit to the general licensing and regulation of the future 'independent radio' network. Capital Radio and LBC in London and Radio Clyde in Glasgow were on air by the end of the year. In 1973, the Independent Broadcasting Authority Act further charged the IBA with the statutory duty to devise and implement a television-style system for the regulation of radio advertising. After another 17 years, it was decided to devolve the administration of the two media to separate statutory bodies. The 1990 Broadcasting Act created the Radio Authority, requiring it to ensure fair and effective competition in the provision of services and to draw up a code which set standards regulated practice in advertising and programme sponsorship. The new body immediately announced its intention to exert a 'lighter touch' than the IBA with respect to the second of these remits, which it duly did: *see* ADVERTISING CONTROL, MINUTAGE. During 1996, the Authority re-advertised the franchises for all 125 ILR (independent local radio) stations and announced the smallest permanent licence yet offered, to serve Ullapool in the north-west of Scotland. During 1997, it will draft guidelines and licence specifications for the introduction of DAB (digital audio broadcasting) transmission alongside the existing analogue system.   (KC)

Radio Marketing Bureau. A body established in 1982 to promote radio as an advertising medium, especially to the 80 per cent of national advertis-

ers who had not yet included ILR in their advertising schedule. It did not always enjoy the wholehearted support of the stations themselves, and was dormant for several years before being formally wound up in 1992. An independent successor, the RADIO ADVERTISING BUREAU, appeared in the same year and has been altogether more successful.   (KC)

radio ratings. The main 'currency' for valuing radio 'AIRTIME'. One radio rating, or RR, represents the achievement of 1 per cent of a station's total potential audience, called its 'universe'. *See also* TV RATINGS.   (KC)

R&D. *See* RESEARCH AND DEVELOPMENT.

raincheck. An American term to describe the practice of promising to supply an out of stock item on the same terms as those prevailing when the customer asked for it. Usually refers to merchandise on special offer.   (MJB)

RAJAR. An acronym, pronounced as a word, for Radio Joint Audience Research. Established in 1992 and funded by the BBC and the commercial radio stations, it replaced JICRAR as the provider of audience data which are accepted as authoritative by all sides of the advertising business. A sample of 160,000 UK listeners fill in weekly listening diaries detailing their choice of station during any daytime quarter-hour or nighttime half-hour. The resulting . data are cross-indexed by the demographic composition of the sample and their consumption of other media. They are made available in print and electronically by subscription, and are a key input to the MEDIA PLANNING process.   (KC)

random assignment. The essential experimental manipulation, whereby other influences that participants bring to experiments are controlled by cancelling each other out by being ignored by the random assignment.   (SKT)

random-digit dialling. Telephone interviewing technique where rather than using lists of subscribers, random numbers (within certain ranges) are used to generate subscriber numbers.   (SKT)

random effects model. In ANALYSIS OF VARIANCE, models used to analyse factors where the particular values of the factor are merely representative of the effects of the factor. This is in contrast to a

FIXED EFFECTS MODEL where the levels of the factor are in the nature of the factor.   (SKT)

random error. Changes in observation due to differences in RESPONDENTS or situations that fluctuate in a random fashion. *Contrast* SYSTEMATIC ERROR.   (SKT)

random factor analysis. A sales forecasting approach in which erratic variations in sales are attributed to random events rather than any underlying trend.   (MJB)

randomized-block design (RBD). In experimental design, procedures which randomly assign objects within each block (defined to be homogeneous by some external criterion) to treatment conditions.   (SKT)

random number list. A published list of random numbers, from a published random number generation process. It is typically used to commence a stratified sampling procedure.   (SKT)

random sample. *See* SAMPLING, RANDOM SAMPLING.

random sampling. The drawing of a SAMPLE in which every member of the POPULATION being sampled has an equal chance of being selected. Other than in controlled experimental situations this is almost impossible to achieve. To begin with one must have a complete SAMPLING FRAME listing every member of the population. While the REGISTER OF ELECTORS is updated every year it is known that approximately 4 per cent of eligible voters will be omitted for one reason or another while over the year many will move or die so that by the end of the year it may be only 80 per cent accurate (even less in areas with a highly mobile population). Further, if one were to seek to interview a random sample drawn from the Register many would not be available at the time of calling or would refuse to cooperate.

For all these reasons most market researchers will use a probabilistic sampling method but based on strata or quotas with defined procedures for replacing 'missing' respondents. *See* SAMPLING.   (MJB)

random walk. Procedure used in interviewing which seeks to provide a degree of randomness within a non-random sampling technique. For example, if one is using a CLUSTER SAMPLING approach one may decide to select a number of representative residential areas to provide a cross

section of the individuals/ households one is interested in. Having selected the area the interviewer will be given a starting point and then call on every *n*th person/house following a random walk or route, e.g. take alternative left and right turns at each intersection within the area boundary.   (MJB)

range branding strategy. The use of separate brand names for families of related products.   (MJB)

ranking. *See* SCALES OF MEASUREMENT.

ratchet effect. The increase in sales achieved by combining sales promotions with advertising so-called because sales promotion is regarded as having a short-term effect while advertising has long-term effects. By combining both in a single campaign a ratchet effect results.   (MJB)

rate card. A document in which MEDIA OWNERS detail their charges for units of ADVERTISING SPACE or ADVERTISING TIME: in effect, their price list. Television CONTRACTING COMPANIES in fact have a statutory obligation to publish one which has been approved by the INDEPENDENT TELEVISION COMMISSION. However, both television and radio CONTRACTING COMPANIES have tended increasingly over recent time to sell time on a case-by-case basis rather than 'off the rate card', and the basic details of their rates are no longer reproduced in BRAD (q.v.). The PRESS, OUTDOOR and CINEMA media continue to publish and use rate cards, though surcharges, discounts and packages mean that almost no advertising is in fact bought at rate-card cost.   (KC)

rate-card cost. The basic price of ADVERTISING SPACE or ADVERTISING TIME, before discounts or surcharges are applied, available from RATE CARDS or in BRAD (q.v.). In the particular case of TELEVISION, there is no single rate-card cost for a given SPOT, but a sliding scale of as many as 18 premium and standard rates that confer increasing protection against PRE-EMPTION by competing bidders for the same spot.   (KC)

ratings. The generic term for the various measures of television and radio audiences. *See* BARB, RAJAR, RADIO RATINGS, TV RATINGS.   (KC)

rating scale. *See* ATTITUDE MEASUREMENT.

ratio analysis. An approach to the analysis of financial information which allows management to monitor changes in the performance of their company from one period to the next or to compare it with other companies. Typical ratios which are calculated and compared include profit/capital employed or current assets/current liabilities. More detailed evaluation of ratios such as production costs/sales turnover, administration costs/sales turnover and selling costs/sales turnover can be used to indicate the relative efficiency of the company in each functional area and changes in that efficiency over time.   (STP)

rational appeals. Persuasive communication aimed at the industrial buyer which is based upon the economic and technical advantages of the product or service to the buyer, rather than emotive appeals which are based upon essentially behavioural factors.   (STP)

rationalization. Generally any action designed to improve efficiency. Specifically, it is a form of ego-defence in which unattainable goals are discarded as undesirable while attainable goals are seen as being more desirable.   (MJB)

ratio scale. *See* SCALING.

raw materials. The term 'raw materials' is often used to describe the physical goods used in manufacturing, without distinguishing between natural raw materials and semi-manufactured or fabricated materials. For example, the raw materials used in the packaging industry – paper, plastics, fibreboard etc. – are the finished goods of other manufacturers in the chemical industry. Natural raw materials include both those such as coal, iron ore and oil which occur in a natural state and are non-renewable, as well as those which occur in a natural state but have been 'adopted' and cultivated by man, which are renewable and whose supply can be increased or decreased through man's efforts – wheat, rubber, wool etc.   (MJB)

raw variable. A variable in a DATA analysis that is in an untransformed state; in contrast to a TRANSFORMED VARIABLE, which might have been regrouped or standardized.   (SKT)

RBD. *See* RANDOMIZED-BLOCK DESIGN.

reach. A quantified measure of the actual audience for a radio or television COMMERCIAL as distinct from the potential audience defined by a station's UNIVERSE or the NET HOMES in its broad-

casting area. It is quantified as the number of people viewing or listening for at least a given number of minutes or hours within a defined period, normally expressed as a percentage of a potential total. Quoted figures may be generalized averages, or specific measures of levels achieved in particular circumstances. Reach is a performance indicator of obvious interest to MEDIA PLANNERS. *See also* COVERAGE and FREQUENCY.   (KC)

reactive bias. BIAS in measurement that is caused by reaction to the measurement process.   (SKT)

reader service card (readers' inquiry card). A detachable pre-paid postcard, typically found in CONTROLLED CIRCULATION PUBLICATIONS, which the reader can return for more information on products and services featured in editorial, ADVERTISING or 'ADVERTORIALS'. Also called, colloquially, 'bingo cards'.   (KC)

readership. The number of people who read a newspaper or magazine, as opposed to the number who actually buy it or subscribe to it, which is CIRCULATION. Readership is measured in Britain by the NATIONAL READERSHIP SURVEY (NRS) and the JOINT INDUSTRY COMMITTEE FOR REGIONAL PRESS RESEARCH (JICREG). MEDIA BUYERS can find the relevant information in BRAD (q.v.), in the form of an absolute figure and a ratio of readers per copy. For example, the listing for the *Manchester Evening News* in late 1996 specified 'Readers per copy 2.8. Average issue readership 551,747. Source JICREG 3/11/1995'; it also provided a basic READERSHIP PROFILE. If there are no readership data for a particular title, media buyers must either rely on the publishers' own statements, which will normally be based selectively on the NRS or JICREG data, or estimate the raw figure by applying standard MULTIPLIERS to the circulation figure. *See also* PRIMARY READERSHIP, SECONDARY READERSHIP.   (KC)

readership profile. A demographic description of the people who read a newspaper or magazine. Ideally, it will further attempt a 'sociographic' description: that is a picture of their social relationships, lifestyle, consumption habits, social values and other personal attributes. Readership profiles are a vital qualitative input to the MEDIA SELECTION decision, augmenting the base quantitative facts transmitted by CIRCULATION and READERSHIP counts or measures of

COVERAGE and FREQUENCY. The raw data for constructing them are available from the continuous research surveys conducted by the NATIONAL READERSHIP SURVEY (NRS) and the JOINT INDUSTRY COMMITTEE FOR REGIONAL PRESS RESEARCH (JICREG). Basic details relating to titles with large circulations are published in BRAD (q.v.). For example, the listing for the *Manchester Evening News* in late 1996 provided a 'profile index' and two COVERAGE figures for all adults, all men, all women, main shoppers (female) and main shoppers (total), cross indexed in each case to the six standard SOCIO-ECONOMIC CLASSIFICATIONS and six age ranges. (KC)

reading-and-noting. A research procedure that measures the average proportion of readers of a newspaper or magazine actively paying attention to separate pages and even individual advertisements. Its origin was in a PhD thesis written in the 1920s by George GALLUP, whose surname subsequently became a household word in connection with opinion polling. After a rival service was set up by Dr Daniel STARCH (*see* HIERARCHY-OF-EFFECTS), reading-and-noting developed into the standard method for post-evaluating ADVERTISING EFFECTIVENESS. It came to Britain in the 1940s.

Participants in a 'reading and noting test' are individually questioned about several publications, soon after the day of issue. The criterion of effectiveness is thus RECALL. They must first prove they did read the issue by spontaneously describing some of its contents. They are then asked a series of specific questions, page by page, the answers to which permit the computation of five separate ratios: 'spread traffic', 'page traffic', 'advertisement noting', 'advertisement reading' and 'name noted'. These express the proportion of the sample who, respectively: noticed anything at all on a spread of two pages; noticed anything on a single page; 'looked at' an advertisement; actually 'read most' of it; noticed the brand name. The description 'reading and noting' is thus somewhat back-to-front, the noting of elements of an advertisement being the more significant measure. MEDIA OWNERS periodically conduct and publish their own 'reading-and-noting scores'. Research results accumulated over time permit computation of comparative performance figures for various advertisement types, all other things being equal. For example, the average noting score for a DOUBLE-PAGE SPREAD in a magazine is 60 to 65 per cent, for a colour page in a magazine 50 to 60 per cent and for a black-and-white page in a newspaper also 50 to 60 per cent. (KC)

real income. Income adjusted for the effects of inflation. (MJB)

recall. An implicit criterion of ADVERTISING EFFECTIVENESS, much used in the testing of television commercials and magazine advertisements (*see* DAY-AFTER RECALL, READING-AND-NOTING). Although ability to recall an advertisement undoubtedly proves that it had some IMPACT in the first place, problems arise when researchers imply that recall is by itself a general indicator of effectiveness. The implication is that a respondent who can recollect particular ingredients of the message or aspects of the treatment is significantly more likely to proceed to purchase (or whatever the advertisement advocates) than one who cannot. This is in reality a highly debatable proposition: *see* HIERARCHY-OF-EFFECTS. It is equally probable that recall represents nothing more than 'repeat attention', voluntarily recalling the original to mind. Nevertheless, advertisers seem willing to accept too readily that good recall scores 'prove' effectiveness. They are furthermore prone to do so even when the advertising objective was actually something else – comprehension, for instance. Commentators have noted the virtual tyranny of 'Burke testing', a proprietary day-after recall measuring procedure, in the USA. Many blame it for an observable lack of 'creativity' in American advertising. It is, after all, easy to earn recall by simply endlessly repeating the product name or a catchphrase which sums up its basic attributes. Much American television advertising does tend to be of this kind, sometimes detectable on British screens because it is so different from the domestic norm. (KC)

receiver. *See* SCHRAMM'S COMMUNICATION MODEL.

receptivity to innovation. The extent to which an organization (or individual) is prepared to consider, evaluate and ultimately buy a new product or process. Receptivity to an innovation can vary considerably between organizations or individuals depending on their individual characteristics, and the characteristics of the innovation. *See* ADOPTION CURVE, ADOPTER CATEGORIES. (STP)

recession. The phase of the business cycle during which increasing unemployment reduces disposable incomes and buying power which results in

reduced demand and further increases in unemployment and a deepening of the recession.
(MJB)

reciprocity. The practice of buying from companies who are also your customers. Reciprocal trading can have a major limiting influence on the discretion of the industrial buyer to source effectively, since the buyer may be forced to buy from important customers who are not necessarily the most appropriate suppliers.   (STP)

recognition agreement. 'Recognition' is awarded to British advertising agencies by the trade associations collectively representing the MEDIA OWNERS: the ASSOCIATION OF INDEPENDENT RADIO CONTRACTORS, the INDEPENDENT TELEVISION COMPANIES ASSOCIATION, the NEWSPAPER PUBLISHERS ASSOCIATION, the PERIODICAL PUBLISHERS ASSOCIATION and the NEWSPAPER SOCIETY. The important thing about recognition is that it confers the exclusive right to receive media COMMISSION. Two main criteria must be met. First, agencies must demonstrate their competence; the trade associations want to be sure that the image of the media will not be jeopardized by slapdash and unprofessional advertising. They cannot control all advertising by this means, since some advertisers will place their offers direct or via non-recognized agencies, but the intent of the criterion is quite understandable. Second, agencies must demonstrate their creditworthiness. This is a precaution against the media owners being left with bad debts if advertisers should bankrupt themselves, for the so-called 'agency' is in fact the principal in financial transactions with the media. Several other less vital criteria must also be met.   (KC)

recognition test. A POST TEST of advertising in which individuals are shown a copy of the advertisement and asked if they recognize it.   (MJB)

recognized advertising agency. See RECOGNITION AGREEMENT.

record. The basic element of a file. Each record is made up of numerous fields. In MARKETING, a sales record may include the following fields: company, address, telephone number, contact person, number of employees, quarterly sales, salesperson, date of last call.   (KRD)

recovery. The phase in the business cycle in which demand begins to grow resulting in

increased employment and disposable income which, in turn, stimulates growth.   (MJB)

redemption rate. A measure of the number of buyers taking advantage of a special promotion, normally expressed as a percentage of all those eligible for the offer.   (MJB)

Reeves, Rosser. American advertising COPYWRITER, co-founder in 1940 of the Ted Bates advertising agency, absorbed into the SAATCHI & SAATCHI world-wide group during the 1980s. The agency's success was based to a large extent on his single-minded pursuit of the UNIQUE SELLING PROPOSITION, a concept to guide advertising strategy explained in his book *Reality in Advertising* (1961). Reeves spent a great deal of time and money on product research to generate and verify the selling propositions to be incorporated in the advertisements he wrote. It is reported that Colgate were persuaded to spend $300,000 to authenticate the claim that washing the face thoroughly for a whole minute with Palmolive soap would improve the skin. Reeves believed in retaining a viable USP almost indefinitely. This philosophy is not always popular with advertisers, who fear that audiences become tired of the same message, and who furthermore enjoy the 'buzz' of developing a new advertising campaign, rather as they might when buying new clothes or redecorating the house. Reeves was also always adamantly opposed to advertising that followed a fashionable genre, particularly as produced by what he called the 'artsy crafty crowd' and especially if he thought the copy was so clever that the message was lost. In *Reality in Advertising,* he says: 'I'm not saying charming, witty, and warm copy won't sell. I'm just saying that I've seen thousands of charming, witty campaigns that didn't. ... Now, what do you want of me? Fine writing? Do you want masterpieces? Do you want glowing things that can be framed by copywriters? Or do you want to see the goddamned sales curve stop moving down and start moving up?'   (KC)

reference groups. When discussing psychological influences upon behaviour the emphasis is upon the individual. But 'no man is an island', and all of us are subjected to the influence of others with whom we come into contact. This influence is particularly strong in the case of what are termed reference groups.

Social psychologists reserve the description group for collections of two or more persons who interact with one another over time. In other words there must be some relationship between the group members which goes beyond collections of persons with common interests such as a theatre audience or passengers in an aeroplane. Bennett and Kassarjian in *Consumer Behavior* cite Krech, Crutchfield and Ballachey's definition from *Individual in Society* (1962), namely: 'a group is (a) persons who are interdependent upon each other, such that each member's behavior potentially influences the behavior of each of the others, and (b) the sharing of an ideology – a set of beliefs, values, and norms – which regulate their mutual conduct'.

Several different types of reference groups may be distinguished, the most basic distinction being between primary and secondary groups. A primary group is one which is small enough for all of the members to communicate with each other face to face (the family, a seminar group, the area sale team), while a secondary group is one where less continuous interaction takes place (professional societies, trade unions, companies etc.).

When a group possesses a specified structure and specified functions then it is termed a formal group, but where the structure and function are unspecified, as in a circle of friends, we have an informal group. Both formal and informal groups have norms which prescribe the pattern of behaviour expected of members and the transmission of these norms to new members is known as socialization. In formal groups the norms are usually much more explicit and readily identified than in informal groups, but the norms of the latter are no less demanding if one wishes to remain in membership of the group. In all cases the influence of the group is towards conformity, and the strength of this tendency will depend upon the pressure the group can bring to bear upon the individual, the importance of the group to the individual and the number of groups to which the individual belongs.

In a marketing context perhaps the most important group of all is the family – specifically the nuclear family of husband, wife and children (the extended family includes grandparents, aunts, uncles, cousins etc.). The nuclear family is frequently referred to as 'the household' in consumer studies, but such usage is often looser and may include any group of persons occupying the same housing unit, as does the official US Census Bureau definition.

As a primary group the family has great influence upon motives, personality and attitudes, and acts as a mediating influence upon external influences which impinge upon it from culture, subculture, social class and other reference groups. Because of this mediating influence, and due to the economic interdependence of its members, family (household) decision making has a profound influence upon purchasing and consumption behaviour. (MJB)

reference prices. Prices which represent the potential buyer's expectation of what a particular product should cost. (MJB)

regional issues. Modified versions of national newspapers or magazines for distribution in a region of the country: for example, the Northern edition of the *Guardian.* Some magazines with world circulations, such as *Reader's Digest* or *The Economist,* use the term to describe editions tailored to whole countries or blocs. (KC)

Regional Newspaper Advertising Bureau (RNAB). From 1980 until late 1990, this was the body which made the case for regional and local evening and weekly newspapers to MEDIA BUYERS. Its remit has been assumed by the JICREG (q.v.), which has rectified the previous lack of a comprehensive readership database.
(KC)

regional press. The collective term for newspapers and, less often, magazines that circulate regionally, e.g. the *Yorkshire Post,* the *Los Angeles Times* or *Young Scot.* The boundaries are blurred between the regional and LOCAL PRESS; the implied contrast is with the NATIONAL PRESS.
(KC)

registered trademark. A name or symbol used to identify an organization or PRODUCT and so differentiate it from other competing firms or products which have been registered (usually with a government agency), so that it may only be used by the registered owner or its appointed agents, e.g. Coca-Cola. (MJB)

Register-MEAL. A research service monitoring total UK advertising volume and expenditure, now subsumed into ACNielsen.MEAL (q.v.).
(KC)

Register of Electors. A listing of all those aged 17 and over who will be entitled to vote in Parliamentary and local elections prior to February 16 in the following year. The Register is updated every year in October and the revisions are published in February the following year or soon thereafter. While there will always be a small percentage of persons not recorded on the Register (approximately 4 per cent), and there will be a concentration of these in the younger and more mobile segments of the population, the Register is the only national sampling frame available and so is widely used for drawing samples of individuals. The Register is built up from a series of booklets – one for each polling district – organized by alphabetical street order in urban districts and name order in rural district.   (MJB)

regression analysis. A statistical analytical procedure for relating a dependent variable to one or more independent variables in order to develop an equation that allows an estimation of the dependent variable.   (GA)

regulatory forces. All those forces which influence and/or control marketing activities. Thus, the existence of regulatory agencies affects MARKET STRUCTURE, CONDUCT AND PERFORMANCE while legislation controls actual behaviour.
                          (MJB)

reinforcement. The degree of satisfaction derived from consuming an object in response to a felt need.   (MJB)

reinforcement advertising. Advertising designed to reassure buyers that they have made the right decision in buying a product thus reducing POST-PURCHASE COGNITIVE DISSONANCE.
                          (MJB)

reinnovation. A term coined by Professor Roy Rothwell to denote successive incremental modifications to a GENERIC PRODUCT to take advantage of emerging technological or MARKET OPPORTUNITIES. Characteristically such modifications are sufficiently large to differentiate the versions of the PRODUCT in use, while not being so radical as to conceal the common source. Among several possible examples, the successive developments of the Boeing 747 wide-bodied aircraft is perhaps the most familiar. *See also* INNOVATION and NEW PRODUCTS.   (KNB)

relational database. With this type of data file there are no predefined links or associations to link files. Relational databases are characterized by two features. First, the file is tabular, with each new record being appended. Records therefore do not need to be ordered within the file, and can be

added, deleted or altered with ease. Secondly, associations are made on the basis of the value or contents of a field, rather than on the basis of addresses. A practical example in MARKETING would be the creation of various status reports. The invoice file would relate to a sales executive file and/or a stockholding file. As the value in one file changes (e.g. 100 units are sold), the associated files are automatically updated (e.g. stockholding is reduced 100 units, and the appropriate sales executive is credited with the sale).
                          (KRD)

relationship marketing. The relationship marketing model can trace its lineage directly to the work of European economists of the 1930s onwards (the Copenhagen School's 'parameter theory'). In turn this theory evolved as an explanation of the working of several free market economies in Europe which seemed quite different from the then dominant UK and USA economies. The existence of two different interpretations of capitalism – Anglo-Saxon which prevailed in the UK and USA, and Germanic-Alpine which existed in many European and other economies – was marked by the Cold War between the major capitalistic and communist countries of the world. As a result of this confrontation between different views on economic (and political) organization, interpretations of the two states – capitalism and communism – tended to polarize into two extreme versions. In the case of capitalism it was the model operating in the USA and, to a lesser extent, the UK, rather than that to be found in many other democratic free market economies. The collapse of communism in Eastern Europe prompted a Frenchman, Michel Albert, to write a book entitled *Capitalisme contre capitalisme* in which he pointed out that the elimination of communism had thrown into relief the fact that there is not a single, monolithic model of capitalism but several. Further, it appears that the Germanic-Alpine model leads to superior economic performance when compared with the alternative Anglo-Saxon model. Relationship Marketing emphasises the essence of the MARKETING CONCEPT, namely, mutually satisfying exchange relationships. This is a win–win view of exchange by contrast with the Anglo-Saxon model as epitomized in the American Marketing Management model which sees competition as a zero-sum game in which there are winners and losers and the objective of marketing is to see that it is not the seller that loses. Thus the

Relationship Marketing model emphasizes controlled competition, interaction, networking and the establishment of long-term relationships as opposed to short-term one-off transactions.

(MJB)

relative frequency. Frequencies expressed as percentages of some total. (SKT)

relative income hypothesis. Holds that expenditures/saving patterns depend upon the relative position of the spending unit on the income scale, and not on the absolute income earned. This hypothesis recognizes the 'keeping up with the Joneses' phenomenon. (MJB)

relative market share. The firm's market share divided by that of its largest competitor. (MJB)

relevance trees. A diagrammatic technique for analysing systems or processes which display distinct levels of complexity. The basic approach disaggregates a system's performance, or a plan's objective, into a hierarchy of subordinate (secondary, tertiary etc.) performance levels or sub-objectives.

The relevance tree (Figure 29) depicts the hierarchical relationship in a tree-like pattern that helps to develop and structure a more complete understanding of a system, or a problem and its proposed solutions. Relevance trees are widely used as tools for planning, coordinating and monitoring progress towards a specific goal. In this application the technique adopts the normative forecasting philosophy of first stating a future goal, and then mapping and timing all the paths to be followed in order to attain the goal. Drawing an analogy with a tree, the goals or objectives comprise the trunk, the branches being represented by the various alternative conditions or developments (paths) required to achieve the objective. As the figure indicates, the relevance tree disaggregates objectives into conditions or developments which in turn define a further set of sub-objectives with which are associated various other conditions or developments. The application of the technique was pioneered by Honeywell. In 1964 it developed the relevance technique PATTERN (Planning Assistance Through Technical Evaluation of Relevance Numbers) which proved to be a powerful tool in planning its aerospace technology development programmes. In this context the relevance tree maps and times all the technological developments necessary to achieve a given technological mission. (DB)

reliability. The extent to which the measurement process devised to measure marketing phenomena is free from random errors. The presence of random errors in any measurement can cause the marketing researcher to reach incorrect conclusions. The major operational approaches to the estimation of reliability are (a) test–retest reliability – applying the same measure to the same objects a second time; (b) split-sample reliability – dividing the sample into two (or more) random subsamples and testing to see if the variation in each of the items of interest comprising the measurement instrument is within the range of sampling error; (c) alternative-forms reliability –

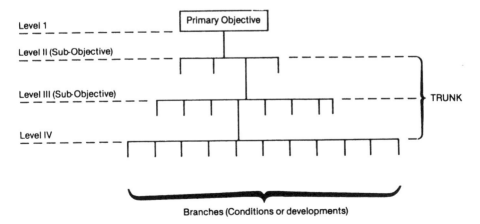

Figure 29: **Relevance tree**

measuring the same objects by two measurement instruments that are designed to be as nearly alike as possible. (GA)

reminder advertising. An advertising strategy aimed at reminding the audience that the product or service still exists, rather than promoting it for the first time or adding a new theme to an existing campaign. It is easy to overlook the importance of maintaining competitiveness after the launch or BRAND LOYALTY between purchases, by means such as this. The OUTDOOR medium is often seen as an ideal vehicle for reminder advertising campaigns. (KC)

remuneration of advertising agencies. *See* MEDIA COMMISSION.

repeat purchasing. Buying the same product or service from the same source of supply over a period of time. A high level of repeat purchasing is a characteristic of many industrial markets, where patterns of inertia in buyer–seller relationships may develop. These established relationships may pose considerable problems for companies which are not already in the market but seeking to enter. (STP)

repeat sales. Sales or business generated by a customer returning to the same retailer to purchase, or returning to any retailer to repurchase the same brand. (AJB)

repertory grid. An approach to the development of scales for evaluating the salience of particular factors within a respondent's perception of and attitude towards a specified object developed by the psychologist G.A. Kelly; hence Kelly Repertory Grid.

Kelly's theory is founded on the hypothesis that every individual seeks to evaluate stimuli in terms of his own personal constructs and that he does so within a grid or framework in which the dimensions are bipolar constructs. However, the approach differs from the SEMANTIC DIFFERENTIAL in which the researcher defines the constructs, and invites the respondent to select the point on the scale which reflects his opinion or attitude, in that the object is used as the stimulus and the respondent is invited to define its characteristics. The method is particularly appropriate both for developing products and for ensuring that the vocabulary used to promote them is meaningful to the intended audience.

Administration of the technique is straightforward and involves presenting the respondent with three cards drawn from a pack which list all the types or brands of product under investigation and known to the respondent, (hence 'Kelly trial' and 'Three Card Trick'). The subject is then asked to select the odd one out of the three and verbalize the basis for this discrimination, e.g. Brand A might be seen as expensive compared with Brands B and C. The cards are then shuffled and the process repeated except that the respondent is not allowed to use price as the basis for discrimination again. Through successive administrations the subject eventually exhausts his vocabulary through which he has been projecting his attitudes and so provides the bipolar constructs on which the products are to be compared. Having defined these the respondent is then invited to rate each individual product in much the same way as he would on a semantic differential test.

By conducting the test with a sample of 30–40 subjects it is possible to select those dimensions which occur most frequently and so may be regarded as salient in the consumer's choice decision. (MJB)

repetition. One feature of a MEDIA SCHEDULE. It is intuitively obvious that the probability of an acceptable proportion of the target audience seeing an ADVERTISEMENT or COMMERCIAL depends on the number of repetitions over a period of time. MEDIA PLANNERS furthermore assume that individuals need to see it more than once before taking it in fully. The challenge is to work out a pattern of repetition that will maximize OPPORTUNITIES-TO-SEE without either costing too much or running the risk that some of the audience will react negatively to perceived over-exposure. *See also* COVERAGE, FREQUENCY, RESPONSE FUNCTIONS, WEAROUT. (KC)

reply card. *See* BUSINESS REPLY SERVICE.

repositioning. Any effort or tactic designed to improve the performance of a product. For example, research may reveal that existing users prefer the product because of a feature which is not mentioned or described in the promotional material – by drawing attention to this feature the seller may reposition the product in the minds of non-users and encourage them to try it. *See also* POSITIONING. (MJB)

request for proposal (RFP). An invitation by an intending buyer to potential suppliers asking them to quote for the supply of specified goods or services. Sometimes referred to as a 'request for quotation' or RFQ. (MJB)

resale price maintenance. The practice of a supplier, who sells to an intermediary conditional upon the setting of a resale price, at the wholesale and/or retail level. Now only legal for the pharmaceutical trade. (AJB)

research. *See* MARKET RESEARCH, MARKETING RESEARCH and RESEARCH AND DEVELOPMENT.

research and development (R&D). A planned search or critical investigation aimed at discovery of new knowledge with the objective that such new knowledge will be translated into a plan, or design for new, modified or improved products and processes. (KAB)

research brief. A summary of an organization's specific requirements from a MARKET RESEARCH project. This should include the research objectives, the information required and the date by which the research report is to be submitted. This forms the basis of the marketing research design and any RESEARCH PROPOSAL prepared by a MARKET RESEARCH agency. (AMW)

research design. The incorporation of those elements of a marketing problem which are to be the subject of a marketing research enquiry into an operational plan, usually for field research. Such a design needs to be prepared to ensure that financial constraints and objectives are clearly agreed. It may be prepared by a research organization for its client, as a proposal or by the client as a specification for tender by research companies. (JAB)

research proposal. The submission prepared by a research agency for a potential client specifying the research to be undertaken, its methodology, sample design, project time-scale and costs. On the basis of the research proposal, the client will select an agency to undertake the research. The proposal then becomes the contract between the agency and the client-company. (AMW)

reseller market. The set of organizations which buy products in order to resell them at a profit. (AJB)

reserve price. A minimum but usually undisclosed price which is the least a seller is willing to accept for the object on offer, e.g. items in an auction, property etc. (MJB)

respondent. One who provides information in an enquiry, either on behalf of him or herself, his or her family, or on behalf of an organization. Typically unpaid, their interest must be safeguarded by the researcher. The Code of Standards of the Industrial Market Research Association and the Market Research Society endeavours to secure the application of suitable standards in the UK. In other countries legal controls often exist. (JAB)

respondent refusal problem. A source of NON-SAMPLING ERROR in survey methodology, caused by RESPONDENTS refusing to be interviewed. A critical question is whether respondents that refuse are in any consistent way different from those who respond. (SKT)

response bias. Error associated with a propensity to respond to an item or a set of items in a stereotyped way, e.g. always selecting yes, or always selecting the first given reason. (SKT)

response category sequence rotation. A procedure to overcome some problems of RESPONSE BIAS by presenting each RESPONDENT with the categories in a differing order, typically by rotating the sequence, so that for the next respondent the category that was read out first will become last and the one that was second will become first etc. (SKT)

response functions. Mathematical formulae used to apply a weighting to each successive occurrence of an advertisement in a campaign schedule. They are normally generated by computer software packages and summarized in user-friendly graphical form, but it is doubtful that more than a handful of MEDIA PLANNERS understand the mathematics well enough to be able to use the results with genuine confidence. Scheduling decisions are still made intuitively, in the main. This is not necessarily a bad thing, for intuition combined with experience may produce more reliable response functions than the unimaginative accuracy of a computer, given the irregular and unpredictable nature of audience response in real life. (KC)

response latency. The time it takes for a RESPONDENT to reply to a question. (SKT)

response rate. In any survey investigation, the response rate is the ratio of people responding to an enquiry to the total number of people approached.   (KAB)

Restrictive Trade Practices Act 1976. UK legislation which governs trading agreements which may be seen as restricting free competition in a way which is contrary to the public interest.
                                                    (MJB)

retail audit. A broad analysis of a retail business which makes a systematic evaluation of the retailer's strategies and marketing activities in relation to his retailing procedures and practices.
                                                    (AJB)

retailer. Any establishment engaged in selling merchandise for personal or household consumption and rendering services incidental to the sale of such goods.   (AJB)

retailer cooperative. A voluntary organization of retailers who have agreed to combine their purchases of commonly-bought merchandise in order to obtain the price advantage of large quantity buying.   (AJB)

retailing cycle. *See* CYCLE MODELS.

retailing functions. The more important retailing functions may be summarized as: (a) the physical movement and storage of goods; (b) the transfer of title to goods; (c) the provision of information concerning the nature and use of goods; (d) the standardization, grading and final processing of goods; (c) the provision of ready availability; (f) the assumption of risk concerning the precise nature and extent of demand; (g) the financing of inventory and the extension of credit to consumers.   (MJB)

retail park. A planned retail development, usually on the outskirts of a major conurbation, with easy access and ample parking with a wide variety of different outlets often linked in an enclosed shopping mall.   (MJB)

retail price index. More often termed the 'cost of living index', it measures changes in the prices of a representative 'shopping basket' of household goods. The composition of the shopping basket is determined from the government's family expenditure survey, is varied on a seasonal basis, and the individual items are weighted to reflect their relative importance to the basket as a whole. Sampling of prices is undertaken on a regional basis enabling comparison to be made between different areas in the UK and the UK national index.   (MJB)

revenue expenditure. Money spent on routine business purchases and expenses. *See* CAPITAL EXPENDITURE.   (GM)

risk. A purchase of a product has two elements which combine to create a certain level of perceived risk: the consequences which follow from a wrong choice, and the certainty or uncertainty about the likelihood of this product choice being a wrong choice. A consumer's tolerance for risk-taking varies amongst individuals and is related to personality and education.   (KF)

risk reduction. In many situations consumers perceive risk and develop their own unique strategies for reducing it. Some of the more common strategies include information seeking, brand loyalty, selection by brand or store image, selection of the most expensive product or those with a warranty or guarantee.   (KF)

Rogers, E.M. American sociologist who has extensively studied the process of the diffusion of innovation, and the characteristics of different categories of adopters. His early publications were based on the study of the adoption of new products amongst farming communities in the Mid-West, from which he identified different categories of adopters and different stages in the adoption process.   (STP)

role. A concept borrowed from the social sciences, used to describe the expected contribution of any member of the marketing channel. The role allows members to predict behaviour and levels of performance of each other in order to cooperate with them.   (AJB)

role expectations. One's expectation about the privileges, rights, duties and responsibilities associated with a particular role.   (MJB)

rolling launch. The phased introduction of a new PRODUCT onto the MARKET. The advantages of a rolling launch are that the seller can use the experience gained in the first submarket to improve and streamline the launch in subsequent submarkets and also that the cash flows generated by the early sales can be used to invest in increased capacity and MARKETING necessary for expansion. The major disadvantage is that by only addressing a part of the potential market the innovator runs the risk of seeing his new product imitated and introduced elsewhere by competitors. (MJB)

roll out. The process of extending the geographical coverage of marketing activity for a product/service from its original and test area base. (JRB)

rom. A MEDIA BUYER'S booking instruction, standing for 'run of month'. It permits the MEDIA OWNER to decide in which issue of a PERIODICAL an advertisement appears, and the advertiser consequently pays the basic RATE-CARD COST. The alternative is to specify a particular issue, which will typically carry a surcharge. (KC)

rop. A MEDIA BUYER'S booking instruction, standing for 'run of paper' or 'run of press'. It permits the MEDIA OWNER to decide where an advertisement will be placed within a newspaper or magazine, wherever the MEDIA OWNER decides, and the advertiser consequently pays the basic RATE-CARD COST. The alternative is to specify a SPECIAL POSITION, at a surcharge. (KC)

Rorschach Test. Projective test of personality named after its inventor in which respondents are asked to describe what they see in a series of abstract shapes created from ink blots. The test has proved to be reliable when interpreted by properly trained analysts who score respondents on the basis of the number, speed, originality and nature of their responses. (MJB)

Rothe, James T. (1943–). American marketing academic. Born in Milwaukee, Wisconsin, in 1943. His education includes a BBA (1965), MBA (1966) and PhD (1968) from the University of Wisconsin. In his research he studied the practices and policies pertaining to the product-line management. His published work includes articles in the *Journal of Marketing, Business Horizons* and *MSU Business Topics.* His present concern is with strategic planning and product portfolio management. (GA)

routinized response behaviour. A habitual purchase response from a known group of alternatives where product attributes and evaluative criteria are predetermined. (KF)

row. A MEDIA BUYER'S booking instruction, standing for 'run of week'. It permits the MEDIA OWNER to decide in which issue of a daily newspaper an advertisement will appear, and the advertiser consequently pays the basic RATE-CARD COST. The alternative is to specify a particular day, which will normally carry a surcharge. (KC)

Rowell, George P. (1839–1908). A major figure in the early days of American advertising. Starting his career as a debt collector for the *Boston Post* newspaper, he saw a business opportunity in buying ADVERTISING SPACE in bulk and reselling it to individual advertisers in the appropriate units. He was thus a 'space broker', like Charles BARKER in Britain. He was also the first advertising intermediary of any kind to guarantee payment to MEDIA OWNERS, instead of making them wait until the advertiser paid the agent. For their part, the publishers were naturally happier to deal with one major customer than dozens or perhaps hundreds of minor ones. Rowell assumed the financial risk in exchange for a standard discount from the media owners, thereby originating the MEDIA COMMISSION convention which is still the most significant element in the remuneration of present-day ADVERTISING AGENCIES. Volney B. PALMER is often credited with the invention of media commission but converted to that form of payment only after Rowell had set the precedent, having previously claimed a fee from the advertiser for his services and no discount from the media owners.

In 1869, Rowell compiled a list of the CIRCULATIONS and ADVERTISING RATES of all 5,500 American newspapers, the direct ancestor of *Standard Rate and Data* in America and BRAD (q.v.) in the UK. This initiative helped to sustain and institutionalize the commission system, for if the standard price of space was officially published, the advertiser could tell that he was indeed receiving the brokerage service 'free'. In 1888, he founded the still extant magazine, *Printer's Ink,* the first in the world to cater exclusively to the advertising business. (KC)

royalty. A payment to the owner of a copyright or trademark for its use by another seller. This is usually an agreed percentage of sales revenue. (MJB)

R-type analysis. A FACTOR or component ANALYSIS based on correlations between RESPONDENTS: in contrast to a Q-TYPE ANALYSIS, where the correlations are between questions. (SKT)

run of month (rom). A MEDIA BUYER'S ordering instruction. The advertisement will appear in whichever issue of a PERIODICAL the MEDIA OWNER chooses and the order will be invoiced AT the basic ADVERTISING RATE. The alternative is to specify a particular issue, which will typically carry a surcharge. (KC)

run of paper (rop). A MEDIA BUYER'S ordering instruction. The advertisement will be positioned within the newspaper or magazine wherever the MEDIA OWNER decides. The order will be invoiced at the basic ADVERTISING RATE. The alternative is to specify a SPECIAL POSITION, at a surcharge. (KC)

run of week (row). A MEDIA BUYER'S ordering instruction. The advertisement will appear in whichever issue of a daily newspaper the MEDIA OWNER chooses. The order will be invoiced at the basic ADVERTISING RATE. The alternative is to specify a particular day, which may carry a surcharge. (KC)

S

Saatchi & Saatchi. A British ADVERTISING AGENCY founded in 1970 by Charles Saatchi, a 27-year-old COPYWRITER, and his brother Maurice, a 25-year-old management trainee. After only nine years, it took over the top ranking among British agencies from J. Walter THOMPSON and became the first such company to become a household name as a result of being appointed by the Conservative Party to run the advertising campaign which played a significant part in Margaret Thatcher's occupation of Number 10 Downing Street. Success at home having been secured, the Saatchis set their sights on America. In 1982, the audacious acquisition of a New York agency, much larger than their own, established the first British-owned advertising agency to make any significant impact on MADISON AVENUE, after 90 years of largely benevolent Americanization of British advertising. Within four years, Saatchi & Saatchi Garland Compton Worldwide had bought three more significant transatlantic agencies and could lay claim to being the largest advertising group in the world, the ambition that fuelled Charles and Maurice Saatchi's expansion strategies since their earliest days in business. Multinational advertising was no longer the exclusive preserve of Americans. It is generally agreed that the architect of this dramatic growth was the chief financial officer, Martin SORRELL, who was subsequently to repeat the performance in even less time on his own account.

In 1983, Saatchi & Saatchi added British Airways to its client list, and created for it the most expensive television commercial ever made: 'Manhattan landing'. Simultaneously, the brothers wholeheartedly embraced the currently fashionable globalization philosophy. They set out to build two global networks, one based on an American agency they had acquired in 1986, Ted Bates (see REEVES, ROSSER), and the other on London office, which was by then employing about 800 staff. At the same time, the group was building itself into a 'one-stop-shop'. By 1988, it comprised, in Britain alone, seven advertising agencies, a design firm, a centralized media buying company, Zenith, and various consultancies. Neither strategy was entirely successful, because many of the formerly autonomous companies that were made to work together had distinctive cultures which could not readily be combined into convincing, saleable entities. Those were at least logical developments, but the failed attempts to take over the Midland Bank and then Hill Samuel struck many contemporary analysts as evidence that what had been a creative 'hot-shop' only twenty years earlier was turning into a meaningless conglomerate.

Nevertheless, Saatchi & Saatchi continued to dominate British and world advertising, now alongside Martin Sorrell's WPP Group. Then, in late 1994, an otherwise relatively insignificant financial manager looked into the principals' remuneration packages and suggested to them that they had a moral responsibility to their shareholders to rein back. Still thinking of the company as his own, the more public Maurice Saatchi resisted such interference. But opinions polarized within the company, and the Saatchis left the ship before they were forced to walk the plank. Followed by several key people and a key client, Gallaher, they immediately set up a new agency, M&C Saatchi. Dixons and British Airways undertook reviews of their agency arrangements soon after, at length and in depth in the case of the latter, and duly became clients of the old team with the new name. Those who stayed at Saatchi & Saatchi meanwhile won new clients to replace the lost ones, and emerged relatively unscathed from the break-up of the empire. In 1996, the holding company was the fifth largest advertising organization in the world, with total BILLINGS of $9.7 billion. Saatchi & Saatchi in London had slipped no further down the UK league table than to 5th, and was still earning impressive revenue: annual billings of £224 million. The wholly-owned Bates Dorland agency occupied 10th place, with another £168.4 million in billings, and Zenith headed the list of 'media independents' at £554.3 million. M&C Saatchi meanwhile climbed from 20th rank in its first year to 8th in 1996, posting billings of £175 million. One name has symbolized the dynamism of the British advertising business for a quarter of a century, and looks set to do so for the foreseeable future.   (KC)

safety needs. *See* MOTIVATION.

safety stock. The minimum level of STOCK considered necessary to enable a firm to satisfy orders within acceptable delivery times. As stockholding ties up capital which could be used for other purposes, most firms keep this to a minimum and many have moved to 'JUST-IN-TIME' methods where stockholding is negligible and the producer or seller depends upon his supplier to deliver just before required use or resale.   (MJB)

Sale of Goods Act (1893). UK act amended by the Supply of Goods (Implied Terms) Act 1973, the act protects the buyers' rights to goods of 'merchantable' quality. A buyer can no longer be induced to give up his rights by signing a warranty card. The remedy now available is to reject goods and have the price returned, with a possible claim for compensation if any subsequent loss or damage resulted from the fault.   (AJB)

sale or return. To help the MARKETING and distribution of certain goods, some manufacturers and distributors make their PRODUCTS available to RETAILERS on a 'sale or return' basis. If the merchandise is sold to ultimate customers the retailer retains a previously agreed proportion of the sales revenue and remits the balance to the supplier. In the event of the merchandise not being sold, after a previously agreed time period, they are returned to the supplier at no charge to the retailer. Some manufacturers and distributors of merchandise are prepared to operate on this basis as they are convinced that once their merchandise is on display to the public it will be purchased. Retailers are willing to accept goods on a 'sale or return' basis as they do not have to pay for items until the merchandise is actually sold. Under a 'sale or return' agreement both supplier and retailer can potentially benefit, although the financial risk is borne by the supplier. 'Sale or return' is a common practice among suppliers of fashionable items of clothing to departmental stores and boutiques, for example, but is also adopted with some perishable foodstuffs. Suppliers have to consider their pricing practices and to calculate whether they will make profits even if a proportion of the merchandise is returned. Many retailers are willing to display and promote items on a 'sale and return' basis rather than run the risks associated with outright purchase, which include having to take more care over merchandise selection and the possibility of being left with outdated or slow-selling STOCKS.   (BRM)

sales agent. A person or organization operating independently to sell products or services on behalf of a company or a third party.   (WD)

sales aids. A term used to categorize all forms of aids used by salespeople to assist their sales presentations. Sales aids can be grouped into two broad types: (a) those which the salesperson uses and carries from one sales presentation to the next; (b) those which are introduced into the sales presentation and then left with the prospective customer. Within the former category sales aids include models of the PRODUCT, photographic displays of the product or service in use, audio-visual presentations, tape recordings or videos. Such sales aids are generally not left with the prospective customer but are taken from presentation to presentation. Sales aids may also include free samples, small novelty items such as penknives, pens, pencils, paperweights identified with the donor which are given to prospective customers as an inducement to purchase. (BRM)

sales analysis. (1) The process of interpreting the pattern of sales orders obtained in the marketplace.

(2) This term may also refer, more widely, to the interpretation of all data – including sales orders – from the marketplace. While such analysis serves the company in a variety of ways, it is particularly useful as a measure of the effectiveness of the salesforce.   (JRB)

sales audit. That part of the marketing audit (*see* AUDIT, MARKETING) which is a formal and comprehensive assessment of sales strategy in terms of meeting sales objectives with the aim of improving the overall effectiveness of the salesforce. (WD)

sales branch. Subunit usually situated at one or more regional locations which is used as a means of decentralizing the sales operation to improve the administration and effectiveness of the sales force. (WD)

sales broker. An agent who does not physically handle the goods with which he deals and very often has little control over the terms of a contract between principal and third party. *See* SALES AGENT. (WD)

sales budget. Usually the sum of money required over a specified time to run a sales department. It is a term also often used to include all marketing expenditures of which selling is only a part. (JRB)

sales call pattern. Pattern of activity in which the field (actively selling) salesman is involved in the process of calling on his customers. Primarily, such a pattern is determined by (a) the universe of target customers and their geographical distribution; (b) the frequency of calls required per customer; (c) the cost-effectiveness of calling; (d) the selling traditions of, and competitive sales pattern in, the specific universe of customers. (JRB)

sales campaign. A preplanned and coordinated sales effort designed to achieve specific sales objectives. (MJB)

sales closing. Also 'closing the sale'. The activity of completing a selling presentation to a customer and achieving the desired (order getting) result. (JRB)

sales conference. A meeting organized by an organization for the purpose of educating, enthusing and motivating sales related personnel. Sales conferences may be of varying duration, can be of regional, national or international dimensions and may include the sponsoring organization's own personnel (sales and services) and/or those of licensees, distributors and agents. Typically, sales conferences are held before the launch of new PRODUCTS or services to introduce them to the SALESFORCE who will be taking

responsibility for selling them; alternatively, they may be held on a regular basis, often annually, to provide personnel who commonly work alone or in widely scattered groups with updates on company and product progress. The locations of sales conferences may be in the organization's own premises, at a special conference centre or hotel, or on occasion in conference facilities in an area of outstanding natural beauty. Sales conferences are used by many organizations as periods of business but also rest and relaxation for their sales staff, and are therefore mostly involved with maintaining and building morale. Programmes for the sales conference, while usually intensive, frequently combine business and social activities. (BRM)

sales contests. A special sales programme offering incentives to sales people to achieve specific targets, usually on a short-term basis. (WD)

sales decline stage. The period in the life of a product or market when sales are falling and will continue to fall unless remedial action is taken. (WD)

sales drive. An additional selling effort to boost sales at particular times (e.g. out of season, off-peak), or to meet particular circumstances (e.g. increased COMPETITION). (MJB)

sales efficiency. A measure of performance to evaluate the relationship between sales volume or value and individual and total selling costs. (WD)

sales-expense forecasting. A method of budgeting the control sales expenses in line with expected sales revenues. (WD)

salesforce compensation. The paying of a salesforce. There has been much contention in marketing/selling circles as to the virtues of the payment-by-result (COMMISSION) system, and a straight-salary system which is not based on results. More progressive companies tend today to favour straight salary with the addition of bonuses as a reward for special effort. (JRB)

salesforce decisions. Measures taken concerning the management of sales people or groups of sales people. (WD)

salesforce efficiency. A measure of performance to evaluate sales or other objectives in relation to personal selling costs. (WD)

salesforce forecasts. Forecasts of the sales made by the sales force; usually by summing the forecasts made by individual (territory) salesmen. Where, as in industrial markets, the salesman is directly in touch with the market such a forecasting system may prove indispensable. As a system it may be much less reliable in consumer goods marketing where the salesforce is not directly in touch with the end-users. Such forecasting tends, inevitably, to be extrapolated from current trends and is thus a passive rather than a dynamic system.   (JRB)

salesforce motivation. That area of administration concerned to improve selling efficiency by increasing salesman morale.   (JRB)

salesforce objectives. Predetermined tasks set by management for sales people in terms of fulfilling organizational goals.   (WD)

salesforce organization. The means by which salesforce people (or groups of people) are deployed, via structure and distribution of personnel, to achieve sale goals.   (WD)

salesforce recruitment. All those activities involved in the hiring of salesforce personnel.   (WD)

salesforce selection. The means of choosing the most qualified applicant for a sales position.   (WD)

salesforce size. The number of people approved by management to perform selling tasks aimed at achieving SALES OBJECTIVES.   (WD)

salesforce supervision. The number of people and the methods employed for controlling and motivating sales personnel in the execution of their duties.   (WD)

salesforce training. The effort expended by an employer to provide the opportunity for a salesperson to improve or modify individual or team skills and attitudes in an effort to achieve improved performance.   (WD)

sales forecasting. The process of estimating the units of product or service that will be sold over a specified future period. The unit sales forecast provides the estimate of future revenue which underlines all company plans. It is also frequently the least reliable prediction the company makes by virtue of the nature of such an activity: guessing future buying decisions.   (JRB)

sales houses. Organizations which sell television and radio ADVERTISING TIME TO MEDIA BUYERS on behalf of the individual stations. Five cover almost all the television options available to British advertisers: Carlton UK Sales, Laser and TSMS collectively represent the ITV network, British Sky Broadcasting and Zierler Media the satellite and cable channels. Four radio sales houses share the UK network on a more or less country-by-country basis. MSM (Media Sales & Marketing) represents more than 70 stations throughout England, another 22 being handled by Katz Radio Sales. SIRS (Scottish and Irish Radio Sales) sells time on all but one of the 19 stations in Scotland and Northern Ireland, and First Choice Radio Sales & Marketing represents 5 in Wales and the Welsh Borders.   (KC)

sales incentive. The offering of a bonus or some other incentive to motivate salespersons to increase their efforts and sales.   (MJB)

sales lead. When a salesman is given basic information or a contact which may help him focus his selling efforts and possibly result in a sale. Sales leads may come from enquiries to advertising, by referral from an existing customer or by following up other information, e.g. offering catering services, mortgages etc. to couples announcing their engagement.   (WD)

sales manager. Managers responsible for some or all of the activities of the sales department of a business.   (JRB)

salesmanship. The arts and sciences of selling.   (JRB)

sales maximization. An alternative theory to that which argues that firms seek to maximize profits. W.J. Baumol (*Economic Theory and Operations Analysis,* 1965) is generally recognized as having first suggested that firms often seek to maximize the money value of their sales, i.e. their sales revenue, subject to a constraint that their profits do not fall short of some minimum level which is just on the borderline of acceptability. In other words, so long as profits are at a satisfactory level, management will devote the bulk of its energy and efforts to the expansion of sales. Such a goal may be explained perhaps by the businessman's desire to maintain his competitive position, which is partly dependent on the sheer size of his enterprise, or it may be a matter of the interested management, since management's salaries may be related more closely to the size of the firm's operation than to its profits, or it may simply be a matter of prestige. It is also Baumol's view that short-run revenue maximization may be consistent with long-run profit maximization, and revenue maximization can be regarded as a long-run goal in many oligopolistic firms. Baumol also reasons that high sales attract customers to the popular product, cause banks to be receptive to the firm's financial needs, encourage distributors, and make it easier to retain and attract good employees. *See* PROFIT MAXIMIZATION and SATISFICING.   (MJB)

sales meetings. Meetings at which salesmen are gathered to further the organization's selling efficiency.   (JRB)

sales-orientated. Orientation towards the selling function as the key organizational activity. One of a triumvirate of company orientations which identify, chronologically, the history of business attitudes towards marketing: (a) production (manufacturing) orientation; (b) sales orientation; (c) marketing orientation.   (JRB)

sales pitch. The reasons and arguments deployed by a salesman to encourage prospective purchasers to buy.   (MJB)

sales potential. Unfulfilled capacity to purchase. Usually of a market or geographic area, with reference to a particular product/ brand or service.   (JRB)

sales promotion. An ingredient of the MARKETING COMMUNICATIONS MIX. Considerable potential for terminological confusion lies in the fact that one of the 'four Ps' of the MARKETING MIX stands for 'promotion', and that the marketing communications mix is therefore often called the 'promotional mix' in practice. Furthermore, the term 'promotions' is generally used as shorthand for 'sales promotion initiatives'. All this so, a novice might well assume that the description 'sales promotion' encompasses any form of 'promotion' intended to sell a product or service. However, PERSONAL SELLING is normally expressly excluded, because it is the sole face-to-face communication technique in the mix. Indeed, many people would see sales promotion as activity in support of the sales force. Convention also treats ADVERTISING and PACK-

AGING as distinct forms of 'promotion' in their own right. As for the rest of the marketing communications mix, grey areas abound between sales promotion and DIRECT MARKETING communications, SPONSORSHIP and PUBLICITY. It is thus a highly elastic term, embracing a host of marketing communications tactics. Within that scope, one could usefully distinguish 'economic incentive' and 'information delivery' forms of sales promotion initiative. The first would include premium offers, money-off deals, banded offers, gifts and some competitions; the second, product literature, exhibitions, sponsorship and free trials. It is worth noting the possibility that an initiative intended only to provide an incentive can accidentally communicate messages in conflict with overall marketing communications objectives. For instance, people may feel that it vulgarizes a prestige service or that there must be something not quite right about a product that is virtually given away.   (KC)

sales quotas. Sales targets given to individual salesmen as their 'quota' from the total sales forecast. Such targets may be given in the form of revenue goals or unit sales goals.   (JRB)

sales reports. A written means of information feedback to sales management on sales performance and salesperson's activities.   (WD)

sales representative. A person who represents his or her organization in a selling capacity. Sales representatives are product or company specialists who spend their time contacting customers and prospective customers and attempting to obtain orders. Sales representatives are the front-line selling operators of an organization who typically work in a territory although the geographical size of the territories can vary considerably between different types of products.   (BRM)

sales response function. The reaction of a prospect to a sales presentation. This can be set as a percentage return on the number and frequency of sales presentations to a particular target market or section of the population. (WD)

sales revenue. The monetary proceeds which an organization receives from the sale of goods and services.   (BRM)

sales targets. A performance standard against which the degree of achievement can be measured. Targets are usually set on a geographical, product or customer basis in either selling quantities or sales performance terms. (WD)

sales techniques. The methods used by salespeople to achieve sales objectives. Such techniques usually apply at one or more stages in the selling process and will vary accordingly, e.g. techniques to overcome objections, techniques to close the sale and so on. (WD)

sales territory. An area of responsibility for an individual salesperson in which to develop sales. Territories can be allocated on a geographical, product or customer basis or on any combination of these, to achieve sales objectives. (WD)

sales territory design. The means of allocating customers or groups of customers as a basis for assignment to a salesperson to achieve sales objectives. This is usually on a geographical, product or market basis or on a combination of these bases. (WD)

sales volume planning. A means of allocating targets, expressed in quantitative terms, to individual salespersons to achieve overall sales volume objectives. (WD)

sales wave planning. A particular means of deploying the sales force at specific time intervals to achieve the desired response from prospective customers. (WD)

salience. A measure of the importance attached to specific attributes of a product or service which influences individual buying decisions. (MJB)

salient beliefs. Strongly held BELIEFS which have a major influence on decision making. (MJB)

sample. A subset of a POPULATION. (MJB)

samples. A trial offer designed to encourage potential buyers to sample the product without risk in the hope that they will then ADOPT it. (MJB)

sample surveys. A fundamental method of marketing and social research is the collection of data from individuals in a sample of the population of interest to produce results which can be generalized to apply to the whole population. The enquiries are QUANTITATIVE, conducted among samples by INTERVIEWS, and the results subject to analysis. (JAB)

sampling. The process of selecting a subgroup of a population of interest for the collection of information which may be generalized to the whole population, as opposed to a census in which information is collected from the entire population. In marketing research, the population is usually of human beings (but may be of shops, cars etc.). Samples are either probability (or random), or non-probability. Measures of statistical error may be readily applied to probability samples, which, however, require the existence or possibility of a list of all members of the population, and the ability to contact a designated member. The ELECTORAL REGISTER is often used in the UK as such a list, and calls made at the addresses given. If a minority group is involved, the method is clearly costly. See RANDOM SAMPLING.

Non-probability samples are selected by researchers or interviewers in accordance either with no rules (purposive) or with rules (quota). The application of rules to sample selection designed to reduce statistical error by making the sample representative of selected subgroups is termed stratification, and the process of concentrating the sample geographically to save travelling for interviews at the expense of increased statistical error is called CLUSTERING. Both are used in complicated surveys to increase efficiency. It should be noted that the statistical computations required to estimate the statistical or sampling errors in these complex samples are themselves complex in calculation, and that the simple formulae appropriate to simple samples will normally underestimate the sampling error. See DESIGN FACTOR. (JAB)

sampling distribution. The statistical distribution of the theoretical drawing of a large number of samples using a defined procedure from the defined POPULATION. (SKT)

sampling error. The error associated with SAMPLING procedures. Such error can be calculated for any probability sample: NON-SAMPLING ERROR is typically larger and cannot be calculated. (SKT)

sampling fraction. The ratio of the sample size to the POPULATION size, usually given as a simple $1:n$ fraction. Such a sampling fraction is useful in SYSTEMATIC SAMPLING where every nth RESPONDENT is sampled. (SKT)

sampling frame. The definition of a population from which a sample is to be drawn, e.g. the REG-

ISTER OF ELECTORS, today's output, all residents of the Strathclyde region etc. A sampling frame needs to be accurate, adequate, complete, up-to-date and relevant to the purposes of the survey for which it is to be used. (MJB)

sampling frame error. NON-SAMPLING ERRORS due to imperfect coverage of the SAMPLING FRAME. If the POPULATION to be sampled is defined by those on the UK electoral register, those who do not appear on the register (for where they are living at the time of the SAMPLE SURVEY, e.g. by moving house and antipathy to form-filling etc.) are not represented by the results because they were not available for SAMPLING. (SKT)

sampling interval. The whole number denominator of the sampling fraction. If the sampling fraction is 1:*n*, *n* is the sampling interval, because every *n*th element on the list is sampled. (SKT)

sampling point. A physical location at which sampling is to be undertaken – outside Marks & Spencer, exit of the paint shop etc. It may also define the origin for a RANDOM WALK. (MJB)

sampling unit. In MULTI-STAGE SAMPLING schemes the clusters (typically areas) that are selected before the final selection of RESPONDENTS. (SKT)

sandwich board. One of a pair of boards which are joined by straps and worn over the front and back of a person who carries them around to display ADVERTISEMENTS or public notices. (MDP)

satisficing. An alternative view of the behaviour of entrepreneurs which states that they seek to make satisfactory profits rather than pursue a goal of PROFIT MAXIMIZATION. The concept owes much to the seminal work of Simon, who observes that the notion of satiation plays no role in classical economic theory, while it enters rather prominently in the treatment of motivation in psychology. In most psychological theories, the motive to act stems from drive, and action terminates when the drive is satisfied. Moreover, the conditions for satisfying drive are not necessarily fixed, but may be specified by an aspiration level that self-adjusts upward or downward on the basis of experience. Simon argues that to explain business behaviour in terms of this theory, we must expect the firm's goals to be not maximiz-

ing profit, but attaining a certain level or rate of profit, holding a certain share of the market, or a certain level of sales. (MJB)

scaling techniques. Widely used in marketing research in order to determine the nature and strength of an individual's attitudes or opinions towards a specific object, concept or idea.

In brief there are four types of scale: nominal, ordinal, interval and ratio, and their properties may be summarized as:

(a) Nominal scales. This is the weakest form of scale in which the number assigned serves only to identify the subjects under consideration. Library classification schemes employ nominal scales, as does the Standard Industrial Classification (SIC) such that members of the same class will be assigned the same number but each class will have a different number. By extending the number it is possible to achieve finer and finer distinctions, until a unique number is assigned to a specific object, e.g. a telephone number.

(b) Ordinal scales seek to impose more structure on objects by rank ordering them in terms of some property which they possess such as height or weight. As with nominal scales, identical objects are given the same number but the ordinal scale has the added property that it can tell us something about the direction or relative standing of one object to another, e.g. 1 may represent the smallest member of a group such that we can safely say that 2 is bigger than 1, 5 is bigger than 2 and 17 is bigger than 5. However, this is all we can say (other than reversing the scale) and in order to be able to draw conclusions about differences between the numbers we must know something about the interval between the numbers.

(c) Interval scales have this property in that they are founded on the assumption of equal intervals between numbers, i.e. the space between 5 and 10 is the same as the space between 45 and 50 and in both cases this distance is five times as great as that between 1 and 2 or 11 and 12 etc. However, it must be stressed that while we may compare the magnitude of the differences between numbers we cannot make statements about them unless the scale possesses an absolute zero, in which case we would have a ratio scale.

(d) Ratio scales are the most powerful and possess all the properties of nominal, ordinal and interval scales, while in addition they permit absolute comparisons of the objects e.g. 6 metres is twice as high as 3 metres and six times as high as 1 metre.

Amongst the more important scaling techniques borrowed by marketers from the behavioural sciences may be distinguished: THURSTONE'S COMPARATIVE JUDGEMENT TECHNIQUE, LIKERT SCALES, GUTTMAN SCALES, SEMANTIC DIFFERENTIAL.   (MJB)

scalogram. A manual alternative to categorizing answers to ATTITUDE SCALES by means of factor analysis or other statistical techniques requiring access to a computer. A board is used to group data by eye into categories as a basis for distinguishing underlying patterns but the method is only possible with a relatively small data base.
                                        (MJB)

scanner data. Information acquired at the point-of-sale from BAR CODES.   (MJB)

scatter diagram. A plot of observed values in two-dimensional space to determine if there are any distinctive patterns or relationships between the variables concerned. Used for CLUSTER ANALYSIS and the measurement of correlation.
                                        (MJB)

scc. *See* SINGLE-COLUMN CENTIMETRE.

scenario. Sequence of events that might possibly occur in the future. In the context of business planning a scenario depicts a particular combination of the interdependent issues, factors or forces (social, economic, competitive, technological, political) that define the future. A scenario depicts a possible future state and should not be taken as a forecast. It does so in a logical and internally consistent manner. A scenario will, therefore, describe the course of events, combination of factors or evolution of trends that is expected to realize one of several plausible alternative futures. Additional scenarios can be constructed to describe a range of possible combinations of the pertinent variables. for example, from optimistic to pessimistic. Multiple scenarios provide a vehicle for environmental analysis and strategic planning. *See also* SCENARIO PLANNING. (DB)

scenario planning. The purpose of business planning is to provide an accessible framework within which the firm's strategic and tactical decisions can be taken. The integrity of the structure demands an understanding of the forces that will shape the future. Traditional approaches to business planning have made the principal assumption that the future can be predicted: these have largely been based on the single-line forecasts made by sophisticated mathematical techniques. A growing realization of the inadequacy of the traditional approaches has necessitated a re-examination of the principal assumption. A contingency approach is now preferred. It makes the assumption that it is not possible to predict or quantify the future, but that it is possible to describe a range of possible alternative futures by combining in various ways the key elements that will determine the future. Second-generation planning systems have moved away from rigid methodology towards a more conceptual or qualitative approach to understanding the future. It is in this context that multiple scenarios are widely used. *See also* ALTERNATIVE FUTURES and SCENARIO.   (DB)

Schramm's communication model. Wilbur Schramm in *The Process and Effects of Mass Communication* (Illinois, University of Illinois Press: 1955) defined communication as 'the process of establishing a commonness or oneness of thought between a sender and a receiver'. Central to this definition is the CONCEPT that for communication to occur, there must be a transfer of information from one party – the sender – which is received and understood by the other party – the receiver. To achieve this, information must be encoded and decoded and both sender and receiver must be linked by a channel of communication and a shared field of experience. This may be represented pictorially as shown in Figure 30.   (MJB)

scientific method. A systematic, objective and logical method of inquiring into and analysing problems in terms of (a) the definition of needs or goals; (b) collection of pertinent data; (c) classification and analysis of data; (d) determination

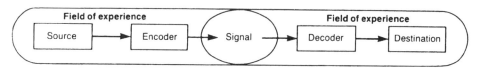

Figure 30: **Schramm's communication model**

of solution on the basis of available data; (e) application of proposed solutions; and (f) checking or follow-up. (GA)

Scottish Health Education Group (SHEG). A division of the Common Services Agency of the Scottish Health Service. Responsible for health education on national level in Scotland. Innovative user and designer of social advertising which has pioneered the transfer of commercial techniques to not-for-profit situations. Now superseded by the Health Education Board for Scotland (HEBS). (MJB)

scrambled merchandising. The stocking and selling of unrelated merchandise. (MJB)

screen. (1) In the context of CINEMA advertising, this is the basic unit of ADVERTISING SPACE available from the MEDIA OWNERS. Since the arrival of MULTIPLEX cinemas, the number of screens bought for a campaign is not necessarily the same as the number of locations. At the end of 1996, there were 2,166 screens at 742 'sites' in the UK.

(2) In the context of PRESS advertising, it is a measure of the density of a HALFTONE reproduction of an original photograph. Because newsprint is rather absorbent paper, newspapers require 'coarse screen' halftones so that the ink will not spread enough to merge even the smaller dots with one another. Magazines are printed on 'coated stock', which can tolerate 'fine screen'. 'Medium screen' is appropriate for the 'matt coated' paper characteristic of colour supplements. Density is measured by the number of dots per centimetre or, among traditionalists, per inch. Coarse screen has between 25 and 34 (64–85 per inch), medium typically 40 (100 per inch), and fine 48, 54 or 60 (120, 133 or 150 per inch). (KC)

screen advertising. An alternative term for CINEMA advertising. (KC)

screening. The second stage in the NEW PRODUCT DEVELOPMENT process. Once the firm has generated a portfolio of ideas for new products, it is essential that these be screened to ensure that only the most promising are subject to thorough analysis. Screening is an essentially subjective procedure in which managers use their knowledge and experience to weed out obvious non-starters. Managers tend to be most confident when applying their knowledge of internal constraints and will eliminate many ideas as being

inconsistent with the firm's product policy and objectives, with the existing skills and resources and so on. In the same way, ideas which are incompatible with the firm's existing markets and its knowledge of its current users and customers, are likely to be screened out at this phase as the firm seeks to build upon its existing strengths. (MJB)

SD. *See* STANDARD DEVIATION.

se. *See* STANDARD ERROR.

sealed bid price. An approach to competitive bidding where the potential suppliers submit their bids to the prospective customers in response to an invitation to bid. All bids are opened at the same time and the lowest bidder is offered the contract as long as he meets the specification set out in the contract. The price is therefore fixed by the bidding process. (STP)

seasonal analysis. The ANALYSIS of DATA on a season-by-season basis to determine the extent and magnitude of any variations in activity attributable to seasonal effects. (MJB)

seasonal demand. Demand which varies according to the season of the year. For example, more soup is consumed during the winter months and ice cream during the summer. (MJB)

seasonal discounts. Offers of a reduced price to encourage purchase and consumption out-of-season. These are particularly popular for Christmas, Spring and Autumn sales to clear seasonal STOCK in retailing and for travel and recreation. (MJB)

seasonality. Variation in sales attributable to the season of the year, e.g. increases sales of electricity in winter in cold climates and in summer in hot climates. (MJB)

secondary data. *See* PRIMARY DATA.

secondary readership. The number of people who read a copy of a newspaper or magazine bought by someone who is not a member of their household or workplace unit. The most familiar case in point is the many people who browse through publications set out in waiting rooms and reception areas. Readers within a household or equivalent unit are defined as the 'primary readership'. Figures for secondary readership can range in practice from very small numbers to totals larger than either CIRCULATION or primary readership. They are bound to be lower than overall 'READERSHIP', normally taken to mean primary plus secondary.   (KC)

secular economic growth. Perhaps the best known of theories of secular economic growth is that put forward by W.V. Rostow (*The Stages of Economic Growth,* 1960) in which he proposes six stages: traditional society; preconditions for take-off; take-off; the drive to technological maturity; the age of high mass consumption; and the search for quality. There would seem to be close parallels between Rostow's stages and the phases of the PRODUCT LIFE CYCLE, particularly in the sense that growth in per capita GNP may be represented by an S-SHAPED CURVE.   (MJB)

segment. A band of television or radio ADVERTISING TIME within which a specific RATE-CARD COST used to apply. Since about 1990, both media have increasingly negotiated the price of time on a case-by-case basis, mainly on the basis of current demand for advertising time and the degree to which the advertiser wishes to fix precise timing. Television CONTRACTING COMPANIES have a statutory duty to publish a rate card and do specify segments, whether or not time is in practice sold that way. They are typically: 'coffee time', 09:25–12:29; 'afternoon', 12:30–17:14; 'early peak', 17:15–19:24; 'late peak', 19:25–23:29; and 'late night', 23:30 to close-down. The RADIO stations in effect recognise only PEAK TIME, normally defined as 'morning drive time'. *See also* PRE-EMPT STRUCTURE.   (KC)

segmentation variable. Any factor which can be used as the basis for SEGMENTING a market.
                    (MJB)

segmenting. The act of disaggregating market demand into a number of discrete sub-markets for the purpose of developing specific marketing mixes for some or all of them. *See* MARKET SEGMENTATION.   (MJB)

selected break. A MEDIA BUYER'S booking instruction, specifying that a COMMERCIAL is to appear in a specified COMMERCIAL BREAK, but not necessarily requesting a FIXED SPOT within that break. The reason is normally to capitalize on the subject matter or general atmosphere of the adja-

cent programme, and the advertiser will pay a surcharge for the privilege.   (KC)

selection bias. BIAS caused by judgemental stages in SAMPLING procedures.   (SKT)

selective attention. The subconscious suppression of most incoming information so that the individual only pays conscious attention to those messages or stimuli which appear to be relevant at a particular point in time. A protective device which protects us from information overload.
                    (MJB)

selective demand. Demand for a particular product or service.   (MJB)

selective distortion. Occurs when an individual is exposed to a stimulus which challenges his predisposition or commitment with the result that the individual seeks to interpret the stimulus in a manner consistent with that predisposition or commitment.   (MJB)

selective distribution. The use of more than one but less than all of the intermediaries who are willing to carry a particular product. The purpose is to ensure that the most fruitful areas of market potential are developed by the best distributors available with less waste of resources.   (AJB)

selective exposure. The avoidance of stimuli which may not be congruent with the intended receiver's self-perception, VALUES or BELIEFS. ZAPPING is a form of selective exposure in that the viewer switches from the communication he wishes to avoid to another channel.   (MJB)

selective perception. The unconscious filtration process that reduces the plethora of sensory stimuli to which the individual is exposed to that small portion which becomes part of personal experience, choosing those stimuli which are rated subjectively as being of relevance. In other words it is a phenomenon whereby individuals screen out stimuli which they do not understand or do not wish to recognize. The classic example of selective perception is that reported by Hastorf and Cantril ('They Saw a Game: A Case History', *Journal of Abnormal and Social Psychology,* vol. 49, 1954) of the perceptions of supporters of two American football teams – Dartmouth and Princeton. The match contained a number of incidents which led to players being injured and penalties being imposed. While most uninvolved viewers felt these were the joint responsibility of both teams, supporters of the two sides were almost unanimous in their view that all the trouble was the fault of the other team.

This tendency to perceive what one wants to see can be traced to several factors. First, there is our ability to screen out or ignore a very large number of stimuli and so enable us to give our full attention to those which have some particular relevance or which strike a discordant note because of the contrast they make with other stimuli. Research has shown that we screen out the vast majority of advertisements to which we are exposed and, in fact, perceive less than 1 per cent of all those we come into contact with. Thus, in order to secure our attention advertisers must use contrasts, e.g. a colour advertisement in a black and white medium, loud noise (or silence) in broadcast media, luxury yacht advertisements in *The Economist,* etc. By the same token we possess perceptual defences which block out stimuli which are offensive, or are otherwise in conflict with our values or attitudes.

The issue of relevance is also important for clearly we will be more likely to perceive stimuli which cater to our needs, both psychological and emotional than those which do not. On occasion physical and emotional needs may generate a conflict (termed COGNITIVE DISSONANCE) such that acquisition of a physical object to satisfy a need (a car for transportation) may generate uncertainty as to the wisdom of that choice. Under these circumstances it has been shown that purchasers of objects pay more attention to advertising or other stimuli relating to the object than do intending purchasers. (MJB, JLD)

selective retention. The tendency to recognize and retain only that information that is congruent and consistent with our existing values and beliefs. (MJB)

self-actualization. *See* MOTIVATION.

self-administered questionnaire. A questionnaire which is completed by the RESPONDENT recording his own answers to the questions. Such questionnaires can be delivered or handed to the respondent for completion. Self-administered questionnaires are most commonly used in mail surveys. *See* MAIL SURVEYS. (AMW)

self-completion. Term used to describe questionnaires which can be completed by the respondent without the assistance of an interviewer. Self-completion questionnaires are essential for mail surveys and possess the twin advantages of low cost and the absence of interviewer bias. Against this must be weighed the disadvantages that the stimulus to respond is less than when faced with an interviewer (although appropriate incentives can help reduce this), that bias may be introduced by respondent self-selection (persons who self-complete questionnaires are different in at least one respect from those that don't!) and that the respondent is able to consider all the questions before answering any of them which may lead to an artificial consistency in the response.

Self-completion questionnaires tend to be most effective when concerned with factual information, particularly when the respondent needs to consult records or check details with others. The design of unambiguous self-completion questionnaires is difficult and adequate pre-testing is essential. (MJB)

self-concept. The sum total of all that a person can call their own – body, traits and abilities; material possessions; family, friends and enemies; vocations and avocations and much else: an amalgam of physical, psychological and mental attitudes and beliefs made up of self-reflected appraisals. (JLD)

self-fulfilling forecast. A forecast that stimulates behaviour that tends to cause itself to be realized. For example, if an influential stockbroker forecasts the movement of a share price, investors begin to act on the belief of such a forecast, their action making it come true. (DB)

self-liquidating promotion. A SALES PROMOTION in which the CONSUMER mails or presents a stipulated number of proofs of purchase along with sufficient money to cover the cost of the manufacturer's purchase, handling and distribution of the premium item. It is also defined by many organizations as any promotion where the customer covers the cost of the merchandise but excludes handling and postage. The use of these promotions has diminished as a result of the growth in discount RETAILERS who can offer the same discounts. (GM)

self liquidator. A sales promotion where the costs involved are met by the person taking advantage of the promotion, e.g. paying a discounted price for cutlery, crockery etc. (MJB)

self-perception theory. The process by which individuals use their own experience as a basis for acquiring attitudes and guiding subsequent action.   (JLD)

self-reference criterion (src). Having sold a product successfully in the domestic market a firm may assume that the product will, without adaptation, also be successful in foreign markets. Frequently this assumption leads to failure. The src refers to the assumption that what is suitable for the home market will be suitable for the foreign market and therefore there is no need to test whether or not the product should be altered.   (CNW)

self-service. A retail selling arrangement which allows shoppers direct access to merchandise which is then carried by the customer for payment to a point of sale or service unit. Effective in reducing store labour costs, but with an increase in theft.   (AJB)

self-service retailer. A retail outlet in which the customers make their own choice from the assortment of goods on offer.   (MJB)

sell-by date. *See* BEST-BEFORE DATE and USE-BY DATE.

sellers' market. Sellers' MARKETS exist where there are shortages of goods and services for general consumption. In wartime conditions and in periods of rationing an economy is said to be operating as a sellers' market. Where such basic items as food, clothing and fuels are in short supply customers buy whatever is available. Design, style and fashion are of little consequence when you are cold in the wintertime and just require a warm coat. Thus where sellers' markets exist, producers do not have to take heed of CONSUMERS' wishes as they are capable of selling all they can make. Thus in a sellers' market there is little need for MARKETING activities as COMPETITION between producers is non-existent. The opposite of a sellers' market is a buyers' market, where consumers have a wide choice, as is the case of Western society today. Manufacturers have to differentiate their PRODUCTS in an attempt to win customers and so marketing activities become important.   (BRM)

selling. *See* PERSONAL SELLING.

selling agent. A type of non-stockholding agent who takes on the whole marketing task for one or more manufacturers, controlling selling, adver-tising, sales promotion and sometimes pricing. May also provide working capital, especially when the reason for his services being required is based on financial difficulty.   (AJB)

selling concept. The achievement of sales and marketing objectives of the firm by the salesperson by providing services and solutions to customers' problems in addition to taking orders.   (WD)

selling formula approach. Stimulus–response method of selling which assumes all prospects are alike or will at least react in a predictable fashion to a set sales presentation.   (WD)

selling situations. The conditions that exist whereby a salesperson can make a sales presentation to a prospect with the potential for a sale to be made.   (WD)

selling tasks. All those activities in addition to order-taking which a salesperson is required to perform, such as display, advice, after-sales services, delivery, collection, stock checks, training or as directed by sales management.   (WD)

semantic differential. A type of attitude measurement test in which a respondent indicates where a brand or company stands on a scale of paired opposites, either descriptive adjectives or phrases, e.g. reliable–unreliable. This SCALING TECHNIQUE was developed by Osgood *et al.* (*Method and Theory in Experimental Psychology*, 1952) and is very widely used, largely because it is much simpler to construct than most other scales and yet yields a very high measure of agreement with these more elaborate measures. The method consists of a series of bipolar adjectives (strong–weak, good–bad etc.) separated usually by between five to nine points. The respondent is asked to check-mark the point which best indicates their attitude. Scale positions are sometimes qualified, for example:
Extremely good. Very good. Fairly good. Neither good nor bad. Fairly bad. Extremely bad.
However, such qualification tends to discourage selection of the extreme positions.
                                                    (MJB)

semantic differential scale. A type of MARKET RESEARCH CLOSED QUESTION, in which the RESPONDENT is asked to select the point on the scale between two bipolar words (e.g.

large/small; old/young), that represents the direction and intensity of their feeling or belief:

Strathclyde University is:
Large ... : x : ... : ... : ... Small

(GM)

semi-display. *See* DISPLAY ADVERTISEMENT.

semiotics. A philosophical concept applied in marketing to the theory of conveying meaning through packaging, promotional signs, symbols, logos, slogans, songs, humour, cartoon and caricature. The three branches of semiotics are syntactics, semantics and pragmatics. (AJB)

semi-solus. A description of a PRESS ADVERTISEMENT or POSTER not quite in a SOLUS POSITION or on a SOLUS SITE, yet not surrounded on all sides by other advertising. (KC)

semi-structured questionnaire. A questionnaire consisting of both open-ended and closed QUESTIONS. It provides greater depth than is possible with a totally structured questionnaire. It is often used when a combination of quantitative and qualitative information is required. *See* OPEN-ENDED QUESTION and CLOSED QUESTION. (AMW)

semi-variable costs. Costs that are composed of two cost components – a fixed component and a variable component. Such costs vary with activity, but not in direct proportion to it. Maintenance, supervision and store-keeping are typical examples of semi-variable costs.

For instance, maintenance can be analysed into time-based maintenance (e.g. weekly, monthly, or annual preventative maintenance) the cost of which is independent of activity and therefore fixed, and activity-based maintenance (e.g. 5,000-mile service for vehicles, and breakdowns due to worn-out parts) the costs of which are wholly dependent on activity and therefore variable. (GA)

sensitivity. The extent to which the variation of a factor or factors may influence an expected outcome. For example, when developing a forecast or plan, it will be necessary to make assumptions about factors such as inflation and exchange rates. To determine how important these assumptions are likely to be on the final outcome, the ANALYSIS should run several times with different values of the relevant factors to determine the forecast/plan's sensitivity to such variations. (MJB)

sensory threshold. The limits above and below which humans are unable to detect changes in sensory stimuli. (MJB)

sentence completion test. A motivational research technique in which the RESPONDENT is invited to complete a sentence on the premise that by imputing the thought to a third person, they will expose their real BELIEFS about the topic which they might not do in response to direct questioning. For example, when instant coffee was first introduced to the MARKET, the sentence 'Women who use instant coffee are ...' was completed by many women with words such as 'lazy', 'poor housekeepers' etc., revealing a deeply held belief that because instant coffee was so easy to prepare, it could not be as good as percolated coffee. Given this insight, the sellers were able to develop communication strategies to overcome this resistance. (MJB)

sequence bias. Bias introduced in the responses to a questionnaire due to the sequence in which the questions are asked. The problem is particularly acute in mail or other self completion questionnaires as the respondent can read all the questions before answering. (MJB)

sequential sampling. A sample whose eventual size depends on a series of stages. If data at the first stage is insufficient to show the desired effect, further stages are conducted until a sample whose size is sufficient is obtained. (SKT)

series discount. A reduction in the RATE-CARD COST given to MEDIA BUYERS who place a single order for a significant series of ADVERTISING SPACES or time SLOTS. *See also* VOLUME DISCOUNT. (KC)

served market. The market defined by the characteristics and/or behaviour of persons actually buying the product or service. The served market will rarely correspond precisely to the target market defined by the organization when developing its marketing plan. Comparison of the intended and served market is important as it may reveal unanticipated opportunities. (MJB)

service charge. A sum of money, or fee, charged to an individual or organization for the provision of a service. (BRM)

service decisions. Decisions concerning the level of service back-up and support to be given to the distributor/buyer pre-sale, at the time of sale and post-sale (after-sales service). As a broad generalization the more complex and durable the object of sale the greater the need for service support, e.g. insurance policies or numerically controlled machine tools.

In many situations, service provision may be the only basis by which buyers can differentiate between suppliers of essentially homogeneous products like chemicals, steel, lubricating oils etc. Similarly, the availability of after-sales service may well influence buyer preference and provide the seller with the opportunity both of maintaining contact with his customers as well as earning a substantial continuing income from the provision of maintenance and repairs, e.g. computers, office equipment.

Service decisions have received increasing attention in the marketing literature in recent years. (MJB)

service department. The section or department within an organization which has the responsibility for providing the after-sales service for the organization's PRODUCTS. At the time of purchase of both domestic and industrial products purchasers are often encouraged to protect their equipment by regular and planned maintenance. This is particularly important where there are moving mechanical parts, as is the case with machinery (cars, lawn-mowers, machine tools, photocopiers, gas and oil burners). It is the personnel of the service department who undertake this work. In the case of cars and lawn-mowers servicing owners are expected to take their equipment to an appropriate service centre for attention. Where this is impractical, as in the case of heavy duty industrial plant, members of the service department travel to the site and transport the necessary tools and equipment with them. Service departments usually work closely with spare parts departments as replacement parts are frequently required by service personnel. In the case of fully integrated MARKETING organization structures the service department becomes part of the overall marketing activity of the organization because of the close liaison service personnel have with the customers. Astute service personnel can advise sales and marketing personnel of obsolete equipment and products nearing the end of their useful life and thus create sales opportunities. (BRM)

service inseparability. *See* INSEPARABILITY.

service intangibility. *See* INTANGIBILITY.

service perishability. *See* PERISHABILITY.

service quality. Given the importance of services in advanced economies considerable effort has been directed to identifying and measuring the factors which define quality from the consumer's perspective. Essentially, however, service quality is a subjective concept which describes the degree to which the service meets the consumer's expectations. Thus people with average expectations receiving good service will perceive the quality as high. Conversely, consumers with high expectations experiencing the same good service may be disappointed as it falls short of what they expected. It follows that the service provider should take care to measure expectations when developing a service and targeting potential users. (MJB)

services. Defined by the American Marketing Association as activities, benefits or satisfactions which are offered for sale, or are provided with the sale of goods. Clearly, this definition is too broad as products also offer benefits and satisfactions to consumers. Accordingly, many authors seek to differentiate physical products from services by defining characteristics which are present in services but absent in physical products, or by the simple expedient of classifying activities or outputs as belonging to either one category or the other. In the case of factors which distinguish products from services, most commentators agree with Stanton, who points out that services possess distinctive characteristics which create marketing problems and result in marketing programmes which are often substantially different from those found in the marketing of products. Among these characteristics Stanton singles out four for particular comment – intangibility, inseparability, heterogeneity, and perishability and fluctuating demand (William J. Stanton, *Fundamentals of Marketing,* 1964). As well as specifying the characteristics which distinguish services from products, Stanton also lists a classification of commercial services as follows: (a) housing; (b) household operations (includes utilities, house repairs, repairs of equipment in the house, landscaping and household cleaning; (c) recreation; (d) personal care which includes services such as laundry, dry-cleaning, beauty care etc.; (e) medical and other health care; (f) private education; (g) business and other professional services, such as legal, accountancy, management consultancy and computer services;

(h) insurance and financial; (i) transportation; (j) communication.

In light of the foregoing comments a possible definition of services might be any activity or benefit performed by individuals and/or organizations where the object of marketing is an intangible, aimed at satisfying the needs and wants of customers and/or industrial users without any acquisition of physical goods arising from the exchange transaction.   (MJB)

sheet. The standard unit of charge for OUTDOOR advertising. The sheet in question is a traditional paper size, 'double crown', still un-metricated at 30 inches x 20 inches. Confusingly, the separate pieces of paper comprising a POSTER are typically 60 inches by 30 inches, the area of 4 'sheets'. Thus, the visible sheet does not correspond to the notional sheet. A few POSTER SITES in the 'transport' subdivision of the medium are double-crown size and posters advertising films are often 'quad crown', which is two double-crowns side by side. The smallest non-transport site is a 'panel' the size of one 4-sheet piece of paper, in PORTRAIT format. Once very widespread, these are steadily being replaced by 6-sheet spaces, typically back illuminated and incorporated into bus shelters. This is the only metricated size: 1.8 metres by 1.2 metres, portrait format, which is roughly 6 feet by 4 feet. The most widespread size of all is the 48-sheet, a LANDSCAPE format measuring 20 feet by 10 feet. Anything larger than that is called a 'supersite', the most familiar of which is the very large 40 foot by 10 foot landscape 96-sheet format. Four other sizes are available but not common: the portrait-format 16-sheet (6 foot 8 inches by 10 feet); the landscape-format 12-sheet (10 feet by 5 feet), 32-sheet (13 feet 4 inches by 10 feet), and 64-sheet (26 feet 8 inches by 10 feet). Notice that 'billboard' does not define any of these sizes. It is simply the American word for an outdoor poster, imported into colloquial British usage but not into the technical vocabulary.   (KC)

shelf life. The total life of a PRODUCT, both organoleptically (taste, flavour, texture, appearance) and microbiologically. Shelf life varies depending on the type of product, e.g. tinned beans, 12 months; frozen peas, 6 months; fresh chicken, 8 days; fresh strawberries, 3 days; fresh bean sprouts, 1 day.   (SD)

shelf talker. A communication (card, sticker, poster etc.) attached to a shelf to draw attention to the goods displayed.   (MJB)

shipping conference. An organization of shipping lines on regular, i.e. 'liner' routes, which meets regularly to agree freight rates, and thus limit the possibility of competitive price cutting. Shipping lines in such conferences often combine the system with deferred rebate schemes which, in general, offer rebates to regular shippers who are still using their services at the time of refund.
(JML)

shopper study. A convenience SAMPLE SURVEY of shoppers at a given location to determine their ATTITUDES, OPINIONS, intentions and/or actual purchase behaviour.   (MJB)

shopping centre. A purpose-designed site containing a variety of retail outlets often under a single roof and with extensive parking facilities. Such centres would normally contain one or more major SUPERMARKETS, chain stores and specialist RETAILERS such as Dixons, as well as a number of boutiques and catering establishments.   (MJB)

shopping goods. Those consumer goods which the customer in the process of selection and purchase characteristically compares on such bases as suitability, quality, price and style. Products in this group are more complex than convenience goods and exhibit a higher degree of differentiation. Usually they are purchased less frequently and are of higher unit value. Many consumer durables fall into this category.   (MJB)

shopping mall. Alternative description of a SHOPPING CENTRE.   (MJB)

shopping mall intercept. The administration of a questionnaire to persons intercepted while shopping in a SHOPPING MALL.   (MJB)

short run. *See* DEMAND, SHORT-RUN.

showcard. A card used in MARKET RESEARCH interviewing listing the alternatives to be considered or rated by the RESPONDENT.   (MJB)

shrinkage. Used in a retailing context as a collective term for the various kinds of STOCK losses which occur. In some contexts shrinkage has become a euphemism for theft.   (BRM)

shrink-wrap. Plastic PACKAGING which moulds to take up the conformation of a PRODUCT.   (SD)

SIC system. *See* STANDARD INDUSTRIAL CLASSIFICATION SYSTEM.

significance. A statistical measure of the likelihood that the result obtained from a sample reflects a true difference rather than a chance occurrence. Usually expressed as a percentage (e.g. 95 per cent) or probabilistically (e.g. 0.99). *See* STANDARD ERROR. (MJB)

simple cluster sampling. A SAMPLING procedure, typically within small POPULATIONS, where a probability sample of clusters is made, followed by a complete enumeration of the population of the cluster. (SKT)

simple random sampling. A SAMPLING procedure where a single list of a POPULATION is drawn up and each element has a known and equal chance of being included in the sample. (SKT)

simple regression. The estimation of a best-fitting line to model the prediction of one variable by another. *Contrast* MULTIPLE REGRESSION.(SKT)

simulated test market. A judgemental procedure claimed to simulate TEST MARKETING. Typically involves conjoint measurement to extract the utilities of existing PRODUCT ATTRIBUTES, followed by the modelling of utilities to purchase patterns and the prediction of purchase patterns for new PRODUCTS. (SKT)

simulation. The use of mathematical formulae to replicate or model processes which describe in a simplified form some aspects of the real world. The use of computers allows the elements of a model to be manipulated with some ease, thus enabling the simulation of a wide range of real-world situations. Econometric forecasters use complex mathematical models to simulate the operation of the economy, so to evaluate the likely impact of government economic policy options. Models which simulate the behaviour of consumer product markets can be used as an alternative to traditional TEST-MARKETING routines. (DB)

single-column centimetre (scc). The basic unit of charge for ADVERTISING SPACE in newspapers. The ADVERTISING RATE per single-column centimetre is the notional price of a space one column wide and one centimetre deep. This 'standard rate' for all national, regional and local newspapers is published in BRAD (q.v.). The price to be paid for a given space relates directly to its area, and can thus be calculated by multiplying the scc rate by the number of columns and the number of centimetres. For example, the *Guardian*'s standard rate in 1996 was £32 per scc. An advertiser would therefore pay £32 x 20 x 2 = £1,280 for one insertion in a double-column space 20 cm deep, assuming no surcharges or discounts. Prices for half-pages, pages and DOUBLE-PAGE SPREADS are normally quoted separately. Magazines do not use the column-centimetre convention, but fractions of a page, even for the smallest display spaces on offer. Both newspapers and magazines charge for CLASSIFIED ADVERTISING SPACE by the line. (KC)

single-item scale. An attitude scale based on a single item or question. (SKT)

single sourcing. The action of buying all the company's requirements for a particular product or service from one source of supply. The advantages of single sourcing are several. A company is able to concentrate its demand on one supplier, and may achieve cost savings through greater negotiating power. There are also fewer problems of supplier management and control, and less 'learning' has to take place for each new order. The major disadvantage is over-reliance on one source of supply. Changes in the market may mean that the supplier's products can become uncompetitive, or that eventually the supplier may go out of business, leaving the buyer with the problem of finding new suppliers. Furthermore, if the buyer is able to split the order between two or more suppliers then he is able to use variations in the amount of order which he allocates to each supplier as a negotiation TOOL. (STP)

site location. *See* STORE LOCATION.

site passage. One unit of measurement of the audience for OUTDOOR advertising. A single site passage represents the presence of one person within what is deemed to be the viewing area of a POSTER SITE. As part of the overall POSTAR research methodology, developed during 1996, participants in a laboratory experiment viewed a series of street scenes, including poster sites, in front of an eye-movement camera. The data were entered into a geometric model that calculated the period of time in which a passer-by has the opportunity to notice a poster, based on such variables as its size and elevation, the angle of vision, its distance from bends in the road, and so on. The outcome was a series of estimated Visibility Adjusted Impacts. These can predict only the outdoor-advertising equivalent of PRESENCE, not the amount of attention given to the poster on the site. Motorists, bus passengers and pedestrians all count equally. 'Total site passages' and 'gross VAI' are thus OPPORTUNITIES-TO-SEE figures, an estimate of the COVERAGE of a campaign.   (KC)

situational analysis. *See* AUDIT, MARKETING.

situation analysis. The broadly based evaluation of the external and internal factors bearing upon a marketing decision. The basis of the SWOT ANALYSIS.   (MJB)

skewed response distribution. The distribution of frequency of responses when not in a normal distribution; typically responses are BIASED towards one end of the spectrum. For example, if you ask hospital in-patients 'What do you think of the nurses?' when still in hospital, they are likely to skew their responses towards the positive.   (SKT)

skimming strategy. A high price policy which aims to 'skim the cream off the market'. This tactic can be appropriate for example when marketing a product with unique characteristics, as consumers will be more willing to pay a premium price for products not aimed at the mass market.   (MDP)

slice-of-life advertising. Advertising which shows people in situations which reflect real life.   (MJB)

slope. In REGRESSION ANALYSIS, a simple linear formula is generated that best fits the observations; the predicted value is calculated by adding to the constant the predictor variable times the slope. Steeper slopes mean more effect of a unit change of the predictor variable on the dependent variable.   (SKT)

slot. *See* SPOT.

Smith, Adam (1723–90). Scottish economist, born at Kirkcaldy, Fife, the posthumous child of a comptroller of customs. He studied at Oxford University for seven years before returning to Scotland where he was one of the brilliant intellectual circle of which David Hume became the best known member. As professor of moral philosophy at Glasgow (1752–64) he gained fame as a lecturer and wrote *Theory of Moral Sentiments* (1759). He travelled in France (1764–6) as tutor

to the young Earl of Buccleuch and in Paris met Turgot and Necker and discussed their economic ideas. In 1776 he settled in London where he joined Dr Johnson's literary circle. In the same year he published his *Inquiry into the Nature and Causes of the Wealth of Nations,* the original source of most future writing on political economy.

He was opposed to the monopolistic mercantilism (e.g. Navigation Acts, trading monopolies such as the East India Company etc.) that had dominated previous economic thinking, but neither was he an uncritical advocate of *laissez-faire.* He believed with Hume that enlightened self-interest would promote public welfare, but insisted in all his works on the maintenance of the link between individual freedom and such moral obligations as kindness, sympathy and justice. Individual freedom releases the energy that produces wealth but the wealth can only fructify by the consumption of goods, not by being hoarded as gold. He also saw that unfettered individual enterprise must be combined with the division of labour (i.e. specialization) to maximize efficiency. Specialization entails the need for markets, which in turn need a common purchasing medium, a conclusion leading to considering methods of determining money values. Thus one by one, he considered the many interlocking factors of political economy. Though some of Adam Smith's conclusions have been assailed or even overthrown, *The Wealth of Nations* has been one of the most influential books ever produced, and Smith has been considered the founder of the study of political economy as a separate discipline.

(Macmillan Reference Biography)

SMP. *See* STRATEGIC MARKETING PLANNING.

snowball sample. A JUDGEMENT SAMPLE in which the interviewer uses the initial respondent to help identify others with similar characteristics. (MJB)

social advertising. Advertising designed to influence the target audiences' social behaviour.   (MJB)

social class. *See* SOCIO-ECONOMIC CLASSIFICATIONS.

social cost. A concept of increased importance with the growth of consumerism and environmentalism. It represents the opportunity cost to society as a whole as the result of any loss attributable to production and not absorbed or paid for by the producer, e.g. the discharge of pollutants into the atmosphere.   (MJB)

social engineering. The application of the social sciences to the development and improvement of a community's social technology, that is its social systems, behaviour and mode of life.   (DB)

social factors. Influences on individual behaviour attributable to the social values and/or behaviour of the groups to which an individual belongs or aspires to belong.   (MJB)

social forecasting. The forecasting of social development and its impact on the systems, behaviour and mode of life of a society, for example, the changing attitudes, values and behaviour of the populace.   (DB)

social group. A social entity which allows individuals to interact with one another in relation to particular phenomena: an aggregate of individuals standing in certain observable relations to each other, e.g. family group, friendship group, work group.   (JLD)

social indicator. Statistical variable that measures and records the patterns of social change which emerge with the development of a society, for example the crime rate, the level of illiteracy and the incidence of alcoholism.   (DB)

social influences. Those factors which mediate and affect the individual components of behaviour: cognition, perception, learning, personality, motivation and attitudes. Social influences originate in and are transmitted by membership of social groups both formal and informal.   (MJB)

socialisation. The process by which the NORMS and VALUES of a society are transmitted.   (MJB)

social marketing. An alternative interpretation of marketing as a purely business-orientated activity which proposes that its philosophical base and justification rests in meeting the needs of society. Accordingly the practice of marketing and its institutions should be conditioned more by a concern for social needs rather than the operational aspects of the marketing function and the pursuit of profit for its own sake.

To a large degree social marketing, or societal marketing as it is sometimes termed, is a reaction to CONSUMERISM, and its articulation may be dated to the late 1960s. Many eminent marketing authors have argued for this 'broadening' of the marketing concept building upon the seminal contribution of Kotler and Levy in 1969 ('Broadening the Concept of Marketing', *Journal of Marketing,* vol. 33). Others are of the view that marketing is a business activity whose effectiveness should be measured in terms of profit with decisions on the distribution and utilization of that profit being left to other social institutions.   (DB)

social mobility. The potential to change one's social class generally via education and/or employment. *See* SOCIO-ECONOMIC CLASSIFICATION.   (MJB)

social responsibility audit. An evaluation or assessment of the policies and practices of an organization to establish how and to what extent it is behaving in a socially responsible manner, e.g. in terms of employment practices, relationships with its local community, environmental protection etc.   (MJB)

social technology. Denotes the procedures which determine and describe the social activity of a society, such as its money system or its social security system. This form of technology is the product of social invention.   (DB)

Social Trends. Compendium of social statistics from a wide range of governmental departments and other organizations presenting a broad picture of British society today and how it has been changing.   (MJB)

societal marketing. *See* SOCIAL MARKETING.

socio-economic classifications. A particularly strong and pervasive, indeed universal, sub-cultural division is that of social class, whereby members of a society are stratified into a number of subdivisions. These subdivisions or classes are based upon many common characteristics, which usually include income, education, occupation and social status or prestige. These characteristics give rise to similar behavioural patterns and activities which can be differentiated from those of other social classes. This latter point is of particular importance to marketers, for the value of such a classification lies in the ability to discriminate between groupings of people and, it is hoped, to predict their behaviour under given conditions.

Many people find the concept of class offensive, because of the intrinsic implication that people can be ordered according to their worth, and argue that all people are equal. Such an argument would appear to be based largely upon an economic interpretation of equality and leads to attempts to distribute wealth more evenly through society. However, it is clear that the redistribution of wealth has relatively little to do with the value attached to the various roles filled by individuals and it is this which is the essence of social stratification. Thus in most societies teachers and priests are accorded relatively high status and prestige but earn incomes more in keeping with members of a lower class; similarly, pop singers earn more than opera singers but their earnings are probably inversely related to their prestige. Thus, while it is true that the status associated with given roles may change over time, it seems highly improbable that there will ever be a truly classless society.

It follows that if we wish to make use of this universal tendency for societies to 'classify' themselves, then we must identify and measure those factors or criteria upon which such a classification rests. In doing so one must not be surprised if different sets of criteria result in a different number of classes. However, most systems used in Western cultures have a close allegiance to the six-class model proposed by W. Lloyd Warner in his celebrated study of a small New England Town (*Social Class in America*, 1960).

Social class membership is classified as:
Upper-upper aristocracy
Lower-upper new rich
Upper-middle successful business and
    professional
Lower-middle white-collar worker
Upper-lower blue-collar worker
Lower-lower unskilled

While this scheme recognizes two more classes than did Centers's 1949 division into upper, middle, working and lower classes, Warner himself saw the issue as a false one, in that the number of divisions is relatively arbitrary and dependent upon whose opinion you are seeking. It should also be noted that in many instances one is as much concerned with differences within classes as between them.

The most widely used system in the United Kingdom is that developed for use in the NATIONAL READERSHIP SURVEY (*see* Figure 31).

Just as the concept of culture is useful for classifying people into broadly similar grouping, so social-class concepts help refine the classification into smaller and more specific segments with greater operational potential for practitioners. Engel *et al.* cite a large number of studies which illustrate the application of social class in helping to interpret and predict consumer behaviour. Social class has been found to be especially useful in predicting preferences for kind, quality and style of clothing, home furnishings, leisure

Social grade	Social status	Occupation	% of population (approx.)
A	Upper middle class	Higher managerial, administrative or professional	2.6
B	Middle class	Middle managerial, administrative or professional	12.7
C1	Lower middle class	Supervisory or clerical, junior management	22.8
C2	Skilled working class	Skilled manual workers	31.2
D	Working class	Semi- and unskilled manual workers	21.0
E	Those at lowest level of subsistence	Pensioners, casual or lowest-grade worker, unemployed	9.7
			100.0

*The breakdown in the table is derived from data published by JICNARS (Joint Industry Committee for National Readership Surveys) and is not dependent on income, i.e. it is based on the occupation of the head of household with limited exception – when the chief wage-earner is used instead.

Figure 31: **Socio-economic groupings***

activities, cars, consumer durables, and use of credit cards. Social class has also been shown to be associated with patterns of media usage, language patterns, source credibility and shopping behaviour. This predictive power is considerably enhanced if one is able to add to it knowledge concerning reference groups, role and family influence.   (MJB)

socio-economic groups. UK method of classifying individuals used by the Registrar General in the analysis of Census of Population material, based entirely on information about the job of the person classified. *See* SOCIO-ECONOMIC CLASSIFICATIONS.   (KF)

soft goods. Household furnishings, clothing etc., as distinct from CONSUMER DURABLES such as washing machines, cookers televisions etc., which are hard goods.   (MJB)

soft sell. A selling approach in which the salesperson determines the prospective customer's needs through dialogue, points out the PRODUCT'S benefits which will satisfy the customer and to persuade him of the wisdom of accepting the salesperson's offer. Contrast with hard selling in which the salesman seeks to dominate the client by means of a forceful presentation and to emphasize what the customer will be missing if he doesn't secure the opportunity now.   (MJB)

sole trader. A person who trades on his or her own account. The individual and the business are legally and financially inseparable. The individual is wholly responsible for any business debts.   (GM)

solus position. An ADVERTISING SPACE not abutted by any other. Therefore, a reader's attention cannot be distracted at the time by a message from another advertiser (though potentially by the surrounding editorial matter).   (KC)

solus site. A POSTER SITE comprising a single 'panel' at a location where no other site is directly in view. Therefore, the attention of a passer-by cannot be distracted at the time by a message from another advertiser (though potentially by any number of other things in the immediate vicinity).   (KC)

Sorrell, Martin (1945–). The son of a businessman who helped to build Britain's biggest chain of consumer electronics retailers, this graduate of Cambridge and the Harvard Business School

entered the advertising business as recently as 1977, yet now owns two of the world's largest and most famous American ADVERTISING AGENCIES. After first working for Mark McCormack, the legendary pioneer of sports sponsorship and management, he returned to the UK to collaborate with James Gulliver in the creation by acquisition of the Argyll Group, a food retailing conglomerate. In 1976, both men began to act as financial and business strategy consultants to the six-year-old SAATCHI & SAATCHI. A year later, Sorrell became its chief financial officer. Over the following ten years, the Saatchi brothers bought four major American advertising agencies to become one of the biggest advertising groups in the world. It was Sorrell who was generally credited with structuring the audacious deals that permitted a relatively small, foreign firm to take over such large and long-established American institutions. In 1985, aiming to build an empire of his own, he bought the majority stake in a small manufacturer of supermarket baskets and animal cages for £400,000, reputedly by persuading its two owners to issue new stock and give him 30 per cent of it on the prospect that the company would be transformed into one of the biggest communications conglomerates in the world. Within 18 months, Wire & Plastic Products (WPP) had bought 15 other companies and increased its stock market valuation exactly one hundred times. Its sixteenth acquisition, after a two-week takeover battle in 1987, was the famous J. Walter THOMPSON agency. Two years later, the almost equally famous Ogilvy & Mather succumbed to an offer of more than $850 million for its shares, and WPP Group had moved up the world rankings to a place just behind Saatchi & Saatchi. In just four years and only a dozen years after entering the business, the man the legendary David OGILVY had branded 'an odious little jerk' during the heat of battle had become one of the most powerful figures in the world-wide business. In 1996, his personal creation was the largest advertising group in the world, with global annual BILLINGS of $24.7 billion. J. Walter THOMPSON and Ogilvy & Mather occupied second and third place in the UK league table, respectively billing £278 and £255 million that year. Martin Sorrell was now beyond doubt the most successful advertising tycoon since James Walter Thompson and David Ogilvy themselves, though much less in the public eye than his own former employer.   (KC)

sort and count. Many advertisements contain an invitation to interested parties to write in to the advertiser for further information, free samples, and so on. By sorting and counting the requests generated by such advertisements the advertiser can obtain much useful information at low cost. Despite the potential bias due to respondent self-selection, this method does give valuable information in relative terms of the pulling power of different media, of different copy platforms and advertisement make-up, and of different sizes and positions within the media. The advertisements are usually keyed, that is given a coding to assist identification, either by including the code in the address, for example Dept DM7 for an edition of the Daily Mail, or by requiring the respondent to clip the coupon on which the information is similarly recorded. As mentioned by OGILVY (in *Confessions of an Advertising Man*), direct mail advertisers have a continuous feedback of the pulling power of their advertisements, which supports his suggestion that those selling through more conventional channels might do well to adopt some of the former's advertising practices, for example the use of long copy. (MJB)

sorting out. Products of nature (agriculture, forestry, fishing, extraction) must be sorted out into types or grades suitable for the purpose of the consumer. The same may also be true of some manufacturing processes where process control is difficult, resulting in output which is not uniform. (AJB)

sound bite. Technically, the information given in a 10- or 20-second time period within a news broadcast. In common usage, any short pithy statement summarizing a point of view but without elaborating on it. (MJB)

source. The originator of a message. (MJB)

source effect. The effect that the source of a MARKETING COMMUNICATIONS message has upon the target audience's perceptions of it and their reactions to it, along with CHANNEL EFFECT, MESSAGE EFFECT and the time effects created by the MEDIA SCHEDULE. An extensive literature of source effect relies heavily on studies in social communication as models for predictions about marketing communications. This transfer is conceptually dubious. First, the source is usually clear-cut in the former but often compound or even ambiguous in the latter: a firm, a presenter, a sales representative, an actor playing a part, a retailer, or various combinations of these.

Second, social-communication experiments assume that respondents can rate sources either credible or not. In the marketing context, an audience can be expected to rate a source neither wholly credible nor wholly non-credible, so a sliding scale of credibility must be visualized. The literature does not appear to recognize these shortcomings in its source material.

With those provisos, there is general agreement that source effect has four interacting components: 'visibility' (high or low profile), 'credibility' (perceived objectivity and expertise), 'attractiveness' (familiarity and perceived congruence with the audience's own values) and 'power' (authority and prestige). Many authors interpret ENDORSEMENT ADVERTISING as a tactic to enhance source effect, by offering a third person as the 'source' in the expectation that he or she will be more positively rated on the dimensions of source effect than the company itself would. However, the endorsers are generally celebrities or actors, and the audience is relatively unlikely to credit them with genuine 'expertise' in the advertised product or service, with 'objectivity', since they are known to be paid for their endorsement, or with authority, because they are acting. Furthermore, one would expect few members of a typical audience to see the perceived values of most celebrities as generally congruent with their own. This leaves only 'visibility', 'familiarity' and perhaps 'prestige'. The explanation is not entirely convincing. (KC)

sourcing strategy. *See* SINGLE SOURCING.

space broker. The nineteenth-century ancestor of present day ADVERTISING AGENCIES, who bought ADVERTISING SPACE in bulk from the MEDIA OWNERS and re-sold it in lots to ADVERTISERS. *See* BARKER, CHARLES; PALMER, VOLNEY B.; ROWELL, GEORGE P.; THOMPSON, J. WALTER. (KC)

span of control. The number of people at one level in an organization who report to someone at the next level up. The concept of span of control is used as one measure of organizational climate. In marketing it has been used as part of the definition of mechanistic and organic organizations. Mechanistic organizations have a relatively narrow span of control and tend to be less rapid than organic organizations (with broader span of control) to become aware of new products or processes. (STP)

Spearhead. The Department of Trade and Industry's Single Market Database. This online service summarizes current and prospective EUROPEAN COMMUNITY measures which will have an effect on British business, and gives full texts of relevant Community legislation. (GM)

specialization. The process whereby particular companies concentrate on the manufacture and marketing of a limited number of products or types of product. (GA)

special position. A MEDIA BUYER'S booking instruction, specifying the location of an ADVERTISEMENT in a newspaper or magazine, either by its position on the page or its relationship to editorial material. The terminology is esoteric: 'FM', 'next-matter', 'title corner', SOLUS POSITION, 'first rhp' (right-hand page), and so on. All special positions carry a surcharge on the standard ADVERTISING RATE. The alternative is to settle for 'run of paper': *see* ROP. (KC)

specialty goods. Consumer goods on which a significant group of buyers characteristically insists and for which they are willing to make a special purchasing effort.

Some critics argue that this is a meaningless category as the 'special purchasing effort' required is due to limited availability and that otherwise such goods would fall into one of the other groups. This argument is rejected on the grounds that brand insistence has a very real bearing on the consumer's patronage of different outlets and therefore on the retailer's stock policy. Thus, although the housewife may be indifferent to the brand of canned peas she buys and will take what is available, she may well change to another store altogether if she cannot find her preferred brand of baby food, cigarette or headache remedy. (MJB)

specialty store. A retail outlet which offers a narrow assortment of product lines but a great depth within those lines. (AJB)

specialty wholesalers. A wholesaler who carries a very limited assortment of product lines but a very great depth within those lines. His stock range appeals to both SPECIALTY RETAILERS and to MASS MERCHANDISERS who usually buy directly from manufacturers of the product lines which form the greater part of their range. (AJB)

speculation. One of three concepts proposed by Louis P. Bucklin ('Postponement, Speculation and the Structure of Distribution Channels',

Journal of Marketing Research, vol. 2, February 1965) which affect the structure of distribution channels, the other two being SUBSTITUTABILITY and POSTPONEMENT. The principle of speculation holds that changes in form, and the movement of goods to forward inventories, should be made at the earliest possible time in the marketing flow in order to reduce the costs of the marketing system. (MJB)

spin-off. This occurs when research results are successfully applied in a context other than the one for which they were developed. Non-stick frying pans and smoother razor blades are the results of spin-off from friction reduction research in NASA's space programme. (KAB)

split-half reliability. The reliability of measurement of a multiple-item scale assessed by measuring the correlation of two scores formed by splitting the scale into half. (SKT)

sponsorship. (1) An ingredient of the MARKETING COMMUNICATION MIX, describing the familiar tactic of gaining exposure for a company's name by associating it with an individual, an entity, an event or an activity, in the expectation of secondary exposure via attribution to the sponsor during associated media coverage.

(2) The explicit association of a television or radio programme with an otherwise unconnected sponsoring company or organization which has met any part of the costs of production or transmission. All television programmes are eligible for sponsorship except news, business and financial reports which contain interpretation or comment, and current affairs programmes containing analysis or discussion. The Independent Television Commission's ITC CODE OF PROGRAMME SPONSORSHIP and the RADIO AUTHORITY ADVERTISING AND SPONSORSHIP CODE explicitly forbid the influencing of the content or scheduling of a programme by its sponsors. (KC)

spot. A unit of ADVERTISING TIME on radio or television that is occupied by a single COMMERCIAL, sometimes called a 'slot'. The price actually paid for the spot occupied by a given commercial is nowadays typically negotiated on a case-by-case basis, depending very much on current demand for advertising time and the degree to which the advertiser wants to fix precise timing. Television commercials typically fill 40-second spots, radio commercials 30-second spots, and cinema commercials 30 or 60 seconds. A variable but finite number of consecutive spots comprises one COMMERCIAL BREAK. (KC)

spot colour. An option offered by MEDIA OWNERS, to add a single, solid colour to an otherwise monochrome press ADVERTISEMENT.   (KC)

spot market. The current market for effecting immediate transactions as contrasted with the FUTURES MARKET.   (MJB)

spot rate. The price of a single SPOT rather than a package of ADVERTISING TIME. The most costly way to buy television, radio or cinema 'AIRTIME'.   (KC)

spreadsheet. An application package for use on a personal computer (PC). It allows text and numerical data to be entered and manipulated on a grid of cells arranged in columns and rows. Complex formulae are supported and any number of 'what if?' scenarios can be examined. Marketing applications include BREAK-EVEN ANALYSIS, forecasting and linear programming. The MARKET LEADER is Lotus 1-2-3, though many similar packages are available.   (KRD)

spurious relationship. The situation where the correlation suggests a relationship between two variables, but interpretation (or deeper statistical analysis) suggests that this is able to be explained away by some other factor.   (SKT)

src. *See* SELF REFERENCE CRITERION.

s-shaped sales response function. Graphical representation of the relationship between sales and the level of marketing expenditure. Usually shown as an 's' shaped curve since the sales return from initial levels of marketing expenditure is likely to be low. As marketing expenditures increase so sales are likely to increase at a higher rate until market saturation, when sales are likely to increase at a slower rate than increases in marketing expenditure.   (STP)

stagflation. Term used to describe the state of an economy in which growth is falling or 'stagnating' while prices are increasing – 'inflation'.   (MJB)

standard costing. A system of costing an item over a period of time by forecasting probable changes of such costs and averaging these out to provide a 'standard' cost. Such a system avoids the hazard that sharp, short-term fluctuations in costs make it difficult to compare financially consecutive periods of company activity or arrive at sensible price-change decisions. The system requires a back-up control system which ensures

that this forecast of cost changes is accurate. Errors in this area can lead to serious losses of profit if the standard cost is under-recovering real costs.   (JRB)

standard deviation (SD). A measure of dispersion in the same units as the original measure, calculated as the square root of the variance. For a normal distribution, about 66 per cent of the observations fall within one standard deviation of the MEAN.   (SKT)

standard error (se). A measure of the margin of confidence associated with a sample statistic. The standard error of a statistic decreases with increasing sample size. Short for 'the standard error of estimate'.   (SKT)

standard error of the regression. A measure of the accuracy of the regression model, calculated as the standard deviation of the residuals. (SKT)

Standard Industrial Classification of Economic Activities (SIC). Is a system of classification of establishments according to industry covering all economic activities. Contains 17 sections, 16 subsections, 60 divisions, 222 groups, 503 classes and 142 sub-classes. Class or subclass are the main level at which detailed data are presented.   (MJB)

Stapel scale. A technique similar to the SEMANTIC DIFFERENTIAL IN WHICH RESPONDENTS are invited to indicate the extent to which a word or phrase might describe an object by assigning a numerical value to each in accordance with a prescribed scale of values.   (MJB)

staples. Products which the consumer buys regularly and routinely, frequently with a hierarchy of brand preference in mind. The consequence is that brand switching may be influenced by availability and convenience.   (AJB)

Starch, Dr Daniel (1883–1979). American pioneer of READERSHIP research (*see* READING-AND-NOTING), who propounded a theory of advertising effect in the process of developing his research technique (*see* HIERARCHY-OF-EFFECTS) and published a textbook, *Principles of Advertising* (1923), to promote both.   (KC)

stars. *See* BUSINESS PORTFOLIO.

station. The everyday description of a television or radio CONTRACTING COMPANY.   (KC)

statistical demand analysis. The procedure of discovering the direct relationship between sales and real demand factors. The procedure consists of expressing sales (Y) as a dependent variable and trying to explain sales variation as a result of variation in a number of independent demand variables (factors) $X_1, X_2, ..., X_n$; that is $Y = f(AX_1, X_2, ..., X_n)$. The demand variables (factors) most commonly analysed are prices, incomes, population and promotion. Statistical demand analysis represents a typical application of MULTIPLE REGRESSION ANALYSIS in demand forecasting problems.   (GA)

statistical design. Sampling and experimental designs based on statistical procedures.   (SKT)

statistical efficiency. The figure used to compare the performance of SAMPLING designs: designs with higher efficiency have lower standard errors of estimate.   (SKT)

statistical regression. In experimental and research designs, the tendency of groups selected as highest (or lowest) on some attribute to 'revert to the MEAN' during the course of a series of measurements. A group selected as high in preference for some product will not be so high on a repeat measurement.   (SKT)

stereotype. A generalized belief or expectation concerning likely behaviour, a relationship or an outcome based upon a person or object's association with a particular group, organization or culture e.g. old people are more set in their ways than young ones; French wine and Swiss watches are of high quality.   (MJB)

stimulus. Any kind or form of change that acts on a sense organ – vision, hearing, taste, smell, touch which includes pressure, pain, cold and warmth, balance, muscle coordination or kinaesthetic sense, and the visceral senses. The stimulus may be chemical, mechanical or physical in nature. See STIMULUS RESPONSE.   (MJB)

stimulus response. The central concept in the behavioural school of psychology which developed out of the work of Pavlov, John Watson, Clark Hull and Edward Tolmen. Behaviourists developed their theories from their observations of animals to the study of human physiology and behaviour and argued that their approach was superior to those which were associated with theories emphasizing the conscious and unconscious

mind on the grounds that these studies were essentially subjective while behaviourism is objective in character. According to the behaviourists every STIMULUS provokes a response and, from the marketing point of view, the key issue is to identify what stimulus will provoke the desired response such as attention, recall, purchase etc.   (MJB)

stimulus–response theory. The pairing of two objects or ideas to create an associative bond; the objects are connected by the prospect of a reward being given as the result of certain actions, or alternatively punishment may follow from specific situations giving rise to the pleasure–pain theory of learning. This theory has been widely researched in laboratory experiments of animal behaviour (e.g. Pavlov's experiments on conditioned reflexes in dogs). In consumer marketing, stimulus–response theory relates to the creation of a link between, for example, brand name and product quality as a means of encouraging the development of routinized patterns of buying behaviour, reducing the influence of perception and insight in the buying decision.   (JLD)

stock. The fund invested in goods used in trade, or in raw materials to be processed and used in trade. The list of units of all the goods kept for trade by a merchant. A capital sum to trade with. Of Anglo-Saxon origin, this term tends to be more widely used in the UK than in the USA, and with a greater range of meaning. See INVENTORY.   (AJB)

stock cover. The ratio of current average weekly sales (units or value) to current STOCK. This expresses the number of weeks which the present stock can be expected to last at the current rate of sale.   (AJB)

stockist. An organization which acts as a holder and distributor of goods from STOCK.   (BRM)

stockless purchasing. Buying and obtaining delivery of goods required for production on demand, where the supplier assumes the responsibility of holding stock of the item, and the buyer guarantees to buy a minimum quantity at a fixed price within a given time period. This has advantages for the buyer in terms of reducing the amount of stock which is held, but can create difficulties if the supplier's production scheduling is not coordinated with the buyer's usage rates.   (STP)

stockout. Literally, an item which is temporarily out of STOCK and unavailable for immediate use or delivery. An increase in the level of stockouts thus implies a decline in the LEVEL OF SERVICE available to customers. In practical terms, usage of the word is usually restricted to circumstances of reporting of actual unfulfilled orders.   (KNB)

stocktaking. A regular check of the goods in a shop, warehouse or factory.   (BRM)

stock to sales method. A method of planning inventory levels that derives beginning-of-month (BOM) inventory from planned sales for that month. The ratio of stock to sales of the same month in the previous year is used as a guide for the plan in the current year.   (AJB)

stockturn rate. A measure of the number of times the average inventory is sold during a year. Preferably the average inventory should be calculated from the beginning inventory and 12 end-of-month inventories, at cost. The sales figure should also be converted to cost by using the 'cost of goods sold', or alternatively both figures should be at selling price.   (AJB)

store audit. *See* RETAIL AUDIT.

store brands. A brand whose copyright belongs to the retailer, though the product may have been produced for him by a supplier. The name may be that of the store, or a name devised by the store (e.g. Safeway) or it may be unnamed but distinguished by the package design.   (AJB)

store image. The overall perception people have of given stores; e.g. Marks & Spencer offers very good value for money.   (MJB)

store layout. The design of a store's interior to encourage people to enter the store and expose them to the maximum variety of merchandise within the space available. For example, some stores have the fresh fruit and vegetable display at the entrance because it is colourful and will attract people in while other stores have fresh foods and the most frequently bought items at the back of the store so people will be exposed to all the other displays when locating them.   (MJB)

store location. The problem of selecting a site for a retail store arises out of differing needs and circumstances. In selecting the best site from the many offered, the retailer attempts to evaluate each site's potential in terms of sales which could be made to a particular target market. A wide range of techniques is available to help but the final judgement often depends on qualitative factors. *See* LOCATION DECISIONS.   (AJB)

store traffic. The volume of shoppers who enter the store whether with intention to purchase or not. Retailers use the ratio of actual purchasers to total traffic to evaluate the efficiency of the store's trading operation.   (AJB)

storyboard. A series of drawings summarising the action in a proposed television COMMERCIAL, accompanied by a script and descriptions of the soundtrack. Storyboards rather resemble strip cartoons, similarly condensing continuous action into a series of frozen moments. They are typically used at an early stage in the development of the commercial, to explain the idea and execution more vividly than would be possible in words alone, without incurring any of the high costs of television production. *See also* ANIMATIC.   (KC)

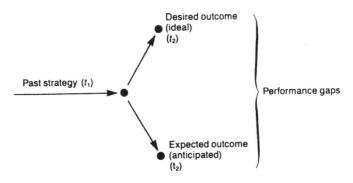

Figure 32: **Strategic gap analysis**

straight rebuy. A situation where the customer repurchases the same product without any further search or evaluation. *See* BUY CLASSES. (MJB)

strapline. A short statement or slogan incorporated into all the firm's advertising, e.g. British Airways 'The world's favourite airline'; Coca-Cola 'It's the real thing'. (MJB)

strategic alliance. An agreement between two or more organizations to collaborate with one another in order to enhance their competitiveness in GLOBAL MARKETS. (MJB)

strategic business unit (strategy centre). This has been defined by Arthur D. Little as a business area with an external marketplace for goods and services, for which management can determine objectives and execute strategies independent of other business areas. It is a business that could probably stand alone if divested. Strategic business units are the 'natural' or homeogeneous businesses of a corporation. (MJB)

strategic fit. A concept which defines the degree to which a future growth strategy is consistent with the firm's existing strengths and the market opportunities available to it. (MJB)

strategic gap analysis. An examination, at a point of time (t^1), of a company's position after following a particular strategy. An alternative strategy is considered which would result, at time t^2, in an ideal outcome. The consideration of this alternative strategy may be the result of any number of factors, e.g. a change in objectives, decision makers or performance levels. The need for change is then examined in the light of the gap between this new ideal outcome at time t^2 and the anticipated outcome at time t^2 if no change is initiated. Management should perceive the gaps as being considerable before the alternative strategy is accepted. Additionally, the decision maker must believe that the gaps can be reduced and must be suitably motivated to achieve this. (KRD)

strategic intent. A future objective to be achieved through the development and implementation of a new strategy. (MJB)

strategic marketing planning (SMP). A recent review by Brownlie would seem to support the view that there is no single universally accepted definition of strategic marketing planning, and he offers the following seven definitions: (a) The answers to two questions, 'What is our business?' and 'What should it be?' implicit to Drucker's early conceptualization of an organization's strategy. (b) Chandler defines strategy as: 'The determination of the basic long-term goals and objectives of an enterprise, and the adoption of courses of action and the allocation of resources necessary for carrying out these goals.' (c) Andrew's definition of strategy combines the ideas of Drucker and Chandler: 'Strategy is the pattern of objectives, purposes or goals and plans for achieving these goals stated in such a way as to define what business the company is in or is to be in, and the kind of company it is to be.' (d) Hofer and Schendel define an organized strategy as: 'The fundamental pattern of present and planned resource deployments and environmental interactions that indicates how the organization will achieve its objectives.' (e) According to Abell, strategic planning involves: 'The management of any business unit in the dual tasks of anticipating and responding to changes which affect the marketplace for their products.' (f) In 1979, Derek Wynne-Jones, Head of the Planning and Strategy Division of PA Management Consultants, considered that strategic planning 'embraces the overall objectives of an organization in defining its strategy and preparing and subsequently implementing its detailed plans.' (g) Christopher Lorenz, late Editor of the Management Page of the *Financial Times,* considered strategic planning to be: 'The process by which top and senior executives decide, direct, delegate and control the generation and allocation of resources within a company.'

While these definitions may differ in the particular, there does appear to be a common thread which is that SMP is concerned with establishing the goal or purpose of an organization and the means chosen for achieving that goal. In the case of the single-product organization, it is felt that the concepts of marketing strategy and strategic marketing planning are synonymous with corporate strategy and corporate planning. However, in the case of a multi-product firm, corporate strategy and corporate planning will apply to the organization as a whole, whereas marketing strategy and strategic marketing planning will be appropriate to the individual STRATEGIC BUSINESS UNITS which comprise it. (MJB)

strategic planning. *See* STRATEGIC MARKETING PLANNING.

strategic thrust. The central theme or principle which informs the firm's STRATEGIC INTENT.

(MJB)

strategic window. A concept developed by Derek Abell ('Strategic Windows', *Journal of Marketing,* July 1978) 'to focus attention on the fact that there are only limited periods during which the "fit" between the key requirements of a market and the particular competencies of a firm competing in that market is at an optimum. Investment in a product line or market area should be timed to coincide with periods in which such a strategic window is open.' The article provides a number of detailed examples to support the argument that firms must anticipate and respond to changes in the marketplace if they are to remain successful. (MJB)

strategy centre. *See* STRATEGIC BUSINESS UNIT.

stratification. Procedures that divide up a POPU-LATION into strata that are probably homogeneous on the attributes of interest. Generally stratification can increase the precision of SAMPLING compared to simple random sampling, if differences between strata correlate with differences on the attributes of interest. (SKT)

stratified sampling. A restricted approach to RANDOM SAMPLING in which a POPULATION is subdivided into subgroups or strata in accordance with a criterion correlated with the factor under study. A simple random sample is then drawn from each stratum. Ideally each stratum should be as homogeneous as possible and distinctive from all other strata. While it may be possible to define strata on some *a priori* basis (e.g. location), it is often necessary to undertake some exploratory research in order to define strata which are both homogeneous and distinctive and also to determine whether SAMPLING should be proportionate or disproportionate. Provided one can define the strata accurately, stratified sampling offers a cost-effective approach to probabilistic sampling. (MJB)

Strong, E.K. (1884–1963). American academic who expounded a HIERARCHY-OF-EFFECTS model of response to sales pitches in his textbook, *The Psychology of Selling* (1925). Dubbed 'AIDA', it was adopted as an explanation of audience response to ADVERTISING messages and has been enthusiastically applied to the planning and evaluation of campaigns ever since, despite serious conceptual shortcomings. He also studied the phenomenon of WEAROUT in MEDIA SCHEDULES.

(KC)

structured question. A question to which the possible answers have been pre-determined by the researcher. (MJB)

style obsolescence. OBSOLESCENCE resulting from a change in the styling of a product which makes earlier versions appear dated. (MJB)

subculture. A group within a culture which possesses certain distinguishing values, beliefs and/or patterns of behaviour which enable it to be identified as a differentiated segment of the population defined by the overall culture of which it is a part. (MJB)

subliminal advertising. A controversial ADVER-TISING strategy that achieved notoriety when case examples were cited in Vance PACKARD'S popular exposé, *The Hidden Persuaders* (Penguin, 1960 and 1981). 'Subliminal' describes a stimulus that is below the threshold of conscious perception. Though there is ample evidence from experimental psychology for the ability of such stimuli to lodge themselves in the subconscious memory, evidence that they can be successfully incorporated into ADVERTISING messages is equivocal to say the least. Indeed, there is an equally popular argument that people employ subconscious perceptual defence mechanisms quite capable of frustrating advertisers' efforts to influence them. Furthermore, the only experiment conducted in a marketing context has never been successfully replicated, though it continues to be reported in textbooks. A psychologist who ran a commercial motivational research company, James Vicary, arranged for the subliminal message 'drink Coca-Cola ... eat popcorn' to be repeated on the screen of a cinema in New Jersey, in 1957. The audience did both. But it is worth noting that the two products are exactly what one would expect people to buy in the foyer of a cinema in any case, and that American cinema audiences are not exposed to overt advertising messages against which they might erect subconscious defences. Despite this lack of hard evidence, the possibility of subliminal techniques being used visually or aurally in print and broadcasting advertising periodically resurfaces as an issue of debate, in both Britain and America. One consequence is that the ITC CODE OF ADVERTISING STANDARDS AND PRACTICE SPECIFIES THAT TELEVISION COMMERCIALS must not 'include any technical device which, by using images of very brief duration or by any other means, exploits the possibility of conveying a message to, or otherwise influencing the minds of, members of an audience without their being aware, or fully aware, of what has been done'. However, neither the RADIO AUTHORITY ADVERTISING AND SPONSORSHIP CODE NOR THE BRITISH CODES OF ADVERTISING AND SALES PROMOTION, covering print and cinema advertising, contains any explicit reference to subliminal advertising. Those who fear its potential for manipulation of audiences subscribe, by implication, to a propaganda model of advertising effect, placing the balance of power firmly on the advertiser's end of the scales. This view is somewhat at odds with current academic thinking about the nature of the relationship between advertisers and their audiences in 'advertising literate' societies. (KC)

subsidiary company. In UK company law, a company is a subsidiary of another company (a) if that company is a member of it and controls the composition of its board of directors; (b) if that other company holds more than half (in nominal value) of its equity share capital; or (c) if it is a subsidiary of any company which is a subsidiary of the first company. (CNW)

subsidy. (1) Money given by one country to another in payment for help of some kind.
(2) Money granted by the government to a service (transport, education) which is important to the public, or to the growers of an important foodstuff (milk, potatoes) to help keep the prices down. (BRM)

subsistence economy. An economy at the lowest level of development where the output of its members is just sufficient to meet their basic physiological needs with no surpluses available for exchange. (MJB)

substantiality. A key requirement of a viable MARKET SEGMENT i.e. that the segment is of sufficient size to justify developing a marketing mix especially for it. (MJB)

substitutability. One of three concepts proposed by Louis P. Bucklin ('Postponement, Speculation and the Structure of Distribution Channels', *Journal of Marketing Research,* vol. 2, February 1965) which affect the structure of distribution channels, the other two being POSTPONEMENT and SPECULATION. In essence, the concept of substitutability states that under competitive conditions institutions of the channel will interchange the

workload among functions, not to minimize the cost of some individual function, but the total costs of the channel. (MJB)

substitute goods. A good which may be substituted for another to a greater (perfect substitute) or lesser (imperfect substitute) degree. Where goods are perfect substitutes, CONSUMERS will be indifferent to the manufacturer's or seller's identity. It is for this reason that sellers seek to differentiate their PRODUCTS both physically and psychologically so that prospective users can be encouraged to distinguish between them (imperfect substitutes) and develop preference and loyalty towards the outputs of a designated seller. (MJB)

summated rating. A value or score computed by summing a respondent's answers to a series of scaled questions intended to measure their attitudes towards the issue under investigation. (MJB)

supermarket. Defined by the UK Institute of Grocery Distribution (IGD) as a self-service store with a selling area of 2,000 to 25,000 square feet with an assortment including fresh meat and produce. (AJB)

supersite. A large POSTER SITE. *See also* SHEET. (KC)

superstore. Defined by the UK Institute of Grocery Distribution (IGD) as a self-service store with a selling area of 25,000 to 50,000 square feet carrying an assortment which includes fresh and packaged foods, and a limited range of non-food, located beside a car parking area. The area is generally on the periphery of a town. (AJB)

supplement. Additional material which is 'supplementary' to a print medium with which it is included. Supplements are issued with many newspapers and magazines and consist of a combination of editorial matter and advertising. Newspaper supplements are often produced to a higher standard than the paper itself and so can make full use of colour making it more attractive to advertisers. Further, because of their magazine, like qualities supplements tend to be read at leisure and so command more attention than advertising in the newspaper itself. (MJB)

supplier-active. The NEW PRODUCT DEVELOPMENT process is said to be supplier-active when it is the manufacturer who: (a) surveys a group of customers to obtain data on needs for new products; (b) analyses the data; (c) develops a product idea; (d) tests the idea against ensuing purchase decisions. (KAB)

supplier development. In some situations there may be only a limited number of suppliers from whom an industrial buyer can source a specific item. To improve the choice of suppliers, the buyer may become involved in supplier development, deliberately encouraging companies which are not currently supplying an item, to consider doing so. In such circumstances the buyer may then actively help the supplier to develop the production knowledge needed to manufacture the item, and guarantee sufficient demand for the supplier to invest in the production capacity which is required. (STP)

supplier management. In some situations the industrial buyer may deliberately attempt to influence the policies of specified suppliers to improve the quality of the service which is received from them. This process, termed supplier management, may extend to making suggestions about the supplier's manufacturing or procurement policies, or about the supplier's general administrative and distribution activities. The supplier will be more or less likely to make such changes depending on the importance of the customer. For example, Marks & Spencer plc have a very active supplier management programme for many of the small to medium-sized companies from which they source specific products. These companies are usually willing to make changes where necessary because of the importance of Marks & Spencer to them as a customer. (STP)

supplier search. The stage in the buying process when the intending buyer seeks to identify those suppliers who, a priori, appear to be able to meet the buyer's needs. (MJB)

supplier selection. The stage in the buying process when the intending buyer chooses the preferred supplier or suppliers from those qualified as suitable during SUPPLIER SELECTION. (MJB)

supply. Technically, a projection of the volume of goods or services which would be made available at any given price. In ordinary usage, the total volume offered for sale in a particular market. (MJB)

survey. The evaluation, analysis and description of a population based upon a sample drawn from it. *See* SAMPLING. (MJB)

survey methods. Generic term which embraces all the methods which may be used in collecting data by means of a SURVEY. (MJB)

survey reports. The Market Research Society has adopted the following standards as constituting the minimum acceptable content of a survey report: (a) the purpose of the survey; (b) for whom and by whom the survey was undertaken; (c) general description of the universe covered; (d) size and nature of the sample, including a description of any weighting methods used; (e) the time when the field work was carried out; (f) the method of interviewing used; (g) adequate description of field staff and any control methods used; (h) a copy of the questionnaire; (i) the factual findings; (j) bases of percentages; (k) geographical distribution of the interviews. (MJB)

sustainable competitive advantage (SCA). A long-term advantage possessed by an organization which is not easily copied or eroded by its competitors. SCA is usually the consequence of distinctive skills and competencies possessed by employees and/or the ownership of a customer franchise developed by RELATIONSHIP MARKETING. (MJB)

SWOT analysis. SWOT is an acronym for strengths, weaknesses, opportunities and threats, and is a popular shorthand for the environmental analysis and marketing audit which comprise such an essential part of formal STRATEGIC MARKETING PLANNING. Specifically, strengths and weaknesses relate to the present and expected future status of the company and are determined through the marketing audit while opportunities and threats exist in the present and future environment in which the organization is to operate. (MJB)

symbol grocer. Independent retail food store which has become a member of a VOLUNTARY CHAIN OR GROUP organized either by wholesalers or by retailers. The owner uses the name and logo of the group, often in preference to his own name, and includes in the brands carried, those of the group. For example a wholesale group – Londis, retail group – Spar. (AJB)

symbolic pricing. A form of PRESTIGE PRICING in which the price is set very high to communicate exclusivity, quality and prestige. (MJB)

syndicated data services. Services offered by companies such as A.C. Neilson, AGB etc. in which they provide data on a regular basis on specific markets of interest to the subscribers, e.g. brand shares in consumer markets. (MJB)

syndicated research. Research, often based on SAMPLES or PANELS, in which all or part of the same results are supplied to different users. (JAB)

synectics. A term taken from the Greek by W.J.J. Gordon (*Synectics: The Development of Creative Capacity,* 1961) to describe 'the joining together of different and apparently irrelevant elements. Synectics theory applies to the integration of diverse individuals into a problem-stating, problem-solving group. It is an operational theory for the conscious use of preconscious psychological mechanisms present in man's creative activity' and is particularly useful in the idea generation stage of NEW PRODUCT DEVELOPMENT.

The synectics process involves two steps – making the strange familiar and making the familiar strange. Making the strange familiar has to do with problem statement for by definition the problem is unfamiliar or else its solution would be known. Thus the purpose is to restate and redefine the problem until it becomes familiar in terms of one's extant knowledge and experience. To make the familiar strange is to distort, invert or transpose the ordinary way of thinking about an object in order to develop new perceptions of it. (MJB)

synergy. This occurs when the combination of separate parts makes up a whole greater than the sum of these parts. (MDP)

systacy. A fundamental drive in the individual which creates a desire to be united in working with others. Applied to the study of channels of distribution, the drive for systacy is strengthened when members realize that more can be accomplished and individual goals reached through cooperation. (AJB)

system. The aggregate representation of a set of interacting units, devices, procedures, rules, programmes, and so on. A system is organized to form an integrated entity which will achieve an overall result. An important feature of a system is its utilization of the FEEDBACK which occurs when one unit of the system is acted upon, causing it in turn to react and thereby have an impact on other parts of the system. (DB)

systematic error. Variation associated with levels of factors; also known as 'constant error'. *Contrast* RANDOM ERROR. (SKT)

systematic sampling. A method of probability SAMPLING in which every nth element of a list is included in the sample after a random start. (SKT)

systems buying. The combination of all those elements necessary to ensure the satisfaction of the customer's need, especially where this requires the combination of a variety of PRODUCTS (e.g. a manufacturing plant) and services (e.g. installation). Sometimes referred to as a turnkey operation. (MJB)

systems selling. In many industrial markets (for example the sale of a mainframe computer), the supplier sells not only the product itself, but also a broader set of benefits to the customer. The product is sold as part of an overall 'system' which will solve the company's problems (in the case of a mainframe computer this might be an accountancy system). This involves the supplier in developing an appropriate solution, in terms of product and associated services. 'Systems selling' is often used to refer to this industrial marketing activity. (STP)

T

tabloid. The smaller of the two page sizes common to almost all British newspapers. The 'type area' of a tabloid page varies considerably, but in most of the familiar national titles is between 330 and 360 mm (13 and 14 inches) and between 260 and 280 mm wide (10 or 11 inches). There are always 7 columns per page in the main sections. Precise dimensions for each title are given in BRAD (q.v.), under 'production specifi- cations'. The tabloid format was originally introduced to ease the task of handling evening newspapers in crowded trains or buses. The dimensions also made such papers look and feel thicker, thereby implying there was 'more in them' than in a broadsheet which in fact con- tained the same amount of material. The format was soon adopted by regional and local weekly papers, and came to be associated with 'popular' rather than 'heavyweight' content. National broadsheet papers suffering falling CIRCULATION, such as the *Daily Mail* and *Daily Express*, changed to tabloid size in the apparent belief that they would thereby acquire more 'popular' appeal and appear 'modern'. Meanwhile, the original national tabloids, such as the *Daily Mirror* and the *Sun*, began to compete with one another and new arrivals such as the *Daily Star* for the most sensational and trivial approach to news, establishing an association between size and stature. Today, 'tabloid' is generally a derogatory description. Nevertheless, 9 of the 10 most read daily and Sunday newspapers in Britain are tabloids, in format at least, and share a total CIRCULATION of 21 million. (KC)

tabulation. Normally the first step in data reduc- tion and analysis in which data is grouped into appropriate categories and compiled into tables. (MJB)

tachistoscope. A device for measuring recogni- tion of visual stimuli exposed ultra-briefly, also called a 'T-scope'. *See* LABORATORY TESTS OF ADVERTISING EFFECT. (KC)

tactical plan. A short-term plan setting out the TACTICS to be used in implementing the longer- term strategy. Often linked to the annual plan and budget. (MJB)

tactics. The methods to be employed in execut- ing the strategic plan. In marketing this invariably involves management of the MARKETING MIX. (MJB)

tare. The weight of a vehicle or container which must be deducted from the gross weight in order to determine the net weight of the contents. (MJB)

target audience. The segment or group of people at whom the sellers direct their selling effort. (MJB)

Target Group Index (TGI). A massive-scale commercial research service which produces annual and semi-annual statistical reports in 34 volumes, linking reading, viewing and listening habits to the consumption of almost 4,000 brands in 500 separate product and service categories. The reports are based on data collected by postal questionnaire from a nation-wide sample of 25,000 individuals, classified by the usual demo- graphic criteria, ACORN (q.v.) and additional lifestyle segmenatation variables. Sub-sample surveys produce 'Youth TGI' (7–19 age bracket), 'TGI Gold' (over–50s) and 'Premier TGI' (adults in socio-demographic classes A and B). The company which conducts the research pro-gramme, BRITISH MARKET RESEARCH BUREAU (BMRB), will run special analyses on behalf of regular TGI subscribers and offers a range of software packages for reading and analysing the data. Some information-technology specialists offer TGI analysis packages as a commercial service. In 1997, TGI also operated in Ireland and Russia, and would in due course become avail-able in six other countries.   (KC)

targeting. The selection of the MARKET SEGMENT or segments which represent the best opportunity for the seller based on their analysis.   (MJB)

target market. Group of prospective users/ con-sumers which is the focus of the firm's marketing effort. Usually identified by means of MARKET SEGMENTATION.   (MJB)

target marketing. Concentration of the firm's marketing effort on a clearly defined TARGET MARKET.   (MJB)

target return on investment (ROI). An earnings target which specifies the monetary return or earnings to be achieved from a given investment.   (MJB)

target return pricing. Setting the price so as to obtain a pre-specified return on the capital employed.   (MJB)

tariffs. Customs duties imposed to yield revenue for governments or to 'protect' home industries. Revenue tariffs often apply mainly to high-value products, though some DEVELOPING COUNTRIES with a rather primitive fiscal machine may use them widely. Protective tariffs have the same purpose as QUOTAS, and since they are designed to limit imports, may be most effective when they bring in least revenue. There are two types of tariff: (a) 'ad valorem', which means the duty is charged as a percentage of the value of the goods; (b) 'specific', where the duty is a stated amount per unit of weight or volume. Compound tariffs may be a mixture of the two. Tariffs may be dis-criminatory in that different rates apply to different countries.

Tariffs were raised by many countries in Europe and America during the Great Depression of the early 1930s in an effort to protect home industries and maintain employment. They have tended to fall in the period of trade liberalization since the Second World War promoted by GATT (*see* GENERAL AGREEMENT ON TARIFFS AND TRADE).   (JK, JML)

tear sheet. A specimen of a press ADVERTISE-MENT, figuratively torn from its actual position in a magazine or, less often, newspaper.   (KC)

teaser advertising. A tactic for gaining the audience's interest and involvement in an ADVER-TISING CAMPAIGN by running incomplete or ambiguous advertisements which give clues to the content of the full version that will eventually appear. It has the same aim as those high-profile poster campaigns in Britain which pose a puzzle to identify the subject of somewhat surreal imagery and gnomic headlines, usually cigarette brands. (There is no accepted generic descrip-tion.) The difference is that teaser advertising does eventually give the audience the answer to the puzzle.   (KC)

technical selling. The sale of products where the technical performance of the product is an impor-tant element in the customer's final buying decision.   (STP)

technological environment. The current and developing technology which characterizes the markets in which the firm competes or hopes to compete. An integral part of the ENVIRONMENTAL and SWOT analyses.   (MJB)

technological forecasting (technology fore-casting). The forecasting of the timing and nature of future potential technological developments. A technological forecast predicts how soon various technologies will be possible and what charac-teristics they are likely to have in terms of technical parameters and attributes. The actual technology that will be used in the future depends on economic, social and political considerations. Technological forecasting, therefore, must plot the likely course of development of a product or idea in its total future environment. In the context of a firm it provides a means of predicting tech-nological change that is likely to have an impact on the firm's products or manufacturing processes. It may also outline possible new areas for technological innovation and suggest routes to follow in developing new products or processes. *See also* MORPHOLOGICAL ANALYSIS and RELEVANCE TREES.   (DB)

technological mapping. The collection and synthesis of information which describes the timing and direction of possible patterns of competitive technological effort.   (DB)

technological mission. A long-term corporate goal couched in terms of technological achievement. It is set after having evaluated the various product-market strategies available to the firm.
(DB)

technological obsolescence. OBSOLESCENCE created through the introduction of new technology.   (MJB)

technology. In the broadest sense, technology denotes the purposeful application of scientific knowledge. It has three constituent elements: hardware – machines, tools, materials; software – processes and procedures; and standards which provide the definitional systems governing the preceding elements. *See also* SOCIAL TECHNOLOGY.   (DB)

technology assessment. The evaluation of a technology in terms of its long- and short-term social, economic and environmental impacts. The term became current in the late 1960s when there developed intense concern in the USA to make the designers and propagators of new or proposed technology accountable for its total impact. In 1972 the US Office of Technology Assessment was established to assist Congress by evaluating the long-range, and often hidden social and environmental impacts of technology.   (DB)

technology forecasting. *See* TECHNOLOGICAL FORECASTING.

technology planning. The development of concepts and routines to direct the implementation of a proposed scheme of TECHNOLOGY TRANSFER.
(DB)

technology transfer. This involves the transfer of a capability to use, adapt, modify or innovate with respect to a product, process, piece of equipment or field of technology. Technology transfer is sometimes seen as a special case of innovation, since in a technology transfer exchange the source, production and application of technology occur in different organizations, whereas in innovation, source, production and application are all under the same managerial control. (KAB)

telemarketing. *See* TELEPHONE SELLING, TELEPHONE MARKETING.

telephone marketing. Marketing activities carried out through the medium of the telephone. The most common activities include telephone marketing research and telephone selling. (GM)

telephone selling. Selling using the telephone as the medium for contacting prospective customers. While some sales may be made over the telephone, it is generally used to arrange for a personal call by the salesmen of products such as insurance, double glazing, fitted kitchens etc.
(MJB)

telephone survey. The execution of a SURVEY using the telephone. Given the very high levels of telephone ownership in most advanced countries this is an acceptable way of conducting a representative survey and possesses particular advantages as data is inputted directly and questions can be dropped from the survey as soon as sufficient data has been collected on a specific point.   (MJB)

teleshopping. Literally 'shopping from a distance'. Currently teleshopping is largely limited to placing orders over the telephone. However, it is anticipated that in the not-too-distant future, shoppers will be able to call up information on their television screens and place orders directly with the supplier. The introduction of HOBS (Home and Office Banking System) by the Bank of Scotland whereby customers can make financial transactions via the television and a modem and a micro computer is clearly the shape of things to come.   (MJB)

teletext. Written data transmitted by television companies which can be received by using a special adapter on an otherwise normal television set. There is no charge for viewing the data. *See also* CEEFAX and ORACLE.   (GM)

telethon. A marathon television programme aimed at giving support to a charity or political candidate. The term originated in the United States, and is simply a combination of the words 'television' and 'marathon'.   (GM)

television. One of the five 'major' ADVERTISING MEDIA in Britain. It is the second-youngest but also ranks second in terms of its share of total ADVERTISING EXPENDITURE. The history of television as a commercially-funded advertising medium paradoxically begins with the BBC's broadcast of the Coronation in 1953, which was watched by 20 million viewers on only 4 million television sets. This evidence that television was a bona fide 'mass medium' to compete with radio, newspapers and magazines lent strong support to the growing lobby for a new service, financed by advertisers, to compete with the BBC, funded by its viewers via the statutory 'licence fee'. The counter-lobbyists wielded political influence, however. Sir Winston Churchill had seen television-with-advertising in America, and predicted that a British equivalent would be a 'tuppenny Punch and Judy show'. Lord Beaverbrook, who owned the *Daily Express* and had an obvious vested interest in keeping advertisers' money where it was, spoke out against it in the Upper House. Others were alarmed by the assumed potential of the new medium, reaching uninvited into the privacy of the home, to exercise special persuasive power over consumers. Parliament eventually responded by requiring formal controls of television advertising as a *quid pro quo* for the award of broadcasting franchises. The Television Act of 1954 established an Independent Television Authority (ITA), and charged it with the statutory duty to devise and implement a system to achieve this. The first British television commercial, for Gibbs SR toothpaste, duly appeared on the new commercially-funded channel at 12 minutes and 7 seconds past 8 on the evening of 22 September 1955. For an account of the subsequent developments in the regulation of advertising in the new medium, *see* INDEPENDENT TELEVISION COMMISSION and ADVERTISING CONTROL.

By 1959, 'independent television' (that is, not dependent on government support through a licence fee) was taking a 20 per cent share of total expenditure on media advertising, that held by the press as a whole having meanwhile fallen from almost 90 per cent to just over 70 per cent. Three years later, its share reached exactly a quarter, overtook the individual figures for both national and regional newspapers, and was four times the combined share of posters, radio and cinema. A vigorous new advertising medium was firmly established. Throughout the 1960s and 1970s, the figures for the new big two more or less stabilized at roughly a quarter and two-thirds respectively. In the 1980s, independent television put on another spurt to settle at a new horizon of just over 30 per cent, while the total press share fell steadily to 60 per cent. It would be simplistic to say, as people did, that 'TV has killed the press', for unit price can affect a percentage figure as well as volume. Furthermore, it is more logical to compare independent television with the constituent parts of the press than with the

whole of it. In 1996, actual revenue figures for each were: television, £6,413 million; regional newspapers, £2,061 million; national press, £1,510; business and professional magazines, £1,018 million: consumer magazines, £583 million. Taking this fact in conjunction with the undoubted impact of sound and moving images combined, it is easy to understand why advertisers seem to treat television as the nation's prime advertising medium, rather than the runner-up. Its share of total national advertising expenditure is about the same as in France and the USA, much lower than in Japan or Italy, but significantly higher than in Germany or the Netherlands.

In its current form, the medium mainly comprises the regionalized ITV ('independent television') network on channel 3, plus national Channel 4 and Channel 5, morning-only national GMTV, 6 of the 26 cable channels and 33 of the 56 satellite channels originating in the UK. The ITV network in turn comprises 14 stations in 13 ITV Regions, London being served by one during the week and another at the weekend. They are, in descending order by share of total ITV advertising revenue: Carlton, Central, LWT, Meridian, Granada, Yorkshire, Anglia, HTV, Scottish, Tyne-Tees, Westcountry, Ulster, Grampian and Border. The three 'terrestrial' channels took 44 per cent of the average weekly total television audience in 1996 versus the BBC's 46 per cent, satellite and cable television accounting for the remainder. Audience research is commissioned jointly with the BBC, via the BROADCASTERS AUDIENCE RESEARCH BOARD (BARB). Typically, ADVERTISING TIME is bought from SALES HOUSES, not from the stations themselves.

Significant developments in DIGITAL TELEVISION broadcasting are on the near horizon at the time of writing, and are expected to add hundreds of additional terrestrial and satellite channels to the 40-odd options on offer to British advertisers at present. Advertisers will be faced by a huge choice and MEDIA PLANNERS by a considerable challenge to the scope of their expertise. In short, television may in effect be more than one medium (as the press to all intents and purposes already is) by the time the fourth edition of this Dictionary appears.   (KC)

Television Advertising Bureau (Surveys) Ltd (TABS). A UK commercial research company which has been running a continuous quantitative survey of television ADVERTISING EFFECTIVENESS since 1976. Viewers recruited to the TABS panel watch programmes of their own choice, and record their reactions to all COMMERCIALS they happen to see by means of specially designed self-completion questionnaires which can be completed very quickly thanks to clever use of 'shaped' scales. The TABS National Brand Standing Monitor delivers to subscribers a monthly measure of advertising visibility and brand standing for 100 brands, derived from weekly interviews with 250 housewives and 200 men. The TABS On-Air Panel continuously monitors 2,000 housewives and 1,500 males in the London ITV broadcasting area, recording the same two performance measures plus emotional reaction to the commercial. (KC)

Television Consumer Audit (TCA). Commercial research service commissioned and subsidized by the seven largest television CONTRACTING COMPANIES. Advertisers spending a stipulated minimum budget with each of the companies can receive four-weekly reports on the consumption of selected product groups in their broadcast area, computed from weekly PANTRY CHECKS in a sample of households. The data are cross-tabulated by intensity of ITV viewing.
(KC)

tendering. *See* COMPETITIVE BIDDING.

terms of trade. (1) The terms under which a seller is willing to sell and, thus, the benefits to and responsibilities of the buyer. Traditionally such terms cover, for example, the period allowed for payment, procedure for faulty product, special discounts for cash/prompt payment, time to be allowed for delivery etc.

(2) The ratio of the price of imports (expressed as a percentage or index number of a base year) to the price of exports. Since UK imports are largely (but not wholly) food and raw materials, British terms of trade tend to move favourably if raw material prices fall, or at least rise more slowly than the price of manufacture, and vice versa. The terms of trade particularly affect the prosperity of the poorer raw material exporting countries whose ability to pay for imports can be seriously impaired by a worsening in the terms of trade. (JRB, JML)

territorial franchise. *See* TERRITORIAL RIGHTS.

territorial potential. The total potential demand for a specific product within a defined area of territory. (AJB)

territorial rights (territorial franchise). A FRANCHISE agreement in which a supplier grants the exclusive right to develop the potential demand in an area for a product to one distributor. The right may be conditional on using approved distribution policies or practices, and the boundaries of the territory will be defined.
(AJB)

testimonial. A special case of ENDORSEMENT ADVERTISING with a long history. An ostensibly unsolicited testimonial from a celebrity, ordinary user or expert aims to exploit SOURCE EFFECT. A famous early user of testimonials in press and poster advertising was Pears Soap. The celebrated beauty Lillie Langtry, mistress of the future Edward VII, was an enthusiastic and frequent endorser. The best known of her many statements is probably 'Since using Pears' Soap for the hands and complexion, I have discarded all others', mercilessly parodied at the time. A generation later, the J. Walter THOMPSON advertising agency routinely wrote testimonials into American radio advertising scripts. (KC)

test instrument. Any technique or method used for eliciting data required to test a hypothesis in MARKETING RESEARCH, e.g. a QUESTIONNAIRE, a psychological test (e.g. THEMATIC APPERCEPTION TEST), or a physiological test (e.g. PSYCHO-GALVANOMETER). (MJB)

test marketing. Basically, test marketing consists of launching the product on a limited scale in a representative market, thus avoiding the costs of a full-scale launch while permitting the collection of market data which may subsequently be used for predictive purposes. In practice the term 'test marketing' tends to be used loosely, and it is important to distinguish the original concept, as outlined above, from two associated techniques commonly confused with it. The first of these is often referred to as PILOT MARKETING, and fulfils the same function for the marketer as the pilot plant does for the production engineer, i.e. it tests the feasibility of the proposed course of action. In many instances companies become so involved with the development of a new product that by the time successful product tests have been completed they feel irrevocably committed, and any course of action other than full-scale marketing is unthinkable. However, companies of this type are usually aware of the critical importance of a well-designed and coordinated MARKETING PLAN, and so test its feasibility in practice prior to full-scale operations. Pilot marketing on a regional basis may also serve to give the firm valuable marketing experience while commissioning new plant to meet the anticipated demands of a national market.

The other practice often confused with test marketing is the testing of mix variables, i.e. measuring the effect of changes in the test variable, all other variables being held constant, e.g. COPY TESTING. Such tests are often used to improve the marketing of existing products, and should not be confused with the true test market in which the collective impact of all variables is being tested, simultaneously.

It is clear that if test market results are to be used to predict the likely outcome of a full-scale national launch, then the test market must constitute a representative SAMPLE of the national market. Despite the claims of various media owners it is equally clear that no such perfect microcosm exists and that test marketing is of dubious value if undertaken for predictive purposes alone. In addition to the dangers inherent in scaling up atypical test market results to derive national sales forecasts, many marketers feel that test marketing increases the risks of aggressive competitive reaction in an attempt to nip the new product in the bud. Test market validity depends heavily on the assumption that trading conditions in the market are 'normal', and it follows that any departure from such conditions will bias the results. Competitors learn quickly of test marketing operations and typically react in one of two ways. If the new product closely resembles existing BRANDS, the manufacturers of these brands will usually step up their ADVERTISING and SALES PROMOTION in the test market to maintain existing brand loyalties and prevent the new entrant getting a foothold. These tactics also ensure the existence of 'abnormal' trading conditions during the test period. Alternatively, if the new product represents a radical departure from existing products, competitors can easily monitor its test market performance while developing their own substitutes. If the test results seem promising the imitative innovator may well enter the national market at the same time as the originator of the idea – if not before!

For these reasons many manufacturers now undertake more exhaustive tests of the mix variables and omit the test market stage altogether. If the new product is launched on a limited scale initially, more often than not it is in the nature of

a feasibility study rather than in the hope of obtaining hard data from which to predict the outcome of a national launch.   (MJB)

test-re-test reliability. A method to assess the reliability of a measure by correlating it with a repeated use of the measuring procedure. (SKT)

test statistic. The value calculated for a SAMPLE while performing a statistical test, e.g. CHI-SQUARE or Student's T.   (SKT)

Theory of Reasoned Action. A theory developed by Martin Fishbein which links attitudes to behavioural intentions to actual behaviour. According to this theory decision makers evaluate the likely consequences of choice behaviour and choose the course of action with the most favourable outcomes. For predictive purposes it is necessary to measure behavioural intentions rather than attitudes because an individual may hold a favourable attitude towards an object without any intention of buying it. *See* ATTITUDE.
(MJB)

third party endorsement. Positive support for an object or organization from a third party who is not directly involved with the making or selling of the object. See SOURCE EFFECT.   (MJB)

Thompson, J. Walter (1847–1928). The founder of the eponymous ADVERTISING AGENCY, in New York in 1867. At that time, American magazines carried almost no advertising (unlike their British counterparts). Thompson succeeded in persuading the publishers of general periodicals and women's magazines that the sale of ADVERTISING SPACE would greatly subsidize their production costs. Having done so, he bought it all up and re-sold it in lots to potential advertisers. He was thus a classic case of the entrepreneurial SPACE BROKER, acting as a sales agent for the MEDIA OWNERS. At the turn of the century, his agency still controlled the sale of almost all the magazine advertising space available. But Thompson was much more than a fast-buck merchant. In a period of advertising history characterized by exaggeration and dishonesty (*see* HOLLOWAY, THOMAS) he released space only to companies he considered reputable. He also treated women seriously as consumers, before the view was generally fashionable, and introduced what would much later be called ACCOUNT PLANNING.

During the early twentieth century, 'JWT' became established as the largest and most important advertising agency in the world, by steadily opening offices overseas. In the 1970s, in a strong echo of the founder's business ethics, it led an industry-wide boycott in America against buying advertising time in unacceptably violent television programmes. That action is credited with being the single most influential factor in the eventual reduction of the level of violence on American television screens. JWT remained the undisputed leader in virtually every country where it operated, until falling victim to a dramatic resurgence in British advertising by losing a takeover battle in 1987 against the upstart WPP Group (*see* SORRELL, MARTIN). Ten years later, J. Walter Thompson's name lives on as one of its constituent agencies of the world's biggest advertising group, ranked 2nd in the UK with annual BILLINGS of £278 million in 1996, and 5th in the USA with $2.6 billion. Little has changed but its nationality.   (KC)

Thurstone scales. Thurstone scales were first introduced by L.L. Thurstone in 1928 and have been very widely used ever since. In essence, a Thurstone scale is an attempt to construct an interval scale by selecting a set of statements about a subject which range from very favourable to very unfavourable expressions of attitude towards the subject with each statement appearing to be equidistant from those on either side of it. Scales may contain 11, 9 or 7 statements, which are chosen by a panel of judges from a pool so as to achieve the property of equal-appearing intervals, and respondents are asked to select the statement which most accurately reflects their attitude. A score is assigned to each statement and is used, often in conjunction with scores for other sets of statements, in order to provide a summary statement of attitude towards the object of inquiry.   (MJB)

time and motion study. Investigations into the actions and motions performed and the time taken in industrial work with a view to cutting out unnecessary movements and activities and so speeding up production. Also called 'work study'.   (BRM)

time of adoption. This is central to the whole concept of diffusion (*see* DIFFUSION PROCESS) and underlies all attempts to describe the diffusion process in mathematical terms.   (MJB)

time-series analysis. A more rigorous approach to estimating the effect of a predictor variable than a simple before-and-after test. In a time series analysis a number of observations are taken on the factor to be predicted at intervals prior to the administration of the predictor variable followed by a similar series of observations after its administration. To reduce the possibility that some intervening variable may have caused any change in the factor to be predicted it is helpful to maintain a control group which will not be subjected to the predictor variable, so that if it remains unchanged the likelihood is that changes in the test group are due to changes in the predictor variable.   (MJB)

time series forecast. The development of forecasts using data collected at regular intervals which is averaged and extrapolated to give a future forecast which takes into account SEASONALITY and other trends.   (MJB)

time to market. Literally, the time taken to bring a new product into the market. Because of increased competition and the effects of accelerating technological change the elapsed time to market launch has become of growing concern to those responsible for NEW PRODUCT DEVELOPMENT with clear evidence that late commercialization results in a significant decline in potential profits. In consequence many firms now skip the TEST MARKETING stage and go directly to a full launch.   (MJB)

time utility. The utility created by the availability of a good or service at the time it is required for consumption. It may be measured in terms of the price premium which the consumer is prepared to pay for such instant availability and will have a significant impact on the producer/distributor's willingness to hold an inventory of physical goods and the service organization's willingness to install sufficient capacity to meet peak demands.   (MJB)

total costs. The total of all fixed and variable costs.   (MJB)

total error. In ANALYSIS OF VARIANCE, the variation of each object's value around the overall MEAN.   (SKT)

total quality management (TQM). An approach to management pioneered in the USA by Deming and Juran during the Second World War to reduce faults in the manufacture of products. Largely neglected by Western manufacturers these techniques were widely adopted by Japanese manufacturers', especially in the auto industry, becoming a major source of their competitive advantage in international markets. TQM involves the entire work force and devolves the responsibility to the individual worker to ensure that the required quality standards are met. (MJB)

total revenue. The product of price times the quantity sold. (MJB)

town hall test. *See* CENTRAL LOCATION TEST.

traceable common costs. Those costs which can be allocated to specific functions. (MJB)

traceable costs. Common or shared costs that can be assigned to individual products or functional areas e.g. electricity consumption. (MJB)

trade deficit. The amount by which the value of a country's imports exceed the value of its exports. (MJB)

trade discount. An allowance offered to defined classes of customers (but excluding ultimate CONSUMERS who are not 'in the trade') as a discount against the published list price. Such discounts are usually related to volume but may also be used to encourage purchase out of season. *See* SEASONAL DISCOUNTS. (MJB)

trade-in. The return of an object in exchange for a discount against a repurchase. Frequently found in MARKETS for industrial machinery and CONSUMER DURABLES, especially cars, where the existence of a buoyant trade-in market is considered vital to the sale of new models. (MJB)

trademark. *See* REGISTERED DESIGN.

trade marketing mix. The variables of the MARKETING MIX when applied to wholesaling or retailing can be seen to have basic similarities. These variables are merchandise – supplies, assortment; services – margin/turnover; promotion; store location. Also called the retailing mix. (AJB)

tradename. The name of an organization, as opposed to a TRADEMARK, which is usually associated with a PRODUCT or SERVICE. (MJB)

trade-offs. The concept that activities which provide benefits also incur disadvantages and vice versa. (JRB)

trade press. Printed material targeted to the needs of a particular industry or trade, e.g. *Farmers Weekly, Campaign.* (MJB)

trade price. The price offered to INTERMEDIARIES which offers a TRADE DISCOUNT against the recommended retail price. (MJB)

Trades Descriptions Acts (1968 and 1972). Replaced and expanded the UK Merchandise Marks Law dealing with misdescriptions of goods in general: its particular purpose is to ensure as far as possible truthful information about goods, prices and services. (JLD)

trade shows. Exhibitions mounted to provide a platform for organizations which participate in a trade, business or profession, for the dissemination of information, for public relations purposes and for taking sales orders. (JRB)

Trades Union Congress (TUC). In the UK, the national centre of the trade union movement is the Trades Union Congress (TUC), which was founded in 1868. The TUC's objects are to promote the interests of its affiliated organizations and to improve the economic and social conditions of working people. Its affiliated membership comprises 69 trade unions which together represent 7.6 million people, or 80 per cent of all trade unionists in Britain, and it exercises power less through a formal structure than through influence. The TUC deals with all general questions which concern trade unions both nationally and internationally and provides a forum in which affiliated unions can collectively determine policy. There are eight TUC regional councils for England and a Wales Trade Union Council.

The annual Congress convenes in September to discuss matters of concern to trade unionists and to employees generally. It elects a General Council which represents it between Congresses and is responsible for carrying out Congress decisions, watching economic and social developments, providing educational and advisory services to unions, and presenting to the Government the trade union viewpoint on economic, social and industrial issues. The council is also empowered to mediate in inter-union disputes in certain circumstances, and uses its authority to deal with unauthorized and unconstitutional stoppages of work, as well as official disputes.

The TUC, as well as many individual unions, conducts extensive educational services for members, mainly concerned with industrial subjects, trade unionism and the principles and practice of industrial relations.

The TUC plays an active part in international trade union activity, through its affiliation to the International Confederation of Free Trade Unions and the European Trade Union Confederation. It also nominates the British workers' delegation to the annual International Labour Conference.

(HMSO)

trade-up. The practice of retail salespersons who show a medium-priced product first and then offer a better quality or larger quantity than the customer had originally intended to purchase. By analogy, the practice of a retail store which is changing its image during times of increasing affluence. (AJB)

trading down. Reducing price (and usually quality) in order to meet the demands of potential customers who cannot afford the prevailing MARKET price or consider it excessive in terms of the satisfaction offered. (MJB)

trading stamps. A promotional technique by which retailers give free stamps with every purchase. When accumulated by the customer these may be exchanged for products or cash. The UK Trading Stamps Act (1964) requires that the cash redemption value be shown on the stamp. (AJB)

trading-up. The practice of trying to persuade an intending buyer to purchase a more expensive article than that originally chosen or offered for sale. (MJB)

traffic. (1) The total number of persons who enter a store, or department of a store.

(2) The total number of persons or cars who pass the frontage of the shop whether they enter or not.

(3) The section of an ADVERTISING AGENCY responsible for managing the flows of materials and documentation that accompany an ADVERTISING CAMPAIGN on its progress from the initial ADVERTISING BRIEF through the execution of CREATIVE STRATEGY and MEDIA STRATEGY, to the buying of the MEDIA SCHEDULE and the delivery of ARTWORK to the MEDIA OWNERS. This bland statement conceals a welter of detail and a daunting need for efficient co-ordination. Advertising agencies tend to hide the Traffic Department's light under a bushel, in practice, but they simply could not function at all without it. (KC)

traffic count. One element of the POSTAR research methodology for estimating the audience for outdoor advertising, developed during 1996. Data gathered by approximately 5,000 local authority traffic surveys were used to compute traffic flows in the vicinity of about 10,000 POSTER SITES in 6,475 locations, and from those to generate estimates for every other site in the country. The results were analysed by a 'neural network' computer program, capable of recognising the patterns in a dataset and of revising its interpretation of them as it received further information. It identified 20 significant variables, and applied them to the construction of four predictive models, for 'conurbation main roads', non-conurbation secondary roads', 'other-area main roads' and 'other-area secondary roads'. In a small scale validation of the estimates, modelled estimates and actual traffic volumes were found to vary by plus or minus 0.5 per cent. The same modelling procedure has also been used to estimate 'pedestrian counts' for all sites from 12-minute observations at 9,000 locations. Validation of those figures yielded the larger margin of error of plus or minus 5 per cent. Pedestrian and vehicular flows past an individual POSTER SITE are monitored continuously over a 24-hour period. *See* JOURNEY MAPPING. (KC)

trailer tests. *See* CARAVAN TESTS.

transaction. An individual act of exchange. The focus of the Marketing Management approach to marketing and the antithesis of RELATIONSHIP MARKETING. (MJB)

transactions cost analysis. An approach to costing transactions within a channel or value chain to establish whether it is more economic to perform functions oneself or sub-contract them to other members of the system. (MJB)

transfer pricing. Prices set for internal transfers within an organization, particularly the subsidiaries of a MULTINATIONAL CORPORATION. In the latter cases, prices are set to minimize tax liabilities and maximize tariff regulations. While transfer prices may maximize the overall profit, they are frequently a source of disagreement between operating divisions who perceive them as diminishing their actual performance. (MJB)

transformed variable. A variable that has been changed from its status before DATA analysis (e.g. by standardization or recoding), in contrast to the original RAW VARIABLE. (SKT)

transport advertising. A subdivision of the OUTDOOR ADVERTISING medium, comprising a considerable variety of MEDIA VEHICLES which can deliver the characteristic audiences reached by ADVERTISING SPACE in and on buses and taxis, in underground and 'overground' stations, and at airports. Transport advertising campaigns can be targeted geographically and demographically. They are characteristically local or regional, at least partly because space bookings for a national campaign would have to be placed with a daunting variety of MEDIA OWNERS. (KC)

transportation (of shoppers). The method used by shoppers to reach a shopping centre. The method used affects the size of the catchment area of the centre and it includes foot, car, train, bus, bicycle. (AJB)

transport model. An application of linear programming to the transportation problem of supplying stated amounts of goods to defined destinations from warehouse origins. The objective may be to supply demand by incurring the lowest transport cost or with some other stated constraint. (AJB)

trend analysis. The process of determining the underlying trend or pattern of growth, stability or decline in the time series of a quantifiable variable (e.g. sales). (GA)

trend extrapolation. The process of projecting the trend pattern (growth, stability or decline) of a quantifiable variable (e.g. sales) identified in past periods into future periods. (GA)

trend fitting. The process of representing the trend component of a time-series of a quantifiable variable (e.g. sales). A trend may be represented by a particular curve form, e.g. first-degree polynomial, second-degree polynomial, logistic, Gompertz, etc., depending on whether the underlying trend or pattern in the time series is that of stability, decline or growth. (GA)

trend identification. *See* TREND ANALYSIS.

trial. The stage in the buying process when the intending customer seeks to assess the performance of a product or service through direct personal experience before coming to a decision whether or not to adopt it on a continuing basis. *See* HIERARCHY-OF-EFFECTS. (MJB)

triangulation. A social RESEARCH methodology where empirical endeavour is seen as only one leg of a three-way approach, the other aspects being participatory observation and DESK RESEARCH. (SKT)

trickle down theory. A theory which claims that the adoption of goods, especially clothing fashions, starts with members of higher socio-economic groups and then trickles down to lower levels. The available evidence does not support this theory. (MJB)

T-scope. The everyday name for a tachistoscope. *See* LABORATORY TESTS OF ADVERTISING EFFECT. (KC)

T-shape. An ADVERTISING SPACE on a double-decker bus, consisting of the BUS SIDE shape plus a vertical stalk covering the windowless lower-deck area corresponding to the staircase. The combination makes a rather distorted version of the letter T. (KC)

T-test. Student's 't' is a sampling distribution used instead of the normal distribution when dealing with small samples of data ($n = 30$). It is a distribution which is used to test means when the population variance has to be estimated from sample data. Its most common application is in testing whether or not the sample means are significantly different. The 't' statistic can be calculated by the following formula:

$$t = \frac{\bar{x} - \mu}{s\sqrt{n}}$$

$\bar{x}$ = sample mean
μ = population mean
s = sample standard deviation
n = sample size (KAB)

turnkey operation. The construction of a complete project, e.g. a power station or car plant, to the point where it is a going operation at which time it is turned over to the owners.

It could be argued that this is simply an export of capital equipment. However, it is not a construction company or one which specializes in large capital works which is involved but a manufacturing company. The firm sells its technical and engineering skills and may also train foreign nationals to run the plant. It gains from the immediate sale and may also profit further from supplying materials and equipment for the operation once turned over to the owner.

Turnkey operations are typical in Communist countries which are short of foreign exchange to buy imports and prefer to control key industries. A good example is Fiat, which in the 1960s effectively delivered producing plant to the USSR and Poland (rather than selling these countries vehicles).   (JK)

turnover. (1) Sales revenue: the money an organization earns through the sale of its product or service.

(2) The rate at which a product sells relative to the stock held (stock turnover), e.g. if a shop normally stocks $50,000 of product and achieves $200,000 of sales in a year it is said to 'turnover stock four times'. It is thus one measure of operating efficiency.   (JRB)

TVR. *See* TV RATINGS.

TV ratings. The main 'currency' for valuing television AIRTIME, regardless of channel or time of day. One TV rating (TVR) represents the achievement of 1 per cent of a station's entire total potential audience, also called its 'universe'. The number of TVRs achieved by a particular COMMERCIAL is abstracted from the continuous audience research data published by the BROADCASTERS' AUDIENCE RESEARCH BOARD (BARB). TVRs can be specified in terms of homes, housewives, adults, children and numerous other population subgroups. For example, a national commercial on Channel 4 rated at '50 dog-owner TVRs' will have reached exactly half the 7.3 million dog-owning households capable of receiving its broadcasts: that is, nearly 3.7 million IMPACTS on the required audience. However, this tells a MEDIA PLANNER only that a set in each household was on and tuned to Channel 4 when the commercial was screened. It gives no indication of how many dog-owners were actually watching it, let alone paying attention to the message.   (KC)

twenty-four hour recall. An alternative term for DAY-AFTER RECALL.   (KC)

two-stage area sampling. Sampling where the clusters (or primary units) are areas, and where they are selected in two stages. For example, the first stage may select the area of the country, and the second might select within strata of areas based on urban versus rural differences.   (SKT)

two-step flow of communication. Early models of communication regarded both impersonal sources (the mass media) and personal sources as establishing direct contact with an audience – the

so-called 'hypodermic effect'. Belief in this model leads to speculation concerning the influence of the mass media upon voting behaviour – thus the undertaking of one of the most celebrated pieces of communication research, reported in Paul F. Lazarsfeld *et al., The People's Choice* (1944).

Lazarsfeld and his colleagues set out to study the influence of the mass media on individual voting behaviour in the 1940 presidential election in the United States. Contrary to expectations, it was found that influence did not flow directly from a medium (press, radio etc.) to an audience but was channelled through an intermediary who was designated the 'OPINION LEADER'. It was this finding which gave rise to the two-step model which has had a significant influence on communication research and practice ever since. However, it must be emphasized that the two-step hypothesis does not exclude the possibility of a direct flow (one step) and its main contribution is in introducing the mediating effect of personal influence on impersonal communications. Thus nowadays the mass media are regarded primarily as information sources and considerable attention is focused upon the nature and behaviour of opinion leaders – how to identify them and how to communicate effectively with them.   (MJB)

two-tailed test. An inferential statistics procedure where the direction of the test is unimportant; the test is merely for a difference, either lower or higher. *Contrast* ONE-TAILED TEST.   (SKT)

two-way table. A table whose cells may contain frequencies, percentages and other statistics, and whose rows and columns represent two categorical variables. An example might be the frequency with which people from different lifestyle groups choose different destinations for their ideal holiday.   (SKT)

tying agreement. An agreement whereby the seller of a product requires a re-seller to take other products in their line which are 'tied' to it but in which the re-seller may have less interest.   (MJB)

type I error. When a hypothesis is true, but has been rejected. A test of significance enables a statistical hypothesis to be accepted or rejected for a particular SAMPLE. When the result of the significance test leads the researcher to reject the hypothesis, but it is in reality, a true hypothesis, this is termed type I error. *See also* TESTS OF SIGNIFICANCE. (GM)

type II error. When a false hypothesis has been accepted. A test of significance enables a statistical hypothesis to be accepted or rejected for a particular SAMPLE. When the result of the significance test leads the researcher to accept the hypothesis but it is, in reality, a false hypothesis, then this is termed type II error. *See also* TESTS OF SIGNIFICANCE. (GM)

typesetting. *See* PHOTOTYPESETTING.

U

unaided recall. The spontaneous recollection of a RESPONDENT to a question. *See* RECALL TESTING.
(MJB)

unawareness set. All those BRANDS, in a multi-brand MARKET, which the CONSUMER is not aware of. The converse of AWARENESS SET. (GKP)

unbiased estimate. A statistical phrase for a sample statistic whose MEAN (over repeated SAMPLING) is equal to the target value in the POPULATION. (SKT)

undifferentiated marketing strategy. One of three basic marketing strategies (the other two being DIFFERENTIATED and CONCENTRATED). An undifferentiated strategy exists when the supplier offers the same or undifferentiated product to all persons or organizations believed to have a demand for a product of that type. Three sets of circumstances suggest themselves as being suited to an undifferentiated strategy: (a) the introduction of an INNOVATION; (b) the mature/decay stage of the PRODUCT LIFE CYCLE; (c) commodity marketing where the conditions most closely approximate the economist's model of PERFECT COMPETITION. When introducing a new product into the marketplace, especially a radically different product, several factors may predicate an undifferentiated strategy. For example it is widely recognized that much of the risk attendant upon a new product launch is uncertainty as to the scope and nature of demand, which may result in a perceptual mismatch between supplier and potential user. Inertia and commitment to the known and safe product or process make it very difficult to forecast just what interpretation prospective users will make of the benefits offered by the innovation. Under such circum-stances, a broad approach may be preferable to an attempt to pre-identify receptive customers as a basis for MARKET SEGMENTATION and the development of either differentiated or concentrated strategies. Similarly, by the time that the product is moving into its decline it is safe to assume that the users/consumers are strongly committed to the product and so there is little need for special marketing effort. In the third case, the essential homogeneity of the commodity militates against either a differentiated or concentrated strategy.
(MJB)

uniform delivered price. A GEOGRAPHIC PRICING POLICY in which the seller offers the same delivered price to customers irrespective of their geographic location. (MJB)

unique selling proposition. *See* REEVES, ROSSER.

unitary demand. Demand which varies proportionately with changes in price. *See* ELASTICITY OF DEMAND. (MJB)

unit pricing. An approach to pricing in which the price per standard measure is provided for all competing brands and pack sizes so enabling the customer to make direct comparisons between them. (MJB)

univariate analysis. Statistical procedures involving only one dependent variable. Contrast MULTIVARIATE ANALYSIS procedures such as FACTOR ANALYSIS, or MULTIVARIATE ANALYSIS OF VARIANCE. (SKT)

Universal Product Code (UPC). System of product identification used in the USA by which a 10-digit number is assigned to each grocery product sold by US producers. The system is also in use in the UK where a 13-digit article number is assigned to each product. The code is printed in a system of black and white bars referred to as a BAR-CODE which can be read by an electronic scanner at the supermarket checkout. *See also* ARTICLE NUMBERING.   (AJB, MDP)

universe. (1) The total number of people or organizations available from which to select a sample.
                                              (BRM)
(2) The maximum potential audience for a radio or television COMMERCIAL, often subdivided demographically in practice. For example, Radio Forth has an overall universe of 1.1 million adults and a 'housewives with child' universe of 168,000. *See also*: ITV REGION; NET HOMES; TV RATINGS.   (KC)

unprompted response. *See* UNAIDED RECALL.

unsought products. Those for which the customer has no felt need. Unsolicited goods sent by suppliers in the hope that the buyers' inertia will result in their keeping them e.g. book and record clubs.   (MJB)

unstructured interview. Often called a DEPTH INTERVIEW. A non-directive interview in which the RESPONDENT is encouraged to talk about the subject, rather than to answer specific questions.

The interviewer uses a topic list, which sets out a list of points that should be covered during the interview; his role is to guide the conversation, rather than to ask formal QUESTIONS. *See* DEPTH INTERVIEW.   (AMW)

UPC. *See* UNIVERSAL PRODUCT CODE.

upper class. *See* SOCIO-ECONOMIC CLASSIFICATIONS.

use-by date. Also known as BEST-BEFORE DATE, but is gradually replacing this term as CONSUMERS find it less confusing.   (SD)

user-active. A term referring to the source of ideas for new industrial products. The new industrial product development process is said to be user-active when it is the customer who: (a) develops the idea for the new product; (b) selects a supplier capable of making the product; (c) takes the initiative to buy the product from the supplier, thus aiding the diffusion of that new product.   (KAB)

USP (unique selling proposition). *See* REEVES, ROSSER.

utility. In economics, the value or satisfaction associated with the acquisition/consumption of a good or service.   (MJB)

V

VAI. *See* VISIBILITY ADJUSTED IMPACT.

valence. *See* ATTITUDE VALENCE.

validity. The extent to which the measurement process devised to measure marketing phenomena is free from systematic errors. In testing the validity of a measurement instrument the researcher might use any or all of the following: (a) content validity, (b) criterion validity, (c) construct validity. (GA)

VALS. An acronym for Values and Lifestyles which is an approach to segmenting a market using psychographic variables developed by the Stanford Research Institute International. (MJB)

value added. The value that is added by an organization to the cost of its inputs and arriving, thus, at the price of its output. A process which turns steel plates into smaller plates adds only a little value. A process which turns steel plates into cars or refrigerators adds a great deal of value. Added value as an economic concept is thus a yardstick which can compare the technological levels and sophistication of process companies, industries and nations. (JRB)

value added tax (VAT). A tax on output, whether at manufacturing, wholesale or retail level, levied throughout the EUROPEAN ECONOMIC COMMUNITY (EEC). In the UK the firm makes its own calculations of tax due, subject to inspection, by HM Customs and Excise Department, and pays at intervals during the year. (AJB)

value adding resellers (VARs). Intermediaries who add value to the product before selling it on.

Sellers of computing equipment who combine various product like processors, VDUs, printers etc. into a system are a good example. (MJB)

value analysis. The systematic evaluation of the individual elements of a manufactured product, which is already on the market, to determine the optimum combination of each element to satisfy the user's needs at minimum cost. Typical questions which are asked in value analysis exercises include: how is the item currently manufactured? What contribution does it make to the overall product? Could it be redesigned to make it cheaper to manufacture or the overall product easier to manufacture? Could it be replaced or eliminated? If so, by what? Value analysis is critical for any company seeking to produce products which remain competitive in price and value terms. (STP)

value-based pricing. Basing prices on the customer's perception of value rather than on cost plus some kind of mark-up. 'Charging what the market will bear'. (MJB)

value chain. A concept which recognizes that there is a continuous link or chain right the way through from the extraction of raw materials to the provision of post-purchase services. Value is added at each stage of the value chain and a major consideration in strategy formulation is to identify where and how value is added as this constitutes a potential source of competitive advantage. (MJB)

value engineering. The same process as VALUE ANALYSIS but conducted at the product's design stage when the ability to make changes in design is far greater. (STP)

values. A major component of culture, which reflects the beliefs of its members concerning what is good (to be encouraged) and bad (to be discouraged). Values exercise considerable influence over behaviour. (MJB)

van sales. Vans, or small covered lorries are stocked with a range of merchandise at a factory or distribution centre and the van driver takes the goods to prospective customers. Orders are taken and fulfilled at the premises of the customers, or in the street, depending upon the PRODUCTS being sold. It is common practice for certain perishable merchandise (bread and other bakery products) to be sold in this manner. Also soft drinks and ice-creams are frequently distributed on a van sales basis. Van sales of industrial goods is less common but there are examples of its being used as in the case of small hand tools being taken by vans to garages and workshops. (BRM)

variable. A basic term indicating that which varies between RESPONDENTS, in other words, measured attributes. (SKT)

variable cost. Those costs which vary directly with the volume of production. (MJB)

variance. A dispersion measure calculated (in one method and approximately) by summing the squared standardized score from each case. (SKT)

variety. A measure of the number of different categories of products offered by a producer or retailer. (MJB)

variety chain store. Retail store offering a wide assortment of products, most of which have a low unit value. Variety chain stores are a form of multiple trading. The term 'chain store' is often used erroneously, as a variety chain store is a type of multiple, but not all multiples are chain stores. The difference lies in the types of merchandise sold. Multiples tend to specialize in one type of product such as shoes, books, clothes, food and so on. Variety chain stores offer a wide range of types of merchandise. They were originally 'bazaar-type' shops. In the USA Woolworth was an original example, but UK variety stores have now developed into different and higher value units (mostly in clothing), with Marks &

Spencer plc being a good example. *See* MASS MERCHANDISER. (AJB, MDP)

variety reduction. The deliberate elimination of the number of variants in a PRODUCT range or line in order to improve efficiency and secure scale economies. Usually accomplished through PARETO ANALYSIS. (MJB)

VAT. *See* VALUE ADDED TAX.

Veblenian social-psychological model. One of the four basic models of buyer behaviour distinguished by Philip Kotler (*Marketing Management,* 1972) in which individual buyer behaviour is explained in terms of social rather than economic influences. According to Veblen, man is a social animal trying to conform to the general norms of his larger culture and to the more specific standards of the subcultures and face-to-face groupings to which he or she is bound. Based upon his 'theory of the leisure class' Veblen hypothesized that much of economic consumption is motivated not by intrinsic needs or satisfactions so much as by prestige seeking. Thus the Veblenian model proposes that man's attitudes and behaviour are conditioned by the norms of the social groupings to which he belongs: CULTURE, subculture, his social class (*see* SOCIO-ECONOMIC CLASSIFICATIONS), REFERENCE GROUPS, and his family affiliations. His model was also the first to suggest the concept of CONSPICUOUS CONSUMPTION, although there is much subsequent work which indicates that the majority of consumers prefer to conform rather than stand out from their peer group. To this extent conspicuous consumption must be distinguished from the more familiar idea of 'keeping up with the Joneses'. (MJB)

vehicle effect. The perceived influence on the recipient of a communications message attributable to the MEDIA VEHICLE used, as opposed to the message content itself. It can be demonstrated that the perception of, or response to, ADVERTISEMENTS and editorial copy are dependent upon matching not only the TARGET MARKET, but also the target's impression of the image of the media vehicle itself. This is particularly relevant as between one newspaper or journal and another, or between one radio or television station and another. (KNB)

vending machine. Vending machines are unmanned dispensers of prepackaged food and drinks usually in response to the insertion of a coin or token. Vending machines are typically located in offices and factories and other places of work, also in public places such as railway stations, airports and sports centres and are easily accessible dispensers of snacks. Vending machines in the UK traditionally dispense coffee and tea (with and without sugar and milk), confectionery and savoury items such as crisps. The quality of some of the drinks is often questionable and in some working environments vending machines have not proved popular.   (BRM)

vendor. Synonym for supplier or seller.   (MJB)

vendor rating. The organizational buyer's evaluation of existing or potential suppliers against criteria which are deemed by the buyer as important if the supplier is to be considered as a potential source of supply. Vendor rating can be conducted formally using a vendor assessment questionnaire which the potential supplier has to complete in order to be considered. The organizational customer may also send an audit team to the supplying company to evaluate it on the criteria which are deemed important. These may include factors such as location, financial stability, manufacturing capacity and technological competence, work-force relations, and general management quality. Suppliers who are deemed unsatisfactory may be asked to make improvements in order to be actively considered as a qualified supplier. *See* SUPPLIER DEVELOPMENT; SUPPLIER MANAGEMENT.   (STP)

venture teams. Such teams are formed to take responsibility for specific NEW PRODUCT DEVELOPMENT projects. While similar to new product committees in the sense that they are usually composed of experts drawn from different areas of the organization, and that they are formed for a specific purpose, the new product committee's role is solely advisory, while a new venture team assumes responsibility for the execution of the proposal too. Thus, members will have to be seconded from their normal duties for the life of the project and the approach may best be thought of as establishing a new business in its own right.   (MJB)

Verified Free Distribution (VFD). A wholly-owned subsidiary of the AUDIT BUREAU OF CIRCULATIONS that certifies the number of FREESHEETS, free magazines and directories delivered to readers by door-to-door distribution in the

UK, averaged over a six-month period. The magazines in question are often called 'profile mags', and are delivered to specific individuals or particular types of address by, for example, estate agents. They therefore resemble CONTROLLED CIRCULATION PUBLICATIONS rather than freesheets, which are distributed universally within a locality. Directories falling within the VFD remit are mainly the Thomson Local series. Certification covers about 80 per cent of all titles in the three categories. BRAD (q.v.) publishes the certified distibution figure in the listing for each one, under the heading 'CIRCULATION'.   (KC)

vertical diversification. *See* VERTICAL INTEGRATION.

vertical integration. The acquisition by a member of a distribution channel of a facility or establishment at a different level in the channel. If the acquisition is farther from the consumer then it is backward integration usually with the purpose of assuring supplies. *See* FORWARD INTEGRATION.   (AJB)

vertical marketing system (VMS). A marketing channel which has achieved some degree of vertical integration involving some central control of operational practices, and programmes. Three types are generally distinguished: corporate, contractual and administered.   (AJB)

vertical publication. One directed at readers who belong to a common location or type of organization but may be diverse in other respects, e.g. *Drapers Record.* The implied alternative is a HORIZONTAL PUBLICATION.   (KC)

VFD. *See* VERIFIED FREE DISTRIBUTION.

Visibility Adjusted Impact (VAI). A measure of COVERAGE developed in 1996 for the OUTDOOR advertising medium. *See* SITE PASSAGE.   (KC)

vision. A vision is a view of the future which represents where an organization would like to be and gives a sense of purpose and direction from which a strategy may be formulated. In the words of Warren Bennis: 'A vision should state what the future of the organisation will be like. It should engage our hearts and our spirits; it is an assertion about what we and our colleagues want to create. It is something worth going for; it provides meaning to the people in the organisation, in the work that they are doing. By its definition, a vision is a little cloudy and grand; if it were clear, it wouldn't be vision. It is a living document that can always be added to; it is a starting place to get more and more levels of specificity.' (MJB)

visual aids. Any processes, activities or materials used to explain, emphasize or advertise. Usually with reference to the making of presentations, lectures and sales pitches. (JRB)

visualizer. An employee of an ADVERTISING AGENCY whose skill is to be able to produce quick visual interpretations from tentative verbal descriptions of an emerging advertising theme or treatment. See ARTWORK. (KC)

visuals. Visual element of an ADVERTISEMENT as distinct from the COPY. For instance: 'The visuals are perfect, but the copy is weak.' (KC)

VMS. See VERTICAL MARKETING SYSTEM.

V/O. See VOICE-OVER.

voice-over. A commentary heard in a TV or cinema COMMERCIAL but not spoken by any of the characters seen on the screen. Often contracted to V/O. Scripts very often specify MVO, which stands for 'male voice-over'. Observation confirms that the great majority of voice-overs are indeed predominantly spoken by men. This may reflect no more than the unthinking perpetuation of a historical stereotype, but seems a curious tactical decision when the product or service implies a predominantly female target audience, as the majority of those advertised on television do. In those cases, it may be an instinctive power ploy, exploiting the authority attributed to male voices by sex-role stereotyping: see SOURCE EFFECT. (KC)

volume discount. A reduction in the RATE CARD COST given to MEDIA BUYERS who order a large volume of ADVERTISING SPACE or ADVERTISING TIME within a relatively short period. See also SERIES DISCOUNT. (KC)

volume segmentation. The segmentation of total DEMAND for a PRODUCT or SERVICE in terms of the volume consumed by individuals, groups or types of individuals, within geographic markets and so on. The primary objective of such segmentation is to identify the HEAVY USER as the basis for developing DIFFERENTIATED MARKETING STRATEGIES for both heavy and light users. See MARKET SEGMENTATION. (MJB)

volumetrics. A technique for making INTERMEDIA COMPARISONS, in which MEDIA WEIGHTS derived from surveys of consumption patterns among subgroups of a target audience are applied to data linking product use and media use, such as the TARGET GROUP INDEX figures. (KC)

voluntary chain or group. Any group of traders who have agreed to make joint purchases in order to attain the benefits of quantity discounts. See SYMBOL GROCER. (AJB)

W

wants. *See* NEED.

warehouse. A storehouse for merchandise, sometimes used to describe a retail system where lower prices are offered with fewer services.

(AJB)

warehouse, automated. A warehouse which has been automated with robotics, conveyors etc. so that orders can be selected and picked automatically using electronically-based information systems.

(MJB)

warranty. Now generally used to mean the same as guarantee. A statement by a seller in which he promises to do certain things should the item bought not perform as specified or prove to be defective in some way within a certain time after being put into use.

(GA)

wastage. That portion of an audience or readership which is of no practical use to an advertiser because it consists of people other than the TARGET MARKET. Wastage depends on the characteristics of the MEDIA VEHICLE and of the product or service advertised, but is almost always high in the case of television and the mass-circulation newspapers.

(KC)

weak signals. An idea proposed by Igor Ansoff that argues that future events are anticipated by weak signals which, if identified, will give advance warning of a forthcoming change. Accordingly scanning for weak signals should be an integral part of ENVIRONMENTAL ANALYSIS. A useful concept difficult to implement.

(MJB)

wearout. A phenomenon connected with the scheduling of ADVERTISING CAMPAIGNS. As long ago as 1912, a series of laboratory experiments conducted by E.K. STRONG suggested there was an optimum scheduling interval. Beyond it, forgetting would occur between consecutive INSERTIONS: below it, no improvement in recall could be detected after each further exposure. This pioneering work was eventually taken up 44 years later by H.H. Zielske, whose carefully controlled field experiment initiated a whole series of related studies and led eventually to the formulation of the 'threshold' and 'wearout' concepts. It is postulated that no beneficial effect is achieved until a threshold level of 'advertising pressure', the number of repetitions within a given period. Thereafter, learning is progressive and new behaviour patterns such as search, trial and purchase may result, until a 'satiation' level' is reached beyond which each further exposure produces fewer improvements in response than the previous one. This is the 'wearout' phenomenon. It is easily confused with simple forgetting, but that is simply a function of the passage of time whereas wearout relates to frequency of re-exposure. The twin concepts were clarified diagrammatically in a thorough review by D.R. Corkindale and J. Newall ('Advertising Thresholds and Wearout', *European Journal of Marketing,* vol. 12, no. 5, 1978).

(KC)

Weber's Law. A view which argues that purchasers are less interested in the absolute characteristics of individual objects than they are in the comparative performance characteristics of like objects which are close SUBSTITUTES for one another.

(MJB)

weighting. A means of attaching greater or lesser importance to a factor or variable. Weights may be assigned judgementally to reflect experience or company policy, e.g. in rating tables for screening new product ideas, or based upon prior knowledge of the incidence with which the variable occurs naturally and which one may wish to modify, e.g. in QUOTA SAMPLING one can emphasize those subgroups in which one is particularly interested by giving greater weight to them.

(MJB)

Weights and Measures Act (1963) (UK). This act consolidates a considerable number of earlier acts in setting out definitions and standards for weight and measurement and deals with the marketing of a wide range of processed and unprocessed goods and merchandise. Enforcement is the responsibility of the local authority.

(AJB)

wheel of retailing. *See* CYCLE MODELS.

Which? A UK consumer testing and advisory magazine published by the CONSUMERS' ASSOCIATION.

(JLD)

white goods. A term used to describe particular types of CONSUMER DURABLES, e.g. washing machines, dishwashers, fridge-freezers. These goods were originally covered in white enamel paint and this is apparently the origin of the term.

(MDP)

wholesaler. An establishment whose business is to buy for resale to retailers or industrial buyers.

(AJB)

width. Defined in terms of the number of different product lines.

(MJB)

wildcats. Another term for 'problem children'. *See* BUSINESS PORTFOLIO.

(MJB)

WOM. *See* WORD OF MOUTH.

word-of-mouth. A narrow interpretation of the effect of personal influence on the flow of mass

communications. In a seminal study (*Personal Influence: The Part Played by People in the Flow of Mass Communication,* 1966) Elihu Katz and Paul F. Lazarsfeld developed what has become known as the 'two-step flow' theory which holds that communications do not move directly from the mass media to the consumer but are translated or transmitted through the intervention of OPINION LEADERS. There is considerable empirical evidence to support this theory but it is difficult to operationalize it as opinion leaders do not possess any distinctive characteristics which apply across the board. Rather, opinion leaders are recognized as such by their peer group by virtue of their perceived expertise and knowledge on a particular subject and it is quite likely that on other topics they will be 'followers' rather than 'leaders'. That said, identifying opinion leaders holds considerable promise for accelerating the DIFFUSION of an innovation if they can be profiled at reasonable cost.

(MJB)

working capital. *See* CAPITAL.

work study. *See* TIME AND MOTION STUDY.

World Trade Organisation (WTO). The WTO was set up on 1 January 1995 to replace the General Agreement on Tariffs and Trade (GATT) which had been established in 1948.

The WTO's aim is to liberalize world trade and it provides the legal and institutional foundation for the promotion of multinational trade. It is responsible for administering 29 existing multilateral agreements covering such areas as agriculture, textiles, clothing etc. The main differences between the WTO and GATT which it has replaced are that the WTO is a permanent organization with a wider remit and stronger powers of enforcement. As of 1995 it had 97 members who contributed a budget of SFr105 million based on their share of world trade.

(MJB)

Y

y-intercept. The position on the x-axis where the regression line crosses. The value that is predicted for y when x is zero; the constant in the regression equation.   (SKT)

Z

zapping. A popular term to describe the behaviour of television viewers who use the remote-control device to sample the alternative viewing available on other channels: also called 'channel switching', 'channel flicking' and, in America, 'channel surfing'. It is a cause for consternation among MEDIA PLANNERS because it is presumed to happen most often during COMMERCIAL BREAKS. This reflects the somewhat masochistic belief in the business that ordinary people resent the interruption of programmes by commercials, no matter how dire the former or how inventive the latter. Furthermore, two studies in America have found that zapping may in fact improve the effectiveness of a commercial. Zufryden and his fellow workers thought the explanation must be that zapping indicates a high level of involvement in general (Zufryden, Pedrick and Sankaralingam, *Journal of Advertising Research*, vol. 33 no. 1, 1993, pp. 58–66). Gilmore and Secunda suggested that commercials half-noticed during zapping were in effect acting as reminders and reinforcers of messages already assimilated to some extent (*Journal of Advertising Research*, vol. 33 no. 6, 1993, pp. 28–38). Whether practitioners' fears are exaggerated or not, the point is that the BROADCASTERS' AUDIENCE RESEARCH BOARD (BARB) counts anyone within viewing range of a TV set for more than half of any quarter-hour as 'audience'. Yet studies have shown that actual PRESENCE during commercial breaks is significantly less than the maximum defined by the BARB data, because people engage in a bewildering variety of distracting activities while 'viewing'. If zapping is nowadays one of those, the gap between 'audience' and 'presence' will be even wider. Further surveys (or preferably controlled experiments) are keenly awaited. (KC)

zero-based budgeting. A form of budgeting in which each item in the budget must be justified before funds are allocated to it. (MJB)

zero defects. The ultimate objective of QUALITY CONTROL SYSTEMS – the elimination of all defects. In practice it is very difficult to attain and is more of a benchmark to work towards. For example, Hewlett Packard has a policy of 'six parts per million'. (MJB)

zero-order association. The simple association (or as measured by a coefficient such as PEARSON'S CORRELATION COEFFICIENT) between two variables without adjustment for any of the effects of any other variables. Higher-order associations, by contrast, are calculated with some such adjustment. (SKT)

zero rating. Goods on which VALUE ADDED TAX (VAT) is not paid by the final CONSUMER but on which the supplier can recover VAT for his inputs. In the UK this includes food, books and several other items, but the government is progressively reducing the number of zero-rated goods. (MJB)

zip code. A five-digit number added to the last line of American postal addresses. Machine operators in sorting offices convert it into a machine-readable code on the envelope, which is then routed to the appropriate delivery office. It does not indicate the addressee's location with as much precision as its British and Canadian counterparts, and is therefore a far less powerful device for DIRECT MAIL targeting. This is equally true of the codes used elsewhere in the world, all of which more or less resemble zip codes. In the mid-1990s, however, the U.S. Postal Service introduced an expanded version called 'ZIP+4', which adds a hyphen and four more digits. When this dictionary went to press, the extended code was hardly in evidence at all on corporate letter-heads or in private addresses, and informal research suggested that very few Americans yet had any idea what it was for. Once the system is properly in use, it will specify the destination address with the same degree of precision as British POSTCODES. Take, for example, 10016-2526. The first three digits identify New York City and the next two the 16th 'delivery office' there. This traditional zip code, still the everyday norm, discloses no more than did the long super-seded 'New York, N.Y. 16', namely that the destination is somewhere in a large area of mid-town Manhattan. Outside the large cities, a whole township is likely to share a single zip code. After the hyphen, 25 identifies a 'delivery sector'. It consists of several city blocks, but could in other locations be a group of streets, a single high-rise apartment or office building, or a smallish geo-graphical area. The final pair of digits denote a 'delivery segment', 26 being one floor of an office building. Elsewhere, that most specific element of the ZIP+4 could be one side of a street between intersecting streets, one department of a large firm or a set of post office boxes. A software package called TIGER ZIP allows market researchers and direct marketers to match ZIP+4 coded addresses to demographic data which can be purchased from the Census Bureau. The process is not yet as sophisticated as the routine use of ACORN and MOSAIC in Britain for socio-demographic market segmentation by postcode, but the addition of four digits to coventional zip codes has greatly increased their potential use-fulness to marketing managers.   (KC)

zone prices. Similar to BASE POINT PRICING in that prices within the zone or area are standardized to share the AVERAGE COSTS of delivery to the area.
(MJB)

z-test. An inferential statistical test used to test the difference between the MEAN of a sample and either the mean of a different independent sample, or a POPULATION mean. Requires at least 30 cases and normally distributed variables.
(SKT)